BLACK
SEA

W9-DGF-821

R. Iris

Cotyora    Trapezus

CHALYBES

ARMENIA

DOCIA

Pyramus
Isus
Syrian Gates
R. Carsus
Myriandus
Amanus
Chalybon
R. Chalus

Carchemish

Charan

MESOPOTAMIA

Nisibis

Nineveh

Larissa    R. Zapatas    Arbela

MEDIA

To Susa

R. Physcus

Thapsacus

R. Euphrates

R. Araxes

R. Tigris

SYRIA

Corsote

ARABIA

Charmande

Pylae    Opis

Sittace

Cunaxa

Babylon

Galilee

Soderberg

40

42

40

38

36

36

34

34

32

32

38    40    42    44

6    38    40    42    44    46    42

# BEGINNING GREEK

# BEGINNING GREEK

## *A Functional Approach*

BY

### STEPHEN W. PAINE

HOUGHTON COLLEGE, NEW YORK

NEW YORK
OXFORD UNIVERSITY PRESS
1961

© 1961 by Oxford University Press, Inc.


Library of Congress Catalog Card Number: 60–13206


Fifth printing, 1971

Manufactured in the United States of America

# PREFACE

THIS elementary Greek textbook employs a more inductive approach to learning the language than has been customary. Emphasis is placed upon reading substantial passages from original literature of the language. Grammar and syntax are introduced as the reading progresses. The pattern thus follows that by which one learns his native language: first using it and then learning its rules. During the past twenty-five years the inductive method has been widely adopted by modern language teachers. This book applies the same principles to the study of Greek, but without the conversational practice so useful with modern languages.

The inductive approach is a break with the traditional method of having students memorize rules and forms, then having them 'solve' problem sentences. Instead the student is asked to read unaltered selections from original Greek literature. Because these reading passages inevitably include some constructions that the student may not have learned, the notes provide immediate and sometimes repeated explanations of those points. These explanations, supplemented by literal (not literary) translations in the appendix, assist the student in learning to *read*, and not merely to *translate* Greek.

The book presents grammar in large units, thus giving the student a more unitary view of it. For example, he sees λύω as an entire verb instead of as a dozen fragments. The usual grammatical appendix is made unnecessary, for all such material is included in the body of the textbook for observation and later reference.

An innovation of this book is its presentation of the κοινή Greek of the New Testament before the more difficult Attic Greek of the classical period. While the student begins with the more recent and simpler dialect and then moves back to the more complex and formal Attic Greek, he is shown the close relationship between the two. He can see that, as Greek emerged to become a world language, the more abstruse inflections disappeared, and a co-ordinative style of construction replaced the more hypotactical style of the earlier period.

The Gospel of St. John has been chosen as ideal for the beginning student. Not only has it the advantages of simplicity, common to κοινή Greek, but it also offers a rather limited, repetitive vocabulary. As Professor A. T. Robertson has said: 'John's vocabulary is somewhat

limited. . . . But the characteristic words are repeated many times.'[1] He
goes on to quote Professor E. A. Abbott's statement; 'He [John] rings
the changes on a small number of elementary words and their synonyms.'[2]
Once the student has mastered the simple grammatical style and restricted vocabulary of St. John, he should be able to learn more easily
the involved style and larger vocabulary of Attic Greek represented by
the passages from Xenophon's *Anabasis* in the latter part of this textbook.

In his volume *The Greek World Under Roman Sway*,[3] published in 1850,
Professor J. P. Mahaffy argued that the principal reason for the persistence of Greek studies was the circumstance that the Gospels are
written in that language. His point could be stated more emphatically
today. In liberal arts colleges a generation ago *Greek* meant *classical
Greek*. A general survey of college Greek courses in 1957 indicated that
about half the students enrolled were studying κοινή Greek. Furthermore,
a large portion of those studying classical Greek are anticipating theo-
logical studies, for which the ability to read the language of the New
Testament is invaluable.

It cannot be said too often that Greek is an evolving language and that
an understanding of ancient Greek includes mastery of both Attic and
κοινή. The former was the language of the great works of history, literature, and philosophy of the classical period that have had such a profound influence on our Western culture. κοινή Greek, on the other hand,
is the dialect of the New Testament writers who recorded the beginnings
of the most significant religious movement of the West. Whatever the
student's or scholar's own particular interests, he cannot fully appreciate
the one without an understanding of the other and of the relationships
between the two. If this book can help beginning students toward such
an understanding, it will have done its work.

## ACKNOWLEDGEMENTS

The author expresses his thanks to the Privilegierte Württembergische
Bibelanstalt for kind permission to use the 1957 Nestle text for the
readings from St. John; to my colleague, Dr. F. Gordon Stockin, for
valued criticisms and suggestions; to my former teaching assistant,

---

[1] A. T. Robertson, *A Grammar of the Greek New Testament*, 4th edn., 1923, pp. 135 f.
[2] *Johannine Vocabulary*, 1905, p. 348. Quoted by Robertson, op. cit., p. 133.
[3] pp. 389 ff. Quoted by Robertson, op. cit., p. 133.

# Preface vii

Miss Helen K. Hubbard, for her careful preparation of the manuscript; and to the staff at the Oxford University Press for their help in the details of editing and production.

S. W. P.

*Houghton, New York*
28 *October* 1960

# CONTENTS

## PART I

### Grammar: Readings from St. John

# Contents

## PART II

### Readings from the *Anabasis*, Book 1

ILLUSTRATIONS

# GRAMMATICAL INDEX

I N this text the rules of syntax are presented in connection with the reading passages, wherever they apply, and they are summarized in an appendix called the *Syntactical Summary* for easy reference or review. The grammar is presented in large units in connection with the first semester lessons, and it has not been thought necessary to repeat these in an appendix. Hence the following grammatical index is given with sufficient detail so that the student may refer quickly to the rules of mechanics or to any of the grammatical forms (sometimes called *paradigms*, from the Greek παράδειγμα, *example*) given in this text.

# INTRODUCTION

T HE Greek language is the historic tongue of the people inhabiting the mainland of Greece, the islands near it, and, to a considerable extent, the other coastal areas surrounding the Aegean sea. Following the discovery of Sanscrit in the 1780's by Sir William Jones, scholars soon realized that Sanscrit, Greek, Latin, Gothic, Celtic, German, Lithuanian, Slavic, Armenian, and Albanian have all without doubt sprung from a parent tongue which was anciently used from India to eastern Europe. These languages are therefore said to belong to the Indo-European family. Sanscrit, ancient language of the sacred Zoroastrian writings called the *Avesta*, is the oldest known representative of this family, followed in antiquity by the Greek.

The Greek language is known to us through extant writings which span some thirty centuries from the epic poetry of Homer to the current literature of modern Greece. The early history of the language was marked by a multiplicity of dialects.

With the conquests of Alexander, the Greek language spread through the known world as a κοινὴ διάλεκτος, or 'common dialect'. The Romans, in turn, gladly made use of this world language to help them in their task of administering a world-wide domain. Scholars generally distinguish five periods in the history of the Greek language. These will be given briefly.

**The Early Period.** Thanks to widespread archaeological interest in Greece and the rest of the Aegean basin, there is a solid and still growing body of information concerning the early period of Greek civilization extending from prehistoric times to the destruction of Troy. The traditional date for the destruction of Troy, set by Alexandrian scholars of the early Christian era, is 1184 B.C., but some scholars today set this event almost a hundred years earlier.

Heinrich Schliemann, the German pioneer in archaeological research, excavated Troy, Mycenae, and Tiryns (1871-85). The exploration of Crete, begun in 1899 by Sir Arthur Evans, has led in very recent years to further discoveries whose full significance is still unfolding. There have been countless other explorations in the Aegean basin, many of them very significant.

These finds, consisting mainly of an abundance of artifacts, enable us to reconstruct a surprisingly accurate picture of everyday life in the periods from which they come, and, taken as a whole, they afford help in piecing together a general schedule of the development of Hellenic civilization. But, at best, they are circumstantial, and so they allow some scope for varying theories.

The year 1400 B.C., or thereabouts, marks an important point in early Aegean history, for this was the time when the city of Mycenae, standing at the head of the 'Argive plain' in the Peloponnesus, was rebuilt upon a grander scale and began an era of prosperity and power which was to last about 300 years. It was also in 1400 that Cnossos in Crete was overcome and its beautiful and elaborate palace destroyed.

It has been customary to attribute the various dialectical and cultural divisions of early Greece to succeeding migrations or population waves coming into Greece proper from the northwest or northeast, principally during the period from 1400 B.C. to the Trojan War and, in the case of the Dorian migration, directly after this war. The Greeks themselves referred to the earliest inhabitants of Greece as Leleges or Pelasgians. Homer mentions the Pelasgians as connected with various specific localities in Greece. They were apparently an Aryan stock.

In explaining the language groups of ancient Greece scholars have spoken of a migration into Euboea and Attica of Greek people, many of whom were later to move across the Aegean and settle along the west coast of Asia Minor. To this group and their dialect is assigned the label Ionian, from Ionia, the name of their section in Asia Minor.

A century or so earlier than the Ionian migration just mentioned, beginning very shortly after the Trojan War, settlers from Thessaly and northeastern Greece had been crossing over to the northern shore of Asia Minor, including the large island of Lesbos, and had been settling in a region which came to be known as Aeolis, with its Aeolian dialect.

The dialect common to Arcadia and the island of Cyprus (called Arcado-Cyprian) is seen as resulting from the southward migration of an Arcadian family into the Peloponnesus, and subsequently to the island of Cyprus, during the period prior to the Trojan War.

An Achaean migration from Thessaly is supposed to account for the settlement in northern Greece known as Achaea, and is envisaged as having moved into the Argive plain in the Peloponnesus. Here the Achaeans are said to have become a part of the Mycenaean people and to have assumed peacefully the dominant role described by Homer in his account of the Trojan War. Certainly at the time of this war the rulers of Mycenae, exemplified by Agamemnon and his family, were Achaeans.

This traditional accounting for the dialects of early Greece as resulting from successive migrations from the north is thought by some scholars to have received a serious challenge, if not a reversal, in very recent years. This comes about because of the decipherment by the late Dr. Michael Ventris and Dr. John Chadwick, in 1953, of the so-called Linear B script used on tablets found earlier in Cnossos, Mycenae, and on the island of Pylos.

This script, antedating the Greek alphabet by some 500 years, and apparently devised originally for a non-Hellenic language, is found to have been the vehicle for a Greek dialect, specifically Achaean. Its decipherment makes available the information carried on four to five thousand clay tablets, relating mostly to current government affairs and inventories in Cnossos as of 1400 B.C., and in Mycenae and Pylos about 1200 B.C.

From the evidence thus released it is deemed clear that at least from 1400 to 1200 B.C., on Crete as well as in the Peloponnesus, one standard language was spoken, that is, Achaean. Some think that it was spoken on Crete as early as 1750 B.C., having been taken there by Achaean invaders from the mainland. There may have been, as a corollary of this unified language, a more or less formal political or military federation such as Homer implies in the *Iliad*, with Achaean Mycenae at its head.

Following this line of reasoning, the dialects known in historical times as Ionic, Aeolic, and Arcado-Cyprian are held to be best understood as differentiations from the Achaean common language, of which the Mycenaean Linear B script was for a considerable period the vehicle. The Greek alphabet proper, Semitic in its origin, was probably introduced into Greece at about the time of the Trojan War or shortly thereafter, perhaps by Phoenician traders. Hence any written records of these dialects fall after the Trojan War and within the historical period of Greek civilization.

Shortly after the conclusion of the Trojan War occurred the invasion, or series of inroads, of the Dorians, who descended into the Greek peninsula from the northwest, fanning out eastward into Thessaly, Boeotia, Phocis, Locris, and Elis, crossing the Corinthian Gulf at Naupactus ('Building of the Ships'), wresting Argos from the Achaeans, sacking Tiryns and Mycenae, settling notably in Laconia, meanwhile also subduing Crete and destroying the Minoan civilization there.

This invasion of course brought into Greece proper the so-called 'northwestern' or Dorian dialects. It also provided a very strong impetus to the movement of earlier Hellenic peoples to Asia Minor, a migration which has already been mentioned as following fairly closely the Trojan War. It should also be added that the Dorians themselves joined this eastward migration of Greek peoples to Asia Minor, settling to the south of Ionia in Halicarnassus, Rhodes, and the adjacent mainland and islands.

Whether or not we follow the newer thinking, growing out of revelations from the Linear B tablets, and conceive of an Achaean language unity up to the time of the Trojan War, certain it is that the dislocations and migrations following the Dorian invasion, or generally contemporary with it, would have ministered in the direction of breaking down any existing unity of speech and of moving toward differentiated dialects.

**The Classical Period** (from Homer to Alexander, about 330 B.C.). The classical period is said to begin with Homer because the *Iliad* and the *Odyssey*, hexameter poems centering about the Trojan War and anciently attributed to the Ionian poet Homer, constitute our earliest examples of Greek literature.

Concerning their traditional author and the date of their composition there has been endless controversy in modern times. We know that they were edited at the order of Pisistratus, the ruler of Athens, about 550 B.C., and so must have existed in finished form at that time. Herodotus wrote of Homer as having done his work not more than 400 years before himself, that is, about 830 B.C. Theopompus, the historian, represented Homer as active in 685 B.C. Aristarchus of Samothrace, writing about A.D. 150, assigned to Homer the date 1044, doubtless relating it to the supposed time of the fall of Troy.

Homer was said to be a native of Chios in Ionia. His poems have frequently been analyzed as having been written in the Ionian dialect, tempered to some extent by the inclusion of Aeolic and Achaean elements.

The composite nature of the language of these ancient poems has called forth elaborate explanations wherein sometimes an Aeolic 'first layer' is said to have been covered over by Ionic modifications and additions, or sometimes both the Ionic and Aeolic elements are seen as having been imposed upon an even earlier dialect. Their so-called 'epic dialect' has been regarded as highly artificial and synthetic, not like any Greek that was ever actually in use.

Scholars espousing the concept of the Achaean language as the common

Greek language for the period culminating in the Trojan War urge that
it is more natural to regard the 'epic dialect' of Homer as a late development of the Achaean, still containing within itself those elements
which would later be observable in the Ionic and Aeolic dialects.

Certain peculiarities of the Achaean language as revealed in studies
of the Linear B tablets seem to bear in this direction, for instance, the
second declension genitive singular ending in -οιο and an often used third
declension noun-ending in -ευς (genitive -εϝος, pronounced -ewos), both
so evident in Homer.

It will be interesting to see what will be the ultimate verdict of scholar-
ship with reference to this newer analytical approach to the *Iliad* and the
*Odyssey*. If it is sustained, and if these poems are taken as a late development of the Achaean language which flourished at least from 1400 to
1200 B.C., yielding soon thereafter to the more differentiated dialects, it
would appear that this would affect to some extent the ideas of scholars as
to the time when the Homeric poems were composed, moving this to
a considerably earlier period than now generally assigned.

The emergence of Athens as the undisputed intellectual and literary
leader of ancient Greece gave to the Attic Greek dialect (in the Ionic
family) a growing pre-eminence over the other dialects which have been
mentioned. Athens's long list of great writers and thinkers includes such
names as those of the tragic poets Aeschylus, Sophocles, and Euripides;
the comic poet Aristophanes; the historians Thucydides and Xenophon; Plato and Aristotle, philosophers; and the orator Demosthenes.
Generally speaking, 'classical Greek' is Attic Greek.

But the Attic dialect itself had to face new and changing times.
Xenophon's *Anabasis*, the account of the march of some 13,000 Greek
mercenaries into Persia with Cyrus the younger in 401 B.C. and their
retreat after the battle of Cunaxa, is itself a good example of Attic Greek.
But as Xenophon tells how Cyrus united in one army Greeks from Parrhasia, Boeotia, the Chersonese, Thessaly, Sparta, Stymphalia, Achaea,
Arcadia, Megara, Syracuse, and Miletus, to say nothing of an Egyptian
pilot, Persian allies, Thracian targeteers, and Cretan bowmen, he gives
an excellent intimation of the inevitability of a common dialect. And the
*Anabasis* itself, with its inclusion of elements foreign to the Attic dialect,
might even be cited as a forerunner.

Alexander himself was taught in Attic Greek, and in connection with
the spread of his domain this language, slightly modified by the languages
with which it came into contact, became the κοινὴ διάλεκτος, or 'common
dialect' of the world.

**Period of the κοινή** (from 330 B.C. to the building of Byzantium by Constantine, A.D. 330). This κοινή, or 'common' Greek, was the vehicle for the Septuagint translation of the Old Testament scriptures, made in Alexandria about 280 B.C. by a group of seventy (hence the name Septuagint) scholars. It was also the vehicle for the New Testament scriptures. Until less than a century ago these were the principal extant monuments of the κοινή Greek of this period, and scholars regarded the κοινή as a debasement of the classic Greek, as a dialect peculiar to the Hebrews and perhaps more Semitic than Greek. A. T. Robertson, in the introduction to his *A Grammar of the Greek New Testament*,[1] gives an excellent discussion of this problem.

But the discovery and publication of large numbers of papyri and inscriptions dating back to the κοινή period rapidly dispelled the theory just mentioned.[2] Robertson cites 186 words formerly supposed to be peculiar to 'Biblical Greek' which the papyri and inscriptions have shown were in common use elsewhere.

Scholarly studies of the Greek language have brought the realization that in every era of its history this language, as any language, has been used for literary and formal discourse on the one hand and, on the other, as a vehicle for ordinary speech, letter-writing, and the like—a vernacular. In the classical period of Greek literature there was a vernacular which to some extent was preserved. For example, in certain of the plays of Aristophanes words were used which were found nowhere else in Greek literature until they were seen again in the non-literary κοινή. They had been in the vernacular all the while.

There were writers of the κοινή period who still affected a pure Attic style. These were called the Atticists. Lucian is perhaps the best example. The historian Polybius wrote in literary κοινή. The Greek of the New Testament is for the most part non-literary κοινή, the everyday language of the people. It is simple and vigorous in its style. It makes much less use of subordinate constructions, more use of co-ordinate clauses (that is, it tends to be paratactical rather than hypotactical). It makes frequent use of the historical present tense and also shows a preference for direct rather than indirect discourse. Robertson[3] lists a number of specific points of grammar and syntax in which the κοινή differs from classical usage. Some of the most important of these are shown in the syntactical summary of this text (p. 266).

**The Byzantine Period** (from Constantine to the fall of Byzantium to the Turks, 1453). Byzantine Greek is, generally speaking, a simple con-

---

[1] Fourth edition, 1923.    [2] Ibid., pp. 65f.    [3] Ibid., pp. 62 ff.

tinuation of the κοινή. There were still occasional writers who clung to a pure, if anachronistic, Attic style. An example of this group was Procopius of Caesarea (518–610) who wrote histories of the time of Justinian and followed Herodotus and Thucydides for his models. But the copious writings of the Church Fathers and of the commentators upon classical authors and of the encyclopaedists and historians were for the most part in literary κοινή. During this period learned activities nearly ceased in Greece proper, and it was in Byzantium and Asia Minor and, for a time, in Alexandria that scholarly studies in Greek were kept alive.

 **The Period of Modern Greek.** Since the fall of Constantinople (old Byzantium) to the Turks in 1453, Greek has continued to be a vehicle for communication in the Orthodox Church. It is also the spoken and written language of the Greek people. As such it still exists both as a non-literary vernacular and also as a language of letters. The Greek newspapers, for example, endeavour to keep to the literary Greek (ἡ καθαρεύουσα). Tendencies already noted in the so-called period of the κοινή have continued and are reflected in the modern Greek. For example, Robertson[1] comments that the use of ἵνα in non-final clauses is 'too common for remark in the modern Greek'.

 By the same token, shifts in pronunciation which have long been a matter of familiar knowledge to paleographers because of their cropping out in mistakes in the copying of ancient manuscripts, are to be seen full-blown in the pronunciation of modern Greek. One such phenomenon is that known as *itacism*, or *iotacism*, by which term is meant the tendency to give the pronunciation of iota (English *e* as in *be*) to a number of other vowels and diphthongs, such as η, υ, ει, οι. ὑμεῖς and ἡμεῖς are alike pronounced 'emees'. (Note also that the rough breathing is not pronounced.)

 Such in brief is the history of this great language which forms such an important part of our own, a history of change and yet of amazing persistence. Despite these continuing modifications which naturally occur in a living language, the Greek of today is surprisingly like its ancient prototype. On the basis of our knowledge of the non-literary Greek of earlier times gained from the papyri, Robertson[2] can declare that 'the modern Greek of popular speech does not differ materially from the vernacular Byzantine', and he quotes Professor G. N. Hatzidakis as saying: 'The language generally spoken today in the towns differs less from the common language of Polybius than this last differs from the language of Homer'.[3]

---

 [1] Ibid., p. 45.  [2] Ibid., p. 44.  [3] Ibid., p. 23.

From K. Brugmann[1] he adduces the opinion: 'With all the changes in this long history the standards of classicity have not varied greatly from Homer till now in the written style, while the Greek vernacular today is remarkably like the earliest known inscriptions of the folk speech in Greece.'

[1] *Griechische Grammatik*, 3 Aufl., 1900, p. 13.

# PART I

## GRAMMAR: READINGS FROM ST. JOHN

# LESSON 1

# The Alphabet

## 1. The letters of the Greek alphabet

| Letter | | Name of letter | Sound |
|---|---|---|---|
| A | α | alpha | f*a*ther |
| B | β | beta | *b*e |
| Γ | γ | gamma | *g*oing |
| Δ | δ | delta | *d*o |
| E | ε | epsilon | *g*et |
| Z | ζ | zeta | ad*z*e |
| H | η | eta | wh*ey* |
| Θ | θ | theta | *th*in |
| I | ι | iota | mach*i*ne, f*i*t |
| K | κ | kappa | *k*in |
| Λ | λ | lambda | *l*ay |
| M | μ | mu | *m*en |
| N | ν | nu | *n*ame |
| Ξ | ξ | xi | wa*x* |
| O | ο | omicron | *o*bey |
| Π | π | pi | *p*in |
| P | ρ | rho | *r*ing |
| Σ | σ, ς | sigma | *s*it |
| T | τ | tau | *t*ell |
| Y | υ | upsilon | gr*ü*n (German) |
| Φ | φ | phi | *ph*ysics |
| X | χ | chi | *Ch*aldean |
| Ψ | ψ | psi | li*ps* |
| Ω | ω | omega | g*o*ld |

## 2. Pronunciation. Vowels and consonants

The pronunciation of each letter is indicated in the pronunciation of the name of that letter. Therefore the student should memorize and practice the names of the Greek letters. To know the names of the letters is to know the pronunciation of the letters.

The vowels in Greek correspond to the English vowels *a*, *e*, *i*, *o*, and *u*, and are as follows: α, ε and η, ι, ο and ω, and υ. ε has a shortened quality of η, ο a similarly restricted quality of ω. Each of the vowels is pronounced as is the corresponding letter in its own name word, e.g. ε is valued as the *e* in g*e*t, which is also its value in its own name word *epsilon*; η is valued as the *e* in wh*e*y, which is also its value in the name word *eta*.

The remaining letters are consonants. Each of these has the same pronunciation as does the opening sound of its own name; e.g. β is the *b* in *beta*, γ is the *g* in *gamma*.

Learn the Greek alphabet, with special attention to the small letters, which are more frequently used than the capitals. Practice writing the Greek letters. The teacher should demonstrate the best way for writing these.

**3. Gamma nasal.** Note that while γ by itself is pronounced like hard *g*, when it is combined with another γ or with κ, χ, or ξ the combination is pronounced like *ng* in si*ng*, *nk* in i*nk*, *nch* in a*nch*or, or the *nx* in ly*nx*.

**4. Diphthongs.** When two vowels are pronounced as one sound the combination is called a diphthong. There are eight proper diphthongs in Greek, pronounced as follows (not necessary to memorize):

αι as *ai* in *aisle*        οι as *oi* in *oil*
αυ as *au* in *kraut*        ου as *ou* in *soup*
ει as *ei* in *vein*         υι as *ui* in *quick*
ευ and ηυ pronounced as *eh-oo* and *ay-oo*

ᾳ, ῃ, and ῳ are called *improper diphthongs*. The iota subscript does not affect their pronunciation.

**5. Breathings.** Each word which begins with a vowel or a diphthong uses also on its first syllable a breathing mark, rough or smooth. The rough breathing (ʻ) is pronounced as *h*; the smooth breathing (ʼ) does not affect the pronunciation of the word at all.

**6. Reading exercise**

Read aloud the Greek in the following passage (*John 1 : 1-7*), practicing the pronunciation of each word:

1:1    Ἐν ἀρχῇ ἦν ὁ λόγος, καὶ ὁ λόγος ἦν πρὸς τὸν θεόν, καὶ θεὸς
2, 3    ἦν ὁ λόγος. οὗτος ἦν ἐν ἀρχῇ πρὸς τὸν θεόν. πάντα δι᾽ αὐτοῦ
4    ἐγένετο, καὶ χωρὶς αὐτοῦ ἐγένετο οὐδὲ ἓν ὃ γέγονεν. ἐν αὐτῷ

5 ζωὴ ἦν, καὶ ἡ ζωὴ ἦν τὸ φῶς τῶν ἀνθρώπων. καὶ τὸ φῶς ἐν τῇ
6 σκοτίᾳ φαίνει, καὶ ἡ σκοτία αὐτὸ οὐ κατέλαβεν. Ἐγένετο ἄνθρω-
7 πος, ἀπεσταλμένος παρὰ θεοῦ, ὄνομα αὐτῷ Ἰωάννης· οὗτος
ἦλθεν εἰς μαρτυρίαν, ἵνα μαρτυρήσῃ περὶ τοῦ φωτός, ἵνα πάντες
πιστεύσωσιν δι᾽ αὐτοῦ.

### 7. Purpose of the daily writing exercises

The writing exercises from day to day are for the purpose of giving the student a minimum of practice in writing with the Greek letters, at the same time causing him to go over items of material which he has already observed, whether in the day's assignment or in some previous lesson.

The exercises are not intended to be problem-solving situations but rather they are designed to require the student to apply quickly and in writing some of the grammar he has already observed. Hence an effort is made in each exercise to indicate clearly the precise clues which are needed for the assignment given. In short, these writing exercises are meant to provide a device for practice writing and quick review which shall not, it is hoped, steal any considerable amount of the student's daily study time.

### 8. Writing exercise for today's lesson

1. Write the small letters of the Greek alphabet three times using ruled paper or lines which have been ruled. Leave enough space between the lines, and between the letters in a line so that corrections may be indicated.

2. After practicing the pronunciation of the reading exercise above (*John I : I–7*), copy *vss. 5 through 7.*

### LESSON 2

# Greek Parts of Speech; Suggestions for Reading

### 9. Greek Parts of Speech

IN Greek literature there are nine distinct kinds of words, called 'parts of speech', as follows: the definite article, nouns, pronouns, adjectives, verbs, adverbs, prepositions, conjunctions, and interjections. The general functions of these parts of speech are given in a preliminary manner below.

**10.** The **definite article** in Greek is the word ὁ with its variations, corresponding to English *the*, and used to modify the application of a noun. The Greek has no indefinite article corresponding to English *a, an*. The effect of the English indefinite article is obtained in Greek by using a noun without article, or modified by the indefinite pronoun τὶς, *any*. The definite article in one of its three genders, ὁ masculine, ἡ feminine, and τό neuter, is regularly used in vocabularies and word lists to indicate the gender of a noun.

**11.** A **noun** is the name of a person, place, thing, quality, action, or idea. Examples: ἄνθρωπος, *man*; πεδίον, *plain*; ἅρμα, *chariot*; ἡ πίστις, (the) *faith*; δρόμος, *running*; φόβος, *a fear*.

**12.** A **pronoun** is a word which may take the place of a noun, e.g. ἐκεῖνος, *that* (man); τοῦτο, *this* (thing). Nouns and pronouns are called *substantives*.

**13.** An **adjective** is a word which qualifies or describes a noun, e.g. ἀγαθός, *good, noble*. The definite article, nouns, pronouns, and adjectives vary their endings to show five uses, or *cases*: nominative (subject of sentence), genitive ('of'), dative ('to' or 'for'), accusative (object of verb), and vocative (person addressed).

**14.** A **verb** denotes *action* or *being*. If a verb takes an object it is called *transitive*, e.g. παίω, *I strike*. If it does not take an object it is called *intransitive*, e.g. βαίνω, *I go*. The Greek verb varies its form to show seven time qualities or *tenses*: present, imperfect (past indefinite), future, aorist (past definite), perfect (action presently complete), pluperfect (action completed in past time), and future perfect (action completed in future time).

**15.** An **adverb** modifies or qualifies a verb, e.g. σχολαίως βαίνειν, *to walk slowly*.

**16.** A **preposition** governs a noun, e.g. πρὸς τὸν ἄνθρωπον, *towards the man*.

**17.** A **conjunction** connects words or phrases, e.g. ἐγὼ καὶ σύ, *I and you*.

BRITISH MUSEUM

## *Manuscript Text from St. John 1*

From the fourth-century *Codex Sinaiticus*, one of the five most important manuscripts containing considerable portions of the entire Bible. This manuscript gets its name from the fact that it was discovered in the Greek Monastery of St. Catharine on Mt. Sinai by Count Tischendorf in 1844. Like all of the oldest manuscripts, it is in uncials—round shaped capitals—with no spacing between words. There are four columns on each page. Now in the British Museum.

**18.** An **interjection** is an exclamatory word expressing feeling, e.g. ὦ, *oh!*

### 19. Suggestions for reading the Greek

In life we learn first how to use our language in an elementary imitative manner and the reasons for it later. This is the intended procedure in this course. At first the student should read simply, with the aid of the daily new word list, the footnotes, and, if needed, the cumulative vocabulary and the daily translations, which begin at 408.

It will be found that nouns, pronouns, and adjectives vary their endings—that is, they are *inflected*—to show number, gender, and case. The daily new word list shows the nominative case of each noun, and also the ending of the genitive (the 'of' case). The noun's gender is also shown by the presence of the article ὁ, ἡ, or τό, as mentioned above. In the case of pronouns and adjectives the endings for all three genders are indicated in the word list.

The student will also observe that, as already stated, the verbs show changes both in their endings and in their beginnings—that is, they are *conjugated*—to show person (*I, you, he,* etc.), number (*singular, plural,* etc.), tense (time), mood (*indicative, subjunctive,* etc.), and voice (*active, passive,* etc.). But for purposes of early translation, knowing the root or primary meaning of the words and, from the translation, how the sentence is supposed to go, the student will be able to fit the words into a meaningful pattern and to make progress in the use of the language.

From the start each new *simple* (i.e. without prefix) verb is listed with its *principal parts*. A complete, or *regular* verb has six principal parts, each being the key to an entire *tense system*. These six, or as many of them as a given verb has, are always given in the same order, namely, (1) *present*, (2) *future*, (3) *aorist* (past definite), (4) *perfect active*, (5) *perfect middle*[1] *and passive*, and (6) *aorist passive*. Some verbs are *defective*, and lack one or more of the principal parts.

If the student is observant, he will be able to tell from which principal part a given verb form comes. Also he will learn to identify the tenses of the principal parts. For instance, he sees the form γέγονε from the verb γίγνομαι (or γίνομαι), *to become*. Looking at γίγνομαι in the word list he notes that it shows only the first four principal parts, lacking the last two. γέγονε compares closely with the fourth principal part γέγονα, the perfect. Hence γέγονε must be perfect. He also notes from the daily

---

[1] Verbs in the middle voice generally represent the subject as acting *upon* or *for* itself.

translation that the word is translated *has become* or *has been made*. Thus he is enabled to place the form.

During this stage it is quite important to memorize faithfully the first form and primary meaning of each new word which is starred for frequency in the daily word list. At the beginning of the course, this includes a large proportion of the words in the new word lists; during the latter part of the course, a small part only. No proper names are starred for memorizing because it is felt that the student can always read these. The importance or frequency of a given word in the reading passages *of this course only* has been the criterion for starring it. Do not memorize the words until after using them in the reading and translation. Write the words in addition to pronouncing them.

It will also be helpful if a solid period of time in each class session can be given to review reading, and to the reading of the advance lesson with the teacher's help. Unison translating by the class has been found a useful device.

Later in the course the student will be shown exactly how the nouns, pronouns, and adjectives are declined, and how the verbs are conjugated. With many of these items careful observation will be sufficient. A few key items will need to be mastered thoroughly to make them available as much-used tools in the later lessons.

The student is also urged to follow carefully the references in the reading footnotes. Otherwise he cannot have a full awareness of what he is doing in his translation work.

With the Greek words shown in the daily word lists the student will often find presented in capital letters an English derivative or related word. It is hoped that in presenting the new word list, preparatory to reading in class the translation passage being assigned for the new lesson, the teacher may be able to suggest briefly the line of relationship between the Greek word and its derivative, or related word.

For example, the word ἀρχή signifies a *being first*. This often relates to time, in the sense of a *beginning*. It sometimes relates to position, in the sense of *rulership*. Hence the relationship to MONARCH, *sole ruler*. Both teacher and student should also observe alertly the relationships of kindred Greek words to one another. Thus the verb ἄρχω, *to rule* or *to begin*, and the nouns ἄρχων, *ruler*, and ἀρχιτρίκλινος, *master of ceremonies*, are easily seen as related to ἀρχή. To point out in the textbook these multiplied relationships would require much space, and it is felt that awareness of them can be effected naturally and quickly through attention on the part of teacher and student.

## 20. New word list

*ἀρχή, -ῆς, ἡ, beginning, supreme power, realm. MONARCHY.

*αὐτός, αὐτή, αὐτό, gen. αὐτοῦ, αὐτῆς, αὐτοῦ, in other than nom., him, her, it; with article ὁ αὐτός, the same; following the word modified, ὁ λόγος αὐτός, intensive, the word itself. AUTOGRAPH.

*γίνομαι or γίγνομαι, γενήσομαι, ἐγενόμην, γέγονα, to be, become, show one's self; ἐγένετο, he, she, or it became or came to be; γέγονε, he, she, or it has come to be. GENESIS.

*διά, with gen., through; with acc., through, on account of. DIATHERMY.

*εἰμί, ἔσομαι, to be; ἦν, he, she, it was.

*εἷς, μία, ἕν, gen. ἑνός, μιᾶς, ἑνός, one.

*ἐν, with dat., in.

*θεός, -οῦ, ὁ, god. THEOLOGY.

*καί, and.

*λόγος, -ου, ὁ, word. THEOLOGY.

*ὁ, ἡ, τό, gen. τοῦ, τῆς, τοῦ, def. article the, sometimes used by itself as pronoun the one, the ones.

*ὅς, ἥ, ὅ, gen. οὗ, ἧς, οὗ, rel. pronoun who, which.

οὐδέ, but not, and not, not even.

*οὗτος, αὕτη, τοῦτο, gen. τούτου, ταύτης, τούτου, this, already mentioned.

*πᾶς, πᾶσα, πᾶν, gen. παντός, πάσης, παντός, the whole, all. PAN-AMERICAN.

*πρός, with gen., from; with dat., at; with acc., to, toward.

χωρίς, with gen., without, apart from.

## 21. Reading passage

Read and translate the following passage (*John 1:1–3*) with the help of the word list:

1:1   Ἐν ἀρχῇ ἦν ὁ λόγος, καὶ ὁ λόγος ἦν πρὸς τὸν θεόν, καὶ θεὸς
2, 3   ἦν ὁ λόγος. οὗτος ἦν ἐν ἀρχῇ πρὸς τὸν θεόν. πάντα δι' αὐτοῦ ἐγένετο, καὶ χωρὶς αὐτοῦ ἐγένετο οὐδὲ ἓν ὃ γέγονεν.

1. ἦν: from εἰμί, to be, in today's word list. πρὸς τὸν θεόν: towards (the) God, or with God. Drop the article in translating. The English does not use it in this way. τόν: definite article, the. See ὁ, ἡ, τό, in word list.

3. πάντα: all things. From πᾶς in today's word list. δι' αὐτοῦ: for διὰ αὐτοῦ, through him. A short final vowel of most prepositions may be dropped when the next word begins with a vowel. The omission is marked by an apostrophe. This is called elision and is particularly frequent with prepositions, like διά, ἐπί, ὑπό, etc. ἐγένετο: see principal parts of γίγνομαι (γίνομαι) in today's word list. This form comes through ἐγενόμην, the aorist (past definite) tense. ἕν: neuter nominative of εἷς (see word list). Because neuter, it has the sense, one thing. Distinguish this from ἐν, in. γέγονεν: see principal parts of γίγνομαι (or γίνομαι) in today's word list. The final -ν is not a regular part of the verb form but is added for euphony and is called ν-movable. It is added to words ending in -σι or to verbs of the third person ending in -ε when the next word begins with a vowel or at the end of a sentence. It will thus be seen very frequently.

## 22. Writing exercise

1. From today's word list copy three nouns each preceded by its definite article (e.g. ἡ ἀρχή) and three pronouns giving three genders for each (nominative cases only).
2. Copy the reading passage for today (*John 1:1–3*).

# LESSON 3

# Syllabication and Accent

R U L E S of accent, or of anything else in Greek, for that matter, are merely attempted descriptions of linguistic process. Not infrequently an exception or apparent exception to the 'rule' is observed, generally showing only that there is a further principle involved, a factor not fully appreciated previously, something further to be explained.

## 23. Syllables

Each word has as many syllables as it has separate vowels and diphthongs. Single consonants, and combinations of consonants which may stand at the beginning of a word, are placed at the beginning of their syllable. The student's ear for English words will serve as a criterion here. Other combinations of consonants are divided. For example, ἄν-θρω-πος, πολ-λά-κις, πίμ-πλη-μι.

A syllable is long by nature when it contains a long vowel or a diphthong. Of the vowels, η and ω are always long, ε and ο always short. α, ι, and υ are sometimes long, sometimes short, and their quantity (i.e. long or short) has to be observed as they are used. The diphthongs are all regularly long.

The last syllable of a word is called the *ultima*; the next to the last is the *penult* (Latin *paene ultima*, 'almost last'), and the third syllable from the end is the *antepenult* (Latin *ante*, 'before the almost last').

## 24. Accents

There are three accents, the *acute* (′) which may stand on any of the last three syllables, the *circumflex* (⌢) which may stand on one of the last two syllables, and the *grave* (`) which stands only on the ultima.

The antepenult cannot be accented if the ultima is long by nature.

The circumflex can stand only on a syllable which is long by nature.

**25. Principles governing the location of accent**

The student will desire to have some understanding as to why the accent falls on a given syllable, and as to what principles determine which particular accent is used. The matter of *location* of accent will be considered first, and in this connection two general principles will be noted.

*The accent on verb forms is recessive*; it moves as far back from the end of the word as the length, or quantity, of the ultima will permit. This means that if the ultima is long by nature the accent will fall on the penult; if it is short, the accent falls on the antepenult (it cannot move back farther than the antepenult). Note, for example, κα-τα-λαμ-βά-νει where the ultima contains a diphthong and is long, but κα-τε-λάμ-βα-νε where the ultima is short.

*The accent of nouns, pronouns, and adjectives is persistent.* It tries to stay on the same syllable on which it starts, and moves therefrom only as long as compelled to. The student learns by observation what is the characteristically accented syllable in a noun, pronoun, or adjective.

For example, the noun ἀρχή, *beginning*, accents the ultima in its first form, the nominative, and this syllable is accented throughout the noun's declension. The noun ἄν-θρω-πος, *man*, characteristically accents the antepenult. But in the genitive, ἀν-θρώ-που, and in the dative, ἀν-θρώ-πῳ, the ultima is long. By rule the antepenult cannot then be accented, so the accent moves to the penult. But with the accusative, ἄν-θρω-πον, the last syllable is again short and the accent returns to its original syllable.

A word with acute accent on the ultima is said to be *oxytone*.

**26. Principles governing the kind of accent used**

If the accent is on the antepenult it is always acute (´).

If the accent is on the penult it is a circumflex (˜) if the penult is long by nature and the ultima short, e.g. δῶ-ρον. Otherwise it is acute, as λό-γος, δώ-ρῳ.

If the accent is on the ultima it is circumflex by special rule, otherwise acute. But the acute accent on a final syllable is replaced by the grave if the word is followed by another word (except an enclitic) in the same sentence without intervening punctuation.

For example, in *John 1:1* in yesterday's lesson ἀρ-χῇ uses the circumflex on the ultima because there is a rule that with feminine nouns of the α-declension, the genitive and dative cases, if accented on the ultima, take a circumflex. καὶ has a grave because followed by another word without intervening punctuation. θε-όν takes acute because followed by a comma. The accent or breathing marks are regularly placed over the vowel or diphthong of the syllable where they occur. In the case of a diphthong, the accent and breathing marks are placed over the second letter of the diphthong.

### 27. Elision

When a word ending in a short vowel immediately precedes a word beginning with a vowel or diphthong, the final vowel of the preceding word is sometimes dropped, or *elided*, and the omission indicated with an apostrophe. For example, ἀπὸ αὐτοῦ, *from him*, may be written ἀπ᾽ αὐτοῦ. When a verb beginning with a vowel or diphthong is compounded by the prefixing of a preposition ending in a vowel, the prefix usually drops its final vowel (no apostrophe is used), as κατεσθίω for κατα-εσθίω, *to devour*.

### 28. Proclitics and enclitics

A *proclitic* ('leaning forward') is a monosyllabic word which has no accent of its own but is pronounced with the following word, as ἐν τῷ πεδίῳ, *in the plain*.

An *enclitic* ('leaning in *or* backward') is a word which has no accent of its own and is pronounced with the preceding word, as ἀρχή τις, *a certain beginning*. Note that a final acute accent does not change to grave when the following word is an enclitic.

### 29. Punctuation marks

The *comma* (,) and the *period* (.) are as in English. The Greek also uses occasionally a *colon*, a point above the line (·). The question mark is like the English semicolon (;).

### 30. New word list

*ἄνθρωπος, -ου, ὁ, man. ANTHROPO-
LOGY.

*ἀποστέλλω (see στέλλω for prin.
parts), *to send forth, send*; ἀπεσταλμένος, *having been sent forth*.
APOSTLE.

·*ζωή, -ῆς, ἡ, *life, means of living*.
ZOOLOGY.

'Ιωάννης, -ου, ὁ, *John*.

*καταλαμβάνω (see λαμβάνω for
prin. parts), *to seize upon, arrest,
discover, grasp*.

*λαμβάνω, λήψομαι or λήμψομαι,
ἔλαβον, εἴληφα, εἴλημμαι, ἐλήφθην, *to take*. EPILEPSY.

*ὄνομα, -ατος, τό, *name*. ONOMATO-
POEIA.

*οὐ, οὐκ, οὐχ, *not*.

*παρά, with gen., *from beside*; with
dat., *beside*; with acc., *to, towards, beyond.* PARATHYROID.
*σκοτία, -ας, ἡ, *darkness.*
*στέλλω, στελῶ, ἔστειλα, ἔσταλκα,
ἔσταλμαι, ἐστάλην, *to send.*

*φαίνω, φανῶ, ἔφηνα, πέφηνα, πέ-
φασμαι, ἐφάνην, *to show, shine*;
mid., *to appear.* PHENOMENON.
φῶς, φωτός, τό, *light.* PHOTOGRAPH.

## 31. Reading passage (*John* 1:4-6)

1:4, 5   Ἐν αὐτῷ ζωὴ ἦν, καὶ ἡ ζωὴ ἦν τὸ φῶς τῶν ἀνθρώπων. καὶ τὸ
φῶς ἐν τῇ σκοτίᾳ φαίνει, καὶ ἡ σκοτία αὐτὸ οὐ κατέλαβεν.
6   Ἐγένετο ἄνθρωπος, ἀπεσταλμένος παρὰ θεοῦ, ὄνομα αὐτῷ
Ἰωάννης.

**4. ἐν:** has no accent because it is a proclitic. καί, ζωή, and τό have changed final acute accents to grave because followed by another word without intervening punctuation. **τῶν:** *of the,* from definite article ὁ in yesterday's word list. It need not be translated here, for the English does not use the definite article referring to *man* or *men* in a generic sense. τῇ in *vs. 5* is also the definite article.

**5. κατέλαβε(ν):** *grasped.* From καταλαμβάνω in today's word list. The principal parts are under the simple form λαμβάνω. (κατ)έλαβε comes through ἔλαβον, which is aorist (past definite) in tense.

**6. ἐγένετο:** from γίγνομαι (γίνομαι). See its principal parts. **ἄνθρωπος:** the nominative case accents the antepenult, whereas in *vs. 4* the related form ἀνθρώπων accents the penult. This is because the latter has a long ultima (-ων) which will not permit the antepenult to be accented. Translate, *a man.* The Greek has no word for the indefinite article, *a, an.* **ἀπεσταλμένος:** *having been sent forth,* perfect passive participle of ἀποστέλλω.

## 32. Writing exercise

1. The following are all verb forms. Accent is therefore *recessive,* and in every instance there is no question whether the ultima (the last syllable) is long or short. Divide each word into syllables, and place an acute accent over the proper syllable in each (example, ἐ-λά-βο-μεν): (*a*) στελλομεν, (*b*) καταλαμβανεις, (*c*) φαινετε, (*d*) ἀποστελλετε, (*e*) ἐσταλκαμεν, (*f*) ἐφανης, (*g*) ἐλαβες, (*h*) κατελαμβανον.

2. The following are noun forms from nouns in today's word list, and have *persistent* accent. The word list shows on which syllables the accent characteristically falls. Divide each word into syllables and accent the proper syllable in each: (*a*) ζωαι, (*b*) ὀνοματι, (*c*) ἀνθρωποις, (*d*) σκοτια (*e*) ἀνθρωπον, (*f*) ζωας, (*g*) σκοτιας, (*h*) ὀνοματων.

# LESSON 4

# Greek Nouns

**33.** A NOUN is a word which serves as the name of a person, place, thing, quality, action, or idea.

## 34. Use of nouns

In normal use a noun may be the subject, direct object, or indirect object of a verb, or it may be the object of a preposition. In modern languages, such as English, the precise use of a noun in a given sentence is usually indicated by its *position* in the sentence, or by the use of prepositions and helping words. Take, for example, the sentence: *John sent his brother a book of stories.*

Here are four nouns: *John, brother, book, stories.* The noun *John* is indicated as the subject of the sentence by the fact that it is placed first, before the verb. The noun *brother* is shown to be the indirect object, the one *to* or *for whom* the action is done, by its position right after the verb. The same thought could have been conveyed by using, instead of this position, the helping word *to*—a preposition. Then the prepositional phrase *to his brother* could have been moved around in the sentence without changing the thought.

The noun *book*, by being placed directly after the verb (except for the indirect object), is indicated to be the direct object of the verb *sent*. The noun *stories* is shown to be a qualification or connection of the preceding noun *book* by being connected to it with the preposition *of*. Thus the intent of the nouns, their use, is shown by their position or by the use of helping words and not by changes in the form of the nouns themselves.

In Greek, however, actual changes are made in the form of a word to indicate just what is its use in a sentence or in a clause. These word-modifications are referred to generally as *inflections*, and Greek and Latin are said to be *inflected* languages, as compared with English and some of the modern languages, which are said to be relatively *uninflected*. The various changes or inflections which take place in nouns, pronouns, and adjectives are called *cases*, and when one gives in order the cases of a noun he is *declining* it or giving its *declension*.

## 35. The cases

There are four cases in common use in Greek, generally recognizable by their endings. These cases are as follows:

1.  The *nominative* case, which usually shows that the word is the subject of its sentence or clause.
2.  The *genitive* case, which indicates that the noun is used to show possession or qualification, often shown in English by the preposition *of* (note the phrase 'a book *of stories*' in the sentence above).
3.  The *dative* case, which generally indicates the indirect object of a verb. The English would often say 'to' or 'for'.
4.  The *accusative* case, showing most often that the noun is used as a direct object.

There is also a *vocative* case which is used for a person or thing being addressed or called. It is often the same in form as is the nominative case and can be noted as the student meets it in actual reading.

A more careful discussion of the cases is given in the syntactical summary (491 ff.) and will be referred to later from time to time. The cases other than the nominative and vocative are called the *oblique*, i.e. collateral, cases. The student should also note that in addition to their grammatical meanings, the cases (particularly the oblique cases) have spatial significance. For example, the genitive case is used to indicate *separation* (is sometimes called *ablative*, i.e. separative). These spatial qualities of the cases are used and emphasized by the prepositions, as will now be indicated.

## 36. Use of nouns with prepositions

In addition to the uses of the cases just noted, in Greek as in English, nouns are used in prepositional phrases, e.g. 'he goes *to the city*' ; 'he comes *from the country*'.

Greek prepositions call for their object sometimes in the genitive, sometimes in the dative, and sometimes in the accusative case. The primary idea of the prepositions is spatial. When a preposition uses a noun in the accusative case the primary idea is usually *motion towards* a place or objective. The dative case with a preposition usually depicts *place where*, and the genitive case with a preposition carries the idea of *place from which*, the thought of separation. The following simple chart will help the student to keep these three basic ideas in mind.

Some prepositions use all three cases as, for example, παρά (cf. our word *parallel*). With the accusative it means *to the side of, to*. With the dative it means *beside*. With the genitive it means *from beside*. Of course, these *basic* meanings quickly lend themselves to more derived ideas. The word εἰς, which means *into*, can also mean *to such an objective*, or *for such a purpose*. περί, which means *around, about*, can refer to a report *from* or *concerning*, just as we say, *I have heard about him*.

## 37. Number in Greek nouns and verbs

The endings of Greek nouns and verbs are capable of indicating three types of number: *singular*, meaning one person or thing; *plural*, meaning more than one; and *dual*, meaning exactly two. The dual number is used chiefly in poetry and will not be emphasized in this text. It can be comprehended quite easily when met in the reading of Greek authors.

## 38. Gender

As before mentioned incidentally, there are three genders in Greek: *masculine, feminine*, and *neuter*. The gender of a Greek noun can often be seen from its endings, but the definite article, ὁ, ἡ, τό, is used in lexicons and word lists where it is desired to indicate gender clearly.

## 39. New word list

*ἀλλά, but.

*εἰς, with acc., *into, to*.

*ἐκεῖνος, ἐκείνη, ἐκεῖνο, gen. ἐκείνου, ἐκείνης, ἐκείνου, demonstr. *that*.

*ἔρχομαι, ἐλεύσομαι, ἦλθον, ἐλήλυθα, to go, come; ἦλθεν, *he, she*, or *it went, came*.

*ἵνα, *that, in order that*.

*μαρτυρέω, μαρτυρήσω, ἐμαρτύρησα, μεμαρτύρηκα, μεμαρτύρημαι, ἐμαρτυρήθην, to *bear witness*;

ἵνα μαρτυρήσῃ, *that he may* or *might bear witness*. MARTYR.

*μαρτυρία, -ας, ἡ, *witness, testimony*.

*περί, with gen., *about, concerning*; with dat., *round, about* (of position); with acc., *around* (of motion). PERISCOPE.

*πιστεύω, πιστεύσω, ἐπίστευσα, πεπίστευκα, πεπίστευμαι, ἐπιστεύθην, to *trust, believe*.

**40. Reading passage** (*John 1:7, 8*)

1:7   Οὗτος ἦλθεν εἰς μαρτυρίαν, ἵνα μαρτυρήσῃ περὶ τοῦ φωτός, ἵνα
  8   πάντες πιστεύσωσιν δι᾽ αὐτοῦ. οὐκ ἦν ἐκεῖνος τὸ φῶς, ἀλλ᾽ ἵνα
     μαρτυρήσῃ περὶ τοῦ φωτός.

7. ἦλθε(ν): from ἔρχομαι, *to go* or *come*. See its principal parts in the vocabulary. This form is aorist (past definite). **εἰς μαρτυρίαν**: *for a witness*. Here the preposition εἰς, *into*, *to*, expresses end or purpose. **πάντες**: *all* (*men*). From πᾶς, πᾶσα, πᾶν, *each*, *all*. **πιστεύσωσι(ν)**: the κοινή frequently uses ν-movable before a word beginning with a consonant (482. 1). Compare 21, note on *vs. 3*, above. **δι᾽ αὐτοῦ**: *through him*. The basic idea of διά is *through*. This may be thought of as motion *towards* or motion *from*. Hence διά uses sometimes accusative, sometimes genitive. Here the genitive gives the idea of *person from whom*, the thought of *source* or *agency*.
8. **τὸ φῶς**: the neuter article τό shows that φῶς is a neuter noun. The gender of a noun is shown by the definite article (ὁ, ἡ, or τό) used with it.

**41. Comprehension exercise**

1. Give the name of the Greek case for each of the following italicized nouns as used: (*a*) The *darkness* was dense. (*b*) He did this for the *man*. (*c*) He wronged his *brother*. (*d*) The *tree* of *life* was there.

2. According to the paragraph on the use of nouns with prepositions, give the Greek *case* which would be needed for the noun in each of the following prepositional phrases: (*a*) He stayed *in the garden*. (*b*) He sent the book *to the city*. (*c*) Several men arrived *from Ephesus*. (*d*) The spear rested *beside the tent*.

# LESSON 5

# Nouns of the *a*-Declension

**42.** O N E family or declension of Greek nouns has case endings which, despite individual exceptions, are characterized by α, and this group of nouns is known as the α-declension.

The nouns of the α-declension end in ᾱ, η, or short -α (feminines), and in ᾱς and ης (masculines). When the stem (i.e. the uninflected portion of the noun) ends in ε, ι, or ρ (as in the word σκοτία, *darkness*) the endings are characterized in both singular and plural by α. When the stem ends in other than ε, ι, or ρ (as in ἀρχή, *beginning*) the endings in the singular are characterized by η, the plurals by ᾱ.

The following are some sample inflections for reference in reading. They need not be memorized at this time.

## 43. Feminines

First to be noticed are those whose singular endings are in η (stems do not end in ε, ι, or ρ) and in ᾱ (stems end in ε, ι, ρ). Note how the definite article 'agrees' with its noun as to case:

|  | *Singulars* |  |  | *Plurals* |  |
|------|-----------|----------------------|------------|-----------|-----------------|
| Nom. | ἡ ἀρχή | the beginning | αἱ ἀρχαί | the beginnings |
| Gen. | τῆς ἀρχῆς | of the beginning | τῶν ἀρχῶν | of the beginnings |
| Dat. | τῇ ἀρχῇ | to or for the beginning | ταῖς ἀρχαῖς | to or for the beginnings |
| Acc. | τὴν ἀρχήν | the beginning | τὰς ἀρχάς | the beginnings |

The stem of ζωή ends in other than ε, ι, or ρ :

| ζωή | a life | ζωαί | lives |
|-----|--------|------|-------|
| ζωῆς | of a life | ζωῶν | of lives |
| ζωῇ | to or for a life | ζωαῖς | to or for lives |
| ζωήν | a life | ζωάς | lives |

The stem of σκοτία ends in ι, and its endings are all characterized by ᾱ:

| σκοτία | darkness | σκοτίαι | darknesses |
|--------|----------|---------|-----------|
| σκοτίας | of darkness | σκοτιῶν | of darknesses |
| σκοτίᾳ | to or for darkness | σκοτίαις | to or for darknesses |
| σκοτίαν | darkness | σκοτίας | darknesses |

Next for attention are the so-called 'short-α nouns'. They end in short -α in the nominative and accusative singular (no matter what the stem ending). But the endings of the genitive and dative singular revert to ᾱ if the stem ends in ε, ι, or ρ—otherwise to η. The plurals are the same as with the ᾱ or η nouns. Short-α nouns may be recognized by the fact that they accent the antepenult in the nominative and accusative singular and in the nominative plural (where the final αι is reckoned short).

τράπεζα ends in short -α in nominative and accusative singular, and the stem ends in other than ε, ι, or ρ :

| τράπεζα | a table | τράπεζαι | tables |
|---------|---------|----------|--------|
| τραπέζης | of a table | τραπεζῶν | of tables |
| τραπέζῃ | to or for a table | τραπέζαις | to or for tables |
| τράπεζαν | a table | τραπέζας | tables |

ἀλήθεια ends in short -α, and the stem ends in ι:

| ἀλήθεια | truth | ἀλήθειαι | truths |
| ἀληθείας | of truth | ἀληθειῶν | of truths |
| ἀληθείᾳ | to or for truth | ἀληθείαις | to or for truths |
| ἀλήθειαν | truth | ἀληθείας | truths |

### 44. Masculines

The masculine nouns of the α-declension have a ς-ending in the nominative singular and the ου-ending in the genitive singular. Otherwise their endings are the same as with the feminines. The masculine article is given, showing the gender.

προφήτης has a stem ending in other than ε, ι, or ρ:

| ὁ προφήτης | the prophet | οἱ προφῆται | the prophets |
| τοῦ προφήτου | of the prophet | τῶν προφητῶν | of the prophets |
| τῷ προφήτῃ | to or for the prophet | τοῖς προφήταις | to or for the prophets |
| τὸν προφήτην | the prophet | τοὺς προφήτας | the prophets |

The stem of 'Ηλίας ends in ι:

| 'Ηλίας | Elias | 'Ηλίᾳ | to or for Elias |
| 'Ηλίου | of Elias | 'Ηλίαν | Elias |

**45.** Note the following observations about these nouns of the α-declension:

1. The genitive plural always has a circumflex on the ultima no matter where the accent falls characteristically.
2. Where the last syllable is characteristically accented, the genitive and dative both singular and plural take the circumflex, as in ζωῆς and ἀρχῇ.
3. Final αι in the nominative plural, though a diphthong, is reckoned short in determining accent. This can be seen in προφῆται and τράπεζαι.
4. The nouns with stems ending in ε, ι, or ρ (as σκοτία, μάχαιρα, 'Ηλίας) are characterized by α-endings throughout. But stems ending otherwise are characterized by η-endings in the singular.
5. τρά-πε-ζα is recognized as a 'short-α' noun by the fact that its accent in the nominative is on the antepenult. The short-α ending occurs only in the nominative and accusative singular.

## 46. New word list

ἀληθινός, -ή, -όν, true.
*γιγνώσκω or γινώσκω, γνώσομαι,
ἔγνων, ἔγνωκα, ἔγνωσμαι, ἐγνώσθην, to know, learn to know.
GNOSTIC, KNOW.
*δέ, postpositive conj., but, and.
*δίδωμι, δώσω, ἔδωκα, δέδωκα,
δέδομαι, ἐδόθην, to give; ἔδωκεν,
he, she, or it gave. DOSE.
ἐξουσία, -ας, ἡ, power, freedom,
right, possibility.
*ἴδιος, ἰδία, ἴδιον, one's own. IDIOM.

*κόσμος, -ου, ὁ, order, ornament,
universe, world. COSMETIC, COSMIC.
*ὅσος, ὅση, ὅσον, as much as, as
many as.
παραλαμβάνω (see λαμβάνω for
prin. parts) to receive; παρέλαβον,
I or they received.
*τέκνον, -ου, τό, child, one born.
φωτίζω, φωτίσω, ἐφώτισα, πεφώτισμαι, ἐφωτίσθην, to enlighten,
illuminate. PHOTOGRAPH.

## 47. Reading passage (*John 1:9–12*)

1:9 Ἦν τὸ φῶς τὸ ἀληθινόν, ὃ φωτίζει πάντα ἄνθρωπον, ἐρχόμενον
10 εἰς τὸν κόσμον. ἐν τῷ κόσμῳ ἦν, καὶ ὁ κόσμος δι᾽ αὐτοῦ ἐγένετο,
11 καὶ ὁ κόσμος αὐτὸν οὐκ ἔγνω. εἰς τὰ ἴδια ἦλθεν, καὶ οἱ ἴδιοι
12 αὐτὸν οὐ παρέλαβον. ὅσοι δὲ ἔλαβον αὐτόν, ἔδωκεν αὐτοῖς
ἐξουσίαν τέκνα θεοῦ γενέσθαι, τοῖς πιστεύουσιν εἰς τὸ ὄνομα
αὐτοῦ.

9. ἦν: imperfect of εἰμί, to be. τὸ φῶς τὸ ἀληθινόν: when an adjective is used as an attributive, or immediate modifier of a noun, it may take one of two positions: either immediately before the noun, as τὸ ἀληθινὸν φῶς, or following the noun with article repeated, as here (489). ὅ: the neuter relative pronoun, from ὅς, ἥ, ὅ, who, which. This ὅ differs from the definite article ὁ in that it is accented. πάντα: accusative singular masculine of πᾶς, all, every. ἐρχόμενον: present participle of ἔρχομαι, to go or come.

10. ἐγένετο: from γίγνομαι (γίνομαι). See its principal parts. ἔγνω: from γιγνώσκω (γινώσκω). See its principal parts in today's word list.

11. τὰ ἴδια: τά, the neuter plural article, has the sense the things. The κοινή sometimes uses the adjective ἴδιος, one's own, as a sort of possessive pronoun (482. 16). Translate, (his) own things. ἦλθε(ν): from ἔρχομαι. οἱ ἴδιοι: here instead of τὰ ἴδια, his own things, occurs the masculine, οἱ ἴδιοι, which has the sense, his own men, or people. παρέλαβον: from (παρα)λαμβάνω. See principal parts of λαμβάνω in the cumulative vocabulary. Prefixed by παρά. The final α of the prefix is dropped, or elided, before the ε of ἔλαβον.

12. ἔδωκεν: from δίδωμι, to give. See today's new word list. γενέσθαι: the infinitive from ἐγενόμην, aorist tense of γίγνομαι (γίνομαι). Translate, to become. τοῖς πιστεύουσιν: as in vs. 11, here the definite article is used as a substantive. It is masculine and is modified by the participle of πιστεύω, to believe. Translate, to the ones believing.

## 48. Writing exercise

Write the following Greek noun forms of a-declension nouns, and give the simple translation for each (example: genitive singular of σκοτία:

σκοτίας, *of darkness*): (*a*) Dative plural of ζωή. (*b*) Genitive singular of
'Ηλίας. (*c*) Genitive plural of ἀλήθεια. (*d*) Accusative plural of ὁ προφήτης.
(*e*) Nominative plural of σκοτία. (*f*) Dative singular of τράπεζα. (*g*) Accusative singular of ζωή. (*h*) Dative plural of ἡ ἀρχή.

## LESSON 6
# Nouns of the *o*-Declension

PRACTICALLY all of the nouns whose endings are characterized by o
are either masculine or neuter in gender. The following are some sample
nouns declined so that the student may recognize accurately these case
endings as he meets them in reading. They need not be memorized here.

Three of these nouns occur in the reading passage for the preceding
lesson, or in today's reading passage. The definite article is shown as
agreeing, both in the masculine and in the neuter gender.

**49. Masculines**

| *Singulars* | | *Plurals* | |
|---|---|---|---|
| ὁ ἄνθρωπος | the man | οἱ ἄνθρωποι | the men |
| τοῦ ἀνθρώπου | of the man | τῶν ἀνθρώπων | of the men |
| τῷ ἀνθρώπῳ | to or for the man | τοῖς ἀνθρώποις | to or for the men |
| τὸν ἄνθρωπον | the man | τοὺς ἀνθρώπους | the men |
| θεός | a god | θεοί | gods |
| θεοῦ | of a god | θεῶν | of gods |
| θεῷ | to or for a god | θεοῖς | to or for gods |
| θεόν | a god | θεούς | gods |

**50. Neuters**

| | | | |
|---|---|---|---|
| τὸ τέκνον | the child | τὰ τέκνα | the children |
| τοῦ τέκνου | of the child | τῶν τέκνων | of the children |
| τῷ τέκνῳ | to or for the child | τοῖς τέκνοις | to or for the children |
| τὸ τέκνον | the child | τὰ τέκνα | the children |
| ἱερόν | a temple | ἱερά | temples |
| ἱεροῦ | of a temple | ἱερῶν | of temples |
| ἱερῷ | to or for a temple | ἱεροῖς | to or for temples |
| ἱερόν | a temple | ἱερά | temples |

**51. Notes on the examples**

Observe that in the o-declension the genitive plural does not invariably take the circumflex accent on the ultima, as in the α-declension (see ἀνθρώπων, τέκνων), but that when the accent does fall on the ultima the genitive and dative of both numbers call for the circumflex on the ultima.

Notice also here the operation of the principle of *persistent accent* in nouns, which was mentioned in 25. In the case of ἄν-θρω-πος it is learned by observation of the nominative singular that the accent falls characteristically on the antepenult. But by rule it cannot stay there if the ultima is long. In the genitive and dative singular the endings are long (-ου, -ῳ), so the accent moves to the penult. In the accusative singular ἄν-θρω-πον the ending is short, so the accent goes back to the antepenult. The same is true in the nominative plural ἄν-θρω-ποι, where the final -οι (just as we saw with final -αι) is reckoned short in determining accent. All the remaining case endings (-ων, -οις, -ους) are long, drawing the accent forward to the penult.

Note that in words where the accent characteristically falls on the penult (τέκ-νον) or on the ultima (θε-ός, ἱ-ε-ρόν) it does not move from its starting position but 'persists' there throughout.

Observe further that in the neuters, both in the singular and in the plural, the nominative and the accusative cases are the same in form.

**52. New word list**

αἷμα, -ατος, τό, blood. HAEMOPHILIA.

*ἀλήθεια, -ας, ἡ, truth.

*ἀνήρ, ἀνδρός, ὁ, man. PHILANDER.

γεννάω, γεννήσω, ἐγέννησα, γεγέννηκα, γεγέννημαι, ἐγεννήθην, to beget, bear; ἐγεννήθησαν, they were born.

*δόξα, -ης, ἡ, glory, good opinion. DOXOLOGY.

*ἐγώ, ἐμοῦ (or μου), I; ἡμεῖς, we; ἡμῖν, to or for us. EGOTIST.

*ἐκ, ἐξ, with gen., out of. ECCENTRIC.

*θεάομαι, θεάσομαι, ἐθεασάμην, τεθέαμαι, to behold. THEATER.

θέλημα, -ατος, τό, will.

μονογενής, μονογενές, only-begotten.

*πατήρ, πατρός, ὁ, father. PATERNAL.

*πλήρης, πλῆρες, full, full of (with gen.).

σάρξ, σαρκός, ἡ, flesh. SARCOPHAGUS.

σκηνόω, σκηνώσω, ἐσκήνωσα, to tent, dwell.

χάρις, -ιτος, ἡ, grace, favor. EUCHARIST.

*ὡς, as. A relative adverb of manner, described more fully in the cumulative vocabulary, back of book.

**53. Reading passage** (*John 1:13, 14*)

1:13    οἳ οὐκ ἐξ αἱμάτων οὐδὲ ἐκ θελήματος σαρκὸς οὐδὲ ἐκ θελήματος
14    ἀνδρὸς ἀλλ' ἐκ θεοῦ ἐγεννήθησαν. Καὶ ὁ λόγος σὰρξ ἐγένετο
καὶ ἐσκήνωσεν ἐν ἡμῖν, καὶ ἐθεασάμεθα τὴν δόξαν αὐτοῦ, δόξαν
ὡς μονογενοῦς παρὰ πατρός, πλήρης χάριτος καὶ ἀληθείας.

13. **οἳ**: different from the definite article οἱ in that it has an accent, and is not proclitic. It is the masculine plural of the relative pronoun ὅς, ἥ, ὅ, *who*. **ἐξ αἱμάτων**: note the final -ων. This is genitive plural. Literally this would translate, *out of bloods*. Note also that when followed by a vowel, the preposition is ἐξ; when followed by a consonant (as ἐκ θελήματος) it uses the form ἐκ. Translate, *of blood*. **ἐγεννήθησαν**: from γεννάω in today's word list, aorist passive.

14. **ἐσκήνωσε(ν)**: aorist tense of σκηνόω in today's list. **ἐν ἡμῖν**: has the sense, *among us*. It is dative plural of the very irregular (because much used) pronoun ἐγώ, *I*. **μονογενοῦς**: genitive singular of the adjective μονογενής. The expansion of this class of adjectives will be studied later. **πλήρης**: agrees with λόγος. **χάριτος καὶ ἀληθείας**: genitives with a word denoting fullness. The English, too, says *full of* (501).

**54. Writing exercise**

Write the following noun forms of o-declension nouns, and give the simple translation for each (example: genitive singular of ὁ ἄνθρωπος: τοῦ ἀνθρώπου, *of the man*): (*a*) Accusative plural of τὸ τέκνον. (*b*) Dative singular of ἄνθρωπος. (*c*) Dative singular of θεός. (*d*) Dative plural of τὸ ἱερόν. (*e*) Nominative plural of ὁ ἄνθρωπος. (*f*) Genitive plural of τέκνον. (*g*) Genitive plural of ὁ θεός. (*h*) Accusative singular of ἱερόν.

# LESSON 7

# Adjectives of the *a*- and *o*-Declensions

**55.** T H E student has had opportunity to observe the inflection of nouns in both the *a*- and *o*-declensions. He has also seen how the definite article agrees with its noun in number, gender, and case. This has been evident as the article has been declined with paradigms in all three genders. It has also been evident in the reading, where such phrases as τὴν δόξαν, *the glory*; περὶ τοῦ φωτός, *concerning the light*; ἐν τῇ σκοτίᾳ, *in the darkness*, have been met.

This all leads naturally to an observation of the declension of that group of adjectives which combines the characteristics of the *a*- and the *o*-declensions.

An adjective, as already intimated, is a word which modifies or qualifies a noun. It agrees with its noun in number, gender, and case. It may be *attributive*, attached closely to its noun. If so it stands either immediately preceding the noun, as τὸ ἀληθινὸν φῶς, *the true light*, or follows it with article repeated, as τὸ φῶς τὸ ἀληθινόν. If it stands elsewhere, it is being used in the *predicate*, as τὸ φῶς ἀληθινὸν ἦν, or ἀληθινὸν τὸ φῶς ἦν, *the light was true*.

Adjectives through use sometimes take on the quality of substantives, usually accompanied by the definite article, as τὰ ἴδια, *his own (things)*; οἱ ἴδιοι, *his own (men)*. This will be mentioned later in discussion of the article. The adjectives in today's lesson need not be memorized now. Later a memory assignment will be made.

**56.** The declension of an adjective follows all three genders, and this usually means three sets of endings. πρῶτος, *first*, is an adjective found in *vs. 15* of today's reading passage.

πρῶτος, *first*

| *Masculine* | *Feminine* | *Neuter* |
|---|---|---|
| πρῶτος | πρώτη | πρῶτον |
| πρώτου | πρώτης | πρώτου |
| πρώτῳ | πρώτῃ | πρώτῳ |
| πρῶτον | πρώτην | πρῶτον |
| πρῶτοι | πρῶται | πρῶτα |
| πρώτων | πρώτων | πρώτων |
| πρώτοις | πρώταις | πρώτοις |
| πρώτους | πρώτας | πρῶτα |

In *John 1:11* occurs the adjective ἴδιος, *one's own*, declined as follows:

| | | |
|---|---|---|
| ἴδιος | ἰδία | ἴδιον |
| ἰδίου | ἰδίας | ἰδίου |
| ἰδίῳ | ἰδίᾳ | ἰδίῳ |
| ἴδιον | ἰδίαν | ἴδιον |
| ἴδιοι | ἴδιαι | ἴδια |
| ἰδίων | ἰδίων | ἰδίων |
| ἰδίοις | ἰδίαις | ἰδίοις |
| ἰδίους | ἰδίας | ἴδια |

**57.** Occasionally there are adjectives of this group which omit the a-declension forms and use the same set of endings to represent both masculine and feminine. An example is αἰώνιος, *eternal,* which appears in the word list with two endings only, and is declined as follows:

| Masculine and Feminine | Neuter |
|---|---|
| αἰώνιος | αἰώνιον |
| αἰωνίου | αἰωνίου |
| αἰωνίῳ | αἰωνίῳ |
| αἰώνιον | αἰώνιον |
| αἰώνιοι | αἰώνια |
| αἰωνίων | αἰωνίων |
| αἰωνίοις | αἰωνίοις |
| αἰωνίους | αἰώνια |

**58.** The middle and passive participles of verbs are really three-ending adjectives just like πρῶτος, -η, -ον, and are so declined. The present participle of ἔρχομαι, *to go* or *come,* is ἐρχόμενος, -η, -ον, *going* (or *coming*). It occurs in *vs. 15* of the reading passage today. Its declension is as follows:

| Masculine | Feminine | Neuter |
|---|---|---|
| ἐρχόμενος | ἐρχομένη | ἐρχόμενον |
| ἐρχομένου | ἐρχομένης | ἐρχομένου |
| ἐρχομένῳ | ἐρχομένῃ | ἐρχομένῳ |
| ἐρχόμενον | ἐρχομένην | ἐρχόμενον |
| ἐρχόμενοι | ἐρχόμεναι | ἐρχόμενα |
| ἐρχομένων | ἐρχομένων | ἐρχομένων |
| ἐρχομένοις | ἐρχομέναις | ἐρχομένοις |
| ἐρχομένους | ἐρχομένας | ἐρχόμενα |

Note that where the stem of an adjective ends in ε, ι, or ρ the feminine forms use α-endings throughout (see ἴδιος) but otherwise η-endings are used in the singular (see πρῶτος, ἐρχόμενος).

**59. New word list**

*ἀντί, with gen., *instead of.* ANTI-PHONAL.

*εἴρω, ἐρῶ, εἶπον, εἴρηκα, εἴρημαι, ἐρρήθην, *to say*; εἶπον, *I* or *they said.*

*ἔμπροσθεν, *before.*

Ἰησοῦς, -οῦ, -οῦ, -οῦν, ὁ, *Jesus.*

κράζω, κράξω, ἔκραξα or ἔκραγον, κέκραγα, *to cry.*

*λέγω, λέξω, ἔλεξα, λέλεγμαι, ἐλέχθην, *to say, call, mean.* DIALECTIC.

Μωϋσῆς, -έως, ὁ, *Moses.*

νόμος, -ου, ὁ, law. NOMOLOGY.

ὀπίσω, *after.*

*ὅτι, conj., *that, for, because.*

πλήρωμα, -ατος, τό, *a filling, fullness.*

*πρῶτος, πρώτη, πρῶτον, *first.* PROTOTYPE.

Χριστός, -οῦ, ὁ, *the Anointed, Christ.*

**60. Reading passage** (*John 1:15–17*)

1:15 Ἰωάννης μαρτυρεῖ περὶ αὐτοῦ καὶ κέκραγεν λέγων· οὗτος ἦν
ὃν εἶπον· ὁ ὀπίσω μου ἐρχόμενος ἔμπροσθέν μου γέγονεν, ὅτι
16 πρῶτός μου ἦν. ὅτι ἐκ τοῦ πληρώματος αὐτοῦ ἡμεῖς πάντες
17 ἐλάβομεν, καὶ χάριν ἀντὶ χάριτος· ὅτι ὁ νόμος διὰ Μωϋσέως
ἐδόθη, ἡ χάρις καὶ ἡ ἀλήθεια διὰ Ἰησοῦ Χριστοῦ ἐγένετο.

15. μαρτυρεῖ: present, while κέκραγε(ν) is perfect. The Greek frequently uses an
historic present for vividness. This can be translated as a past tense or it can be kept
present without being out of place, as *John witnesses about him, and he has cried* . . . .
κέκραγε(ν): *has cried*; see principal parts of κράζω in today's word list. For ν-movable
before a consonant see 482. 1. ὅν: from the relative ὅς, ἥ, ὅ. Translate, *whom*, or *he (of)*
*whom*. The antecedent (pronoun) of a relative pronoun is often omitted. εἶπον: see
principal parts of εἴρω in today's word list. ὁ . . . ἐρχόμενος: here again is the definite
article with a participle. Translate, *the one coming*. ὀπίσω μου . . . πρῶτός μου:
ὀπίσω, *after, behind*, is an adverb of place, and is here used with the genitive of separation (508). πρῶτος, *first*, is an adjective used to imply comparison, and it takes here the
genitive of comparison (507). The ideas of *comparison* and *separation* are closely related.
Translate, *after me . . . before me*. For the use of the superlative (πρῶτος) instead of
a comparative see 482. 14. As to accent, μου is enclitic (see 28). When an enclitic
follows a word with the acute accent on the antepenult (as ἔμπροσθεν) or with the
circumflex on the penult (as πρῶτος) this preceding word receives an additional acute
accent on the ultima. Recall also that before an enclitic a final acute does not change
to grave.
16. ἡμεῖς: *we*. Nominative plural of ἐγώ, *I*.
17. ἐδόθη: from δίδωμι, *to give*. It is passive (see the last principal part), *was given*.
ἡ χάρις, ἡ ἀλήθεια: abstract qualities, like *grace* and *truth*, often use the definite article
in the Greek. Leave off the article when translating, as the English does not use it.

**61. Writing exercise**

An adjective modifier should agree with its noun in number, gender,
and case. Join with each noun form below the appropriate number,
gender, and case of the adjective shown in parenthesis, to form the thought
indicated in translation. The adjective modifiers are placed in one of the
two attributive positions: (*a*) τὴν (ἀληθινός) δόξαν, *the true glory*. (*b*) τοῦ
(ἐρχόμενος) ἀνθρώπου, *of the coming man*. (*c*) τῷ τέκνῳ τῷ (πρῶτος), *for the
first child*. (*d*) τῆς (αἰώνιος) σκοτίας, *of the eternal darkness*. (*e*) τοῖς (ἴδιος)
λόγοις, *for one's (or the) own words*. (*f*) τῶν (ἀληθινός) νόμων, *of the true laws*.
(*g*) τὴν σκοτίαν τὴν (ἐρχόμενος), *the coming darkness*. (*h*) τῇ (ἴδιος) ἀρχῇ, *for*
*one's (the) own beginning*.

## LESSON 8
# Pronouns General

**62.** A **pronoun** is a word which may stand in place of a *noun*. For example, when we hold up an apple and say 'Who wants *this*?' or 'Who wants *that*?' the word *this* and the word *that*, being demonstrative or 'pointing' pronouns, take the place of the word *apple*. Other pronouns are *relative* (like *who* or *which*), *interrogative* (like *who?* or *which?*), *personal* (like *he, she, his, her*), *reflexive* (as 'he shot *himself*'), and so on. These words do not call by name the person or thing to which they refer.

Most pronouns, in addition to being able to stand alone as substantives, can also be used like adjectives to modify nouns. So that we can say, 'This apple', 'That fruit', 'Which way?' The usage in Greek pronouns is very similar. For further discussion of the pronouns, see 537–41.

Several of the most frequently used Greek pronouns, some of which have already occurred in the reading, and some of which are in today's reading passage, are declined very nearly like the three-ending adjectives observed in the last lesson. Various slight irregularities and differences occur, however, so that it is necessary to observe particularly the declension of some of them. These pronouns need not be memorized.

**63.** Attention is now called to the declension of the definite article ὁ, ἡ, τό, *the*, which is like the pronouns, though in English grammar not counted one of them. The definite article is often used by itself somewhat as a demonstrative pronoun, *the one* or *the ones*. For example, οἱ ἀγαθοί means *the good* (ones) and οἱ ἐν τῷ ἱερῷ, *those in the temple*. The definite article has occurred frequently in the reading passages already and it is declined as follows:

ὁ, ἡ, τό, *the*

| *Singulars* | | | *Plurals* | | |
|---|---|---|---|---|---|
| ὁ | ἡ | τό | οἱ | αἱ | τά |
| τοῦ | τῆς | τοῦ | τῶν | τῶν | τῶν |
| τῷ | τῇ | τῷ | τοῖς | ταῖς | τοῖς |
| τόν | τήν | τό | τούς | τάς | τά |

**64.** The relative pronoun ὅς, ἥ, ὅ, *who* or *which*, is very similar in form to the definite article. It carries the initial rough breathing throughout instead of introducing initial τ-, and it has no proclitic forms. All forms have their own accent.

ὅς, ἥ, ὅ, *who or which*

| | | | | | |
|---|---|---|---|---|---|
| ὅς | ἥ | ὅ | οἵ | αἵ | ἅ |
| οὗ | ἧς | οὗ | ὧν | ὧν | ὧν |
| ᾧ | ᾗ | ᾧ | οἷς | αἷς | οἷς |
| ὅν | ἥν | ὅ | οὕς | ἅς | ἅ |

**65.** As we come to the demonstrative ὅδε, ἥδε, τόδε, *this, the following*, it is important to comment upon the mechanics of its use, and this will apply also to οὗτος, *this, the foregoing*, and to ἐκεῖνος, *that*, declined below. These pronouns may, of course, stand alone as substantives, and they may be used as adjective modifiers of a noun or other substantive, e.g. τὰ αὐτὰ ταῦτα, ἐκεῖνοι οἱ ἄριστοι. When used in this latter sense, they always occupy the *predicate position* with relationship to the noun and its article (see again 55), as ἐκεῖνοι οἱ λόγοι or οἱ λόγοι ἐκεῖνοι, *those words*; τάδε τὰ τέκνα or τὰ τέκνα τάδε, *the following children*. As to form, ὅδε, ἥδε, τόδε is exactly the same as the definite article plus -δε (but for accents of the masculine and feminine nominatives).

ὅδε, ἥδε, τόδε, *this, the following*

| | | | | | |
|---|---|---|---|---|---|
| ὅδε | ἥδε | τόδε | οἵδε | αἵδε | τάδε |
| τοῦδε | τῆσδε | τοῦδε | τῶνδε | τῶνδε | τῶνδε |
| τῷδε | τῇδε | τῷδε | τοῖσδε | ταῖσδε | τοῖσδε |
| τόνδε | τήνδε | τόδε | τούσδε | τάσδε | τάδε |

**66.** The pronoun αὐτός, αὐτή, αὐτό has three distinct uses, as follows: (1) it may be an intensive adjective pronoun and as such generally occupies the predicate position (see 55, 489) with reference to its noun and accompanying definite article, as αὐτὸς ὁ ἄνθρωπος or ὁ ἄνθρωπος αὐτός, *the man himself*; (2) preceded by the article, it means *the same*, as ὁ αὐτὸς ἄνθρωπος, *the same man*; (3) in its oblique cases, it is used as a third personal pronoun for, *him, her, it*, etc. As to forms it is very nearly like πρῶτος, -η, -ον, only deviating from it in the neuter nominative and accusative singular. It is as follows:

αὐτός, αὐτή, αὐτό, *self, himself, him*

| | | | | | |
|---|---|---|---|---|---|
| αὐτός | αὐτή | αὐτό | αὐτοί | αὐταί | αὐτά |
| αὐτοῦ | αὐτῆς | αὐτοῦ | αὐτῶν | αὐτῶν | αὐτῶν |
| αὐτῷ | αὐτῇ | αὐτῷ | αὐτοῖς | αὐταῖς | αὐτοῖς |
| αὐτόν | αὐτήν | αὐτό | αὐτούς | αὐτάς | αὐτά |

Note: ἄλλος, -η, -ο, *other*, is declined the same as αὐτός.

**67.** The demonstrative pronoun οὗτος, αὕτη, τοῦτο, *this, the foregoing*, needs closer watching. It follows the analogy of the article in having a rough breathing and no initial τ in the nominatives masculine and feminine. Its stem uses αυ instead of ου wherever α or η appears in the final syllable.

οὗτος, αὕτη, τοῦτο, *this, the foregoing*

| οὗτος | αὕτη | τοῦτο | οὗτοι | αὗται | ταῦτα |
|---|---|---|---|---|---|
| τούτου | ταύτης | τούτου | τούτων | τούτων | τούτων |
| τούτῳ | ταύτῃ | τούτῳ | τούτοις | ταύταις | τούτοις |
| τοῦτον | ταύτην | τοῦτο | τούτους | ταύτας | ταῦτα |

**68.** The demonstrative pronoun ἐκεῖνος, -η, -ο, *that*, is like αὐτός in its declension, being as follows:

ἐκεῖνος, -η, -ο, *that*

| ἐκεῖνος | ἐκείνη | ἐκεῖνο | ἐκεῖνοι | ἐκεῖναι | ἐκεῖνα |
|---|---|---|---|---|---|
| ἐκείνου | ἐκείνης | ἐκείνου | ἐκείνων | ἐκείνων | ἐκείνων |
| ἐκείνῳ | ἐκείνῃ | ἐκείνῳ | ἐκείνοις | ἐκείναις | ἐκείνοις |
| ἐκεῖνον | ἐκείνην | ἐκεῖνο | ἐκείνους | ἐκείνας | ἐκεῖνα |

**69. New word list**

*εἰ, *if, whether.*
ἐξηγέομαι (see ἡγέομαι for prin. parts), *to lead out, declare.* EXEGESIS.
*ἐρωτάω, ἐρωτήσω, ἠρώτησα, ἠρώτηκα, ἠρώτημαι, ἠρωτήθην, *to ask.*
*ἡγέομαι, ἡγήσομαι, ἡγησάμην, ἥγημαι, *to lead, be in command of*; of mental action, *to consider.*
*ἱερεύς, -έως, ὁ, *priest.*
Ἱεροσόλυμα, -ων, τά, *Jerusalem.*
Ἰουδαῖος, -α, -ον, *Jewish*; as a substantive, *a Jew.*
κόλπος, -ου, ὁ, *bosom.*

Λευείτης, -ου, ὁ, *Levite.*
*ὁράω, ὄψομαι, εἶδον, ἑώρακα, ἑώραμαι or ὦμμαι, ὤφθην, *to see.* (εἶδον is borrowed from εἴδω.) OPTICAL.
*ὅτε, *when.*
*οὐδείς, οὐδεμία, οὐδέν, gen. οὐδενός, οὐδεμιᾶς, οὐδενός, *no one, none.*
πώποτε, *ever, ever yet.*
*σύ, σοῦ, *thou, you.*
*τίς, τί, interrogative *who? what?*
τί sometimes means *why?*
ὤν, pres. act. partic. of εἰμί, *being.*

**70. Reading passage** (*John 1:18, 19*)

1:18 Θεὸν οὐδεὶς ἑώρακεν πώποτε· μονογενὴς θεὸς ὁ ὢν εἰς τὸν κόλπον τοῦ πατρός, ἐκεῖνος ἐξηγήσατο.

18. ἑώρακε(ν): perfect active tense of ὁράω, *to see*. Note its principal parts in today's word list. Here again is ν-movable before a consonant (482. 1). ὁ ὤν: masculine definite article with the present participle of εἰμί, *to be*. Translate, *the one being*. εἰς τὸν κόλπον: irregular for the idea of *place where*. More regular would have been ἐν τῷ κόλπῳ, *in the bosom*.

19  Καὶ αὕτη ἐστὶν ἡ μαρτυρία τοῦ Ἰωάννου, ὅτε ἀπέστειλαν πρὸς
αὐτὸν οἱ Ἰουδαῖοι ἐξ Ἱεροσολύμων ἱερεῖς καὶ Λευείτας ἵνα
ἐρωτήσωσιν αὐτόν· σὺ τίς εἶ;

19. ἐστί(ν) and εἶ: from εἰμί, *I am*, which in the present singular is conjugated εἰμί
(*I am*), εἶ (*you are*), ἐστί (*he is*). ἀπέστειλαν: aorist tense of ἀποστέλλω, *to send forth*.
See principal parts of στέλλω in the cumulative vocabulary.

**71. Writing exercise**

Use today's pronouns (as shown in the brackets) as modifiers of the
noun forms given below, making them agree with the noun forms in
number, gender, and case : (*a*) τῆς ζωῆς (αὐτός), *of the life itself.* (*b*) (ὅδε)
οἱ ἄνθρωποι, *the following men.* (*c*) (ἐκεῖνος) τῇ μαρτυρίᾳ, *for that witness.*
(*d*) (οὗτος) τῶν νόμων, *of these laws.* (*e*) (ὁ) τέκνα (ὅ) . . . *the children who.* . . .
(*f*) τοῦ (αὐτός) κόλπου, *of the same bosom.*

# LESSON 9

# Personal Pronouns

CONTINUING the observation of some of the pronouns whose inflection
lies within the orbit of the a- and o-declensions, the student considers
today some of the most frequently used pronouns referring to persons.

**72.** First note the inflection of two pronouns occurring in today's reading
passage, ἐγώ, *I*, and σύ, *you*, where both masculine and feminine are
included in one set of forms. Included also is the third personal pronoun
οὗ, *of him*, somewhat rare in occurrence.

The pronouns ἐγώ, σύ, and οὗ are declined as follows :

| | | |
|---|---|---|
| ἐγώ | σύ | |
| ἐμοῦ or μοῦ | σοῦ | οὗ |
| ἐμοί or μοί | σοί | οἷ |
| ἐμέ or μέ | σέ | ἕ |
| ἡμεῖς | ὑμεῖς | σφεῖς |
| ἡμῶν | ὑμῶν | σφῶν |
| ἡμῖν | ὑμῖν | σφίσι |
| ἡμᾶς | ὑμᾶς | σφᾶς |

The forms μοῦ, μοί, μέ, σοῦ, σοί, σέ, οὗ, οἷ, ἕ are often used as enclitics.
But οὗ, οἷ, ἕ, etc., are seldom used as third personal pronouns (the oblique

cases of αὐτός filling this need). Instead they are most often used as *indirect reflexives*, that is, standing in the subordinate clause of a sentence but referring to the subject of the main verb, as 'he asked for the cities to be given *to him*'. Thus used, they are not enclitics, but have their own accent.

**73.** The reflexive personal pronouns below are essentially the personal pronouns plus the intensive αὐτός, *self*. The pronouns of this group, with very infrequent exception, are used as direct reflexives; that is, they reflect the action to the subject of the clause *in which they stand*, as ὁρῶμαι ἐμαυτόν, *I see myself*. Because of their reflexive function they have no nominatives. The plurals are compound forms. First comes ἐμαυτοῦ. ἐμαυτῆς, *of myself*, which inflects as follows:

| *Masculine* | *Feminine* |
|---|---|
| ἐμαυτοῦ | ἐμαυτῆς |
| ἐμαυτῷ | ἐμαυτῇ |
| ἐμαυτόν | ἐμαυτήν |
| ἡμῶν αὐτῶν | ἡμῶν αὐτῶν |
| ἡμῖν αὐτοῖς | ἡμῖν αὐταῖς |
| ἡμᾶς αὐτούς | ἡμᾶς αὐτάς |

The second personal reflexive pronoun σεαυτοῦ, σεαυτῆς, *of yourself*, combines the accusative σέ with the forms of the intensive pronoun αὐτός, *self*. Contraction sometimes occurs to make it σαυτοῦ, σαυτῆς, etc. Sometimes the contracted single forms are carried into the plurals.

| *Masculine* | *Feminine* |
|---|---|
| σεαυτοῦ | σεαυτῆς |
| σεαυτῷ | σεαυτῇ |
| σεαυτόν | σεαυτήν |
| ὑμῶν αὐτῶν | ὑμῶν αὐτῶν |
| ὑμῖν αὐτοῖς | ὑμῖν αὐταῖς |
| ὑμᾶς αὐτούς | ὑμᾶς αὐτάς |

The third personal reflexive pronoun ἑαυτοῦ, ἑαυτῆς, ἑαυτοῦ, *of himself, of herself, of itself*, combines the accusative of the pronoun οὗ, οἷ, ἕ with the oblique cases of αὐτός. Contraction sometimes occurs to make it αὑτοῦ, αὑτῆς, αὑτοῦ. The κοινή sometimes uses ἑαυτῶν, etc., for the plurals of the first and second personal reflexive pronouns above (see 482. 19).

## *The Parthenon in Athens*

The Parthenon, or temple of Athena Parthenos, occupies the commanding position on the Acropolis, or fortified hill, of Xenophon's home city, the city which carried the name of the 'virgin goddess'. Preceded by at least two simpler structures, the Parthenon was begun in 447 B.C. and dedicated in 438 B.C. Designed by the architects Ictinus and Callicrates, and supervised by the sculptor Phidias, it was the crowning architectural triumph of the Age of Pericles. It is conceded to be the most perfect example of the Doric order. A giant gold and ivory statue of Athena stood at its center until the 5th century A.D. During a siege of the Acropolis in 1687 it was used for the storage of gunpowder. An explosion of this magazine caused the heavy damage to its central portion.

| Masculine | Feminine | Neuter |
|-----------|----------|--------|
| ἑαυτοῦ | ἑαυτῆς | ἑαυτοῦ |
| ἑαυτῷ | ἑαυτῇ | ἑαυτῷ |
| ἑαυτόν | ἑαυτήν | ἑαυτό |
| ἑαυτῶν | ἑαυτῶν | ἑαυτῶν |
| ἑαυτοῖς | ἑαυταῖς | ἑαυτοῖς |
| ἑαυτούς | ἑαυτάς | ἑαυτά |
| or | | or |
| σφῶν αὐτῶν | σφῶν αὐτῶν | |
| σφίσιν αὐτοῖς | σφίσιν αὐταῖς | |
| σφᾶς αὐτούς | σφᾶς αὐτάς | |

**74.** The reciprocal pronoun ἀλλήλων, *of one another*, is found only in the oblique cases of the plural. Its declension goes thus:

| Masculine | Feminine | Neuter |
|-----------|----------|--------|
| ἀλλήλων | ἀλλήλων | ἀλλήλων |
| ἀλλήλοις | ἀλλήλαις | ἀλλήλοις |
| ἀλλήλους | ἀλλήλας | ἄλληλα |

**75. Memory assignment**

At this point, having observed the declension of several characteristic nouns, pronouns, adjectives, and participles whose endings follow (with minor deviations) the general pattern of the a- and o-declensions, the student is required to memorize and from this point to be responsible for the declension of the a- and o-declension adjective πρῶτος, -η, -ον, *first*, whose endings are felt to be characteristic of the group. See 56 for this declension.

**76. New word list**

*ἀποκρίνω (see κρίνω for prin. parts), *to reply, answer*.
ἀπόκρισις, -εως, ἡ, *a reply*.
ἀρνέομαι, ἀρνήσομαι, ἠρνησάμην, ἤρνημαι, ἠρνήθην, *to deny*.
*βοάω, βοήσω, ἐβόησα, βεβόηκα, βεβόημαι, ἐβώσθην, *to shout*.
*ἐρῆμος, -ου, ἡ, *desert*. HERMIT.
εὐθύνω, ηὔθυνα, *to make straight*.
Ἠλίας, -ου, ὁ, *Elias, Elijah*.

Ἡσαΐας, -ου, ὁ, *Esaias, Isaiah*.
*καθώς, *according as, as*.
*κρίνω, κρινῶ, ἔκρινα, κέκρικα, κέκριμαι, ἐκρίθην, *to judge*.
κύριος, -ου, ὁ, *lord*; vocative κύριε often *sir*.
*ὁδός, -ου, ἡ, *road, way*. EXODUS.
*ὁμολογέω, ὁμολογήσω, ὡμολόγησα, ὡμολόγηκα, ὡμολόγημαι, ὡμολογήθην, *to agree, confess*. HOMOLOGOUS.

*οὖν, postpositive, *then, therefore.*
*πέμπω, πέμψω, ἔπεμψα, πέπομφα,
πέπεμμαι, ἐπέμφθην, *to send.*
POMP.
προφήτης, -ου, ὁ, prophet. PROPHET.

*σεαυτοῦ, σεαυτῆς, also σαυτοῦ,
σαυτῆς, *of yourself.*
*φημί, φήσω, ἔφησα, *to say.* EUPHEM-
ISM.
φωνή, -ῆς, ἡ, *sound, voice.* PHONETIC.

**77. Reading passage** (*John 1:20–23*)

1:20  Καὶ ὡμολόγησεν καὶ οὐκ ἠρνήσατο, καὶ ὡμολόγησεν ὅτι ἐγὼ οὐκ
21   εἰμὶ ὁ χριστός. καὶ ἠρώτησαν αὐτόν· τί οὖν; Ἠλίας εἶ σύ; καὶ
22   λέγει· οὐκ εἰμί. ὁ προφήτης εἶ σύ; καὶ ἀπεκρίθη· οὔ. εἶπαν οὖν
     αὐτῷ· τίς εἶ; ἵνα ἀπόκρισιν δῶμεν τοῖς πέμψασιν ἡμᾶς· τί λέγεις
23   περὶ σεαυτοῦ; ἔφη· ἐγὼ φωνὴ βοῶντος ἐν τῇ ἐρήμῳ· εὐθύνατε
     τὴν ὁδὸν κυρίου, καθὼς εἶπεν Ἠσαΐας ὁ προφήτης.

20. **ὡμολόγησε(ν)**: aorist tense of ὁμολογέω. See its third principal part in today's
word list. **ἠρνήσατο**: aorist tense of ἀρνέομαι. See its third principal part in today's word list.
21. **ἠρώτησαν**: aorist of ἐρωτάω, *to ask.* See this verb in the vocabulary. **ἀπεκρίθη**:
from ἀποκρίνω, *to reply.* Its principal parts are seen under κρίνω in today's word list.
22. **εἶπαν**: aorist of εἴρω, as is εἶπε(ν) in vs. 23. See this verb in the vocabulary.
**δῶμεν**: a subjunctive form from δίδωμι, *to give.* Translate, *we may give.* **τοῖς πέμψασι(ν)**:
*to those having sent.* πέμψασι is an aorist active participle of πέμπω, *to send.*
23. **ἔφη**: imperfect of φημί in today's word list. **ἐγὼ φωνή**: understand εἰμί, *am.*
**βοῶντος**: genitive of the present participle of βοάω. Translate, *of (one) shouting.* **εὐθύνατε**:
aorist imperative of εὐθύνω in today's word list.

**78. Writing exercise**

Insert in each of the following sentences the proper form of the indicated
pronoun to give the translated thought: (*a*) πιστεύομεν (σύ), *we trust you*
(dative plural). (*b*) φωτίζετε τὴν ἀρχὴν (σεαυτοῦ), *you are lighting the realm
of yourselves.* (*c*) γινώσκομεν (ἐμαυτοῦ), *we know ourselves.* (*d*) διδόασι νόμους
(ἀλλήλων), *they give laws to one another* (masculine). (*e*) ἐρωτᾷς (ἐγώ), *you
are asking* (or *you ask*) *me.*

# LESSON 10¹

# Synopsis of λύω

**79. The synopsis of a verb**

A CENTRAL item in beginning Greek is the inflection, or *conjugation*, of
the regular verb ending in ω. Vs. 27 of the reading passage today brings

¹ This lesson is given as one lesson in the interest of unity, but because of its length
it is suggested that it be given two class periods, breaking before the reading passage.

to view the verb λύω, *to loose* or *destroy*, which is a frequently used example of the regular verb in ω.

In the chart in section 82, the student has before him what is called the *synopsis* of this verb. The synopsis is a shortened presentation which gives just the first person singular (that is, *I*) or the first form (in the imperative, for example, this will be the second person singular, *you*) of each tense–mood grouping.

In the next lesson will be presented a full development of λύω in all three persons, singular and plural (*I, you, he*; *we, you, they*), but for the present the student is asked to note from the synopsis some general principles which it is believed will greatly increase his feeling for the verb. The quantity of the stem vowel *υ* is noted in this chart for the various systems. It is long in the present, future, and first aorist systems and in the future perfect. In the remainder of the verb it is short.

## 80. The voices

There are three voices in Greek verbs: *active, passive,* and *middle.* As in English, the active voice represents the subject as *acting,* and the passive voice represents the subject as *being acted upon.* The middle voice in Greek, except in the future and aorist tenses, has exactly the same forms as the passive. The middle voice represents the subject as acting *on* or *for itself.*

## 81. The principal parts as index to the synopsis

Attention has already been called to the seven tenses of the Greek verb. It now needs to be noted that these tenses, with their active, middle, and passive voices, are customarily grouped into six *tense systems,* the forms within a given tense system being similar in their essential structure. One of the six principal parts (previously mentioned in 19) of the regular verb stands at the beginning of each tense system. Below are listed the principal parts of λύω, *to loose.* After each principal part is given the name of its tense system. Then follows a statement of the tenses and voices comprising the given tense system. In the synopsis chart these tense systems are shown in detail. The seldom used future perfect is not shown.

The principal parts of λύω, and the names and composition of the respective tense systems follow:

| *Principal part* | *Name of tense system* | *Content of tense system* |
|---|---|---|
| λύω | present system | present and imperfect, all voices |
| λύσω | future system | future, active and middle voice |

| *Principal part* | *Name of tense system* | *Content of tense system* |
|---|---|---|
| ἔλυσα | first aorist system | first aorist, active and middle |
| λέλυκα | first perfect active system | perfect and pluperfect, active |
| λέλυμαι | perfect middle and passive system | perfect, pluperfect, and future perfect, middle and passive |
| ἐλύθην | first passive system | aorist and future, passive |

It is well to become familiar with the principal parts of a verb, and particularly when the verb has irregularities. Knowing the principal parts of a verb, one has the index to each tense system of that verb. Later the principal parts of certain verbs will be assigned for memorization.

[*For section 82 see pp. 38–39*]

**83. The moods**

Properly speaking, there are but four moods, the indicative, subjunctive, optative, and imperative. These are sometimes called the *finite* (i.e. definite, determinate as to *person*) moods to distinguish them from the infinitive and the participle. For a more complete discussion of the moods in Greek, see 556 ff.

The *indicative* mood is the mood of simple statement. The main verb of a sentence is usually in this mood. For example, in the sentence, *I fear that I may die*, the verb *fear* is the main verb and is indicative in *mood* or *feeling*. The phrase *that I may die* is subordinate and has a feeling of lesser positiveness. This calls for a verb in another mood; in Greek, the subjunctive.

The *subjunctive* and *optative* moods are rarely used for the main verb of a sentence. To assign them shades of meaning like *I may loose, I might loose*, could give an inaccurate impression unless this is remembered.

Later there will be specific rules for the use of these moods, but for now it can be said that in general the subjunctive is used subordinately after a main verb in the present tense, while the optative is used subordinately after a main verb in a past tense.

The English language provides for a comparable distinction. For example, as already noted, one of the subordinate uses calling for one or other of these moods is in clauses expressing fear. Let us take a sentence

## 82. Synopsis of λύω in all tense systems

| | | Present | | | Future | |
|---|---|---|---|---|---|---|
| *Active* | Ind. | λύω | *I loose* | λύσω | *I shall loose* | |
| | Imp. | ἔλῡον | *I was loosing* | | | |
| | Subj. | λύω | *I may be loosing* | | | |
| | Opt. | λύοιμι | *I might be loosing* | λύσοιμι | *I might loose* | |
| | Imv.* | λῦε | *you* (sing.) *loose!* | | | |
| | Inf. | λύειν | *to loose* | λύσειν | *to be about to loose* | |
| | Partic. | λύων | *loosing* | λύσων | *being about to loose* | |

| | | | | | | |
|---|---|---|---|---|---|---|
| *Middle* | Ind. | λύομαι | *I loose (for myself)* | λύσομαι | *I shall loose (for myself)* | |
| | Imp. | ἐλῡόμην | *I was loosing (for myself)* | | | |
| | Subj. | λύωμαι | *I may be loosing (for myself)* | | | |
| | Opt. | λῡοίμην | *I might be loosing (for myself)* | λῡσοίμην | *I might loose (for myself)* | |
| | Imv.* | λύου | *loose (for yourself)!* | | | |
| | Inf. | λύεσθαι | *to loose (for one's self)* | λύσεσθαι | *to be going to loose (for one's self)* | |
| | Partic. | λῡόμενος | *loosing (for one's self)* | λῡσόμενος | *being about to loose (for one's self)* | |

| | | | | | First passive | |
|---|---|---|---|---|---|---|
| *Passive* | Ind. | λύομαι | *I am being loosed* | λυθήσομαι | *I shall be loosed* | |
| | Imp. | ἐλῡόμην | *I was being loosed* | | | |
| | Subj. | λύωμαι | *I may be being loosed* | | | |
| | Opt. | λῡοίμην | *I might be being loosed* | λυθησοίμην | *I might be loosed* | |
| | Imv.* | λύου | *be loosed!* | | | |
| | Inf. | λύεσθαι | *to be loosed* | λυθήσεσθαι | *to be going to be loosed* | |
| | Partic. | λῡόμενος | *being loosed* | λυθησόμενος | *being about to be loosed* | |

* Abbreviation for imperative, as distinguished from imperfect.

**82** *(cont.)*

|  |  | First aorist |  |  | First perfect active |  |
|---|---|---|---|---|---|---|
| *Active* | Ind. | ἔλῡσα | I loosed | λέλυκα | I have loosed | |
| | | | | Plup. ἐλελύκη | I had loosed | |
| | Subj. | λύσω | I may loose | λελύκω* | I may have loosed | |
| | Opt. | λύσαιμι | I might loose | λελύκοιμι* | I might have loosed | |
| | Imv. | λῦσον | you (sing.) loose! | λελυκὼς ἴσθι | be having loosed!† loosed!* | |
| | Inf. | λῦσαι | to have loosed | λελυκέναι | to have loosed | |
| | Partic. | λύσας | having loosed | λελυκώς | having loosed | |

|  |  |  |  | Perfect middle and passive‡ |  |
|---|---|---|---|---|---|
| *Middle* | Ind. | ἐλῡσάμην | I loosed (for myself) | λέλυμαι | I have loosed (for myself) |
| | | | | Plup. ἐλελύμην | I had loosed (for myself) |
| | Subj. | λύσωμαι | I may loose (for myself) | λελυμένος ὦ | I may have loosed (for myself) |
| | Opt. | λῡσαίμην | I might loose (for myself) | λελυμένος εἴην | I might have loosed (for myself) |
| | Imv. | λῦσαι | Loose (for yourself)! | λέλυσο | be having loosed (for yourself)!† |
| | Inf. | λύσασθαι | to have loosed (for one's self) | λελύσθαι | to have loosed (for one's self) |
| | Partic. | λῡσάμενος | having loosed (for one's self) | λελυμένος | having loosed (for one's self) |

|  |  | First passive |  |  |  |
|---|---|---|---|---|---|
| *Passive* | Ind. | ἐλύθην | I was loosed | λέλυμαι | I have been loosed |
| | | | | Plup. ἐλελύμην | I had been loosed |
| | Subj. | λυθῶ | I may be loosed | λελυμένος ὦ | I may have been loosed |
| | Opt. | λυθείην | I might be loosed | λελυμένος εἴην | I might have been loosed |
| | Imv. | λύθητι | be loosed! | λέλυσο | be loosed!† |
| | Inf. | λυθῆναι | to have been loosed | λελύσθαι | to have been loosed |
| | Partic. | λυθείς | having been loosed | λελυμένος | having been loosed |

\* The perfect active often uses periphrastic forms consisting of the participle plus forms of εἰμί, *to be,* for the subjunctive (λελυκὼς ὦ, etc.) and the optative (λελυκὼς εἴην, etc.).

† The English has no form to express a command in perfect tense.

‡ The perfect middle and passive system also includes a future perfect passive which is rarely used.

expressing fear after a present tense, and one involving past tense as follows:

> Present: He *fears* that he *may* be robbed (subjunctive idea).
> Past: He *feared* that he *might* be robbed (optative idea).

Now let us take a sentence expressing purpose, in the same manner.

> Present: He *labors* that he *may* succeed (subjunctive idea).
> Past: He *labored* that he *might* succeed (optative idea).

The *imperative* mood is used for expressing a command. It uses only the second person (e.g. *you loose!*) and the third person (e.g. *let him loose!*), singular and plural.

The *infinitive*, as in English, expresses the idea *to do, to loose*.

The *participle* is in reality an adjective in three genders, used as in English. For example, *a loosing motion*.

## 84. Few optatives in the New Testament

While it is felt that the student should even now have a feeling for the place of the optative mood of the Greek verb, yet he should also realize that by the time the New Testament was written, the functions of the optative mood had been largely taken over by the subjunctive. Hence the optative mood will not be encountered in the readings from St. John's gospel.

## 85. Tense suffixes and tense signs

Each tense system has a distinctive suffix which it adds to the simple stem of the verb before the personal endings of the various forms. Properly speaking this *tense suffix* includes all the letters standing between the end of the stem (λυ- in the present case) and the personal endings.

In the present lesson the student will be given for each tense system a distinctive 'tense sign' to serve as an aid in identifying the tense system. These 'tense signs' also are added to the verb stem λυ- and hence are really a part of the tense suffix for the various tense systems.

For the purposes of accuracy and of future reference there will be indicated in addition to the 'tense sign' the remaining letters of the tense suffix. In some cases these will involve 'alternate letters'. For example, in the present tense system the mention of the so-called *variable vowel* o/ε will indicate that some of the personal endings are preceded by o and some by ε. This will be treated further in the next lesson.

The student is asked to memorize at this time the tense signs of each of these tense systems and to note their use in the synopsis chart.

## 86. Present system

Tense sign: plain stem of verb (λυ- in this case), plus the variable vowel o/ε, with personal endings added.

The imperfect tense is considered part of the present system. The ε which is prefixed to the stem of the imperfect (e.g. ἔ-λυον) is called a *syllabic augment*. It occurs also with the aorist and the pluperfect, the two other tenses comprising, with the imperfect, the *secondary tenses*. Augment is used only in the indicative mood.

The present system depicts action as *present* or *continuing*. The imperfect represents *past continuing action*.

## 87. Future system

Tense sign: σ added to the stem (λυ-), plus variable vowel o/ε, before the personal endings (e.g. λύ-σ-ω).

The future system has no forms in the subjunctive or the imperative moods.

The future system as such includes only the active and middle voices.

## 88. First aorist system

Tense sign: σα added to the augmented stem (ἐλυ-) before the personal endings (e.g. ἔλυσα). σα is the complete tense suffix for this system.

In the subjunctive and the imperative forms shown the a of the σα tense sign is not immediately apparent. It can be sensed better in the other persons of these categories.

The aorist signifies *simple action* in past time. Its *simple action* is contrasted with the *continuing action* of the present system. In the subjunctive, optative, and imperative moods of the aorist, the idea of *past action* is forgotten and the idea of *simple action* is what is left. Note the synopsis chart on this point. Perhaps it is this tenseless quality which gave rise to the name of the tense, ἀόριστος (a-privative, plus ὁρίζω, *to bound*), *without boundaries*.

Like the future system, the first aorist system proper includes only the active and middle voices.

## 89. First perfect active system

Note here that the initial letter is doubled with an ε inserted. So the stem λυ- becomes λελυ-. This is called *reduplication* and is characteristic of the perfect systems.

Tense sign: κ added to the reduplicated stem (λελυ-), plus a/ε, before the personal endings (e.g. λέλυκα). The subjunctive, optative, and imperative moods are often formed by using the perfect active participle plus the corresponding moods of εἰμί in the present tense.

The perfect denotes *presently completed action*; the pluperfect, *action completed in past time*. Note that the pluperfect has in addition to the reduplication an initial syllabic augment (e.g. ἐ-λε-λύκη).

**90. Perfect middle and passive system**

Tense sign: personal endings added directly to the reduplicated stem λελυ- (e.g. λέλυμαι). The perfect middle and passive has no tense suffix, but the future perfect tense suffix is σο/ε.

**91. First passive system**

Tense sign: θη added to stem before the personal endings (e.g. ἐλύθην). The future passive adds σο/ε to make its tense suffix. Because of their distinctive tense sign, the future and aorist passives have their own tense system.

In the first aorist passive imperative (for euphony) the typical imperative ending -θι is changed to -τι after -θη-. Hence λύθητι is for λύθηθι.

**92. New word list**

*ἄξιος, -α, -ον, *worthy, worth* (often with gen. of value). AXIOM.

βαπτίζω, βαπτίσω, ἐβάπτισα, βεβάπτισμαι, ἐβαπτίσθην, to *baptize*. BAPTIZE.

Βηθανία, -ας, ἡ, *Bethany*.

*εἴδω, εἴσομαι, εἶδον, οἶδα, to *see*; οἶδα (perfect as pres.; ἤδη pluperf. as past), to *know*.

ἱμάς, ἱμάντος, ὁ, *thong, lacing*.

Ἰορδάνης, -ου, ὁ, *Jordan*.

*ἵστημι, στήσω, ἔστησα or ἔστην, ἔστηκα, ἔσταμαι, ἐστάθην, to *set*, to *stand*. STAND.

*λύω, λύσω, ἔλυσα, λέλυκα, λέλυμαι, ἐλύθην, to *loose, destroy*. ANALYSIS.

*μέσος, -η, -ον, *middle, in the middle*. MESOPOTAMIA.

*ὅπου, *where, wherever*.

πέραν, *beyond, on the other side of*, usually with gen.

στήκω, to *stand* (an inferior Greek word taken from ἔστηκα, perfect of ἵστημι).

*ὕδωρ, ὕδατος, τό, *water*. HYDRAULIC.

ὑπόδημα, -ματος, τό, *sandal, shoe*.

Φαρισαῖος, -ου, ὁ, *Pharisee*.

**93. Reading passage** (*John 1:24–28*)

1:24, 25 Καὶ ἀπεσταλμένοι ἦσαν ἐκ τῶν Φαρισαίων. καὶ ἠρώτησαν αὐτὸν καὶ εἶπαν αὐτῷ· τί οὖν βαπτίζεις εἰ σὺ οὐκ εἶ ὁ χριστὸς οὐδὲ

24. **ἀπεσταλμένοι**: perfect middle and passive participle from ἀποστέλλω, to *send forth*. See principal parts of στέλλω and note from which of these principal parts this comes. With the verb ἦσαν, *they were*, it forms the pluperfect of ἀποστέλλω and translates, *they had been sent*.

25. **ἠρώτησαν**: aorist of ἐρωτάω. **εἶπαν**: aorist of εἴρω. **εἶ**: second person singular present indicative of εἰμί, to *be*.

26  Ἠλίας οὐδὲ ὁ προφήτης; ἀπεκρίθη αὐτοῖς ὁ Ἰωάννης λέγων·
    ἐγὼ βαπτίζω ἐν ὕδατι· μέσος ὑμῶν στήκει ὃν ὑμεῖς οὐκ οἴδατε,
27  ὁ ὀπίσω μου ἐρχόμενος, οὗ οὐκ εἰμὶ ἐγὼ ἄξιος ἵνα λύσω αὐτοῦ
28  τὸν ἱμάντα τοῦ ὑποδήματος. Ταῦτα ἐν Βηθανίᾳ ἐγένετο πέραν
    τοῦ Ἰορδάνου, ὅπου ἦν ὁ Ἰωάννης βαπτίζων.

26. **ἀπεκρίθη**: from ἀποκρίνω, *to reply*. See principal parts of κρίνω and note from which of these principal parts it comes. **ὑμῶν, ὑμεῖς**: from the personal pronoun σύ (72). **ὅν**, also **οὖ** in *vs.* 27: from the relative pronoun ὅς, ἥ, ὅ (64). The Greek often combines both antecedent and relative idea in one relative pronoun. We would say *he whom*, or *one whom*. **οἴδατε**: from εἴδω in today's word list. οἶδα, a perfect, is used with present significance. Indeed the perfect tense in Greek emphasizes what is *presently true* on account of that which has taken place.

27. **ὁ . . . ἐρχόμενος**: *the one coming*. **λύσω**: not the future indicative here, but aorist subjunctive (see today's chart) with ἵνα, *that, in order that*, in a sort of purpose clause which translates, *worthy that I may loose*, or *worthy to loose*.

28. **ταῦτα**: from οὗτος. See 67. **ἐγένετο**: second aorist of γίγνομαι. A neuter plural subject (ταῦτα) usually has its verb in the singular. **ἦν . . . βαπτίζων**: *was baptizing*. Perhaps a periphrasis, or circumlocution, for ἐβάπτιζε, imperfect. The κοινή frequently uses periphrases (482. 9).

**94. Comprehension exercise**

After learning the distinctive signs of the six tense systems, inspect the following verb forms for these tense signs, and indicate to which of the six tense systems each verb form belongs: (*a*) ἐφώτισα (from φωτίζω). (*b*) ἐγεννήθην (from γεννάω). (*c*) πιστεύσομαι (from πιστεύω). (*d*) στελλοίμην (from στέλλω). (*e*) πιστευθήσομαι (from πιστεύω). (*f*) μεμαρτύρημαι (from μαρτυρέω).

LESSON 11¹
# Further Development of λύω

**95.** THE chart in 97 presents the total conjugation of the regular verb in -ω, using λύω as the example. In the synopsis of λύω in the previous lesson the student observed the distinctive signs of the various tense systems. The chart in today's lesson gives the complete expansion of each tense–mood group.

The indicative, subjunctive, and optative moods use first, second, and third persons in both singular and plural—six forms in each tense–mood group. The imperative uses second and third persons, singular and plural —four forms in each tense system where the imperative occurs.

Person and number are not labeled in this chart. The traditional arrangement is followed and will be introduced by the teacher. The infinitive and the participle do not have personal endings.

¹ The teacher will of course use his judgement as to the time needed for covering this rather lengthy lesson,

## 96. The thematic vowel

In the preceding lesson, mention was made of certain vowels or variable vowel combinations forming part of the tense suffixes of the different tense systems. It should be added that these are but one form of the vowel implementation for the endings of Greek verbs, which is called in general the *thematic vowel*. The subjunctive and the optative moods make characteristic use of vowels in what are called their 'mood suffixes'. (The imperatives follow closely the corresponding indicative tenses as to thematic vowels.)

With reference again to the variable vowel $o/\epsilon$ which forms a part of the tense suffix in the present and future systems and in the future and future perfect passive tenses it will now be worth while to note that this variable vowel is $o$ before $\mu$ and $\nu$, and elsewhere it is $\epsilon$. This makes a pattern which holds constant in the tenses and tense systems just mentioned, in both active and middle/passive groupings, as follows:

| Person | Singular | Plural |
|--------|----------|--------|
| 1 | $o$ | $o$ |
| 2 | $\epsilon$ | $\epsilon$ |
| 3 | $\epsilon$ | $o$ |

The student is asked to check the accuracy of this observation by reference to these tense systems and tenses in today's chart.

The subjunctive forms its mood suffix by simply lengthening the thematic vowel $o/\epsilon$ to form the variable thematic vowel $\omega/\eta$. This is the distinctive mark of the subjunctive mood, and it follows the pattern just noted, in every tense where the subjunctive occurs, in all voices. This lengthened thematic vowel is distributed as follows:

| Person | Singular | Plural |
|--------|----------|--------|
| 1 | $\omega$ | $\omega$ |
| 2 | $\eta$ | $\eta$ |
| 3 | $\eta$ | $\omega$ |

The student is asked to observe the use of this thematic vowel in the subjunctives shown in the chart.

The optative forms its mood suffix by using $\iota$ or $\iota\eta$, combining with the variable vowel $o/\epsilon$ to form $o\iota$, or with $(\sigma)a$ of the aorist to form $a\iota$, or with $(\theta)\eta$ or with the forms of $\epsilon\dot{\iota}\mu\dot{\iota}$, *to be*, to form $\epsilon\iota$. This mood suffix of the optative tends not to vary within a given tense grouping. The student is asked to follow the optatives in the chart, noting how the mood suffix always contains $\iota$ ($o\iota$, $a\iota$, $\epsilon\iota$).

[*For section 97 see pp. 46–47*]

## 98. Primary and secondary personal endings

Passing reference has already been made to the fact that the present, future, perfect, and future perfect tenses are called the *primary* tenses; while the imperfect, aorist, and pluperfect tenses are called the *secondary* tenses. In the previous lesson it was noted that the secondary tenses have in common the fact that they receive an initial *augment*. Attention is now called to the similarity in the personal endings within the two groups. The *primary endings*, active and middle/passive, are given as follows:

| Person | Active Singular | Active Plural | Middle/Passive Singular | Middle/Passive Plural |
|---|---|---|---|---|
| 1 | -μι, -ω | -μεν | -μαι | -μεθα |
| 2 | -s | -τε | -σαι, -ι | -σθε |
| 3 | -σι, -ι | -ωσι, -ουσι | -ται | -νται |

The active singular endings are of involved analysis. Their applicability is not always evident. These primary endings are used by the subjunctive throughout, following its variable vowel ω/η. Sometimes the ι of the personal ending appears as ι-subscript. The student should follow these endings in the present, future, perfect, and future perfect indicative groupings, and in all tenses of the subjunctive. Despite a few apparent lapses, the general applicability is readily apparent. The *secondary endings*, active and middle/passive, are as follows:

| Person | Active Singular | Active Plural | Middle/Passive Singular | Middle/Passive Plural |
|---|---|---|---|---|
| 1 | -ν | -μεν | -μην | -μεθα |
| 2 | -s | -τε | -σο, -ο | -σθε |
| 3 | – | -ν,- σαν | -το | -ντο |

The optative (with the apparent exception of the -μι often used as ending in the first person singular actives) uses these secondary endings throughout. It will be helpful to refer once more to the chart and to follow these endings in the imperfect, aorist, and pluperfect indicative (active and middle/passive), and in the optatives, all tenses and voices.

## 99. Apparent irregularities in accents

To one who has firmly in mind the recessive principle in the accent of verbs the appearance, in the λύω chart, of the infinitives λελυκέναι

## 97. Total conjugation of λύω, to loose

### Active

| | Present system | Future system | First aorist system | First perfect active system |
|---|---|---|---|---|
| **Indicative** | λύω   λύομεν <br> λύεις   λύετε <br> λύει   λύουσι | λύσω   λύσομεν <br> λύσεις   λύσετε <br> λύσει   λύσουσι | ἔλυσα   ἐλύσαμεν <br> ἔλυσας   ἐλύσατε <br> ἔλυσε   ἔλυσαν | λέλυκα   λελύκαμεν <br> λέλυκας   λελύκατε <br> λέλυκε   λελύκασι |
| (Imperfect) | ἔλυον   ἐλύομεν <br> ἔλυες   ἐλύετε <br> ἔλυε   ἔλυον | | | (Pluperfect) <br> ἐλελύκη   ἐλελύκεμεν <br> ἐλελύκης   ἐλελύκετε <br> ἐλελύκει   ἐλελύκεσαν |
| **Subjunctive** | λύω   λύωμεν <br> λύῃς   λύητε <br> λύῃ   λύωσι | | λύσω   λύσωμεν <br> λύσῃς   λύσητε <br> λύσῃ   λύσωσι | λελύκω*   λελύκωμεν <br> λελύκῃς   λελύκητε <br> λελύκῃ   λελύκωσι |
| **Optative** | λύοιμι   λύοιμεν <br> λύοις   λύοιτε <br> λύοι   λύοιεν | λύσοιμι   λύσοιμεν <br> λύσοις   λύσοιτε <br> λύσοι   λύσοιεν | λύσαιμι   λύσαιμεν <br> λύσειας   λύσαιτε <br> λύσειε   λύσειαν | λελύκοιμι†   λελύκοιμεν <br> λελύκοις   λελύκοιτε <br> λελύκοι   λελύκοιεν |
| **Imperative** | λῦε   λύετε <br> λυέτω   λυόντων | | λῦσον   λύσατε <br> λυσάτω   λυσάντων | λελυκὼς ἴσθι   λελυκότες ἔστε <br> λελυκὼς ἔστω   λελυκότες ὄντων |
| **Infinitive** | λύειν | λύσειν | λῦσαι | λελυκέναι |
| **Participle** | λύων, λύουσα, λῦον | λύσων, λύσουσα, λῦσον | λύσας, λύσασα, λῦσαν | λελυκώς, -υῖα, -ός |

### Middle

| | Present system | Future system | First aorist system | Perfect mid. and pass. system |
|---|---|---|---|---|
| **Indicative** | λύομαι   λυόμεθα <br> λύει   λύεσθε <br> λύεται   λύονται | λύσομαι   λυσόμεθα <br> λύσει   λύσεσθε <br> λύσεται   λύσονται | ἐλυσάμην   ἐλυσάμεθα <br> ἐλύσω   ἐλύσασθε <br> ἐλύσατο   ἐλύσαντο | λέλυμαι   λελύμεθα <br> λέλυσαι   λέλυσθε <br> λέλυται   λέλυνται |
| (Imperfect) | ἐλυόμην   ἐλυόμεθα <br> ἐλύου   ἐλύεσθε <br> ἐλύετο   ἐλύοντο | | | (Pluperfect) <br> ἐλελύμην   ἐλελύμεθα <br> ἐλέλυσο   ἐλέλυσθε <br> ἐλέλυτο   ἐλέλυντο |
| **Subjunctive** | λύωμαι   λυώμεθα <br> λύῃ   λύησθε <br> λύηται   λύωνται | | λύσωμαι   λυσώμεθα <br> λύσῃ   λύσησθε <br> λύσηται   λύσωνται | λελυμένος ὦ   λελυμένοι ὦμεν <br> λελυμένος ᾖς   λελυμένοι ἦτε <br> λελυμένος ᾖ   λελυμένοι ὦσι |

## Middle

**Optative**

| λυοίμην | λυοίμεθα |
|---|---|
| λύοιο | λύοισθε |
| λύοιτο | λύοιντο |

**Imperative**

| λύου | λύεσθε |
|---|---|
| λυέσθω | λυέσθων |

**Infinitive**

λύεσθαι

**Participle**

λυόμενος, -η, -ον

---

| λυσοίμην | λυσοίμεθα |
|---|---|
| λύσοιο | λύσοισθε |
| λύσοιτο | λύσοιντο |

λύσεσθαι

λυσόμενος, -η, -ον

---

| λυσαίμην | λυσαίμεθα |
|---|---|
| λύσαιο | λύσαισθε |
| λύσαιτο | λύσαιντο |

| λῦσαι | λύσασθε |
|---|---|
| λυσάσθω | λυσάσθων |

λύσασθαι

λυσάμενος, -η, -ον

---

Perfect passive same forms as middle voice

| λέλυσο | |
|---|---|
| λελύσθω | λελύσθων |

λελύσθαι

λελυμένος, -η, -ον

---

*Future perfect passive*‡‡

| λελυμένος εἴην | λελυμένοι εἶμεν |
|---|---|
| λελυμένος εἴης | λελυμένοι εἶτε |
| λελυμένος εἴη | λελυμένοι εἶεν |

λελυμένος, -η, -ον

| λελύσομαι | λελυσόμεθα |
|---|---|
| λελύσει | λελύσεσθε |
| λελύσεται | λελύσονται |

| λελυσοίμην | λελυσοίμεθα |
|---|---|
| λελύσοιο | λελύσοισθε |
| λελύσοιτο | λελύσοιντο |

λελύσεσθαι

λελυσόμενος, -η, -ον

## Passive

**First passive system**

*(Future)*     *(Aorist)*

**Indicative**

| λυθήσομαι | λυθησόμεθα |
|---|---|
| λυθήσει | λυθήσεσθε |
| λυθήσεται | λυθήσονται |

| ἐλύθην | ἐλύθημεν |
|---|---|
| ἐλύθης | ἐλύθητε |
| ἐλύθη | ἐλύθησαν |

Present passive same forms as middle voice

**Subjunctive**

| λυθῶ | λυθῶμεν |
|---|---|
| λυθῇς | λυθῆτε |
| λυθῇ | λυθῶσι |

**Optative**

| λυθησοίμην | λυθησοίμεθα |
|---|---|
| λυθήσοιο | λυθήσοισθε |
| λυθήσοιτο | λυθήσοιντο |

| λυθείην | λυθεῖμεν |
|---|---|
| λυθείης | λυθεῖτε |
| λυθείη | λυθεῖεν |

**Imperative**

| λύθητι | λύθητε |
|---|---|
| λυθήτω | λυθέντων |

**Infinitive**

λυθήσεσθαι

λυθῆναι

**Participle**

λυθησόμενος, -η, -ον

λυθείς, λυθεῖσα, λυθέν

---

\* Often replaced by the periphrastic forms λελυκὼς ὦ, ῇς, ῇ; λελυκότες ὦμεν, ἦτε, ὦσι.

† Often replaced by λελυκὼς εἴην, εἴης, εἴη; λελυκότες εἴμεν, εἴτε, εἶεν. This general principle will not be restated with subsequent verb charts.

‡‡ The future perfect is, with only rare exceptions, a passive tense, and is so shown here. Because forms in the future perfect are so seldom encountered, this tense is not shown in the other verb charts in this text.

(perfect active), λελύσθαι (perfect middle/passive), and λυθῆναι (aorist passive) will perhaps have given a shock. But it must always be remembered that while they partake of the action-nature of the verb, the infinitive is really a verbal noun, and the participle a verbal adjective. The following rules concerning the accent of infinitives are offered:

1. All infinitives in -ναι accent the penult (λελυκέναι, λυθῆναι).
2. The perfect middle and passive infinitive always accents the penult (λελύσθαι).

The following rules concerning the accent of participles will prove helpful:

1. All consonant declension participles in *s* (except the aorist active participle) take the acute accent on the ultima (a word so accented is called an *oxytone*). This takes in λελυκώς and λυθείς. (Note: the cases of this declension will be observed later.)
2. The perfect middle and passive participle always takes the acute accent on the penult (called a *paroxytone*). This covers λελυμένος and is the distinctive mark of the perfect middle/passive participle.

It must also be noted that final -οι and -αι in optative forms receive their normal value as diphthongs and are counted *long* in determining the accent of the verb forms in which they occur, as λύσοι.

## 100. Notes on the future and aorist

Note that in the future and aorist tense systems proper there are no passive forms. The passive forms of these tenses are characteristically different from the forms of the active and middle voices and are placed in a tense system of their own called the *passive system*.

Note that the future system has no subjunctives or imperatives, nor has the future passive or the future perfect.

## 101. Second aorist

Some verbs have an aorist which is not characterized by the σ and the α in the ending. These are called *second aorists*. Hence the designation *first aorist* is used for regular verbs like λύω. The same type of observation applies to the passive system with its θη characteristic as seen in λύω.

## 102. Memory assignment

It is felt that the student will be handicapped if he does not have by memory the regular verb λύω, thus giving him a good point of reference as he meets the varying formations presented by other verbs to be encountered. Therefore in connection with today's lesson the student is asked to memorize the forms of the present and future systems of λύω as seen in the chart.

## 103. New word list

*αἴρω, ἀρῶ, ἦρα, ἦρκα, ἦρμαι, ἤρθην, to lift up, take away.
ἁμαρτία, -ας, ἡ, error, sin.
ἀμνός, -οῦ, ὁ or ἡ, lamb.
*βαίνω, βήσομαι, ἔβην, βέβηκα, βέβαμαι, ἐβάθην, to go. ANABASIS.
*βλέπω, βλέψω, ἔβλεψα, to look, see.
ἐπαύριον, on the morrow.
*ἐπί, with gen., on, upon; with dat., on, at; with acc., upon, against. EPIGLOTTIS.
Ἰσραήλ, ὁ, indecl., Israel.
καταβαίνω (see βαίνω for prin.

parts), to come or go down, descend.
*μένω, μενῶ, ἔμεινα, μεμένηκα, to remain. REMAIN.
οὐρανός, -οῦ, ὁ, heaven. URANUS.
περιστερά, -ᾶς, ἡ, dove.
*πνεῦμα, -ατος, τό, breath, spirit. PNEUMATIC.
*ὑπέρ, with gen., over, concerning, for the sake of; with acc., over, more than, beyond. HYPERTROPHY.
φανερόω, φανερώσω, ἐφανέρωσα, πεφανέρωκα, πεφανέρωμαι, ἐφανερώθην, to show.

## 104. Reading passage (*John 1:29–32*)

1:29  Τῇ ἐπαύριον βλέπει τὸν Ἰησοῦν ἐρχόμενον πρὸς αὐτόν, καὶ λέγει·
30  ἴδε ὁ ἀμνὸς τοῦ θεοῦ ὁ αἴρων τὴν ἁμαρτίαν τοῦ κόσμου. οὗτός
       ἐστιν ὑπὲρ οὗ ἐγὼ εἶπον· ὀπίσω μου ἔρχεται ἀνὴρ ὃς ἔμπροσθέν
31  μου γέγονεν, ὅτι πρῶτός μου ἦν. κἀγὼ οὐκ ᾔδειν αὐτόν, ἀλλ' ἵνα
       φανερωθῇ τῷ Ἰσραήλ, διὰ τοῦτο ἦλθον ἐγὼ ἐν ὕδατι βαπτίζων.

29. τῇ ἐπαύριον: τῇ understands ἡμέρᾳ, on the day, dative of time when (526). ἐπαύριον is an adverb where we would have used an adjective. Translate, on the next day. ἴδε: aorist imperative of ὁράω. It comes from εἶδον, the third principal part. The unaugmented stem of εἶδον is ἰδ-. Add the second person singular imperative ending ε and ἴδε results. Translate, see, behold. Note that it does not take a direct object when used in this way. ἀμνός is nominative. The sense is elliptical: behold, (here is) the lamb. Translate simply, behold, the lamb.

30. οὗτός, ἔμπροσθέν: a word preceding an enclitic sometimes receives an additional acute accent on the ultima. ὑπὲρ οὗ: literally, concerning whom. The antecedent he is not expressed. εἶπον: from εἴρω. γέγονε(ν): from γίγνομαι.

31. κἀγώ: a shortened form for καὶ ἐγώ. This is called crasis (Gr. κρᾶσις, mixing), a blending of two words into one. ᾔδειν: pluperfect of εἴδω, to see (perf., to know), translated as imperfect. οἶδα, the perfect, translates as present. See the vocabulary. ἵνα φανερωθῇ: the form φανερωθῇ is the aorist passive subjunctive of φανερόω, to manifest. This is a purpose clause using ἵνα with the subjunctive (562). The aorist tense in the subjunctive denotes simple action as contrasted with continuing action, which would have been indicated by the present subjunctive. ἦλθον: from ἔρχομαι.

32 Καὶ ἐμαρτύρησεν Ἰωάννης λέγων ὅτι τεθέαμαι τὸ πνεῦμα καταβαῖνον ὡς περιστερὰν ἐξ οὐρανοῦ καὶ ἔμεινεν ἐπ᾽ αὐτόν.

**32. ἐμαρτύρησε(ν):** aorist of μαρτυρέω, *to witness.* Notice that it would compare with
ἔλυσε(ν) from λύω. See chart of λύω in 97. **λέγων ὅτι:** the N.T. often uses ὅτι, *that,*
to introduce a direct statement, as here. **τεθέαμαι:** from θεάομαι. θ when reduplicated
is τεθ-. So here is the perfect middle, *I have beheld* or *seen.* **καταβαῖνον:** a present participle in the neuter gender. Note the third form of the present active participle of
λύω in the chart in 97. **ἔμεινε(ν):** aorist of μένω. See today's word list. **ἐπ᾽ αὐτόν:** involves an idea of motion not generally associated with the verb *to remain.* Translate the
whole phrase, *he came to rest upon him.*

## 105. Writing exercise

In *Lesson 10* there was given only the first person singular (*I*) of each
tense–mood group of λύω, and the translated significance of each of these
forms was also given. Today each tense–mood group of λύω is given in
full—all six forms (*I, you* (sing.), *he; we, you* (pl.), *they*). Using this information, find by using first the chart in 82 and then today's more complete chart of λύω the forms which would give the following meanings
(for example, *I shall loose* calls for λύσω): (*a*) *We loose* (*for ourselves*).
(*b*) *They have loosed.* (*c*) *You* (sing.) *were loosed.* (*d*) *We have loosed* (*for ourselves*). (*e*) *You* (pl.) *shall be loosed.* (*f*) *He was loosing.* (*g*) *You* (pl.) *loose!*

# LESSON 12

# Augment and Reduplication

IN the treatment of λύω it was seen that the verb receives an *augment* in
the secondary tenses (imperfect, aorist, and pluperfect) of the indicative,
and that it receives a *reduplication* in the perfect. There is need to follow
a little further the matter of augment and reduplication in Greek verbs,
and in order to do so, it is necessary to study that group of consonants
called *mutes.*

## 106. Classes of mutes

Nine of the Greek consonants are relatively unvoiced and are called
*mutes* or *stops.* It is important to discern three classes of these mutes,
because the classes involve slightly different problems as they blend with
other letters in a given verb form. These three classes of mutes are

grouped according to the organs of speech predominant in their pronunciation, these being the lips, the palate, and the tongue tip. Hence the classes are:

| | *Orders.* | | |
| --- | --- | --- | --- |
| *Classes* | *Smooth* | *Hard, or middle* | *Aspirated or rough* |
| Labials (lips), or π-mutes | π | β | φ |
| Palatals (roof of mouth), or κ-mutes | κ | γ | χ |
| Linguals (tip of tongue), or τ-mutes | τ | δ | θ |

Note that in each class there is one mute which is close-clipped in pronunciation, or *smooth*, one which is hard (called *middle*), and one which is aspirated (given more breath) and is called *rough*. The three consonants in a given class are said to be *cognate* or *related* to each other, and the three groups of smooth, or middle, or rough consonants are said each to contain mutes of the same *order*, or *co-ordinate* mutes.

## 107. Augment

In the indicative mood, the secondary tenses of verbs receive an augment (or enlargement) at the beginning. Augment is of two kinds, *syllabic* and *temporal*. Syllabic augment consists in prefixing ε to verbs beginning with a consonant. This was noted in λύω where the imperfect is ἔλυον; aorist, ἔλυσα; and pluperfect, ἐλελύκη.

Temporal augment, on the other hand, lengthens the first syllable of verbs beginning with a vowel or diphthong. For example, ἀρνέομαι, *I deny*, becomes in the imperfect, ἠρνούμην, *I denied*. Here is the way in which the initial vowels and diphthongs are affected by being augmented:

| *Unaugmented* | | *Augmented* |
| --- | --- | --- |
| α or ε | becomes | η |
| ι | becomes | ῑ |
| ο | becomes | ω |
| υ | becomes | ῡ |
| αι or ᾳ | becomes | ῃ |
| οι | becomes | ῳ |

The verb ἔχω augments irregularly and has the imperfect εἶχον.

When a preposition is prefixed to a simple verb, the resulting compound verb uses an augment *between the prefix and the simple verb*. When this brings two vowels together the first vowel is usually elided. For example, ἀπο-στέλλω, *to send forth*, has the imperfect ἀπ-έστελλον. It should also be added that when elision occurs within a compound verb for any reason, if the simple verb begins with a rough breathing, the consonant of the prefix is changed to the related rough consonant. So κατα-ἵστημι becomes καθίστημι. (Note: περί and πρό do not elide.)

## 108. Reduplication

The perfect systems of verbs regularly use in all moods a *reduplication*, this being the sign of completed action.

Like augment, reduplication is of two kinds, syllabic and temporal. Verbs beginning with a single consonant (except ρ) are reduplicated by prefixing the initial consonant followed by ε. So λύω becomes λέλυκα. The pluperfect prefixes to the reduplication of the perfect a syllabic augment, ε, e.g. ἐλελύκη.

In most cases where verbs begin with two consonants, with a double consonant (ξ, ψ, or ζ), or with ρ the reduplication is a simple ε, as στέλλω, *to send*, which in the perfect active becomes ἔσταλκα. No further syllable is then prefixed for the pluperfect, which for στέλλω would be ἐστάλκη.

Where a verb begins with a rough consonant (see above chart), the reduplication uses the related smooth mute. For example, θεάομαι, *to behold*, has for its perfect τεθέαμαι. Similarly φωτίζω, *to enlighten*, has the perfect middle πεφώτισμαι.

In most verbs beginning with vowels or diphthongs the reduplication is just like augment, and no additional augment is added in the pluperfect.

With compound verbs the reduplication comes between the prefix and the simple verb. For example, ἀπο-κρίνω, *to reply*, becomes ἀπο-κέκρικα in the perfect. Where two vowels are thus brought together the first is usually elided, as with ἀπο-στέλλω, where the perfect is ἀπ-έσταλκα. The student should remember that περί and πρό do not elide.

## 109. Memory assignment

Memorize the first aorist, the first perfect active, the perfect middle and passive, and the first passive systems of λύω from the chart in 97. The student will be responsible for the complete conjugation of the regular verb λύω from now on.

## 110. Writing exercise

1. Using the principles given in today's lesson for augmenting and/or reduplicating verbs beginning with consonants or vowels, augment the

following verb stems: (a) κριν- (from κρίνω). (b) ἐρωτα- (from ἐρωτάω).
(c) ὁρα- (from ὁράω). (d) ἀρνε- (from ἀρνέομαι).
   2. Reduplicate the following verb stems: (a) πομπ- (from πέμπω).
(b) σκην- (from σκηνόω). (c) γεννη- (from γεννάω). (d) θεα- (from θεάομαι).
   3. Augment the following compound stems: (a) καταβαιν- (from
καταβαίνω). (b) ἀποστελλ- (from ἀποστέλλω). (c) παραλαμβαν- (from
παραλαμβάνω).


# LESSON 13

# The τ-Mute Verb βαπτίζω

## 111. Conjugation of the τ-mute verb

HAVING observed the mood and tense endings of the verb λύω, a verb
whose stem (λυ-) ends in a vowel and very readily accepts the tense suffixes and personal endings, consider now the synopsis of βαπτίζω, a verb
occurring in today's reading passage. Verbs in -ίζω tend to have their real
stem in δ. The stem of βαπτίζω is βαπτιδ-. It ends in δ, which belongs to
the lingual or τ- mutes (see again the chart showing the classes of mutes
in 106).

   The synopsis of βαπτίζω illustrates how *all of the τ-mutes* (τ, δ, and θ)
adapt to the tense signs and personal endings. The synopsis is expanded
sufficiently so that these adaptations can be noted. The student should
trace these carefully on the synopsis chart, as follows:

   *Future and first aorist.* The tense sign of the future is σ and of the first
aorist σα. Note that when these are added to the stem βαπτιδ- the final
letter of the stem (δ) is dropped and the σ of the tense sign remains. The
endings then run regularly as with λύω.

   *First perfect.* βαπτίζω does not have a perfect active, but one is here
given by way of illustration. Note that when the κ of the perfect is added
to the stem βαπτιδ-, the final letter of the stem is again dropped and the κ
of the ending remains. The endings then run regularly as with λύω.

   *Perfect middle and passive.* Here in the various personal endings of the
perfect and pluperfect indicative the stem βαπτιδ- has to blend with μ, σ,
τ, and θ of the endings. It does this by changing δ to σ, or by dropping
δ when the ending begins with σ. Then the endings run regularly.

Note that the perfect and pluperfect third person plurals use forms compounded of the perfect participle (no augment for pluperfect) with the present and imperfect respectively of εἰμί. This is unlike the vowel-stem verb λύω, which uses λέλυνται and ἐλέλυντο.

*First passive.* Where the stem βαπτιδ- meets the θη of the first passive system, it again changes δ to σ so as to make the junction with the best possible euphony. The endings run regularly.

**112. Accent of βαπτίσαι**

The first aorist active infinitive regularly accents the penult. Note that, beginning with this lesson, the synopsis sheet does not label regularly the voices and moods. A somewhat standard tabulation is followed and the student should by now be familiar with this arrangement.

[*For section 113 see opposite*]

**114. New word list**

ἅγιος, -α, -ον, *holy.* HAGIOLATRY.

*ἀκολουθέω, ἀκολουθήσω, ἠκολού-θησα, ἠκολούθηκα, to follow,* with dat. ANACOLUTHON.

*ἀκούω, ἀκούσομαι, ἤκουσα, ἀκήκοα, ἠκούσθην, to hear.* ACOUSTIC.

διδάσκαλος, -ου, ὁ, *teacher.*

δύο, gen. and dat. δυοῖν, *two.* DUAL.

ἐμβλέπω (see βλέπω for prin. parts), *to look upon.*

*ζητέω, ζητήσω, ἐζήτησα, ἐζήτηκα, ἐζητήθην, to seek, ask.*

*λαλέω, λαλήσω, ἐλάλησα, λελάληκα, λελάλημαι, ἐλαλήθην, to converse, talk, say.*

*μαθητής, -οῦ, ὁ, learner, disciple.* POLYMATH.

μεθερμηνεύω, μεθερμηνεύσω, *to trans-late, interpret.*

*πάλιν, again, back.* PALINDROME.

πατέω, πατήσω, ἐπάτησα, πεπά-τηκα, πεπάτημαι, *to tread, walk.*

*περιπατέω* (see πατέω for prin. parts), *to walk about, walk.* PERI-PATETIC.

*ποῦ, where?*

ῥαββί, *rabbi, honorable sir.*

*στρέφω, στρέψω, ἔστρεψα, ἔστροφα, ἔστραμμαι, ἐστράφην, to turn, twist.* STREPTOCOCCUS.

*υἱός, -οῦ, ὁ, son.*

**115. Reading passage** (*John 1:33–38*)

1:33 Κἀγὼ οὐκ ᾔδειν αὐτόν, ἀλλ' ὁ πέμψας με βαπτίζειν ἐν ὕδατι, ἐκεῖνός μοι εἶπεν· ἐφ' ὃν ἂν ἴδῃς τὸ πνεῦμα καταβαῖνον καὶ μένον

33. **κἀγὼ οὐκ ᾔδειν**: see the note on *vs. 31* in 104. **πέμψας**: aorist active participle of πέμπω, *to send.* Compare λύσας in 97. **ἐν ὕδατι**: *in* or *with water.* For instrumental use of ἐν by the κοινή see 482. 15. **εἶπε(ν)**: second aorist of εἴρω. See its principal parts. **ἐφ' ὃν**: for ἐπὶ ὅν, *upon whom.* The final ι of ἐπί is elided before a vowel beginning the

## 113. Partially expanded synopsis of τ-mute verb βαπτίζω, *to baptize.*

| *Present* | *Future* | *First aorist* | *First perfect active* | *Perfect middle and passive* |
|---|---|---|---|---|
| βαπτίζω | βαπτίσω | ἐβάπτισα | (βεβάπτικα) | βεβάπτισμαι |
| ἐβάπτιζον | | | (ἐβεβαπτίκη) | βεβάπτισαι |
| βαπτίζω | | βαπτίσω | (βεβαπτίκω) | βεβάπτισται |
| βαπτίζοιμι | βαπτίσοιμι | βαπτίσαιμι | (βεβαπτίκοιμι) | |
| βάπτιζε | | βάπτισον | (βεβαπτικὼς ἴσθι) | βεβαπτίσμεθα |
| βαπτίζειν | βαπτίσειν | βαπτίσαι | (βεβαπτικέναι) | βεβάπτισθε |
| βαπτίζων, -ουσα, -ον | βαπτίσων, -ουσα, -ον | βαπτίσας, -ασα, -αν | (βεβαπτικώς, -κυῖα, -κός) | βεβαπτισμένοι εἰσί |
| | | | | |
| βαπτίζομαι | βαπτίσομαι | ἐβαπτισάμην | | ἐβεβαπτίσμην |
| | | | | ἐβεβάπτισο |
| | | | | ἐβεβάπτιστο |
| | | | | |
| ἐβαπτιζόμην | | | | ἐβεβαπτίσμεθα |
| | | | | ἐβεβάπτισθε |
| | | | | βεβαπτισμένοι ἦσαν |
| | | | | |
| βαπτίζομαι | βαπτίσομαι | βαπτίσομαι | | βεβαπτισμένος ὦ |
| βαπτιζοίμην | βαπτισοίμην | βαπτισαίμην | | βεβαπτισμένος εἴην |
| βαπτίζου | | βάπτισαι | | βεβάπτισο |
| βαπτίζεσθαι | βαπτίσεσθαι | βαπτίσασθαι | | βεβαπτίσθαι |
| βαπτιζόμενος, -η, -ον | βαπτισόμενος, -η, -ον | βαπτισάμενος, -η, -ον | | βεβαπτισμένος, -η, -ον |

*First passive*

| *Future* | *First aorist* |
|---|---|
| βαπτισθήσομαι | ἐβαπτίσθην |
| | βαπτισθῶ |
| βαπτισθησοίμην | βαπτισθείην |
| | βαπτίσθητι |
| βαπτισθήσεσθαι | βαπτισθῆναι |
| βαπτισθησόμενος, etc. | βαπτισθείς, -εῖσα, -έν |

Present — Passive same forms as middle voice

First perfect active / Perfect middle and passive — Passive same forms as middle voice

34  ἐπ᾽ αὐτόν, οὗτός ἐστιν ὁ βαπτίζων ἐν πνεύματι ἁγίῳ. κἀγὼ
    ἑώρακα, καὶ μεμαρτύρηκα ὅτι οὗτός ἐστιν ὁ υἱὸς τοῦ θεοῦ.
35  Τῇ ἐπαύριον πάλιν εἱστήκει ὁ Ἰωάννης καὶ ἐκ τῶν μαθητῶν
36  αὐτοῦ δύο, καὶ ἐμβλέψας τῷ Ἰησοῦ περιπατοῦντι λέγει· ἴδε ὁ
37  ἀμνὸς τοῦ θεοῦ. καὶ ἤκουσαν οἱ δύο μαθηταὶ αὐτοῦ λαλοῦντος καὶ
38  ἠκολούθησαν τῷ Ἰησοῦ. στραφεὶς δὲ ὁ Ἰησοῦς καὶ θεασάμενος
    αὐτοὺς ἀκολουθοῦντας λέγει αὐτοῖς· τί ζητεῖτε; οἱ δὲ εἶπαν
    αὐτῷ· ῥαββί (ὃ λέγεται μεθερμηνευόμενον διδάσκαλε), ποῦ μένεις;

next word, and because the following vowel has a rough breathing, the π is changed to
its cognate rough mute φ. **ἐφ᾽ ὅν ἂν ἴδῃς** . . . **οὗτός ἐστιν:** here is a *conditional relative*
sentence. Conditional and conditional relative sentences form one of the most important subjects in Greek syntax. Read carefully 593 and 594 by way of definition.
Then in 599 note the structure of the present general condition, and of the corresponding conditional relative. Next note that the sentence at hand here is constructed as
follows: protasis, relative (ὅν) plus ἂν with subjunctive (ἴδῃς is subjunctive of εἶδον,
second aorist of ὁράω, *to see*); apodosis, present indicative (ἐστιν). Observe how this
corresponds to the rule as stated in 599. Translate, *upon whom(ever) you see . . . this one
is . . . .*
    34. **ἑώρακα:** from ὁράω. **μεμαρτύρηκα:** from μαρτυρέω, a regular verb.
    35. **Τῇ ἐπαύριον:** see 104, note on *vs. 29*. **εἱστήκει:** pluperfect of ἵστημι, to stand.
See principal parts of ἵστημι in the cumulative vocabulary, and locate the perfect
ἕστηκα. The lengthening of initial ε to ει is a *temporal augment* since the pluperfect is
a secondary tense. εἱστήκει is often translated as an imperfect, *he stood.*
    36. **ἐμβλέψας:** first aorist active participle of ἐμβλέπω, *to look upon.* Like λύσας in the
λύω chart (97).
    37. **ἤκουσαν:** aorist active of ἀκούω. See its principal parts. ἀκούω, *to hear,* often takes
the genitive of the one heard. See 499.
    38. **στραφεὶς:** aorist passive participle of στρέφω, *to turn, twist.* It translates literally,
*having been turned.* It comes from the last principal part of στρέφω. Refer to the chart of
λύω in 97 and note how its aorist passive participle is formed. **ἀκολουθοῦντας:**
accusative plural of the present participle ἀκολουθῶν, *following.* **ὃ λέγεται:** literally,
*which is said.* Translate, *which is to say.* **διδάσκαλε:** this is the vocative case (singular) of
διδάσκαλος. It is used in addressing a person.

### 116. Writing exercise

Using as a pattern the conjugation chart of λύω in 97, and getting the
first form in each tense–mood group from today's synopsis of βαπτίζω,
make a chart showing the full conjugation of βαπτίζω in the future and
in the first aorist systems.

# LESSON 14
# The κ-Mute Verb ἄγω

**117. Conjugation of the κ-mute verb**

It has been observed that when the stem of the Greek verb ends in a consonant, this calls for certain adaptations as the tense signs and personal endings are affixed. The student has noted the three classes of mute consonants, called respectively π-mutes, κ-mutes, and τ-mutes, and has observed the development of a τ-mute verb, βαπτίζω, with stem ending in δ.

Today attention is called to those verbs whose stems end in a κ-mute. It will be recalled that the three κ-mutes all use the back part of the palate in pronunciation. They are palatal mutes, and include κ, γ, and χ. In the reading passage for today occurs an excellent example of this group, the verb ἄγω, to lead, with stem ending in γ. Verbs with stems ending in κ or χ would be developed just as ἄγω in the matter of the blending of tense signs and endings to the verb stem. In 118 is presented the synopsis of ἄγω, somewhat expanded to show how the endings are joined to it.

The verb ἄγω also gives an opportunity to follow the development of the *second aorist system*, which has not been studied up to this point. The student should follow the ensuing observations carefully, tracing each one in the synopsis chart.

*Present system.* Note that for this verb ἄγω, beginning as it does with a vowel, the augment for the imperfect tense (also the second aorist) is provided by a lengthening of the initial α to η. This is a case of *temporal augment*, where a verb beginning with a consonant would have used *syllabic augment* by adding an initial ε (e.g. ἔλυον). Both α and ε usually augment to η. Sometimes ε augments to ει. This has been discussed more fully in 107.

*Future system.* Verbs with stems ending in κ, γ, or χ combine this final letter of the stem with the σ of the future to make ξ (κs). The σ is still there and is recognized in the double consonant ξ.

*First perfect active.* The κ, γ, or χ of the stem combines with the κ of the perfect system to make χ. In the letter χ the presence of the tense sign κ is still to be recognized. But for this modification the endings run the same as with λύω (λέλυκα, etc.).

Note also that the lengthening of initial α to η suffices for reduplication and, with the pluperfect, for both reduplication and augment.

*Perfect middle and passive.* The κ, γ, or χ of the stem combines with μ by becoming (or remaining) γ. They combine with σ by becoming ξ. They combine with τ by becoming (or remaining) κ. And they combine with θ by becoming (or remaining) χ. Follow this in the chart. Note that the third person plural of the perfect and of the pluperfect are again compound forms, thus differing from λέλυνται and ἐλέλυντο of λύω.

*First passive system.* In order to articulate with the θ of the tense sign θη, the γ (or κ) of the stem becomes χ. Otherwise the endings are just as we have seen them in the first passive system of λύω.

[*For section 118 see opposite*]

**119. Second aorist system — accents**

Some verbs do not have a first aorist system with its σα but instead use a modified stem, with the same endings as the imperfect so far as the indicative mood is concerned (other types of second aorist will be noted later). Second aorists thus following the analogy of the imperfect assume generally the endings of the various moods in the *present system*, to which the imperfect belongs. The student should observe the following rules of accent for second aorist forms:

1. The second aorist active infinitive and the second person singular of the second aorist imperative, because of contraction, receive the circumflex accent on the ultima (a word so accented is called *perispomenon*). This includes ἀγαγεῖν and ἀγαγοῦ.
2. The second aorist active participle, in the masculine and neuter, receives an acute on the ultima (i.e. it is *oxytone*). This applies to ἀγαγών.
3. The second aorist middle infinitive takes the acute on the penult (i.e. it is *paroxytone*), as ἀγαγέσθαι.

**120. New word list**

*ἄγω, ἄξω, ἤγαγον, ἦχα, ἦγμαι, ἤχθην, to lead, drive.
*ἀδελφός, -οῦ, ὁ, brother. PHILA-DELPHIA.
Ἀνδρέας, -οῦ, ὁ, Andrew.
δέκατος, -η, -ον, tenth.

ἑρμηνεύω, ἑρμηνεύσω, to explain, interpret. HERMENEUTICS.
*εὑρίσκω, εὑρήσω, ηὗρον, ηὕρηκα, ηὕρημαι, ηὑρέθην (often with augment or reduplication εὑ-), to find. EUREKA.

## 118. Partially expanded synopsis of κ-mute verb ἄγω, to lead

| Present | Future | Second aorist | First perfect |
|---|---|---|---|
| ἄγω | ἄξω ἄξομεν <br> ἄξεις ἄξετε <br> ἄξει ἄξουσι | ἦγαγον ἠγάγομεν <br> ἤγαγες ἠγάγετε <br> ἤγαγε ἤγαγον | ἦχα ἤχαμεν <br> ἦχας ἤχατε <br> ἦχε ἤχασι <br> ἦχα, ἦχης, ἦχει, etc. |
| ἦγον | | | |
| ἄγω | ἄξοιμι | ἀγάγω, -ῃς, -ῃ, etc. <br> ἀγάγοιμι, -οις, -οι, etc. <br> ἄγαγε, -έτω; -ετε, -όντων <br> ἀγαγεῖν <br> ἀγαγών, -οῦσα, -όν | ἤχω <br> ἤχοιμι <br> ἦχ ὼς ἴσθι <br> ἠχέναι <br> ἠχώς, -χυῖα, -χός |
| ἄγοιμι | | | |
| ἄγε | ἄξειν | | |
| ἄγειν | ἄξων, -ουσα, -ον | | |
| ἄγων, -ουσα, -ον | | | |

### Perfect middle and passive

| Present | Future | Second aorist | First perfect |
|---|---|---|---|
| ἄγομαι | ἄξομαι | ἠγαγόμην ἠγαγόμεθα <br> ἠγάγου ἠγάγεσθε <br> ἠγάγετο ἠγάγοντο | ἦγμαι ἤγμεθα <br> ἦξαι ἦχθε <br> ἦκται ἠγμένοι εἰσί |
| ἠγόμην | | | ἤγμην ἤγμεθα <br> ἦξο ἦχθε <br> ἦκτο ἠγμένοι ἦσαν |
| ἄγωμαι | ἀξοίμην | ἀγάγωμαι, -ῃ, -ηται, etc. <br> ἀγαγοίμην, -οιο, -οιτο, etc. <br> ἀγαγοῦ, -έσθω; -εσθε, -έσθων <br> ἀγαγέσθαι <br> ἀγαγόμενος, -η, -ον | ἠγμένος ὦ <br> ἠγμένος εἴην <br> ἦξο, ἦχθω; ἦχθε, ἤχθων <br> ἦχθαι <br> ἠγμένος, -η, -ον |
| ἀγοίμην | | | |
| ἄγου | ἄξεσθαι | | |
| ἄγεσθαι | ἀξόμενος, -η, -ον | | |
| ἀγόμενος, -η, -ον | | | |

Passive same forms as middle voice      Passive same forms as middle voice

### First passive

| | Future | First passive | |
|---|---|---|---|
| | ἀχθήσομαι | ἤχθην | |
| | ἀχθησοίμην | ἀχθῶ <br> ἀχθείην <br> ἄχθητι <br> ἀχθῆναι | |
| | ἀχθήσεσθαι <br> ἀχθησόμενος, -η, -ον | ἀχθείς, -θεῖσα, -θέν | |

*ἡμέρα, -ας, ἡ, day.* EPHEMERAL.
*καλέω, καλῶ, ἐκάλεσα, κέκληκα,*
*κέκλημαι, ἐκλήθην, to call.* CALL.
*Κηφᾶς, -ᾶ, ὁ, Cephas.*

*Μεσσίας, -ου, ὁ, Messiah.*
*Πέτρος, -ου, ὁ, Peter.*
*Σίμων, -ωνος, ὁ, Simon.*
*ὥρα, -ας, ἡ, hour.* HOROSCOPE.

**121. Reading passage** (*John 1:39–42*)

1:39 Λέγει αὐτοῖς· ἔρχεσθε καὶ ὄψεσθε. ἦλθαν οὖν καὶ εἶδαν ποῦ μένει, καὶ παρ᾽ αὐτῷ ἔμειναν τὴν ἡμέραν ἐκείνην· ὥρα ἦν ὡς δεκάτη.

40 Ἦν Ἀνδρέας ὁ ἀδελφὸς Σίμωνος Πέτρου εἷς ἐκ τῶν δύο τῶν
41 ἀκουσάντων παρὰ Ἰωάννου καὶ ἀκολουθησάντων αὐτῷ· εὑρίσκει οὗτος πρῶτον τὸν ἀδελφὸν τὸν ἴδιον Σίμωνα καὶ λέγει αὐτῷ· εὑρήκαμεν τὸν Μεσσίαν (ὅ ἐστιν μεθερμηνευόμενον χριστός).

42 ἤγαγεν αὐτὸν πρὸς τὸν Ἰησοῦν. ἐμβλέψας αὐτῷ ὁ Ἰησοῦς εἶπεν· σὺ εἶ Σίμων ὁ υἱὸς Ἰωάννου, σὺ κληθήσῃ Κηφᾶς (ὅ ἑρμηνεύεται Πέτρος).

39. **ἔρχεσθε**: note how the present middle imperative of λύω is formed. See chart in 97. **ὄψεσθε**: from ὁράω, *to see.* See its principal parts. **ἦλθαν, εἶδαν**: these two second aorists are respectively from ἔρχομαι and ὁράω. One would have expected ἦλθον and εἶδον, as these are second aorists (compare the expansion of ἄγω in today's lesson). But the N.T. sometimes follows the Alexandrian usage of substituting a as the personal ending vowel in the second aorist (482. 7). **ἔμειναν**: first aorist of μένω, *to remain.* From the principal parts of μένω (see cumulative vocabulary) the aorist is seen to be ἔμεινα. This is a verb with stem ending in a liquid consonant ν. Its structure will be studied later. It regularly uses the same endings as the first aorist of λύω but without the σ. Hence ἔμειναν is considered a first aorist like ἔλυσαν. **τὴν ἡμέραν ἐκείνην**: *during that day.* Extent of time or space is usually indicated in Greek by the accusative case without a preposition (531). **ὡς**: translate, *about.*

40. **εἰς**: distinguish from εἰς, *into.* **ἀκουσάντων, ἀκολουθησάντων**: aorist active participles from ἀκούω and ἀκολουθέω. Note the σα tense sign in each. These are in the genitive plural masculine. The nominatives are ἀκούσας, ἀκολουθήσας. Compare λύσας in the chart of λύω in 97.

41. **εὑρήκαμεν**: perfect active of εὑρίσκω in today's word list. **μεθερμηνευόμενον**: present middle and passive participle of μεθερμηνεύω. Its use is here passive. It is neuter, agreeing with ὅ, *which.* See ἐρχόμενος as developed in 58.

42. **ἤγαγε(ν)**: second aorist of ἄγω. Locate this form in today's chart. **εἶπε(ν)**: second aorist of εἴρω. See this verb in vocabulary. **εἶ**: from εἰμί. See note on *vs. 18* in 70. **κληθήσῃ**: from καλέω, *to call,* in today's word list. Locate the form λυθήσει in the chart of λύω in 97, and compare with this form. Classical Greek (especially the tragic poets), as well as the κοινή, sometimes uses the ending -ῃ instead of -ει for the second person singular, middle and passive (482. 3).

**122. Writing exercise**

Using as a model the conjugation chart of λύω in 97, construct a chart showing the full conjugation of ἄγω in the second aorist, first perfect active, and in the perfect middle and passive systems. The student will find an indication of the expansion of several of the tense–mood groups in today's chart of ἄγω and can follow the chart of λύω for the rest if necessary.

LESSON 15

## The π-Mute Verb γράφω

### 123. Conjugation of the π-mute verb

THE development of verbs with stems ending in the lingual mutes (τ, δ, θ), and in the palatal mutes (κ, γ, χ), has now been studied. Today attention is given to the labial or π-mute stems. The verb γράφω, *to write*, which occurs in *vs. 45* of today's reading passage, is an example. The somewhat expanded synopsis of γράφω is given in the chart in 124. The student should consult this chart carefully as he reads each of the following observations:

*Present system.* Note that γράφω, beginning with a consonant, receives the simple syllabic augment of the prefixed ε- in the imperfect (also aorist and pluperfect) indicative.

*Future and first aorist systems.* The φ of the stem blends with the σ of the future and with the σα of the first aorist to form ψ. A final π or β in the stem would be treated just the same.

*Second perfect active.* The perfect active, γέγραφα, is called a *second perfect*, because it fits the personal endings -α, -ας, -ε, etc., directly to the reduplicated stem γεγραφ-. But there is a sense in which it can be said that verbs with stems ending in π, β, or φ unite that final letter with the κ of the perfect to form φ. For example, the perfect active of πέμπ-ω is πέπομφα, of τρίβ-ω, τέτριφα. Note that with these labials, regularly the π, β, or φ becomes or remains φ.

More irregular is λείπω, whose second perfect λέλοιπα does not even have the roughened φ as a reminder that the final π of the stem was combined with κ of the perfect. The κ is simply lost. λέλοιπα is, of course, a second perfect.

The personal endings of the second perfect active are just like those of the first perfect active, but without κ.

*Perfect middle and passive.* The φ (or π or β) of the stem is changed to μ when it joins with μ in the personal endings, or to ψ when combined with σ, or to π when it precedes τ. Preceding θ it remains rough φ to match rough θ (π or β would change to φ). Third person plurals, both perfect and pluperfect, are compound forms, and not single forms like λέλυνται, the perfect, and ἐλέλυντο, the pluperfect, middle and passive, of λύω.

*Second passive.* In the passive system, γράφω, like a few other Greek verbs, omits the θ which has been noted in the θη of the first passive system. The student is alerted to this by the form of the last principal part, ἐγράφην. The system is called the *second passive system*. Note that its personal endings do not otherwise differ from those seen in the first passive system of λύω except that the aorist passive imperative starts with γράφηθι (λύω uses λύθητι). Review the comment on this in 91.

[*For section 124 see opposite*]

## 125. New word list

*ἀγαθός, -ή, -όν, good, brave.*
ἀληθῶς, *truly.*
*ἀπό, with gen., from.* APOSTATE.
Βηθσαϊδά, ἡ, indecl. except acc.
    Βηθσαϊδάν, *Bethsaida.*
Γαλιλαία, -ας, ἡ, *Galilee.*
*γράφω, γράψω, ἔγραψα, γέγραφα,*
    *γέγραμμαι, ἐγράφην, to write.*
    TELEGRAPH.
δόλος, -ου, ὁ, *deceit, treachery.*
*δύναμαι, δυνήσομαι, δεδύνημαι,*
    *ἐδυνήθην, to be able, be worth.*
    DYNAMO.

*ἐθέλω, ἐθελήσω, ἠθέλησα, ἠθέληκα,*
    *to be willing, wish.*
*ἐξέρχομαι (see ἔρχομαι for prin.*
    parts), *to come or go out.*
'Ισραηλείτης, -ου, ὁ, *Israelite.*
'Ιωσήφ, ὁ, indecl., *Joseph.*
Ναζαρέθ, ἡ, indecl., *Nazareth.*
Ναθαναήλ, ὁ, indecl., *Nathanael.*
*πόλις, πόλεως, ἡ, city.* METRO-
    POLIS.
*τὶς, τὶ, gen. τινὸς or του, anyone,*
    *anything, someone, something.*
Φίλιππος, -ου, ὁ, *Philip.*

## 126. Reading passage (*John 1:43–47*)

1:43  Τῇ ἐπαύριον ἠθέλησεν ἐξελθεῖν εἰς τὴν Γαλιλαίαν, καὶ εὑρίσκει
  44  Φίλιππον. καὶ λέγει αὐτῷ ὁ 'Ιησοῦς· ἀκολούθει μοι. ἦν δὲ ὁ
      Φίλιππος ἀπὸ Βηθσαϊδά, ἐκ τῆς πόλεως Ἀνδρέου καὶ Πέτρου.

43. **τῇ ἐπαύριον**: see note on *vs. 29* in 104. **ἠθέλησε(ν)**: aorist active of ἐθέλω in today's word list. **ἐξελθεῖν**: second aorist infinitive of ἐξέρχομαι, *to go out.* Drop the prefix, for the purpose of analysis, and look up the principal parts of ἔρχομαι. The third principal part is found to be ἦλθον (a second aorist like ἤγαγον). Drop the augment, and the stem is seen to be ἐλθ-. Add the ending -εῖν, as with the second aorist ἀγαγεῖν (118). **ἀκολούθει**: second person singular present imperative active of ἀκολουθέω, *to follow.* This verb is called a *contract verb in* ε (from its ending -εω) and the development of this type of verb will be presented later. The contract verbs differ, in the present system, from verbs like λύω. The corresponding imperative in λύω would be λῦε (see the chart in 97).

## 124. Partially expanded synopsis of π-mute verb γράφω, *to write*

| Present | Future | First aorist | Second perfect active |
|---|---|---|---|
| γράφω | γράψω | ἔγραψα | γέγραφα, γέγραφας, γέγραφε, etc. |
| ἔγραφον | | | ἐγεγράφη, ἐγεγράφης, ἐγεγράφει, etc. |
| γράφω | γράψοιμι | γράψω | γεγράφω |
| γράφοιμι | | γράψαιμι | γεγράφοιμι |
| γράφε | γράψειν | γράψον | γεγραφὼς ἴσθι |
| γράφειν | | γράψαι | γεγραφέναι |
| γράφων, -ουσα, -ον | γράψων, -ουσα, -ον | γράψας, -ασα, -αν | γεγραφώς, -φυῖα, -φός |

### Perfect middle and passive

| | | | |
|---|---|---|---|
| | | | γέγραμμαι　γεγράμμεθα |
| | | | γέγραψαι　γέγραφθε |
| | | | γέγραπται　γεγραμμένοι εἰσί |
| | | | ἐγεγράμμην　ἐγεγράμμεθα |
| | | | ἐγέγραψο　ἐγέγραφθε |
| | | | ἐγέγραπτο　γεγραμμένοι ἦσαν |
| | | | γεγραμμένος ὦ |
| | | | γεγραμμένος εἴην |
| | | | γέγραψο, γεγράφθω; γέγραφθε, γεγράφθων |
| | | | γεγράφθαι |
| | | | γεγραμμένος, -η, -ον |

| Present | Future | First aorist | |
|---|---|---|---|
| γράφομαι | γράψομαι | ἐγραψάμην | |
| γράφωμαι | γραψοίμην | γράψωμαι | |
| γραφοίμην | | γραψαίμην | |
| γράφου | γράψεσθαι | γράψαι | |
| γράφεσθαι | γραψόμενος, -η, -ον | γράψασθαι | |
| γραφόμενος, -η, -ον | | γραψάμενος, -η, -ον | |

### Second passive

| | | | |
|---|---|---|---|
| Passive same forms as middle voice | γραφήσομαι | ἐγράφην | |
| | γραφησοίμην | γραφῶ | |
| | | γραφείην | |
| | γραφήσεσθαι | γράφηθι, γραφήτω, etc. | |
| | γραφησόμενος, etc. | γραφῆναι | |
| | | γραφείς, -εῖσα, -έν | |

Passive same forms as middle voice

45  εὑρίσκει Φίλιππος τὸν Ναθαναὴλ καὶ λέγει αὐτῷ· ὃν ἔγραψεν
Μωϋσῆς ἐν τῷ νόμῳ καὶ οἱ προφῆται εὑρήκαμεν, Ἰησοῦν υἱὸν
46  τοῦ Ἰωσὴφ τὸν ἀπὸ Ναζαρέθ. καὶ εἶπεν αὐτῷ Ναθαναήλ· ἐκ
Ναζαρὲθ δύναταί τι ἀγαθὸν εἶναι; λέγει αὐτῷ ὁ Φίλιππος· ἔρχου
47  καὶ ἴδε. εἶδεν Ἰησοῦς τὸν Ναθαναὴλ ἐρχόμενον πρὸς αὐτὸν καὶ
λέγει περὶ αὐτοῦ· ἴδε ἀληθῶς Ἰσραηλείτης, ἐν ᾧ δόλος οὐκ
ἔστιν.

45. **ὅν**: from ὅς, ἥ, ὅ, the relative pronoun. Locate this form in the expansion in 64.
**ἔγραψε(ν)**: aorist active of γράφω in today's word list. **εὑρήκαμεν**: from εὑρίσκω. See
its principal parts.
46. **δύναται**: present indicative of δύναμαι in today's word list. Translate, *is able, can*.
**τι**: the forms of τίς, τὶ are enclitic. Thus the preceding word, δύναται, receives a secondary accent. See note on *vs. 15* in 60. **εἶναι**: present infinitive of εἰμί, *to be*. **ἔρχου**:
present imperative of ἔρχομαι. Compare with λύου in the chart of λύω (97). **ἴδε**: see
note on *vs. 29* in 104. (So also in *vs. 47* below).
47. **εἶδε(ν)**: from ὁράω. **ᾧ**: from the relative ὅς, ἥ, ὅ. See 64. **ἔστιν**: third person
singular present indicative of εἰμί, *to be*.

**127. Writing exercise**

Expand γράφω fully in the second passive system, referring to λύω in
the first passive system (97). Allow extra space after each form, and write
in the translation of each form. The λύω synopsis in 82 will suggest the
translation for the first person singular in each tense–mood group.

# LESSON 16

# The Verb εἰμί

**128. Conjugation of the verb εἰμί**

SEVERAL of the forms of the verb εἰμί, *to be*, have been presented individually in the word lists. Its complete expansion is now presented in
the chart in 132. Note that the verb has forms in two tense systems
only, the present and the future. The present forms are active; the future
forms are middle.

*Enclitic forms of* εἰμί. It should further be noted that all of the forms
of the present indicative of εἰμί are enclitics except εἶ. The third person
singular ἐστί takes ν-movable like words ending in -σι. Review the paragraph on enclitics (28).

ἐστί becomes ἔστι, losing its character as an enclitic, under certain
circumstances such as the following:

1. At the beginning of a sentence.
2. When signifying existence (*there is*) or possibility (*it is possible*).
3. Following οὐκ, μή, εἰ, ὡς, ἀλλά, καί, and τοῦτο.

**129. Variations in accent of enclitics**

While enclitics generally lose their accent to the word preceding, yet in certain cases, as already observed with εἰμί, they retain it. The Greeks felt it awkward to pronounce several syllables in succession without accenting any of them. They also disliked to place acute accents upon adjoining syllables in the same word. Consequently the student needs to note the following:

1. When a dissyllabic enclitic follows a word with acute on the penult, the enclitic retains its accent, as λόγοι τινές *certain words*, to avoid three unaccented syllables.
2. When an enclitic follows a word with acute on the antepenult or circumflex on the penult, the preceding word receives a secondary accent, as ἄνθρωπός τις, *a certain man*; δῶρά τινα, *certain gifts*.
3. Further, an enclitic retains its accent if the preceding syllable is elided, as τοῦτ' ἐστὶ τὸ τέλος, *this is the end*.
4. A proclitic or enclitic, when followed by an enclitic, receives an acute accent, as ἔν γε τῷ φανερῷ, *at least in the open*.

**130. Memory assignment**

The student is asked to memorize the complete conjugation of εἰμί and to be responsible for it from now on in the course.

**131. Deponent verbs**

Before leaving for a while the study of the verbs, notice is given to the nature of *deponent verbs*. Some verbs occur only in middle or passive form, even though they may be active in meaning, for example γίγνομαι (or γίνομαι), *to become*; δύναμαι, *to be able*; ἔρχομαι, *to go, come*. Such are called *deponent verbs*, as in Latin.

A regular deponent verb has four principal parts (present, future, aorist, perfect) and is recognized as a *middle deponent* or a *passive deponent* according to whether the *aorist middle* or the *aorist passive* is shown in the principal parts. For example, with θεάομαι, θεάσομαι, ἐθεασάμην, τεθέαμαι, the presence of the aorist middle ἐθεασάμην shows that θεάομαι, *to behold*, is a middle deponent. But note δύναμαι, δυνήσομαι, δεδύνημαι, ἐδυνήθην. The presence of the aorist passive ἐδυνήθην shows that δύναμαι, *to be able*, is a passive deponent.

Some deponent verbs are irregular and have both the aorist middle and the aorist passive. Some have active forms in certain tense systems, as γέγονα, the perfect of γίγνομαι, or ἦλθον, the second aorist of ἔρχομαι. Also some verbs in -ω are deponent in certain tense systems, and are thus irregular, for example βαίνω, βήσομαι, etc. εἰμί, *to be*, is deponent in its future system.

[*For section 132 see opposite*]

## 133. New word list

*ἄγγελος, -ου, ὁ, messenger, angel.* ANGEL.

*ἀμήν, verily, surely, certainly.* AMEN.

*ἀναβαίνω (see βαίνω for prin. parts), to go up, ascend.* ANABASIS.

ἀνοίγω, ἀνοίξω, ἀνέῳξα, ἀνέῳγα, ἀνέῳγμαι, ἀνεῴχθην, *to open.*

*βασιλεύς, -έως, ὁ, king.* BASIL.

*μείζων, -ον (comp. of μέγας), greater.*

*πόθεν, whence.*

*πρό, with gen., before.* PROSCENIUM.

συκῆ, -ῆς, ἡ, *fig tree.* SYCOPHANT.

*ὑπό, with gen., under of place where; with acc., under of place to which.* HYPODERMIC.

ὑποκάτω, *below, underneath.*

φωνέω, φωνήσω, ἐφώνησα, ἐφώνήθην, *to speak, call.* EUPHONIC.

## 134. Reading passage (*John 1:48–51*)

1:48 Λέγει αὐτῷ Ναθαναήλ· πόθεν με γινώσκεις; ἀπεκρίθη Ἰησοῦς καὶ εἶπεν αὐτῷ· πρὸ τοῦ σε Φίλιππον φωνῆσαι ὄντα ὑπὸ τὴν

48. με: accusative singular of ἐγώ, *I*. It has no accent but is enclitic. Turn to the declension of ἐγώ in 72 and note that in the genitive, dative, and accusative singular there are alternate shortened forms μου, μοι, με which are often used as enclitics. Note also in 72 that the singular forms of σύ are often used as enclitics. This applies to σοι in *vs. 50* below. ἀπεκρίθη: from ἀποκρίνω. See principal parts of κρίνω. εἶπε(ν): from εἴπω, *to say*. So also for *vs. 50* below. πρὸ τοῦ σε Φίλιππον φωνῆσαι: as to the form of φωνῆσαι, by reference to the principal parts of φωνέω, *to call*, or by noting the σα of its ending and comparing it mentally with λῦσαι (see the chart in 97), the student will place this as the first aorist active infinitive of φωνέω, *to call*. Now note that with it comes the article τοῦ (neuter). We have here an *articular infinitive*, that is, an infinitive which is shown by the definite article to have substantive or noun force. τὸ φωνῆσαι is *the to call*, *the calling* (see 572). Both the subject and the object of such an infinitive, if it has them, are generally in the accusative case. Here Φίλιππον is the subject and σε (see 72 for this form) the object. This substantive clause is object of the preposition πρό, *before*, which takes its object in the genitive case. Thus the article is genitive in form. The literal translation of πρὸ τοῦ σε Φίλιππον φωνῆσαι would be, *before the Philip to call you*. Since the English has no parallel usage, translate, *before Philip called you*. ὄντα: from ὤν, *being*, the present active participle of εἰμί. It is accusative singular masculine agreeing with σε.

## 132. Conjugation of εἰμί, *to be*

| Present | | Future | First aorist | First perfect |
|---|---|---|---|---|
| εἰμί | ἐσμέν | | | |
| εἶ | ἐστέ | | | |
| ἐστί | εἰσί | | | |
| | | | | |
| ἦν | ἦμεν | | | |
| ἦσθα | ἦτε | | | |
| ἦν | ἦσαν | | | |
| | | | | |
| ὦ | ὦμεν | | | |
| ᾖς | ἦτε | | | |
| ᾖ | ὦσι | | | |
| | | | | |
| εἴην | εἶμεν | | | |
| εἴης | εἶτε | | | |
| εἴη | εἶεν or | | | |
| | εἴησαν | | | |
| ἴσθι | ἔστε | | | |
| ἔστω | ἔστων | | | |
| | | | | |
| εἶναι | | | | |
| | | | | |
| ὤν, οὖσα, ὄν | | | | |

*Perf. mid. and pass.*

ἔσομαι     ἐσόμεθα
ἔσει       ἔσεσθε
ἔσται      ἔσονται

ἐσοίμην    ἐσοίμεθα
ἔσοιο      ἔσοισθε
ἔσοιτο     ἔσοιντο

ἔσεσθαι

ἐσόμενος, -η, -ον

*First passive*

49   συκῆν εἶδόν σε. ἀπεκρίθη αὐτῷ Ναθαναήλ· ῥαββί, σὺ εἶ ὁ υἱὸς τοῦ
50   θεοῦ, σὺ βασιλεὺς εἶ τοῦ Ἰσραήλ. ἀπεκρίθη Ἰησοῦς καὶ εἶπεν
     αὐτῷ· ὅτι εἶπόν σοι ὅτι εἶδόν σε ὑποκάτω τῆς συκῆς, πιστεύεις;
51   μείζω τούτων ὄψῃ. καὶ λέγει αὐτῷ· ἀμὴν ἀμὴν λέγω ὑμῖν,
     ὄψεσθε τὸν οὐρανὸν ἀνεῳγότα καὶ τοὺς ἀγγέλους τοῦ θεοῦ
     ἀναβαίνοντας καὶ καταβαίνοντας ἐπὶ τὸν υἱὸν τοῦ ἀνθρώπου.

48. **εἶδον**: from ὁράω. 50. **μείζω**: a shortened form of the neuter plural μείζονα, *greater (things)*. **τούτων**: genitive plural neuter of οὗτος. See 67. The idea of comparison is expressed by the genitive case. It is called *genitive of comparison* (507). Translate, *than these (things)*. **ὄψῃ**: from ὁράω. See its principal parts. This form is the second person singular of the future (middle). One might have expected ὄψει (like λύσει in 97). For the η ending see 482. 3. ὄψεσθε in the next verse is second person plural.

51. **ὑμῖν**: from σύ. See 72. **ἀνεῳγότα**: by looking at the principal parts of ἀνοίγω, *to open*, the student will see that ἀνεῳγότα is apparently taken from the form ἀνέῳγα, and is thus perfect active. Following the analogy of the other verbs so far, it is evident that the perfect active participle would then be ἀνεῳγώς, *having opened*. The form ἀνεῳγότα is the masculine accusative singular of ἀνεῳγώς. In this same verse ἀναβαίνοντας and καταβαίνοντας are the masculine accusative plural of the present participles ἀναβαίνων and καταβαίνων.

### 135. Writing exercise

1. From today's chart of εἰμί, *to be*, write the proper form of εἰμί to give the sense of the translated phrases below (recall from the synopsis chart of λύω in 82 that we have somewhat arbitrarily translated the subjunctive mood as *may*, and the optative as *might*): (*a*) *You* (pl.) *were*. (*b*) *I may be.* (*c*) *You* (sing.) *might* (now) *be.* (*d*) *We shall be.* (*e*) *To be.* (*f*) *They are.*

2. List the principal parts of the following deponent verbs, and say whether each verb is a passive or a middle deponent: (*a*) ἡγέομαι (*to lead*). (*b*) ἐπίσταμαι (*to know*). (*c*) δέχομαι (*to receive*). Consult the vocabulary at rear of book.

## LESSON 17

## Review

**136.** REVIEW the meanings of all starred words in the word lists up to this point.

Review the translation of the entire first chapter of St. John's gospel.

Review the declension of the adjective πρῶτος, -η, -ον (56).

Review the conjugation of the regular verb λύω (97).

Review the conjugation of the verb εἰμί (132).

## LESSON 18
# Consonant Declension Nouns

### 137. Nouns of the consonant declension

EARLIER in the course the declension of nouns of the two so-called vowel declensions, the α- and the ο-declensions, has been studied. There is a third general group, containing principally nouns with stems ending in consonants, and thus called the *consonant declension*.

### 138. Syncopated stems

In the reading passage today the word μήτηρ, *mother*, occurs three times. ἡ μήτηρ belongs to a small group within the consonant declension whose stems end in ερ, and which, instead of carrying this syllable throughout, tend to cut it off (syncopate). So while the genitive of μήτηρ, if used in full, would be μητέρος, it is cut down to μητρός. The student need not be concerned about these internal matters, but should carefully observe this noun in its generally used form. The accents appear irregular and have to be learned by observation. The three most commonly used nouns from this group are here presented in full:

| ἡ μήτηρ, mother | ὁ πατήρ, father | ὁ ἀνήρ, man |
|---|---|---|
| μητρός | πατρός | ἀνδρός |
| μητρί | πατρί | ἀνδρί |
| μητέρα | πατέρα | ἄνδρα |
| | | |
| μητέρες | πατέρες | ἄνδρες |
| μητέρων | πατέρων | ἀνδρῶν |
| μητράσι | πατράσι | ἀνδράσι |
| μητέρας | πατέρας | ἄνδρας |

### 139. Stems in ς

Next for attention is a small group of nouns in the consonant declension usually referred to as 'stems in ς'. The final σ of the original stem drops out in all but the nominative singular and leaves the vowel of the stem to contract with the vowel of the ending (e.g. ἔτος, *year*, stem ἐτεσ-, genitive ἐτε[σ]ος or ἔτεος or ἔτους). κέρας, *horn*, has forms showing a τ-stem (κερατ-), also shorter forms indicating the dropped σ. Here are four examples with the original stems indicated:

| | |
|---|---|
| τὸ κρέας (κρεασ-), *meat* | τὸ ἔτος (ἐτεσ-), *year* |
| κρέως | ἔτους or ἔτεος |
| κρέαι or κρέᾳ | ἔτει |
| κρέας | ἔτος |
| | |
| κρέα | ἔτη (for -εα) |
| κρεῶν | ἐτῶν or ἐτέων |
| κρέασι | ἔτεσι |
| κρέα | ἔτη |
| | |
| τὸ κέρας (κερᾱτ-, κερασ-), *horn* | ἡ τριήρης (τριηρεσ-), *trireme* |
| κέρατος or κέρως | τριήρους |
| κέρατι or κέραι | τριήρει |
| κέρας | τριήρη (-εα) |
| | |
| κέρατα or κέρα | τριήρεις (ε-ες) |
| κεράτων or κερῶν | τριήρων |
| κέρασι | τριήρεσι |
| κέρατα or κέρα | τριήρεις (-εας) |

## 140. Generalizations as to endings

As can be seen, there are quite a few variations within this group, but still a general pattern can be discerned in the endings as given above (not every one of the characteristics is observable in the examples just given. Some will be noted in later examples).

| | Singular | Plural |
|---|---|---|
| Nom. | ς, ν, or ρ (liquids), α (neut.) | ες, εις, η or α (neut.) |
| Gen. | ος, ους, έως | ων |
| Dat. | ι | σι |
| Acc. | α, ν, ς or α (neut.) | ας, εις, η or α (neut.) |

Look through the examples given in today's lesson rather carefully, observing how the endings correspond to those in the chart just suggested.

## 141. New word list

γάμος, -ου, ὁ, *wedding, marriage.*
  POLYGAMY.
*γυνή, γυναικός, ἡ, *woman, wife.*
  GYNECOLOGY.
διάκονος, -ου, ὁ or ἡ, *servant, minister.* DEACON.

*ἐκεῖ, *there, in that place.*
*ἔχω, ἕξω, ἔσχον, ἔσχηκα, ἔσχημαι, (imperfect εἶχον), *to have, hold.*
*ἥκω, ἥξω, ἧξα, ἧκα, *to have come, come, be present.*
Κανά, ἡ, indecl., *Cana.*

*μήτηρ, μητρός, ἡ, mother. MATER-
NAL.
*οἶνος, -ου, ὁ, wine. WINE.
*ὅστις, ἥτις, ὅ τι, gen. οὗτινος,
ἧστινος, οὗτινος, whoever, anyone
who, whatever.
*οὔπω, not yet.

*ποιέω, ποιήσω, ἐποίησα, πεποίηκα,
πεποίημαι, ἐποιήθην, to make, do.
POET.
*τρίτος, -η, -ον, third.
ὑστερέω, ὑστερήσω, ὑστέρησα,
ὑστέρηκα, ὑστερήθην, to be behind,
be deficient, insufficient.

**142. Reading Passage** (*John* 2:1–5)

2:1  Καὶ τῇ ἡμέρᾳ τῇ τρίτῃ γάμος ἐγένετο ἐν Κανὰ τῆς Γαλιλαίας,
2  καὶ ἦν ἡ μήτηρ τοῦ Ἰησοῦ ἐκεῖ· ἐκλήθη δὲ καὶ ὁ Ἰησοῦς καὶ οἱ
3  μαθηταὶ αὐτοῦ εἰς τὸν γάμον. καὶ ὑστερήσαντος οἴνου λέγει ἡ
4  μήτηρ τοῦ Ἰησοῦ πρὸς αὐτόν· οἶνον οὐκ ἔχουσιν. καὶ λέγει αὐτῇ ὁ
5  Ἰησοῦς· τί ἐμοὶ καὶ σοί, γύναι; οὔπω ἥκει ἡ ὥρα μου. λέγει ἡ
μήτηρ αὐτοῦ τοῖς διακόνοις· ὅ τι ἂν λέγῃ ὑμῖν, ποιήσατε.

1. **τῇ ἡμέρᾳ τῇ τρίτῃ**: dative of time when (526). **ἐγένετο**: second aorist of γίγνομαι
(N.T. γίνομαι). The basic meaning *to become* easily yields the thought *to take place*,
as here.
2. **ἐκλήθη**: from καλέω. See its principal parts. Compare with ἐλύθη in the chart of
λύω in 97. **καὶ ... καὶ**: where used double, as here, the sense is usually *both . . . and*.
3. **ὑστερήσαντος οἴνου**: ὑστερήσαντος is the genitive singular masculine of the aorist
active participle ὑστερήσας, *having been deficient*, or *run out*. Its subject οἴνου is also in the
genitive. This introduces a much used Greek construction, the *genitive absolute*, where
a noun or pronoun subject and a participle, both in the genitive case, are translated
independently of the sentence. It is like the ablative absolute in Latin. Consult 582
for its various possible meanings. The context helps to indicate which shade of meaning
is implied in a given case. Here the genitive absolute ὑστερήσαντος οἴνου is probably
best understood as referring to time, *wine having run short* or *when wine had run short*.
4. **τί ἐμοὶ καὶ σοί**: understand ἐστίν, *what is it* or *that?* See 72 for ἐμοί and σοί. These
are datives of advantage (517). **γύναι**: vocative case of γυνή, *woman*.
5. **ὅ τι ἂν λέγῃ ὑμῖν, ποιήσατε**: another conditional relative sentence. Read again
593, 594 for a review of the general concept. Then read 603 which describes the construction of the future more vivid conditional relative. Now look at the sentence in
hand, which is formed as follows: protasis, relative (ὅ τι) plus ἂν plus subjunctive
(λέγῃ); apodosis, an imperative (ποιήσατε, *do* (*it*)!) which, of course, refers to the future
and is thus the equivalent, in time value, of a future indicative. Here, then, is a conditional relative with future more vivid supposition. Translate, *whatever he says* (*shall
say*) *to you, do* (*it*).

## 143. Writing exercise

Using today's examples or *paradigms*, and the pronouns in 63–67,
write the Greek words to give the following indicated meanings:
(*a*) *Of the fathers themselves.* (*b*) *These* (the foregoing) *triremes* (accusative; use definite article immediately preceding noun). (*c*) *Of that* (use

article immediately preceding noun) *year.* (*d*) *To* or *for these* (the following) *mothers* (use definite article preceding the noun). (*e*) *The men who . . .* (nom.). (*f*) *To* or *for that* (use article immediately preceding noun) *darkness.*

## LESSON 19
# Mute- and Liquid- Stem Nouns

### 144. The mute-stem nouns

ANOTHER family of nouns in the consonant declension, and a rather numerous one, is the group of nouns whose stems end in one of the three classes of mute consonants. The endings of these nouns are substantially the same as those noted in the last lesson. In order to find the true stem of nouns in this group, go to the genitive singular and drop the final -ος. The stem cannot be identified as accurately from the nominative singular.

### 145. π- and κ-mute nouns

First is presented the declension of the π-mute stem ὁ κλώψ, *thief*; and of the two κ-mute nouns, ἡ σάρξ, *flesh*, and ἡ γυνή, *woman*. These are as follows:

| ὁ κλώψ, *thief* | ἡ σάρξ, *flesh* | ἡ γυνή, *woman* |
|---|---|---|
| κλωπός | σαρκός | γυναικός |
| κλωπί | σαρκί | γυναικί |
| κλῶπα | σάρκα | γυναῖκα |
| κλῶπες | σάρκες | γυναῖκες |
| κλωπῶν | σαρκῶν | γυναικῶν |
| κλωψί | σαρξί | γυναιξί |
| κλῶπας | σάρκας | γυναῖκας |

The accent of γυνή is somewhat irregular. That of κλώψ and σάρξ and most of the nouns in this group is regular. The rule of persistent accent for nouns holds in the background (see 25). But note that in this group a noun *with a monosyllabic stem* regularly accents the last syllable in the genitive and dative of both numbers, the genitive plural taking the circumflex.

Note also that one determines the true stem of a noun in the consonant declension by dropping the -ος from the end of the genitive singular. For example, dropping final -ος from the genitive singular of

## *Cana of Galilee*

The village of Kefr Kenna is the traditional Cana of Galilee, where Jesus' first miracle, recorded in John 2, was performed. Near the right is the modern Greek church commemorating this miracle. In the foreground is the ancient walled spring from which the servants may have filled their earthen water-jars to supply the wedding-feast.

κλώψ, κλωπός, one sees that the stem is κλωπ-. Since this is a single syllable, the genitive and dative of both numbers will accent the ultima.

### 146. τ-mute nouns

Next follows the declension of some nouns with τ-mute stems. This class includes many neuters.

| ἡ χάρις, *grace* | ἡ ἀσπίς, *shield* | ὁ ἄρχων, *leader* |
|---|---|---|
| χάριτος | ἀσπίδος | ἄρχοντος |
| χάριτι | ἀσπίδι | ἄρχοντι |
| χάριν | ἀσπίδα | ἄρχοντα |
| χάριτες | ἀσπίδες | ἄρχοντες |
| χαρίτων | ἀσπίδων | ἀρχόντων |
| χάρισι | ἀσπίσι | ἄρχουσι |
| χάριτας | ἀσπίδας | ἄρχοντας |

| τὸ ὕδωρ, *water* | τὸ ἅρμα, *chariot* |
|---|---|
| ὕδατος | ἅρματος |
| ὕδατι | ἅρματι |
| ὕδωρ | ἅρμα |
| ὕδατα | ἅρματα |
| ὑδάτων | ἁρμάτων |
| ὕδασι | ἅρμασι |
| ὕδατα | ἅρματα |

### 147. The liquid-stem nouns

The so-called liquid consonants, or 'singing consonants', are λ, μ, ν, and ρ. Some nouns with liquid stems are now observed. The endings are very similar to those of the other nouns noted in the consonant declension.

| ὁ ἀγών, *contest* | ὁ μήν, *month* | ὁ Σίμων, *Simon* |
|---|---|---|
| ἀγῶνος | μηνός | Σίμωνος |
| ἀγῶνι | μηνί | Σίμωνι |
| ἀγῶνα | μῆνα | Σίμωνα |
| ἀγῶνες | μῆνες | |
| ἀγώνων | μηνῶν | |
| ἀγῶσι | μησί | |
| ἀγῶνας | μῆνας | |

Note that as far as the nominatives are concerned, ἀγών might easily be assumed to be developed just as ἄρχων in 146 above. But by looking at the genitive singular of each it is found that the stem of ἄρχων is ἀρχοντ- while that of ἄγων is ἀγων-.

## 148. New word list

*ἀνά, with gen., *on board*; with acc., *up, throughout*. ANALYSIS.

ἀντλέω, ἀντλήσω, ἤντλησα, ἤντληκα, to bail out, draw out.

ἄνω, *up, upwards, on high*.

ἀρχιτρίκλινος, -ου, ὁ, *toastmaster, master of ceremonies*.

γεμίζω, γεμιῶ, ἐγέμισα, ἐγεμίσθην, to fill, load.

γεύω, γεύσω, ἔγευσα, γέγευμαι, to give a taste; mid., to taste. DISGUST.

*ἕξ, indecl., *six*. HEXAGON.

*ἕως, *until*.

*ἤ, *or, than*.

καθαρισμός, -οῦ, ὁ, a cleansing, purifying. CATHARTIC.

*κατά, with gen., *down from, down upon*; with acc., *down along, accord-

ing to*. CATACLYSM.

*κεῖμαι, κείσομαι, to lie, be situated*.

λίθινος, -η, -ον, *of stone, stony*. PALEOLITHIC.

μετρητής, -οῦ, ὁ, *a measure*, (about 9 gallons).

νυμφίος, -ου, ὁ, *bridegroom, husband*. NYMPH.

*νῦν, *now*.

ὑδρία, -ας, ἡ, *water pot, water jar*.

*φέρω, οἴσω, ἤνεγκα, ἐνήνοχα, ἐνήνεγμαι, ἠνέχθην, to carry. PHOSPHORUS.

χωρέω, χωρήσω, ἐχώρησα, κεχώρηκα, κεχώρημαι, ἐχωρήθην, to make room for, hold, contain.

ὡς, conj., of time, *as, when*. Discussed more fully in cumulative vocabulary.

## 149. Reading passage (*John 2:6–9*)

2:6   Ἦσαν δὲ ἐκεῖ λίθιναι ὑδρίαι ἓξ κατὰ τὸν καθαρισμὸν τῶν Ἰουδαίων

7   κείμεναι, χωροῦσαι ἀνὰ μετρητὰς δύο ἢ τρεῖς. λέγει αὐτοῖς ὁ Ἰησοῦς· γεμίσατε τὰς ὑδρίας ὕδατος. καὶ ἐγέμισαν αὐτὰς ἕως

8   ἄνω. καὶ λέγει αὐτοῖς· ἀντλήσατε νῦν καὶ φέρετε τῷ ἀρχιτρικλίνῳ.

9   οἱ δὲ ἤνεγκαν. ὡς δὲ ἐγεύσατο ὁ ἀρχιτρίκλινος τὸ ὕδωρ οἶνον γεγενημένον, καὶ οὐκ ᾔδει πόθεν ἐστίν, οἱ δὲ διάκονοι ᾔδεισαν οἱ ἠντληκότες τὸ ὕδωρ, φωνεῖ τὸν νυμφίον ὁ ἀρχιτρίκλινος.

6. κείμεναι: present participle of κεῖμαι. Compare with ἐρχόμενος as developed in 58. χωροῦσαι: present active participle of χωρέω. A 'contract verb'; its development will be presented later. ἀνά: probably carries here the basic idea *at the rate of*. The thought is that each pitcher held this much, and it can best be translated by saying *each*.

7. γεμίσατε (also ἀντλήσατε in *vs. 8*): compare with the aorist active imperative βάπτισον in 113 and the more particularized λύσατε in the chart of λύω in 97. ὕδατος: from ὕδωρ. Genitive with a verb denoting fullness (501).

8. ἤνεγκαν: see principal parts of φέρω in today's word list.

9. ἐγεύσατο: aorist middle of γεύω. Compare with ἐλύσατο in the chart of λύω in 97. γεγενημένον: see principal parts of γίγνομαι. This is a perfect participle. Note its

accent. ἤδει, ἤδεισαν: pluperfect of εἴδω, *to see* (perf., *to know*), with the force of an imperfect. ἠντληκότες: in the chart of λύω in 97, note how the perfect active participle is formed. For ἀντλέω (note its principal parts in today's word list) this would be ἠντληκώς, *having drawn out*. From this is developed the plural form used in this verse.

### 150. Writing exercise

Using today's paradigms, the definite article (in 63), and the adjectives in 56–58, write the Greek words to give the following: (*a*) *For a coming thief.* (*b*) *Of one's* (Gk., *the*) *own flesh.* (*c*) *The first woman* (acc.). (*d*) *The eternal waters* (nom.). (*e*) *Of coming leaders.* (*f*) *Of the first month.*

# LESSON 20
# Diphthong-Stem Nouns

### 151. Nouns with diphthong stems

CERTAIN nouns of the consonant declension have stems ending in diphthongs. These are included in the consonant declension because, even though they have diphthong stems, the endings are those of the consonant declension. As these nouns are declined, the stem endings suffer a certain amount of distortion. While it is hard to make rules concerning these alterations, yet the observation of some typical examples will help the student to follow more intelligently the nouns in this class.

| ὁ or ἡ βοῦς, *ox or cow* | ὁ ἱερεύς, *priest* | ἡ ναῦς, *ship* |
|---|---|---|
| βοός | ἱερέως | νεώς |
| βοΐ | ἱερεῖ | νηΐ |
| βοῦν | ἱερέα | ναῦν |
| βόες | ἱερεῖς | νῆες |
| βοῶν | ἱερέων | νεῶν |
| βουσί | ἱερεῦσι | ναυσί |
| βοῦς | ἱερέας or ἱερεῖς | ναῦς |

### 152. Nouns with stems in ι and υ

Certain other nouns with stems ending in ι and υ have endings like those of the consonant declension and are classified with this declension. ἡ πόλις, *city*; ἡ ἀπόκρισις, *reply*; and ὁ ἰχθύς, *fish*:

| ἡ πόλις, *city* | ἡ ἀπόκρισις, *reply* | ὁ ἰχθύς, *fish* |
|---|---|---|
| πόλεως | ἀποκρίσεως | ἰχθύος |
| πόλει | ἀποκρίσει | ἰχθύϊ |
| πόλιν | ἀπόκρισιν | ἰχθύν |
| πόλεις | ἀποκρίσεις | ἰχθύες |
| πόλεων | ἀποκρίσεων | ἰχθύων |
| πόλεσι | ἀποκρίσεσι | ἰχθύσι |
| πόλεις | ἀποκρίσεις | ἰχθῦς |

Note that genitives in -εως and -εων of nouns in -ις and -υς allow the acute accent on the antepenult despite the long ultima.

### 153. New word list

*ἄρτι, exactly, just now.*

βοῦς, βοός, ὁ or ἡ, *ox* or *cow.*
BOSPORUS.

*ἐγγύς, near* (often with gen.).

*ἐλάττων, ἔλαττον,* or *ἐλάσσων, ἔλασσον, lesser, smaller, fewer, worse.*

*ἱερόν, -οῦ, τό, sacred place, temple.*
HIERARCHY.

*κάθημαι, καθήσομαι, to sit, be seated.*

*καλός, -ή, -όν, beautiful, good, fine.*
CALLIGRAPHY.

Καφαρναούμ, ἡ, indecl., *Capernaum.*

κερματιστής, -οῦ, ὁ, *money changer.*

μεθύσκω, μεθύσω, ἐμέθυσα, μεμέθυσμαι, ἐμεθύσθην, *to intoxicate, make drunk.*

*μετά, with* gen., *with*; with acc., *after.* METAPHYSICS.

πάσχα, τό, indecl., *passover, paschal lamb.* PASCHAL.

*πολύς, πολλή, πολύ,* gen. πολλοῦ, πολλῆς, πολλοῦ, *much, many.* POLYGAMY.

πρόβατον, -ου, τό, *sheep*; pl., *cattle.*

πωλέω, πωλήσω, ἐπώλησα, πεπώλημαι, ἐπωλήθην, *to barter, sell.*

*σημεῖον, -ου, τό, sign, proof.* SEMANTICS.

τηρέω, τηρήσω, ἐτήρησα, τετήρηκα, τετήρημαι, ἐτηρήθην, *to keep.*

*τίθημι, θήσω, ἔθηκα, τέθηκα* or *τέθεικα, τέθειμαι, ἐτέθην, to set, place.* EPITHET.

### 154. Reading passage (*John* 2:10–14)

2:10  Καὶ λέγει αὐτῷ· πᾶς ἄνθρωπος πρῶτον τὸν καλὸν οἶνον τίθησιν,
καὶ ὅταν μεθυσθῶσιν τὸν ἐλάσσω· σὺ τετήρηκας τὸν καλὸν οἶνον

10. **τίθησι(ν):** third person singular present indicative active of the μι- verb τίθημι, *to set.* The development of this group of verbs will be studied later in the course.
**ὅταν μεθυσθῶσιν τὸν ἐλάσσω** (understand τίθησιν) : ὅταν stands for the relative adverb ὅτε, *when*, plus ἄν. μεθυσθῶσι is from the last principal part of μεθύσκω, which is ἐμεθύσθην, *I was made drunk.* It has no augment, and the ω in the ending shows it to be subjunctive. So here is another conditional relative sentence in which the protasis has a relative (ὅτε), plus ἄν, plus subjunctive, and the apodosis has the present indicative

11 ἕως ἄρτι. Ταύτην ἐποίησεν ἀρχὴν τῶν σημείων ὁ Ἰησοῦς ἐν
Κανὰ τῆς Γαλιλαίας καὶ ἐφανέρωσεν τὴν δόξαν αὐτοῦ, καὶ
ἐπίστευσαν εἰς αὐτὸν οἱ μαθηταὶ αὐτοῦ.

12 Μετὰ τοῦτο κατέβη εἰς Καφαρναοὺμ αὐτὸς καὶ ἡ μήτηρ αὐτοῦ
καὶ οἱ ἀδελφοὶ καὶ οἱ μαθηταὶ αὐτοῦ, καὶ ἐκεῖ ἔμειναν οὐ πολλὰς
ἡμέρας.

13 Καὶ ἐγγὺς ἦν τὸ πάσχα τῶν Ἰουδαίων, καὶ ἀνέβη εἰς Ἱεροσό-
14 λυμα ὁ Ἰησοῦς. καὶ εὗρεν ἐν τῷ ἱερῷ τοὺς πωλοῦντας βόας καὶ
πρόβατα καὶ περιστερὰς καὶ τοὺς κερματιστὰς καθημένους.

(τίθησι). This gives a conditional relative sentence with present general supposition
(599). It translates, *when they are made drunk, (he sets forth) the inferior (wine)*. ἐλάσσω:
accusative singular masculine of the adjective ἐλάσσων or ἐλάττων, *inferior*. The
development of this type of adjective is yet to be studied. τετήρηκας: from τηρέω in
today's word list.

12. κατέβη: from καταβαίνω, *to go down*. See βαίνω for principal parts. αὐτός:
intensive here, *himself*. ἔμειναν: from μένω, *to remain*. See its principal parts. πολλὰς
ἡμέρας: accusative of extent of time (531).

13. ἀνέβη: from ἀναβαίνω, *to go up*. Compare κατέβη in *vs. 12.*

14. εὗρε(ν): from εὑρίσκω, *to find*. It omits the augment, as is often done in verbs
beginning with ευ-. πωλοῦντας: present active participle of πωλέω, *to sell*. βόας: alternate form for βοῦς, the accusative plural. καθημένους: present participle of κάθημαι in
today's word list.

## 155. Writing exercise

Using today's nouns, the definite article (63), and the adjectives in
56–58, plus καλός, -ή, -όν, *beautiful* (declined like πρῶτος, 56), and ἄξιος,
-α, -ον, *worthy* (declined like ἴδιος, 56), write out the Greek for the following: (*a*) *Of beautiful ships.* (*b*) *To* or *for the first priest.* (*c*) *The eternal city*
(acc.). (*d*) *The worthy replies* (nom.). (*e*) *Of the* (one's) *own ox.* (*f*) *The
coming fish(es)*(acc.).

# LESSON 21

# Consonant and *a*-Declension Adjectives

## 156. Adjectives of the consonant and a-declension

THERE is an important family of Greek adjectives which have their
masculine and neuter forms declined just as the nouns of the consonant
declension, whereas the feminine is declined as the nouns of the a-
declension whose nominative and accusative singular end in short -a. See
ἡ τράπεζα, *table*, and ἡ ἀλήθεια, *truth*, in 43.

Three adjectives of this group are presented, πᾶς, *every, all*; βαθύς, *deep*; and εἷς *one*. The last is a cardinal numeral, but is often used as an adjective. Its feminine is irregular as to stem but the endings are regular.

πᾶς, *every, all*

| πᾶς | πᾶσα | πᾶν |
|---|---|---|
| παντός | πάσης | παντός |
| παντί | πάσῃ | παντί |
| πάντα | πᾶσαν | πᾶν |
| πάντες | πᾶσαι | πάντα |
| πάντων | πασῶν | πάντων |
| πᾶσι | πάσαις | πᾶσι |
| πάντας | πάσας | πάντα |

βαθύς, *deep*

| βαθύς | βαθεῖα | βαθύ |
|---|---|---|
| βαθέος | βαθείας | βαθέος |
| βαθεῖ | βαθείᾳ | βαθεῖ |
| βαθύν | βαθεῖαν | βαθύ |
| βαθεῖς | βαθεῖαι | βαθέα |
| βαθέων | βαθειῶν | βαθέων |
| βαθέσι | βαθείαις | βαθέσι |
| βαθεῖς | βαθείας | βαθέα |

εἷς, *one*

| εἷς | μία | ἕν |
|---|---|---|
| ἑνός | μιᾶς | ἑνός |
| ἑνί | μιᾷ | ἑνί |
| ἕνα | μίαν | ἕν |

## 157. Adjectives of the consonant declension

Just as with the o-declension there were a few adjectives of two endings only (like αἰώνιος, -ον, 57), where one set of forms in -ος represented both masculine and feminine, so in the consonant declension there are a few adjectives, developed as are the consonant-stem nouns, and having both masculine and feminine represented by one set of forms. When such are presented in the word lists, the fact that two endings only are given (instead of three) helps the student to recognize them as belonging to this group. We present εὐδαίμων, *fortunate*; ἀληθής, *true*; and ἡδίων, *sweeter*.

εὐδαίμων, *fortunate, prosperous*

| εὐδαίμων | εὔδαιμον |
|---|---|
| εὐδαίμονος | εὐδαίμονος |
| εὐδαίμονι | εὐδαίμονι |
| εὐδαίμονα | εὔδαιμον |
| εὐδαίμονες | εὐδαίμονα |
| εὐδαιμόνων | εὐδαιμόνων |
| εὐδαίμοσι | εὐδαίμοσι |
| εὐδαίμονας | εὐδαίμονα |

ἀληθής, *true*

| ἀληθής | ἀληθές |
|---|---|
| ἀληθοῦς | ἀληθοῦς |
| ἀληθεῖ | ἀληθεῖ |
| ἀληθῆ | ἀληθές |
| ἀληθεῖς | ἀληθῆ |
| ἀληθῶν | ἀληθῶν |
| ἀληθέσι | ἀληθέσι |
| ἀληθεῖς | ἀληθῆ |

Note the very close relationship between ἀληθής and some of the nouns grouped under 'stems in s' (139), particularly τὸ ἔτος, *the year*, and ἡ τριήρης, *the trireme*.

ἡδίων, *sweeter*

| | |
|---|---|
| ἡδίων | ἥδιον |
| ἡδίονος | ἡδίονος |
| ἡδίονι | ἡδίονι |
| ἡδίονα or ἡδίω | ἥδιον |
| | |
| ἡδίονες or ἡδίους | ἡδίονα or ἡδίω |
| ἡδιόνων | ἡδιόνων |
| ἡδίοσι | ἡδίοσι |
| ἡδίονας or ἡδίους | ἡδίονα or ἡδίω |

The short forms ἡδίω (for ἡδίονα) and ἡδίους (for ἡδίονες or ἡδίονας) are frequently used. For example, recall the form τὸν ἐλάσσω used in *John 2:10*. The note explained that ἐλάσσω is accusative singular masculine of ἐλάσσων, *inferior*. ἐλάσσων declines just as does ἡδίων, and the form ἐλάσσω is the short form for ἐλάσσονα, the accusative singular masculine (and also the nominative or accusative plural neuter).

## 158. The pronouns τίς, τὶς, and ὅστις

The interrogative pronoun τίς, *who?* is declined like a two-ending adjective of the consonant declension. Very similar to it, but for accent, is the indefinite pronoun τὶς, *anyone*, *someone*, which is enclitic in all its forms. The two are presented herewith:

τίς, *who? what?*           τὶς, *someone, a certain*

| τίς | τί | τὶς | τὶ |
|---|---|---|---|
| τίνος or τοῦ | τίνος or τοῦ | τινός or του | τινός or του |
| τίνι or τῷ | τίνι or τῷ | τινί or τῳ | τινί or τῳ |
| τίνα | τί | τινά | τὶ |
| | | | |
| τίνες | τίνα | τινές | τινά |
| τίνων | τίνων | τινῶν | τινῶν |
| τίσι | τίσι | τισί | τισί |
| τίνας | τίνα | τινάς | τινά |

The student has already noted the relative pronoun ὅς, ἥ, ὅ. This pronoun combines with the indefinite τὶς, τὶ to form ὅστις, *whoever, anyone who*. It is declined as follows:

| ὅστις | ἥτις | ὅ τι |
|---|---|---|
| οὗτινος or ὅτου | ἧστινος | οὗτινος or ὅτου |
| ᾧτινι or ὅτῳ | ᾗτινι | ᾧτινι or ὅτῳ |
| ὅντινα | ἥντινα | ὅ τι |
| | | |
| οἵτινες | αἵτινες | ἅτινα or ἅττα |
| ὧντινων or ὅτων | ὧντινων | ὧντινων or ὅτων |
| οἷστισι or ὅτοις | αἷστισι | οἷστισι or ὅτοις |
| οὕστινας | ἅστινας | ἅτινα or ἅττα |

## 159. Memory assignment

In order to have a good degree of control over the consonant declension nouns and the consonant and α-declension adjectives, the student is asked, in connection with today's lesson, to memorize the adjective πᾶς, πᾶσα, πᾶν as shown above.

## 160. New word list

ἀνατρέπω (see τρέπω for prin. parts), *to overturn.*

*βάλλω, βαλῶ, ἔβαλον, βέβληκα, βέβλημαι, ἐβλήθην, to throw.*

*ἐκβάλλω (see βάλλω for prin. parts), to throw out.*

ἐκχέω (see χέω for prin. parts), *to pour out.*

ἐμπόριον, -ου, τό, *market place, merchandise.* EMPORIUM.

*ἐντεῦθεν, from there, thence.*

*ἐσθίω, ἔδομαι or φάγομαι, ἔφαγον, ἐδήδοκα, ἐδήδεσμαι, ἠδέσθην, to eat.* ESOPHAGUS.

ζῆλος, -ου, ὁ, *jealousy, zeal.* ZEAL.

κατεσθίω (see ἐσθίω for prin. parts), *to devour, eat up.*

κέρμα, -ατος, τό, *small change, coins.*

κολλυβιστής, -οῦ, ὁ, *money changer.*

*μή, not.* Used to negate commands and purpose clauses. Also introduces clauses of fearing.

*μιμνήσκω, μνήσω, ἔμνησα, μέμνημαι, ἐμνήσθην, to remind; mid. and pass., to remember.* MNEMONICS.

οἶκος, -ου, ὁ, *house, abode.* ECONOMY.

σχοινίον, -ου, τό, *rope, cord.*

*τε, postpositive, and.*

τράπεζα, -ης, ἡ, *table.* TRAPEZE.

*τρέπω, τρέψω, ἔτρεψα, τέτροφα, τέτραμμαι, ἐτράπην, to turn.* HELIOTROPE.

φραγέλλιον, -ου, τό, *scourge.*

χέω, χεῶ, ἔχεα, κέχυκα, ἐχύθην, *to pour, let flow.*

## 161. Reading passage (*John 2:15-17*)

2:15 Καὶ ποιήσας φραγέλλιον ἐκ σχοινίων πάντας ἐξέβαλεν ἐκ τοῦ ἱεροῦ, τά τε πρόβατα καὶ τοὺς βόας, καὶ τῶν κολλυβιστῶν

15. **ποιήσας**: aorist participle of ποιέω. Compare λύσας in the chart of λύω (97). **ἐξέβαλε(ν)**: from ἐκβάλλω, *to throw out.* See principal parts of βάλλω in today's word list. **τε . . . καί**: *both . . . and.* **βόας**: for the accusative plural, βοῦς. **ἐξέχεε(ν)**:

16  ἐξέχεεν τὰ κέρματα καὶ τὰς τραπέζας ἀνέτρεψεν, καὶ τοῖς τὰς
    περιστερὰς πωλοῦσιν εἶπεν· ἄρατε ταῦτα ἐντεῦθεν, μὴ ποιεῖτε
17  τὸν οἶκον τοῦ πατρός μου οἶκον ἐμπορίου. ἐμνήσθησαν οἱ
    μαθηταὶ αὐτοῦ ὅτι γεγραμμένον ἐστίν· ὁ ζῆλος τοῦ οἴκου σου
    καταφάγεταί με.

aorist of ἐκχέω in today's list. ἀνέτρεψε(ν): from ἀνατρέπω. See principal parts of
τρέπω. 16. πωλοῦσι(ν): present active participle of πωλέω, *to sell*. Dative plural. ἄρατε:
aorist imperative active of αἴρω. See its principal parts. ποιεῖτε: present imperative
active of ποιέω. The development of the present system of this verb has not yet been
presented. 17. ἐμνήσθησαν: from μιμνήσκω in today's word list. γεγραμμένον ἐστίν: a periphrasis for γέγραπται. See chart of γράφω in 124. For the frequency of periphrases
in the κοινή, see 482. 9. καταφάγεται: from κατεσθίω. See principal parts of ἐσθίω in
today's word list.

## 162. Writing exercise

Using today's adjectives and the nouns in 43 f. and 49 f., write the
Greek forms which will give the meanings indicated below: (*a*) *For all the
men* (use predicate position for πᾶς, see 490). (*b*) *Of one god*. (*c*) *For a certain
true prophet* (*certain* comes right after *prophet*, in the Greek. Also note that
when a dissyllabic enclitic follows a word with the acute on the penult, the
enclitic retains its accent). (*d*) *Whatever table* (acc.). (*e*) *Of prosperous
beginnings* (also means *realms*). (*f*) *What man?* (nom.). (*g*) *For certain children*
(*children* comes first. And remember the rule cited under (*c*) above).

## LESSON ·22

# The Contract Verb in -εω

## 163. The contract verb in -εω

THERE is a rather large and important group of verbs whose present
stems end in a vowel which is blended with the vowels of the personal
endings and which are therefore called *contract verbs*. Those observed
today use the vowel ε at the end of the present stem. In today's reading
passage several of these will be noted, such as ποιέω, *to make*; οἰκοδομέω,
*to build*; and θεωρέω, *to behold*.

Because it is important to know exactly what is the contract vowel in
each of these verbs as they are used, they are regularly referred to and
shown in the word lists in their uncontracted first form (e.g. ποιέω) even

though it is not this form but the contracted form (e.g. ποιῶ) which always appears in actual use. And it is in the present system only that these contractions take place. The other tense systems regularly add the personal endings just as does λύω.

In the present system the vowels or diphthongs of the endings are ω, ει or ε, ο or ου, η or ῃ, and οι. The vowel ε combines with these vowels or diphthongs as follows:

ε+ω = ω; ε+ει or ε = ει; ε+ο or ου = ου; ε + η or ῃ = η or ῃ; ε + οι = οι.

The accent of the contracted verb remains on the same syllable on which it was found in the uncontracted form. And when the original accent would have been on the first of the two combining syllables, the resulting contracted syllable carries the circumflex accent.

By way of illustration, here is the manner in which the syllables are contracted in the present indicative active of ποιέω, *to do*. The uncontracted forms are in parentheses.

| | | | |
|---|---|---|---|
| (ποιέω) | ποιῶ | (ποιέομεν) | ποιοῦμεν |
| (ποιέεις) | ποιεῖς | (ποιέετε) | ποιεῖτε |
| (ποιέει) | ποιεῖ | (ποιέουσι) | ποιοῦσι |

Note that here the accent invariably falls on the first of the two contracting syllables. Hence all the contract forms are circumflexed.

The imperfect indicative active runs as follows:

| | | | |
|---|---|---|---|
| (ἐποίεον) | ἐποίουν | (ἐποιέομεν) | ἐποιοῦμεν |
| (ἐποίεες) | ἐποίεις | (ἐποιέετε) | ἐποιεῖτε |
| (ἐποίεε) | ἐποίει | (ἐποίεον) | ἐποίουν |

Here in the singular forms the original accent was not on one of the contracting syllables. Therefore it is not on the contracted syllable in the final form, and it stays acute.

It is felt not to be necessary for the student to work his way through the mechanics of all of these contractions. Simply observe carefully the final contracted forms as shown in the expanded synopsis on the following page. The endings are not greatly dissimilar to those of λύω (except in the optative active, where the endings follow the analogy of εἰμί rather than λύω. See 132). The circumflex accent is, of course, used very frequently.

[*For section 164 see p. 84*]

## 165. Other tense systems of the contract verb

This group of verbs, as a rule, uses the vowel contractions *in the present system only*. In the other tense systems the contract vowel (ε in today's

**164. Partially expanded synopsis of the ε-contract verb ποιέω, *to do***

| Present | Future | First aorist | First perfect active |
|---|---|---|---|
| ποιῶ ποιοῦμεν<br>ποιεῖς ποιεῖτε<br>ποιεῖ ποιοῦσι | ποιήσω | ἐποίησα | πεποίηκα<br>ἐπεποιήκη |
| ἐποίουν ἐποιοῦμεν<br>ἐποίεις ἐποιεῖτε<br>ἐποίει ἐποίουν | ποιήσοιμι | ποιήσω<br><br>ποιήσαιμι | πεποιήκω<br><br>πεποιήκοιμι |
| ποιῶ ποιῶμεν<br>ποιῇς ποιῆτε<br>ποιῇ ποιῶσι | ποιήσειν | ποίησον<br><br>ποιῆσαι | πεποιηκὼς ἴσθι<br><br>πεποιηκέναι |
| ποιοίην ποιοῖμεν<br>ποιοίης ποιοῖτε<br>ποιοίη ποιοῖεν | ποιήσων | ποιήσας | πεποιηκώς, -κυῖα,<br>-κός |

| Present | Future | First aorist | Perf. mid. and pass. |
|---|---|---|---|
| ποίει ποιεῖτε<br>ποιείτω ποιούντων<br><br>ποιεῖν<br><br>ποιῶν, -οῦσα, -οῦν | ποιήσομαι | ἐποιησάμην | πεποίημαι<br><br>ἐπεποιήμην |
| ποιοῦμαι ποιούμεθα<br>ποιεῖ ποιεῖσθε<br>ποιεῖται ποιοῦνται | ποιησοίμην | ποιήσωμαι<br><br>ποιησαίμην | πεποιημένος ὦ<br><br>πεποιημένος εἴην |
| ἐποιούμην ἐποιούμεθα<br>ἐποιοῦ ἐποιεῖσθε<br>ἐποιεῖτο ἐποιοῦντο | ποιήσεσθαι | ποίησαι<br><br>ποιήσασθαι | πεποίησο<br><br>πεποιῆσθαι |
| ποιῶμαι ποιώμεθα<br>ποιῇ ποιῆσθε<br>ποιῆται ποιῶνται | ποιησόμενος | ποιησάμενος | πεποιημένος,<br>-η, -ον |

**First passive**

| | | |
|---|---|---|
| ποιοίμην ποιοίμεθα<br>ποιοῖο ποιοῖσθε<br>ποιοῖτο ποιοῖντο | ποιηθήσομαι | ἐποιήθην<br><br>ποιηθῶ |
| ποιοῦ ποιεῖσθε<br>ποιείσθω ποιείσθων<br><br>ποιεῖσθαι<br><br>ποιούμενος, -η, -ον | ποιηθησοίμην<br><br>ποιηθήσεσθαι<br><br>ποιηθησόμενος | ποιηθείην<br><br>ποιήθητι<br><br>ποιηθῆναι<br><br>ποιηθείς, etc. |

Passive same forms as middle

Passive same<br>forms as middle

study) simply lengthens and remains a part of the stem. So the stem of ποιέω in all but the present system is ποιη-. This makes it a simple vowel stem like that of λύω and the tense signs and personal endings are added with no alterations whatever. Thus the contract verbs are among the easiest to develop, once the present system has become familiar.

The synopsis of ποιέω is not expanded in the tense systems other than the present, as these run perfectly regularly, just as does λύω.

## 166. Memory assignment

In order that he may have a working knowledge of the contract verb, the student is expected to memorize the present system of ποιέω, and to be responsible for it from this point in the course.

## 167. New word list

*γάρ, postpositive, *for.*

*γραφή, -ῆς, ἡ, *writing, scripture.* GRAPH.

*δείκνυμι or δεικνύω, δείξω, ἔδειξα, δέδειχα, δέδειγμαι, ἐδείχθην, *to show.* EPIDEICTIC.

*ἐγείρω, ἐγερῶ, ἤγειρα, ἐγρήγορα, ἐγήγερμαι, ἠγέρθην, *to raise, arouse.*

ἑορτή, -ῆς, ἡ, *feast, festival.*

*ἔτος, ἔτους, τό, *year.*

*θεωρέω, θεωρήσω, ἐθεώρησα, τε-

θεώρηκα, τεθεώρημαι, ἐθεωρή-θην, *to behold, review.* THEORY.

ναός, -οῦ, ὁ, *temple.*

*νεκρός, -ά, -όν, *dead.* NECROTIC.

οἰκοδομέω, οἰκοδομήσω, ᾠκοδόμησα, ᾠκοδόμημαι, ᾠκοδομήθην, *to build.*

*σῶμα, -ατος, τό, *body.* SOMATIC.

τεσσαράκοντα, *forty.*

*τρεῖς, τρία, gen. τριῶν, τριῶν, *three.* TRIGONOMETRY.

χρεία, -ας, ἡ, *advantage, use, need.*

## 168. Reading passage (*John 2:18–25*)

2:18 Ἀπεκρίθησαν οὖν οἱ Ἰουδαῖοι καὶ εἶπαν αὐτῷ· τί σημεῖον δεικνύ-
19 εις ἡμῖν, ὅτι ταῦτα ποιεῖς; ἀπεκρίθη Ἰησοῦς καὶ εἶπεν αὐτοῖς·
λύσατε τὸν ναὸν τοῦτον, καὶ ἐν τρισὶν ἡμέραις ἐγερῶ αὐτόν.
20 εἶπαν οὖν οἱ Ἰουδαῖοι· τεσσαράκοντα καὶ ἓξ ἔτεσιν οἰκοδομήθη

18. **ἀπεκρίθησαν**: from ἀποκρίνω. So also for ἀπεκρίθη in *vs. 19.* **εἶπαν**: for εἶπον, as noted previously (482. 7). **ἡμῖν**: from ἐγώ. See 72.

19. **λύσατε**: see chart on λύω (97). **τρισί(ν)**: dative plural of τρεῖς.

20. **ἔτεσι(ν)**: see development of τὸ ἔτος in 139. One might well have expected the accusative of duration of time (*for forty-six years*) rather than the dative of time when (*in forty-six years*) as here. Note, however, that the verb form is appropriate. οἰκοδομήθη is aorist, denoting a simple act, rather than an imperfect to imply continuing action. This verb form here irregularly omits the augment, which would have made it ᾠκοδο-μήθη. This tendency is characteristic of the κοινή (482. 10). **ἐγερεῖς**: see principal parts of ἐγείρω in today's word list.

21 ὁ ναὸς οὗτος, καὶ σὺ ἐν τρισὶν ἡμέραις ἐγερεῖς αὐτόν; ἐκεῖνος δὲ
22 ἔλεγεν περὶ τοῦ ναοῦ τοῦ σώματος αὐτοῦ. ὅτε οὖν ἠγέρθη ἐκ
νεκρῶν, ἐμνήσθησαν οἱ μαθηταὶ αὐτοῦ ὅτι τοῦτο ἔλεγεν, καὶ
ἐπίστευσαν τῇ γραφῇ καὶ τῷ λόγῳ ὃν εἶπεν ὁ Ἰησοῦς.
23 Ὡς δὲ ἦν ἐν τοῖς Ἱεροσολύμοις ἐν τῷ πάσχα ἐν τῇ ἑορτῇ,
πολλοὶ ἐπίστευσαν εἰς τὸ ὄνομα αὐτοῦ, θεωροῦντες αὐτοῦ τὰ
24 σημεῖα ἃ ἐποίει· αὐτὸς δὲ Ἰησοῦς οὐκ ἐπίστευεν αὐτὸν αὐτοῖς
25 διὰ τὸ αὐτὸν γινώσκειν πάντας, καὶ ὅτι οὐ χρείαν εἶχεν ἵνα τις
μαρτυρήσῃ περὶ τοῦ ἀνθρώπου· αὐτὸς γὰρ ἐγίνωσκεν τί ἦν ἐν τῷ
ἀνθρώπῳ.

22. **ἠγέρθη**: see again principal parts of ἐγείρω. **νεκρῶν**: here used as a substantive, *of* or *from (the) dead* (544). **ἐμνήσθησαν**: from μιμνήσκω.

23. **ὡς**: *as, when*. **θεωροῦντες**: nominative plural masculine of θεωρῶν (compare ποιῶν in today's chart), the present participle of θεωρέω. **ἃ**: from ὅς, ἥ, ὅ, the relative pronoun. See 63.

24. **αὐτός**: intensive, *himself*. **αὐτόν**: reflexive (note the rough breathing), shortened form of ἑαυτόν, *himself*. See 73. **διὰ τὸ αὐτὸν γινώσκειν πάντας**: here is an articular infinitive (see note on *John 1:48* in 134) used as an accusative after διά, *because of*. αὐτόν is the subject of the infinitive γινώσκειν, and πάντας is the direct object. Literally, *on account of (the) him to know (knowing) all (men)*.

25. **εἶχε(ν)**: imperfect of ἔχω. **ἵνα ... μαρτυρήσῃ**: a sort of purpose clause, ἵνα with subjunctive (562). The κοινή sometimes uses ἵνα with subjunctive where the idea of *purpose* is weak or absent (482. 18). **περὶ τοῦ ἀνθρώπου**: as with abstract qualities, so with *man* in the generic sense, the definite article is here used. Omit it in translation.

### 169. Writing exercise

Using ποιέω as a pattern, make a chart showing the complete conjugation of the present system of θεωρέω, *to behold*.

# LESSON 23

# The Contract Verb in -αω

**170.** ANOTHER group of contract verbs is of those ending in -αω. In today's reading passage the verb γεννάω, *to beget* or *bear*, is frequently used. The verb ἐρωτάω, *to ask*, and the verb ζάω, *to live*, have also been seen in the reading passages.

The vowel α of the present stem combines with the o-sounds (o, ω, ου, οι) to give ω. It combines with the ε- sounds (ε, η, ει, η) to give α. Where the combining syllables included an ι or ι-subscript, the resulting contracted syllable will have ι-subscript.

The chart in 173 gives a synopsis of γεννάω, expanded in the present system to show the contracted endings. Observe these, and compare them mentally with the endings of the present system of λύω.

In the other tense systems than the present, γεννάω lengthens the stem to γεννη- and takes the tense signs and personal endings just as does λύω. Hence the other tenses are not expanded in today's chart.

### 171. New word list

ἄνωθεν, *from above, anew.*

*ἄρχων, ἄρχοντος, ὁ, *leader, commander.*

βασιλεία, -ας, ἡ, *kingdom.*

γέρων, γέροντος, ὁ, *old man.*

*δεῖ, δεήσει, ἐδέησε, third person verb, *it is necessary.*

*δεύτερος, -α, -ον, *second.* DEUTERONOMY.

εἰσέρχομαι (see ἔρχομαι for prin. parts), *to go* or *come in* or *into, enter.*

*θαυμάζω, θαυμάσομαι, ἐθαύμασα, τεθαύμακα, ἐθαυμάσθην, *to wonder, be surprised.*

*θέλω, θελήσω, shortened form of ἐθέλω, *to desire, be willing.*

κοιλία, -ας, ἡ, *belly, womb.*

Νικόδημος, -ου, ὁ, *Nicodemus.*

*νύξ, νυκτός, ἡ, *night.* NYCTALOPIA.

*οὕτως or οὕτω, *thus, in this way.*

πνέω, πνεύσομαι, ἔπνευσα, πέπνευκα, πέπνευσμαι, ἐπνεύσθην, *to breathe, blow.* PNEUMATIC.

*πῶς, *how?*

ὑπάγω (see ἄγω for prin. parts), *to lead* or *go slowly, to go.*

### 172. Reading passage (*John 3:1–11*)

3:1  Ἦν δὲ ἄνθρωπος ἐκ τῶν Φαρισαίων, Νικόδημος ὄνομα αὐτῷ,

2  ἄρχων τῶν Ἰουδαίων· οὗτος ἦλθεν πρὸς αὐτὸν νυκτὸς καὶ εἶπεν αὐτῷ· ῥαββί, οἴδαμεν ὅτι ἀπὸ θεοῦ ἐλήλυθας διδάσκαλος· οὐδεὶς γὰρ δύναται ταῦτα τὰ σημεῖα ποιεῖν ἃ σὺ ποιεῖς, ἐὰν μὴ ᾖ ὁ θεὸς

3  μετ' αὐτοῦ. ἀπεκρίθη Ἰησοῦς καὶ εἶπεν αὐτῷ· ἀμὴν ἀμὴν λέγω σοι, ἐὰν μή τις γεννηθῇ ἄνωθεν, οὐ δύναται ἰδεῖν τὴν βασιλείαν

1. αὐτῷ: dative of possessor, literally, *name to him* (see 518).

2. ἦλθε(ν): from ἔρχομαι. νυκτός: the genitive is used to denote the *time within which* an action occurs (510). The colloquial statement 'He liked to sit and read *of an evening*' is our English approximation of this usage. οἴδαμεν: from εἴδω. So also in *vs. 11* below, and for οἶδας in *vs. 8*. ἐλήλυθας: see again principal parts of ἔρχομαι. ᾖ: locate this form in the chart of εἰμί in 132. οὐδεὶς γὰρ δύναται ταῦτα τὰ σημεῖα ποιεῖν ... ἐὰν μὴ ᾖ ὁ θεὸς μετ' αὐτοῦ: a straight conditional (not conditional relative) sentence with apodosis preceding the protasis. Observe the structure of the present general conditional sentence in 599. Now note the elements in the sentence at hand, taking the protasis, or condition, first. It is analyzed as follows: protasis, ἐάν (negatived by μή, it translates, *if not* or *unless*) plus subjunctive (ᾖ); apodosis, present indicative (δύναται). Translate, keeping the normal order for the time, *unless (if not) God is with him, no one is able to do these signs.*

3. γεννηθῇ: aorist passive subjunctive of γεννάω. Follows the form γεννηθῶ. See today's chart. ἐὰν μή τις γεννηθῇ ... οὐ δύναται ...: apply the rule of the present general conditional sentence to this sentence. ἰδεῖν: from εἶδον, second aorist of ὁράω, *to see.* Compare ἀγαγεῖν in the chart of ἄγω (118).

4  τοῦ θεοῦ. λέγει πρὸς αὐτὸν ὁ Νικόδημος· πῶς δύναται ἄνθρωπος
   γεννηθῆναι γέρων ὤν; μὴ δύναται εἰς τὴν κοιλίαν τῆς μητρὸς
5  αὐτοῦ δεύτερον εἰσελθεῖν καὶ γεννηθῆναι; ἀπεκρίθη Ἰησοῦς·
   ἀμὴν ἀμὴν λέγω σοι, ἐὰν μή τις γεννηθῇ ἐξ ὕδατος καὶ πνεύματος,
6  οὐ δύναται εἰσελθεῖν εἰς τὴν βασιλείαν τοῦ θεοῦ. τὸ γεγεννημένον
   ἐκ τῆς σαρκὸς σάρξ ἐστιν, καὶ τὸ γεγεννημένον ἐκ τοῦ πνεύματος
7  πνεῦμά ἐστιν. μὴ θαυμάσῃς ὅτι εἶπόν σοι· δεῖ ὑμᾶς γεννηθῆναι
8  ἄνωθεν. τὸ πνεῦμα ὅπου θέλει πνεῖ, καὶ τὴν φωνὴν αὐτοῦ ἀκούεις,
   ἀλλ' οὐκ οἶδας πόθεν ἔρχεται καὶ ποῦ ὑπάγει· οὕτως ἐστὶν πᾶς ὁ
9  γεγεννημένος ἐκ τοῦ πνεύματος. ἀπεκρίθη Νικόδημος καὶ εἶπεν
10 αὐτῷ· πῶς δύναται ταῦτα γενέσθαι; ἀπεκρίθη Ἰησοῦς καὶ εἶπεν
   αὐτῷ· σὺ εἶ ὁ διδάσκαλος τοῦ Ἰσραὴλ καὶ ταῦτα οὐ γινώσκεις;
11 ἀμὴν ἀμὴν λέγω σοι ὅτι ὃ οἴδαμεν λαλοῦμεν καὶ ὃ ἑωράκαμεν
   μαρτυροῦμεν, καὶ τὴν μαρτυρίαν ἡμῶν οὐ λαμβάνετε.

4. **γεννηθῆναι**: see chart of γεννάω in today's lesson. **ὤν**: see chart of εἰμί (132).
**μὴ δύναται**: μή is here used simply as the sign of a question, like the Latin *num*. It need
not be translated in words. **εἰσελθεῖν**: from εἰσέρχομαι. See principal parts of ἔρχομαι.
ἐλθεῖν is the infinitive from the second aorist ἦλθον. Dropping the augment, the second
aorist has the stem ἐλθ-.

6. **τὸ γεγεννημένον**: find γεγεννημένος in today's chart of γεννάω. τὸ γεγεννημένον is
the neuter of this and is used as a substantive, *that having been born.*

7. **μὴ θαυμάσῃς**: the aorist subjunctive with μή is often used to express prohibitions
(559). **ὑμᾶς**: see declension of σύ in 72.

8. **τὸ πνεῦμα**: note the play on this word, which can mean either *breath*, *wind*, or
*spirit.*

9. **γενέσθαι**: from ἐγενόμην, second aorist of γίγνομαι. The augment is dropped.
Compare ἀγαγέσθαι in the chart of ἄγω in 118.

11. **ἑωράκαμεν**: see principal parts of ὁράω. **ἡμῶν**: see declension of ἐγώ in 72.

[*For section 173 see opposite*]

## 174. Writing exercise

Lay out in chart form the present system of βοάω, *to shout*, which is
conjugated just the same as γεννάω in today's lesson.

**173.** **Partially expanded synopsis of the contract verb** γεννάω, to bear, beget

| Present | | Future | First aorist | First perfect active |
|---|---|---|---|---|
| γεννῶ | γεννῶμεν | γεννήσω | ἐγέννησα | γεγέννηκα |
| γεννᾷς | γεννᾶτε | | | |
| γεννᾷ | γεννῶσι | | | ἐγεγεννήκη |
| ἐγέννων | ἐγεννῶμεν | | γεννήσω | γεγεννήκω |
| ἐγέννας | ἐγεννᾶτε | | | |
| ἐγέννα | ἐγέννων | γεννήσοιμι | γεννήσαιμι | γεγεννήκοιμι |
| γεννῶ | γεννῶμεν | | γέννησον | γεγεννηκὼς ἴσθι |
| γεννᾷς | γεννᾶτε | | | |
| γεννᾷ | γεννῶσι | γεννήσειν | γεννῆσαι | γεγεννηκέναι |
| γεννῴην | γεννῷμεν | γεννήσων | γεννήσας | γεγεννηκώς |
| γεννῴης | γεννῷτε | | | |
| γεννῴη | γεννῷεν | | | |
| γέννα | γεννᾶτε | | | *Perf. mid. and pass.* |
| γεννάτω | γεννώντων | γεννήσομαι | ἐγεννησάμην | γεγέννημαι |
| γεννᾶν | | | | ἐγεγεννήμην |
| γεννῶν, γεννῶσα, γεννῶν | | | γεννήσωμαι | γεγεννημένος ὦ |
| γεννῶμαι | γεννώμεθα | | | |
| γεννᾷ | γεννᾶσθε | γεννησοίμην | γεννησαίμην | γεγεννημένος εἴην |
| γεννᾶται | γεννῶνται | | γέννησαι | γεγέννησο |
| ἐγεννώμην | ἐγεννώμεθα | | | |
| ἐγεννῶ | ἐγεννᾶσθε | γεννήσεσθαι | γεννήσασθαι | γεγεννῆσθαι |
| ἐγεννᾶτο | ἐγεννῶντο | | | |
| γεννῶμαι | γεννώμεθα | γεννησόμενος | γεννησάμενος | γεγεννημένος |
| γεννᾷ | γεννᾶσθε | | | |
| γεννᾶται | γεννῶνται | *First passive* | | |
| γεννῴμην | γεννῴμεθα | γεννηθήσομαι | ἐγεννήθην | |
| γεννῷο | γεννῷσθε | | | |
| γεννῷτο | γεννῷντο | | γεννηθῶ | Passive same |
| γεννῶ | γεννᾶσθε | γεννηθησοίμην | γεννηθείην | forms as |
| γεννάσθω | γεννάσθων | | | middle |
| γεννᾶσθαι | | | γεννήθητι | |
| γεννώμενος, -η, -ον | | γεννηθήσεσθαι | γεννηθῆναι | |
| Passive same forms as middle | | γεννηθησόμενος | γεννηθείς | |

# LESSON 24

## The Contract Verb in -οω

**175.** TODAY the student considers the group of contract verbs which end in -οω. The word ὑψόω, *to lift up*, which occurs in *vs. 14* of today's reading passage, is an example of the group. In paragraph 177 will be found a synopsis of this verb, expanded in the present system. The forms for the first perfect system and for the perfect middle and passive system are in brackets because ὑψόω does not actually use these tenses, although most contract verbs in -οω do so.

The endings of ὑψόω contract according to the following principles:

ο+ε or ο or ου = ου
ο+η or ω = ω
ο+ι-diphthong (ει, οι, η) = οι (except infinitive, ὑψοῦν).

The tenses other than those in the present system of ὑψόω call for a lengthening of the final ο of the stem to ω, and then take the tense signs and endings regularly, just as does λύω. This can readily be seen by noting the various tense systems in the chart which follows.

## 176. New word list

ἀγαπάω, ἀγαπήσω, ἠγάπησα, ἠγάπηκα, ἠγάπημαι, ἠγαπήθην, to *love spiritually*. AGAPĒ.

*αἰώνιος, -ον, *eternal*.

*ἀπόλλυμι, ἀπολῶ or ἀπολέσω, ἀπώλεσα or ἀπωλόμην, ἀπολώλεκα or ἀπόλωλα, to *destroy*; mid. and pass., to *perish*. APOLLYON.

ἐλέγχω, ἐλέγξω, ἤλεγξα, ἐλήλεγμαι, ἠλέγχθην, to *refute, convict, reprove*.

ἐπίγειος, -ον, *on* or *of the earth, earthly*.

ἐπουράνιος, -α, -ον, *of* or *in heaven, heavenly*.

ἐργάζομαι, ἐργάσομαι, εἰργασάμην, εἴργασμαι, to *work*.

*ἔργον, -ου, τό, *work, deed*. ERG, ENERGY.

*ἤδη, *already, now*.

κρίσις, -εως, ἡ, *decision, judgment*. CRISIS.

*μᾶλλον, *more, rather*.

μισέω, μισήσω, ἐμίσησα, μεμίσηκα, μεμίσημαι, ἐμισήθην, to *hate*. MISANTHROPE.

ὄφις, -εως, ὁ, *serpent*.

πονηρός, -ά, -όν, *painful, evil*.

*πράττω or πράσσω, πράξω, ἔπραξα, πέπραχα, πέπραγμαι, ἐπράχθην, to *do*. PRACTICAL.

σκότος, σκότους, τό, *darkness*.

*σώζω, σώσω, ἔσωσα, σέσωκα, σέσωμαι or σέσωσμαι, ἐσώθην, to *save*. (N.T. omits ι-subscript).

ὑψόω, ὑψώσω, ὕψωσα, ὑψώθην, to *lift up, exalt*.

φαῦλος, -η, -ον, *trivial, bad*.

*ὥστε, *so that, so as*.

**177. Partially expanded synopsis of the o-contract verb ὑψόω,** *to lift up*

| | Present | Future | First aorist | First perfect active |
|---|---|---|---|---|
| ὑψῶ<br>ὑψοῖς<br>ὑψοῖ | ὑψοῦμεν<br>ὑψοῦτε<br>ὑψοῦσι | ὑψώσω | ὕψωσα | (ὕψωκα)<br>(ὑψώκη) |
| ὕψουν<br>ὕψους<br>ὕψου | ὑψοῦμεν<br>ὑψοῦτε<br>ὕψουν | ὑψώσοιμι | ὑψώσω<br>ὑψώσαιμι | (ὑψώκω)<br>(ὑψώκοιμι) |
| ὑψῶ<br>ὑψοῖς<br>ὑψοῖ | ὑψῶμεν<br>ὑψῶτε<br>ὑψῶσι | ὑψώσειν | ὕψωσον<br>ὑψῶσαι | (ὑψωκὼς ἴσθι)<br>(ὑψωκέναι) |
| ὑψοίην<br>ὑψοίης<br>ὑψοίη | ὑψοῖμεν<br>ὑψοῖτε<br>ὑψοῖεν | ὑψώσων | ὑψώσας | (ὑψωκώς) |

| | Present | Future | First aorist | First perfect active |
|---|---|---|---|---|
| ὕψου<br>ὑψούτω | ὑψοῦτε<br>ὑψούντων | | | *Perf. mid. and pass.* |
| ὑψοῦν | | ὑψώσομαι | ὑψωσάμην | (ὕψωμαι)<br>(ὑψώμην) |
| ὑψῶν, -οῦσα, -οῦν | | | ὑψώσωμαι | (ὑψωμένος ὦ) |
| ὑψοῦμαι<br>ὑψοῖ<br>ὑψοῦται | ὑψούμεθα<br>ὑψοῦσθε<br>ὑψοῦνται | ὑψωσοίμην | ὑψωσαίμην | (ὑψωμένος εἴην) |
| ὑψούμην<br>ὑψοῦ<br>ὑψοῦτο | ὑψούμεθα<br>ὑψοῦσθε<br>ὑψοῦντο | ὑψώσεσθαι | ὕψωσαι<br>ὑψώσασθαι | (ὕψωσο)<br>(ὑψῶσθαι) |
| ὑψῶμαι<br>ὑψοῖ<br>ὑψῶται | ὑψώμεθα<br>ὑψῶσθε<br>ὑψῶνται | ὑψωσόμενος | ὑψωσάμενος | (ὑψωμένος) |
| | | | *First passive* | |
| ὑψοίμην<br>ὑψοῖο<br>ὑψοῖτο | ὑψοίμεθα<br>ὑψοῖσθε<br>ὑψοῖντο | ὑψωθήσομαι | ὑψώθην<br>ὑψωθῶ | |
| ὑψοῦ<br>ὑψούσθω | ὑψοῦσθε<br>ὑψούσθων | ὑψωθησοίμην | ὑψωθείην | Passive same<br>forms as<br>middle |
| ὑψοῦσθαι | | | ὑψώθητι | |
| ὑψούμενος, -η, -ον | | ὑψωθήσεσθαι | ὑψωθῆναι | |
| Passive same forms as middle | | ὑψωθησόμενος | ὑψωθείς | |

**178. Reading passage** (*John 3 : 12–21*)

3:12  Εἰ τὰ ἐπίγεια εἶπον ὑμῖν καὶ οὐ πιστεύετε, πῶς ἐὰν εἴπω ὑμῖν
13    τὰ ἐπουράνια πιστεύσετε; καὶ οὐδεὶς ἀναβέβηκεν εἰς τὸν οὐρανὸν
14    εἰ μὴ ὁ ἐκ τοῦ οὐρανοῦ καταβάς, ὁ υἱὸς τοῦ ἀνθρώπου. καὶ καθὼς
       Μωϋσῆς ὕψωσεν τὸν ὄφιν ἐν τῇ ἐρήμῳ, οὕτως ὑψωθῆναι δεῖ τὸν
15    υἱὸν τοῦ ἀνθρώπου, ἵνα πᾶς ὁ πιστεύων ἐν αὐτῷ ἔχῃ ζωὴν
16    αἰώνιον. οὕτως γὰρ ἠγάπησεν ὁ θεὸς τὸν κόσμον, ὥστε τὸν υἱὸν
       τὸν μονογενῆ ἔδωκεν, ἵνα πᾶς ὁ πιστεύων εἰς αὐτὸν μὴ ἀπόληται
17    ἀλλ᾽ ἔχῃ ζωὴν αἰώνιον. οὐ γὰρ ἀπέστειλεν ὁ θεὸς τὸν υἱὸν εἰς
       τὸν κόσμον ἵνα κρίνῃ τὸν κόσμον, ἀλλ᾽ ἵνα σωθῇ ὁ κόσμος δι᾽
18    αὐτοῦ. ὁ πιστεύων εἰς αὐτὸν οὐ κρίνεται· ὁ μὴ πιστεύων ἤδη
       κέκριται, ὅτι μὴ πεπίστευκεν εἰς τὸ ὄνομα τοῦ μονογενοῦς υἱοῦ
19    τοῦ θεοῦ. αὕτη δέ ἐστιν ἡ κρίσις, ὅτι τὸ φῶς ἐλήλυθεν εἰς τὸν
       κόσμον καὶ ἠγάπησαν οἱ ἄνθρωποι μᾶλλον τὸ σκότος ἢ τὸ φῶς·
20    ἦν γὰρ αὐτῶν πονηρὰ τὰ ἔργα. πᾶς γὰρ ὁ φαῦλα πράσσων μισεῖ
       τὸ φῶς καὶ οὐκ ἔρχεται πρὸς τὸ φῶς, ἵνα μὴ ἐλεγχθῇ τὰ ἔργα

12. **εἰ τὰ ἐπίγεια εἶπον ὑμῖν**...: protasis of a past particular supposition, whose
structure is described in 598. The apodosis of this conditional sentence is not given;
it is lost in another conditional sentence immediately following. Translate, *if I told you
earthly things* .... **ἐὰν εἴπω ὑμῖν τὰ ἐπουράνια, (πῶς) πιστεύσετε**; : this conditional
sentence is analyzed as follows: protasis, *ἐάν* with subjunctive (*εἴπω* is subjunctive of
*εἶπον*, second aorist of *εἴρω*); apodosis, future indicative (*πιστεύσετε*). Refer again to
603, if necessary, for this supposition. Translate, *if I tell (shall tell) you the heavenly
things, how will you believe?*
13. **ἀναβέβηκε(ν)**: from ἀναβαίνω. See principal parts of βαίνω. **εἰ μή**: *unless* (literally, *if not*). **καταβάς**: participle of κατέβην, second aorist of καταβαίνω.
14. **ὕψωσε, ὑψωθῆναι**: see synopsis of ὑψόω, *to lift up*, in today's chart.
15. **ἵνα ... ἔχῃ**: *in order that* ... *may have*, a purpose clause using the subjunctive
(562). **πᾶς ὁ πιστεύων**: note that here and in *vs. 16* πᾶς occupies predicate position (490).
16. **ἠγάπησε(ν)**: from ἀγαπάω in today's list. Compare ἐγέννησε in the chart of
γεννάω (173). So also for ἠγάπησαν in *vs. 19* below. **ἔδωκε(ν)**: see principal parts of
δίδωμι, *to give*. **μονογενῆ**: from the adjective μονογενής, -ές. Compare the expansion of
ἀληθής (157). Note also the form μονογενοῦς, found in *vs. 18* below. **ἵνα ... μὴ ἀπόληται**: a negative purpose clause using the subjunctive. ἀπόληται is from ἀπωλόμην, second
aorist of ἀπόλλυμι. Compare the form ἀγάγηται in the chart of ἄγω (118).
17. **ἀπέστειλε(ν)**: from ἀποστέλλω. See principal parts of στέλλω. **σωθῇ**: see principal
parts of σῴζω. Compare with λυθῇ in the chart of λύω (97).
18. **κέκριται**: see principal parts of κρίνω. **μή**: basically οὐ negates fact while μή
negates ideas, opinions. The phrase ὁ μὴ πιστεύων, *the one not believing*, is not a specific
reference but a generality, a concept, a supposed situation. Hence it is negated with the
use of μή. The same reasoning extends to μὴ πεπίστευκεν. **πεπίστευκε(ν)**: see principal
parts of πιστεύω.
19. **ἐλήλυθε(ν)**: see principal parts of ἔρχομαι. **ἦν ... τὰ ἔργα**: note again how the
neuter plural noun often takes a singular verb.
20. **ἐλεγχθῇ**: see principal parts of ἐλέγχω in today's word list.

21   αὐτοῦ· ὁ δὲ ποιῶν τὴν ἀλήθειαν ἔρχεται πρὸς τὸ φῶς, ἵνα φανερωθῇ αὐτοῦ τὰ ἔργα ὅτι ἐν θεῷ ἐστιν εἰργασμένα.

21. **ἐστιν εἰργασμένα**: a periphrasis for εἴργασται, perfect of ἐργάζομαι in today's
word list. Literally, *they are having been wrought*, which amounts to saying, *they have been
wrought* (482. 9).

## 179. Writing exercise

Make a chart showing the conjugation of the present system of σκηνόω,
*to tent*. This is an o-contract verb and inflects just as does ὑψόω in today's
chart. The student should remember, though, that as ὑψόω begins with
a vowel, it is augmented simply by lengthening this vowel. But σκηνόω,
beginning with a consonant, uses syllabic augment and reduplication
(see 107, 108).

# LESSON 25
# Declension of the Active Participles

**180.** THE active participles of the ω-verbs are declined like the consonant
and α-declension adjectives. The endings are very regular. Notice first
the word ὤν, *being*, the present active participle of εἰμί.

| | | |
|---|---|---|
| ὤν | οὖσα | ὄν |
| ὄντος | οὔσης | ὄντος |
| ὄντι | οὔσῃ | ὄντι |
| ὄντα | οὖσαν | ὄν |
| | | |
| ὄντες | οὖσαι | ὄντα |
| ὄντων | οὐσῶν | ὄντων |
| οὖσι | οὔσαις | οὖσι |
| ὄντας | οὔσας | ὄντα |

**181.** Very similar to this is λύων, *loosing*, the present active participle of
λύω. The future participle λύσων is identical in its endings. Only the s
is inserted.

| | | |
|---|---|---|
| λύων | λύουσα | λῦον |
| λύοντος | λυούσης | λύοντος |
| λύοντι | λυούσῃ | λύοντι |
| λύοντα | λύουσαν | λῦον |

| | | |
|---|---|---|
| λύοντες | λύουσαι | λύοντα |
| λυόντων | λυουσῶν | λυόντων |
| λύουσι | λυούσαις | λύουσι |
| λύοντας | λυούσας | λύοντα |

**182.** Observe next the declension of λύσας, *having loosed*, the aorist active participle of λύω. Note the σα throughout. The case endings are the same as those of ὤν and λύων.

| | | |
|---|---|---|
| λύσας | λύσασα | λῦσαν |
| λύσαντος | λυσάσης | λύσαντος |
| λύσαντι | λυσάσῃ | λύσαντι |
| λύσαντα | λύσασαν | λῦσαν |
| | | |
| λύσαντες | λύσασαι | λύσαντα |
| λυσάντων | λυσασῶν | λυσάντων |
| λύσασι | λυσάσαις | λύσασι |
| λύσαντας | λυσάσας | λύσαντα |

**183.** The declension of the perfect active participle λελυκώς, *having loosed*, is as follows:

| | | |
|---|---|---|
| λελυκώς | λελυκυῖα | λελυκός |
| λελυκότος | λελυκυίας | λελυκότος |
| λελυκότι | λελυκυίᾳ | λελυκότι |
| λελυκότα | λελυκυῖαν | λελυκός |
| | | |
| λελυκότες | λελυκυῖαι | λελυκότα |
| λελυκότων | λελυκυιῶν | λελυκότων |
| λελυκόσι | λελυκυίαις | λελυκόσι |
| λελυκότας | λελυκυίας | λελυκότα |

**184.** The aorist passive uses active endings throughout. Hence the aorist passive participle λυθείς, *having been loosed*, is included with the active participles here.

| | | |
|---|---|---|
| λυθείς | λυθεῖσα | λυθέν |
| λυθέντος | λυθείσης | λυθέντος |
| λυθέντι | λυθείσῃ | λυθέντι |
| λυθέντα | λυθεῖσαν | λυθέν |
| | | |
| λυθέντες | λυθεῖσαι | λυθέντα |
| λυθέντων | λυθεισῶν | λυθέντων |
| λυθεῖσι | λυθείσαις | λυθεῖσι |
| λυθέντας | λυθείσας | λυθέντα |

## 185. New word list

Αἰνών, ἡ, indecl., Aenon.

*ἀληθής, ἀληθές, true.

ἀπειθέω, ἀπειθήσω, ἠπείθησα, to be unbelieving, disobedient.

αὐξάνω, αὐξήσω, ηὔξησα, ηὔξηκα, ηὔξημαι, ηὐξήθην, trans. to augment; intrans. (late Gk.) to grow. AUGMENT.

*γῆ, γῆς, ἡ, earth, land. GEOGRAPHY.

*διατρίβω (see τρίβω for prin. parts), to wear away, spend time, discourse. DIATRIBE.

ἐλαττόω or ἐλασσόω, ἠλάττωσα, ἠλάττωκα, ἠλάττωμαι, ἠλαττώθην, to make less or inferior, decrease.

ἐπάνω, above.

ζήτησις, -εως, ἡ, inquiry.

μέτρον, -ου, τό, measure. METER.

νύμφη, -ης, ἡ, bride. NYMPH.

ὀργή, -ῆς, ἡ, anger, wrath.

παραγίγνομαι or παραγίνομαι (see γίγνομαι for prin. parts), to become near, be present, come.

*πληρόω, πληρώσω, ἐπλήρωσα, πεπλήρωκα, πεπλήρωμαι, ἐπληρώθην, to fill, fulfill.

ῥῆμα, -ατος, τό, saying, word.

Σαλείμ, τό, indecl., Salim.

σφραγίζω, σφραγίσω, ἐσφράγισα, ἐσφράγικα, ἐσφράγισμαι, to seal, confirm.

τρίβω, τρίψω, ἔτριψα, τέτριφα, τέτριμμαι, ἐτρίβην, rub, wear.

*φίλος, -ου, ὁ, friend. ANGLOPHILE.

*φυλακή, -ῆς, ἡ, guard, jail. PROPHYLACTIC.

χαίρω, χαιρήσω, ἐχάρησα, κεχάρηκα, κεχάρημαι, ἐχάρην, to rejoice, be of good cheer.

χαρά, -ᾶς, ἡ, joy, delight.

*χείρ, -ός, ἡ, hand. CHIROPRACTOR.

## 186. Reading passage (John 3 : 22–36)

3:22 Μετὰ ταῦτα ἦλθεν ὁ Ἰησοῦς καὶ οἱ μαθηταὶ αὐτοῦ εἰς τὴν Ἰουδαίαν γῆν, καὶ ἐκεῖ διέτριβεν μετ' αὐτῶν καὶ ἐβάπτιζεν.

23 ἦν δὲ καὶ Ἰωάννης βαπτίζων ἐν Αἰνὼν ἐγγὺς τοῦ Σαλείμ, ὅτι

24 ὕδατα πολλὰ ἦν ἐκεῖ, καὶ παρεγίνοντο καὶ ἐβαπτίζοντο· οὔπω

25 γὰρ ἦν βεβλημένος εἰς τὴν φυλακὴν Ἰωάννης. Ἐγένετο οὖν ζήτησις ἐκ τῶν μαθητῶν Ἰωάννου μετὰ Ἰουδαίου περὶ καθαρι-

26 σμοῦ. καὶ ἦλθον πρὸς τὸν Ἰωάννην καὶ εἶπαν αὐτῷ· ῥαββί, ὃς ἦν μετὰ σοῦ πέραν τοῦ Ἰορδάνου, ᾧ σὺ μεμαρτύρηκας, ἴδε οὗτος

22. ἦλθε(ν): see principal parts of ἔρχομαι. διέτριβε(ν): imperfect of διατρίβω in today's list.

23. ἐγγὺς τοῦ Σαλείμ: ἐγγύς is properly an adverb meaning near. The genitive τοῦ Σαλείμ is a genitive of separation (508). Literally the expression translates, near from Salim. We would say, near to Salim. ὕδατα πολλὰ ἦν: note that here again the neuter plural noun uses a verb in the singular. παρεγίνοντο: imperfect of παραγίνομαι (classical, παραγίγνομαι).

24. βεβλημένος: see principal parts of βάλλω. Compare with λελυμένος of λύω (97). ἦν βεβλημένος is periphrastic for ἐβέβλητο, he had been thrown (482. 9).

25. Ἐγένετο: see principal parts of γίγνομαι.

26. ἴδε: imperative from εἶδον, second aorist of ὁράω. Compare ἄγαγε from the chart of ἄγω (118).

27  βαπτίζει καὶ πάντες ἔρχονται πρὸς αὐτόν. ἀπεκρίθη Ἰωάννης καὶ
    εἶπεν· οὐ δύναται ἄνθρωπος λαμβάνειν οὐδὲν ἐὰν μὴ ᾖ δεδομένον
28  αὐτῷ ἐκ τοῦ οὐρανοῦ. αὐτοὶ ὑμεῖς μοι μαρτυρεῖτε ὅτι εἶπον· οὐκ
    εἰμὶ ἐγὼ ὁ χριστός, ἀλλ᾽ ὅτι ἀπεσταλμένος εἰμὶ ἔμπροσθεν
29  ἐκείνου. ὁ ἔχων τὴν νύμφην νυμφίος ἐστίν· ὁ δὲ φίλος τοῦ νυμ-
    φίου, ὁ ἑστηκὼς καὶ ἀκούων αὐτοῦ, χαρᾷ χαίρει διὰ τὴν φωνὴν
30  τοῦ νυμφίου. αὕτη οὖν ἡ χαρὰ ἡ ἐμὴ πεπλήρωται. ἐκεῖνον δεῖ
31  αὐξάνειν, ἐμὲ δὲ ἐλαττοῦσθαι. Ὁ ἄνωθεν ἐρχόμενος ἐπάνω
    πάντων ἐστίν· ὁ ὢν ἐκ τῆς γῆς ἐκ τῆς γῆς ἐστιν καὶ ἐκ τῆς γῆς
32  λαλεῖ. ὁ ἐκ τοῦ οὐρανοῦ ἐρχόμενος ἐπάνω πάντων ἐστίν· ὃ ἑώρακεν
    καὶ ἤκουσεν, τοῦτο μαρτυρεῖ, καὶ τὴν μαρτυρίαν αὐτοῦ οὐδεὶς
33  λαμβάνει. ὁ λαβὼν αὐτοῦ τὴν μαρτυρίαν ἐσφράγισεν ὅτι ὁ θεὸς
34  ἀληθής ἐστιν. ὃν γὰρ ἀπέστειλεν ὁ θεὸς τὰ ῥήματα τοῦ θεοῦ λαλεῖ·
35  οὐ γὰρ ἐκ μέτρου δίδωσιν τὸ πνεῦμα. ὁ πατὴρ ἀγαπᾷ τὸν υἱόν, καὶ
36  πάντα δέδωκεν ἐν τῇ χειρὶ αὐτοῦ. ὁ πιστεύων εἰς τὸν υἱὸν ἔχει
    ζωὴν αἰώνιον· ὁ δὲ ἀπειθῶν τῷ υἱῷ οὐκ ὄψεται ζωήν, ἀλλ᾽ ἡ
    ὀργὴ τοῦ θεοῦ μένει ἐπ᾽ αὐτόν.

27. οὐδέν: from οὐδείς, declined just as is εἷς, μία, ἕν, one. See 156. οὐ δύναται . . .
ἐὰν μὴ ᾖ . . .: present general conditional sentence (599). ᾖ δεδομένον: see principal
parts of δίδωμι. Cf. λελυμένος ᾖ, in 97.
28. ἀπεσταλμένος εἰμί: N.T. circumlocution for ἀπέσταλμαι from ἀποστέλλω. See
principal parts of στέλλω. εἰμί, a dissyllabic enclitic following a word with acute accent
on penult, retains its own accent. Cf. νυμφίος ἐστίν (vs. 29) and πάντων ἐστίν (vs. 31).
See 129.
29. ἑστηκώς: see principal parts of ἵστημι. Compare with λελυκώς in the chart of
λύω (97). χαρᾷ: dative of manner, with joy, with delight (522). πεπλήρωται: see principal
parts of πληρόω.
30. ἐλαττοῦσθαι: from ἐλαττόω in today's list. Compare ὑψοῦσθαι in the chart of
ὑψόω (177). αὐξάνειν: our word increase can be transitive ('to increase profits') or
intransitive ('profits increase'). So to the transitive verb αὐξάνω late Greek added the
intransitive sense observed here.
32. ἑώρακε(ν): see principal parts of ὁράω.
33. λαβών: participle from ἔλαβον, second aorist of λαμβάνω. Compare with ἀγαγών
in the chart of ἄγω (118). ἐσφράγισε(ν): a gnomic aorist, which denotes a general truth
(555). Translates as a present.
34. ἀπέστειλε(ν): from ἀποστέλλω. See principal parts of στέλλω. δίδωσι(ν): third
person singular present indicative active of δίδωμι, to give.
35. δέδωκε(ν): see principal parts of δίδωμι.
36. ὄψεται: see principal parts of ὁράω.

**187. Writing exercise**

Using the participles in today's lesson and the pronouns (and definite
article) declined in 63 ff., 72 ff., write out the Greek to give the meanings
indicated: (a) The ones (masc.) having been loosed (nom.) (b) Of these (the
foregoing, fem.) being. (c) For those (demonstrative, masc.) having loosed

(aor.). (*d*) . . . *us* (acc.) *having loosed* (perf.). (*e*) . . . *them* (masc.) *loosing.* (*f*)
*For you* (pl.) *being.*

## LESSON 26

# Irregular Greek Adjectives

**188.** THE student needs to be made aware of certain irregular but
frequently used Greek adjectives. The first is πολύς, *much* or *many*, which
is very much like the α- and o-adjective.

| | | |
|---|---|---|
| πολύς | πολλή | πολύ |
| πολλοῦ | πολλῆς | πολλοῦ |
| πολλῷ | πολλῇ | πολλῷ |
| πολύν | πολλήν | πολύ |
| πολλοί | πολλαί | πολλά |
| πολλῶν | πολλῶν | πολλῶν |
| πολλοῖς | πολλαῖς | πολλοῖς |
| πολλούς | πολλάς | πολλά |

**189.** Next is μέγας, *great*, whose stem develops in an unusual manner, but
whose endings again largely run true to the α- and o-declension pattern.

| | | |
|---|---|---|
| μέγας | μεγάλη | μέγα |
| μεγάλου | μεγάλης | μεγάλου |
| μεγάλῳ | μεγάλῃ | μεγάλῳ |
| μέγαν | μεγάλην | μέγα |
| μεγάλοι | μεγάλαι | μεγάλα |
| μεγάλων | μεγάλων | μεγάλων |
| μεγάλοις | μεγάλαις | μεγάλοις |
| μεγάλους | μεγάλας | μεγάλα |

**190.** Another important irregular adjective, developed in the fashion of
the consonant and α-declension adjectives, is χαρίεις, *graceful.*

| | | |
|---|---|---|
| χαρίεις | χαρίεσσα | χαρίεν |
| χαρίεντος | χαριέσσης | χαρίεντος |
| χαρίεντι | χαριέσσῃ | χαρίεντι |
| χαρίεντα | χαρίεσσαν | χαρίεν |

| χαρίεντες | χαρίεσσαι | χαρίεντα |
|---|---|---|
| χαριέντων | χαριεσσῶν | χαριέντων |
| χαρίεσι | χαριέσσαις | χαρίεσι |
| χαρίεντας | χαριέσσας | χαρίεντα |

**191.** Finally, the adjective μέλας, *black*, is presented. This adjective is declined as follows:

| μέλας | μέλαινα | μέλαν |
|---|---|---|
| μέλανος | μελαίνης | μέλανος |
| μέλανι | μελαίνῃ | μέλανι |
| μέλανα | μέλαιναν | μέλαν |
| μέλανες | μέλαιναι | μέλανα |
| μελάνων | μελαινῶν | μελάνων |
| μέλασι | μελαίναις | μέλασι |
| μέλανας | μελαίνας | μέλανα |

## 192. New word list

ἀγοράζω, ἀγοράσω, ἠγόρασα, ἠγόρακα, ἠγοράσθην, *to buy.*

ἀπέρχομαι, (see ἔρχομαι for prin. parts), *to go away*; ἀπεληλύθεισαν is pluperfect active.

ἀφίημι (see ἵημι for prin. parts), *to send forth, let go, leave.*

διέρχομαι (see ἔρχομαι for prin. parts), *to pass through, come frequently.*

ἕκτος, -η, -ον, *sixth.*

'Ιακώβ, ὁ, indecl., *Jacob.*

*ἵημι, ἥσω, ἧκα, εἷκα, εἷμαι, εἵθην, *to send, throw.*

καθέζομαι, same as καθίζω.

καθίζω, καθιῶ, ἐκάθισα, κεκάθικα, *to seat*; mid., *be seated.*

καίτοιγε, *and yet, although.*

κοπιάω, κοπιάσω, ἐκοπίασα, κεκοπίακα, *to be weary, to labor.*

ὁδοιπορία, -ας, ἡ, *journey.*

*πηγή, -ῆς, ἡ, *spring, well.*

πίνω, πίομαι, ἔπιον, πέπωκα, πέπομαι, ἐπόθην, *to drink*; πεῖν is for πιεῖν, second aorist infinitive. POTION.

*πλείων, πλεῖον (also πλέων, πλέον), gen. πλείονος, πλείονος, comparative of πολύς, *more.* PLEONASM.

πλησίος, -α, -ον, *near*; as adv., πλησίον, *near by*; with gen., *near from* (the English would put it, *near to*).

Σαμαρεία, -ας, ἡ, *Samaria.*

Συχάρ, ἡ, indecl., *Sychar.*

τροφή, -ῆς, ἡ, *food.* HYPERTROPHY.

*χωρίον, -ου, τό, *place.*

## 193. Reading passage (*John 4: 1–8*)

4:1    Ὡς οὖν ἔγνω ὁ κύριος ὅτι ἤκουσαν οἱ Φαρισαῖοι ὅτι 'Ιησοῦς

1. **ἔγνω**: third person singular of the second aorist indicative active of γιγνώσκω. Grouped under the designation of 'second aorist' are a number of rather irregularly

2  πλείονας μαθητὰς ποιεῖ καὶ βαπτίζει ἢ Ἰωάννης,—καίτοιγε
3  Ἰησοῦς αὐτὸς οὐκ ἐβάπτιζεν ἀλλ' οἱ μαθηταὶ αὐτοῦ,—ἀφῆκεν
4  τὴν Ἰουδαίαν καὶ ἀπῆλθεν πάλιν εἰς τὴν Γαλιλαίαν. Ἔδει δὲ
5  αὐτὸν διέρχεσθαι διὰ τῆς Σαμαρείας. ἔρχεται οὖν εἰς πόλιν τῆς
   Σαμαρείας λεγομένην Συχάρ, πλησίον τοῦ χωρίου ὃ ἔδωκεν
6  Ἰακὼβ τῷ Ἰωσὴφ τῷ υἱῷ αὐτοῦ· ἦν δὲ ἐκεῖ πηγὴ τοῦ Ἰακώβ.
   ὁ οὖν Ἰησοῦς κεκοπιακὼς ἐκ τῆς ὁδοιπορίας ἐκαθέζετο οὕτως
7  ἐπὶ τῇ πηγῇ· ὥρα ἦν ὡς ἕκτη. ἔρχεται γυνὴ ἐκ τῆς Σαμαρείας
8  ἀντλῆσαι ὕδωρ. λέγει αὐτῇ ὁ Ἰησοῦς· δός μοι πεῖν. οἱ γὰρ μαθηταὶ
   αὐτοῦ ἀπεληλύθεισαν εἰς τὴν πόλιν, ἵνα τροφὰς ἀγοράσωσιν.

developed types, not frequent in occurrence, which can be considered individually
as they are met. ἔγνων is one of these. Its conjugation in the indicative runs ἔγνων,
ἔγνως, ἔγνω; ἔγνωμεν, ἔγνωτε, ἔγνωσαν. **πλείονας**: from πλείων. Compare ἡδίων (157).

3. **ἀφῆκε(ν)**: first aorist of ἀφίημι, in today's list, using -κα instead of -σα. See third
principal part of of ἵημι. This first aorist is usually found only in the singular forms
of the indicative active: ἧκα, ἧκας, ἧκε. Second aorist forms are used for the rest of
the system. **ἀφῆκε(ν), ἀπῆλθε(ν)**: ν-movable before a consonant again (482. 1).

4. **ἔδει**: imperfect of δεῖ, impersonal verb meaning in the present, *it is necessary.*

5. **πλησίον**: used with a noun in the genitive, this adverb is sometimes called a preposition. **ἔδωκε(ν)**: first aorist of δίδωμι, *to give.* See its third principal part. The
observation on ἵημι in the note on ἀφῆκε(ν), *vs. 3*, applies also to δίδωμι.

6. **κεκοπιακώς**: from κοπιάω in today's word list. Perfect active participle, like
λελυκώς of λύω (97). **ὡς**: *as, about.*

7. **ἀντλῆσαι**: from ἀντλέω. Compare with ποιῆσαι in the chart of ποιέω (164). Infinitive
of purpose (576). **δός**: second aorist imperative of δίδωμι. The development of these
μι-verbs will be studied later. **πεῖν**: from πίνω in today's word list. This also is an infinitive of purpose. It is several times repeated in this chapter.

8. **ἀπεληλύθεισαν**: from ἀπέρχομαι. See principal parts of ἔρχομαι. The regular form
would be ἀπεληλύθεσαν. Compare ἐλελύκεσαν under λύω (97). **ἀγοράσωσι(ν)**: from
ἀγοράζω. Compare λύσωσι in the chart of λύω in 97. This is a purpose clause employing
ἵνα with the aorist subjunctive (562).

## 194. Writing exercise

Using the adjectives in today's lesson and the nouns declined in 138 f.
and 145 ff., write the Greek words to give the meanings indicated : (*a*) *For
a graceful woman.* (*b*) *The black triremes* (acc.). (*c*) *Of many years.* (*d*) *The great
leaders* (nom.). (*e*) *For many thieves.* (*f*) *Of black waters.*

# LESSON 27

# Declension of the Contract Participles

**195.** THE present active participles of the contract verbs in -εω, -αω, and
-οω follow the regular rules of development when one takes into account

the processes of contraction which they embody. But since they are always seen in their contracted forms, it is well for the student to observe these.

Note that the case endings follow the regular progression seen in the adjectives of the consonant and α-declension and in the active participles of the uncontracted verbs. As a result of their contract nature, the circumflex accent is much in evidence. First observe the ε-contract participle ποιῶν, *making*:

| | | |
|---|---|---|
| ποιῶν | ποιοῦσα | ποιοῦν |
| ποιοῦντος | ποιούσης | ποιοῦντος |
| ποιοῦντι | ποιούσῃ | ποιοῦντι |
| ποιοῦντα | ποιοῦσαν | ποιοῦν |
| | | |
| ποιοῦντες | ποιοῦσαι | ποιοῦντα |
| ποιούντων | ποιουσῶν | ποιούντων |
| ποιοῦσι | ποιούσαις | ποιοῦσι |
| ποιοῦντας | ποιούσας | ποιοῦντα |

Consider next the α-contract participle γεννῶν, *bearing*:

| | | |
|---|---|---|
| γεννῶν | γεννῶσα | γεννῶν |
| γεννῶντος | γεννώσης | γεννῶντος |
| γεννῶντι | γεννώσῃ | γεννῶντι |
| γεννῶντα | γεννῶσαν | γεννῶν |
| | | |
| γεννῶντες | γεννῶσαι | γεννῶντα |
| γεννώντων | γεννωσῶν | γεννώντων |
| γεννῶσι | γεννώσαις | γεννῶσι |
| γεννῶντας | γεννώσας | γεννῶντα |

Finally, the o-contract ὑψῶν, *lifting up*, is presented. Note that it works out the same as ποιῶν.

| | | |
|---|---|---|
| ὑψῶν | ὑψοῦσα | ὑψοῦν |
| ὑψοῦντος | ὑψούσης | ὑψοῦντος |
| ὑψοῦντι | ὑψούσῃ | ὑψοῦντι |
| ὑψοῦντα | ὑψοῦσαν | ὑψοῦν |
| | | |
| ὑψοῦντες | ὑψοῦσαι | ὑψοῦντα |
| ὑψούντων | ὑψουσῶν | ὑψούντων |
| ὑψοῦσι | ὑψούσαις | ὑψοῦσι |
| ὑψοῦντας | ὑψούσας | ὑψοῦντα |

## 196. New word list

*αἰτέω, αἰτήσω, ᾔτησα, ᾔτηκα, ᾔτη-
μαι, to ask, demand, beg.

αἰών, -ῶνος, ὁ, age, eternity. EON.

ἅλλομαι, ἁλοῦμαι, ἡλάμην or ἡλόμην, to leap, spring up.

ἄντλημα, -ατος, τό, bucket, vessel for
drawing water.

βαθύς, -εῖα, -ύ, deep. BATHY-
SCAPHE.

διψάω, διψήσω, ἐδίψησα, δεδίψηκα,
to thirst, suffer from thirst. DIPSO-
MANIAC.

δωρεά, -ᾶς, ἡ, gift.

*ἐνθάδε, thither, here.

ζάω, ζήσω, ἔζησα, ἔζηκα, to live.

θρέμμα, -ατος, τό, creature; pl.,
domestic animals, cattle.

*καλῶς, well.

*πέντε, indecl., five. PENTAGON.

Σαμαρίτης, -ου, ὁ, a Samaritan.

Σαμαρῖτις, -ιδος, ἡ, Samaritan woman.

συνχράομαι or συγχράομαι (see
χράομαι for prin. parts), to use
jointly, have dealings with (with
dat.).

φρέαρ, φρέατος, τό, well.

*χράομαι, χρήσομαι, ἐχρησάμην,
κέχρημαι, ἐχρήσθην, to use (with
dat.).

## 197. Reading passage (*John 4 : 9–18*)

4:9   Λέγει οὖν αὐτῷ ἡ γυνὴ ἡ Σαμαρῖτις· πῶς σὺ Ἰουδαῖος ὢν παρ'
ἐμοῦ πεῖν αἰτεῖς γυναικὸς Σαμαρίτιδος οὔσης; οὐ γὰρ συνχρῶνται

10   Ἰουδαῖοι Σαμαρίταις. ἀπεκρίθη Ἰησοῦς καὶ εἶπεν αὐτῇ· εἰ ᾔδεις
τὴν δωρεὰν τοῦ θεοῦ, καὶ τίς ἐστιν ὁ λέγων σοι· δός μοι πεῖν,

11   σὺ ἂν ᾔτησας αὐτὸν καὶ ἔδωκεν ἄν σοι ὕδωρ ζῶν. λέγει αὐτῷ·
κύριε, οὔτε ἄντλημα ἔχεις καὶ τὸ φρέαρ ἐστὶν βαθύ. πόθεν οὖν

9. **πεῖν**: second aorist infinitive of *πίνω, to drink*. In the moods other than the indicative, the chief significance of the aorist tense is not of *past action* but of *simple action*.
So the aorist infinitive need not be translated *to have drunk*, but simply *to drink*. **οὔσης**:
see development of the participle *ὤν, being*, in 180. These genitives modify *ἐμοῦ* and
agree in case with it. **συνχρῶνται**: from *συνχράομαι* in today's list. Compare with
*γεννῶνται* in the chart of *γεννάω* (173).

10. **εἰ ᾔδεις τὴν δωρεὰν . . . ἂν ᾔτησας . . . καὶ ἔδωκεν ἄν**: a conditional sentence
implying that the condition stated in its protasis is not fulfilled. These are called
*contrary-to-fact* suppositions. Refer to 601, 602, and note the structure of the straight
conditional sentence, contrary-to-fact, in both present and past time. Observe that for
this condition in present time the imperfect indicative is used; in past time, the aorist
indicative. Now analyze the sentence at hand as follows: protasis, *εἰ* with imperfect
indicative (*ᾔδεις*, pluperfect of *εἴδω, to know*, has the force of an imperfect indicative—
see 199 below); apodosis (a double conclusion), *ἄν* with aorist indicative (*ᾔτησας*,
aorist of *αἰτέω, to ask*), and *ἄν* with aorist indicative (*ἔδωκε*, aorist of *δίδωμι, to give*). So
the protasis is contrary to fact in present time, *if you knew (right now)* . . ., and the apodosis is contrary to fact in past time, *you would (in the past, or already) have asked . . . and
he would have given*. **ζῶν**: note the neuter forms in the declension of *γεννῶν* in today's
lesson. This is neuter accusative singular.

11. **κύριε**: vocative singular of *κύριος, lord or sir*. The vocative signifies the person
called or addressed. **οὔτε**: regularly used with co-ordinate negative clauses, here it
is paired with *καί* and an affirmative. **βαθύ**: observe the declension of *βαθύς* in 156.

12  ἔχεις τὸ ὕδωρ τὸ ζῶν; μὴ σὺ μείζων εἶ τοῦ πατρὸς ἡμῶν Ἰακώβ,
    ὃς ἔδωκεν ἡμῖν τὸ φρέαρ, καὶ αὐτὸς ἐξ αὐτοῦ ἔπιεν καὶ οἱ υἱοὶ
13  αὐτοῦ καὶ τὰ θρέμματα αὐτοῦ; ἀπεκρίθη Ἰησοῦς καὶ εἶπεν αὐτῇ·
14  πᾶς ὁ πίνων ἐκ τοῦ ὕδατος τούτου διψήσει πάλιν. ὃς δ' ἂν πίῃ
    ἐκ τοῦ ὕδατος οὗ ἐγὼ δώσω αὐτῷ, οὐ μὴ διψήσει εἰς τὸν αἰῶνα.
    ἀλλὰ τὸ ὕδωρ ὃ δώσω αὐτῷ γενήσεται ἐν αὐτῷ πηγὴ ὕδατος ἀλλο-
15  μένου εἰς ζωὴν αἰώνιον. λέγει πρὸς αὐτὸν ἡ γυνή· κύριε, δός μοι
    τοῦτο τὸ ὕδωρ, ἵνα μὴ διψῶ μηδὲ διέρχωμαι ἐνθάδε ἀντλεῖν.
16  λέγει αὐτῇ· ὕπαγε φώνησον τὸν ἄνδρα σου καὶ ἐλθὲ ἐνθάδε.
17  ἀπεκρίθη ἡ γυνὴ καὶ εἶπεν· οὐκ ἔχω ἄνδρα. λέγει αὐτῇ ὁ Ἰησοῦς·
18  καλῶς εἶπες ὅτι ἄνδρα οὐκ ἔχω. πέντε γὰρ ἄνδρας ἔσχες, καὶ νῦν
    ὃν ἔχεις οὐκ ἔστιν σου ἀνήρ· τοῦτο ἀληθὲς εἴρηκας.

12. **μή**: simply a sign of a question with negative answer expected. **εἶ**: see chart of εἰμί in 132. **τοῦ πατρός**: genitive of comparison, *than our father* (507). **ἔπιε(ν)**: second aorist of πίνω, *to drink*.

13. **πᾶς ὁ πίνων**: note that πᾶς here occupies predicate position (490).

14. **ὃς δ' ἂν πίῃ . . . οὐ μὴ διψήσει**: here is a conditional relative sentence as follows: protasis, relative ὅς plus ἄν plus subjunctive πίῃ (second aorist of πίνω); apodosis, future indicative διψήσει. Refer again to 603, if necessary, to identify this conditional relative. **οὗ ἐγὼ δώσω**: one would have expected ὅ (accusative) . . . δώσω as later in this same verse. οὗ is said to be *attracted* to the case of its antecedent ὕδατος (541). **οὐ μή**: intensive form of the negative with future indicative (561). **γενήσεται**: see principal parts of γίγνομαι.

15. **διψῶ, διέρχωμαι**: subjunctives in a negative clause of purpose (562).

16. **φώνησον**: from φωνέω, *to call*. Compare λῦσον in chart of λύω (97). **ἐλθέ**: from ἦλθον, second aorist of ἔρχομαι. Compare ἄγαγε in chart of ἄγω (118). ἐλθέ is one of five second aorist imperatives which irregularly accent the final syllable in the second person singular.

18. **ἔσχες**: see principal parts of ἔχω. **εἴρηκας**: see principal parts of εἴρω.

### 198. Writing exercise

Write the declension of the present active participles of the contract verbs, καλέω, *to call*; διψάω, *to thirst*; and σκηνόω, *to tent*.

# LESSON 28

# Second Perfect System of εἴδω

**199.** THE irregular verb εἴδω, *to see*, is related to the Latin *video*. Its second aorist, εἴδον, is used frequently to supply the aorist for ὁράω, *to see*. Of the other tense systems only the second perfect, οἶδα, *I have seen*, hence *I know*, is used very often. Its development is as follows:

## Second perfect system of εἴδω

| Indicative | οἶδα | ἴσμεν or οἴδαμεν |
|---|---|---|
| | οἶσθα | ἴστε or οἴδατε |
| | οἶδε | ἴσασι |
| (Pluperfect) | ᾔδη | ᾖσμεν |
| | ᾔδησθα or ᾔδεις | ᾖστε |
| | ᾔδει | ᾖσαν or ᾔδεσαν |
| Subjunctive | εἰδῶ | εἰδῶμεν |
| | εἰδῇς | εἰδῆτε |
| | εἰδῇ | εἰδῶσι |
| Optative | εἰδείην | εἰδεῖμεν |
| | εἰδείης | εἰδεῖτε |
| | εἰδείη | εἰδεῖεν |
| Imperative | ἴσθι | ἴστε |
| | ἴστω | ἴστων |
| Infinitive | εἰδέναι | |
| Participle | εἰδώς, εἰδυῖα, εἰδός | |

As has been said before, the perfect οἶδα is translated as present, *I know*, and the pluperfect ᾔδη is translated as imperfect, *I knew*.

## 200. New word list

*ἀγγέλλω, ἀγγελῶ, ἤγγειλα, ἤγγελκα, ἤγγελμαι, ἠγγέλθην, to announce. EVANGELIZE.

*ἀλλήλων, ἀλλήλοις, etc., *of, to one another*, etc.

ἀναγγέλλω (see ἀγγέλλω for prin. parts), *to carry back tidings, report.*

*ἅπας, ἅπασα, ἅπαν, strengthened form of πᾶς, *quite all, all together.*

βρῶμα, -ατος, τό, *food*. BROMA.

βρῶσις, -εως, ἡ, *meat, food.*

δεῦτε, pl. of δεῦρο, *hither! come hither!* perhaps for δεῦρ' ἴτε).

μέντοι, *however.*

μεταξύ, *between*; τὸ μεταξύ, *the time or space between, the meantime.*

μήτι, interrog. particle, often untranslated. Expects a negative, often with sense, *can it be that . . . ?*

*ὄρος, ὄρους, τό, *mountain*. OROGRAPHY.

προσκυνέω, προσκυνήσω, προσεκύνησα, προσκεκύνηκα, προσεκυνήθην, to *worship, adore.*

προσκυνητής, -οῦ, ὁ, *worshiper.*

σωτηρία, -ας, ἡ, *salvation, safety.*

τελειόω, τελειώσω, ἐτελείωσα, τετελείωκα, τετελείωμαι, ἐτελειώθην, *to finish, perfect.*

*τοιοῦτος, τοιαύτη, τοιοῦτο, gen. -ου, -ης, -ου, *of this kind, such.*

*τόπος, -ου, ὁ, *place*. TOPOGRAPHY.

## 201. Reading passage (*John 4 : 19–34*)

4 : 19,20 Λέγει αὐτῷ ἡ γυνή· κύριε, θεωρῶ ὅτι προφήτης εἶ σύ. οἱ πατέρες
ἡμῶν ἐν τῷ ὄρει τούτῳ προσεκύνησαν· καὶ ὑμεῖς λέγετε ὅτι ἐν
21     Ἱεροσολύμοις ἐστὶν ὁ τόπος ὅπου προσκυνεῖν δεῖ. λέγει αὐτῇ ὁ
Ἰησοῦς· πίστευέ μοι, γύναι, ὅτι ἔρχεται ὥρα ὅτε οὔτε ἐν τῷ ὄρει
22     τούτῳ οὔτε ἐν Ἱεροσολύμοις προσκυνήσετε τῷ πατρί. ὑμεῖς
προσκυνεῖτε ὃ οὐκ οἴδατε, ἡμεῖς προσκυνοῦμεν ὃ οἴδαμεν, ὅτι
23     ἡ σωτηρία ἐκ τῶν Ἰουδαίων ἐστίν· ἀλλὰ ἔρχεται ὥρα καὶ νῦν
ἐστιν, ὅτε οἱ ἀληθινοὶ προσκυνηταὶ προσκυνήσουσιν τῷ πατρὶ
ἐν πνεύματι καὶ ἀληθείᾳ· καὶ γὰρ ὁ πατὴρ τοιούτους ζητεῖ τοὺς
24     προσκυνοῦντας αὐτόν· πνεῦμα ὁ θεός, καὶ τοὺς προσκυνοῦντας
25     ἐν πνεύματι καὶ ἀληθείᾳ δεῖ προσκυνεῖν. λέγει αὐτῷ ἡ γυνή· οἶδα
ὅτι Μεσσίας ἔρχεται, ὁ λεγόμενος χριστός· ὅταν ἔλθῃ ἐκεῖνος,
26     ἀναγγελεῖ ἡμῖν ἅπαντα. λέγει αὐτῇ ὁ Ἰησοῦς· ἐγώ εἰμι, ὁ λαλῶν
27     σοι. Καὶ ἐπὶ τούτῳ ἦλθαν οἱ μαθηταὶ αὐτοῦ, καὶ ἐθαύμαζον ὅτι
μετὰ γυναικὸς ἐλάλει· οὐδεὶς μέντοι εἶπεν· τί ζητεῖς ἢ τί λαλεῖς
28     μετ' αὐτῆς; ἀφῆκεν οὖν τὴν ὑδρίαν αὐτῆς ἡ γυνὴ καὶ ἀπῆλθεν εἰς
29     τὴν πόλιν, καὶ λέγει τοῖς ἀνθρώποις· δεῦτε ἴδετε ἄνθρωπον ὃς
30     εἶπέν μοι πάντα ἃ ἐποίησα· μήτι οὗτός ἐστιν ὁ χριστός; ἐξῆλθον
31     ἐκ τῆς πόλεως καὶ ἤρχοντο πρὸς αὐτόν. Ἐν τῷ μεταξὺ ἠρώτων
32     αὐτὸν οἱ μαθηταὶ λέγοντες· ῥαββί, φάγε. ὁ δὲ εἶπεν αὐτοῖς· ἐγὼ

19. **κύριε**: vocative singular of κύριος, *lord* or *sir*.

20. **ὄρει**: from τὸ ὄρος. Compare ἔτει in declension of τὸ ἔτος (139). **ἡμῶν, ὑμῶν**: see again ἐγώ and σύ (72). **προσεκύνησαν**: from προσκυνέω. This verb is used several times in today's lesson.

21. **γύναι**: vocative singular of γυνή, *woman*. **οὔτε . . . οὔτε**: *neither . . . nor.*

22. **οἴδατε, οἴδαμεν**: the classical forms would be ἴστε and ἴσμεν, as in chart of οἶδα in today's lesson.

23. **καὶ γάρ**: an elliptical expression a bit hard to translate. Literally it means *and for.* It generally implies an emphasizing of the idea immediately to be expressed by referring it to the preceding idea. In the present context, Jesus has just said, 'True worshipers shall worship the Father in spirit and in truth'. The καὶ γάρ could be translated, 'And well they may, for . . .' Then comes the following idea, 'the Father seeks such as his worshipers'. **τοὺς προσκυνοῦντας**: *those worshiping, the worshipers.*

24. **πνεῦμα ὁ θεός**: understand ἐστι.

25. **ὅταν ἔλθῃ ἐκεῖνος, ἀναγγελεῖ . . .**: ὅταν is for the relative adverb ὅτε (*when*) plus ἄν. ἔλθῃ is subjunctive of ἦλθον, second aorist of ἔρχομαι. ἀναγγελεῖ is future (see principal parts of ἀγγέλλω). Refer again to 603, if necessary, to identify this conditional relative. **ἅπαντα**: from ἅπας, declined like πᾶς. Find πάντα in declension of πᾶς (156).

27. **ἦλθαν**: for ἦλθον from ἔρχομαι (482. 7).

28. **ἀφῆκε(ν)**: from ἀφίημι. See principal parts of ἵημι.

29. **ἴδετε**: from εἶδον, second aorist of ὁράω. See ἀγάγετε in chart of ἄγω (118).

30. **ἤρχοντο**: imperfect of ἔρχομαι.

31. **ἠρώτων**: from ἐρωτάω. Compare ἐγέννων in chart of γεννάω (173). **φάγε**: see principal parts of ἐσθίω. So also for φαγεῖν in next verse. This φαγεῖν is used in *vs. 32* and again in *vs. 33* as an infinitive of purpose (576).

33 βρῶσιν ἔχω φαγεῖν ἣν ὑμεῖς οὐκ οἴδατε. ἔλεγον οὖν οἱ μαθηταὶ
34 πρὸς ἀλλήλους· μή τις ἤνεγκεν αὐτῷ φαγεῖν; λέγει αὐτοῖς ὁ
᾽Ιησοῦς· ἐμὸν βρῶμά ἐστιν ἵνα ποιῶ τὸ θέλημα τοῦ πέμψαντός με
καὶ τελειώσω αὐτοῦ τὸ ἔργον.

33. ἤνεγκε(ν): see principal parts of φέρω.
34. ποιῶ ... τελειώσω: present subjunctive of ποιέω and aorist subjunctive of
τελειόω in a double purpose clause after ἵνα. The former denotes continuing action,
the latter simple action. The idea of purpose here is weak (482. 18).

**202. Writing exercise**

1. Using the table on οἶδα above, give the forms to indicate the following meanings: (a) *You* (pl.) *know.* (b) *They knew.* (c) *That we may know*
(use ἵνα). (d) *Let him know!*
2. Referring to the declension of the perfect active participle of λύω in
183, decline the perfect active participle of οἶδα.

## LESSON 29

# The Liquid-Stem Verb φαίνω

**203.** IN the chart in 205 is presented the synopsis of φαίνω, *to show.* This
verb has a stem ending in the liquid consonant ν. It will be recalled that
the liquids are λ, μ, ν, and ρ.

The future, φανῶ, is conjugated throughout just as is the present
system of the ε-contract verb ποιέω. Verbs whose future is handled in this
way are easily distinguished by means of their second principal part.
If middle, it will have the circumflexed ending -οῦμαι (θνῄσκω, θανοῦμαι,
*to die*; τρέχω, δραμοῦμαι, *to run*). Other verbs of this group, with active
endings in the future, are the following: σπείρω, σπερῶ, *to sow*; βάλλω,
βαλῶ, *to throw*; εἴρω, ἐρῶ, *to speak*; καλέω, καλῶ, *to call* (because καλέω
is itself an ε-contract verb, its present forms are the same as its future
forms, and the context must be consulted to show which is meant); μένω,
μενῶ, *to remain*; ἐλαύνω, ἐλῶ, *to march, drive*; ἀπόλλυμι, ἀπολῶ, *to destroy.*
Note that all these have stems ending in λ, μ, ν, or ρ.

The first aorist of φαίνω is ἔφηνα. It lacks the σ usually found in the
first aorist, but otherwise its endings follow exactly those of ἔλυσα
(see the chart in 97). Similarly, the liquid-stem verb μένω has the first
aorist ἔμεινα, and σπείρω has the first aorist ἔσπειρα. Some of the liquid-
stem verbs use a second aorist with endings just like those of ἤγαγον, the

second aorist of ἄγω (118). These include βάλλω (ἔβαλον), εἴρω (εἶπον), τρέχω (ἔδραμον). The principal parts always show clearly whether a liquid-stem verb uses a first or a second aorist.

The second perfect of φαίνω is πέφηνα. This tense system lacks the κ of the regular first perfect, but otherwise its endings follow those of λέλυκα completely. The second perfect means *have appeared*. A rarely used first perfect, πέφαγκα (not shown), means *have shown*.

Its perfect middle and passive system calls for certain adaptations as the ν of the stem blends with the personal endings.

Its second passive ἐφάνην, etc., lacks the θ usually found in the tense sign of the first passive system, but otherwise the endings follow those of ἐλύθην, etc. (For the -θι ending of imperative see 91.) The student should follow these characteristics carefully in the chart. The second aorist passive means *appeared*; a rarely used first aorist passive, ἐφάνθην, means *was shown*.

## 204. New word list

*ἄλλος, -η, -ο, other, another.* ALLO-
PATHY.
Γαλιλαῖος, -α, -ον, *Galilean*; also
subst., *a Galilean.*
*δέχομαι, δέξομαι, ἐδεξάμην, δέδε-
γμαι, *to receive.*
ἐκεῖθεν, *from there, thence.*
ἐπαίρω (see αἴρω for prin. parts), *to
lift up.*
*ἔτι, *yet, again, still.*
θερίζω, *to reap, harvest.*
θερισμός, -οῦ, ὁ, *a reaping, harvest.*
καρπός, -οῦ, ὁ, *fruit.* POLYCARP.
κόπος, -ου, ὁ, *labor.*
λαλιά, -ᾶς, ἡ, *speech, talk.*
λευκός, -ή, -όν, *brilliant, white.*
λευκός, -ή, -όν, *brilliant, white.*
LEUKEMIA.

*μισθός, -οῦ, ὁ, pay, wages.*
ὁμοῦ, *together, in like manner.*
*οὐκέτι, *no longer, not yet.*
ὀφθαλμός, -οῦ, ὁ, *eye.* OPHTHALMO-
LOGY.
πατρίς, -ίδος, ἡ, *native  country.*
PATRIOTIC.
σός, σή, σόν, *your, yours.*
σπείρω, σπερῶ, ἔσπειρα, ἔσπαρμαι,
ἐσπάρην, *to sow.* DISPERSE.
συνάγω (see ἄγω for prin. parts), *to
gather.* SYNAGOGUE.
σωτήρ, σωτῆρος, ὁ, *savior.* SOTERIO-
LOGY.
τετράμηνος, -ον, *of four months.*
τιμή, -ῆς, ἡ, *honor, value.* TIMOTHY.
χώρα, -ας, ἡ, *country, farm.*

*[For section 205 see opposite]*

## 206. Reading passage (*John 4 : 35–45*)

4:35  Οὐχ ὑμεῖς λέγετε ὅτι ἔτι τετράμηνός ἐστιν καὶ ὁ θερισμὸς ἔρχεται;
ἰδοὺ λέγω ὑμῖν, ἐπάρατε τοὺς ὀφθαλμοὺς ὑμῶν καὶ θεάσασθε τὰς

35. **ἰδού**: from εἶδον, second aorist of ὁράω. Locate the form ἀγαγοῦ in the chart of ἄγω in 118. The accent of ἰδού differs slightly from the classical usage, where the cir-cumflex is used. The idea of ἰδού, as compared with the active form ἴδε, is *see for yourself*, but in the run of conversation *behold* is probably near enough. **ἐπάρατε**: from ἐπαίρω. See principal parts of αἴρω, which is a liquid-stem verb. Note the aorist ἦρα.

## 205. Partially expanded synopsis of liquid-stem verb φαίνω,
### to show

| Present | Future | First aorist | Second perfect active |
|---------|--------|--------------|----------------------|
| φαίνω | φανῶ　φανοῦμεν<br>φανεῖς　φανεῖτε<br>φανεῖ　φανοῦσι | ἔφηνα　ἐφήναμεν<br>ἔφηνας　ἐφήνατε<br>ἔφηνε　ἔφηναν | πέφηνα　πεφήναμεν<br>πέφηνας　πεφήνατε<br>πέφηνε　πεφήνασι |
| ἔφαινον | | | ἐπεφήνη, etc. |
| φαίνω | | φήνω | πεφήνω or πεφηνὼς ὦ |
| φαίνοιμι | φανοίην*　φανοῖμεν<br>φανοίης　φανοῖτε<br>φανοίη　φανοῖεν | φήναιμι | πεφήνοιμι or πεφηνὼς εἴην |
| φαῖνε | | φῆνον | (Imperative missing) |
| φαίνειν | φανεῖν | φῆναι | πεφηνέναι |
| φαίνων | φανῶν, -οῦσα, -οῦν | φήνας | πεφηνώς |

| | | | Perf. mid. and pass. |
|---------|--------|--------------|----------------------|
| φαίνομαι | φανοῦμαι, etc. | ἐφηνάμην, etc. | πέφασμαι　πεφάσμεθα<br>πέφανσαι†　πέφανθε<br>πέφανται　πεφασμένοι<br>εἰσί |
| ἐφαινόμην | | | ἐπεφάσμην　ἐπεφάσμεθα<br>ἐπέφανσο†　ἐπέφανθε<br>ἐπέφαντο　πεφασμένοι<br>ἦσαν |
| φαίνωμαι | | φήνωμαι | πεφασμένος ὦ, etc. |
| φαινοίμην | φανοίμην, etc. | φηναίμην | πεφασμένος εἴην, etc. |
| φαίνου | | φῆναι | πέφανσο,† etc. |
| φαίνεσθαι | φανεῖσθαι | φήνασθαι | πεφάνθαι |
| φαινόμενος | φανούμενος | φηνάμενος | πεφασμένος |

| | | Second passive | |
|---------|--------|--------------|----------------------|
| Passive<br>same<br>forms as<br>middle | φανήσομαι | ἐφάνην | Passive same<br>forms as middle |
| | | φανῶ, -ῇς, -ῇ, etc. | |
| | φανησοίμην | φανείην | |
| | | φάνηθι | |
| | φανήσεσθαι | φανῆναι | |
| | φανησόμενος | φανείς | |

\* Alternative singular forms : φανοῖμι, φανοῖς, φανοῖ.

† Forms ending -νσαι, -νσο, not considered euphonic, were replaced by periphrasis (participle with forms of εἰμί) : πεφασμένος εἶ, ἦσθα, ἴσθι.

36 χώρας, ὅτι λευκαί εἰσιν πρὸς θερισμόν. ἤδη ὁ θερίζων μισθὸν
   λαμβάνει καὶ συνάγει καρπὸν εἰς ζωὴν αἰώνιον, ἵνα ὁ σπείρων
37 ὁμοῦ χαίρῃ καὶ ὁ θερίζων. ἐν γὰρ τούτῳ ὁ λόγος ἐστὶν ἀληθινὸς
38 ὅτι ἄλλος ἐστὶν ὁ σπείρων καὶ ἄλλος ὁ θερίζων. ἐγὼ ἀπέστειλα
   ὑμᾶς θερίζειν ὃ οὐχ ὑμεῖς κεκοπιάκατε· ἄλλοι κεκοπιάκασιν, καὶ
39 ὑμεῖς εἰς τὸν κόπον αὐτῶν εἰσεληλύθατε. Ἐκ δὲ τῆς πόλεως
   ἐκείνης πολλοὶ ἐπίστευσαν εἰς αὐτὸν τῶν Σαμαριτῶν διὰ τὸν λόγον
40 τῆς γυναικὸς μαρτυρούσης ὅτι εἶπέν μοι πάντα ἃ ἐποίησα. ὡς
   οὖν ἦλθον πρὸς αὐτὸν οἱ Σαμαρῖται, ἠρώτων αὐτὸν μεῖναι παρ᾽
41 αὐτοῖς· καὶ ἔμεινεν ἐκεῖ δύο ἡμέρας. καὶ πολλῷ πλείους ἐπίστευσαν
42 διὰ τὸν λόγον αὐτοῦ, τῇ τε γυναικὶ ἔλεγον ὅτι οὐκέτι διὰ τὴν
   σὴν λαλιὰν πιστεύομεν· αὐτοὶ γὰρ ἀκηκόαμεν, καὶ οἴδαμεν ὅτι
   οὗτός ἐστιν ἀληθῶς ὁ σωτὴρ τοῦ κόσμου.
43 Μετὰ δὲ τὰς δύο ἡμέρας ἐξῆλθεν ἐκεῖθεν εἰς τὴν Γαλιλαίαν.
44 αὐτὸς γὰρ Ἰησοῦς ἐμαρτύρησεν ὅτι προφήτης ἐν τῇ ἰδίᾳ πατρίδι
45 τιμὴν οὐκ ἔχει. ὅτε οὖν ἦλθεν εἰς Γαλιλαίαν, ἐδέξαντο αὐτὸν
   οἱ Γαλιλαῖοι, πάντα ἑωρακότες ὅσα ἐποίησεν ἐν Ἱεροσολύμοις ἐν
   τῇ ἑορτῇ. καὶ αὐτοὶ γὰρ ἦλθον εἰς τὴν ἑορτήν.

Dropping augment gives the stem ἀρ-. Compare with λύσατε in chart of λύω (97).
**θεάσασθε**: from θεάομαι a middle deponent. See its principal parts. Compare this form
with λύσασθε in the λύω chart (97).
36. **ἵνα . . . χαίρῃ**: purpose clause with subjunctive (562).
37. **ἄλλος . . . ἄλλος**: one . . . . another.
38. **ἀπέστειλα**: see principal parts of στέλλω. Here is another liquid verb. Compare
ἔστειλα with ἔφηνα in the chart of φαίνω in today's lesson. **κεκοπιάκατε, κεκοπιάκασι(ν)**:
see principal parts of κοπιάω. **εἰσεληλύθατε**: from εἰσέρχομαι. See principal parts of
ἔρχομαι.
39. **μαρτυρούσης**: from μαρτυρῶν, present participle of μαρτυρέω. See development
of ποιῶν in 195. Locate ποιούσης.
40. **ἠρώτων**: imperfect of ἐρωτάω. Compare ἐγέννων in chart of γεννάω (173).
**μεῖναι, ἔμεινε(ν)**: see principal parts of μένω, another liquid-stem verb. Compare with
φῆναι, ἔφηνε in the chart of φαίνω in today's lesson.
41. **πολλῷ**: from the adjective πολύς (188). This is a dative of degree of difference,
more by much, or many more (524). **πλείους**: for πλείονες from the adjective πλείων.
Compare ἡδίους in the expansion of ἡδίων (157).
42. **ἀκηκόαμεν**: see principal parts of ἀκούω. **οἴδαμεν**: see principal parts of εἴδω,
also 199.
45. **ἐδέξαντο**: see principal parts of δέχομαι. **ἑωρακότες**: see principal parts of ὁράω.
Compare λελυκώς as expanded in 183. **καὶ αὐτοὶ γάρ**: and (they would have seen him there)
for (they) themselves . . . .

## 207. Writing exercise

Expand φαίνω fully in the first aorist system, the second perfect active
system, and in the perfect middle and passive system. Some of the con-
jugations are already indicated. For the rest, follow the model of λύω (97).

# LESSON 30

# Expansions in βαίνω and γιγνώσκω

**208.** In today's lesson occurs the second aorist of καταβαίνω (*vss. 47, 49*). In the New Testament βαίνω, *to go*, occurs frequently but only in compounds, as here. In Attic prose the simple verb occurs only in the present and in the perfect active. Its synopsis is given in 211.

The little used future active βήσω (not shown) had causal force, *to make go*. This is reflected in βήσομαι, *I shall make myself go*, hence *I shall go*. Generally intransitive in its simple form, βαίνω has compounds which are transitive (e.g. παραβαίνω, *to transgress*). Hence the passive forms are shown.

The second aorist, ἔβην, is similar to second aorists of μι- verbs, to be studied later. The circumflex accents in this tense are because of contraction, and remain even where the verb is lengthened by being made a compound, as καταβῶ. The rest of the verb, though irregular, presents no special difficulties.

## 209. Second aorist of γιγνώσκω (N.T., γινώσκω), *to know*

The second aorist of γιγνώσκω is ἔγνων. This system develops somewhat unusually and its inflection is therefore noted:

| Indicative | ἔγνων | ἔγνωμεν |
|---|---|---|
| | ἔγνως | ἔγνωτε |
| | ἔγνω | ἔγνωσαν |
| Subjunctive | γνῶ | γνῶμεν |
| | γνῷς | γνῶτε |
| | γνῷ | γνῶσι |
| Optative | γνοίην | γνοῖμεν |
| | γνοίης | γνοῖτε |
| | γνοίη | γνοῖεν |
| Imperative | γνῶθι | γνῶτε |
| | γνώτω | γνόντων |
| Infinitive | γνῶναι | |
| Participle | γνούς, γνοῦσα, γνόν | |

## 210. New word list

*ἀποθνῄσκω (see θνῄσκω for prin. parts), *to die off, die*.

ἀσθενέω, ἠσθένησα, ἠσθένηκα, *to be infirm, sick*. NEURASTHENIA.

βασιλικός, -οῦ, ὁ, *nobleman*.

δοῦλος, -ου, ὁ, *slave*.

ἕβδομος, -η, -ον, *seventh*. HEBDOMADAL.

ἐχθές, *yesterday.*

θνῄσκω, θανοῦμαι, ἔθανον, τέθνηκα, *to die.* THANATOPSIS.

ἰάομαι, ἰάσομαι, ἰασάμην, ἴαμαι, ἰάθην, *to heal, cure.* IATRIC, PEDIATRICS.

κομψός, -ή, -όν, *fine, elegant, well* (of health).

κομψότερος, -α, -ον, *better* (of health), comparative of κομψός.

*μέλλω, μελλήσω, ἐμέλλησα, *to intend, be going to do something.*

*οἰκία, -ας, ἡ, *house, household.* OECOLOGY or ECOLOGY.

ὅλος, -η, -ον, *whole, entire.* HOLO-CAUST.

παιδίον, -ου, τό, *child.*

*παῖς, παιδός, ὁ *or* ἡ, *child.* PAEDIA-TRICS or PEDIATRICS.

*πορεύομαι, πορεύσομαι, ἐπορευσά-μην, πεπόρευμαι, ἐπορεύθην, *to proceed.*

*πρίν, *before, until;* sometimes with ἄν plus subjunctive, sometimes with infin.

*πυνθάνομαι, πεύσομαι, ἐπυθόμην, πέπυσμαι, *to inquire, learn.*

πυρετός, -οῦ, ὁ, *heat, fever.* PYRETIC.

τέρας, -ατος, τό, *sign, wonder.*

ὑπαντάω, ὑπαντήσομαι, ὑπήντησα, *to meet, go to meet* (often with dative).

[*For section 211 see opposite*]

**212. Reading passage** (*John* 4 : 46–54)

4:46    ῏Ηλθεν οὖν πάλιν εἰς τὴν Κανὰ τῆς Γαλιλαίας, ὅπου ἐποίησεν τὸ ὕδωρ οἶνον. Καὶ ἦν τις βασιλικὸς οὗ ὁ υἱὸς ἠσθένει ἐν Καφαρ-

47    ναούμ· οὗτος ἀκούσας ὅτι Ἰησοῦς ἥκει ἐκ τῆς Ἰουδαίας εἰς τὴν Γαλιλαίαν, ἀπῆλθεν πρὸς αὐτὸν καὶ ἠρώτα ἵνα καταβῇ καὶ

48    ἰάσηται αὐτοῦ τὸν υἱόν· ἤμελλεν γὰρ ἀποθνῄσκειν. εἶπεν οὖν ὁ Ἰησοῦς πρὸς αὐτόν· ἐὰν μὴ σημεῖα καὶ τέρατα ἴδητε, οὐ μὴ

49    πιστεύσητε. λέγει πρὸς αὐτὸν ὁ βασιλικός· κύριε, κατάβηθι πρὶν

46. **οὗ**: from the relative pronoun ὅς, ἥ, ὅ. See 64. **ἠσθένει**: from ἀσθενέω. Compare ἐποίει from ποιέω (164).

47. **ἠρώτα**: from ἐρωτάω. Compare ἐγέννα from γεννάω (173). **ἵνα καταβῇ καὶ ἰάσηται**: this use of a purpose clause to express an indirect statement is characteristically N.T. and not classical (482. 18). Note καταβῇ from καταβαίνω. The second aorist of βαίνω is ἔβην. In the chart of βαίνω in today's lesson find the form βῇ. **ἤμελλε(ν)**: irregular for ἔμελλε(ν), imperfect of μέλλω.

48. **ἐὰν μὴ σημεῖα καὶ τέρατα ἴδητε, οὐ μὴ πιστεύσητε**: the use of οὐ μή with the subjunctive in the N.T. constitutes a strong negative statement of futurity (561). It is the equivalent of the future indicative in its idea of time. οὐ μὴ πιστεύσητε means, 'You will never believe'. Hence in this conditional sentence are the following: protasis, ἐάν plus subjunctive ἴδητε (from εἶδον, second aorist of ὁράω); apodosis, equivalent of future indicative. See 603, if necessary, to identify this conditional sentence.

49. **κατάβηθι**: from καταβαίνω. Locate βῆθι in today's expansion of βαίνω. **πρὶν**: often takes the infinitive. Here τὸ παιδίον is the subject of the infinitive ἀποθανεῖν (from ἀπέθανον, second aorist of ἀποθνῄσκω, *to die*). Translate, *before my child dies* (575).

**211. Partially expanded synopsis of βαίνω,** *to go*

| Present | Future | Second aorist | | First perfect active |
|---|---|---|---|---|
| βαίνω | | ἔβην    ἔβημεν | | βέβηκα |
| | | ἔβης    ἔβητε | | |
| ἔβαινον | | ἔβη    ἔβησαν | | ἐβεβήκη |
| βαίνω | | βῶ    βῶμεν | | βεβήκω |
| | | βῇς    βῆτε | | |
| βαίνοιμι | | βῇ    βῶσι | | βεβήκοιμι |
| βαῖνε | | βαίην    βαῖμεν | | βεβηκὼς ἴσθι |
| | | βαίης    βαῖτε | | |
| βαίνειν | | βαίη    βαῖεν | | βεβηκέναι |
| βαίνων | | βῆθι    βῆτε | | βεβηκώς |
| | | βήτω    βάντων | | *Perf. mid. and pass.* * |
| βαίνομαι | βήσομαι | βῆναι | | βέβαμαι |
| ἐβαινόμην | | βάς, βᾶσα, βάν | | ἐβεβάμην |
| βαίνωμαι | | | | βεβαμένος ὦ |
| βαινοίμην | βησοίμην | | | βεβαμένος εἴην |
| βαίνου | | No aorist middle forms | | βέβασο |
| βαίνεσθαι | βήσεσθαι | | | βεβάσθαι |
| βαινόμενος | βησόμενος | | | βεβαμένος |
| | | *First passive** | | |
| | βαθήσομαι | ἐβάθην | | |
| Passive same | | βαθῶ | | Passive same |
| forms as | βαθησοίμην | βαθείην | | forms as |
| middle | | βάθητι | | middle |
| | βαθήσεσθαι | βαθῆναι | | |
| | βαθησόμενος | βαθείς, -θεῖσα, -θέν | | |

\* Forms in the perfect middle and passive and the first passive system are found only rarely.

50 ἀποθανεῖν τὸ παιδίον μου. λέγει αὐτῷ ὁ Ἰησοῦς· πορεύου· ὁ υἱός
   σου ζῇ. ἐπίστευσεν ὁ ἄνθρωπος τῷ λόγῳ ὃν εἶπεν αὐτῷ ὁ Ἰησοῦς,
51 καὶ ἐπορεύετο. ἤδη δὲ αὐτοῦ καταβαίνοντος οἱ δοῦλοι ὑπήντησαν
52 αὐτῷ λέγοντες ὅτι ὁ παῖς αὐτοῦ ζῇ. ἐπύθετο οὖν τὴν ὥραν παρ᾽
   αὐτῶν ἐν ᾗ κομψότερον ἔσχεν· εἶπαν οὖν αὐτῷ ὅτι ἐχθὲς ὥραν
53 ἑβδόμην ἀφῆκεν αὐτὸν ὁ πυρετός. ἔγνω οὖν ὁ πατὴρ ὅτι ἐκείνῃ
   τῇ ὥρᾳ ἐν ᾗ εἶπεν αὐτῷ ὁ Ἰησοῦς· ὁ υἱός σου ζῇ· καὶ ἐπίστευσεν
54 αὐτὸς καὶ ἡ οἰκία αὐτοῦ ὅλη. Τοῦτο [δὲ] πάλιν δεύτερον σημεῖον
   ἐποίησεν ὁ Ἰησοῦς ἐλθὼν ἐκ τῆς Ἰουδαίας εἰς τὴν Γαλιλαίαν.

50. **πορεύου**: from the deponent verb πορεύομαι. Compare with λύου from λύω (97).
**ζῇ**: ζάω irregularly conjugates the present indicative: ζῶ, ζῇς, ζῇ; ζῶμεν, ζῆτε, ζῶσι instead of using α as might have been expected.

51. **αὐτοῦ καταβαίνοντος**: a genitive absolute. See the discussion on the genitive absolute in 582. Here the implication seems to be that of attendant circumstances, *he going down* or *while he was going down*. **ὑπήντησαν**: see ὑπαντάω in today's word list.

52. **ἐπύθετο**: see principal parts of πυνθάνομαι in today's word list. **κομψότερον ἔσχεν**: the Greek uses an adverb plus the verb ἔχω to express the idea of *being* in a certain state. Compare our usage, 'to keep one's self well'. καλῶς ἔχειν means *to be well*. The neuter singular of a comparative adjective is used as the comparative adverb. κομψότερον is thus the comparative adverb *better* (of health). In this idiom an aorist has the idea of entering into a state. The phrase κομψότερον ἔσχεν is translated, *he got*, or *became better*. **ἀφῆκε**: from ἀφίημι. See 193, note on vs. 3, for aorist conjugation.

53. **ἔγνω**: from ἔγνων, the second aorist of γιγνώσκω. See its development in today's lesson. **ἐκείνῃ τῇ ὥρᾳ**: dative of time when (526). Understand also ἦν, *it was*. **ἡ οἰκία . . . ὅλη**: note that ὅλη here occupies predicate position (490).

54. **ἐλθών**: participle from ἦλθον, second aorist of ἔρχομαι.

### 213. Writing exercise

Expand βαίνω fully in the first passive system (cf. λύω, 97).

## LESSON 31
# The Verb ἵστημι

**214.** IN 216 is presented the expanded synopsis of the μι-verb ἵστημι, *to stand*. There are comparatively few of the μι-verbs in common use in Greek. The present and the second aorist systems are the ones demanding closest attention. The student will notice that the personal endings in these two systems run very nearly parallel in most of the tense–mood groups. The first aorist, ἔστησα, *set, caused to stand*, because quite regular, is omitted in favor of the second aorist, ἔστην, *stood*.

The student should go through this expanded synopsis carefully. This table will serve as a later reference when forms of ἵστημι are met.

But the student will need to be familiar enough with this chart to be able
to recognize the forms of ἵστημι as coming from that verb.

## 215. New word list

ἀσθενεία, -ας, ἡ, *weakness, infirmity,
sickness.* ASTHENIC.

Βηθζαθά, ἡ, indecl., *Bethzatha* or
*Bethesda.*

δήποτε, *once, ever.*

Ἑβραϊστί, *in the Hebrew tongue.*

ἐκδέχομαι, (see δέχομαι for prin.
parts), *to receive, expect, await.*

ἐμβαίνω (see βαίνω for prin. parts),
*to enter, go in.*

ἔξεστι, impersonal, *it is possible,
permissible.*

ἐπιλέγω (see λέγω for prin. parts), *to
call by name, say further.* EPILOGUE.

εὐθέως, *straightway, at once.*

θεραπεύω, θεραπεύσω, ἐθεράπευσα,
τεθεράπευμαι, ἐθεραπεύθην, *to
serve, heal.* THERAPEUTIC.

*καιρός, -οῦ, ὁ, *right time, due time,
time.*

κατάκειμαι (see κεῖμαι for prin.
parts), *to recline, lie down.*

κατέχω (see ἔχω for prin. parts), *to
restrain, hold completely.*

κίνησις, -εως, ἡ, *a moving, motion.*
KINETIC.

κολυμβήθρα, -ας, ἡ, *swimming pool,
bath.*

κράβατος, -ου, ὁ, *couch, mat.*

νόσημα, -ατος, τό, *sickness, malady.*
NOSOLOGY.

ξηρός, -ά, -όν, *dry, withered.* XERO-
DERMA.

*ὀκτώ, indecl., *eight.* OCTAGON.

*πλῆθος, -ους, τό, *crowd.* PLETHORA.

προβατικός, -ή, -όν, *of or for sheep* ; ἡ
προβατική, *sheep gate.*

σάββατον, -ου, τό, *sabbath.*

στοά, -ᾶς, ἡ, *portico, cloister.* STOIC.

ταράττω or ταράσσω, ταράξω,
ἐτάραξα, τετάραχα, τετάραγμαι,
ἐταράχθην, *to disturb, trouble.*

ταραχή, -ῆς, ἡ, *disturbance, troubling.*

τριάκοντα, indecl., *thirty.*

τυφλός, -ή, -όν, *blind.* TYPHLOSIS.

ὑγιής, -ές, *sound, healthy, well.*
HYGIENE.

*χρόνος, -ου, ὁ, *time.* CHRONOLOGY.

χωλός, -ή, -όν, *lame, crippled.*

[For section 216 see p. 114]

## 217. Reading passage (John 5 : 1-12)

5:1   Μετὰ ταῦτα ἦν ἑορτὴ τῶν Ἰουδαίων, καὶ ἀνέβη Ἰησοῦς εἰς
2   Ἱεροσόλυμα. ἔστιν δὲ ἐν τοῖς Ἱεροσολύμοις ἐπὶ τῇ προβατικῇ
   κολυμβήθρα, ἡ ἐπιλεγομένη Ἑβραϊστὶ Βηθζαθά, πέντε στοὰς
3   ἔχουσα. ἐν ταύταις κατέκειτο πλῆθος τῶν ἀσθενούντων, τυφλῶν,

1. ἀνέβη: from ἀναβαίνω. See development of βαίνω in 211. Find the form ἔβη.
2. ἔστι(ν): this form is usually enclitic. But enclitics retain their accent under certain
circumstances (see 128). Here the verb signifies existence ('there is') and so retains an
accent on the first syllable.
3. κατέκειτο: imperfect of κατάκειμαι.

# 216. Partially expanded synopsis of ἵστημι, *to stand*

| Present | | Future | Second aorist | | Second* perfect active | |
|---|---|---|---|---|---|---|
| ἵστημι | ἵσταμεν | στήσω | ἔστην | ἔστημεν | (ἕστηκα) | ἕσταμεν |
| ἵστης | ἵστατε | | ἔστης | ἔστητε | (ἕστηκας) | ἕστατε |
| ἵστησι | ἱστᾶσι | | ἔστη | ἔστησαν | (ἕστηκε) | ἑστᾶσι |
| ἵστην | ἵσταμεν | | | | (εἱστήκη) | ἕσταμεν |
| ἵστης | ἵστατε | | | | (εἱστήκης) | ἕστατε |
| ἵστη | ἵστασαν | | | | (εἱστήκει) | ἕστασαν |
| ἱστῶ | ἱστῶμεν | | στῶ | στῶμεν | ἑστῶ | ἑστῶμεν |
| ἱστῇς | ἱστῆτε | | στῇς | στῆτε | ἑστῇς | ἑστῆτε |
| ἱστῇ | ἱστῶσι | | στῇ | στῶσι | ἑστῇ | ἑστῶσι |
| ἱσταίην | ἱσταῖμεν | στήσοιμι | σταίην | σταῖμεν | ἑσταίην | ἑσταῖμεν |
| ἱσταίης | ἱσταῖτε | | σταίης | σταῖτε | ἑσταίης | ἑσταῖτε |
| ἱσταίη | ἱσταῖεν | | σταίη | σταῖεν | ἑσταίη | ἑσταῖεν |
| ἵστη | ἵστατε | | στῆθι | στῆτε | ἔσταθι | ἔστατε |
| ἱστάτω | ἱστάντων | | στήτω | στάντων | ἑστάτω | ἑστάντων |
| ἱστάναι | | στήσειν | στῆναι | | ἑστάναι | |
| ἱστάς, -ᾶσα, -άν | | στήσων | στάς, στᾶσα, στάν | | ἑστώς, ἑστῶσα, ἑστός or ἑστώς | |

| | | | | | Perfect mid. and pass. | |
|---|---|---|---|---|---|---|
| ἵσταμαι | ἱστάμεθα | στήσομαι | | | ἕσταμαι | ἑστάμεθα |
| ἵστασαι | ἵστασθε | | | | ἕστασαι | ἕστασθε |
| ἵσταται | ἵστανται | | | | ἕσταται | ἕστανται |
| ἱστάμην | ἱστάμεθα | | | | | |
| ἵστασο | ἵστασθε | | | | | |
| ἵστατο | ἵσταντο | | | | Further forms | |
| ἱστῶμαι | ἱστώμεθα | | No second | | from this | |
| ἱστῇ | ἱστῆσθε | | aorist middle | | system seldom | |
| ἱστῆται | ἱστῶνται | | | | found | |
| ἱσταίμην | ἱσταίμεθα | στησοίμην | | | | |
| ἱσταῖο | ἱσταῖσθε | | | | | |
| ἱσταῖτο | ἱσταῖντο | | | | | |
| ἵστασο | ἵστασθε | | | | | |
| ἱστάσθω | ἱστάσθων | | | | | |
| ἵστασθαι | | στήσεσθαι | | | | |
| ἱστάμενος | | στησόμενος | | | | |

| Passive same forms as middle | First passive | | Passive same forms as middle |
|---|---|---|---|
| | σταθήσομαι | ἐστάθην, etc. | |
| | regular | regular | |

\* First perfect forms generally used are bracketed. Also sometimes used are pluperfect εἱστήκεμεν, εἱστήκετε, εἱστήκεσαν, and participle ἑστηκώς.

4 χωλῶν, ξηρῶν [ἐκδεχομένων τὴν τοῦ ὕδατος κίνησιν. ἄγγελος
  γὰρ κατὰ καιρὸν κατέβαινεν ἐν τῇ κολυμβήθρᾳ καὶ ἐτάρασσε τὸ
  ὕδωρ· ὁ οὖν πρῶτος ἐμβὰς μετὰ τὴν ταραχὴν τοῦ ὕδατος ὑγιὴς
5 ἐγένετο, ᾧ δήποτε κατείχετο νοσήματι]. ἦν δέ τις ἄνθρωπος ἐκεῖ
6 τριάκοντα καὶ ὀκτὼ ἔτη ἔχων ἐν τῇ ἀσθενείᾳ αὐτοῦ· τοῦτον ἰδὼν
  ὁ Ἰησοῦς κατακείμενον, καὶ γνοὺς ὅτι πολὺν ἤδη χρόνον ἔχει,
7 λέγει αὐτῷ· θέλεις ὑγιὴς γενέσθαι; ἀπεκρίθη αὐτῷ ὁ ἀσθενῶν·
  κύριε, ἄνθρωπον οὐκ ἔχω, ἵνα ὅταν ταραχθῇ τὸ ὕδωρ βάλῃ με εἰς
  τὴν κολυμβήθραν· ἐν ᾧ δὲ ἔρχομαι ἐγώ, ἄλλος πρὸ ἐμοῦ κατα-
8 βαίνει. λέγει αὐτῷ ὁ Ἰησοῦς· ἔγειρε ἆρον τὸν κράβατόν σου
9 καὶ περιπάτει. καὶ εὐθέως ἐγένετο ὑγιὴς ὁ ἄνθρωπος, καὶ ἦρεν
  τὸν κράβατον αὐτοῦ καὶ περιεπάτει. Ἦν δὲ σάββατον ἐν ἐκείνῃ
10 τῇ ἡμέρᾳ. ἔλεγον οὖν οἱ Ἰουδαῖοι τῷ τεθεραπευμένῳ· σάββατόν
11 ἐστιν, καὶ οὐκ ἔξεστίν σοι ἆραι τὸν κράβατον. ὃς δὲ ἀπεκρίθη
  αὐτοῖς· ὁ ποιήσας με ὑγιῆ, ἐκεῖνός μοι εἶπεν· ἆρον τὸν κράβατόν
12 σου καὶ περιπάτει. ἠρώτησαν αὐτόν· τίς ἐστιν ὁ ἄνθρωπος ὁ
  εἰπών σοι· ἆρον καὶ περιπάτει;

4. This verse is included in brackets for continuity in the verse numbering. It has
been omitted from the Nestle text, 1957 edition, because not found in the best manuscripts of the N.T. **κατέβαινε(ν)**: the imperfect of *καταβαίνω.* The idea is that of continuing or customary action, *he went down, he used to go down.* **ἐτάρασσε**: imperfect of
*ταράττω* in today's list. **ἐμβάς**: from *ἐμβαίνω.* Find *βάς* in the chart of *βαίνω* in 211.
**ᾧ**: the antecedent is *τοῦ νοσήματος, from the disease,* but is omitted and must be understood from what follows. **ᾧ** . . . **νοσήματι**: dative of means (520). Literally, *by what
disease.* **κατείχετο**: from *κατέχω.* *εἴχετο* is imperfect passive of *ἔχω.* Translate, *he was
held.*

5. **ἔτη**: from *τὸ ἔτος.* See its development in 139. This is accusative of extent of time.
So also *πολύν* . . . *χρόνον* in *vs.* 6 below (531). **ἔχων**: translate, *being.* Cf. 212, note on
*vs. 52.*

6. **γνούς**: from *ἔγνων,* second aorist of *γιγνώσκω.* See its development in 209.
**ἔχει**: *he is.* Understand *οὕτως, in this case* or *condition.* **γενέσθαι**: see principal parts of
*γίγνομαι.* Compare with *ἀγαγέσθαι* in the chart of *ἄγω* (118).

7. **ὅταν ταραχθῇ**: here are *ὅτε* plus *ἄν* plus subjunctive as a protasis, and the present
indicative (*ἔχω*) as apodosis. A present general conditional relative sentence (see 599).
**ταραχθῇ**: from *ταράττω* in today's list. **βάλῃ**: see principal parts of *βάλλω.* Compare
with second aorist *ἀγάγῃ* in the chart of *ἄγω* (118). **ἐν ᾧ**: carries the idea of time *in
which.* Translate, *while.*

8. **ἆρον**: from *ἦρα,* aorist of *αἴρω.* See its principal parts. Without the augment, the
stem is *ἀρ-.* Find *λῦσον,* the comparable form of *λύω,* in 97. **περιπάτει**: find *ποίει,* the
comparable form of *ποιέω,* in 164.

9. **ἦρε(ν)**: from *αἴρω.* Compare with *ἔλυσε(ν)* from *λύω* (97).

10. **τεθεραπευμένῳ**: see principal parts of *θεραπεύω* in today's list. This is the perfect
passive participle. **ἆραι**: see notes on *ἆρον* and *ἦρε(ν)* under *vss.* 8 and 9 above. *ἆραι*
compares with *λῦσαι* of *λύω* (97).

11. **ὃς δέ**: the Greek sometimes uses a relative pronoun as the subject of a new
sentence where the English would use a demonstrative pronoun. Translate, *but he* . . . .
**ὑγιῆ**: for the form see expansion of *ἀληθής* (157).

**218. Writing exercise**

Decline fully the future and the second aorist active participles of ἵστημι. Refer to 181 and 182. For the endings of στάς, follow λύσας. For its accent in the feminine gender, note ὤν, οὖσα, ὄν.

## LESSON 32
### The Verb δείκνυμι

**219.** THE reading passage today has used a couple of forms from the μι-verb δείκνυμι, *to show*. This μι-verb has a present stem ending in υ and should have special notice. Hence in 222 is presented a synopsis of δείκνυμι which has been expanded in the present system. The other systems are not expanded beyond the dimensions of the usual synopsis, as they are quite regular.

The aorist forms are in the usual first aorist pattern rather than in a second aorist as is often the case with μι-verbs. The first perfect active uses the periphrastic or compound forms for the subjunctive and optative moods (see again λύω, 97, with footnote).

Perhaps it should be said that in addition to the μι-forms the N.T. also makes use of present forms developed from δεικνύω, which is conjugated like λύω in the present and is used as an equivalent of the μι-verb δείκνυμι in the present system.

Follow the synopsis of δείκνυμι, observing the manner in which this important μι-verb is inflected.

**220. New word list**

ἁμαρτάνω, ἁμαρτήσω, ἡμάρτησα or ἥμαρτον, ἡμάρτηκα, ἡμάρτημαι, ἡμαρτήθην, *to err, miss, sin*. HAMARTIOLOGY.

ἀνάστασις, -εως, ἡ, *resurrection*. ANASTASIA.

*ἀποκτείνω (see κτείνω for prin. parts), *to kill*.

*διώκω, διώξω, ἐδίωξα, δεδίωχα, ἐδιώχθην, *to pursue, persecute*.

ἐκνεύω, ἐκνεύσω, ἐξένευσα, *to 'bow out', slip away*.

ἐκπορεύομαι (see πορεύομαι for prin. parts), *to go forth*.

ζωοποιέω (see ποιέω for prin.

parts), *to make alive, quicken*.

θάνατος, -ου, ὁ, *death*. THANATOPSIS.

ἴσος, -η, -ον, *equal, the same as*. ISOSCELES.

*κτείνω, κτενῶ, ἔκτεινα, ἔκτονα, *to kill*. Usually in compounds, ἔκτονα always so.

μεταβαίνω (see βαίνω for prin. parts), *to pass over, cross over*.

μνημεῖον, -ου, τό, *monument, tomb*.

*μόνος, -η, -ον, *only, alone*; μόνον as adv., *only*. MONOLOGUE.

ὁμοίως, *similarly*. HOMOEOPATHY.

ὄχλος, -ου, ὁ, *throng, crowd*. OCHLOCRACY.

*τιμάω, τιμήσω, ἐτίμησα, τετίμηκα,   χείρων, -ον, worse, comp. of κακός.
τετίμημαι, ἐτιμήθην, to honor, value.   *ὥσπερ, just as.

## 221. Reading passage (*John 5 : 13–29*)

5:13   Ὁ δὲ ἰαθεὶς οὐκ ᾔδει τίς ἐστιν· ὁ γὰρ Ἰησοῦς ἐξένευσεν ὄχλου
14   ὄντος ἐν τῷ τόπῳ. μετὰ ταῦτα εὑρίσκει αὐτὸν ὁ Ἰησοῦς ἐν τῷ
     ἱερῷ καὶ εἶπεν αὐτῷ· ἴδε ὑγιὴς γέγονας· μηκέτι ἁμάρτανε, ἵνα μὴ
15   χεῖρόν σοί τι γένηται. ἀπῆλθεν ὁ ἄνθρωπος καὶ εἶπεν τοῖς
16   Ἰουδαίοις ὅτι Ἰησοῦς ἐστιν ὁ ποιήσας αὐτὸν ὑγιῆ. καὶ διὰ τοῦτο
     ἐδίωκον οἱ Ἰουδαῖοι τὸν Ἰησοῦν, ὅτι ταῦτα ἐποίει ἐν σαββάτῳ.
17   ὁ δὲ ἀπεκρίνατο αὐτοῖς· ὁ πατήρ μου ἕως ἄρτι ἐργάζεται, κἀγὼ
18   ἐργάζομαι· διὰ τοῦτο οὖν μᾶλλον ἐζήτουν αὐτὸν οἱ Ἰουδαῖοι
     ἀποκτεῖναι, ὅτι οὐ μόνον ἔλυεν τὸ σάββατον, ἀλλὰ καὶ πατέρα
19   ἴδιον ἔλεγεν τὸν θεόν, ἴσον ἑαυτὸν ποιῶν τῷ θεῷ. Ἀπεκρίνατο
     οὖν ὁ Ἰησοῦς καὶ ἔλεγεν αὐτοῖς· ἀμὴν ἀμὴν λέγω ὑμῖν, οὐ δύναται
     ὁ υἱὸς ποιεῖν ἀφ' ἑαυτοῦ οὐδέν, ἂν μή τι βλέπῃ τὸν πατέρα ποι-
20   οῦντα· ἃ γὰρ ἂν ἐκεῖνος ποιῇ, ταῦτα καὶ ὁ υἱὸς ὁμοίως ποιεῖ. ὁ γὰρ
     πατὴρ φιλεῖ τὸν υἱὸν καὶ πάντα δείκνυσιν αὐτῷ ἃ αὐτὸς ποιεῖ, καὶ
21   μείζονα τούτων δείξει αὐτῷ ἔργα, ἵνα ὑμεῖς θαυμάζητε. ὥσπερ γὰρ
     ὁ πατὴρ ἐγείρει τοὺς νεκροὺς καὶ ζῳοποιεῖ, οὕτως καὶ ὁ υἱὸς οὓς
22   θέλει ζῳοποιεῖ. οὐδὲ γὰρ ὁ πατὴρ κρίνει οὐδένα, ἀλλὰ τὴν κρίσιν

13. **ἰαθείς**: see principal parts of ἰάομαι. This form compares with λυθείς in the chart of λύω (97). **ᾔδει**: pluperfect of εἴδω. See development of οἶδα (199). Translate as an imperfect. **ἐξένευσε(ν)**: see principal parts of ἐκνεύω in today's word list. **ὄχλου ὄντος**: genitive absolute of cause or perhaps of attendant circumstances (582). ὄντος is from ὤν, participle of εἰμί. See 180.
14. **γέγονας**: from γίγνομαι. So also of γένηται. **ἵνα μή** . . .: negative clause of purpose with subjunctive (562). Translate, *that not, lest* . . . .
18. **ἀποκτεῖναι**: from ἀποκτείνω. See principal parts of κτείνω. κτεῖναι corresponds to φῆναι in the chart of φαίνω (205). **ἔλεγε(ν)**: from λέγω. Translate here, *called.*
19. **οὐ δύναται ὁ υἱὸς ποιεῖν ἀφ' ἑαυτοῦ οὐδέν, ἂν μή τι βλέπῃ τὸν πατέρα ποιοῦντα**: ἄν here is a shortened form of ἐάν, *if*. Hence in this conditional sentence are found the following: protasis, ἐάν (or ἄν) with subjunctive βλέπῃ; apodosis, present indicative δύναται. Consult 599, if necessary, to identify. **ἃ γὰρ ἂν ἐκεῖνος ποιῇ, ταῦτα καὶ ὁ υἱὸς ὁμοίως ποιεῖ**: here a conditional relative sentence composed as follows: protasis, relative (ἅ) plus ἄν plus subjunctive ποιῇ; apodosis, present indicative ποιεῖ. Consult 599, if necessary, to identify.
20. **δείκνυσι(ν)** and **δείξει**: see chart of δείκνυμι in today's lesson. **μείζονα**: from μείζων, comparative of μέγας, *great*. See ἡδίονα in ἡδίων (157). **τούτων**: genitive of comparison (507).
22. **οὐδένα**: from οὐδείς. See expansion of εἷς, μία, ἕν in 156. Note the double negative in this sentence, something regularly found in Greek although not in English. **τὴν κρίσιν πᾶσαν**: note that πᾶσαν occupies predicate position (490).

23 πᾶσαν δέδωκεν τῷ υἱῷ, ἵνα πάντες τιμῶσι τὸν υἱὸν καθὼς τιμῶσι
τὸν πατέρα. ὁ μὴ τιμῶν τὸν υἱὸν οὐ τιμᾷ τὸν πατέρα τὸν πέμψαντα
24 αὐτόν. Ἀμὴν ἀμὴν λέγω ὑμῖν ὅτι ὁ τὸν λόγον μου ἀκούων καὶ
πιστεύων τῷ πέμψαντί με ἔχει ζωὴν αἰώνιον, καὶ εἰς κρίσιν οὐκ
25 ἔρχεται ἀλλὰ μεταβέβηκεν ἐκ τοῦ θανάτου εἰς τὴν ζωήν. ἀμὴν
ἀμὴν λέγω ὑμῖν ὅτι ἔρχεται ὥρα καὶ νῦν ἐστιν ὅτε οἱ νεκροὶ
ἀκούσουσιν τῆς φωνῆς τοῦ υἱοῦ τοῦ θεοῦ καὶ οἱ ἀκούσαντες
26 ζήσουσιν. ὥσπερ γὰρ ὁ πατὴρ ἔχει ζωὴν ἐν ἑαυτῷ, οὕτως καὶ τῷ
27 υἱῷ ἔδωκεν ζωὴν ἔχειν ἐν ἑαυτῷ. καὶ ἐξουσίαν ἔδωκεν αὐτῷ
28 κρίσιν ποιεῖν, ὅτι υἱὸς ἀνθρώπου ἐστίν. μὴ θαυμάζετε τοῦτο, ὅτι
ἔρχεται ὥρα ἐν ᾗ πάντες οἱ ἐν τοῖς μνημείοις ἀκούσουσιν τῆς
29 φωνῆς αὐτοῦ καὶ ἐκπορεύσονται οἱ τὰ ἀγαθὰ ποιήσαντες εἰς
ἀνάστασιν ζωῆς, οἱ τὰ φαῦλα πράξαντες εἰς ἀνάστασιν κρίσεως.

**δέδωκε(ν)**: see principal parts of δίδωμι. So also for ἔδωκε(ν) in *vs. 26* below.
23. **τιμῶσι . . . τιμῶσι**: note that the first is subjunctive, the second indicative.
Check the chart of γεννάω in 173 to compare the present indicative with the subjunctive
forms.
24. **μεταβέβηκε(ν)**: from μεταβαίνω. See principal parts of βαίνω.
29. **ἐκπορεύσονται**: a comma could well be placed after this word. **ποιήσαντες,
πράξαντες**: aorist active participles from ποιέω and πράττω (πράσσω). Compare with
λύσαντες in 182.

[*For section 222 see opposite*]

## 223. Writing exercise

Expand δείκνυμι fully in the future system and the perfect middle and
passive system. From today's chart it can be observed that the stem of
δείκνυμι is δεικ-, ending in the palatal mute κ. It will be recalled that
ἄγω (stem ἀγ-) was presented as an example of the development of palatal
mute-stem verbs. A comparison with ἄγω (118) will be helpful in working
out these systems of δείκνυμι.

## 222. Partially expanded synopsis of δείκνυμι, *to show*

| Present | | Future | First aorist | First perfect active |
|---|---|---|---|---|
| δείκνῡμι δείκνῡμεν | | δείξω | ἔδειξα | δέδειχα |
| δείκνῡς δείκνυτε | | | | |
| δείκνῡσι δεικνύᾱσι | | | | ἐδεδείχη |
| ἐδείκνῡν ἐδείκνυμεν | | | δείξω | δεδειχὼς ὦ |
| ἐδείκνῡς ἐδείκνυτε | | | | |
| ἐδείκνῡ ἐδείκνυσαν | | δείξοιμι | δείξαιμι | δεδειχὼς εἴην |
| δεικνύω δεικνύωμεν | | | δεῖξον | (Imperative missing) |
| δεικνύῃς δεικνύητε | | | | |
| δεικνύῃ δεικνύωσι | | δείξειν | δεῖξαι | δεδειχέναι |
| δεικνύοιμι δεικνύοιμεν | | δείξων | δείξας | δεδειχώς, -υῖα, -ός |
| δεικνύοις δεικνύοιτε | | | | |
| δεικνύοι δεικνύοιεν | | | | |

| | | | |
|---|---|---|---|
| δείκνῡ δείκνυτε | | | **Perf. mid. and pass.** |
| δεικνύτω δεικνύντων | | | |
| | δείξομαι | ἐδειξάμην | δέδειγμαι |
| δεικνύναι | | | |
| | | | ἐδεδείγμην |
| δεικνῡς, δεικνῦσα, δεικνύν | | | |
| | | δείξωμαι | δεδειγμένος ὦ |
| δείκνυμαι δεικνύμεθα | | | |
| δείκνυσαι δείκνυσθε | δειξοίμην | δειξαίμην | δεδειγμένος εἴην |
| δείκνυται δείκνυνται | | | |
| | | δεῖξαι | δέδειξο |
| ἐδεικνύμην ἐδεικνύμεθα | | | |
| ἐδείκνυσο ἐδείκνυσθε | δείξεσθαι | δείξασθαι | δεδεῖχθαι |
| ἐδείκνυτο ἐδείκνυντο | | | |
| | δειξόμενος | δειξάμενος | δεδειγμένος, -η, -ον. |
| δεικνύωμαι δεικνυώμεθα | | | |
| δεικνύῃ δεικνύησθε | | | |
| δεικνύηται δεικνύωνται | | *First passive* | |

| | | | |
|---|---|---|---|
| δεικνυοίμην δεικνυοίμεθα | δειχθήσομαι | ἐδείχθην | |
| δεικνύοιο δεικνύοισθε | | | |
| δεικνύοιτο δεικνύοιντο | | δειχθῶ | |
| | | | Passive same |
| δείκνυσο δείκνυσθε | δειχθησοίμην | δειχθείην | forms as |
| δεικνύσθω δεικνύσθων | | | middle |
| | | δείχθητι | |
| δείκνυσθαι | | | |
| | δειχθήσεσθαι | δειχθῆναι | |
| δεικνύμενος, -η, -ον | | | |
| | δειχθησόμενος | δειχθείς | |
| Passive same forms as middle | | | |

# LESSON 33
# The Verb δίδωμι

**224.** APPEARING in today's lesson, and frequently in John's gospel, are forms of the μι-verb, δίδωμι, *to give*, which is another of the important μι-verbs. In today's lesson is presented a synopsis of δίδωμι, with the present and second aorist systems expanded. The student should observe this synopsis and note the pattern of inflection of δίδωμι, particularly in these two tense systems. As with many of the μι-verbs, the perfect active uses the periphrastic forms for the subjunctive and optative moods and omits the imperative.

## 225. New word list

ἀγαλλιάω, ἀγαλλιάσομαι, ἠγαλλίασα, ἠγαλλιάθην, *to gladden, rejoice.*

ἀγάπη, -ης, ἡ, *divine love, love, affection.* AGAPĒ.

γράμμα, -ατος, τό, *a written character, letter.* GRAMMAR.

*δίκαιος, -α, -ον, *just, right.*

*δοκέω, δόξω, ἔδοξα, δέδογμαι, ἐδόχθην, *to consider, think, seem*; impers., δοκεῖ, *it seems best, is decided, is voted.* DOGMA.

εἶδος, -ους, τό, *form, species.*

ἐλπίζω, ἐλπιῶ, ἤλπισα, ἤλπικα, ἤλπισμαι, ἠλπίσθην, *to hope, expect.*

ἐραυνάω or ἐρευνάω, ἠρεύνησα, *to search.*

καίω, καύσω, ἔκαυσα, κέκαυκα, κέκαυμαι, ἐκαύθην, *to burn.* CAUSTIC.

κατηγορέω, κατηγορήσω, κατηγόρησα, *to accuse*, often with gen. of the crime. CATEGORIZE.

λύχνος, -ου, ὁ, *light, lamp.*

## 226. Reading passage (*John 5:30–47*)

5:30  Οὐ δύναμαι ἐγὼ ποιεῖν ἀπ' ἐμαυτοῦ οὐδέν· καθὼς ἀκούω κρίνω, καὶ ἡ κρίσις ἡ ἐμὴ δικαία ἐστίν, ὅτι οὐ ζητῶ τὸ θέλημα τὸ ἐμὸν
31  ἀλλὰ τὸ θέλημα τοῦ πέμψαντός με. Ἐὰν ἐγὼ μαρτυρῶ περὶ
32  ἐμαυτοῦ, ἡ μαρτυρία μου οὐκ ἔστιν ἀληθής· ἄλλος ἐστὶν ὁ μαρτυρῶν περὶ ἐμοῦ, καὶ οἶδα ὅτι ἀληθής ἐστιν ἡ μαρτυρία ἣν
33  μαρτυρεῖ περὶ ἐμοῦ. ὑμεῖς ἀπεστάλκατε πρὸς Ἰωάννην, καὶ
34  μεμαρτύρηκεν τῇ ἀληθείᾳ· ἐγὼ δὲ οὐ παρὰ ἀνθρώπου τὴν μαρτυρίαν λαμβάνω, ἀλλὰ ταῦτα λέγω ἵνα ὑμεῖς σωθῆτε. ἐκεῖνος ἦν ὁ
35  λύχνος ὁ καιόμενος καὶ φαίνων, ὑμεῖς δὲ ἠθελήσατε ἀγαλλιαθῆναι

31. **ἐὰν ἐγὼ μαρτυρῶ περὶ ἐμαυτοῦ, ἡ μαρτυρία μου οὐκ ἔστιν ἀληθής**: here is a conditional sentence composed as follows: protasis, ἐάν plus subjunctive μαρτυρῶ; apodosis, present indicative ἔστι. Consult 599, if necessary, to identify.

33. **ἀπεστάλκατε**: from ἀποστέλλω. See στέλλω for principal parts. So also for ἀπέσταλκε(ν) in *vs. 36*, and ἀπέστειλε(ν) in *vs. 38* below.

34. **σωθῆτε**: see σώζω. And in the chart of λύω (97), find the comparable form λυθῆτε.

35. **ἀγαλλιαθῆναι**: see principal parts of ἀγαλλιάω in today's list. This form compares with λυθῆναι in the chart of λύω (97). **πρὸς ὥραν**: idiomatic, *in terms of* or *for an hour.*

36  πρὸς ὥραν ἐν τῷ φωτὶ αὐτοῦ. ἐγὼ δὲ ἔχω τὴν μαρτυρίαν μείζω
    τοῦ Ἰωάννου· τὰ γὰρ ἔργα ἃ δέδωκέν μοι ὁ πατὴρ ἵνα τελειώσω
    αὐτά, αὐτὰ τὰ ἔργα ἃ ποιῶ, μαρτυρεῖ περὶ ἐμοῦ ὅτι ὁ πατήρ με
37  ἀπέσταλκεν. καὶ ὁ πέμψας με πατήρ, ἐκεῖνος μεμαρτύρηκεν περὶ
    ἐμοῦ. οὔτε φωνὴν αὐτοῦ πώποτε ἀκηκόατε οὔτε εἶδος αὐτοῦ
38  ἑωράκατε, καὶ τὸν λόγον αὐτοῦ οὐκ ἔχετε ἐν ὑμῖν μένοντα, ὅτι
39  ὃν ἀπέστειλεν ἐκεῖνος, τούτῳ ὑμεῖς οὐ πιστεύετε. ἐραυνᾶτε τὰς
    γραφάς, ὅτι ὑμεῖς δοκεῖτε ἐν αὐταῖς ζωὴν αἰώνιον ἔχειν· καὶ
40  ἐκεῖναί εἰσιν αἱ μαρτυροῦσαι περὶ ἐμοῦ· καὶ οὐ θέλετε ἐλθεῖν
41  πρός με ἵνα ζωὴν ἔχητε. Δόξαν παρὰ ἀνθρώπων οὐ λαμβάνω,
42  ἀλλὰ ἔγνωκα ὑμᾶς ὅτι τὴν ἀγάπην τοῦ θεοῦ οὐκ ἔχετε ἐν ἑαυτοῖς.
43  ἐγὼ ἐλήλυθα ἐν τῷ ὀνόματι τοῦ πατρός μου, καὶ οὐ λαμβάνετέ με·
44  ἐὰν ἄλλος ἔλθῃ ἐν τῷ ὀνόματι τῷ ἰδίῳ, ἐκεῖνον λήμψεσθε. πῶς
    δύνασθε ὑμεῖς πιστεῦσαι, δόξαν παρὰ ἀλλήλων λαμβάνοντες, καὶ
45  τὴν δόξαν τὴν παρὰ τοῦ μόνου θεοῦ οὐ ζητεῖτε; μὴ δοκεῖτε ὅτι
    ἐγὼ κατηγορήσω ὑμῶν πρὸς τὸν πατέρα· ἔστιν ὁ κατηγορῶν
46  ὑμῶν Μωϋσῆς, εἰς ὃν ὑμεῖς ἠλπίκατε. εἰ γὰρ ἐπιστεύετε Μωϋ-
47  σεῖ, ἐπιστεύετε ἂν ἐμοί· περὶ γὰρ ἐμοῦ ἐκεῖνος ἔγραψεν. εἰ δὲ
    τοῖς ἐκείνου γράμμασιν οὐ πιστεύετε, πῶς τοῖς ἐμοῖς ῥήμασιν
    πιστεύσετε;

36. **μείζω**: for μείζονα. See declension of ἡδίων (157). **δέδωκε(ν)**: from δίδωμι.
37. **ἀκηκόατε**: from ἀκούω. **ἑωράκατε**: from ὁράω.
39. **ἐραυνᾶτε**: this compares with γεννᾶτε which occurs in two places in the present
system of γεννάω (173). Hence the two possible meanings here, *search!*, or *you search*
*(are searching)*. **μαρτυροῦσαι**: present participle of μαρτυρέω. Find ποιοῦσαι in the
declension of ποιῶν (195).
42. **ἔγνωκα**: from γιγνώσκω. **ἑαυτοῖς**: irregular for σεαυτοῖς (73). The κοινή sometimes
uses ἑαυτῶν, etc., for the other persons of the reflexive pronoun (482. 19).
43. **ἐλήλυθα**: from ἔρχομαι. **ἐὰν ἄλλος ἔλθῃ ἐν τῷ ὀνόματι τῷ ἰδίῳ, ἐκεῖνον λήμψεσθε**:
the form λήμψεσθε is used in place of the more regular λήψεσθε, future of λαμβάνω. In
the conditional sentence here are found the following: protasis, ἐάν plus subjunctive
ἔλθῃ (from ἦλθον second aorist of ἔρχομαι); apodosis, future indicative λήμψεσθε.
Consult 603 for identification if necessary.
45. **ἠλπίκατε**: from ἐλπίζω.
46. **εἰ γὰρ ἐπιστεύετε Μωϋσεῖ, ἐπιστεύετε ἂν ἐμοί**: here is a conditional sentence
formed as follows: protasis, εἰ plus imperfect indicative ἐπιστεύετε; apodosis, ἄν plus
imperfect indicative ἐπιστεύετε. See 601 for identification if necessary.
47. **εἰ δὲ τοῖς ἐκείνου γράμμασιν οὐ πιστεύετε, πῶς τοῖς ἐμοῖς ῥήμασιν πιστεύσετε;**:
here is a *present particular condition*. It calls simply for εἰ with the present indicative in the
protasis. The apodosis may have any tense of the indicative. This sentence has the
following: protasis, εἰ plus present indicative πιστεύετε; apodosis, future indicative
πιστεύσετε. It translates, *but if you do not believe the writings of that one, how will you believe*
*my sayings?* See 597 for this construction. **ῥήμασι**: from τὸ ῥῆμα. Compare with the
form ἅρμασι in the declension of τὸ ἅρμα, in 146.

## 227. Partially expanded synopsis of δίδωμι, *to give*

| | Present | Future | Second* aorist | | First perfect active |
|---|---|---|---|---|---|
| δίδωμι | δίδομεν | δώσω | (ἔδωκα) | ἔδομεν | δέδωκα |
| δίδως | δίδοτε | | (ἔδωκας) | ἔδοτε | |
| δίδωσι | διδόᾱσι | | (ἔδωκε) | ἔδοσαν | |
| | | | | | |
| ἐδίδουν | ἐδίδομεν | | | | ἐδεδώκη |
| ἐδίδους | ἐδίδοτε | | | | |
| ἐδίδου | ἐδίδοσαν | | | | |
| | | | | | |
| διδῶ | διδῶμεν | | δῶ | δῶμεν | δεδωκὼς ὦ |
| διδῷς | διδῶτε | | δῷς | δῶτε | |
| διδῷ | διδῶσι | | δῷ | δῶσι | |
| | | | | | |
| διδοίην | διδοῖμεν | δώσοιμι | δοίην | δοῖμεν | δεδωκὼς εἴην |
| διδοίης | διδοῖτε | | δοίης | δοῖτε | |
| διδοίη | διδοῖεν | | δοίη | δοῖεν | |
| | | | | | |
| δίδου | δίδοτε | | δός | δότε | (Imperative ι |
| διδότω | διδόντων | | δότω | δόντων | missing) |
| | | | | | |
| διδόναι | | δώσειν | δοῦναι | | δεδωκέναι |
| | | | | | |
| διδούς, -οῦσα, -όν | | δώσων | δούς, δοῦσα, δόν | | δεδωκώς |

*Perf. mid. and pass.*

| | | | | | |
|---|---|---|---|---|---|
| δίδομαι | διδόμεθα | δώσομαι | ἐδόμην | ἐδόμεθα | δέδομαι |
| δίδοσαι | δίδοσθε | | ἔδου | ἔδοσθε | |
| δίδοται | δίδονται | | ἔδοτο | ἔδοντο | |
| | | | | | |
| ἐδιδόμην | ἐδιδόμεθα | | | | ἐδεδόμην |
| ἐδίδοσο | ἐδίδοσθε | | | | |
| ἐδίδοτο | ἐδίδοντο | | | | |
| | | | | | |
| διδῶμαι | διδώμεθα | | δῶμαι | δώμεθα | δεδομένος ὦ |
| διδῷ | διδῶσθε | | δῷ | δῶσθε | |
| διδῶται | διδῶνται | | δῶται | δῶνται | |
| | | | | | |
| διδοίμην | διδοίμεθα | δωσοίμην | δοίμην | δοίμεθα | δεδομένος εἴην |
| διδοῖο | διδοῖσθε | | δοῖο | δοῖσθε | |
| διδοῖτο | διδοῖντο | | δοῖτο | δοῖντο | |
| | | | | | |
| δίδοσο | δίδοσθε | | δοῦ | δόσθε | δέδοσο |
| διδόσθω | διδόσθων | | δόσθω | δόσθων | |
| | | | | | |
| δίδοσθαι | | δώσεσθαι | δόσθαι | | δεδόσθαι |
| | | | | | |
| διδόμενος, -η, -ον | | δωσόμενος | δόμενος, -η, -ον | | δεδομένος |

| Passive same forms as middle | First passive | | Passive same forms as middle |
|---|---|---|---|
| | δοθήσομαι | ἐδόθην | |
| | The rest of the system is regular | | |

\* The first aorist forms, which are generally used where shown, are in brackets.

**228. Writing exercise**

Expand δίδωμι fully in the first passive system. Since, as can be observed from today's synopsis of δίδωμι, its stem is δο-, a vowel stem, the verb λύω (97) will provide the most helpful reference.

# LESSON 34
## The Verb τίθημι

**229.** THE synopsis of the μι-verb τίθημι, *to place*, is given on p. 124, with the present and second aorist systems expanded. The other tense systems are conjugated quite regularly.

**230. New word list**

ἀνάκειμαι (see κεῖμαι for prin. parts), *to recline at table, dine.*

ἀναπίπτω (see πίπτω for prin. parts), *to fall back, lie back, recline* (for a meal).

ἀναχωρέω (see χωρέω for prin. parts), *to go back, withdraw, retire.*

ἀνέρχομαι (see ἔρχομαι for prin. parts), *to ascend, go up.*

*ἀριθμός, -οῦ, ὁ, number.* ARITH-METIC.

ἀρκέω, ἀρκέσω, ἤρκεσα, ἤρκεσμαι, ἠρκέσθην, *to ward off, be strong enough, suffice.*

*ἁρπάζω, ἁρπάσω, ἥρπασα, ἥρπακα, ἥρπασμαι, ἡρπάσθην, to seize, plunder, carry off.* HARPY.

ἄρτος, -ου, ὁ, *a wheat loaf, loaf of bread, bread.*

βιβρώσκω, βρώσομαι, βέβρωκα, βέβρωμαι, ἐβρώθην, *to eat.*

βραχύς, -εῖα, -ύ, *short, little, few.* BRACHYLOGY.

δηνάριον, -ου, τό, *denarius*, a Roman coin.

διαδίδωμι (see δίδωμι for prin. parts), *to distribute.*

διακόσιοι, -αι, -α, *two hundred.*

δώδεκα, indecl., *twelve.* DODECA-NESE.

ἐμπίπλημι (for ἐμπίμπλημι; see πίμπλημι for prin. parts), *to fill up, fill to the full.* In the present system all but the imperfect tenses use the stem ἐμπιπ-, dropping the second μ for the sake of euphony.

εὐχαριστέω, ηὐχαρίστησα, *to give thanks.* EUCHARIST.

*θάλαττα (or θάλασσα), -ης, ἡ, sea.*

κλάσμα, -ατος, τό, *fragment, piece, morsel.*

κόφινος, -ου, ὁ, *basket.* COFFIN.

κρίθινος, -η, -ον, *made of barley.*

*μέγας, μεγάλη, μέγα, great.* MEGA-PHONE.

ὀψάριον, -ου, τό, *small fish, sardine.*

παιδάριον, -ου, τό, *little boy, lad.* Diminutive of παῖς.

πειράζω, ἐπείρασα, πεπείρασμαι, ἐπειράσθην, *to make trial of, test.*

πεντακισχίλιοι, -αι, -α, *five thousand.*

περισσεύω, περισσεύσω, ἐπερίσσευθην, *to abound, exceed, be over* or *remain.*

πίμπλημι, πλήσω, ἔπλησα, πέπληκα, πέπλησμαι, ἐπλήσθην, *to fill.*

πίπτω, πεσοῦμαι, ἔπεσον, πέπτωκα, *to fall.*

*τοσοῦτος, τοσαύτη, τοσοῦτο, this much, so much.*

χόρτος, -ου, ὁ, *pasture, grass.*

ὧδε, adv. from ὅδε, *as follows, hither, here.*

| Present | | Future | Second* aorist | | First perfect active |
|---|---|---|---|---|---|
| τίθημι | τίθεμεν | θήσω | (ἔθηκα) | ἔθεμεν | τέθηκα† |
| τίθης | τίθετε | | (ἔθηκας) | ἔθετε | |
| τίθησι | τιθέᾱσι | | (ἔθηκε) | ἔθεσαν | |
| ἐτίθην | ἐτίθεμεν | | | | ἐτεθήκη |
| ἐτίθεις | ἐτίθετε | | | | |
| ἐτίθει | ἐτίθεσαν | | | | |
| τιθῶ | τιθῶμεν | | θῶ | θῶμεν | τεθηκὼς ὦ |
| τιθῇς | τιθῆτε | | θῇς | θῆτε | |
| τιθῇ | τιθῶσι | | θῇ | θῶσι | |
| τιθείην | τιθεῖμεν | θήσοιμι | θείην | θεῖμεν | τεθηκὼς εἴην |
| τιθείης | τιθεῖτε | | θείης | θεῖτε | |
| τιθείη | τιθεῖεν | | θείη | θεῖεν | |
| τίθει | τίθετε | | θές | θέτε | (Imperative |
| τιθέτω | τιθέντων | | θέτω | θέντων | missing) |
| τιθέναι | | θήσειν | θεῖναι | | τεθηκέναι |
| τιθείς, -εῖσα, -έν | | θήσων | θείς, θεῖσα, θέν | | τεθηκώς, -κυῖα, -κός |

|  |  |  |  |  | Perf. mid. and pass. |
|---|---|---|---|---|---|
| τίθεμαι | τιθέμεθα | θήσομαι | ἐθέμην | ἐθέμεθα | τέθειμαι |
| τίθεσαι | τίθεσθε | | ἔθου | ἔθεσθε | |
| τίθεται | τίθενται | | ἔθετο | ἔθεντο | |
| ἐτιθέμην | ἐτιθέμεθα | | | | ἐτεθείμην |
| ἐτίθεσο | ἐτίθεσθε | | | | |
| ἐτίθετο | ἐτίθεντο | | | | |
| τιθῶμαι | τιθώμεθα | | θῶμαι | θώμεθα | τεθειμένος ὦ |
| τιθῇ | τιθῆσθε | | θῇ | θῆσθε | |
| τιθῆται | τιθῶνται | | θῆται | θῶνται | |
| τιθείμην | τιθείμεθα | θησοίμην | θείμην | θείμεθα | |
| τιθεῖο | τιθεῖσθε | | θεῖο | θεῖσθε | τεθειμένος εἴην |
| τιθεῖτο | τιθεῖντο | | θεῖτο | θεῖντο | |
| τίθεσο | τίθεσθε | | θοῦ | θέσθε | τέθεισο |
| τιθέσθω | τιθέσθων | | θέσθω | θέσθων | |
| τίθεσθαι | | θήσεσθαι | θέσθαι | | τεθεῖσθαι |
| τιθέμενος, -η, -ον | | θησόμενος | θέμενος | | τεθειμένος, -η, -ον |

| Passive same forms as middle | | First passive | | Passive same forms as middle |
|---|---|---|---|---|
| | | τεθήσομαι | ἐτέθην | |
| | | The rest of the system is regular | | |

\* Bracket forms are first aorists.      † Later alternative form, τέθεικα.

**231. Reading passage** (*John 6: 1–15*)

6:1    Μετὰ ταῦτα ἀπῆλθεν ὁ Ἰησοῦς πέραν τῆς θαλάσσης τῆς

2    Γαλιλαίας τῆς Τιβεριάδος. ἠκολούθει δὲ αὐτῷ ὄχλος πολύς, ὅτι

3    ἑώρων τὰ σημεῖα ἃ ἐποίει ἐπὶ τῶν ἀσθενούντων. ἀνῆλθεν δὲ εἰς

4    τὸ ὄρος Ἰησοῦς, καὶ ἐκεῖ ἐκάθητο μετὰ τῶν μαθητῶν αὐτοῦ. ἦν

5    δὲ ἐγγὺς τὸ πάσχα, ἡ ἑορτὴ τῶν Ἰουδαίων. ἐπάρας οὖν τοὺς

     ὀφθαλμοὺς ὁ Ἰησοῦς καὶ θεασάμενος ὅτι πολὺς ὄχλος ἔρχεται πρὸς

     αὐτόν, λέγει πρὸς Φίλιππον· πόθεν ἀγοράσωμεν ἄρτους ἵνα

6    φάγωσιν οὗτοι; τοῦτο δὲ ἔλεγεν πειράζων αὐτόν· αὐτὸς γὰρ ᾔδει

7    τί ἔμελλεν ποιεῖν. ἀπεκρίθη αὐτῷ ὁ Φίλιππος· διακοσίων δηναρίων

8    ἄρτοι οὐκ ἀρκοῦσιν αὐτοῖς, ἵνα ἕκαστος βραχύ τι λάβῃ. λέγει

     αὐτῷ εἷς ἐκ τῶν μαθητῶν αὐτοῦ, Ἀνδρέας ὁ ἀδελφὸς Σίμωνος

9    Πέτρου· ἔστιν παιδάριον ὧδε ὃς ἔχει πέντε ἄρτους κριθίνους καὶ

10   δύο ὀψάρια· ἀλλὰ ταῦτα τί ἐστιν εἰς τοσούτους; εἶπεν ὁ Ἰησοῦς·

     ποιήσατε τοὺς ἀνθρώπους ἀναπεσεῖν. ἦν δὲ χόρτος πολὺς ἐν τῷ

     τόπῳ. ἀνέπεσαν οὖν οἱ ἄνδρες τὸν ἀριθμὸν ὡς πεντακισχίλιοι.

11   ἔλαβεν οὖν τοὺς ἄρτους ὁ Ἰησοῦς καὶ εὐχαριστήσας διέδωκεν τοῖς

12   ἀνακειμένοις, ὁμοίως καὶ ἐκ τῶν ὀψαρίων ὅσον ἤθελον. ὡς δὲ

     ἐνεπλήσθησαν, λέγει τοῖς μαθηταῖς αὐτοῦ· συναγάγετε τὰ περισ-

13   σεύσαντα κλάσματα, ἵνα μή τι ἀπόληται. συνήγαγον οὖν, καὶ

     ἐγέμισαν δώδεκα κοφίνους κλασμάτων ἐκ τῶν πέντε ἄρτων τῶν

14   κριθίνων ἃ ἐπερίσσευσαν τοῖς βεβρωκόσιν. Οἱ οὖν ἄνθρωποι

1. **ἀπῆλθε(ν)**: from ἀπέρχομαι, See ἔρχομαι for principal parts.
2. **ἠκολούθει**: from ἀκολουθέω. Compare ἐποίει in ποιέω (164). **ἑώρων**: from ὁράω. Compares with ἐγέννων from γεννάω (173). ὁράω characteristically shows an additional syllabic augment in the imperfect, ἑώρων.
3. **ἀνῆλθε(ν)**: from ἀνέρχομαι. See ἔρχομαι for principal parts. **ἐκάθητο**: from κάθημαι.
5. **ἐπάρας**: from ἐπαίρω. See αἴρω for principal parts. **ἀγοράσωμεν**: aorist subjunctive active of ἀγοράζω. The subjunctive is sometimes used independently to express deliberation (560). πόθεν ἀγοράσωμεν . . . presents a deliberative subjunctive, and translates, *whence are we to buy . . .?* **φάγωσι**: see ἐσθίω. This is the second aorist subjunctive active in a purpose clause (562).
6. **ᾔδει**: see development of the second perfect system of εἴδω (199).
7. **διακοσίων δηναρίων**: genitive of price or value (503).
10. **ἀναπεσεῖν**: from ἀναπίπτω. The second aorist of πίπτω is ἔπεσον. Its active infinitive is πεσεῖν. **ἀνέπεσαν**: N.T. for ἀνέπεσον (482. 7), from the same principal part of πίπτω as is ἀναπεσεῖν, above. **τὸν ἀριθμόν**: accusative of specification (529). It may be translated, *as to number*, or *in number*.
11. **διέδωκε**: from διαδίδωμι. See δίδωμι (227).
12. **ἐνεπλήσθησαν**: from ἐμπίπλημι in today's word list. **συναγάγετε**: from συνάγω. See expansion of ἄγω in 118. **περισσεύσαντα**: from περισσεύω in today's word list. See expansion of λύσας in 182, and locate the form λύσαντα. **ἀπόληται**: subjunctive passive of ἀπωλόμην, second aorist of ἀπόλλυμι.
13. **κλασμάτων**: genitive with a verb denoting fullness (501). **βεβρωκόσι(ν)**: from βιβρώσκω in today's list. See also the declension of λελυκώς in 183.

ἰδόντες ὃ ἐποίησεν σημεῖον ἔλεγον ὅτι οὗτός ἐστιν ἀληθῶς ὁ
15 προφήτης ὁ ἐρχόμενος εἰς τὸν κόσμον. Ἰησοῦς οὖν γνοὺς ὅτι
μέλλουσιν ἔρχεσθαι καὶ ἁρπάζειν αὐτὸν ἵνα ποιήσωσιν βασιλέα,
ἀνεχώρησεν πάλιν εἰς τὸ ὄρος αὐτὸς μόνος.

14. **ἰδόντες**: from ἰδών, second aorist participle of ὁράω.
15. **γνούς**: see expansion of the second aorist of γιγνώσκω in 209. **ἀνεχώρησε(ν)**: from ἀναχωρέω in today's list. For principal parts see χωρέω.

### 232. Writing exercise

Expand the first passive system of τίθημι, both future and aorist, and give the English translation of each form. Use the complete chart of λύω (97) for word form comparisons, and the synopsis chart of λύω (82) for translation comparisons.

## LESSON 35

# Certain Irregular μι-Verbs

**233.** ON the page opposite are presented the present systems of four irregular verbs in -μι which the student will meet and should observe. Some of these verbs have other tenses, but the present forms are the most used. The following general observations should be noted:

1. εἰμί and φημί have no present middle and passive.
2. The present indicative forms of φημί are all enclitics except ῾φής.
3. κεῖμαι is deponent and has no active forms.
4. ἵημι, as can be seen, has forms in all voices.

### 234. New word list

ἄνεμος, -ου, ὁ, wind. ANEMOMETER.
διεγείρω (see ἐγείρω for prin. parts), to rouse thoroughly.
*εἴκοσι, indecl., twenty.
*ἐλαύνω, ἐλῶ, ἤλασα, ἐλήλακα, ἐλήλαμαι, ἠλάθην, to ride, drive, march.
μάννα, τό, indecl., manna.
ὄψιος, -α, -ον, late; ὀψία (sc. ὥρα), the latter part of the day, evening.
πάντοτε, always.
πλοιάριον, -ου, τό, a skiff, boat.

Dimin. of πλοῖον.
πλοῖον, -ου, τό, boat, pontoon.
πότε, interrog. adv., when?
*στάδιον, -ου, τό, a stade, six hundred Greek feet. In the plural also οἱ στάδιοι. STADIUM.
*φοβέω, φοβήσω, ἐφόβησα, ἐφοβήθην, to frighten, terrify; pass., to be frightened, be afraid. PHOBIA.
χορτάζω, χορτάσω, ἐχόρτασα, ἐχορτάσθην, to feed to the full, fatten.

| εἰμί, *to go* | | φημί, *to say* | | ἵημι, *to send, let go* | |
|---|---|---|---|---|---|
| εἶμι | ἴμεν | φημί | φαμέν | ἵημι | ἵεμεν |
| εἶ | ἴτε | φῄς | φατέ | ἵης | ἵετε |
| εἶσι | ἴᾱσι | φησί | φᾱσί | ἵησι | ἱᾶσι |
| | | | | | |
| ᾖα or ᾔειν | ᾖμεν | ἔφην | ἔφαμεν | ἵην | ἵεμεν |
| ᾔεις | ᾖτε | ἔφησθα or ἔφης | ἔφατε | ἵεις | ἵετε |
| ᾔει | ᾖσαν or ᾔεσαν | ἔφη | ἔφασαν | ἵει | ἵεσαν |
| | | | | | |
| ἴω | ἴωμεν | φῶ | φῶμεν | ἱῶ | ἱῶμεν |
| ἴῃς | ἴητε | φῇς | φῆτε | ἱῇς | ἱῆτε |
| ἴῃ | ἴωσι | φῇ | φῶσι | ἱῇ | ἱῶσι |
| | | | | | |
| ἴοιμι or ἰοίην | ἴοιμεν | φαίην | φαῖμεν* | ἱείην | ἱεῖμεν |
| ἴοις | ἴοιτε | φαίης | φαῖτε | ἱείης | ἱεῖτε |
| ἴοι | ἴοιεν | φαίη | φαῖεν | ἱείη | ἱεῖεν |
| | | | | | |
| ἴθι | ἴτε | φαθί or φάθι | φάτε | ἵει | ἵετε |
| ἴτω | ἰόντων | φάτω | φάντων | ἱέτω | ἱέντων |
| | | | | | |
| ἰέναι | | φάναι | | ἱέναι | |
| | | | | | |
| ἰών, ἰοῦσα, ἰόν | | φάς, φᾶσα, φάν† | | ἱείς, ἱεῖσα, ἱέν | |

| κεῖμαι, *to lie, be situated* | | | |
|---|---|---|---|
| κεῖμαι | κείμεθα | ἵεμαι | ἱέμεθα |
| κεῖσαι | κεῖσθε | ἵεσαι | ἵεσθε |
| κεῖται | κεῖνται | ἵεται | ἵενται |
| | | | |
| ἐκείμην | ἐκείμεθα | ἱέμην | ἱέμεθα |
| ἔκεισο | ἔκεισθε | ἵεσο | ἵεσθε |
| ἔκειτο | ἔκειντο | ἵετο | ἵεντο |
| | | | |
| κέωμαι | κεώμεθα | ἱῶμαι | ἱώμεθα |
| κέῃ | κέησθε | ἱῇ | ἱῆσθε |
| κέηται | κέωνται | ἱῆται | ἱῶνται |
| | | | |
| κεοίμην | κεοίμεθα | ἱείμην | ἱείμεθα |
| κέοιο | κέοισθε | ἱεῖο | ἱεῖσθε |
| κέοιτο | κέοιντο | ἱεῖτο | ἱεῖντο |
| | | | |
| κεῖσο | κεῖσθε | ἵεσο | ἵεσθε |
| κείσθω | κείσθων | ἱέσθω | ἱέσθων |
| | | | |
| κεῖσθαι | | ἵεσθαι | |
| | | | |
| κείμενος | | ἱέμενος | |

* Alternative plural forms: φαίημεν, φαίητε, φαίησαν.
† Attic Greek prose regularly uses the frequentative φάσκων for the participle.

128 **Grammar: Readings from St. John** LESSON 35

**235. Reading passage** (*John 6 : 16–34*)

6:16 Ὡς δὲ ὀψία ἐγένετο, κατέβησαν οἱ μαθηταὶ αὐτοῦ ἐπὶ τὴν θάλασ-
17 σαν, καὶ ἐμβάντες εἰς πλοῖον ἤρχοντο πέραν τῆς θαλάσσης εἰς
Καφαρναούμ. καὶ σκοτία ἤδη ἐγεγόνει καὶ οὔπω ἐληλύθει πρὸς
18 αὐτοὺς ὁ Ἰησοῦς, ἥ τε θάλασσα ἀνέμου μεγάλου πνέοντος
19 διεγείρετο. ἐληλακότες οὖν ὡς σταδίους εἴκοσι πέντε ἢ τριάκοντα
θεωροῦσιν τὸν Ἰησοῦν περιπατοῦντα ἐπὶ τῆς θαλάσσης καὶ
20 ἐγγὺς τοῦ πλοίου γινόμενον, καὶ ἐφοβήθησαν. ὁ δὲ λέγει αὐτοῖς·
21 ἐγώ εἰμι, μὴ φοβεῖσθε. ἤθελον οὖν λαβεῖν αὐτὸν εἰς τὸ πλοῖον,
καὶ εὐθέως ἐγένετο τὸ πλοῖον ἐπὶ τῆς γῆς εἰς ἣν ὑπῆγον.
22 Τῇ ἐπαύριον ὁ ὄχλος ὁ ἑστηκὼς πέραν τῆς θαλάσσης εἶδον
ὅτι πλοιάριον ἄλλο οὐκ ἦν ἐκεῖ εἰ μὴ ἕν, καὶ ὅτι οὐ συνεισῆλθεν
τοῖς μαθηταῖς αὐτοῦ ὁ Ἰησοῦς εἰς τὸ πλοῖον ἀλλὰ μόνοι οἱ
23 μαθηταὶ αὐτοῦ ἀπῆλθον· ἄλλα ἦλθεν πλοιάρια ἐκ Τιβεριάδος
ἐγγὺς τοῦ τόπου ὅπου ἔφαγον τὸν ἄρτον εὐχαριστήσαντος τοῦ
24 κυρίου. ὅτε οὖν εἶδεν ὁ ὄχλος ὅτι Ἰησοῦς οὐκ ἔστιν ἐκεῖ οὐδὲ οἱ
μαθηταὶ αὐτοῦ, ἐνέβησαν αὐτοὶ εἰς τὰ πλοιάρια καὶ ἦλθον εἰς
25 Καφαρναοὺμ ζητοῦντες τὸν Ἰησοῦν. καὶ εὑρόντες αὐτὸν πέραν
26 τῆς θαλάσσης εἶπον αὐτῷ· ῥαββί, πότε ὧδε γέγονας; ἀπεκρίθη
αὐτοῖς ὁ Ἰησοῦς καὶ εἶπεν· ἀμὴν ἀμὴν λέγω ὑμῖν, ζητεῖτέ με
οὐχ ὅτι εἴδετε σημεῖα, ἀλλ᾽ ὅτι ἐφάγετε ἐκ τῶν ἄρτων καὶ

16. **κατέβησαν**: from καταβαίνω. For the form ἔβησαν and also for βάς (ἐμβάντες in vs. *17*) see the expansion of βαίνω in the second aorist, 211.
17. **ἤρχοντο**: imperfect of ἔρχομαι. Like ἐλύοντο of λύω. **ἐγεγόνει**: from γίγνομαι. This form is like ἐλελύκει (97). The same observation applies to ἐληλύθει, which is from ἔρχομαι.
18. **ἀνέμου . . . πνέοντος**: a genitive absolute denoting cause (see 582). πνέοντος is from πνέω, and is seen to be uncontracted. πνέω and a few other dissyllabic verbs in -εω contract only εε and εει. **διεγείρετο**: imperfect middle and passive of διεγείρω in today's list.
19. **ἐληλακότες**: from ἐλαύνω. Like λελυκώς, which is declined in 183. **ἐφοβήθησαν**: from φοβέω.
21. **ἤθελον**: imperfect of ἐθέλω. **ἐγένετο . . . ἐπί**: γίγνεσθαι ἐπί with genitive sometimes means *to become* or *change* (direction) *towards*. **ὑπῆγον**: imperfect of ὑπάγω.
22. **ἑστηκώς** see chart of ἵστημι (216, footnote). Here the word carries the idea, *to stay, to remain*. **συνεισῆλθεν**: from συνεισέρχομαι. Principal parts are under ἔρχομαι. Similarly for ἀπῆλθον.
23. **ἔφαγον**: from ἐσθίω. So also in vss. *26* and *31* below. **εὐχαριστήσαντος τοῦ Κυρίου**: genitive absolute denoting time (582).
24. **εἶδεν**: from ὁράω. **ἐνέβησαν**: from ἐμβαίνω. See the second aorist of βαίνω (211).
25. **εὑρόντες**: participle from ηὗρον, second aorist of εὑρίσκω. **γέγονας**: see γίγνομαι.
26. **εἴδετε**: from ὁράω. **ἐχορτάσθητε**: from χορτάζω in today's word list. This form is like ἐλύθητε (97).

27 ἐχορτάσθητε. ἐργάζεσθε μὴ τὴν βρῶσιν τὴν ἀπολλυμένην, ἀλλὰ
τὴν βρῶσιν τὴν μένουσαν εἰς ζωὴν αἰώνιον, ἣν ὁ υἱὸς τοῦ ἀνθρώ-
28 που ὑμῖν δώσει· τοῦτον γὰρ ὁ πατὴρ ἐσφράγισεν ὁ θεός. εἶπον
οὖν πρὸς αὐτόν· τί ποιῶμεν ἵνα ἐργαζώμεθα τὰ ἔργα τοῦ θεοῦ;
29 ἀπεκρίθη Ἰησοῦς καὶ εἶπεν αὐτοῖς· τοῦτό ἐστιν τὸ ἔργον τοῦ
30 θεοῦ, ἵνα πιστεύητε εἰς ὃν ἀπέστειλεν ἐκεῖνος. εἶπον οὖν αὐτῷ·
τί οὖν ποιεῖς σὺ σημεῖον, ἵνα ἴδωμεν καὶ πιστεύσωμέν σοι;
31 τί ἐργάζῃ; οἱ πατέρες ἡμῶν τὸ μάννα ἔφαγον ἐν τῇ ἐρήμῳ, καθώς
ἐστιν γεγραμμένον· ἄρτον ἐκ τοῦ οὐρανοῦ ἔδωκεν αὐτοῖς φαγεῖν.
32 Εἶπεν οὖν αὐτοῖς ὁ Ἰησοῦς· ἀμὴν ἀμὴν λέγω ὑμῖν, οὐ Μωϋσῆς
δέδωκεν ὑμῖν τὸν ἄρτον ἐκ τοῦ οὐρανοῦ, ἀλλ᾽ ὁ πατήρ μου
33 δίδωσιν ὑμῖν τὸν ἄρτον ἐκ τοῦ οὐρανοῦ τὸν ἀληθινόν· ὁ γὰρ
ἄρτος τοῦ θεοῦ ἐστιν ὁ καταβαίνων ἐκ τοῦ οὐρανοῦ καὶ ζωὴν
34 διδοὺς τῷ κόσμῳ. εἶπον οὖν πρὸς αὐτόν· κύριε, πάντοτε δὸς
ἡμῖν τὸν ἄρτον τοῦτον.

27. ἀπολλυμένην: present passive participle of ἀπόλλυμι. δώσει: from δίδωμι.
ἐσφράγισε(ν): from σφραγίζω.
28. τί ποιῶμεν;: deliberative subjunctive, *what are to we do?* (560).
30. ἴδωμεν: subjunctive of εἶδον, second aorist of ὁράω. ἐργάζῃ: alternative to ἐργάζει
(482. 3).
31. ἐστιν γεγραμμένον: perfect passive participle of γράφω. See chart in 124. This is
a circumlocution for γέγραπται of classical usage (482. 9). ἔδωκε(ν): from δίδωμι. See
chart in 227. This also applies to δέδωκε(ν) and δίδωσι in *vs. 32*, διδούς in *vs. 33*, δός
in *vs. 34*, etc.

## 236. Writing exercise

From the verbs listed in today's chart, give the forms to make the
English meanings indicated below. Use ἵνα with subjunctive or optative
where 'may' or 'might' are called for. The student may wish to refer to
the meanings shown with the synopsis of λύω (82). (*a*) *You* (pl.) *are sent*
(*let go*). (*b*) *That he might go.* (*c*) *Let them say.* (*d*) *To recline* (*lie*). (*e*) *He
hurls* (*sends*). (*f*) *That you may go.* (*g*) *We were saying.* (*h*) *They were charging*
(*sending themselves*).

# LESSON 36
# Comparison of Adjectives and Adverbs

## 237. The comparison of Greek adjectives

T H E English language regularly forms the comparison of adjectives by
adding *-er* for the comparative degree and *-est* for the superlative degree
(for example, *fine, finer, finest*). In a few cases—in general, whenever the
pronunciation of a polysyllabic adjective would be awkward—the

auxiliary words *more* and *most* are used (e.g. *agreeable, more agreeable, most agreeable*). Then with some adjectives there is a change in the basic structure of the word to indicate degrees of comparison (e.g. *good, better, best*).

In Greek, most adjectives add -τερος to their full stem to form the comparative degree, and they add -τατος for the superlative, as with the following:

| Positive degree | Comparative degree | Superlative degree |
|---|---|---|
| κόμψος (κομψο-), *well* | κομψότερος | κομψότατος |
| ἅγιος (ἁγιο-), *holy* | ἁγιώτερος | ἁγιώτατος |
| πλήρης (πληρεσ-), *full* | πληρέστερος | πληρέστατος |

Note that in the case of ἅγιος the comparative and superlative degrees have changed the o to ω. Where the penult of the full stem is *long by nature* or where its vowel is followed by two consonants or a double consonant (as in κόμψος above), the o of the stem remains o. Otherwise the o is lengthened to ω as in the case of ἅγιος.

Comparatives and superlatives like those just shown are declined as a- and o-declension adjectives (56 ff.).

Some adjectives, chiefly those in -υς and -ρος, form the comparative and superlative by changing these endings to -ιων, -ιστος, as follows.

| Positive degree | Comparative degree | Superlative degree |
|---|---|---|
| ἡδύς, *sweet* | ἡδίων | ἥδιστος |
| βαθύς, *deep* | βαθίων | βάθιστος |
| αἰσχρός, *shameful* | αἰσχίων | αἴσχιστος |

For the declension of this group, note that the superlatives are declined as the regular a- and o-declension adjectives, while the comparatives are declined as two-ending consonant-stem adjectives (see declension of ἡδίων in 157).

## 238. Certain irregular comparisons

A few adjectives are quite irregular and their comparison must be noted specially. The most important of these are the following:

| Positive degree | Comparative degree | Superlative degree |
|---|---|---|
| ἀγαθός, *good* | ἀμείνων | ἄριστος |
| | βελτίων | βέλτιστος |
| | κρείττων | κράτιστος |
| κακός, *bad* | κακίων | κάκιστος |
| | χείρων | χείριστος |
| | ἥττων | ἥκιστα (adv. only) |

| Positive degree | Comparative degree | Superlative degree |
|---|---|---|
| καλός, beautiful | καλλίων | κάλλιστος |
| μέγας, great | μείζων | μέγιστος |
| μικρός, small | μείων | |
| (also regular) | μικρότερος | μικρότατος |
| ὀλίγος, little, few | ἐλάττων | ἐλάχιστος |
| πολύς, much, many | πλείων or πλέων | πλεῖστος |
| ῥᾴδιος, easy | ῥᾴων | ῥᾷστος |

## 239. The Greek adverb

Greek adverbs are regularly formed from the *genitive plural neuter* of the corresponding adjective, changing its final -ν to -ς, the accent remaining the same, as follows:

| Adjective | Genitive plural neuter | Adverb |
|---|---|---|
| ἡδύς, sweet | ἡδέων | ἡδέως |
| ἀληθής, true | ἀληθῶν | ἀληθῶς |
| καλός, beautiful | καλῶν | καλῶς |

The comparative degree of the adverb is formed by using the *accusative singular neuter* of the comparative degree of the adjective, e.g. πιστότερον, *more faithfully*.

The superlative degree of the adverb is formed by using the *accusative plural neuter* of the superlative of the adjective, e.g. κάλλιστα, *most beautifully*.

## 240. New word list

ἀνίστημι (see ἵστημι for prin. parts), to make stand up, raise up, arouse; mid., to stand up.

γογγύζω, ἐγόγγυσα, to murmur, grumble, mutter.

διδακτός, -ή, -όν, taught. DIDACTIC.

ἕλκω or ἑλκύω, ἑλκύσω, εἵλκυσα, εἵλκυκα, εἵλκυσμαι, εἱλκύσθην, to draw, drag.

*ἔξω, outside. EXOTERIC.

*ἔσχατος, -η, -ον, furthest, utmost, last. ESCHATOLOGY.

*μανθάνω, μαθήσομαι, ἔμαθον, μεμάθηκα, to learn. MATHEMATICS.

*μάχομαι, μαχοῦμαι, ἐμαχεσάμην, μεμάχημαι, to fight (with), quarrel. LOGOMACHY.

πεινάω, πεινήσω or πεινάσω, ἐπείνησα or ἐπείνασα, πεπείνηκα, to hunger.

**241. Reading passage** (*John* 6: 35-52)

6:35 Εἶπεν αὐτοῖς ὁ Ἰησοῦς· ἐγώ εἰμι ὁ ἄρτος τῆς ζωῆς· ὁ ἐρχόμενος πρὸς ἐμὲ οὐ μὴ πεινάσῃ, καὶ ὁ πιστεύων εἰς ἐμὲ οὐ μὴ διψήσει

36 πώποτε. Ἀλλ' εἶπον ὑμῖν ὅτι καὶ ἑωράκατέ [με] καὶ οὐ πιστεύετε.

37 πᾶν ὃ δίδωσίν μοι ὁ πατὴρ πρὸς ἐμὲ ἥξει, καὶ τὸν ἐρχόμενον πρός

38 με οὐ μὴ ἐκβάλω ἔξω, ὅτι καταβέβηκα ἀπὸ τοῦ οὐρανοῦ οὐχ ἵνα ποιῶ τὸ θέλημα τὸ ἐμὸν ἀλλὰ τὸ θέλημα τοῦ πέμψαντός με.

39 τοῦτο δέ ἐστιν τὸ θέλημα τοῦ πέμψαντός με, ἵνα πᾶν ὃ δέδωκέν μοι μὴ ἀπολέσω ἐξ αὐτοῦ, ἀλλὰ ἀναστήσω αὐτὸ ἐν τῇ ἐσχάτῃ

40 ἡμέρᾳ. τοῦτο γάρ ἐστιν τὸ θέλημα τοῦ πατρός μου, ἵνα πᾶς ὁ θεωρῶν τὸν υἱὸν καὶ πιστεύων εἰς αὐτὸν ἔχῃ ζωὴν αἰώνιον, καὶ

41 ἀναστήσω αὐτὸν ἐγὼ ἐν τῇ ἐσχάτῃ ἡμέρᾳ. Ἐγόγγυζον οὖν οἱ Ἰουδαῖοι περὶ αὐτοῦ ὅτι εἶπεν· ἐγώ εἰμι ὁ ἄρτος ὁ καταβὰς ἐκ

42 τοῦ οὐρανοῦ, καὶ ἔλεγον· οὐχ οὗτός ἐστιν Ἰησοῦς ὁ υἱὸς Ἰωσήφ, οὗ ἡμεῖς οἴδαμεν τὸν πατέρα καὶ τὴν μητέρα; πῶς νῦν λέγει ὅτι

43 ἐκ τοῦ οὐρανοῦ καταβέβηκα; ἀπεκρίθη Ἰησοῦς καὶ εἶπεν αὐτοῖς·

44 μὴ γογγύζετε μετ' ἀλλήλων. Οὐδεὶς δύναται ἐλθεῖν πρός με ἐὰν μὴ ὁ πατὴρ ὁ πέμψας με ἑλκύσῃ αὐτόν, κἀγὼ ἀναστήσω αὐτὸν

45 ἐν τῇ ἐσχάτῃ ἡμέρᾳ. ἔστιν γεγραμμένον ἐν τοῖς προφήταις· καὶ ἔσονται πάντες διδακτοὶ θεοῦ· πᾶς ὁ ἀκούσας παρὰ τοῦ πατρὸς

46 καὶ μαθὼν ἔρχεται πρὸς ἐμέ. οὐχ ὅτι τὸν πατέρα ἑώρακέν τις, εἰ

47 μὴ ὁ ὢν παρὰ τοῦ θεοῦ, οὗτος ἑώρακεν τὸν πατέρα. ἀμὴν ἀμὴν

48 λέγω ὑμῖν, ὁ πιστεύων ἔχει ζωὴν αἰώνιον. Ἐγώ εἰμι ὁ ἄρτος τῆς

49 ζωῆς. οἱ πατέρες ὑμῶν ἔφαγον ἐν τῇ ἐρήμῳ τὸ μάννα καὶ

50 ἀπέθανον· οὗτός ἐστιν ὁ ἄρτος ὁ ἐκ τοῦ οὐρανοῦ καταβαίνων, ἵνα

35. οὐ μὴ πεινάσῃ ... οὐ μὴ διψήσει: both are statements of futurity. In Greek, οὐ μή with subjunctive (πεινάσῃ is aorist subjunctive of πεινάω) or future indicative is often used to denote strong negative futurity (561). διψήσει is future indicative of διψάω. ἑωράκατε: from ὁράω.

37. ἥξει: from ἥκω. ἐκβάλω: from ἐκβάλλω. See principal parts of βάλλω. This is second aorist subjunctive. The future indicative would be ἐκβαλῶ.

39. ἀπολέσω: from ἀπόλλυμι. This is first aorist subjunctive. ἀναστήσω: from ἀνίστημι. See principal parts of ἵστημι. This could be future indicative or first aorist subjunctive. In vs. 40 the same situation applies, while in vs. 44 the form is clearly future indicative.

40. πᾶς ὁ θεωρῶν: here, as with πᾶς ὁ ἀκούων in vs. 45, πᾶς occupies predicate position (490).

41. ἐγόγγυζον: imperfect of γογγύζω in today's list. καταβάς: from καταβαίνω. Find βάς in the chart of βαίνω (211).

45. ἔστιν γεγραμμένον: periphrastic form of the perfect middle and passive of γράφω. Frequently used in the N.T. (482. 9). The classical would have used γέγραπται (see 124). ἔσονται: from εἰμί, *to be* (132). μαθών: from the second aorist active of μανθάνω.

46. ἑώρακε(ν): from ὁράω, *to see*.

49. ἔφαγον: from ἐσθίω, *to eat*, so also for φάγῃ and φαγεῖν below. ἀπέθανον (and ἀποθάνῃ, *vs. 50*): from ἀποθνήσκω. See θνήσκω for principal parts.

51 τις ἐξ αὐτοῦ φάγῃ καὶ μὴ ἀποθάνῃ. ἐγώ εἰμι ὁ ἄρτος ὁ ζῶν ὁ ἐκ
τοῦ οὐρανοῦ καταβάς· ἐάν τις φάγῃ ἐκ τούτου τοῦ ἄρτου, ζήσει
εἰς τὸν αἰῶνα· καὶ ὁ ἄρτος δὲ ὃν ἐγὼ δώσω ἡ σάρξ μού ἐστιν
52 ὑπὲρ τῆς τοῦ κόσμου ζωῆς. Ἐμάχοντο οὖν πρὸς ἀλλήλους οἱ
Ἰουδαῖοι λέγοντες· πῶς δύναται οὗτος ἡμῖν δοῦναι τὴν σάρκα
φαγεῖν;

51. **ζήσει**: from ζάω, *to live.* **δώσω**: from δίδωμι. See the expansion of δίδωμι in 227.
So also for δοῦναι, *vs. 52.* **ὑπέρ**: carries here the significance, *for the sake of.*

### 242. Writing exercise

1. Referring to ἴδιος (56), decline in full the adjective κομψότερος,
*better* (of health).
2. Referring to πρῶτος (56), decline the adjective ἄριστος, *best, noblest.*
Remember that the accent of ἄριστος is persistent, and will be moved
only when the final syllable is long.
3. Referring to ἡδίων (157), decline the comparative adjective καλ-
λίων, *more beautiful.*

## LESSON 37
# Contract Nouns and Adjectives

### 243. Contract nouns of the vowel declensions

A SMALL group of nouns having stems ending with a vowel are declined
with the case endings of the α- or the ο-declension, the vowel of the stem
being contracted in the process, and the contraction being indicated
generally by a circumflex accent on the contracted forms. For practical
purposes the student can note that the endings of such nouns are just
like those of ἀρχή or σκοτία (43) or (except for nominative and accusative
singular) ἄνθρωπος (49) but with circumflex accents throughout. In this
group are included ὁ νοῦς, *the mind* (for νόος, an ο-contract); ἡ μνᾶ, *the mina*
(for μνάα, an α-contract); and ἡ γῆ, *the earth* (for γέα, an ε-contract) as
follows:

| ὁ νοῦς, mind | ἡ μνᾶ, mina. | ἡ γῆ, earth |
|---|---|---|
| νοῦ | μνᾶς | γῆς |
| νῷ | μνᾷ | γῇ |
| νοῦν | μνᾶν | γῆν |
| νοῖ | μναῖ | |
| νῶν | μνῶν | |
| νοῖς | μναῖς | |
| νοῦς | μνᾶς | |

## 244. Contract adjectives of the vowel declensions

Similarly there are a few adjectives having stems ending in vowels which use the endings of the α- and o-declensions. The student can observe that the endings are the same as with πρῶτος or ἴδιος (except for their -ος and -ον forms. See 56) but for the accents, which are all circumflex on the final syllable. Three are given here : χρυσοῦς, *golden* (for χρύσεος) ; ἀργυροῦς, *silver* (for ἀργύρεος) ; and ἁπλοῦς, *simple, sincere* (for ἁπλόος), as follows :

### χρυσοῦς, *golden*

| | | |
|---|---|---|
| χρυσοῦς | χρυσῆ | χουσοῦν |
| χρυσοῦ | χρυσῆς | χρυσοῦ |
| χρυσῷ | χρυσῇ | χρυσῷ |
| χρυσοῦν | χρυσῆν | χρυσοῦν |
| | | |
| χρυσοῖ | χρυσαῖ | χρυσᾶ |
| χρυσῶν | χρυσῶν | χρυσῶν |
| χρυσοῖς | χρυσαῖς | χρυσοῖς |
| χρυσοῦς | χρυσᾶς | χρυσᾶ |

### ἀργυροῦς, *silver* (note the ρ of the stem)

| | | |
|---|---|---|
| ἀργυροῦς | ἀργυρᾶ | ἀργυροῦν |
| ἀργυροῦ | ἀργυρᾶς | ἀργυροῦ |
| ἀργυρῷ | ἀργυρᾷ | ἀργυρῷ |
| ἀργυροῦν | ἀργυρᾶν | ἀργυροῦν |
| | | |
| ἀργυροῖ | ἀργυραῖ | ἀργυρᾶ |
| ἀργυρῶν | ἀργυρῶν | ἀργυρῶν |
| ἀργυροῖς | ἀργυραῖς | ἀργυροῖς |
| ἀργυροῦς | ἀργυρᾶς | ἀργυρᾶ |

### ἁπλοῦς, *simple, sincere*

| | | |
|---|---|---|
| ἁπλοῦς | ἁπλῆ | ἁπλοῦν |
| ἁπλοῦ | ἁπλῆς | ἁπλοῦ |
| ἁπλῷ | ἁπλῇ | ἁπλῷ |
| ἁπλοῦν | ἁπλῆν | ἁπλοῦν |
| | | |
| ἁπλοῖ | ἁπλαῖ | ἁπλᾶ |
| ἁπλῶν | ἁπλῶν | ἁπλῶν |
| ἁπλοῖς | ἁπλαῖς | ἁπλοῖς |
| ἁπλοῦς | ἁπλᾶς | ἁπλᾶ |

## 245. New word list

διάβολος, -ου, ὁ, slanderer, the devil.
DIABOLIC, DEVIL.

*διδάσκω, διδάξω, ἐδίδαξα, δεδίδαχα,
δεδίδαγμαι, ἐδιδάχθην, to teach.
DIDACTIC.

ἐκλέγω (see λέγω below for prin.
parts), to choose, pick out. EC-
LECTIC.

Ἰούδας, gen. -α, dat. -ᾳ, acc. -αν, ὁ,
Judas.

Ἰσκαριώτης, -ου, ὁ, Iscariot, citizen
of Carioth in Judaea.

*λέγω, ἔλεξα, εἴλοχα, εἴλεγμαι,
ἐλέγην, to choose, gather. Practically always in compound form.
SELECT.

παραδίδωμι (see δίδωμι for prin.
parts), to give over, surrender, betray.

πόσις, πόσεως, ἡ, a drinking, drink.
POTION.

πρότερος, -α, -ον, former, earlier,
preceding; adverbially, πρότερον
and τὸ πρότερον, before, in time past.

σκανδαλίζω, ἐσκανδάλισα, ἐσκανδαλίσθην, to cause to stumble, offend.
SCANDALIZE.

σκληρός, -ά, -όν, hard, harsh, austere,
stern. SCLEROSIS.

συναγωγή, -ῆς, ἡ, synagogue. SYNA-
GOGUE.

τρώγω, τρώξω, ἔτρωξα, τέτρωγμαι,
to chew, eat.

*ὠφελέω,    ὠφελήσω,    ὠφέλησα,
ὠφέληκα, ὠφέλημαι, ὠφελήθην, to
help, be of use or service, sometimes
with double accusative.

## 246. Reading passage (*John 6 : 53-71*)

6:53   Εἶπεν οὖν αὐτοῖς ὁ Ἰησοῦς· ἀμὴν ἀμὴν λέγω ὑμῖν, ἐὰν μὴ φάγητε
        τὴν σάρκα τοῦ υἱοῦ τοῦ ἀνθρώπου καὶ πίητε αὐτοῦ τὸ αἷμα, οὐκ
  54   ἔχετε ζωὴν ἐν ἑαυτοῖς. ὁ τρώγων μου τὴν σάρκα καὶ πίνων μου τὸ
        αἷμα ἔχει ζωὴν αἰώνιον, κἀγὼ ἀναστήσω αὐτὸν τῇ ἐσχάτῃ ἡμέρᾳ.
  55   ἡ γὰρ σάρξ μου ἀληθής ἐστιν βρῶσις, καὶ τὸ αἷμά μου ἀληθής
  56   ἐστιν πόσις. ὁ τρώγων μου τὴν σάρκα καὶ πίνων μου τὸ αἷμα
  57   ἐν ἐμοὶ μένει κἀγὼ ἐν αὐτῷ. καθὼς ἀπέστειλέν με ὁ ζῶν πατὴρ
        κἀγὼ ζῶ διὰ τὸν πατέρα, καὶ ὁ τρώγων με κἀκεῖνος ζήσει δι᾽
  58   ἐμέ. οὗτός ἐστιν ὁ ἄρτος ὁ ἐξ οὐρανοῦ καταβάς, οὐ καθὼς ἔφαγον
        οἱ πατέρες καὶ ἀπέθανον· ὁ τρώγων τοῦτον τὸν ἄρτον ζήσει εἰς
  59   τὸν αἰῶνα. Ταῦτα εἶπεν ἐν συναγωγῇ διδάσκων ἐν Καφαρναούμ.
  60   Πολλοὶ οὖν ἀκούσαντες ἐκ τῶν μαθητῶν αὐτοῦ εἶπαν· σκληρός
  61   ἐστιν ὁ λόγος οὗτος· τίς δύναται αὐτοῦ ἀκούειν; εἰδὼς δὲ ὁ
        Ἰησοῦς ἐν ἑαυτῷ ὅτι γογγύζουσιν περὶ τούτου οἱ μαθηταὶ αὐτοῦ,

53. πίητε: from πίνω, to drink. ἑαυτοῖς: from the third personal reflexive pronoun
ἑαυτοῦ. Used here for second person (482. 19).
54. τῇ ἐσχάτῃ ἡμέρᾳ: dative of time when (526).
57. ἀπέστειλε(ν): from ἀποστέλλω, to send forth. κἀκεῖνος: crasis for καὶ ἐκεῖνος.
58. καταβάς: from καταβαίνω, to go or come down.
61. εἰδώς: perfect participle of εἶδω, to see (perf., to know). See 199 for the development of this tense. So also for the form ᾔδει in vs. 64.

62 εἶπεν αὐτοῖς· τοῦτο ὑμᾶς σκανδαλίζει; ἐὰν οὖν θεωρῆτε τὸν υἱὸν
63 τοῦ ἀνθρώπου ἀναβαίνοντα ὅπου ἦν τὸ πρότερον; τὸ πνεῦμά
ἐστιν τὸ ζωοποιοῦν, ἡ σὰρξ οὐκ ὠφελεῖ οὐδέν· τὰ ῥήματα ἃ ἐγὼ
64 λελάληκα ὑμῖν πνεῦμά ἐστιν καὶ ζωή ἐστιν. ἀλλ' εἰσὶν ἐξ ὑμῶν
τινες οἳ οὐ πιστεύουσιν. ᾔδει γὰρ ἐξ ἀρχῆς ὁ Ἰησοῦς τίνες εἰσὶν
65 οἱ μὴ πιστεύοντες καὶ τίς ἐστιν ὁ παραδώσων αὐτόν. καὶ ἔλεγεν·
διὰ τοῦτο εἴρηκα ὑμῖν ὅτι οὐδεὶς δύναται ἐλθεῖν πρός με ἐὰν μὴ
ᾖ δεδομένον αὐτῷ ἐκ τοῦ πατρός.
66 Ἐκ τούτου πολλοὶ τῶν μαθητῶν αὐτοῦ ἀπῆλθον εἰς τὰ ὀπίσω
67 καὶ οὐκέτι μετ' αὐτοῦ περιεπάτουν. εἶπεν οὖν ὁ Ἰησοῦς τοῖς
68 δώδεκα· μὴ καὶ ὑμεῖς θέλετε ὑπάγειν; ἀπεκρίθη αὐτῷ Σίμων
Πέτρος· κύριε, πρὸς τίνα ἀπελευσόμεθα; ῥήματα ζωῆς αἰωνίου
69 ἔχεις· καὶ ἡμεῖς πεπιστεύκαμεν καὶ ἐγνώκαμεν ὅτι σὺ εἶ ὁ ἅγιος
70 τοῦ θεοῦ. ἀπεκρίθη αὐτοῖς ὁ Ἰησοῦς· οὐκ ἐγὼ ὑμᾶς τοὺς δώδεκα
71 ἐξελεξάμην; καὶ ἐξ ὑμῶν εἷς διάβολός ἐστιν· ἔλεγεν δὲ τὸν
Ἰούδαν Σίμωνος Ἰσκαριώτου· οὗτος γὰρ ἔμελλεν παραδιδόναι
αὐτόν, εἷς ἐκ τῶν δώδεκα.

62. **ἐὰν οὖν θεωρῆτε**: supply τί, *what?* A rhetorical question. This is an elliptical form
of the future more vivid condition. Understand, *what* (*will you do*) *if. . .?*
63. **ζωοποιοῦν**: from ζωοποιέω. See the present participle of ποιέω in 195. **λελάληκα**:
from λαλέω, *to speak.*
64. **παραδώσων**: from παραδίδωμι. See 227 for the development of δίδωμι. Locate
δώσων.
65. **εἴρηκα**: from εἴρω. **ἐλθεῖν**: from ἔρχομαι. **ᾖ δεδομένον**: from δίδωμι. See 227 for
δεδομένος ὦ.
66. **εἰς τὰ ὀπίσω**: an idiom meaning *backward, back.* **περιεπάτουν**: from περιπατέω.
67. **μή**: sign of a question with negative answer expected. Need not be translated.
68. **ἀπελευσόμεθα**: from ἀπέρχομαι. See ἔρχομαι for the principal parts.
69. **ἐγνώκαμεν**: from γιγνώσκω (see 209).
70. **ἐξελεξάμην**: from ἐκλέγω in today's word list.
71. **ἔλεγε(ν)**: from λέγω, *to say, call, mean*; here used in the sense, *to mean.* **παραδιδόναι** from παραδίδωμι. See 227 for the expansion of δίδωμι. Locate διδόναι. **εἰς
. . . δώδεκα**: ὤν to be understood.

## 247. Writing exercise

Using today's paradigms and the nouns in 151, 152, indicate the
forms to give the following meanings: (*a*) *Of* (*a*) *simple mind.* (*b*) *Silver
minas* (acc.). (*c*) *For the sincere priests.* (*d*) *Of the golden fish*(*es*). (*e*) *To* (or *for*)
*the silver city.* (*f*) *The sincere replies* (nom.).

## LESSON 38
# Review

**248.**

1. REVIEW the starred words in all word lists thus far.
2. Review the reading passages for the semester.
3. Review the complete conjugation of λύω as found in the chart in 97.
4. Review the conjugation of εἰμί as found in the chart in 132.
5. Review the conjugation of ποιέω in the present system. See the chart in 164.
6. Know the declension of the a- and o-declension adjective πρῶτος (56).
7. Know the declension of the consonant and a-declension adjective πᾶς, πᾶσα, πᾶν (156).

# PART II

# READINGS FROM THE *ANABASIS*
## BOOK I

# Introduction to Second Part

**249.** THE second semester will be given to reading from the *Anabasis* of Xenophon, a book which tells of the expedition of Cyrus the Younger inland from Sardis to Babylon in an effort to wrest from his older brother, Artaxerxes, the throne of the Persian Empire.

Cyrus had a profound admiration for the soldierly qualities of the Greek fighting men. He pinned large hopes for the success of his expedition, which left Sardis in 401 b.c., upon his contingent of some thirteen thousand Greek soldiers, most of them heavy-armed infantrymen or hoplites, led by several Greek generals for whom fighting was a career.

Faced with overwhelming numerical odds in the battle which took place near the little village of Cunaxa in Babylonia, the Greeks twice routed their foes, but unfortunately for them their leader and patron, Cyrus, was killed in the battle, and thus their cause was lost.

After some negotiations with the king for safe-conduct out of his realm five of the Greek generals were treacherously seized while at a parley under truce, and four of them were slain. At first dismayed, the Greeks elected new leaders, one of whom was Xenophon the Athenian.

This man was a pupil and friend of the philosopher Socrates and has left to the world a tribute to his great teacher in his little volume of recollections commonly called the *Memorabilia*.

Xenophon had come along on the expedition as an observer and as a friend of Proxenus, one of the murdered generals. To Xenophon's lot now fell the command of the rearguard, a most important post in a retreat. And he it was who chronicled the memorable feat of the Ten Thousand in retreating successfully from the heart of the Persian Empire through exceedingly rough and hostile country along the upper reaches of the Tigris, and in the dead of winter, finally coming out on the Black Sea at Trapezus, the modern Trebizond.

The *Anabasis*, or 'Journey Up-Country', is a model of clear and concise Greek composition, which fact, in addition to its interesting narrative, has made it a favorite reading piece for students beginning Greek. Our readings will be from *Book 1*, which describes the inland march of Cyrus and his Persian and Greek forces, culminating in victory for the Greeks but death for Cyrus in the battle of Cunaxa.

## 250. The Greek of the 'Anabasis'

The student should keep in mind the fact that the Greek language of the *Anabasis* comes from the golden period in Greek literature. It is 'classical' Greek, antedating by four or five centuries the Greek of the New Testament, which is commonly referred to as the κοινή or common conversational Greek of that much later period.

In the *Anabasis* the student will have opportunity to see the Greek language in a much more highly and regularly organized form than as seen in the *Gospel of John*. The optative mood, with its many uses, will come alive. And the vocabulary will bring a slightly altered and more rounded view of some words already met, introducing also many new words.

This experience with more difficult and exacting Greek is needed by the student even though his ultimate objective is to work entirely with the Greek of the New Testament. Just as the piano or organ student who wishes to specialize finally in hymns will gain from the more technical and classical type of music a mastery also of hymns which could not have been achieved through the exclusive playing of hymn literature, so an acquaintance with the more demanding and less familiar classical Greek writers will yield a rich reward of mastery even in the New Testament field.

The length of the assigned daily reading passages varies somewhat, an effort being made to limit the number of new words in a given lesson to between twenty and thirty. The numbering which appears in the left margin of each reading passage will readily be seen to refer only to the lines as they appear in each individual reading lesson in this text. The numbers which appear in the right margin give the traditional paragraphing used in general references to the *Anabasis*. The heading of each reading passage gives the traditional reference for that passage, including the number for book, chapter, paragraph, and line (the last referring to the lines as set in this text).

The student will be required, as a part of each lesson, to memorize the principal parts of one commonly used irregular Greek verb, and there should also be periodic review of the principal parts already learned. These are an absolute 'must' for any student planning to do further work in either classical or New Testament Greek.

# LESSON 39

## Darius nears the End of Life

### 251. New word list

*ἀθροίζω, ἀθροίσω, ἤθροισα, ἤθροικα, ἤθροισμαι, ἠθροίσθην, to collect, gather, muster.

ἀμφότερος, -α, -ον, both.

ἀποδείκνυμι (see δείκνυμι for prin. parts), to appoint.

Ἀρταξέρξης, -ου, ὁ, Artaxerxes, king of Persia.

*βίος, -ου, ὁ, life. BIOLOGY.

*βούλομαι, βουλήσομαι, βεβούλημαι, ἐβουλήθην, to wish, will.

Δαρεῖος, -ου, ὁ, Darius.

Ἕλλην, -ος, ὁ, a Hellene, a Greek. HELLENIC.

*ἐπεί, when, since.

Καστωλός, -οῦ, ἡ, Castolus, a village near Sardis.

Κῦρος, -ου, ὁ, Cyrus.

*μέν ... δέ, particles used to set off contrasting items. In English the contrast is often expressed by mere emphasis in the reading.

*μεταπέμπω (see πέμπω for prin. parts), to send for.

νέος, -α, -ον, new, young; comp. νεώτερος. NEON, NEW.

Ξενίας, -ου, ὁ, Xenias, a Greek general in Cyrus' army.

*ὁπλίτης, -ου, ὁ, a hoplite, heavy-armed soldier.

*πάρειμι (see εἰμί for prin. parts), to be present, come.

Παρράσιος, -ου, ὁ, a Parrhasian, from Parrhasia, a district in Arcadia.

Παρύσατις, -ιδος, ἡ, Parysatis, wife of Darius.

*πεδίον, -ου, τό, plain.

πρεσβύτερος, -α, -ον, older, elder. PRESBYTER.

*σατράπης, -ου, ὁ, satrap, viceroy.

*στρατηγός, -οῦ, ὁ, general. STRATEGY.

τελευτή, -ῆς, ἡ, end.

Τισσαφέρνης, -ους, ὁ, Tissaphernes, a Persian noble.

τριακόσιοι, -αι, -α, three hundred.

*τυγχάνω, τεύξομαι, ἔτυχον, τετύχηκα, to hit the mark, attain, happen.

ὑποπτεύω, ὑποπτεύσω, ὑπώπτευσα, ὑπωπτεύθην, to suspect, be suspicious.

### 252. Principal parts to be memorized

γίγνομαι (or γίνομαι), γενήσομαι, ἐγενόμην, γέγονα, to become, be.

### 253. Reading passage (Anabasis 1.1.1.1—1.1.2.7)

Chapter 1. Δαρείου καὶ Παρυσάτιδος γίγνονται παῖδες δύο,   1
πρεσβύτερος μὲν Ἀρταξέρξης, νεώτερος δὲ Κῦρος· ἐπεὶ δὲ

1. Δαρείου καὶ Παρυσάτιδος: genitive of source, a form of the genitive of separation (509). γίγνονται: an historical present (547). These occur frequently and, since the same usage is found in English, they may occasionally be translated in their original tense. γίγνομαι, to become, is here used in the sense to be born.

ἠσθένει Δαρεῖος καὶ ὑπώπτευε τελευτὴν τοῦ βίου, ἐβούλετο 2
τὼ παῖδε ἀμφοτέρω παρεῖναι. ὁ μὲν οὖν πρεσβύτερος παρὼν
5 ἐτύγχανε· Κῦρον δὲ μεταπέμπεται ἀπὸ τῆς ἀρχῆς ἧς αὐτὸν
σατράπην ἐποίησε. καὶ στρατηγὸν δὲ αὐτὸν ἀπέδειξε πάντων
ὅσοι εἰς Καστωλοῦ πεδίον ἀθροίζονται. ἀναβαίνει οὖν ὁ Κῦρος
λαβὼν Τισσαφέρνην ὡς φίλον, καὶ τῶν Ἑλλήνων ἔχων ὁπλίτας ἀνέβη τριακοσίους, ἄρχοντα δὲ αὐτῶν Ξενίαν Παρράσιον.

3. **ἠσθένει**: from ἀσθενέω. **ὑπώπτευε**: from ὑποπτεύω in today's list.
4. **τὼ παῖδε ἀμφοτέρω**: an example of dual number, seldom found in the *Anabasis*. These are accusatives. Translate, *both of the two boys* or *sons*. **παρεῖναι**: from πάρειμι. Find εἶναι in the development of εἰμί (132). **παρὼν ἐτύγχανε**: literally, *happened being present* (παρών is present participle of πάρειμι). Translate, *happened to be present* (583).
5. **ἧς**: from the relative pronoun ὅς, ἥ, ὅ (see 64).
6. **σατράπην, στρατηγόν**: predicate accusatives with a verb signifying *to appoint* or *make* (see 533). **ἐποίησε**: referring to action prior to that of the historical present μεταπέμπεται, aorists ἐποίησε and ἀπέδειξε are logically pluperfects. **ἀπέδειξε**: from ἀποδείκνυμι. See δείκνυμι for principal parts.
8. **λαβών**: from λαμβάνω. λαβών is like ἀγαγών in the chart of ἄγω (118). **ὡς φίλον**: *as friend*. Often, as here, ὡς implies the thought behind an action. Cyrus thought Tissaphernes a friend. **καὶ . . . δέ**: has the sense *and . . . moreover, also*.
9. **ἀνέβη**: from ἀναβαίνω. Find ἔβη in the chart of βαίνω (211).

## 254. Writing exercise

1. In *l. 3* of today's reading occurs the form ἠσθένει. Write out the full conjugation of the present system of the verb of which this form is a part, and underscore this particular form where it occurs (cf. ποιέω, 164).
2. Complete the declensions of Ξενίαν (*l. 9*) and σατράπην (*l. 6*) and underscore these particular forms where they occur. (See nouns in 44.)

# LESSON·40
# Trouble between Cyrus and Artaxerxes

## 255. New word list

ἀποπέμπω (see πέμπω for prin. parts), *to send back, send away.*

ἄρχω, ἄρξω, ἦρξα, ἦρχα, ἦργμαι, ἤρχθην, *to be first, begin, rule, be in command* (often with gen.). MONARCH.

ἀτιμάζω, ἀτιμάσω, ἠτίμασα, ἠτί-μακα, ἠτίμασμαι, ἠτιμάσθην, *to dishonor, disgrace.*

*ἀφικνέομαι (see ἱκνέομαι for prin. parts), *to arrive at, come to, reach.*

*βάρβαρος, -ον, *not Greek, foreign*;

as subst., *a barbarian, Persian.* BARBARIAN.

*βασιλεύω, βασιλεύσω, *to be king, reign.*

*βουλεύω, βουλεύσω, ἐβούλευσα, βεβούλευκα, βεβούλευμαι, ἐβου-λεύθην, *to plan*; mid., *to consider.*

*δή, postpositive emphatic particle, *indeed*, etc. Sometimes not translated by words.

διαβάλλω (see βάλλω for prin. parts), *to slander, accuse.* DIABOLIC, DEVIL.

διατίθημι (see τίθημι for prin. parts), *to arrange, treat.* DIATHESIS.

*ἑαυτοῦ, -ῆς, -οῦ, *of himself, herself, itself* (73).

ἐξαιτέω (see αἰτέω for prin. parts), *to demand of one*; mid., *to intercede for, beg off.*

*ἐπιβουλεύω (see βουλεύω for prin. parts), *to plot against,* with dat.

ἐπιμελέομαι, ἐπιμελήσομαι, ἐπιμεμέλημαι, ἐπεμελήθην, *to take care*; with gen., *to take care of, attend to.*

εὐνοϊκῶς, *with good will*; with ἔχειν, *to be well disposed.*

ἤν, a form of ἐάν, *if.*

ἱκανός, -ή, -όν, *sufficient, able.*

*ἱκνέομαι, ἵξομαι, ἱκόμην, ἷγμαι, *to come, go.*

καθίστημι (see ἵστημι for prin. parts), *to set down, station, appoint*; second aor. and pluperf., *to succeed, begin to reign.*

κινδυνεύω, κινδυνεύσω, ἐκινδύνευσα, κεκινδύνευκα, κεκινδύνευμαι, ἐκινδυνεύθην, *to face danger, run a risk.*

μήποτε, *never.*

*ὅπως, *in what way, how.* Also in purpose clauses, same as ἵνα, ὡς, *in order that, that.*

*πείθω, πείσω, ἔπεισα, πέπεικα or πέποιθα, πέπεισμαι, ἐπείσθην, *to persuade*; mid. and pass., *to be persuaded, obey,* often with dat.

*πολεμέω, πολεμήσω, ἐπολέμησα, πεπολέμηκα, πεπολέμημαι, ἐπολεμήθην, *to make war.* POLEMIC.

συλλαμβάνω (see λαμβάνω for prin. parts), *to arrest.*

τελευτάω, τελευτήσω, ἐτελεύτησα, τετελεύτηκα, ἐτελευτήθην, *to end, die.*

ὑπάρχω (see ἄρχω for prin. parts), *to begin, be under as a foundation*; with dat., *to support.*

*φιλέω, φιλήσω, ἐφίλησα, πεφίληκα, πεφίλημαι, ἐφιλήθην, *to love,* as a friend. PHILIP.

*ὡς, *as, in order that, that,* same as ἵνα, ὅπως.

## 256. Principal parts to be memorized

ἵστημι, στήσω, ἔστησα or ἔστην, ἔστηκα, ἔσταμαι, ἐστάθην, *to make stand, set*; in second aorist and perfect active, *to stand.*

## 257. Reading passage (*Anabasis 1.1.3.1–1.1.5.5*)

Ἐπεὶ δὲ ἐτελεύτησε Δαρεῖος καὶ κατέστη εἰς τὴν βασι-  3
λείαν Ἀρταξέρξης, Τισσαφέρνης διαβάλλει τὸν Κῦρον πρὸς
τὸν ἀδελφὸν ὡς ἐπιβουλεύοι αὐτῷ. ὁ δὲ πείθεται καὶ συλ-
λαμβάνει Κῦρον ὡς ἀποκτενῶν· ἡ δὲ μήτηρ ἐξαιτησαμένη

1. **κατέστη**: from καθίστημι. For the form ἔστη see development of ἵστημι (216).

2. **διαβάλλει**: another historical present. Translate in the past tense, *slandered,* this time on account of the indirect discourse following.

3. **ἐπιβουλεύοι**: when a statement or thought is quoted indirectly after ὅτι or ὡς after a verb of quotation in past tense, the quoted verb in the indicative usually changes to the optative mood. Tense remains the same as in the original statement. Here present optative shows the original verb was present, ἐπιβουλεύει, *Cyrus is plotting.* See 589.

4. **ὡς ἀποκτενῶν**: future participle of ἀποκτείνω, literally means *being about to kill.*

5   αὐτὸν ἀποπέμπει πάλιν ἐπὶ τὴν ἀρχήν. ὁ δ᾽ ὡς ἀπῆλθε 4
    κινδυνεύσας καὶ ἀτιμασθείς, βουλεύεται ὅπως μήποτε ἔτι
    ἔσται ἐπὶ τῷ ἀδελφῷ, ἀλλά, ἢν δύνηται, βασιλεύσει ἀντ᾽
    ἐκείνου. Παρύσατις μὲν δὴ ἡ μήτηρ ὑπῆρχε τῷ Κύρῳ,
    φιλοῦσα αὐτὸν μᾶλλον ἢ τὸν βασιλεύοντα Ἀρταξέρξην. ὅστις 5
10  δ᾽ ἀφικνεῖτο᾽ τῶν παρὰ βασιλέως πρὸς αὐτόν, πάντας οὕτω
    διατιθεὶς ἀπεπέμπετο ὥστε αὐτῷ μᾶλλον φίλους εἶναι ἢ
    βασιλεῖ. καὶ τῶν παρ᾽ ἑαυτῷ δὲ βαρβάρων ἐπεμελεῖτο ὡς
    πολεμεῖν τε ἱκανοὶ εἴησαν καὶ εὐνοϊκῶς ἔχοιεν αὐτῷ.

Future participle often denotes purpose (581). Translate, *to kill*. The particle ὡς, *that*, can replace ὅτι in introducing an indirect statement, or it is equivalent to ἵνα, *in order that, to*, in a purpose clause. **ἐξαιτησαμένη**: from ἐξαιτέω. See principal parts of αἰτέω. This form is like λυσάμενος, -η, -ον, in the chart of λύω (97).

6. **κινδυνεύσας**: from κινδυνεύω. Similar to λύσας in λύω. **ἀτιμασθείς**: from ἀτιμάζω. Similar to λυθείς in λύω. **ὅπως . . . ἔσται**: from εἰμί (see chart in 132). ὅπως with the future indicative is often used to express purpose. This is called an *object clause* (554).

7. **ἐπὶ τῷ ἀδελφῷ**: idiomatic, *in the power of his (the) brother*. We speak colloquially of a man's being 'on' (dependent upon) his friends. **ἢν (ἐὰν) δύνηται . . . βασιλεύσει**: see 603 if necessary for identification of this conditional sentence. Note also that the deponent verb δύναμαι, which basically follows ἵστημι (216) in the present middle, differs from ἵστημι in that it adheres to *recessive accent* in the subjunctive and optative forms of the present tense.

8. **ὑπῆρχε**: from ὑπάρχω in today's word list. It is here imperfect, not perfect (see principal parts of ἄρχω). **τῷ Κύρῳ**: dative after a compound verb (515).

9. **φιλοῦσα**: from φιλέω. See declension of ποιῶν in 195.

11. **διατιθείς**: from διατίθημι in today's list. See expansion of τίθημι (229). Find τιθείς. **αὐτῷ**; dative with word denoting friendliness or hostility (514). So also in *l. 13*.

12. **βασιλεῖ**: from βασιλεύς (see ἱερεύς, 151). This word, when used to refer to the great king of Persia, regularly omits the definite article. But good English would call for its use in translation, *the king*. **παρ᾽ ἑαυτῷ**: like the French *chez lui, with him, at his home, in his own court*. **ὡς . . . εἴησαν καὶ . . . ἔχοιεν**: purpose after a present tense verb is expressed by ἵνα, ὡς, or ὅπως plus subjunctive; after a past tense the optative mood is regularly used for purpose clauses in classical Greek (568); εἴησαν is an alternative form for εἶεν, present optative of εἰμί (see 132).

13. **εὐνοϊκῶς ἔχοιεν**: recall that the Greek uses the adverb with ἔχω to express a state of being. Translate *(that they might) be well disposed*.

## 258. Writing exercise

1. In *l. 1* of today's reading lesson is found the second aorist form κατέστη. Give the complete conjugation of this verb in the second aorist active (see ἵστημι, 216). It will be helpful to note the discussion of augment in compound verbs under the heading 'Augment' in 107.

2. In *l. 4* occurs the aorist middle participle ἐξαιτησαμένη, from ἐξαιτέω. Referring to the development of the present middle and passive participle ἐρχόμενος (58), decline this participle in all genders, singular and plural, underscoring today's form where it occurs.

# LESSON 41

## Cyrus arms against the King

### 259. New word list

*αἰσθάνομαι, αἰσθήσομαι, ἠσθόμην, ἤσθημαι, to perceive, learn, observe, sense. AESTHETIC.

ἀπαράσκευος, -ον, unprepared.

ἀρχαῖος, -α, -ον, ancient, from of old; τὸ ἀρχαῖον, formerly. ARCHAIC.

ἀφίστημι (see ἵστημι for prin. parts), transitive, to separate; intrans., to revolt.

*βέλτιστος, -η, -ον, best, noblest, bravest; superl. of ἀγαθός.

δύναμις, -εως, ἡ, power, force, army. DYNAMIC.

ἕκαστος, -η, -ον, each, every, all.

Ἑλληνικός, -ή, -όν, Greek. HELLENIC.

ἐπικρύπτω (see κρύπτω for prin. parts), to conceal thoroughly; mid., to do secretly.

Ἰωνικός, -ή, -όν, Ionic, of Ionia.

κρύπτω, κρύψω, ἔκρυψα, κέκρυμμαι, ἐκρύφθην, to hide, conceal. CRYPTOGRAM.

*μάλα, very, exceedingly; μάλιστα, superl. of μάλα; ὡς μάλιστα, as much as possible.

Μίλητος, -ου, ἡ, Miletus, a Greek coastal city in Ionia.

ὅποσος, -η, -ον, how much, how many, as much as, as many as.

παραγγέλλω (see ἀγγέλλω for prin. parts), to send word.

Πελοποννήσιος, -α, -ον, Peloponnesian.

*πλεῖστος, -η, -ον, most, superl. of πολύς.

*πλήν, with gen., except, other than; as conjunction, except that.

προαισθάνομαι (see αἰσθάνομαι for prin. parts), to perceive beforehand, foresee.

συλλογή, -ῆς, ἡ, a gathering, levy. SYLLOGE.

*τότε, then, at that time.

φρούραρχος, -ου, ὁ, commander.

### 260. Principal parts to be memorized

κτείνω, κτενῶ, ἔκτεινα, ἔκτονα, to kill. (Usually found in compounds, ἔκτονα always so.)

### 261. Reading passage (Anabasis 1.1.6.1–1.1.7.3)

Τὴν δὲ Ἑλληνικὴν δύναμιν ἤθροιζεν ὡς μάλιστα ἐδύνατο 6 ἐπικρυπτόμενος, ὅπως ὅτι ἀπαρασκευότατον λάβοι βασιλέα. ὧδε οὖν ἐποιεῖτο τὴν συλλογήν. ὁπόσας εἶχε φυλακὰς ἐν

1. ἤθροιζε(ν): see ἀθροίζω. ὡς μάλιστα: see μάλα in today's word list.
2. ὅπως ... λάβοι: another purpose clause after a past tense (568). λάβοι is from ἔλαβον, the second aorist of λαμβάνω. ὅτι ἀπαρασκευότατον: ὅτι, like ὡς, often emphasizes a superlative. Translate simply, as unprepared as possible.

5  ταῖς πόλεσι παρήγγειλε τοῖς φρουράρχοις ἑκάστοις λαμβάνειν
   ἄνδρας Πελοποννησίους ὅτι πλείστους καὶ βελτίστους, ὡς
   ἐπιβουλεύοντος Τισσαφέρνους ταῖς πόλεσι. καὶ γὰρ ἦσαν αἱ
   Ἰωνικαὶ πόλεις Τισσαφέρνους τὸ ἀρχαῖον, ἐκ βασιλέως
   δεδομέναι, τότε δὲ ἀφειστήκεσαν πρὸς Κῦρον πᾶσαι πλὴν
   Μιλήτου· ἐν Μιλήτῳ δὲ Τισσαφέρνης προαισθόμενος τὰ αὐτὰ  7
10 ταῦτα βουλευομένους, ἀποστῆναι πρὸς Κῦρον, τοὺς μὲν
   ἀπέκτεινε τοὺς δ' ἐξέβαλεν.

4. **πόλεσι**: see declension of *πόλις* in 152. **παρήγγειλε**: from *παραγγέλλω* in today's
list. See *ἀγγέλλω* for principal parts.
5. **ὅτι πλείστους καὶ βελτίστους**: see the note on *l. 2* above. **ὡς**: *as, on the grounds that*.
6. **ἐπιβουλεύοντος Τισσαφέρνους**: genitive absolute expressing cause (582). **ταῖς**
**πόλεσι**: the definite article expresses possession, *his cities* (487). **καὶ γάρ**: understand *and*
*(this was plausible) for* . . . .
7. **Τισσαφέρνους**: a genitive of possession used as predicate (493). **τὸ ἀρχαῖον**:
adverbial accusative, *of old* (530).
8. **δεδομέναι**: see *δίδωμι* (227) for *δεδομένος*. **ἀφειστήκεσαν**: from *ἀφίστημι*. Find
*εἱστήκεσαν* in the chart of *ἵστημι* (216, footnote). So also for *ἀποστῆναι* in *l. 10* below,
note the form *στῆναι* in this chart of *ἵστημι*.
9. **προαισθόμενος τὰ αὐτὰ ταῦτα βουλευομένους**: indirect discourse using the participle in place of the original verb of the statement or thought. See 591 for this construction. Here the verb of quotation is expressed in the participle *προαισθόμενος* (from
*προαισθάνομαι*; see *αἰσθάνομαι* for principal parts), *foreseeing*. The original idea which
he foresaw was *βουλεύουσι, they are planning*. This present indicative is changed into
the present participle *βουλευομένους*. Were the subject expressed, it would also be
accusative in case, *αὐτούς*, *them*. Thus we have *προαισθόμενος (αὐτοὺς) βουλευομένους,*
*foreseeing them planning*, or *foreseeing that they were planning these same things*.
10. **τοὺς μὲν** . . . **τοὺς δέ**: *some* . . . *others*.
11. **ἀπέκτεινε**: from *ἀποκτείνω*. See *κτείνω* for principal parts. **ἐξέβαλε(ν)**: from
*ἐκβάλλω*. See *βάλλω* for principal parts.

## 262. Writing exercise

1. In *l. 11* of today's passage is seen the form *ἀπέκτεινε, he killed*. By
reference to the principal parts of *κτείνω*, also given today, identify the
tense system of *ἀπέκτεινε* (it is not here imperfect). Now conjugate this
entire system (see *φαίνω*, 205). If further detail as to personal endings is
needed, see *λύω* (97). Underscore *ἀπέκτεινε* where it occurs. Remember
that the forms will begin with *ἀπο-* where no augment is used.

2. Write out the declension of the definite article ὁ, ἡ, τό, used frequently
in today's lesson.

# LESSON 42

## A Ruse to deceive the King

### 263. New word list

*ἀμφί with gen., about, concerning; with acc., about, upon. Very much like περί. AMPHITHEATER.

ἀξιόω, ἀξιώσω, ἠξίωσα, ἠξίωκα, ἠξίωμαι, ἠξιώθην, to deem proper, expect, ask as right. AXIOM.

*αὖ, again, furthermore.

ἄχθομαι, ἀχθέσομαι, ἠχθέσθην, to be distressed, angry.

δαπανάω, δαπανήσω, ἐδαπάνησα, δεδαπάνηκα, δεδαπάνημαι, ἐδαπανήθην, to spend.

δασμός, -οῦ, ὁ, tax, tribute.

ἐκπίπτω (see πίπτω for prin. parts), to fall out, be exiled.

ἐπιβουλή, -ῆς, ἡ, plot.

κατάγω (see ἄγω for prin. parts), to lead down, bring to port, restore.

*νομίζω, νομιῶ, ἐνόμισα, νενόμικα, νενόμισμαι, ἐνομίσθην, to consider, think.

πειράομαι, πειράσομαι, ἐπειρασάμην, πεπείραμαι, ἐπειράθην, to attempt, try. EMPIRICAL, PIRATE.

*πίπτω, πεσοῦμαι, ἔπεσον, πέπτωκα, to fall.

πολιορκέω, πολιορκήσω, ἐπολιόρκησα, πεπολιόρκημαι, ἐπολιορκήθην, to besiege, blockade.

πρόφασις, -εως, ἡ, excuse, pretext.

*στράτευμα, -ατος, τό, army.

*συλλέγω (see λέγω, to choose, gather, for prin. parts), to gather, collect.

συμπράττω (see πράττω for prin. parts), to help in doing or effecting, with dat. of the one helped.

ὑπολαμβάνω (see λαμβάνω for prin. parts), to take up the conversation, reply, to receive under one's protection.

*φεύγω, φεύξομαι or φευξοῦμαι, ἔφυγον, πέφευγα, to flee, be exiled. FUGITIVE.

### 264. Principal parts to be memorized

λαμβάνω, λήψομαι or λήμψομαι, ἔλαβον, εἴληφα, εἴλημμαι, ἐλήφθην, to take, receive.

### 265. Reading passage (*Anabasis 1.1.7.4–1.1.8.9*)

Ὁ δὲ Κῦρος ὑπολαβὼν τοὺς φεύγοντας, συλλέξας στράτευμα ἐπολιόρκει Μίλητον καὶ κατὰ γῆν καὶ κατὰ θάλατταν, καὶ

---

1. **ὑπολαβών**: from ὑπολαμβάνω in today's list. λαβών from λαμβάνω is like ἀγαγών from ἄγω (118). **συλλέξας**: from συλλέγω in today's list. See λέγω for principal parts. This form compares with λύσας in λύω.

ἐπειρᾶτο κατάγειν τοὺς ἐκπεπτωκότας. καὶ αὕτη αὖ ἄλλη
πρόφασις ἦν αὐτῷ τοῦ ἀθροίζειν στράτευμα. πρὸς δὲ βασιλέα 8
5 πέμπων ἠξίου ἀδελφὸς ὢν αὐτοῦ δοθῆναι οἷ ταύτας τὰς πόλεις
μᾶλλον ἢ Τισσαφέρνην ἄρχειν αὐτῶν, καὶ ἡ μήτηρ συνέπρατ-
τεν αὐτῷ ταῦτα· ὥστε βασιλεὺς τὴν μὲν πρὸς ἑαυτὸν ἐπι-
βουλὴν οὐκ ᾐσθάνετο, Τισσαφέρνει δὲ ἐνόμιζε πολεμοῦντα
αὐτὸν ἀμφὶ τὰ στρατεύματα δαπανᾶν· ὥστε οὐδὲν ἤχθετο
10 αὐτῶν πολεμούντων. καὶ γὰρ ὁ Κῦρος ἀπέπεμπε τοὺς γιγνομένους δασμοὺς βασιλεῖ ἐκ τῶν πόλεων ὧν Τισσαφέρνους
ἐτύγχανεν ἔχων.

3. ἐκπεπτωκότας: from ἐκπίπτω in today's list. See principal parts of πίπτω to locate
its tense. Then see declension of λελυκώς in 183. Find the form λελυκότας.

4. τοῦ ἀθροίζειν: articular infinitive, *of collecting* or *for collecting* (572).

5. ἠξίου: from ἀξιόω. Find the imperfect form ὕψου in the conjugation of ὑψόω (177).
δοθῆναι: from δίδωμι. This form is like λυθῆναι of λύω. οἷ: see the declension of οὗ in 72.
The pronoun is used here as an indirect reflexive, i.e. it is not in the main clause, yet
refers to the subject of the main verb.

8. ᾐσθάνετο: from αἰσθάνομαι. ἐνόμιζε . . . αὐτὸν . . . δαπανᾶν: for the form δαπανᾶν
compare γεννᾶν from γεννάω (173). Often a verb quoted in indirect discourse is changed
to the same tense of the infinitive, its subject being accusative (590). So here, *he thought
him to be spending,* or *that he was spending.* Τισσαφέρνει . . . πολεμοῦντα: (because)
*warring with Tissaphernes* (581). For the form of the noun, see declension of τριήρης (139).
It is dative with a word implying disagreement (525 A). For πολεμοῦντα, see declension
of ποιῶν (195).

9. οὐδέν: from οὐδείς, *no one* (cf. εἷς, 156), here used adverbially: *he was nothing, no
whit, distressed* (530). ἤχθετο: imperfect of ἄχθομαι in today's list. Compare ἐλύετο
of λύω.

10. αὐτῶν πολεμούντων: genitive absolute expressing cause, *because they were warring*
(582). καὶ γάρ: understand *and (well he might be satisfied) for . . . .* τοὺς γιγνομένους
δασμούς: *the tribute moneys becoming* or *accruing.*

11. ὧν: from ὅς the relative pronoun (64). It is attracted to the case of πόλεων, its
antecedent (541). One might have expected ἅς, the accusative.

12. ἐτύγχανεν ἔχων: *he happened having* or *to have* (583).

## 266. Writing exercise

1. Today's verb for principal parts memorization is λαμβάνω. Its
compound ὑπολαμβάνω, *to take under one's protection,* is seen in *l. 1* of the
reading passage in the participial form ὑπολαβών. Pick out the second
aorist principal part, corresponding to this, and write out the conjugation of the second aorist system of λαμβάνω. Use ἤγαγον, second aorist of
ἄγω (118), as a model, but keep in mind that λαμβάνω uses *syllabic,* not
temporal augment as does ἄγω. Underscore λαβών where it occurs.

2. The perfect participle ἐκπεπτωκότας (from ἐκπίπτω, *to fall out, be
exiled*) is seen in *l. 3* today. Give its declension in full (see the perfect
active participle of λύω, 183). Underscore the form which occurs in
today's passage.

# LESSON 43

## Cyrus' Friendship with Clearchus

### 267. New word list

Ἄβυδος, -ου, ἡ, Abydus, a city of Troas.

ἄγαμαι, ἠγασάμην, ἠγάσθην, to admire.

ἀντιπέρας or ἀντιπέραν, over against, on the opposite side of, sometimes with κατά.

δαρεικός, -οῦ, ὁ, daric, a Persian gold coin worth about 10 dollars (1955).

*ἑκών, -οῦσα, -όν, willing. Often best translated adverbially, willingly.

Ἑλλησποντιακός, -ή, -όν, of the Hellespont.

Θρᾷξ, -κός, ὁ, a Thracian.

Κλέαρχος, -ου, ὁ, Clearchus, one of Cyrus' Greek generals.

Λακεδαιμόνιος, -ου, ὁ, a Lacedemonian, Spartan.

*λανθάνω, λήσω, ἔλαθον, λέληθα, λέλησμαι, to lie hidden, escape the notice of; with partic., to be secret, forgotten. LETHE.

*μύριοι, -αι, -α, ten thousand. MYRIAD.

*οἰκέω, οἰκήσω, ᾤκησα, ᾤκηκα, ᾤκημαι, ᾠκήθην, to dwell, inhabit. ECUMENICAL.

οἴκοι, at home.

ὁρμάω, ὁρμήσω, ὥρμησα, ὥρμηκα, ὥρμημαι, ὡρμήθην, to start out, rush. HORMONE.

*στρατιώτης, -ου, ὁ, soldier.

συγγίγνομαι (see γίγνομαι for prin. parts), to be with, meet, become acquainted with.

συμβάλλω (see βάλλω for prin. parts), to throw together, contribute, collect. SYMBOLIZE.

*τρέφω, θρέψω, ἔθρεψα, τέτροφα, τέθραμμαι, ἐθρέφθην or ἐτράφην, to nurture, nourish, feed, support. DYSTROPHY.

*τρόπος, -ου, ὁ, a turning, way, manner, character. TROPICS.

φυγάς, -άδος, ὁ, exile. REFUGEE.

Χερρόνησος, -ου, ἡ, the Chersonese, a Thracian peninsula.

*χρῆμα, -ατος, τό, a thing of use, goods; τὰ χρήματα, often money.

χρυσίον, -ου, τό, gold, money. CHRYSALIS.

### 268. Principal parts to be memorized

βάλλω, βαλῶ, ἔβαλον, βέβληκα, βέβλημαι, ἐβλήθην, to throw.

### 269. Reading passage (Anabasis 1.1.9.1–1.1.9.10)

Ἄλλο δὲ στράτευμα αὐτῷ συνελέγετο ἐν Χερρονήσῳ τῇ   9
κατ' ἀντιπέρας Ἀβύδου τόνδε τὸν τρόπον. Κλέαρχος Λακε-

---

1. συνελέγετο: imperfect passive of συλλέγω. Compares with ἐλύετο of λύω. τῇ κατ' ἀντιπέρας Ἀβύδου: literally, the (Chersonese) along the opposite of, or along over against, Abydus. Drop one of the prepositions and translate, that over against Abydus.

2. τόνδε τὸν τρόπον: adverbial accusative (530).

δαιμόνιος φυγὰς ἦν· τούτῳ συγγενόμενος ὁ Κῦρος ἠγάσθη
τε αὐτὸν καὶ δίδωσιν αὐτῷ μυρίους δαρεικούς. ὁ δὲ λαβὼν τὸ
5 χρυσίον στράτευμα συνέλεξεν ἀπὸ τούτων τῶν χρημάτων καὶ
ἐπολέμει ἐκ Χερρονήσου ὁρμώμενος τοῖς Θρᾳξὶ τοῖς ὑπὲρ
Ἑλλήσποντον οἰκοῦσι καὶ ὠφέλει τοὺς Ἕλληνας· ὥστε καὶ
χρήματα συνεβάλλοντο αὐτῷ εἰς τὴν τροφὴν τῶν στρατιωτῶν αἱ Ἑλλησποντιακαὶ πόλεις ἑκοῦσαι. τοῦτο δ' αὖ οὕτω
10 τρεφόμενον ἐλάνθανεν αὐτῷ τὸ στράτευμα.

3. **συγγενόμενος**: from συγγίγνομαι. γενόμενος is from ἐγενόμην, second aorist of
γίγνομαι. **ἠγάσθη**: from ἄγαμαι in today's list.
4. **δίδωσι(ν)**: see the conjugation of δίδωμι (227). **λαβών**: participle from ἔλαβον,
second aorist of λαμβάνω.
5. **συνέλεξε(ν)**: from συλλέγω. See principal parts of λέγω.
6. **ὁρμώμενος**: present middle participle of ὁρμάω. Find γεννώμενος in the chart of
γεννάω (173). **τοῖς Θρᾳξί**: dative with a word implying disagreement (525A). **ὑπὲρ
Ἑλλήσποντον οἰκοῦσι**: use of accusative here shows that the idea of *motion towards* must
be implied, i.e. *those going and dwelling above the Hellespont*. For the form οἰκοῦσι, compare
ποιοῦσι in the present active participle of ποιέω (195).
7. **ὠφέλει**: imperfect of ὠφελέω. Like ἐποίει in the chart of ποιέω (164).
8. **συνεβάλλοντο**: from συμβάλλω. Imperfect middle, like ἐλύοντο of λύω. **εἰς τὴν
τροφήν**: *to the support*, or *for the support*, expressive of purpose.
9. **ἑκοῦσαι**: from ἑκών in today's list. This is a somewhat irregular adjective which
declines like the participle ὤν, οὖσα, ὄν, *being*. See 180 and find οὖσαι, the corresponding
form. Translate ἑκοῦσαι adverbially, *willingly*. **τοῦτο**: goes with τὸ στράτευμα, *this
army*.
10. **τρεφόμενον ἐλάνθανε**: λανθάνω frequently uses a participle (583). Literally, *being
supported escaped notice*. A bit more smooth is the rendering, *was secretly supported*.

### 270. Writing exercise

1. The form ἠγάσθη, *he admired*, occurs in *l. 3* of today's story. It is
aorist passive in form, from the deponent verb ἄγαμαι (see principal
parts in today's word list). Write out its first passive system, both aorist
and future. Use λύω as a model (97), but remember that ἄγαμαι uses
*temporal* augment for the aorist indicative. Underscore ἠγάσθη in the
resulting chart.

2. *L. 2* carries the phrase τόνδε τὸν τρόπον, adverbial accusative,
translating, *in this* (the following) *manner*. Decline the entire phrase (see
ὅδε, 65, and ὁ ἄνθρωπος, 49). Underscore the forms as seen in *l. 2*.

## LESSON 44

## The Contingent in Thessaly

### 271. New word list

ἀντιστασιώτης, -ου, ὁ, one of the opposite faction, political opponent.

Ἀρίστιππος, -ου, ὁ, Aristippus, a Thessalian mercenary general.

Ἀχαιός, -οῦ, ὁ, an Achaean.

Βοιώτιος, -ου, ὁ, a Boeotian, a Greek from Boeotia.

*δέω, δεήσω, ἐδέησα, δεδέηκα, δεδέημαι, ἐδεήθην, to lack, need; as passive deponent, δέομαι, to desire, request.

δισχίλιοι, -αι, -α, two thousand.

Θετταλός, -οῦ, ὁ, a Thessalian.

καταλύω (see λύω for prin. parts), to dissolve, end, make peace. CATALYST.

*κελεύω, κελεύσω, ἐκέλευσα, κεκέλευκα, κεκέλευσμαι, ἐκελεύσθην, to command, bid.

μήν, μηνός, ὁ, month. MOON.

Μιλήσιος, -ου, ὁ, a Milesian.

*ξένος, -ου, ὁ, a foreigner, guest-friend, mercenary soldier. XENOPHON, XENOPHOBIA.

παρέχω (see ἔχω for prin. parts), to afford, provide, offer.

περιγίγνομαι (see γίγνομαι for prin.

parts), to be superior, get the better of, with gen.

πιέζω, πιέσω, ἐπίεσα, ἐπιέσθην, to press hard.

Πισίδαι, -ῶν, οἱ, the Pisidians.

*πρᾶγμα, -ατος, τό, an affair, doing, business; in a bad sense, πράγματα παρέχειν, to cause trouble. PRAGMATIC.

Πρόξενος, -ου, ὁ, Proxenus, a Boeotian friend of Cyrus.

*πρόσθεν, earlier, before; πρόσθεν . . . ἤ or πρόσθεν . . . πρίν, sooner than, before.

Σοφαίνετος, -ου, ὁ, Sophaenetus of Stymphalus in Arcadia, a friend of Cyrus.

*στρατεύω, στρατεύσω, ἐστράτευσα, ἐστράτευμαι, to make an expedition, take the field.

Στυμφάλιος, -ου, ὁ, a Stymphalian, native of Stymphalus.

*συμβουλεύω (see βουλεύω for prin. parts), to advise, counsel; mid., to consult with, ask advice.

Σωκράτης, -ους, ὁ, Socrates, an Achaean friend of Cyrus.

τετρακισχίλιοι, -αι, -α, four thousand.

### 272. Principal parts to be memorized

δίδωμι, δώσω, ἔδωκα, δέδωκα, δέδομαι, ἐδόθην, to give.

### 273. Reading passage (Anabasis 1.1.10.1–1.1.11.8)

Ἀρίστιππος δὲ ὁ Θετταλὸς ξένος ὢν ἐτύγχανεν αὐτῷ, καὶ    10
πιεζόμενος ὑπὸ τῶν οἴκοι ἀντιστασιωτῶν ἔρχεται πρὸς τὸν

1. ὢν ἐτύγχανεν: happened being, happened to be (583).

2. ὑπὸ τῶν ἀντιστασιωτῶν: by his party opponents. Agency is frequently expressed by ὑπό with the genitive.

Κῦρον καὶ αἰτεῖ αὐτὸν εἰς δισχιλίους ξένους καὶ τριῶν μηνῶν
μισθόν, ὡς οὕτως περιγενόμενος ἂν τῶν ἀντιστασιωτῶν. ὁ
5   δὲ Κῦρος δίδωσιν αὐτῷ εἰς τετρακισχιλίους καὶ ἓξ μηνῶν
μισθόν, καὶ δεῖται αὐτοῦ μὴ πρόσθεν καταλῦσαι πρὸς τοὺς
ἀντιστασιώτας πρὶν ἂν αὐτῷ συμβουλεύσηται. οὕτω δὲ αὖ
τὸ ἐν Θετταλίᾳ ἐλάνθανεν αὐτῷ τρεφόμενον στράτευμα. Πρό-    11
ξενον δὲ τὸν Βοιώτιον ξένον ὄντα ἐκέλευσε λαβόντα ἄνδρας
10   ὅτι πλείστους παραγενέσθαι, ὡς εἰς Πισίδας βουλόμενος
στρατεύεσθαι, ὡς πράγματα παρεχόντων τῶν Πισιδῶν τῇ
ἑαυτοῦ χώρᾳ. Σοφαίνετον δὲ τὸν Στυμφάλιον καὶ Σωκράτην
τὸν Ἀχαιόν, ξένους ὄντας καὶ τούτους, ἐκέλευσεν ἄνδρας
λαβόντας ἐλθεῖν ὅτι πλείστους, ὡς πολεμήσων Τισσαφέρνει
15   σὺν τοῖς φυγάσι τοῖς Μιλησίων. καὶ ἐποίουν οὕτως οὗτοι.

3. **αἰτεῖ αὐτὸν ... ξένους**: αἰτέω often takes accusative of the thing asked plus
accusative of the person from whom asked. He asks him (for) mercenaries (532). **εἰς
δισχιλίους**: to two thousand. We would say, up to two thousand or about two thousand.
4. **ὡς οὕτως περιγενόμενος ἂν τῶν ἀντιστασιωτῶν**: understand λέγων, saying. This
is a future less vivid ('should—would') condition in indirect discourse, using a participle for its main verb (i.e. the verb of the apodosis). See 604 for the structure of the
future less vivid condition, noting particularly its adaptation to indirect discourse with
the participle (ἔχον). In the sentence at hand the protasis is implied in the adverb
οὕτως, thus, in that case, which carries the sense εἰ διδοίη ξένους, if he should give mercenaries.
The apodosis, which was originally περιγενοίμην ἂν (second aorist optative of περιγίγνομαι), I would get the better of . . ., is changed into the same tense (second aorist) of
the participle, with ἂν remaining. Translate, (saying) that thus he would get the better of his
party opponents. **τῶν ἀντιστασιωτῶν**: genitive with verb meaning to surpass (505).
5. **δίδωσι(ν)**: see the conjugation of δίδωμι (227).
6. **δεῖται**: middle. See δέω in today's list. **μὴ ... καταλῦσαι**: the negative of an infinitive is always expressed with μή except in the indirect statement construction.
7. **πρὶν ἂν αὐτῷ συμβουλεύσηται**: πρὶν plus ἂν plus subjunctive is of the nature of
a conditional relative with future more vivid condition implied (603): before he consults
(shall consult) with him. With συμβουλεύσηται cf. the aorist middle subjunctive λύση-
ται (97).
8. **ἐλάνθανε(ν) ... τρεφόμενον**: similar to ὢν ἐτύγχανεν in l. 1 above. Translate, was
secretly supported (583).
9. **λαβόντα**: from ἔλαβον, second aorist of λαμβάνω. Declines just as ὤν, οὖσα, ὄν,
being (180).
10. **παραγενέσθαι**: from παραγίγνομαι. γενέσθαι is from ἐγενόμην, second aorist of
γίγνομαι. Compares with ἀγαγέσθαι from ἄγω (118). **ὡς βουλόμενος**: as wishing. Here
again the particle ὡς, as, implies an indirectly stated or represented idea.
11. **ὡς πράγματα παρεχόντων τῶν Πισιδῶν**: the genitive absolute (without ὡς)
would translate, the Pisidians causing trouble. ὡς, as, brings in the idea of a saying or
representing. It could well be rendered on the grounds that, and the genitive absolute
translated as though it were a straight statement with a finite verb, the Pisidians were
causing trouble.
14. **ἐλθεῖν**: from ἦλθον, second aorist of ἔρχομαι. Compares with ἀγαγεῖν in ἄγω (118).
**ὡς πολεμήσων**: future participle. Translate, as being about to make war, or as he was going
to make war.

**274. Writing exercise**

1. Today's principal parts for memorization are those of δίδωμι, *to give*. Copy the present middle and passive conjugation of this verb (227); then complete the conjugation of its perfect middle and passive system, noting the points of similarity (compare λύω, 97).

2. Write out the declension of the neuter noun of which πράγματα (*l. 11* today) is a part (cf. τὸ ἅρμα, 146). Underscore πράγματα in the same case as found in today's lesson.

# LESSON 45

# Massing for the Big Push

**275. New word list**

ἀκρόπολις, -εως, ἡ, *upper city, citadel.* ACROPOLIS.

ἀλλάττω, ἀλλάξω, ἤλλαξα, ἤλλαχα, ἤλλαγμαι, ἠλλάχθην or ἠλλάγην, *to change, reconcile.* HYPALLAGE.

Ἀρκάς, -άδος, ὁ, *Arcadian, native of Arcadia.*

*βαρβαρικός, -ή, -όν, barbarian,* i.e. *Persian*; τὸ βαρβαρικόν, *the Persian force of Cyrus.* BARBARIC.

*ἐνταῦθα, in that place, there.*

ἡδέως, *gladly,* adverb from ἡδύς.

καταπράττω (see πράττω for prin. parts), *to accomplish.*

ξενικός, -ή, -όν, *foreign, mercenary.*

οἴκαδε, *homeward, home.*

*ὅπλον, -ου, τό, instrument, weapon.*

PANOPLY, HOPLITE.

παντάπασι, *altogether, wholly.*

*παύω, παύσω, ἔπαυσα, πέπαυκα, πέπαυμαι, ἐπαύθην, to make cease, stop*; mid., *to cease, stop.* PAUSE.

προΐστημι (see ἵστημι for prin. parts), *to put in command*; in intrans. tenses, *be in command.*

Σάρδεις, -εων, αἱ, *Sardis,* capital of Lydia.

συναλλάττω (see ἀλλάττω for prin. parts), *to change, reconcile with.*

*ὑπισχνέομαι, ὑποσχήσομαι, ὑπεσχόμην, ὑπέσχημαι, to promise.*

*φυλάττω, φυλάξω, ἐφύλαξα, πεφύλαχα, πεφύλαγμαι, ἐφυλάχθην, to keep watch, guard.* PROPHYLACTIC.

**276. Principal parts to be memorized**

ἄγω, ἄξω, ἤγαγον, ἦχα, ἦγμαι, ἤχθην, *to lead.*

**277. Reading passage** (*Anabasis 1.2.1.1–1.2.2.6*)

*Chapter 2.* Ἐπεὶ δ᾽ ἐδόκει αὐτῷ ἤδη πορεύεσθαι ἄνω, τὴν μὲν πρό-    1
φασιν ἐποιεῖτο ὡς Πισίδας βουλόμενος ἐκβαλεῖν παντάπασιν

2. ὡς... βουλόμενος: *that he wished.* Literally, *as wishing.* ἐκβαλεῖν: from ἐκβάλλω. See principal parts of βάλλω. This is a liquid-stem verb whose future forms are like the

ἐκ τῆς χώρας· καὶ ἀθροίζει ὡς ἐπὶ τούτους τό τε βαρβαρικὸν καὶ τὸ Ἑλληνικόν. ἐνταῦθα καὶ παραγγέλλει τῷ τε
5 Κλεάρχῳ λαβόντι ἥκειν ὅσον ἦν αὐτῷ στράτευμα, καὶ τῷ
Ἀριστίππῳ συναλλαγέντι πρὸς τοὺς οἴκοι ἀποπέμψαι πρὸς
ἑαυτὸν ὃ εἶχε στράτευμα· καὶ Ξενίᾳ τῷ Ἀρκάδι, ὃς αὐτῷ
προειστήκει τοῦ ἐν ταῖς πόλεσι ξενικοῦ, ἥκειν παραγγέλλει
λαβόντα τοὺς ἄλλους πλὴν ὁπόσοι ἱκανοὶ ἦσαν τὰς ἀκροπόλεις
10 φυλάττειν. ἐκάλεσε δὲ καὶ τοὺς Μίλητον πολιορκοῦντας, καὶ     2
τοὺς φυγάδας ἐκέλευσε σὺν αὐτῷ στρατεύεσθαι, ὑποσχόμενος
αὐτοῖς, εἰ καλῶς καταπράξειεν ἐφ᾽ ἃ ἐστρατεύετο, μὴ πρόσθεν παύσασθαι πρὶν αὐτοὺς καταγάγοι οἴκαδε. οἱ δὲ ἡδέως
ἐπείθοντο· ἐπίστευον γὰρ αὐτῷ· καὶ λαβόντες τὰ ὅπλα
15 παρῆσαν εἰς Σάρδεις.

present tense forms of ποιέω. So judged by its form, (ἐκ)βαλεῖν could be the future
infinitive active (like ποιεῖν from ποιέω) or second aorist infinitive active (like ἀγαγεῖν
from ἄγω,). However, the aorist infinitive would be the usual expectation after a verb
of wishing, as here.

3. **τό τε βαρβαρικὸν . . . τὸ Ἑλληνικόν:** understand στράτευμα, army, in each case.
This is a regular usage in the *Anabasis*.

5. **ὅσον ἦν αὐτῷ στράτευμα:** dative of possessor, *as great an army as there was to him*
or *as much an army as he had* (518).

6. **συναλλαγέντι:** aorist passive participle of συναλλάττω. See principal parts of
ἀλλάττω in today's list. This is the second aorist passive participle ἀλλαγείς, and
declines just as does λυθείς (184). **πρὸς τοὺς οἴκοι:** *towards those at home* (486).

7. **αὐτῷ:** dative of advantage, *for him* (517).

8. **προειστήκει:** from προΐστημι in today's list. See the pluperfect of ἵστημι (216). The
pluperfect of ἵστημι is often used as an imperfect, as is the case here. **τοῦ . . . ξενικοῦ:**
genitive with verbs signifying to *rule, lead, direct* (506). Understand στρατεύματος, *army*.

11. **ὑποσχόμενος:** from ὑπισχνέομαι in today's list. Note that the second aorist is
ὑπεσχόμην. Removing the augment on ἐσχόμην, we have ὑποσχ- as the stem. This form
is like ἀγαγόμενος in the chart of ἄγω (118).

12. **καταπράξειε(ν):** from καταπράττω in today's list. See principal parts of πράττω,
Like λύσειε in λύω. **εἰ καλῶς καταπράξειεν . . . μὴ πρόσθεν παύσασθαι . . .:** here is
a future more vivid condition quoted indirectly after a past tense (ἐκέλευσε . . . ὑποσχόμενος, *he commanded . . . promising . . .*). The future force of the apodosis is derived from
the words ὑποσχόμενος . . . μὴ παύσασθαι, *promising not to cease* (in future). The student
should review at this time the construction of the complex sentence quoted indirectly
after a verb in a secondary tense (589). Remember that a conditional sentence is
a complex sentence, whose protasis is the dependent clause (like ἐπεὶ οἱ φίλοι τιμῶνται
in the example) and whose apodosis is the main clause of the sentence. Note that the
dependent verb usually changes to same tense of optative. So the second aorist optative
here, καταπράξειε, represents an original second aorist subjunctive (and in first person
singular) καταπράξω. εἰ would have been ἐάν, *if I* (*shall*) *accomplish . . . .* Now see 603,
noting the example of a future more vivid sentence quoted indirectly after a secondary
tense. The apodosis uses an infinitive (though not a future infinitive, it has future sense
because used with the word *promising*). Translate this sentence, *promising them, if he accomplished well . . . not to cease before . . . .* **ἐφ᾽ ἃ:** antecedent, ταῦτα, omitted (540).

13. **πρὶν αὐτοὺς καταγάγοι οἴκαδε:** we have seen that πρίν plus ἄν plus subjunctive

is like a conditional relative with future more vivid supposition. So when quoted indirectly after a past tense, ἄν drops (as when ἐάν changed to εἰ) and the subjunctive verb (καταγάγω) changes to same tense of optative (καταγάγοι). Translate, *until he led them back home*. In the chart of ἄγω (118) locate the forms ἀγάγω, and ἀγάγοι.

15. παρῆσαν: from πάρειμι, conjugates like εἰμί (132).

## 278. Writing exercise

1. The form καταγάγοι (*l. 13* today) is the second aorist optative of κατάγω, whose conjugation involves the prefixing of κατ(α)- to the forms of ἄγω whose principal parts are to be memorized in connection with today's lesson. Conjugate the tense system of κατάγω in which this particular form occurs, underscoring this form (cf. ἄγω, 118).

2. Decline the noun of which ἀκροπόλεις (*l. 9*) is a part (see 152). Underscore this form where it occurs. To determine its case, consult its use in the sentence where it is found.

## LESSON 46

# The Roster of the Troops

## 279. New word list

ἀντιπαρασκευάζομαι (see παρα-σκευάζω for prin. parts), *to prepare one's self in return, make counter-preparation.*

γυμνής, -ῆτος, or γυμνήτης, -ου, ὁ, *light-armed foot soldier.* A general term including slingers, bowmen, javelin throwers, and even shield-carrying peltasts. GYM-NAST.

*ἱππεύς, -έως, ὁ, *a horseman, cavalryman.*

κατανοέω (see νοέω for prin. parts), *to observe, perceive.*

Μεγαρεύς, -έως, ὁ, *a Megarian,* from Megara, a Greek city between Athens and Corinth.

νοέω, νοήσω, ἐνόησα, νενόηκα, νενόημαι, ἐνοήθην, *to observe, think, plan.*

*παρασκευάζω, παρασκευάσω, παρ-εσκεύασα, παρεσκεύασμαι, παρ-

εσκευάσθην, *to provide for, prepare, be ready for.*

παρασκευή, -ῆς, ἡ, *preparation.*

Πασίων, -ωνος, ὁ, *Pasion* of Megara, one of Cyrus' Greek generals.

*πελταστής, -οῦ, ὁ, *peltast,* a light-armed soldier carrying a small shield or target, probably several spears for throwing or hand use, and perhaps a sword.

πεντακόσιοι, -αι, -α, *five hundred.*

*στόλος, -ου, ὁ, *an expedition,* from στέλλω, *to send, dispatch.* APOSTLE.

*ταχύς, -εῖα, -ύ, *quick, swift*; as adv., ταχύ, *speedily*; θᾶττον, *faster*; τάχιστα, *most swiftly.* TACHO-METER, TACHYGRAPHY.

*χίλιοι, -αι, -α, *a thousand.* KILOGRAM.

*ὡς, used as equivalent of εἰς, *to, into.* Discussed more fully in cumulative vocabulary.

## 280. Principal parts to be memorized

ἀκούω, ἀκούσομαι, ἤκουσα, ἀκήκοα, ἠκούσθην, to hear.

## 281. Reading passage (*Anabasis 1.2.3.1–1.2.5.2*)

Ξενίας μὲν δὴ τοὺς ἐκ τῶν πόλεων λαβὼν παρεγένετο εἰς     3
Σάρδεις ὁπλίτας εἰς τετρακισχιλίους, Πρόξενος δὲ παρῆν
ἔχων ὁπλίτας μὲν εἰς πεντακοσίους καὶ χιλίους, γυμνῆτας δὲ
πεντακοσίους, Σοφαίνετος δὲ ὁ Στυμφάλιος ὁπλίτας ἔχων χι-
5   λίους, Σωκράτης δὲ ὁ Ἀχαιὸς ὁπλίτας ἔχων ὡς πεντακοσίους,
Πασίων δὲ ὁ Μεγαρεὺς τριακοσίους μὲν ὁπλίτας, τριακοσίους
δὲ πελταστὰς ἔχων παρεγένετο· ἦν δὲ καὶ οὗτος καὶ ὁ Σωκράτης τῶν ἀμφὶ Μίλητον στρατευομένων. οὗτοι μὲν εἰς
Σάρδεις αὐτῷ ἀφίκοντο. Τισσαφέρνης δὲ κατανοήσας ταῦτα,     4
10   καὶ μείζονα ἡγησάμενος εἶναι ἢ ὡς ἐπὶ Πισίδας τὴν παρα-
σκευήν, πορεύεται ὡς βασιλέα ᾗ ἐδύνατο τάχιστα ἱππέας
ἔχων ὡς πεντακοσίους. καὶ βασιλεὺς μὲν δὴ ἐπεὶ ἤκουσε     5
Τισσαφέρνους τὸν Κύρου στόλον, ἀντιπαρεσκευάζετο.

1. **παρεγένετο**: from παραγίγνομαι. See γίγνομαι for principal parts. This word means *to become present*, hence *to come*.

2. **εἰς τετρακισχιλίους**: εἰς and its equivalent, ὡς, are used several times in this passage with the idea *to, up to, about* (of numbers). **παρῆν**: from πάρειμι. See εἰμί (132.) The sense is *to be present* or *to come*.

3. **γυμνῆτας**: the -ας ending of the accusative plural of the α-declension is always long; the -ας of the accusative plural in the consonant declension is short. The accent of γυμνῆτας shows that the ultima is short. Thus this form comes from γυμνής, -ῆτος of the consonant declension, rather than from the related γυμνήτης, -ου.

7. **ἦν δὲ καὶ οὗτος καὶ ὁ Σωκράτης**: with a compound subject the English regularly uses a plural verb. In Greek a singular verb is often put with one member of a compound subject, leaving the other member without a verb expressed. Translate ἦν as though plural. **καὶ ... καί**: *both ... and*.

9. **ἀφίκοντο**: from ἀφικνέομαι. See principal parts of ἱκνέομαι.

10. **ἡγησάμενος**: from ἡγέομαι. Here the meaning is *to consider*.

11. **ὡς βασιλέα**: here again ὡς is the equivalent of εἰς. **ᾗ ἐδύνατο τάχιστα**: ᾗ understands ὁδῷ, *by what way*, dative of means (520).

13. **Τισσαφέρνους**: for the case of this noun see declension of τριήρης (139). Verbs of *hearing* and *learning* may take the accusative of the thing heard and the genitive of the person heard from (500).

## 282. Writing exercise

1. *L. 2* of today's account contains παρῆν, *he was present* or *he came*, from πάρειμι a compound of παρ(ά) with εἰμί, *to be*. Complete the conjugation of the present system, underlining the form in question. Consult the chart of εἰμί (132) for the endings. For accent, follow the rule on recessive accent, modified by these three principles: (*a*) In a compound verb, the

accent never precedes the augment (this will affect the imperfect indicative). (*b*) Infinitive endings in -ναι always accent the penult. (*c*) The participle ὤν retains its accent even when it occurs in compounds.

2. The word γυμνής, used in *l. 3*, is in the consonant declension. As today's word list shows, it has a companion form γυμνήτης which is an α-declension noun. Decline both γυμνής, γυμνῆτος (cf. ἄρχων, 146, and for accent, ἀγών, 147) and γυμνήτης, -ου (cf. προφήτης, 44). Underscore today's form where it occurs.

## LESSON 47

# The Expedition reaches Celaenae in Phrygia

### 283. New word list

Αἰνιάν, -ᾶνος, ὁ, an Aenianian, from southwestern Thessaly.

γέφυρα, -ας, ἡ, bridge.

*διαβαίνω (see βαίνω for prin. parts), to cross over.

Δόλοψ, -οπος, ὁ, a Dolopian. Dolopia was a small country near Aetolia in Greece.

*ἐξελαύνω (see ἐλαύνω for prin. parts), to march forth, march on, drive out.

ἔπειμι (see εἰμί for prin. parts), to be on or upon.

*ἑπτά, indecl., seven. HEPTAGON.

*εὐδαίμων, εὔδαιμον, fortunate, prosperous. EUDAEMONISM.

*εὖρος, -ους, τό, width.

ζεύγνυμι, ζεύξω, ἔζευξα, ἔζευγμαι, ἐζεύχθην or ἐζύγην, to yoke, bind together, fasten. ZEUGMA.

Κελαιναί, -ῶν, αἱ, Celaenae, a flourishing city of Phrygia at the sources of the Marsyas and the Maeander rivers.

Κολοσσαί, -ῶν, αἱ, Colossae, a city on the Lycus river in Phrygia. One of the early Christian

churches was here, addressed by Paul in his epistle to the Colossians.

Λυδία, -ας, ἡ, Lydia.

Μαίανδρος, -ου, ὁ, the Maeander, a winding river rising in Celaenae and flowing through Phrygia, between Lydia and Caria, to the Aegean sea. MEANDER.

Μένων, -ωνος, ὁ, Menon, one of Cyrus' Greek generals.

Ὀλύνθιος, -ου, ὁ, an Olynthian. Olynthus was an Athenian colony on the peninsula of Chalcidice adjoining Macedonia.

*παρασάγγης, -ου, ὁ, a parasang, Persian road measure equal to thirty stadia or 18,000 Greek feet, roughly 3½ miles.

*πλέθρον, -ου, τό, plethron, a measure equal to 100 Greek feet, about 97 feet, 1 inch.

*ποταμός, -οῦ, ὁ, river. HIPPOPOTAMUS.

*σταθμός, -οῦ, ὁ, a stopping-place, day's march, a stage.

Φρυγία, -ας, ἡ, Phrygia.

## 284. Principal parts to be memorized

εἴρω, ἐρῶ, εἶπον, εἴρηκα, εἴρημαι, ἐρρήθην, to say, mention.

## 285. Reading passage (*Anabasis 1.2.5.3–1.2.7.3*)

Κῦρος δὲ ἔχων οὓς εἴρηκα ὡρμᾶτο ἀπὸ Σάρδεων· καὶ
ἐξελαύνει διὰ τῆς Λυδίας σταθμοὺς τρεῖς παρασάγγας εἴκοσι
καὶ δύο ἐπὶ τὸν Μαίανδρον ποταμόν. τούτου τὸ εὖρος δύο
πλέθρα· γέφυρα δὲ ἐπῆν ἑπτὰ ἐζευγμένη πλοίοις. τοῦτον δια-    6
5   βὰς ἐξελαύνει διὰ Φρυγίας σταθμὸν ἕνα παρασάγγας ὀκτὼ εἰς
Κολοσσάς, πόλιν οἰκουμένην, εὐδαίμονα καὶ μεγάλην. ἐνταῦθα
ἔμεινεν ἡμέρας ἑπτά· καὶ ἧκε Μένων ὁ Θετταλὸς ὁπλίτας
ἔχων χιλίους καὶ πελταστὰς πεντακοσίους, Δόλοπας καὶ
Αἰνιᾶνας καὶ Ὀλυνθίους. ἐντεῦθεν ἐξελαύνει σταθμοὺς τρεῖς    7
10  παρασάγγας εἴκοσιν εἰς Κελαινάς, τῆς Φρυγίας πόλιν οἰκουμένην, μεγάλην καὶ εὐδαίμονα.

1. **ἔχων**: circumstantial participle denoting *attendant circumstances* (581). **εἴρηκα**: from
εἴρω. **ὡρμᾶτο**: from ὁρμάω. Like ἐγεννᾶτο in the chart of γεννάω (173).
2. **σταθμούς, παρασάγγας**: the accusative is used to indicate extent of time or
space (531).
3. **τὸ εὖρος**: understand ἐστί.
4. **ἐπῆν**: from ἔπειμι in today's list. See the development of εἰμί (132). Understand
αὐτοῦ, genitive after the ἐπί of ἐπῆν. **ἑπτὰ ἐζευγμένη πλοίοις**: for ἐζευγμένη see
ζεύγνυμι in today's list. ἑπτὰ . . . πλοίοις is dative of means (520). Literally, *joined together
with seven boats.* **διαβάς**: from διαβαίνω in today's list. Locate βάς in the chart of βαίνω
(211).
5. **ἕνα**: see declension of εἷς (156).
6. **πόλιν οἰκουμένην**: *an inhabited city,* as distinguished from the 'ghost towns',
πόλεις ἔρημοι.
7. **ἔμεινε(ν)**: from μένω.

## 286. Writing exercise

1. As shown by the principal parts of εἴρω today, the form εἴρηκα
(*l. 1*) is the first perfect active of this verb. Complete the conjugation of
εἴρω in the first perfect active system and in the perfect middle and passive system, using λέλυκα and λέλυμαι (97) as models. Note from the
principal parts of εἴρω that its initial ει serves as both augment (εἶπον)
and reduplication (εἴρηκα, εἴρημαι). Review 108 in this connection.

2. Decline the participle διαβάς (seen in *l. 4*). Get the nominative
singular forms, using the βαίνω chart (211). Then see λύσας (182) for the
case endings. As to βάς, the α in this stem carries the accent throughout its
declension except in the genitive plural feminine. The same is true for
διαβάς. Remember that throughout the feminine forms the stem α is

*long by nature*, but the α in the endings of the nominative and accusative singular is short. Note again the rule for the circumflex accent as given in 26.

# LESSON 48

## The Palace and Game Preserve at Celaenae

### 287. New word list

ἄγριος, -α, -ον, *wild*.

ἄντρον, -ου, τό, *cave*. ANTRUM.

Ἀπόλλων, -ωνος, ὁ, *Apollo*.

ἀποχωρέω (see χωρέω for prin. parts), *to withdraw, retreat*.

*βασίλειος, -ον, royal; τὰ βασίλεια, palace*.

γυμνάζω, γυμνάσω, ἐγύμνασα, ἐγύμνακα, γεγύμνασμαι, ἐγυμνάσθην, *to exercise*. GYMNASIUM.

δέρμα, -ατος, τό, *skin, hide*. DERMATOLOGY.

δέρω, δερῶ, ἔδειρα, δέδαρμαι, ἐδάρην, *to flay, skin*.

ἐκδέρω (see δέρω for prin. parts), *to strip off the skin, flay*.

Ἑλλάς, -άδος, ἡ, *Hellas, Greece, the Greek mainland*.

ἐμβάλλω (see βάλλω for prin. parts), *to throw in, empty, attack*. EMBOLISM.

ἐρίζω, ἤρισα, *to strive, vie with*. ERISTIC.

ἐρυμνός, -ή, -όν, *fortified*.

ἡττάομαι, ἡττήσομαι, ἥττημαι, ἡττήθην, *to be inferior, be defeated*.

θηρεύω, θηρεύσω, ἐθήρευσα, ἐθηρεύθην, *to hunt*.

θηρίον, -ου, τό, *beast, animal*.

*ἵππος, -ου, ὁ, horse*. HIPPOPOTAMUS.

κρεμάννυμι, κρεμῶ, ἐκρέμασα, ἐκρεμάσθην, *to hang*.

Μαρσύας, -ου, ὁ, *the Marsyas*, a river of Phrygia named from the satyr Marsyas.

*μάχη, -ης, ἡ, battle, fight*. LOGOMACHY.

*νικάω, νικήσω, ἐνίκησα, νενίκηκα, νενίκημαι, ἐνικήθην, to conquer, surpass*.

Ξέρξης, -ου, ὁ, *Xerxes*.

ὅθεν, *whence, from whence*.

*ὁπότε, whenever*.

παράδεισος, -ου, ὁ, *a park, game preserve*. PARADISE.

πούς, ποδός, ὁ, *foot*. In measure about 11·65 inches. PODIATRY.

ῥέω, ῥεύσομαι, ἔρρευσα, ἐρρύηκα, ἐρρύην, *to flow*. RHEUMATIC.

σοφία, -ας, ἡ, *wisdom, skill*. PHILOSOPHY.

### 288. Principal parts to be memorized

καλέω, καλῶ, ἐκάλεσα, κέκληκα, κέκλημαι, ἐκλήθην, *to call*.

**289. Reading passage** (*Anabasis 1.2.7.4–1.2.9.3*)

> Ἐνταῦθα Κύρῳ βασίλεια ἦν καὶ παράδεισος μέγας ἀγρίων
> θηρίων πλήρης, ἃ ἐκεῖνος ἐθήρευεν ἀπὸ ἵππου ὁπότε γυμνάσαι
> βούλοιτο ἑαυτόν τε καὶ τοὺς ἵππους. διὰ μέσου δὲ τοῦ παρα-
> δείσου ῥεῖ ὁ Μαίανδρος ποταμός· αἱ δὲ πηγαὶ αὐτοῦ εἰσιν ἐκ
> 5 τῶν βασιλείων· ῥεῖ δὲ καὶ διὰ τῆς Κελαινῶν πόλεως. ἔστι   8
> δὲ καὶ μεγάλου βασιλέως βασίλεια ἐν Κελαιναῖς ἐρυμνὰ ἐπὶ
> ταῖς πηγαῖς τοῦ Μαρσύου ποταμοῦ ὑπὸ τῇ ἀκροπόλει· ῥεῖ δὲ
> καὶ οὗτος διὰ τῆς πόλεως καὶ ἐμβάλλει εἰς τὸν Μαίανδρον· τοῦ
> δὲ Μαρσύου τὸ εὖρός ἐστιν εἴκοσι καὶ πέντε ποδῶν. ἐνταῦθα
> 10 λέγεται Ἀπόλλων ἐκδεῖραι Μαρσύαν νικήσας ἐρίζοντά οἱ περὶ
> σοφίας, καὶ τὸ δέρμα κρεμάσαι ἐν τῷ ἄντρῳ ὅθεν αἱ πηγαί· διὰ
> δὲ τοῦτο ὁ ποταμὸς καλεῖται Μαρσύας. ἐνταῦθα Ξέρξης, ὅτε   9
> ἐκ τῆς Ἑλλάδος ἡττηθεὶς τῇ μάχῃ ἀπεχώρει, λέγεται οἰκοδο-
> μῆσαι ταῦτά τε τὰ βασίλεια καὶ τὴν Κελαινῶν ἀκρόπολιν.

1. **Κύρῳ**: dative of possessor, *there was to Cyrus* (518).

2. **θηρίων**: genitive with word denoting fullness (501). **ἐκεῖνος ἐθήρευεν . . . ὁπότε γυμνάσαι βούλοιτο . . .**: a conditional relative with past general supposition, encountered here for the first time in the course. This is like a present general supposition in past time. In 600 observe the structure of the past general supposition, particularly as seen in the conditional relative form. Then note that the sentence at hand is analyzed as follows: protasis, relative (ὁπότε) plus optative (βούλοιτο); apodosis, imperfect indicative (ἐθήρευε). Translate, *he hunted (used to hunt) . . . whenever he wished to exercise.* . . . **ἀπὸ ἵππου**: *from horse, on horseback.*

4. **ῥεῖ**: from ῥέω.

5. **ἔστι**: signifies existence, *there is.* For the accent of this form, which is usually enclitic, see 128.

7. **ὑπό**: with dative means place where, *under, at the foot of.* **δὲ καὶ οὗτος**: *and this also.*

8. **ἐμβάλλει**: from ἐμβάλλω, a transitive verb. Understand ἑαυτόν, *itself.*

9. **ποδῶν**: genitive of measure (502).

10. **ἐκδεῖραι**: from ἐκδέρω. See principal parts of δέρω in today's word list. δεῖραι is like φῆναι in the chart of φαίνω (205). **οἱ**: the third personal pronoun, *with him.* Here it is used as an enclitic. Compare οἷ in 265, *l. 5*, where it is used as a regularly accented word. It is used here as an *indirect reflexive*, placed in a subordinate clause, yet referring to the subject of the main verb.

11. **κρεμάσαι**: from κρεμάννυμι in today's list. This form is like λῦσαι in the chart of λύω (97). So also for οἰκοδομῆσαι in *l. 13* below. **αἱ πηγαί**: understand εἰσί.

13. **ἡττηθείς**: from ἡττάομαι in today's list. This form is like λυθείς in λύω. **τῇ μάχῃ**: generally considered a dative of manner, *in (the) battle* (522). **ἀπεχώρει**: from ἀποχωρέω in today's list. ἐχώρει is like ἐποίει in the chart of ποιέω (164).

## 290. Writing exercise

1. In *l. 10* today occurs the liquid first aorist form ἐκδεῖραι, *to have flayed.* Dropping the prefix, write out the conjugation of δέρω, *to flay,* in the first aorist system. It follows the same pattern as that seen in φαίνω

(205). If more detail as to personal endings is needed, see λύω (97). Underscore δεῖραι in the conjugation.

2. Decline πούς, *foot*, from which the form ποδῶν (*l. 9*) is developed. Note its genitive singular in the word list, then use ἀσπίς (146) as a model. Recall that monosyllabic stems in the consonant declension accent the ultima of the genitive and dative, singular and plural.

## LESSON 49
# The Halt at Celaenae

### 291. New word list

*ἀγορά, -ᾶς, ἡ, market, market place.
ἀγών, -ῶνος, ὁ, an assembly, game, contest. AGONIZE.
ἆθλον, -ου, τό, prize. ATHLETE.
*ἅμα, at the same time.
*ἐξέτασις, -εως, ἡ, examination, inspection, review.
θύω, θύσω, ἔθυσα, τέθυκα, τέθυμαι, ἐτύθην, to sacrifice, celebrate with sacrifices, kill.
Κεράμων ἀγορά, -ᾶς, ἡ, Ceramonagora, a town in Phrygia. The name means 'Market of the Ceramians'.
Κρής, -τός, ὁ, a Cretan.
Λύκαια, -ων, τά, the Lycaea, a festival of the Arcadians in honor of Zeus.

Μύσιος, -α, -ον, Mysian, of Mysia, a country in Asia Minor between Lydia and Phrygia.
ὀκτακόσιοι, -αι, -α, eight hundred.
Πέλται, -ῶν, αἱ, Peltae, a city in Phrygia on the Maeander river.
στλεγγίς, -ίδος, ἡ, a flesh scraper, used by athletes.
σύμπας, -ασα, -αν, all together, all taken collectively.
Συρακόσιος, -ον, ὁ, a Syracusan, native of Syracuse.
Σῶσις, -ιος, ὁ, Sosis, a Greek from Syracuse.
*τοξότης, -ου, ὁ, a bowman, archer.
*χρυσοῦς, -ῆ, -οῦν, of gold, golden. CHRYSANTHEMUM.

### 292. Principal parts to be memorized

μένω, μενῶ, ἔμεινα, μεμένηκα, to remain.

### 293. Reading passage (*Anabasis 1.2.9.4–1.2.10.7*)

Ἐνταῦθα ἔμεινε Κῦρος ἡμέρας τριάκοντα· καὶ ἧκε Κλέαρχος ἔχων ὁπλίτας χιλίους καὶ πελταστὰς Θρᾷκας ὀκτακοσίους καὶ τοξότας Κρῆτας διακοσίους. ἅμα δὲ καὶ Σῶσις παρῆν ὁ

1. ἔμεινε: see μένω and its principal parts as shown above.
3. δὲ καί: and also. παρῆν: from πάρειμι.

Συρακόσιος ἔχων ὁπλίτας τριακοσίους, καὶ Σοφαίνετος ὁ
5  Ἀρκὰς ἔχων ὁπλίτας χιλίους. καὶ ἐνταῦθα Κῦρος ἐξέτασιν
καὶ ἀριθμὸν τῶν Ἑλλήνων ἐποίησεν ἐν τῷ παραδείσῳ, καὶ
ἐγένοντο οἱ σύμπαντες ὁπλῖται μὲν μύριοι καὶ χίλιοι, πελ-
τασταὶ δὲ ἀμφὶ τοὺς δισχιλίους. ἐντεῦθεν ἐξελαύνει στα-     10
θμοὺς δύο παρασάγγας δέκα εἰς Πέλτας, πόλιν οἰκουμένην.
10  ἐνταῦθ᾽ ἔμεινεν ἡμέρας τρεῖς· ἐν αἷς Ξενίας ὁ Ἀρκὰς τὰ
Λύκαια ἔθυσε καὶ ἀγῶνα ἔθηκε· τὰ δὲ ἆθλα ἦσαν στλεγγίδες
χρυσαῖ· ἐθεώρει δὲ τὸν ἀγῶνα καὶ Κῦρος. ἐντεῦθεν ἐξελαύνει
σταθμοὺς δύο παρασάγγας δώδεκα εἰς Κεράμων ἀγοράν,
πόλιν οἰκουμένην ἐσχάτην πρὸς τῇ Μυσίᾳ χώρᾳ.

4. **καὶ Σοφαίνετος**: understand παρῆν.
7. **ἐγένοντο οἱ σύμπαντες**: *the entire number became*, or *proved to be*. For the form ἐγένοντο
see γίγνομαι.
10. **αἷς**: from ὅς, ἥ, ὅ the relative pronoun (64). **τὰ Λύκαια ἔθυσε**: *sacrificed the Lycaea*
or *celebrated with sacrifices the Lycaean festival*. The Lycaea was a yearly festival to Zeus
Lycaeus celebrated by the Arcadians in the spring. For the form ἔθυσε see θύω in
today's word list.
11. **ἔθηκε**: see τίθημι as expanded in 229. It has the sense here *to set up, to hold*.

## 294. Writing exercise

1. Today's special study verb is μένω, *to remain*. Expand this verb in the
future system. Note again what is said in 203 about the future of the
liquid stem verbs.

2. In *l. 11* is seen the word στλεγγίδες, *flesh scrapers*. Complete the
declension of this word using ἀσπίς (146) as model.

# LESSON 50

# A Financial Crisis

## 295. New word list

ἀνιάω, ἀνιάσω, ἠνίασα, ἠνιάθην, *to
grieve, distress.*
ἀπαιτέω (see αἰτέω for prin. parts),
*to ask from, ask back, demand.*
ἀποδίδωμι (see δίδωμι for prin.
parts), *to give back, deliver, pay
off, pay.* APODOSIS.
Ἀσπένδιος, -ον, ὁ, *an Aspendian,*

native of Aspendus, a Greek
colony in Pamphylia.
*δῆλος, -η, -ον, plain, evident, manifest.*
διάγω (see ἄγω for prin. parts), *to
pass or spend time, tarry.*
*εἶμι, imperf. ᾖειν or ᾖα, to go.*
The stem is ι, pres. partic., ἰών,
ἰοῦσα, ἰόν.

ἐλπίς, -ίδος, ἡ, *hope.*
'Επύαξα, -ης, ἡ, *Epyaxa.*
θύρα, -ας, ἡ, *a door*; pl., *a residence,
headquarters.*
Καΰστρου πεδίον, τό, *Cayster-plain,*
or *Cayster-field.* A crossroads city
in Phrygia.
Κίλιξ, -ικος, ὁ, *a Cilician.*
Κίλισσα, -ης, ἡ, *a Cilician woman.*

ὀφείλω, ὀφειλήσω, ὠφείλησα or
ὤφελον, ὠφείληκα, ὠφειλήθην, *to
owe.*
πολλάκις, *many times, often.*
*στρατιά, -ᾶς, ἡ, *army.*
Συέννεσις, -ιος, ὁ, *Syennesis,* king or
viceroy of Cilicia, probably an
hereditary title, used by Xenophon as a proper name.
*τέτταρες, -α, *four.* TETRAGON.

**296. Principal parts to be memorized**

ἱκνέομαι, ἵξομαι, ἱκόμην, ἷγμαι. *to come.*

**297. Reading passage** (*Anabasis 1.2.11.1–1.2.12.6*)

'Εντεῦθεν ἐξελαύνει σταθμοὺς τρεῖς παρασάγγας τριά-      11
κοντα εἰς Καΰστρου πεδίον, πόλιν οἰκουμένην. ἐνταῦθ'
ἔμεινεν ἡμέρας πέντε· καὶ τοῖς στρατιώταις ὠφείλετο μισθὸς
πλέον ἢ τριῶν μηνῶν, καὶ πολλάκις ἰόντες ἐπὶ τὰς θύρας
5   ἀπῄτουν. ὁ δὲ ἐλπίδας λέγων διῆγε καὶ δῆλος ἦν ἀνιώμενος·
οὐ γὰρ ἦν πρὸς τοῦ Κύρου τρόπου ἔχοντα μὴ ἀποδιδόναι.
ἐνταῦθα ἀφικνεῖται 'Επύαξα ἡ Συεννέσιος γυνὴ τοῦ Κιλίκων     12
βασιλέως παρὰ Κῦρον· καὶ ἐλέγετο Κύρῳ δοῦναι χρήματα
πολλά. τῇ δ' οὖν στρατιᾷ τότε ἀπέδωκε Κῦρος μισθὸν τετ-
10   τάρων μηνῶν. εἶχε δὲ ἡ Κίλισσα φυλακὴν περὶ αὐτὴν Κίλι-
κας καὶ Ἀσπενδίους· ἐλέγετο δὲ καὶ συγγενέσθαι Κῦρον τῇ
Κιλίσσῃ.

2. Καΰστρου πεδίον: *Cayster-plain.* Cf. our *Springfield, Middlefield,* and so on.
4. ἰόντες: present participle of εἶμι, *to go.* See 233.
5. ἀπῄτουν: from ἀπαιτέω in today's list, imperfect tense. ᾖτουν compares with
ἐποίουν from ποιέω (164). διῆγε: from διάγω in today's list. For ᾖγε, find ᾖγον in the
synopsis of ἄγω (118). δῆλος ἦν ἀνιώμενος: the form ἀνιώμενος is from ἀνιάω in today's
list and compares with γεννώμενος from γεννάω (173). Literally, *he was evident being
distressed,* or more freely, *he was evidently distressed.*
6. πρὸς τοῦ . . . τρόπου: *from the character,* or *in accord with the character* . . . . ἀποδιδόναι: from ἀποδίδωμι in today's list. For διδόναι and δοῦναι in *l. 8* below, see chart of
δίδωμι (227). Also for the ἔδωκε of ἀπέδωκε in *l. 9.*
7. Συεννέσιος: genitive of Συέννεσις in today's list.
8. βασιλέως: see declension of ἱερεύς (151).
9. δ' οὖν: *at any rate.*
10. αὐτήν: shortened form of ἑαυτήν. See 73.
11. συγγενέσθαι: from συγγίγνομαι, here implying sexual relations. See γίγνομαι for
principal parts. This is second aorist infinitive comparing with ἀγαγέσθαι in the chart
of ἄγω (118).

**298. Writing exercise**

1. As can be seen from its principal parts, ἱκνέομαι has the stem ἱκ-.
This is a palatal mute (κ, γ, χ). The verb ἄγω (118) has the same sort

of stem. Conjugate the perfect middle and passive system of ἱκνέομαι. Note that the ι- of the perfect stem is long, as is shown by its circumflex accent in the principal parts.

2. In *l. 10* today occurs the form αὑτήν, *herself*, a contracted form of the third personal reflexive pronoun ἑαυτοῦ, ἑαυτῆς, ἑαυτοῦ (73). Write out the entire declension of this pronoun in its contracted form. Omit the compound forms.

# LESSON 51

## Review of the Armies at Tyriaeum

### 299. New word list

\*ἅρμα, -ατος, τό, *chariot.*
ἁρμάμαξα, -ης, ἡ, *closed carriage.*
\*ἀσπίς, -ίδος, ἡ, *shield.*
\*δεξιός, -ά, -όν, *right, right side.* DEXTROUS.
εἶτα, *then, afterwards.*
ἐκκαλύπτω (see καλύπτω for prin. parts), *to uncover.*
ἐπιδείκνυμι (see δείκνυμι for prin. parts), *to show, display.* EPIDEICTIC.
\*εὐώνυμος, -ον, *left, left side.* Lit., *of good name* or *omen,* euphemism for the side of ill omen, the left.
Θύμβριον, -ου, τό, *Thymbrium,* a city of southern Phrygia.
ἴλη, -ης, ἡ, *a troop, band, company.*
καλύπτω, καλύψω, ἐκάλυψα, κεκάλυμμαι, ἐκαλύφθην, *to cover, veil.* APOCALYPSE.
κεράννυμι, ἐκέρασα, κέκραμαι, ἐκεράσθην or ἐκράθην, *to mix, dilute.* CRASIS.

κνημίς, -ῖδος, ἡ, *greave, shin armor.*
κράνος, -ους, τό, *helmet.* CRANIUM.
κρήνη, -ης, ἡ, *spring, fountain.*
Μίδας, -ου, ὁ, *Midas,* king of the Phrygians.
παρελαύνω (see ἐλαύνω for prin. parts), *to march along, ride past.*
Σάτυρος, -ου, ὁ, *the satyr Silenus.* The satyrs were wood sprites specially associated with Dionysus.
\*συντάττω (see τάττω for prin. parts), *to form together, marshal.* SYNTAX.
\*τάξις, -εως, ἡ, *an arrangement, division, station.* PARATAXIS.
\*τάττω, τάξω, ἔταξα, τέταχα, τέταγμαι, ἐτάχθην, *to arrange, draw up, marshal, assign, order.* TACTICS.
Τυριαῖον, Τυραῖον, or Τυριάειον, -ου, τό, *Tyriaeum,* a city in Phrygia.
φοινικοῦς, -ῆ, -οῦν, *purple, dark red.*
Φρύξ, -υγός, ὁ, *a Phrygian.*
\*χαλκοῦς, -ῆ, -οῦν, *bronze.*
χιτών, -ῶνος, ὁ, *undergarment, tunic.*

### 300. Principal parts to be memorized

τάττω, τάξω, ἔταξα, τέταχα, τέταγμαι, ἐτάχθην, *to arrange, draw up.*

**301. Reading passage** (*Anabasis 1.2.13.1–1.2.16.6*)

Ἐντεῦθεν ἐξελαύνει σταθμοὺς δύο παρασάγγας δέκα εἰς　13
Θύμβριον, πόλιν οἰκουμένην. ἐνταῦθα ἦν παρὰ τὴν ὁδὸν
κρήνη ἡ Μίδου καλουμένη τοῦ Φρυγῶν βασιλέως, ἐφ᾽ ᾗ
λέγεται Μίδας τὸν Σάτυρον θηρεῦσαι οἴνῳ **κεράσας** αὐτήν.

5　ἐντεῦθεν ἐξελαύνει σταθμοὺς δύο παρασάγγας δέκα εἰς　14
Τυριαῖον, πόλιν οἰκουμένην. ἐνταῦθα ἔμεινεν ἡμέρας τρεῖς.
καὶ λέγεται δεηθῆναι ἡ Κίλισσα Κύρου ἐπιδεῖξαι τὸ στράτευμα αὐτῇ· βουλόμενος οὖν ἐπιδεῖξαι ἐξέτασιν ποιεῖται ἐν
τῷ πεδίῳ τῶν Ἑλλήνων καὶ τῶν βαρβάρων. ἐκέλευσε δὲ　15
10　τοὺς Ἕλληνας ὡς νόμος αὐτοῖς εἰς μάχην οὕτω ταχθῆναι καὶ
στῆναι, συντάξαι δ᾽ ἕκαστον τοὺς ἑαυτοῦ. ἐτάχθησαν οὖν
ἐπὶ τεττάρων· εἶχε δὲ τὸ μὲν δεξιὸν Μένων καὶ οἱ σὺν αὐτῷ,
τὸ δὲ εὐώνυμον Κλέαρχος καὶ οἱ ἐκείνου, τὸ δὲ μέσον οἱ ἄλλοι
στρατηγοί. ἐθεώρει οὖν ὁ Κῦρος πρῶτον μὲν τοὺς βαρβά-　16
15　ρους· οἱ δὲ παρήλαυνον τεταγμένοι κατὰ ἴλας καὶ κατὰ
τάξεις· εἶτα δὲ τοὺς Ἕλληνας, παρελαύνων ἐφ᾽ ἅρματος καὶ ἡ
Κίλισσα ἐφ᾽ ἁρμαμάξης. εἶχον δὲ πάντες κράνη χαλκᾶ καὶ
χιτῶνας φοινικοῦς καὶ κνημῖδας καὶ τὰς ἀσπίδας ἐκκεκαλυμμένας.

2. **παρὰ τὴν ὁδόν:** simple *place where* would be indicated by the dative case. The use of the accusative implies motion. The spring (and its outlet) were *along the side of the road*.

3. **κρήνη ἡ Μίδου καλουμένη:** for the participle καλουμένη compare ποιουμένη in the chart of ποιέω (164). Literally this would translate, *a spring, the (spring) called Midas'*. Translate, *the so-called spring of Midas*. **ἐφ᾽ ᾗ:** for ἐπὶ ᾗ. The ι of ἐπί is elided here before the vowel η, and the π of ἐπί becomes rough φ because of the rough breathing of the ᾗ. The form ᾗ is from the relative pronoun ὅς, ἥ, ὅ (64).

4. **θηρεῦσαι:** from θηρεύω. Like λῦσαι from λύω (97). **κεράσας:** from κεράννυμι. See principal parts; like λύσας from λύω. **οἴνῳ:** dative of means (520).

7. **δεηθῆναι:** from δέω. Like λυθῆναι of λύω. **Κύρου:** genitive of source (509). **ἐπιδεῖξαι:** from ἐπιδείκνυμι in today's list. Find δεῖξαι in the chart of δείκνυμι (222).

8. **αὐτῇ:** shortened form of ἑαυτῇ. See 73.

10. **ὡς νόμος αὐτοῖς:** understand ἦν. αὐτοῖς is dative of possessor (518). **ταχθῆναι:** for this form and συντάξαι, also ἐτάχθησαν in *l. 11* and τεταγμένοι in *l. 15*, see the principal parts of τάττω, and then locate the corresponding forms of λύω (97) which would be λυθῆναι, λῦσαι, ἐλύθησαν, λελυμένος.

11. **στῆναι:** from ἵστημι (216). **ἕκαστον:** understand στρατηγόν. **τοὺς ἑαυτοῦ:** understand στρατιώτας. The substantive denoting *men* or *things* is often omitted (486).

12. **ἐπὶ τεττάρων:** *upon fours, four deep.* **τὸ . . . δεξιόν:** understand κέρας, *wing*. So also with εὐώνυμον and μέσον below.

15. **παρήλαυνον:** from παρελαύνω in today's list. Here in the case of the soldiers it means *to march by.* In the case of Cyrus in *l. 16* it means *to ride by.* **κατά:** *according to, by.*

16. **εἶτα δὲ τοὺς Ἕλληνας:** understand ἐθεώρει.

17. **κράνη:** for the declension of τὸ κράνος in today's list, see τὸ ἔτος (139).

18. **ἐκκεκαλυμμένας:** from ἐκκαλύπτω. See principal parts of καλύπτω in today's list.

## 302. Writing exercise

1. Today's special verb is τάττω, *to arrange*. In *l. 10* the form ταχθῆναι and in *l. 11* the form ἐτάχθησαν focus attention upon the first passive system. Write out the conjugation of τάττω in this system, using λύω as model (97). Underscore these two forms where they occur.

2. In *l. 17* the noun form κράνη, *helmets*, is seen. Decline the noun of which this form is a part, using ἔτος (139) for reference. Underscore κράνη where it occurs. Is it nominative or accusative?

# LESSON 52
# Military Prestige of the Greeks

## 303. New word list

αὐτόματος, -η, -ον, *self-impelled, spontaneous*; ἀπό or ἐκ τοῦ αὐτομάτου, *unbidden, of own accord, by chance*. AUTOMATIC.

γέλως, -ωτος, ὁ, *laughter*.

δρόμος, -ου, ὁ, *a running, run, race, gallop, 'double-quick'.* PALINDROME.

*ἐπειδή, *when, after, since.*

*ἔπειμι, *to go on, move forward, charge, attack.* From εἶμι, *to go.*

ἐπιχωρέω (see χωρέω for prin. parts), *to move forward, move against, charge.*

*ἑρμηνεύς, -έως, ὁ, *interpreter, herald.* HERMENEUTICS.

*ἥδομαι, ἡσθήσομαι, ἥσθην, *to be glad, delight in, enjoy.* HEDONISM.

*θᾶττον, *faster*, comparative adv. of ταχύς.

καταλείπω (see λείπω for prin. parts), *to leave behind, abandon.*

*κραυγή, -ῆς, ἡ, *shout, outcry.*

λαμπρότης, -τητος, ἡ, *brightness, splendor.* LAMP.

*λείπω, λείψω, ἔλιπον, λέλοιπα, λέλειμμαι, ἐλείφθην, *to leave.* ELLIPSE.

Πίγρης, -ητος, ὁ, *Pigres*, Cyrus' herald and interpreter.

προβάλλω (see βάλλω for prin. parts), *to throw before*; mid., *to hold in front of one's self.*

πρόειμι (see εἶμι), *to go forward.*

προεῖπον (2nd aorist only; cf. εἶπον from εἴρω), *to tell before, give orders.*

σαλπίζω, ἐσάλπιγξα, *to blow the trumpet*; impers., *the trumpet sounds.*

*σκηνή, -ῆς, ἡ, *awning, tent.* SCENE.

*φάλαγξ, -αγγος, ἡ, *an armed division or formation, battle line.* PHALANX.

φόβος, -ου, ὁ, *fear, terror.* PHOBIA.

ὤνιος, -α, -ον, *for sale, saleable*; τὰ ὤνια, *wares.*

## 304. Principal parts to be memorized

ἐλαύνω, ἐλῶ, ἤλασα, ἐλήλακα, ἐλήλαμαι, ἠλάθην, *to ride, drive, march.*

**305. Reading passage** (*Anabasis 1.2.17.1.–1.2.18.6*)

Ἐπειδὴ δὲ πάντας παρήλασε, στήσας τὸ ἅρμα πρὸ τῆς     17
φάλαγγος μέσης, πέμψας Πίγρητα τὸν ἑρμηνέα παρὰ τοὺς
στρατηγοὺς τῶν Ἑλλήνων ἐκέλευσε προβαλέσθαι τὰ ὅπλα
καὶ ἐπιχωρῆσαι ὅλην τὴν φάλαγγα. οἱ δὲ ταῦτα προεῖπον τοῖς
5   στρατιώταις· καὶ ἐπεὶ ἐσάλπιγξε, προβαλλόμενοι τὰ ὅπλα
ἐπῇσαν. ἐκ δὲ τούτου θᾶττον προϊόντων σὺν κραυγῇ ἀπὸ τοῦ
αὐτομάτου δρόμος ἐγένετο τοῖς στρατιώταις ἐπὶ τὰς σκηνάς,
τῶν δὲ βαρβάρων φόβος πολύς, καὶ ἥ τε Κίλισσα ἔφυγεν ἐπὶ     18
τῆς ἁρμαμάξης καὶ οἱ ἐκ τῆς ἀγορᾶς καταλιπόντες τὰ ὤνια
10   ἔφυγον. οἱ δὲ Ἕλληνες σὺν γέλωτι ἐπὶ τὰς σκηνὰς ἦλθον. ἡ
δὲ Κίλισσα ἰδοῦσα τὴν λαμπρότητα καὶ τὴν τάξιν τοῦ στρατεύματος ἐθαύμασε. Κῦρος δὲ ἥσθη τὸν ἐκ τῶν Ἑλλήνων εἰς
τοὺς βαρβάρους φόβον ἰδών.

1. **παρήλασε**: from παρελαύνω. See principal parts of ἐλαύνω above. **στήσας**: from ἵστημι. The first aorist active participle, like λύσας from λύω. Note that ἵστημι has a first and a second aorist. Translate, *having stopped*, or *stopping*. **πρὸ τῆς φάλαγγος μέσης**: *before the middle battle line* or *in front of the middle of the battle line*.

2. **πέμψας**: like λύσας in λύω. **ἑρμηνέα**: for declension of ἑρμηνεύς see ἱερεύς (151).

3. **προβαλέσθαι**: from προβάλλω in today's list. See principal parts of βάλλω. βαλέσθαι is like ἀγαγέσθαι of ἄγω (118).

4. **ὅλην τὴν φάλαγγα**: note that ὅλην occupies predicate position (490). **προεῖπον**: from προείρω in today's list. For εἶπον see principal parts of εἴρω.

5. **ἐπεὶ ἐσάλπιγξε**: impersonal, *when the trumpet sounded*.

6. **ἐπῇσαν**: from ἔπειμι. See expansion of εἶμι, *to go*, in 233. **ἐκ δὲ τούτου**: *and out of this* or *thereupon*. **θᾶττον**: see ταχύς in the cumulative vocabulary. **προϊόντων**: from πρόειμι; present participle. With τῶν στρατιωτῶν understood, this is a genitive absolute signifying attendant circumstances: *as (the soldiers) went forward more rapidly.*

7. **δρόμος ἐγένετο τοῖς στρατιώταις**: ἐγένετο is from γίγνομαι. This phrase translates literally, *a running became to the soldiers. More freely, the soldiers broke into a run.*

8. **φόβος πολύς**: understand ἦν. **ἔφυγε(ν)**: this and ἔφυγον in *l. 10* are from φεύγω.

9. **καταλιπόντες**: from καταλείπω. See principal parts of λείπω in today's word list. The second aorist participle of λείπω is λιπών, λιποῦσα, λιπόν. This declines just as ὤν, οὖσα, ὄν (180).

11. **ἰδοῦσα**: from ὁράω, of which the second aorist is εἶδον and the second aorist participle ἰδών, ἰδοῦσα, ἰδόν. So also for ἰδών in *l. 13* below.

12. **ἥσθη**: from ἥδομαι in today's word list. This form is like ἐλύθη in λύω. **τὸν ἐκ τῶν Ἑλλήνων εἰς τοὺς βαρβάρους φόβον**: *the fear from the Greeks to the barbarians,* or more freely, *the fear caused by the Greeks upon the barbarians.*

**306. Writing exercise**

1. Today's verb for memorization is ἐλαύνω, whose first aorist is seen to be ἤλασα. The related form παρήλασε in *l. 1* comes from its compound παρελαύνω, *to march* or *ride past*. Conjugate παρελαύνω in its first aorist system, referring to λύω (97). Follow the recessive rule as to accent, except in the active infinitive. The first aorist active infinitive regularly

accents the penult. The stem -α in the first aorist is short, ἤλᾰσα. Underscore παρήλασε where it occurs.

2. *L. 11* contains the word ἰδοῦσα, feminine of ἰδών, from εἶδον, second aorist of ὁράω. This participle inflects like ὤν, οὖσα, ὄν from εἰμί (180), and carries the accents on the same syllables as do the forms of ὤν. Give the declension of ἰδών, underscoring ἰδοῦσα.

## LESSON 53

# The March through Lycaonia and Cappadocia

### 307. New word list

αἰτιάομαι, αἰτιάσομαι, ᾐτιασάμην, ᾐτίαμαι, *to blame, accuse.*

Δάνα, -ων, τά, *Dana*, also *Tyana*, a city of Cappadocia north of Tarsus, on the highway to Cilicia and Syria.

διαρπάζω (see ἁρπάζω for prin. parts), *to plunder thoroughly, sack.*

δυνάστης, -ου, ὁ, *a mighty man, nobleman.* DYNASTY.

ἐπιτρέπω (see τρέπω for prin. parts), *to turn over to, entrust.*

*ἕτερος, -α, -ον, *the other, another, other.* HETERODOX.

Ἰκόνιον, -ου, ὁ, *Iconium,* a city anciently in Phrygia near the border, later on the edge of Lycaonia. Paul and Barnabas ministered here on their first missionary journey.

Καππαδοκία, -ας, ἡ, *Cappadocia,* a country in central Asia Minor.

Κιλικία, -ας, ἡ, *Cilicia,* the country in Asia Minor of which Tarsus, birthplace of the apostle Paul, was the chief city.

Λυκαόνια, -ας, ἡ, *Lycaonia,* a country north of Cilicia in Asia Minor.

Μεγαφέρνης, -ου, ὁ, *Megaphernes.*

Πέρσης, -ου, ὁ, *a Persian.*

*πολέμιος, -α, -ον, *hostile*; οἱ πολέμιοι, *the enemy.*

συμπέμπω (see πέμπω for prin. parts), *to send with.*

*τάχιστος, -η, -ον, *quickest, most rapid,* superl. of ταχύς.

ὕπαρχος, -ου, ὁ, *underofficer, lieutenant.*

φοινικιστής, -οῦ, ὁ, *a wearer of the purple.*

### 308. Principal parts to be memorized

τρέπω, τρέψω, ἔτρεψα, τέτροφα, τέτραμμαι, ἐτράπην, *to turn.*

### 309. Reading passage (*Anabasis 1.2.19.1–1.2.20.9*)

Ἐντεῦθεν ἐξελαύνει σταθμοὺς τρεῖς παρασάγγας εἴκοσιν  19
εἰς Ἰκόνιον, τῆς Φρυγίας πόλιν ἐσχάτην. ἐνταῦθα ἔμεινε τρεῖς

ἡμέρας. ἐντεῦθεν ἐξελαύνει διὰ τῆς Λυκαονίας σταθμοὺς
πέντε παρασάγγας τριάκοντα. ταύτην τὴν χώραν ἐπέτρεψε
5    διαρπάσαι τοῖς Ἕλλησιν ὡς πολεμίαν οὖσαν. ἐντεῦθεν Κῦρος    20
τὴν Κίλισσαν εἰς τὴν Κιλικίαν ἀποπέμπει τὴν ταχίστην ὁδόν·
καὶ συνέπεμψεν αὐτῇ τοὺς στρατιώτας οὓς Μένων εἶχε καὶ
αὐτόν. Κῦρος δὲ μετὰ τῶν ἄλλων ἐξελαύνει διὰ Καππαδοκίας
σταθμοὺς τέτταρας παρασάγγας εἴκοσι καὶ πέντε πρὸς Δάνα,
10    πόλιν οἰκουμένην, μεγάλην καὶ εὐδαίμονα. ἐνταῦθα ἔμειναν
ἡμέρας τρεῖς· ἐν ᾧ Κῦρος ἀπέκτεινεν ἄνδρα Πέρσην Μεγα-
φέρνην, φοινικιστὴν βασίλειον, καὶ ἕτερόν τινα τῶν ὑπάρχων
δυνάστην, αἰτιασάμενος ἐπιβουλεύειν αὐτῷ.

4. ἐπέτρεψε: from ἐπιτρέπω in today's word list. See today's τρέπω for the principal
parts.
5. διαρπάσαι: infinitive of purpose (576). From διαρπάζω in today's list. Like λῦσαι
from λύω. οὖσαν: see the declension of ὤν, participle of εἰμί, in 180.
6. τὴν ταχίστην ὁδόν: adverbial accusative, *the quickest way* (530).
7. καὶ αὐτόν: understand Μένωνα.
11. ἐν ᾧ: understand χρόνῳ, *in which time*. ἀπέκτεινε(ν): from ἀποκτείνω. See principal
parts of κτείνω.
12. ἕτερόν: understand ἀπέκτεινε. Note the secondary accent upon ἕτερόν because
the enclitic here follows a word with acute accent on the antepenult (see 129). τινα:
see the declension of τὶς (158). It is enclitic.
13. αἰτιασάμενος: from αἰτιάομαι. Being a participle, this form has no augment as does
the aorist indicative form in the principal parts. The word αὐτούς is understood here.

## 310. Writing exercise

1. Conjugate τρέπω, today's verb, in the second perfect active, referring to γράφω (124) for guidance. For further detail as to personal
endings, consult the complete chart of λύω (97). After each form, write in
the English translation. The synopsis of λύω in 82 may be helpful for this.

2. Complete the declension of ὁ Ἕλλην, *the Greek*, underscoring the
form τοῖς Ἕλλησι, which appears in *l. 5* today. For the noun endings,
cf. μήν (147). The definite article is given in 63.

# LESSON 54

# Syennesis abandons the Cilician Pass

## 311. New word list

*ἄκρος, -α, -ον, *at the peak, highest*;
τὸ ἄκρον, *height, summit*. AKRON.

(Note: Akron, Ohio, is in Summit Co.)

ἀμαξιτός, -όν, *for wagons.*

ἀμήχανος, -ον, *impossible, impractic-able.* MECHANICAL.

ἄμπελος, -ου, ἡ, *vine.*

δένδρον, -ου, τό, *tree.* PHILODEN-DRON.

διό, *for* διὰ ὅ, *on account of which, wherefore.*

εἰσβάλλω (see βάλλω for prin. parts), *to throw into, invade*; of rivers, *to empty.*

εἰσβολή, -ῆς, ἡ, *an inroad, invasion, a pass.*

εἴσω, *inside.* ESOTERIC.

ἐπίρρυτος, -ον, *well watered.*

ἰσχυρῶς, *strongly, harshly, extremely, very.*

᾿Ιωνία, -ας, ἡ, *Ionia,* the Greek territory of coastal Asia Minor from Phocaea south to Miletus, generally considered.

κέγχρος, -ου, ὁ, *millet grass,* useful as fodder.

κριθή, -ῆς, ἡ, *barley,* plural in the Anabasis.

*κωλύω, κωλύσω, ἐκώλυσα, κεκώ-λυκα, κεκώλυμαι, ἐκωλύθην, *to hinder.*

μελίνη, -ης, ἡ, *millet,* a kind of grain.

ὄρθιος, -α, -ον, *straight up, steep.*

οὗ, *where.*

παντοδαπός, -ή, -όν, *manifold, of all sorts.*

περιπλέω (see πλέω for prin. parts), *to sail around.*

πλέω, πλεύσομαι or πλευσοῦμαι, ἔπλευσα, πέπλευκα, πέπλευσμαι, *to sail.*

πυρός, -οῦ, ὁ, *wheat,* generally plural.

σήσαμον, -ου, τό, *the sesame,* an oriental plant from which is made an oil useful for food and for medicine.

σύμπλεως, -ων, gen. -ω, *quite full,* with gen.

*τριήρης, -ους, ἡ, *a trireme, galley, warship* propelled by three banks of oarsmen, an estimated total of 174 men.

ὑστεραῖος, -α, -ον, *later, following.*

## 312. Principal parts to be memorized

λείπω, λείψω, ἔλιπον, λέλοιπα, λέλειμμαι, ἐλείφθην, *to leave.*

## 313. Reading passage (*Anabasis* 1.2.21.1–1.2.22.6)

᾿Εντεῦθεν ἐπειρῶντο εἰσβάλλειν εἰς τὴν Κιλικίαν· ἡ δὲ    21 εἰσβολὴ ἦν ὁδὸς ἁμαξιτὸς ὀρθία ἰσχυρῶς καὶ ἀμήχανος εἰσ-ελθεῖν στρατεύματι, εἴ τις ἐκώλυεν. ἐλέγετο δὲ καὶ Συέννεσις εἶναι ἐπὶ τῶν ἄκρων φυλάττων τὴν εἰσβολήν· διὸ ἔμειναν

1. ἐπειρῶντο: from πειράομαι. Like ἐγεννῶντο from γεννάω (173).

2. ἀμήχανος εἰσελθεῖν: *difficult to enter.* εἰσελθεῖν is from εἰσέρχομαι. See principal parts of ἔρχομαι. This infinitive, used to complete the meaning of ἀμήχανος, is called an *epexegetic infinitive* (574).

3. στρατεύματι: *for an army.* Dative of disadvantage (517). ἐκώλυε(ν): imperfect of κωλύω in today's list. εἴ τις ἐκώλυεν has the force of a past particular supposition. See 598 for this.

*The Cilician Gates on the Royal Road*

Darius I, who reigned over the Persian Empire from 521 to 486 B.C., improved the ancient highway from Susa to Sardis and called it the Royal Road. The pass through the Taurus Mountains into Tarsus was called 'The Cilician Gates'. The Royal Road was marked accurately every parasang ($3\frac{2}{5}$ miles). At intervals of about 4 parasangs were stages, or stopping places, with posting stations and good inns. The ordinary traveler could go the 1530 miles from Sardis to Susa in ninety days; the king's posts—by relay—in a week. The Persian invasions of Asia Minor and Greece, the Ten Thousand of Cyrus, the phalanxes of Alexander, and the Roman armies of a later day used this great highway.

5   ἡμέραν ἐν τῷ πεδίῳ. τῇ δ' ὑστεραίᾳ ἧκεν ἄγγελος λέγων ὅτι
λελοιπὼς εἴη Συέννεσις τὰ ἄκρα, ἐπεὶ ᾔσθετο ὅτι τὸ Μένωνος
στράτευμα ἤδη ἐν Κιλικίᾳ ἦν εἴσω τῶν ὀρέων, καὶ ὅτι
τριήρεις ἤκουε περιπλεούσας ἀπ' Ἰωνίας εἰς Κιλικίαν τὰς
Λακεδαιμονίων καὶ αὐτοῦ Κύρου. Κῦρος δ' οὖν ἀνέβη ἐπὶ τὰ   22
10   ὄρη οὐδενὸς κωλύοντος, καὶ εἶδε τὰς σκηνὰς οὗ οἱ Κίλικες
ἐφύλαττον. ἐντεῦθεν δὲ κατέβαινεν εἰς πεδίον μέγα καὶ καλόν,
ἐπίρρυτον, καὶ δένδρων παντοδαπῶν σύμπλεων καὶ ἀμπέλων·
πολὺ δὲ καὶ σήσαμον καὶ μελίνην καὶ κέγχρον καὶ πυροὺς καὶ
κριθὰς φέρει.

5. τῇ δ' ὑστεραίᾳ: understand ἡμέρᾳ. ἧκεν ἄγγελος λέγων ὅτι λελοιπὼς εἴη Συέννεσις: λελοιπὼς εἴη is a compound form, the equivalent of the perfect optative active
λελοίποι. Usually the single form is used for the active, while the perfect optative middle
and passive is compound. The statement here is quoted indirectly after a past tense.
Hence the original statement, λέλοιπε Συέννεσις, *Syennesis has left*, is changed to same
tense of the optative, ὅτι λελοιπὼς εἴη Συέννεσις, *that Syennesis had (has) left*. See 589.
6. ᾔσθετο: see αἰσθάνομαι.
7. ἦν: according to the rule in 589 main verbs in the indicative mood without ἄν,
quoted indirectly with ὅτι after a secondary tense, usually change to their same tense
in the optative. ἦν, quoted after the second aorist ᾔσθετο, *he perceived*, is one of the cases
which do not so change. It would otherwise be εἴη.
8. ἤκουε: this may be considered as an indirect quotation with ὅτι after ᾔσθετο in
*l.* 6, parallel with ὅτι τὸ Μένωνος στράτευμα ἦν, or the second ὅτι may be translated
*because*, making ἤκουε a dependent verb. The translation in 458 treats it in this latter
way. In a dependent clause secondary tenses of the indicative (regardless of ἄν) do
not change to optatives (589). Translate, *and because he heard . . . .* τριήρεις ἤκουε
περιπλεούσας: *he heard warships sailing around.* Another example of indirect discourse
using a participle. See 591. Translate, *he heard that warships were sailing around.* For
the absence of contraction in περιπλεούσας note that πλέω, *to sail*, is one of a small
group of dissyllabic verbs in -εω which contract only εε and εει.
9. ἀνέβη: from ἀναβαίνω. See development of βαίνω (211).
10. οὐδενὸς κωλύοντος: a genitive absolute indicating attendant circumstances
(582). οὐδενός is from οὐδείς. See declension of εἷς (156). εἶδε: see ὁράω. οὗ: probably originally from the relative ὅς, ἥ, ὅ, but in use as an adverb, *where.*
12. σύμπλεων: neuter of the rarely used adjective σύμπλεως in today's list. The words
around it are genitives used with a word denoting fullness (501).

## 314. Writing exercise

1. The second aorist of λείπω, *to leave*, is ἔλιπον, *I left.* Conjugate λείπω
in the second aorist system, following the model of ἄγω (118). Note that
ἄγω has temporal augment, while that of λείπω is syllabic. Note that in
the infinitive and participle active, and the imperative and infinitive
middle, the accent departs from the recessive principle. Again write the
English meanings after each form. See the λύω synopsis (82) if needed.
2. In *l.* 3 occurs the form στρατεύματι, *for an army.* Complete the
declension of this noun (cf. ἅρμα, 146), underscoring this particular form.

# LESSON 55

## Cyrus finds Tarsus Deserted

### 315. New word list

*ἑκατόν, indecl., *one hundred*.

ἐκλείπω (see λείπω for prin. parts), *to leave off, abandon*. ECLIPSE.

*ἔνθα, *where, whither, there, thereupon*.

ἐνοικέω (see οἰκέω for prin. parts), *to inhabit, dwell*.

Ἰσσοί, -ῶν, οἱ, *Issus*, a large city in southeastern Cilicia, site of the defeat of Darius by Alexander in 333 B.C.

καπηλεῖον, -ου, τό, *a shop, store*.

*κατακόπτω (see κόπτω for prin. parts), *to cut down, cut to pieces*.

κόπτω, κόψω, ἔκοψα, κέκοφα, κέκομμαι, ἐκόπην, *to cut, knock*. SYNCOPATE.

Κύδνος, -ου, ὁ, *the Cydnus*, a river rising in the Taurus mountains and flowing through Cilicia. Tarsus was on this river.

λόχος, -ου, ὁ, *a company*, generally about 100 men, sometimes less.

ὄλεθρος, -ου, ὁ, *destruction, death, loss*.

ὀργίζω, ὀργιοῦμαι, ὤργισα, ὤργισμαι, ὠργίσθην, *to anger*; mid. and pass., *to be angry*.

ὀχυρός, -ά, -όν, *impregnable, strong*.

πάντῃ, *everywhere, on all sides*.

περιέχω (see ἔχω for prin. parts), *to surround, hem in*.

πλανάω, πλανήσω, ἐπλάνησα, πεπλάνημαι, ἐπλανήθην, *to cause to stray, deceive*; mid., *to wander, straggle*. PLANET.

*πρότερος, -α, -ον, *former, earlier, preceding*; πρότερον, *before*.

Σόλοι, -ων, οἱ, *Soli*, a Cilician coastal city.

συστρατιώτης, -ου, ὁ, *fellow soldier*.

Ταρσοί, -ῶν, οἱ, *Tarsus*, the capital of Cilicia, birthplace of St. Paul.

ὑπερβολή, -ῆς, ἡ, *a passing* or *a pass over, an exceeding*. HYPERBOLE.

ὑπολείπω (see λείπω for prin. parts), *to leave behind*.

ὑψηλός, -ή, -όν, *lofty, high*.

### 316. Principal parts to be memorized

εὑρίσκω, εὑρήσω, ηὗρον, ηὕρηκα, ηὕρημαι, ηὑρέθην, *to find*.

### 317. Reading passage (*Anabasis 1.2.22.7–1.2.26.3*)

Ὄρος δ' αὐτὸ περιέχει ὀχυρὸν καὶ ὑψηλὸν πάντῃ ἐκ θαλάττης εἰς θάλατταν. καταβὰς δὲ διὰ τούτου τοῦ πεδίου ἤλασε 23
σταθμοὺς τέτταρας παρασάγγας πέντε καὶ εἴκοσιν εἰς Ταρσούς, τῆς Κιλικίας πόλιν μεγάλην καὶ εὐδαίμονα, ἔνθα ἦν τὰ
5 Συεννέσιος βασίλεια· διὰ μέσου δὲ τῆς πόλεως ῥεῖ ποταμὸς

1. ὄρος: this mountain is Mt. Taurus. αὐτό: refers to πεδίον above.
2. καταβάς: from καταβαίνω. Find βάς in the development of βαίνω (211). ἤλασε: see ἐλαύνω.

Κύδνος ὄνομα, εὖρος δύο πλέθρων. ταύτην τὴν πόλιν ἐξέλι-    24
πον οἱ ἐνοικοῦντες μετὰ Συεννέσιος εἰς χωρίον ὀχυρὸν ἐπὶ
τὰ ὄρη πλὴν οἱ τὰ καπηλεῖα ἔχοντες· ἔμειναν δὲ καὶ οἱ παρὰ
τὴν θάλατταν οἰκοῦντες ἐν Σόλοις καὶ ἐν Ἰσσοῖς. Ἔπραξα δὲ
10   ἡ Συεννέσιος γυνὴ προτέρα Κύρου πέντε ἡμέραις εἰς Τάρσους
ἀφίκετο· ἐν δὲ τῇ ὑπερβολῇ τῶν ὀρέων τῇ εἰς τὸ πεδίον δύο
λόχοι τοῦ Μένωνος στρατεύματος ἀπώλοντο· οἱ μὲν ἔφασαν
ἁρπάζοντάς τι κατακοπῆναι ὑπὸ τῶν Κιλίκων, οἱ δὲ ὑπο-
λειφθέντας καὶ οὐ δυναμένους εὑρεῖν τὸ ἄλλο στράτευμα οὐδὲ
15   τὰς ὁδοὺς εἶτα πλανωμένους ἀπολέσθαι· ἦσαν δ᾽ οὖν οὗτοι
ἑκατὸν ὁπλῖται. οἱ δ᾽ ἄλλοι ἐπεὶ ἧκον, τήν τε πόλιν διήρπα-    26
σαν, διὰ τὸν ὄλεθρον τῶν συστρατιωτῶν ὀργιζόμενοι, καὶ τὰ
βασίλεια τὰ ἐν αὐτῇ.

6. **ὄνομα, εὖρος**: accusatives of specification : *as to name . . . as to width* (529). **δύο πλέ-θρων** : genitive of measure (502). **ἐξέλιπον**: from ἐκλείπω. See principal parts of λείπω.
7. **οἱ ἐνοικοῦντες**: *the ones dwelling in, the inhabitants.* From ἐνοικέω. οἰκοῦντες is like the present participle ποιοῦντες from ποιέω. See its declension in 195. So also οἰκοῦντες in *l. 9* below. **εἰς χωρίον**: understand ἰόντες.
8. **ὄρη**: from ὄρος. Compare with declension of τὸ ἔτος (139). So also ὀρέων in *l. 11.*
10. **προτέρα Κύρου**: Κύρου is genitive of comparison, *sooner than Cyrus* (507). **πέντε ἡμέραις**: dative of degree of difference, *by five days* (524).
11. **ἀφίκετο**: from ἀφικνέομαι. See principal parts of ἱκνέομαι.
12. **ἀπώλοντο**: from ἀπόλλυμι. See principal parts. **οἱ μὲν . . . οἱ δέ**: *some . . . others.* **ἔφασαν**: imperfect indicative of φημί, *to say.* See 233. **ἔφασαν (αὐτοὺς) ἁρπά-ζοντάς τι κατακοπῆναι**: indirect discourse using the infinitive in the same tense as that of the original statement. Hence the original was ἁρπάζοντές τι κατεκόπησαν, *they were cut down (while) plundering something.* Quoted after a past tense, *some said that plundering something they had been cut down.* κατακοπῆναι is from κατακόπτω. See κόπτω for the principal parts. This is an aorist passive infinitive just like γραφῆναι from γράφω (124).
13. **οἱ δέ**: understand ἔφασαν. Same kind of sentence as the preceding one. **ὑπολει-φθέντας**: from ὑπολείπω in today's word list. This form is like λυθείς from λύω. See 184.
14. **εὑρεῖν**: from ηὗρον, second aorist of εὑρίσκω. Like ἀγαγεῖν of ἄγω (118). **τὸ ἄλλο στράτευμα**: *the other army* or *the rest of the army.*
15. **ἀπολέσθαι**: from ἀπωλόμην, second aorist of ἀπόλλυμι. **δ᾽οὖν**: *but certainly, at any rate.* δέ, adversative, indicates, *Whatever the case about the preceding.*
16. **διήρπασαν**: from διαρπάζω. See principal parts of ἁρπάζω.
17. **καὶ τὰ βασίλεια**: goes with διήρπασαν above.

### 318. Writing exercise

1. The form εὑρεῖν in *l. 14* is the infinitive of ηὗρον, second aorist of today's verb εὑρίσκω, *to find.* Conjugate the second aorist system of εὑρίσκω, writing out the English meaning for each form. Underscore εὑρεῖν.

2. In *ll. 1, 8,* and *11* occur forms of τὸ ὄρος, *the mountain.* Decline this noun with its article, referring if necessary to ἔτος, *year* (139). Underscore the three forms found in today's lesson, where they occur.

# LESSON 56

## Cyrus and Syennesis reach an Agreement

### 319. New word list

*ἀκινάκης, -ου, ὁ, a short-sword.

ἀνδράποδον, -ου, τό, slave, captured person, captive.

ἀπολαμβάνω (see λαμβάνω for prin. parts), to take from, take or receive back, recover.

ἀφαρπάζω (see ἁρπάζω for prin. parts), to plunder, pillage.

βιάζομαι, βιάσομαι, ἐβιασάμην, βεβίασμαι, to compel.

*δῶρον, -ου, τό, gift. DOROTHY, THEODORE.

εἰσελαύνω (see ἐλαύνω for prin. parts), to march into.

ἐντυγχάνω (see τυγχάνω for prin. parts), to chance upon, find.

κρείττων, -ον, better, braver, comparative of ἀγαθός.

*μηκέτι, no longer.

*μισθόω, μισθώσω, ἐμίσθωσα, μεμίσθωκα, μεμίσθωμαι, ἐμισθώθην, to let out, hire.

Περσικός, -ή, -όν, Persian.

πίστις, -εως, ἡ, trust, trustworthiness, a pledge, assurance.

που, anywhere.

πρόσω or τοῦ πρόσω, forward.

πω, yet. Used after a negative.

στολή, -ῆς, ἡ, a garment, robe. STOLE.

*στρεπτός, -ή, -όν, twisted; ὁ στρεπτός, necklace, collar. STREPTO-COCCUS.

τίμιος, -α, -ον, esteemed, precious, honored. TIMOCRACY.

*ὑποζύγιον, -ου, τό, baggage animal.

χρυσοχάλινος, -ον, gold-bridled.

ψέλιον or ψέλλιον, -ου, τό, armlet.

### 320. Principal parts to be memorized

ἔρχομαι, ἐλεύσομαι, ἦλθον, ἐλήλυθα, to go, come.

### 321. Reading passage (Anabasis 1.2.26.4–1.3.1.6)

Κῦρος δὲ ἐπεὶ εἰσήλασεν εἰς τὴν πόλιν, μετεπέμπετο τὸν Συέννεσιν πρὸς ἑαυτόν. ὁ δ᾽ οὔτε πρότερον οὐδενί πω κρείττονι ἑαυτοῦ εἰς χεῖρας ἐλθεῖν ἔφη οὔτε τότε Κύρῳ ἰέναι

1. **εἰσήλασε(ν)**: from εἰσελαύνω in today's list. Check ἤλασε(ν) against the principal parts of ἐλαύνω. **μετεπέμπετο**: imperfect middle of μεταπέμπω. Like ἐλύετο.

2. **οὔτε πρότερον ... ἐλθεῖν ἔφη**: here is an indirect statement using the infinitive ἐλθεῖν, introduced by ἔφη, he said. When there is no subject expressed for the infinitive, the subject of the infinitive is usually understood to be the same as the subject of the verb of quotation. Instead of ἐλθεῖν the original statement was aorist indicative, οὔτε πρότερον ... ἦλθον, neither previously did I come. . . . So translate, he said that neither previously had he come. . . . οὐδενί ... κρείττονι ... εἰς χεῖρας: into the hands of (to) anyone superior. οὐδενί is dative singular of οὐδείς, denoting advantage (517).

3. **ἔφη**: see development of φημί in 233. οὔτε τότε Κύρῳ ἰέναι ἤθελε: for ἰέναι see development of εἶμι (233). ἤθελε is imperfect of ἐθέλω, to be willing. Logically this is part of the indirect statement of the first half of the sentence. Structurally it is outside the

ἤθελε, πρὶν ἡ γυνὴ αὐτὸν ἔπεισε καὶ πίστεις ἔλαβε. μετὰ δὲ 27
5 ταῦτα ἐπεὶ συνεγένοντο ἀλλήλοις, Συέννεσις μὲν ἔδωκε Κύρῳ
χρήματα πολλὰ εἰς τὴν στρατιάν, Κῦρος δὲ ἐκείνῳ δῶρα ἃ
νομίζεται παρὰ βασιλεῖ τίμια, ἵππον χρυσοχάλινον καὶ στρεπτὸν χρυσοῦν καὶ ψέλια καὶ ἀκινάκην χρυσοῦν καὶ στολὴν
Περσικήν, καὶ τὴν χώραν μηκέτι ἀφαρπάζεσθαι· τὰ δὲ
10 ἡρπασμένα ἀνδράποδα, ἤν που ἐντυγχάνωσιν, ἀπολαμβάνειν.
Chapter 3. Ἐνταῦθα ἔμεινε Κῦρος καὶ ἡ στρατιὰ ἡμέρας 1
εἴκοσιν· οἱ γὰρ στρατιῶται οὐκ ἔφασαν ἰέναι τοῦ πρόσω·
ὑπώπτευον γὰρ ἤδη ἐπὶ βασιλέα ἰέναι· μισθωθῆναι δὲ οὐκ
ἐπὶ τούτῳ ἔφασαν. πρῶτος δὲ Κλέαρχος τοὺς αὑτοῦ στρατιώ-
15 τας ἐβιάζετο ἰέναι· οἱ δὲ αὐτόν τε ἔβαλλον καὶ τὰ ὑποζύγια τὰ
ἐκείνου, ἐπεὶ ἄρξαιντο προϊέναι.

quotation and is parallel with ἔφη. So, taken with the preceding statement, a literal translation would be, *he said that neither before had he come . . . nor at that time was he willing to go (into the hands of) Cyrus.*

4. ἔπεισε: from πείθω.

5. συνεγένοντο: from συγγίγνομαι. See principal parts of γίγνομαι. ἔδωκε: see chart of δίδωμι (227).

6. Κῦρος δέ: understand ἔδωκε.

7. ἃ νομίζεται: singular verb with neuter plural subject, as elsewhere. παρὰ βασιλεῖ: translate, *at court.*

9. τὴν χώραν μηκέτι ἀφαρπάζεσθαι: infinitive used as substantive, as also ἀπολαμβάνειν below. Note the middle voice of the infinitive, giving the sense, *to plunder for themselves.*

10. ἡρπασμένα: from ἁρπάζω. ἤν (ἐάν) που ἐντυγχάνωσιν: ἐάν with subjunctive introduces a present general or a future more vivid condition depending on whether the apodosis is present or future. Here the apodosis is found in the idea ἔδωκε . . . ἀπολαμβάνειν, *he gave (granted) to take back* . . . . This clearly has future significance. So the condition is future more vivid.

12. οὐκ ἔφασαν: see chart of φημί (233). The negative here really belongs with ἰέναι, *to go*, rather than with ἔφασαν, *they said.* But just as in the English statement, 'I don't think I'll go,' the negation is transferred illogically from the *going* to the *thinking,* so in Greek. Translate, *for the soldiers said they would not go forward.* The present tense of εἶμι sometimes has future significance, as here in ἰέναι (550). τοῦ πρόσω: an instance of the genitive of place, found mostly in poetry (511).

13. ὑπώπτευον . . . ἰέναι: no subject is expressed for ἰέναι. Therefore it has the same subject as does ὑπώπτευον. Translate, *they suspected that (they) were going.* μισθωθῆναι: like λυθῆναι of λύω. Literally, *to have been hired.* After οὐκ ἔφασαν, *they said that they had not been hired.* Same as in *l. 12,* above.

15. ἐβιάζετο: the imperfect sometimes carries the sense of attempted (conative) action (549). Here *he was forcing* clearly means *he was trying to force.* αὐτόν . . . ἔβαλλον . . . ἐπεὶ ἄρξαιντο προϊέναι: here is a conditional relative sentence made up as follows: protasis, relative (ἐπεί) plus optative (ἄρξαιντο); apodosis, imperfect indicative (ἔβαλλον). It is thus a past general supposition (600): *they pelted him . . . when(ever) they (he and the baggage animals) started to go forward.*

16. ἄρξαιντο: from ἄρχω. The first aorist is ἦρξα. Removing the augment and using the optative endings gives ἄρξαιμι, etc. It is like λύσαιμι in λύω (97).

## 322. Writing exercise

1. In *l. 16* occurs the form ἄρξαιντο, first aorist optative middle of ἄρχω, *to rule, begin*. Conjugate this verb in the first aorist system. λύω may be used as model, but remember that the σ of ἔλυσα, etc., is found in the ξ of ἦρξα. Also note that the stem α in ἄρχω is short, which will make a difference in certain accents. Underscore the form ἄρξαιντο where it occurs.

2. In *l. 2* occurs the form οὐδενί, dative of οὐδείς, *no one*. Decline this in all three genders, singular number (see εἷς, 156). Except for masculine singular nominative it accents just as εἷς. The rough breathing disappears. In the feminine, prefix οὐδε- instead of οὐδ-.

# LESSON 57

# Speech of Clearchus to his Men

## 323. New word list

\*αἱρέω, αἱρήσω, εἷλον, ἥρηκα, ἥρημαι, ἡρέθην, *to take, seize*; mid., *to choose, prefer*. HERESY.

ἀνάγκη, -ης, ἡ, *necessity, distress*; ἀνάγκη ἐστί, or with ἐστί understood, *it is necessary*.

ἀφαιρέω (see αἱρέω for prin. parts), *to take away*. Sometimes with acc. of thing taken and acc. of person deprived.

δακρύω, δακρύσω, ἐδάκρυσα, δεδάκρυμαι, *to weep*.

ἐκκλησία, -ας, ἡ, *an assembly, meeting, church*. ECCLESIASTICAL.

ἐκφεύγω (see φεύγω for prin. parts), *to evade, escape*.

εὖ, *well*. EUPHONY.

καθηδυπαθέω, καθηδυπάθησα, *to waste in luxury*.

καταπετρόω (see πετρόω for prin. parts), *to stone to death*.

κατατίθημι (see τίθημι for prin. parts), *to put down, deposit, lay up*.

\*μικρός, -ά, -όν, *small*; as adv., μικρόν, *by a little, just*. MICROSCOPE.

\*οὔποτε, *never*.

\*πάσχω, πείσομαι, ἔπαθον, πέπονθα, *to experience, suffer, be treated*. PATHOLOGY.

πετρόω, ἐπέτρωσα, ἐπετρώθην, *to turn to stone*; pass., *to be stoned*. PETRIFY.

προδίδωμι (see δίδωμι for prin. parts), *to give over, abandon, desert*.

σιωπάω, σιωπήσομαι, ἐσιώπησα, σεσιώπηκα, ἐσιωπήθην, *to be silent*.

συμπορεύομαι (see πορεύομαι for prin. parts), *to go along with, accompany, proceed with*.

τιμωρέω, τιμωρήσομαι, ἐτιμωρησάμην, τετιμώρημαι, *to avenge, take vengeance on, punish*.

τοιόσδε, τοιάδε, τοιόνδε, *of this kind, as follows*.

ὕστερος, -α, -ον, later, following;
ὕστερον, afterwards, later.
*φιλία, -ας, ἡ, friendship, affection,
tendency. HEMOPHILIA.
*χαλεπῶς, harshly, with difficulty;

χαλεπῶς φέρειν, to be grieved at.
ψεύδω, ψεύσω, ἔψευσα, ἔψευσμαι,
ἐψεύσθην, to lie, cheat, deceive,
behave falsely. PSEUDONYM.

### 324. Principal parts to be memorized

ὁράω, ὄψομαι, εἶδον, ἑώρακα, ἑώραμαι or ὦμμαι, ὤφθην, to see.

### 325. Reading passage (Anabasis 1.3.2.1–1.3.5.7)

Κλέαρχος δὲ τότε μὲν μικρὸν ἐξέφυγε μὴ καταπετρωθῆναι,    2
ὕστερον δ᾽, ἐπεὶ ἔγνω ὅτι οὐ δυνήσεται βιάσασθαι, συνήγαγεν
ἐκκλησίαν τῶν αὑτοῦ στρατιωτῶν. καὶ πρῶτον μὲν ἐδάκρυε
πολὺν χρόνον ἑστώς· οἱ δὲ ὁρῶντες ἐθαύμαζον καὶ ἐσιώπων·
5   εἶτα δὲ ἔλεξε τοιάδε. Ἄνδρες στρατιῶται, μὴ θαυμάζετε ὅτι    3
χαλεπῶς φέρω τοῖς παροῦσι πράγμασιν. ἐμοὶ γὰρ ξένος
Κῦρος ἐγένετο καί με φεύγοντα ἐκ τῆς πατρίδος τά τε
ἄλλα ἐτίμησε καὶ μυρίους ἔδωκε δαρεικούς· οὓς ἐγὼ λαβὼν
οὐκ εἰς τὸ ἴδιον κατεθέμην ἐμοὶ οὐδὲ καθηδυπάθησα,
10   ἀλλ᾽ εἰς ὑμᾶς ἐδαπάνων. καὶ πρῶτον μὲν πρὸς τοὺς Θρᾷκας    4
ἐπολέμησα, καὶ ὑπὲρ τῆς Ἑλλάδος ἐτιμωρούμην μεθ᾽ ὑμῶν,
ἐκ τῆς Χερρονήσου αὐτοὺς ἐξελαύνων βουλομένους ἀφαιρεῖ-

1. μικρόν: adverbial accusative, narrowly, by a little (530). ἐξέφυγε: from ἐκφεύγω in today's list. See principal parts of φεύγω. καταπετρωθῆναι: from καταπετρόω in today's list. This is like λυθῆναι in λύω. Note the μή which gives a double negative idea. Omit it in translating.

2. ἔγνω: see second aorist of γιγνώσκω (209). ὅτι οὐ δυνήσεται: here is a place where the verb δυνήσεται though quoted after a past tense (ἔγνω) does not follow the usual pattern of changing to the same tense of the optative. συνήγαγε(ν): from συνάγω. Find ἤγαγε in the chart of ἄγω (118).

4. πολὺν χρόνον: accusative of extent of time (531). ἑστώς: see development of ἵστημι (216). The perfect of ἵστημι is sometimes used with present significance.

5. ἔλεξε: from λέγω. τοιάδε: the following, as follows. From τοιόσδε in today's word list. θαυμάζετε: present imperative of θαυμάζω. Like λύετε in λύω (97).

6. τοῖς παροῦσι πράγμασιν: dative of cause (521). παροῦσι is present participle of πάρειμι, to be present. See declension of ὤν (180).

7. ἐγένετο: from γίγνομαι. τά τε ἄλλα: accusative of specification, both in other things or respects (529).

8. ἐτίμησε: from τιμάω. ἔδωκε: see chart of δίδωμι (227).

9. τὸ ἴδιον: translate, personal use. κατεθέμην: from κατατίθημι, to lay up. See development of τίθημι (229). Locate the form ἐθέμην.

11. ὑπὲρ τῆς Ἑλλάδος: concerning Greece, or for the sake of Greece. ἐτιμωρούμην: imperfect of τιμωρέω. Understand αὐτούς.

12. ἐξελαύνων: the verb is here transitive, to drive out. ἀφαιρεῖσθαι: takes double

σθαι τοὺς ἐνοικοῦντας Ἕλληνας τὴν γῆν. ἐπειδὴ δὲ Κῦρος
ἐκάλει, λαβὼν ὑμᾶς ἐπορευόμην, ἵνα εἴ τι δέοιτο ὠφελοίην
15  αὐτὸν ἀνθ᾽ ὧν εὖ ἔπαθον ὑπ᾽ ἐκείνου. ἐπεὶ δὲ ὑμεῖς οὐ     5
βούλεσθε συμπορεύεσθαι, ἀνάγκη δή μοι ἢ ὑμᾶς προδόντα
τῇ Κύρου φιλίᾳ χρῆσθαι ἢ πρὸς ἐκεῖνον ψευσάμενον μεθ᾽
ὑμῶν εἶναι. εἰ μὲν δὴ δίκαια ποιήσω οὐκ οἶδα, αἱρήσομαι δ᾽
οὖν ὑμᾶς καὶ σὺν ὑμῖν ὅ τι ἂν δέῃ πείσομαι. καὶ οὔποτε ἐρεῖ
20  οὐδεὶς ὡς ἐγώ, Ἕλληνας ἀγαγὼν εἰς τοὺς βαρβάρους, προ-
δοὺς τοὺς Ἕλληνας τὴν τῶν βαρβάρων φιλίαν εἱλόμην.

accusative here, accusative of the thing taken away and of the people deprived (532).
In form it is like ποιεῖσθαι in ποιέω (164).

14. **ἵνα εἴ τι δέοιτο ὠφελοίην αὐτόν**: a mixture involving the protasis of a future less
vivid condition, εἰ plus optative δέοιτο, *if he should need anything*, (see 604), together
with a purpose clause after a past tense, ἵνα plus optative ὠφελοίην, *in order that I might
help him* (see 568). Putting these together: *in order that, if he should need anything, I might
help him.*

15. **ἀνθ᾽ ὧν**: for ἀντὶ ὧν, *instead of what things* or *in return for the things which* . . . . **ἔπαθον**:
from πάσχω, *to suffer, be treated*. See its principal parts. **ὑπ᾽ ἐκείνου**: *by him (that one)*.
The genitive with ὑπό is often used to denote *agent*, with passive verbs.

16. **ἀνάγκη**: understand ἐστί. **προδόντα**: in 227, note that the second aorist active
participle of δίδωμι is δούς, δοῦσα, δόν. This would be developed as follows:

| | | | |
|---|---|---|---|
| Genitive | δόντος | δούσης | δόντος |
| Dative | δόντι | δούσῃ | δόντι |
| Accusative | δόντα | δοῦσαν | δόν |

17. **τῇ . . . φιλίᾳ χρῆσθαι**: χράομαι has its (apparent) object in the dative because its
accurate sense is, *to serve one's self by*. Thus in reality it uses a dative of instrument
or means. Translate as though a direct object (520). **χρῆσθαι**: present infinitive of
χράομαι. **ψευσάμενον**: see ψεύδω in today's word list.

18. **εἰ**: *whether*. **οἶδα**: from εἴδω. **αἱρήσομαι**: from αἱρέω. **δ᾽ οὖν**: *at any rate.*

19. **ὅ τι ἂν δέῃ πείσομαι**: for tense of πείσομαι see principal parts of πάσχω. Here
is a conditional relative set up as follows: protasis, relative (ὅ τι) plus ἄν plus subjunctive (δέῃ); apodosis, future indicative (πείσομαι). See 603, if necessary, in order
to identify. **ἐρεῖ**: see εἴρω. **οὔποτε . . . οὐδείς**: *never shall no one*. The Greeks frequently
used a double negative with simple negative meaning intended.

20. **ἀγαγών**: find this form in the chart of ἄγω (118). **προδούς**: see the note on προδόντα in *l. 16* above.

21. **εἱλόμην**: from αἱρέω. See its principal parts.

## 326. Writing exercise

1. Conjugate ὁράω, *to see*, in the future system (middle voice only), and
in the perfect middle and passive system, using λύω for reference.

2. Decline σύ, *you*, several of whose forms appear in today's lesson.

# LESSON 58

## Double-talking Orator

### 327. New word list

*ἀδικέω, ἀδικήσω, ἠδίκησα, ἠδίκηκα, ἠδίκημαι, ἠδικήθην, to do wrong, wrong, harm.

αἰνέω, αἰνέσω, ᾔνεσα, ᾔνεκα, ᾔνημαι, ᾐνέθην, to praise.

αἰσχύνω, αἰσχυνῶ, ᾔσχυνα, ᾐσχύνθην, to dishonor, shame; mid., to be ashamed.

ἀλέξω, ἀλέξομαι, ἠλεξάμην, to ward off; mid., to defend. ALEXANDER.

*ἀπορέω, ἀπορήσω, ἠπόρησα, ἠπόρηκα, ἠπόρημαι, ἠπορήθην, to be at a loss, be puzzled.

*γε, enclitic postpositive, at least, at any rate, even.

γνώμη, -ης, ἡ, opinion, intention, mind, idea. GNOMIC.

*δείδω, δείσομαι, ἔδεισα, δέδοικα or δέδια, to fear, perf. used as pres.

δίκη, -ης, ἡ, justice, punishment, penalty.

ἐπαινέω (see αἰνέω for prin. parts), to praise, approve, applaud.

ἐπιτίθημι (see τίθημι for prin. parts), to put upon, set upon, attack, inflict upon. EPITHET.

*ἕπομαι, ἕψομαι, ἑσπόμην, to follow, with dat.

*ἔρημος, -η, -ον, also -ος, -ον, deserted, deprived of, through desert, desert-. HERMIT.

ἐχθρός, -οῦ, ὁ, enemy, personal foe.

ἡμέτερος, -α, -ον, our, ours.

θαρρέω, θαρρήσω, ἐθάρρησα, τεθάρρηκα, to be of courage, be of good cheer.

λάθρᾳ, secretly; with gen., without the knowledge of.

λυπέω, λυπήσω, ἐλύπησα, λελύπημαι, ἐλυπήθην, to grieve, vex, give pain.

*μέγιστος, -η, -ον, greatest, superl. of μέγας.

μισθοδότης, -ου, ὁ, paymaster, employer.

*οἴομαι or οἶμαι, οἰήσομαι, ᾠήθην, to think, believe.

ὅπη, whithersoever, wherever.

προσέρχομαι (see ἔρχομαι for prin. parts), to go over to, join.

σκευοφόρος, -ον, baggage-carrying; τὰ σκευοφόρα, the baggage animals.

*στρατοπεδεύω, ἐστρατοπεδευσάμην, ἐστρατοπέδευμαι, to pitch camp.

*σύμμαχος, -ον, allied; ὁ σύμμαχος, -ου, ally.

συνέπομαι (see ἕπομαι for prin. parts), to follow with.

σύνοιδα (see εἴδω for prin. parts), to share in knowledge; with reflexive pron., to be conscious.

### 328. Principal parts to be memorized

νομίζω, νομιῶ, ἐνόμισα, νενόμικα, νενόμισμαι, ἐνομίσθην, to consider, think.

## 329. Reading passage (*Anabasis 1.3.6.1–1.3.10.5*)

Ἀλλ' ἐπεὶ ὑμεῖς ἐμοὶ οὐκ ἐθέλετε πείθεσθαι, ἐγὼ σὺν ὑμῖν    6
ἕψομαι καὶ ὅ τι ἂν δέῃ πείσομαι. νομίζω γὰρ ὑμᾶς ἐμοὶ εἶναι
καὶ πατρίδα καὶ φίλους καὶ συμμάχους, καὶ σὺν ὑμῖν μὲν ἂν
οἶμαι εἶναι τίμιος ὅπου ἂν ὦ, ὑμῶν δὲ ἔρημος ὢν οὐκ ἂν ἱκανὸς
5  εἶναι οὔτ' ἂν φίλον ὠφελῆσαι οὔτ' ἂν ἐχθρὸν ἀλέξασθαι. ὡς
ἐμοῦ οὖν ἰόντος ὅπῃ ἂν καὶ ὑμεῖς, οὕτω τὴν γνώμην ἔχετε.
ταῦτα εἶπεν· οἱ δὲ στρατιῶται οἵ τε αὐτοῦ ἐκείνου καὶ οἱ    7
ἄλλοι ταῦτα ἀκούσαντες ἐπῄνεσαν· παρὰ δὲ Ξενίου καὶ
Πασίωνος πλείους ἢ δισχίλιοι λαβόντες τὰ ὅπλα καὶ τὰ
10  σκευοφόρα ἐστρατοπεδεύσαντο παρὰ Κλέαρχον. Κῦρος δὲ
τούτοις ἀπορῶν τε καὶ λυπούμενος μετεπέμπετο τὸν Κλέαρ-
χον· ὁ δὲ ἰέναι μὲν οὐκ ἤθελε, λάθρᾳ δὲ τῶν στρατιωτῶν
πέμπων αὐτῷ ἄγγελον ἔλεγε θαρρεῖν ὡς καταστησομένων

2. **ἕψομαι**: from ἕπομαι in today's word list. **ὅ τι ἂν δέῃ πείσομαι**: see note on *l. 19* in 325 above. **εἶναι**: see chart of εἰμί (132).

3. **σὺν ὑμῖν μὲν ἂν οἶμαι εἶναι τίμιος**: οἶμαι, *I think*, here introduces a long indirect statement which is essentially of the structure of two future less vivid conditions. The protasis of the first is implied in σὺν ὑμῖν, *with you* (*if I should have you*). The apodosis is ἂν εἶναι, where the infinitive with ἂν represents the optative plus ἂν, *that I would be . . . .* The protasis of the second part is implied in ὑμῶν δὲ ἔρημος ὤν, *but being deprived of you* (*if I should be deprived of you*). The apodosis is οὐκ ἂν ἱκανὸς εἶναι, *that I would not be able . . . .* The ensuing infinitives, ὠφελῆσαι, ἀλέξασθαι, are complementary infinitives after ἱκανός, *able.* While ἂν appears with these, it is an unnecessary repetition of the ἂν with ἂν ἱκανὸς εἶναι, and would better have been omitted. See 604, last example.

4. **ὅπου ἂν ὦ**: *wherever I am.* This is the protasis of a future more vivid conditional relative. See 603.

5. **ὡς ἐμοῦ οὖν ἰόντος**: genitive absolute, *in terms (as) of my going, then . . . .* An unusual case where the genitive absolute carries the idea of *purpose* usually expressed by a future tense circumstantial participle (581). ἰόντος (present participle of εἶμι, 233) has future force here (550).

6. **ὅπῃ ἂν καὶ ὑμεῖς**: understand ἴητε, *wherever you also (go).* Relative (ὅπῃ) plus ἂν plus subjunctive (ἴητε): protasis of a conditional relative. The apodosis, *I will go,* is implied in the preceding genitive absolute. Hence it is future more vivid. **τὴν γνώμην ἔχετε**: may be translated as a present imperative, *have the idea.* Or as present indicative it could mean, *you have my intention.*

8. **ἐπῄνεσαν**: from ἐπαινέω. See principal parts of αἰνέω in today's word list.

9. **πλείους**: short for πλείονες. Cf. ἡδίων (157).

10. **παρὰ Κλέαρχον**: *over to* or *on Clearchus' side,* or *with Clearchus.* The accusative is used because motion is implied.

11. **τούτοις**: dative of cause, *because of these things* (521). **μετεπέμπετο**: imperfect middle of μεταπέμπω.

12. **ἰέναι**: see expansion of εἶμι (233). **ἤθελε**: imperfect of ἐθέλω. **τῶν στρατιωτῶν**: really genitive of separation, *secretly from the soldiers* (508).

13. **ὡς καταστησομένων τούτων**: a genitive absolute of cause, *as these things would take their place* or *turn out . . .* (582).

τούτων εἰς τὸ δέον. μεταπέμπεσθαι δ᾽ ἐκέλευεν αὐτόν· αὐτὸς
15 δ᾽ οὐκ ἔφη ἰέναι. μετὰ δὲ ταῦτα συναγαγὼν τούς θ᾽ ἑαυτοῦ    9
στρατιώτας καὶ τοὺς προσελθόντας αὐτῷ καὶ τῶν ἄλλων τὸν
βουλόμενον, ἔλεξε τοιάδε. Ἄνδρες στρατιῶται, τὰ μὲν δὴ
Κύρου δῆλον ὅτι οὕτως ἔχει πρὸς ἡμᾶς ὥσπερ τὰ ἡμέτερα
πρὸς ἐκεῖνον· οὔτε γὰρ ἡμεῖς ἐκείνου ἔτι στρατιῶται, ἐπεί
20 γε οὐ συνεπόμεθα αὐτῷ, οὔτε ἐκεῖνος ἔτι ἡμῖν μισθοδότης.
ὅτι μέντοι ἀδικεῖσθαι νομίζει ὑφ᾽ ἡμῶν οἶδα· ὥστε καὶ    10
μεταπεμπομένου αὐτοῦ οὐκ ἐθέλω ἐλθεῖν, τὸ μὲν μέγιστον
αἰσχυνόμενος ὅτι σύνοιδα ἐμαυτῷ πάντα ἐψευσμένος αὐτόν,
ἔπειτα καὶ δεδιὼς μὴ λαβών με δίκην ἐπιθῇ ὧν νομίζει ὑπ᾽
25 ἐμοῦ ἠδικῆσθαι.

14. **εἰς τὸ δέον**: δέον is present neuter participle of δέω, *to need*. With the article it is used in the sense of *the needful, the good*. **αὐτός:** *he himself*.

15. **οὐκ ἔφη ἰέναι**: see the note on 321, *l. 12.* **θ᾽**: for τε, with ε elided before a vowel, and τ changed to θ because the following vowel is rough, or aspirated.

16. **προσελθόντας**: from προσέρχομαι in today's list. ἐλθόντας is the participle from ἦλθον and is declined like ὤν, οὖσα, ὄν (180).

17. **τὰ μὲν δὴ Κύρου**: accusative of specification (understand πράγματα), *as to the affairs (relationships) of Cyrus indeed* (529).

18. **δῆλον**: understand ἐστί. **οὕτως ἔχει**: *they are thus, this way* or *the same.*

19. **ἡμεῖς**: understand ἐσμέν.

20. **ἐκεῖνος**: understand ἐστί.

22. **μεταπεμπομένου αὐτοῦ**: genitive absolute denoting concession, *although he summons*, or *continues to summon* (582). **ἐλθεῖν**: infinitive from ἦλθον, second aorist of ἔρχομαι. **τὸ μὲν μέγιστον**: adverbial accusative, *most* or *chiefly* (530).

23. **πάντα**: accusative of specification, *as to all things* or *in all respects* (529). **ἐψευσμένος**: from ψεύδω.

24. **δεδιώς**: from δέδια, second perfect of δείδω, *to fear.* Translate as though a present participle, *fearing.* **μὴ . . . ἐπιθῇ**: a clause of fearing after primary tense (563). ἐπιθῇ is from ἐπιτίθημι, *to inflict.* See development of τίθημι (229). Locate θῇ. **ὧν**: *of what things* or *for what things.* The genitive is used with verbs of judicial action to indicate the crime for which the action is taken (497).

25. **ἠδικῆσθαι**: from ἀδικέω. Like λελύσθαι from λύω (97).

## 330. Writing exercise

1. Today's verb νομίζω (stem νομιδ-) is similar to βαπτίζω (113). Conjugate νομίζω in the first passive system. The λύω chart gives more details as to endings, if needed.

2. πλείους in today's passage (*l. 9*) is a contracted alternative form in the declension of πλείων, *more* (comparative of πολύς, *much*). Decline πλείων (cf. ἡδίων, 157), showing the alternative contracted forms. Underscore πλείους, determining from its use in the reading passage whether it is nominative or accusative.

# LESSON 59

## Clearchus warns of Cyrus' Wrath

### 331. New word list

ἀμελέω, ἀμελήσω, ἠμέλησα, ἠμέληκα, to neglect, be negligent of.

ἄνευ, without.

ἀπάγω (see ἄγω for prin. parts), to lead back, lead away.

ἄπειμι (from εἶμι), to go away.

ἀποπλέω (see πλέω for prin. parts), to sail away.

ἀπορία, -ας, ἡ, difficulty.

*ἄριστος, -η, -ον, finest, noblest, bravest, superl. of ἀγαθός. ARISTOCRACY.

*ἀσφαλής, -ές, safe, secure, 'non-slipping'; comp., ἀσφαλέστερος; superl., ἀσφαλέστατος.

αὐτοῦ, here.

ἐγκέλευστος, prompted.

ἐπίσταμαι, ἐπιστήσομαι, ἠπιστήθην, to know, know how. EPISTEMOLOGY.

*ἐπιτήδειος, -α, -ον, suitable, fitting; τὰ ἐπιτήδεια, provisions, supplies.

*ἕως, as long as; with ἄν plus subjunctive, until.

ἡγεμών, -όνος, ὁ, leader, guide. HEGEMONY.

ἰδιώτης, -ου, ὁ, private soldier, person in private status. IDIOT.

ἱππικός, -ή, -όν, on horse, cavalry.

καθεύδω, καθευδήσω, ἐκαθεύδησα, κεκαθεύδηκα, to sleep, go to sleep.

ναυτικός, -ή, -όν, naval. NAUTICAL.

οἷος, -α, -ον, such as, of such a kind as, of what sort.

ὄφελος, τό (nom. and acc. sing. only), help, advantage, use.

πεζός, -ή, -όν, on foot, infantry.

πόρρω, afar, far off, far from.

προσποιέομαι (see ποιέω for prin. parts), to pretend.

σκεπτέος, -α, -ον, to be enquired or deliberated, verbal adjective of σκέπτομαι.

σκέπτομαι, σκέψομαι, ἐσκεψάμην, ἔσκεμμαι, to view, search out, deliberate. SCEPTIC.

σπεύδω, σπεύσω, ἔσπευσα, to urge, be eager, hasten.

συσκευάζω, to pack up.

χαλεπός, -ή, -όν, difficult, harsh, grievous; superlative, χαλεπώτατος.

*χρή, χρήσει (imperf. ἐχρῆν or χρῆν), impersonal, it is necessary.

### 332. Principal parts to be memorized

γιγνώσκω, γνώσομαι, ἔγνων, ἔγνωκα, ἔγνωσμαι, ἐγνώσθην, to know, be convinced.

### 333. Reading passage (Anabasis 1.3.11.1–1.3.14.8)

Ἐμοὶ οὖν δοκεῖ οὐχ ὥρα εἶναι ἡμῖν καθεύδειν οὐδ'    11
ἀμελεῖν ἡμῶν αὐτῶν, ἀλλὰ βουλεύεσθαι ὅ τι χρὴ ποιεῖν ἐκ
τούτων. καὶ ἕως τε μένομεν αὐτοῦ σκεπτέον μοι δοκεῖ εἶναι

2. ἡμῶν αὐτῶν: plural of ἐμαυτοῦ (73). ἀμελέω often takes the genitive. ἐκ τούτων: from these things or next.

3. σκεπτέον μοι δοκεῖ εἶναι: verbal adjectives in -τέος, -τέα, -τέον denote necessity.
A verbal adjective may agree with a noun, as ὁ ποταμὸς διαβατέος ἐστί, the river must be

ὅπως ὡς ἀσφαλέστατα μένωμεν, εἴ τε ἤδη δοκεῖ ἀπιέναι,
5    ὅπως ὡς ἀσφαλέστατα ἄπιμεν, καὶ ὅπως τὰ ἐπιτήδεια
ἕξομεν· ἄνευ γὰρ τούτων οὔτε στρατηγοῦ οὔτε ἰδιώτου
ὄφελος οὐδέν. ὁ δ' ἀνὴρ πολλοῦ μὲν ἄξιος φίλος ᾧ ἂν φίλος ᾖ,        12
χαλεπώτατος δ' ἐχθρὸς ᾧ ἂν πολέμιος ᾖ, ἔχει δὲ δύναμιν καὶ
πεζήν καὶ ἱππικὴν καὶ ναυτικὴν ἣν πάντες ὁμοίως ὁρῶμέν τε
10   καὶ ἐπιστάμεθα· καὶ γὰρ οὐδὲ πόρρω δοκοῦμέν μοι αὐτοῦ
καθῆσθαι. ὥστε ὥρα λέγειν ὅ τι τις γιγνώσκει ἄριστον
εἶναι. ταῦτα εἰπὼν ἐπαύσατο. ἐκ δὲ τούτου ἀνίσταντο οἱ        13
μὲν ἐκ τοῦ αὐτομάτου, λέξοντες ἃ ἐγίγνωσκον, οἱ δὲ καὶ ὑπ'
ἐκείνου ἐγκέλευστοι, ἐπιδεικνύντες οἵα εἴη ἡ ἀπορία ἄνευ τῆς
15   Κύρου γνώμης καὶ μένειν καὶ ἀπιέναι. εἰς δὲ δὴ εἶπε, προσ-        14
ποιούμενος σπεύδειν ὡς τάχιστα πορεύεσθαι εἰς τὴν Ἑλλάδα,
στρατηγοὺς μὲν ἑλέσθαι ἄλλους ὡς τάχιστα, εἰ μὴ βούλεται
Κλέαρχος ἀπάγειν· τὰ δ' ἐπιτήδει' ἀγοράζεσθαι—ἡ δ' ἀγορὰ
ἦν ἐν τῷ βαρβαρικῷ στρατεύματι—καὶ συσκευάζεσθαι·
20   ἐλθόντας δὲ Κῦρον αἰτεῖν πλοῖα, ὡς ἀποπλέοιεν· ἐὰν δὲ μὴ

crossed; or it may be used impersonally, σκεπτέον ἐστί, it must be inquired (literally, it is to
be inquired). The dative of agent is often used with a verbal adjective in -τέος (519).
Translate the above, it seems to me that it must be deliberated.
    4. ὅπως . . . μένωμεν: a purpose clause, ὅπως plus the subjunctive. ὡς ἀσφαλέστατα:
ὡς is often used with the superlative adjective or adverb to mean, as here, as safely as
possible. ἀπιέναι: from ἄπειμι. See εἶμι (233).
    5. ὅπως . . . ἄπιμεν: an object clause. Verbs signifying to care for, strive for, effect
often take an object clause consisting of ὅπως plus the future indicative (554). ἄπειμι
(from εἶμι) has no future in form, but the present often has a future sense. For ἄπιμεν
see development of εἶμι (233). Translate, that we shall depart. The following clause,
ὅπως . . . ἕξομεν, is also a regular object clause. ἕξομεν is future of ἔχω, to have. Translate, that we shall have.
    7. ὄφελος οὐδέν: understand ἐστί, there is no use. . . . πολλοῦ . . . ἄξιος: worth much.
πολλοῦ is genitive of value (503). ἄξιος φίλος (ἐστὶ) ᾧ ἂν φίλος ᾖ: a conditional relative sentence set up as follows: protasis (follows apodosis), relative (ᾧ) plus ἂν plus
subjunctive; apodosis, present indicative (ἐστί understood). Hence a present general
condition is implied. The following sentence is similar in its construction (599).
    8. ᾖ: see chart of εἰμί (132).
    10. καὶ γάρ: and (well we may) for . . . .
    11. καθῆσθαι: present infinitive of κάθημαι, to sit, be situated. ὥρα: understand ἐστί.
    12. ἐκ δὲ τούτου: and thereupon. ἀνίσταντο: from ἀνίστημι. Find ἵσταντο in the chart
of ἵστημι (216). οἱ μὲν . . . οἱ δέ: some . . . others.
    13. λέξοντες: future participle of λέγω, expressing purpose (581). Translate, to say.
    14. ἐπιδεικνύντες: from ἐπιδείκνυμι. The present active participle of δείκνυμι (222)
is δεικνύς, -ῦσα, -ύν, (genitives) δεικνύντος, δεικνύσης, δεικνύντος, and so on.
    16. ὡς τάχιστα: see ταχύς. With ὡς, as quickly as possible.
    17. ἑλέσθαι: from αἱρέω. See principal parts. Second aorist indicative is εἷλον.
The unaugmented stem is ἑλ-. Active infinitive is ἑλεῖν; middle infinitive, ἑλέσθαι, to
choose.
    20. ἐλθόντας: from ἦλθον, second aorist of ἔρχομαι. Declined like ὤν, οὖσα, ὄν (180).

διδῷ ταῦτα, ἡγεμόνα αἰτεῖν Κῦρον ὅστις διὰ φιλίας τῆς χώρας ἀπάξει.

Understand αὐτούς, (*for*) *them going* . . . . **Κῦρον αἰτεῖν πλοῖα**: αἰτέω, *to demand*, takes double accusative (532). **ὡς ἀποπλέοιεν**: purpose clause using ὡς with optative (568). ἀποπλέοιεν here is uncontracted. Recall note on 313, *l. 8*.

21. **διδῷ**: see chart of δίδωμι (227).
22. **ἀπάξει**: from ἀπάγω.

### 334. Writing exercise

1. In *l. 12* today occurs the verb form ἀνίσταντο, *they stood*. It is a part of ἀνίστημι, a compound of ἵστημι (216). Conjugate ἀνίστημι in the present system, underscoring ἀνίσταντο.

2. The adverb ἀσφαλέστατα in *ll. 4* and *5* today is really the neuter plural of the superlative of ἀσφαλής, *safe*. Locating a similar form as model (237), give the comparison of ἀσφαλής—positive, comparative, and superlative.

3. Give all the comparisons also of the adjective in whose comparison ἄριστον, *best*, in *l. 11* belongs. Consult 238.

# LESSON 60

# The Democratic Process

### 335. New word list

ἄκων, -ουσα, -ον, *unwilling*.

ἀναρπάζω (see ἁρπάζω for prin. parts), *to snatch up, carry off as booty*.

δυνατός, -ή, -όν, *able, possible*.

*δύω, δύσω, ἔδυσα or ἔδυν, δέδυκα, δέδυμαι, ἐδύθην, *to enter, put on, sink*; of the sun, *to set*.

ἐμβαίνω (see βαίνω for prin. parts), *to enter, embark*.

ἐνοράω (see ὁράω for prin. parts), *to see in* something.

εὐήθεια, -ας, ἡ, *foolishness, silliness*.

εὐήθης, -ες, *foolish, silly*.

καταδύω (see δύω for prin. parts), *to sink, make sink*.

λυμαίνομαι, λυμανοῦμαι, ἐλυμηνάμην, λελύμασμαι, ἐλυμάνθην, *to outrage, spoil*.

μηδέ, *and not, not even, neither*.

ὀκνέω, ὀκνήσω, ὤκνησα, *to hesitate, dread*.

ποιητέος, -α, -ον, *to be made or done, necessary to do*, verbal adj. from ποιέω.

πρᾶξις, -εως, ἡ, *a doing, undertaking, enterprise*. PRAXIS.

προκαταλαμβάνω (see λαμβάνω for prin. parts), *to seize before or first*.

# 188     *Readings from the* Anabasis     LESSON 60

*στρατηγέω, στρατηγήσω, ἐστρα-
τήγησα, ἐστρατήγηκα, to be general,
be in command of, manage.
στρατηγία, -ας, ἡ, plan of command.
STRATEGY.

τοιοῦτος, τοιαύτη, τοιοῦτο, of this
kind, such as this.
*φθάνω, φθήσομαι, ἔφθην or ἔφθασα,
to get the start of, do first, usually
with participle.

### 336. Principal parts to be memorized

αἱρέω, αἱρήσω, εἷλον, ᾕρηκα, ᾕρημαι, ᾑρέθην, to seize; middle, to choose.

### 337. Reading passage (*Anabasis 1.3.14.9–1.3.17.6*)

Ἐὰν δὲ μηδὲ ἡγεμόνα διδῷ, συντάττεσθαι τὴν ταχίστην,
πέμψαι δὲ καὶ προκαταληψομένους τὰ ἄκρα, ὅπως μὴ
φθάσωσι μήτε Κῦρος μήτε οἱ Κίλικες καταλαβόντες, ὧν
πολλοὺς καὶ πολλὰ χρήματα ἔχομεν ἀνηρπακότες. οὗτος μὲν     15
5   τοιαῦτα εἶπε· μετὰ δὲ τοῦτον Κλέαρχος εἶπε τοσοῦτον. Ὡς
μὲν στρατηγήσοντα ἐμὲ ταύτην τὴν στρατηγίαν μηδεὶς ὑμῶν
λεγέτω· πολλὰ γὰρ ἐνορῶ δι' ἃ ἐμοὶ τοῦτο οὐ ποιητέον· ὡς
δὲ τῷ ἀνδρὶ ὃν ἂν ἕλησθε πείσομαι ᾗ δυνατὸν μάλιστα, ἵνα
εἰδῆτε ὅτι καὶ ἄρχεσθαι ἐπίσταμαι ὥς τις καὶ ἄλλος μάλιστα

1. **τὴν ταχίστην**: understand ὁδόν. Adverbial accusative, *the quickest way, as quickly
as possible* (530).
2. **πέμψαι δὲ καὶ (τοὺς) προκαταληψομένους τὰ ἄκρα**: λήψομαι and ληψόμενος its
participle are future of λαμβάνω. The form προκαταληψομένους is a future participle
expressing purpose (581). Translate the above, *and also to send (those) being about to seize
first the heights*, or to send *(men) to seize first the heights*. **ὅπως μὴ φθάσωσι**: a negative purpose clause. φθάσωσι is from φθάνω in today's vocabulary.
4. **ἀνηρπακότες**: from ἀναρπάζω. See principal parts of ἁρπάζω. ἡρπακότες is like
λελυκότες from λύω. See 183.
6. **στρατηγήσοντα . . . ταύτην τὴν στρατηγίαν**: here we have the object (στρατηγίαν)
repeating the idea of its verb (the participle στρατηγήσοντα). This kind of accusative is
called a *cognate*, or *related*, accusative (528). The phrase means literally, *being about to
general this generalship*, or more freely, *being about to take charge of this plan of command*.
7. **λεγέτω**: third person singular imperative of λέγω. Like λυέτω of λύω. **ποιητέον**:
understand ἐστί. Here ποιητέον, a verbal adjective expressing *necessity*, is used personally,
and agrees in number, gender, and case with τοῦτο. ἐμοί is dative of agent, *by me* (519).
**ὡς δέ**: understand λεγέτω, *let him say.*
8. **τῷ ἀνδρὶ ὃν ἂν ἕλησθε πείσομαι**: ἕλησθε is second aorist subjunctive middle of
αἱρέω and signifies *to choose*. πείσομαι is future middle of πείθω and means *to obey*. Here
is a conditional relative as follows: protasis, relative (ὅν) plus ἄν plus subjunctive
(ἕλησθε); apodosis, future indicative (πείσομαι). It is therefore future more vivid, *the
man whom you (shall) choose, I will obey* (603). **ᾗ**: understand ὁδῷ, *in what way*. **δύνατον**:
understand ἐστί.
9. **εἰδῆτε**: see development of οἶδα, *to know*, perfect of εἴδω (199). The perfect is used
as a present.

10  ἀνθρώπων. μετὰ τοῦτον ἄλλος ἀνέστη, ἐπιδεικνὺς μὲν τὴν   16
εὐήθειαν τοῦ τὰ πλοῖα αἰτεῖν κελεύοντος, ὥσπερ πάλιν τὸν
στόλον Κύρου ποιουμένου, ἐπιδεικνὺς δὲ ὡς εὔηθες εἴη ἡγεμόνα αἰτεῖν παρὰ τούτου ᾧ λυμαινόμεθα τὴν πρᾶξιν. εἰ δὲ
καὶ τῷ ἡγεμόνι πιστεύσομεν ὃν ἂν Κῦρος δῷ, τί κωλύει καὶ
15  τὰ ἄκρα ἡμῖν κελεύειν Κῦρον προκαταλαβεῖν; ἐγὼ γὰρ   17
ὀκνοίην μὲν ἂν εἰς τὰ πλοῖα ἐμβαίνειν ἃ ἡμῖν δοίη, μὴ ἡμᾶς
ταῖς τριήρεσι καταδύσῃ, φοβοίμην δ' ἂν τῷ ἡγεμόνι ᾧ δοίη
ἕπεσθαι, μὴ ἡμᾶς ἀγάγῃ ὅθεν οὐκ ἔσται ἐξελθεῖν· βουλοίμην
δ' ἂν ἄκοντος ἀπιὼν Κύρου λαθεῖν αὐτὸν ἀπελθών· ὃ οὐ
20  δυνατόν ἐστιν.

10. ἀνέστη: from ἀνίστημι. Find ἔστη in the chart of ἵστημι (216). ἐπιδεικνύς: see present system of δείκνυμι (222).
12. Κύρου ποιουμένου: genitive absolute expressing condition, *if* (582). With ὥσπερ, *just as if Cyrus were making . . . .* A contrary-to-fact idea. εἴη: see chart of εἰμί (132). Optative in indirect discourse with ὅτι or ὡς after a past tense.
13. ᾧ: dative of disadvantage, *for whom* (517).
14. ὃν ἂν Κῦρος δῷ: for δῷ see the chart of δίδωμι (227). Here is a relative (ὅν) plus ἄν plus subjunctive, the protasis for a future more vivid conditional relative, the context being future (603).
16. ὀκνοίην μὲν ἂν εἰς τὰ πλοῖα ἐμβαίνειν ἃ ἡμῖν δοίη: conditional relative as follows: protasis (follows apodosis), relative (ἅ) plus optative (δοίη); apodosis, ἄν plus optative ὀκνοίην. This is future less vivid, *I would dread to enter into the ships which he should give us.* So also for the sentence φοβοίμην δ' ἄν, etc. (see 604).
18. ἔσται: future of εἰμί. Here signifies possibility. βουλοίμην δ' ἄν: *and I would wish*, a potential optative (ἄν plus optative, 567). Very similar to the apodosis of a future less vivid condition. The participle ἀπιών, *departing* or *if I should depart*, stands in the place of the condition or protasis.
19. ἄκοντος Κύρου: understand ὄντος, *Cyrus (being) unwilling*. ἄκων, *unwilling*, is really ἀ-έκων. The adjective ἑκών means *willing*. In Greek an a is sometimes prefixed to a word to negate or reverse its force. This is called *alpha privative*. λαθεῖν αὐτὸν ἀπελθών: λαθεῖν is second aorist infinitive of λανθάνω, *to escape the notice of*. So translate, *to escape the notice of him departing*, or *to depart unknown to him* (583). ἀπελθών is second aorist participle of ἀπέρχομαι.

### 338. Writing exercise

1. Conjugate αἱρέω in the second aorist system, underscoring the form ἔλησθε, which occurs in *l. 8* today. Use the second aorist of ἄγω (118) for reference if needed.

2. Decline ἀπελθών, second aorist participle of ἀπέρχομαι, referring to ὤν, οὖσα, ὄν as needed. This form occurs in *l. 19* of today's lesson.

## LESSON 61

# Collective Bargaining

### 339. New word list

Ἀβροκόμας, -α, ὁ, Abrocomas, satrap of Phoenicia and Syria and commander of one-fourth of Darius' army, some 300,000 men.

αἱρετός, -ή, -όν, chosen.

*ἀπαγγέλλω (see ἀγγέλλω for prin. parts), to bring back word.

*ἀπέχω (see ἔχω for prin. parts), to be distant.

ἀσφαλῶς, safely.

*δεῦρο, hither, here.

ἐπικίνδυνος, -ον, dangerous; comp., ἐπικινδυνότερος.

ἐπίπονος, -ον, toilsome; comp., ἐπιπονώτερος.

ἡμιδαρεικόν, -οῦ, τό, a half-daric.

ἡμιόλιος, -α, -ον, half as much again, half more.

*κακός, -ή, -όν, bad, cowardly, dastardly; comp., κακίων; superl., κάκιστος. CACOPHONY.

μείζων, -ον, greater, comp. of μέγας.

οἷόσπερ, -απερ, -όνπερ, just such as.

*ὅμως, nevertheless.

παραπλήσιος, -α, -ον, like, resembling.

*πρόθυμος, -ον, willing, eager.

προσαιτέω (see αἰτέω for prin. parts), to ask more, beg.

συναναβαίνω (see βαίνω for prin. parts), to march inland with.

ὑποψία, -ας, ἡ, suspicion.

*φανερός, -ά, -όν, evident; ἐν τῷ φανερῷ, in the open.

φλυαρία, -ας, ἡ, folly, foolishness.

χρῄζω, to need, desire.

### 340. Principal parts to be memorized

πείθω, πείσω, ἔπεισα, πέπεικα or πέποιθα, πέπεισμαι, ἐπείσθην, to persuade; middle, obey.

### 341. Reading passage (Anabasis 1.3.18.1–1.3.21.7)

Ἀλλ' ἐγώ φημι ταῦτα μὲν φλυαρίας εἶναι· δοκεῖ δέ μοι   18
ἄνδρας ἐλθόντας πρὸς Κῦρον οἵτινες ἐπιτήδειοι σὺν Κλεάρχῳ
ἐρωτᾶν ἐκεῖνον τί βούλεται ἡμῖν χρῆσθαι· καὶ ἐὰν μὲν ἡ
πρᾶξις ᾗ παραπλησία οἷάπερ καὶ πρόσθεν ἐχρῆτο τοῖς ξένοις,
5    ἕπεσθαι καὶ ἡμᾶς καὶ μὴ κακίους εἶναι τῶν πρόσθεν τούτῳ
συναναβάντων· ἐὰν δὲ μείζων ἡ πρᾶξις τῆς πρόσθεν φαίνηται   19

2. οἵτινες ἐπιτήδειοι: understand εἰσί.

3. χρῆσθαι: present infinitive of χράομαι.

4. ᾗ: see chart of εἰμί (132). οἷάπερ: to just such (an undertaking) as . . . . Dative of likeness (516).

5. κακίους: short form for κακίονας (see ἡδίων, 157). τῶν . . . συναναβάντων: genitive of comparison, than those having gone up-country with . . . (507).

καὶ ἐπιπονωτέρα καὶ ἐπικινδυνοτέρα, ἀξιοῦν ἢ πείσαντα
ἡμᾶς ἄγειν ἢ πεισθέντα πρὸς φιλίαν ἀφιέναι· οὕτω γὰρ καὶ
ἑπόμενοι ἂν φίλοι αὐτῷ καὶ πρόθυμοι ἐποίμεθα καὶ ἀπιόντες
10   ἀσφαλῶς ἂν ἀπίοιμεν· ὅ τι δ᾽ ἂν πρὸς ταῦτα λέγῃ ἀπαγγεῖλαι δεῦρο· ἡμᾶς δ᾽ ἀκούσαντας πρὸς ταῦτα βουλεύεσθαι.
ἔδοξε ταῦτα, καὶ ἄνδρας ἑλόμενοι σὺν Κλεάρχῳ πέμπουσιν   20
οἳ ἠρώτων Κῦρον τὰ δόξαντα τῇ στρατιᾷ. ὁ δ᾽ ἀπεκρίνατο
ὅτι ἀκούει Ἀβροκόμαν ἐχθρὸν ἄνδρα ἐπὶ τῷ Εὐφράτῃ ποταμῷ
15   εἶναι, ἀπέχοντα δώδεκα σταθμούς· πρὸς τοῦτον οὖν ἔφη
βούλεσθαι ἐλθεῖν· κἂν μὲν ᾖ ἐκεῖ, τὴν δίκην ἔφη χρῄζειν
ἐπιθεῖναι αὐτῷ, ἢν δὲ φεύγῃ, ἡμεῖς ἐκεῖ πρὸς ταῦτα βουλευσό-
μεθα. ἀκούσαντες δὲ ταῦτα οἱ αἱρετοὶ ἀγγέλλουσι τοῖς   21
στρατιώταις· τοῖς δὲ ὑποψία μὲν ἦν ὅτι ἄγει πρὸς βασιλέα,
20   ὅμως δὲ ἐδόκει ἕπεσθαι. προσαιτοῦσι δὲ μισθόν· ὁ δὲ Κῦρος
ὑπισχνεῖται ἡμιόλιον πᾶσι δώσειν οὗ πρότερον ἔφερον, ἀντὶ
δαρεικοῦ τρία ἡμιδαρεικὰ τοῦ μηνὸς τῷ στρατιώτῃ· ὅτι δὲ
ἐπὶ βασιλέα ἄγοι οὐδὲ ἐνταῦθα ἤκουσεν οὐδεὶς ἔν γε τῷ
φανερῷ.

7. ἀξιοῦν: from ἀξιόω, *to ask*. See development of ὑψόω (177). This infinitive, as well
as those which follow in this sentence, depends upon δοκεῖ, *it seems best*, in *l. 1*.
8. πρὸς φιλίαν: *on terms of friendship*. ἀφιέναι: from ἀφίημι, *to let go, send away*. See development of ἵημι in 233. Find ἰέναι.
9. ἑπόμενοι . . . ἀπιόντες: equivalent to εἰ ἐποίμεθα . . . εἰ ἀπίοιμεν in a future less
vivid sequence.
10. ἀπαγγεῖλαι: from ἀπαγγέλλω. See principal parts of ἀγγέλλω.
12. ἔδοξε, δόξαντα (*l. 13*): from ἔδοξα, aorist of δοκέω, *to seem best, be voted*. ἑλόμενοι:
from αἱρέω.
13. ἠρώτων: from ἐρωτάω. ἀπεκρίνατο: from ἀποκρίνω, *to reply*. See principal parts
of κρίνω.
14. ἀκούει: one might have expected to find this changed to present optative, since
it is quoted indirectly after ὅτι after a past tense.
16. κἂν μὲν ᾖ ἐκεῖ: the thought goes into direct discourse here. κἂν is καὶ ἐάν.
Followed by the subjunctive ᾖ (see εἰμί), it is the protasis of a future more vivid condition, *and if he be there . . . .*
17. ἐπιθεῖναι: from ἐπιτίθημι, *to inflict upon*. See development of τίθημι (229). Find
θεῖναι.
19. τοῖς δέ: dative of possessor: *and to them was a suspicion* or *they had a suspicion* (518).
21. οὗ: genitive of comparison, *than that which*, used after ἡμιόλιον, which carries the
idea *half more*.
22. τοῦ μηνός: genitive of time within which, *within the month* or *each month* (510).
τῷ στρατιώτῃ: the definite article sometimes has distributive force (see 488). Translate,
*to each soldier*.

## 342. Writing exercise

1. ἀξιοῦν in *l. 7* is present infinitive active of the o-contract verb
ἀξιόω, *to ask, deem worthy*. Conjugate this in the present system (cf.

ὑψόω, 177). Remember to augment, changing α to η, for the imperfect. Underscore ἀξιοῦν where it occurs.

2. In *l. 5* is seen the form κακίους, *more cowardly, worse*, comparative of κακός. Decline κακίων, using ἡδίων (157) as model. Give also the alternative shortened forms and underscore κακίους. Is it nominative or accusative? Consult its context.

## LESSON 62

# Arrival of Reinforcements at Issus

### 343. New word list

Αἰγύπτιος, -ου, ὁ, *an Egyptian.*

βία, -ας, ἡ, *force, violence.*

ἑπτακόσιοι, -αι, -α, *seven hundred.*

ἔσωθεν, *from inside*; τὸ ἔσωθεν, *the inside.*

Ἔφεσος, -ου, ἡ, *Ephesus*, oldest of the twelve ancient cities of Ionia, famed for its temple of Ephesian Artemis, and scene of missionary activities of St. Paul.

Κάρσος or Κέρσος, -ου, ὁ, *the Carsus* or *Cersus river*, between Syria and Cilicia.

μετάπεμπτος, -ον, *summoned.*

*μισθοφόρος, -ου, ὁ, *a mercenary.*

ναύαρχος, -ου, ὁ, *fleet commander, admiral.*

ὁρμέω, ὁρμήσω, *to be moved, come to anchor.*

παρέρχομαι (see ἔρχομαι for prin. parts), *to pass by, pass through.*

Πελοπόννησος, -ου, ἡ, *the Peloponnesus, southern portion of Greece.*

πεντεκαίδεκα, indecl., *fifteen.*

Πυθαγόρας, -ου, ὁ, *Pythagoras*, a Spartan admiral.

*πύλη, -ης, ἡ, *gate, pass.* PYLON.

Πύραμος, -ου, ὁ, *the Pyramus*, a large river rising in Cappadocia and flowing through Cilicia to the sea.

Συρία, -ας, ἡ, *Syria.*

*συστρατεύομαι (see στρατεύω for prin. parts), *to take the field with, join an expedition.*

Ταμώς, Ταμώ, ὁ, *Tamos*, an Egyptian pilot.

τεῖχος, -ους, τό, *wall.*

Χειρίσοφος, -ου, ὁ, *Chirisophus*, a Spartan general of Cyrus' mercenary force.

Ψάρος, -ου, ὁ, *the Psarus*, a river rising in Cataonia and flowing through Cilicia to the sea.

### 344. Principal parts to be memorized

ἡγέομαι, ἡγήσομαι, ἡγησάμην, ἥγημαι, *to lead, be in command of.*

**345. Reading passage** (*Anabasis 1.4.1.1–1.4.4.7*)

*Chapter 4.* Ἐντεῦθεν ἐξελαύνει σταθμοὺς δύο παρασάγγας δέκα     1
ἐπὶ τὸν Ψάρον ποταμόν, οὗ ἦν τὸ εὖρος τρία πλέθρα. ἐντεῦθεν ἐξελαύνει σταθμὸν ἕνα παρασάγγας πέντε ἐπὶ τὸν Πύρα-
μον ποταμόν, οὗ ἦν τὸ εὖρος στάδιον. ἐντεῦθεν ἐξελαύνει
5  σταθμοὺς δύο παρασάγγας πεντεκαίδεκα εἰς Ἰσσούς, τῆς
Κιλικίας ἐσχάτην πόλιν ἐπὶ τῇ θαλάττῃ οἰκουμένην, μεγάλην
καὶ εὐδαίμονα. ἐνταῦθα ἔμειναν ἡμέρας τρεῖς· καὶ Κύρῳ     2
παρῆσαν αἱ ἐκ Πελοποννήσου νῆες τριάκοντα καὶ πέντε καὶ
ἐπ᾿ αὐταῖς ναύαρχος Πυθαγόρας Λακεδαιμόνιος. ἡγεῖτο δ᾿
10  αὐταῖς Ταμὼς Αἰγύπτιος ἐξ Ἐφέσου, ἔχων ναῦς ἑτέρας
Κύρου πέντε καὶ εἴκοσιν, αἷς ἐπολιόρκει Μίλητον. παρῆν δὲ     3
καὶ Χειρίσοφος Λακεδαιμόνιος ἐπὶ τῶν νεῶν, μετάπεμπτος
ὑπὸ Κύρου, ἑπτακοσίους ἔχων ὁπλίτας, ὧν ἐστρατήγει παρὰ
Κύρῳ. αἱ δὲ νῆες ὥρμουν παρὰ τὴν Κύρου σκηνήν. ἐνταῦθα καὶ
15  οἱ παρὰ Ἀβροκόμα μισθοφόροι Ἕλληνες ἀποστάντες ἦλθον
παρὰ Κῦρον τετρακόσιοι ὁπλῖται καὶ συνεστρατεύοντο ἐπὶ
βασιλέα. ἐντεῦθεν ἐξελαύνει σταθμὸν ἕνα παρασάγγας πέντε     4
ἐπὶ πύλας τῆς Κιλικίας καὶ τῆς Συρίας. ἦσαν δὲ ταῦτα δύο
τείχη, καὶ τὸ μὲν ἔσωθεν τὸ πρὸ τῆς Κιλικίας Συέννεσις εἶχε
20  καὶ Κιλίκων φυλακή, τὸ δὲ ἔξω τὸ πρὸ τῆς Συρίας βασιλέως
ἐλέγετο φυλακὴ φυλάττειν. διὰ μέσου δὲ ῥεῖ τούτων ποταμὸς
Κάρσος ὄνομα, εὖρος πλέθρου. ἅπαν δὲ τὸ μέσον τῶν τειχῶν
ἦσαν στάδιοι τρεῖς· καὶ παρελθεῖν οὐκ ἦν βία.

6. **οἰκουμένην**: *inhabited*, almost in the sense of *situated*.

8. **νῆες**: see declension of *ναῦς* (151). Also for *ναῦς* in *l. 10*, *νεῶν* in *l. 12*.

9. **ἐπ᾿ αὐταῖς**: *over them*. **ἡγεῖτο δ᾿ αὐταῖς**: *ἡγέομαι, to lead, guide*, is often followed by the dative when the idea of advantage is prominent, as here. When the idea of rank is prominent, as *to be the leader of an army*, the genitive is more often used (506, 514).

11. **αἷς**: *with which*, dative of means (520).

13. **παρὰ Κύρῳ**: literally *by the side of Cyrus*. Translated, *for Cyrus*.

14. **ὥρμουν**: imperfect of *ὁρμέω* in today's list. **παρὰ τὴν Κύρου σκηνήν**: with the accusative, motion is implied. (*They*) *came to anchor beside the tent of Cyrus.*

15. **Ἀβροκόμα**: a Doric genitive, rarely used in Attic Greek and then usually in connection with foreign names.

22. **ὄνομα**: *by name, as to name*. Accusative of specification (529). **τὸ μέσον**: *the space* or *distance between*.

23. **ἦσαν**: the verb is attracted to the plural number of the predicate noun *στάδιοι*.
**οὐκ ἦν**: the verb here signifies possibility, negated of course by *οὐκ*.

**346. Writing exercise**

1. *ἡγέομαι, to lead*, is a deponent verb with all its forms in the middle voice. Give its conjugation in the present and in the future middle

systems, all moods. For the present system, since it is an ε-contract verb, see ποιέω (164). Its initial η is not altered by augment in the imperfect. For the future, start with its future principal part and follow λύω. Underscore ἡγεῖτο, which occurs in *l. 9* today.

2. Complete the declension of νῆες, *ships*, which occurs in *l. 8*, with the feminine definite article (see 63, 151). Underscore νῆες.

## LESSON 63

# The Strange Retreat of Abrocomas

### 347. New word list

ἁλίσκομαι, ἁλώσομαι, ἑάλων or ἥλων, ἑάλωκα or ἥλωκα, *to be caught, captured.*

ἀναστρέφω (see στρέφω for prin. parts), *to turn back, reverse.* ANASTROPHE.

*ἄξιος, -α, -ον, *worthy, worth,* with gen. of value. AXIOM.

ἀπελαύνω (see ἐλαύνω for prin. parts), *to march away.*

ἀποβιβάζω (see βιβάζω for prin. parts), *to cause to go off, land.*

αὐτόθι, *in this* or *that place, there.*

ἀφανής, -ές, *out of sight, hidden, doubtful.*

βιβάζω, βιβάσω or βιβῶ, ἐβίβασα, causal of βαίνω, *to make go, push.*

δειλός, -ή, -όν, *cowardly.*

διέρχομαι (see ἔρχομαι for prin. parts), *to go through, be circulated.*

*ἐάω, ἐάσω, εἴασα, εἴακα, εἴαμαι, εἰάθην, *to permit, allow.*

*ἕνεκα, with gen., *because of.*

ἐντίθημι (see τίθημι for prin. parts), *to put in* or *into.*

εὔχομαι, εὔξομαι, εὐξάμην or ηὐξάμην, *to pray, wish for.*

ἐφίστημι (see ἵστημι for prin. parts), *to make stop, set in command*; perf. and pluperf. act., *to stand, be set.*

ἠλίβατος, -ον, *high, steep.*

καθήκω (see ἥκω for prin. parts), *to come* or *extend down.*

Μυρίανδος, -ου, ἡ, *Myriandus,* a Syrian city on the gulf of Issus.

μυριάς, -άδος, ἡ, *a ten thousand.* MYRIAD.

οἰκτείρω, οἰκτερῶ, ᾤκτειρα, *to pity, feel sorry for.*

ὁλκάς, -άδος, ἡ, *merchant ship, freighter.*

ὅσπερ, ἥπερ, ὅπερ, intensive for ὅς, ἥ, ὅ, *who indeed, which indeed.*

πάροδος, -ου, ἡ, *passage, roadway.*

πέτρα, -ας, ἡ, *rock, cliff.* PETRIFY.

στενός, -ή, -όν, narrow. STENOGRAPHY.

Σύριος, -α, -ον, *Syrian.*

ὕπερθεν, *from above, overhead.*

φιλοτιμέομαι, φιλοτιμήσομαι, πεφιλοτίμημαι, ἐφιλοτιμήθην, *to be jealous, feel piqued.*

Φοινίκη, -ης, ἡ, *Phoenicia.*

Φοῖνιξ, -ικος, ὁ, *a Phoenician.*

## 348. Principal parts to be memorized

βαίνω, βήσομαι, ἔβην, βέβηκα, βέβαμαι, ἐβάθην, *to go.*

## 349. Reading passage (*Anabasis* 1.4.4.8–1.4.7.9)

Ἦν γὰρ ἡ πάροδος στενὴ καὶ τὰ τείχη εἰς τὴν θάλατταν
καθήκοντα, ὕπερθεν δ᾽ ἦσαν πέτραι ἠλίβατοι· ἐπὶ δὲ τοῖς
τείχεσιν ἀμφοτέροις ἐφειστήκεσαν πύλαι. ταύτης ἕνεκα τῆς    5
παρόδου Κῦρος τὰς ναῦς μετεπέμψατο, ὅπως ὁπλίτας ἀπο-
5   βιβάσειεν εἴσω καὶ ἔξω τῶν πυλῶν βιασομένους τοὺς πολεμίους εἰ φυλάττοιεν ἐπὶ ταῖς Συρίαις πύλαις, ὅπερ ᾤετο
ποιήσειν ὁ Κῦρος τὸν Ἀβροκόμαν, ἔχοντα πολὺ στράτευμα.
Ἀβροκόμας δὲ οὐ τοῦτ᾽ ἐποίησεν, ἀλλ᾽ ἐπεὶ ἤκουσε Κῦρον
ἐν Κιλικίᾳ ὄντα, ἀναστρέψας ἐκ Φοινίκης παρὰ βασιλέα
10  ἀπήλαυνεν, ἔχων, ὡς ἐλέγετο, τριάκοντα μυριάδας στρατιᾶς.
ἐντεῦθεν ἐξελαύνει διὰ Συρίας σταθμὸν ἕνα παρασάγγας    6
πέντε εἰς Μυρίανδον, πόλιν οἰκουμένην ὑπὸ Φοινίκων ἐπὶ τῇ
θαλάττῃ· ἐμπόριον δ᾽ ἦν τὸ χωρίον καὶ ὥρμουν αὐτόθι
ὁλκάδες πολλαί. ἐνταῦθ᾽ ἔμειναν ἡμέρας ἑπτά· καὶ Ξενίας    7
15  ὁ Ἀρκὰς καὶ Πασίων ὁ Μεγαρεὺς ἐμβάντες εἰς πλοῖον καὶ
τὰ πλείστου ἄξια ἐνθέμενοι ἀπέπλευσαν, ὡς μὲν τοῖς πλεί-
στοις ἐδόκουν, φιλοτιμηθέντες ὅτι τοὺς στρατιώτας αὐτῶν

2. **ἐπὶ δὲ τοῖς τείχεσιν ἀμφοτέροις**: *and commanding both walls.*
3. **ἐφειστήκεσαν**: from (ἐφ)ίστημι. This is an alternative form for the pluperfect
ἑστάσαν. See development of ἵστημι (216). Translate as an imperfect.
4. **ἀποβιβάσειε(ν)**: see principal parts of βιβάζω in today's new word list. In the
chart of λύω (97), locate the corresponding form λύσειε. This is an optative in a purpose
clause after a past tense (568).
5. **βιασομένους**: future participle expressing purpose, *to force* (581).
6. **εἰ φυλάττοιεν**: in the discussion of purpose just preceding, the idea of mental
action has been built up. So Cyrus' original thought, εἰ φυλάττουσι, *if they are guarding,*
or ἐὰν φυλάττωσι, *if they are (shall be) guarding* (ἐάν would become εἰ, 589), is changed to
an optative after the implied indirect discourse. Translate, *if they were guarding.* ᾤετο
ποιήσειν: ᾤετο, imperfect of οἴομαι, introduces the indirect statement. ποιήσειν, future
infinitive of ποιέω, shows that the original statement was future, ποιήσει, *he will do.*
Translate, *he thought that Abrocomas would do.*
8. **Κῦρον ὄντα**: *Cyrus being, that Cyrus was.*
13. **ὥρμουν**: from ὁρμέω. Like ἐποίουν from ποιέω (164).
15. **ἐμβάντες**: from ἐμβαίνω. Find βάς in the development of βαίνω (211). For its
declension see λύσας (182). The accent of λύσας differs, of course.
16. **ἐνθέμενοι**: from ἐντίθημι. See development of τίθημι (229). Find θέμενος.
**ἀπέπλευσαν**: from ἀποπλέω. See πλέω for principal parts.
17. **φιλοτιμηθέντες**: from φιλοτιμέομαι in today's word list. Like λυθέντες from λυθείς
(184).

τοὺς παρὰ Κλέαρχον ἀπελθόντας ὡς ἀπιόντας εἰς τὴν Ἑλλάδα πάλιν καὶ οὐ πρὸς βασιλέα εἶα Κῦρος τὸν Κλέαρχον
20  ἔχειν. ἐπεὶ δ᾽ ἦσαν ἀφανεῖς, διῆλθε λόγος ὅτι διώκοι αὐτοὺς
Κῦρος τριήρεσι· καὶ οἱ μὲν ηὔχοντο ὡς δειλοὺς ὄντας αὐτοὺς
ληφθῆναι, οἱ δ᾽ ᾤκτειρον εἰ ἁλώσοιντο.

18. **ἀπελθόντας**: from ἀπέρχομαι. **ἀπιόντας**: from ἄπειμι. Present participle with
future significance (550).
19. **εἶα**: imperfect of ἐάω. Note that the augment is εἰ- rather than the usual ἠ-.
20. **διῆλθε**: from διέρχομαι in today's word list. **διώκοι**: present optative showing that
the rumor was in present tense, διώκει, *Cyrus is pursuing*. Translate, *that Cyrus was
pursuing* . . . .
21. **τριήρεσι**: for the declension of τριήρης see 139. This is a dative of means (520).
**οἱ μὲν . . . οἱ δέ**: *some . . . others*. **ηὔχοντο**: imperfect of εὔχομαι.
22. **ληφθῆναι**: aorist passive infinitive of λαμβάνω, *to take, catch*. **ᾤκτειρον**: imperfect
indicative active of οἰκτείρω. **εἰ ἁλώσοιντο**: the verb *to pity* implies mental action,
and is here in the past tense. ἁλώσοιντο is *future* optative, so the original statement must have been in the future tense and could only have been indicative, εἰ
ἁλώσονται, *if they shall be caught* (see principal parts of ἁλίσκομαι in today's word list).
Here then is a case where a future more vivid condition is introduced by εἰ with
future indicative, rather than by ἐάν with subjunctive. Translate, *if they should be
caught* (see 603, note).

## 350. Writing exercise

1. The participle ἐμβάντες in *l. 15* is from the second aorist system
of ἐμβαίνω, a compound of βαίνω, *to go*. Conjugate ἐμβαίνω, *to enter*, in
the second aorist system (see 211). When the prefix precedes a vowel it is
ἐν-; before a labial mute (π, β, φ) it is ἐμ-. Use recessive accent except for
the infinitive (infinitives in -ναι accent the penult) and the participle,
which retains the accent on the same syllable as with the uncompounded
βαίνω.

2. Decline the participle ἐμβάς, underscoring the form ἐμβάντες, which
appears in *l. 15*. Get the nominative singular forms, using the βαίνω chart
(211). Then see λύσας (182) for the form of the case endings. As to βάς,
the α in this stem carries the accent throughout its declension except in
the genitive plural feminine. The same will be true for ἐμβάς. Remember
this stem α is *long by nature*, while the final α in the nominative and accusative feminine is *short*. Final -αι is regularly reckoned short.

# LESSON 64

## Cyrus tactfully spares the Deserters

### 351. New word list

ἄθυμος, -ον, dispirited, discouraged; comp., ἀθυμότερος.

ἀνάβασις, -εως, ἡ, an expedition up-country, into the interior. ANABASIS.

ἀποδιδράσκω, ἀποδράσομαι, ἀπέδραν, ἀποδέδρακα, to run away, get fully away.

*ἀπολείπω (see λείπω for prin. parts), to desert, abandon.

ἀποσυλάω (see συλάω for prin. parts), to despoil, plunder.

ἀποφεύγω (see φεύγω for prin. parts), to flee away, make an escape.

ἀρετή, -ῆς, ἡ, valor, loyalty, goodness.

ἔγωγε, emphatic for ἐγώ; I for my part.

ζώνη, -ης, ἡ, belt, girdle, 'girdle money' or 'pin money'. ZONE.

ἥδιον, more gladly, comp. of ἡδέως.

ἰχθύς, -ύος, ὁ, fish. ICHTHYOLOGY.

*κώμη, -ης, ἡ, village.

μά, introduces a negative oath no or not, by . . . !

οἴχομαι, οἰχήσομαι, to be gone, to have gone.

πρᾷος, -εῖα, -ον, tame, mild.

στερέω, στερήσω, ἐστέρησα, ἐστέρηκα, ἐστέρημαι, ἐστερήθην, to deprive of, rob.

συγκαλέω (see καλέω for prin. parts), to call together.

συλάω, συλήσω, ἐσύλησα, ἐσυλήθην, to spoil, strip off the spoil.

Σύρος, -ου, ὁ, a Syrian.

Τράλλεις, -εων, οἱ, Tralles, a city in northern Caria.

*φρουρέω, φρουρήσω, ἐφρούρησα, πεφρούρημαι, ἐφρουρήθην, to guard, watch.

Χάλος, -ου, ὁ, the Chalus, a river in the northern part of Syria.

### 352. Principal parts to be memorized

ἐάω, ἐάσω, εἴασα, εἴακα, εἴαμαι, εἰάθην, to allow.

### 353. Reading passage (Anabasis 1.4.8.1–1.4.9.8)

Κῦρος δὲ συγκαλέσας τοὺς στρατηγοὺς εἶπεν· Ἀπολελοί-   8
πασιν ἡμᾶς Ξενίας καὶ Πασίων. ἀλλ' εὖ γε μέντοι ἐπιστάσθων ὅτι οὔτε ἀποδεδράκασιν, οἶδα γὰρ ὅπη οἴχονται· οὔτε

1. συγκαλέσας: from συγκαλέω. Like λύσας from λύω. Ἀπολελόιπασι(ν): see ἀπολείπω in today's list.

2. ἐπιστάσθων: ἐπίσταμαι, to know, is a deponent verb whose active form would have been ἐπίστημι and whose present system is conjugated just as the present middle and passive of ἵστημι. See development of ἵστημι in 216 and find the corresponding form, ἱστάσθων.

3. ἀποδεδράκασι(ν): from ἀποδιδράσκω in today's word list.

ἀποπεφεύγασιν, ἔχω γὰρ τριήρεις ὥστε ἑλεῖν τὸ ἐκείνων
5    πλοῖον. ἀλλὰ μὰ τοὺς θεοὺς οὐκ ἔγωγε αὐτοὺς διώξω, οὐδ᾽
ἐρεῖ οὐδεὶς ὡς ἐγὼ ἕως μὲν ἂν παρῇ τις χρῶμαι, ἐπειδὰν
δὲ ἀπιέναι βούληται, συλλαβὼν καὶ αὐτοὺς κακῶς ποιῶ καὶ
τὰ χρήματα ἀποσυλῶ. ἀλλὰ ἰόντων, εἰδότες ὅτι κακίους
εἰσὶ περὶ ἡμᾶς ἢ ἡμεῖς περὶ ἐκείνους. καίτοι ἔχω γε αὐτῶν
10   καὶ τέκνα καὶ γυναῖκας ἐν Τράλλεσι φρουρούμενα· ἀλλ᾽ οὐδὲ
τούτων στερήσονται, ἀλλ᾽ ἀπολήψονται τῆς πρόσθεν ἕνεκα
περὶ ἐμὲ ἀρετῆς. καὶ ὁ μὲν ταῦτα εἶπεν· οἱ δὲ ῞Ελληνες, εἴ τις        9
καὶ ἀθυμότερος ἦν πρὸς τὴν ἀνάβασιν, ἀκούοντες τὴν Κύρου
ἀρετὴν ἥδιον καὶ προθυμότερον συνεπορεύοντο. μετὰ ταῦτα
15   Κῦρος ἐξελαύνει σταθμοὺς τέτταρας παρασάγγας εἴκοσιν
ἐπὶ τὸν Χάλον ποταμόν, ὄντα τὸ εὖρος πλέθρου, πλήρη δ᾽
ἰχθύων μεγάλων καὶ πραέων, οὓς οἱ Σύροι θεοὺς ἐνόμιζον
καὶ ἀδικεῖν οὐκ εἴων, οὐδὲ τὰς περιστεράς. αἱ δὲ κῶμαι ἐν
αἷς ἐσκήνουν Παρυσάτιδος ἦσαν εἰς ζώνην δεδομέναι.

4. **ἀποπεφεύγασι(ν)**: from ἀποφεύγω in today's list. **ἑλεῖν**: second aorist infinitive of
αἱρέω.

5. **τοὺς θεούς**: the accusative follows the adverb of swearing, μά (534).

6. **ἐρεῖ**: from εἴρω. See its principal parts. **ἕως . . . ἂν παρῇ τις χρῶμαι**: conditional
relative sentence. Protasis, relative (ἕως) plus ἄν plus subjunctive (παρῇ, from πάρειμι);
apodosis, present indicative. See 599 if necessary. Note also the remaining part of the
sentence, where ἐπειδάν equals ἐπειδή plus ἄν.

7. **συλλαβών**: from συλλαμβάνω. **κακῶς ποιῶ**: *I do ill, injure.*

8. **ἰόντων**: find this form in the expansion of εἰμι (233). It is not a participle here.
**εἰδότες**: locate the nominative singular of this participle in the expansion of the perfect
system of εἴδω, *to know* (199). It is expanded like λελυκώς (183). **κακίους**: shortened
form of κακίονες, comparative of κακός (cf. ἡδίων, 157).

10. **φρουρούμενα**: from φρουρέω in today's list. Translate, *being guarded,* or *under guard.*

11. **στερήσονται**: future middle used as a passive. **ἀπολήψονται**: from ἀπολαμβάνω.

13. **ἀθυμότερος**: the comparative sometimes carries the sense of *rather, somewhat.*
Translate, *somewhat discouraged.*

14. **ἥδιον καὶ προθυμότερον**: recall that the neuter singular of the comparative adjective is used to form the comparative adverb (239).

18. **εἴων**: imperfect of ἐάω. Like ἐγέννων from γεννάω (173).

19. **ἐσκήνουν**: imperfect of σκηνόω. **εἰς ζώνην**: *for* (*her*) *girdle* or *for her girdle money,*
with the idea of *for her small change.* Cf. our expression *pin money.* **δεδομέναι**: see δίδωμι
(227).

## 354. Writing exercise

1. In *l. 18* occurs the form εἴων, imperfect of ἐάω, *to allow.* Conjugate
ἐάω in the present system. It is an a-contract like γεννάω (173). It augments in the secondary tenses by lengthening ε- to ει-. Underscore εἴων
where it occurs in same sense as in *l. 18.* Decide whether it is first person
singular or third person plural.

2. Decline the perfect participle of οἶδα, *to know*, of which εἰδότες (*l. 8*) is a part. Get the nominatives of the participle from οἶδα (199), and develop them as with λελυκώς (183). Underscore εἰδότες.

# LESSON 65
# The Crossing of the Euphrates

## 355. New word list

ἀνωτέρω, *higher than, higher, above.*

Ἀράξης, -ου, ὁ, *the Araxes*, a river flowing into the Euphrates between Thapsacus and Corsote.

Βέλεσυς, -υος, ὁ, *Belesys*, satrap of Syria, and Assyria.

βρέχω, βρέξω, βέβρεγμαι, ἐβρέχθην, *to wet.*

Δάρδας, -ατος, *the Dardas*, a little river in Syria.

διαβατός, -ή, -όν, *crossable, fordable.*

ἐκκόπτω (see κόπτω for prin. parts), *to cut out, cut down.*

*ἐννέα, indecl., *nine.*

*ἐπισιτίζομαι, ἐπισιτιοῦμαι, ἐπεσιτισάμην, *to collect supplies, forage.*

Εὐφράτης, -ου, ὁ, *the Euphrates*, the great river of western Asia, rising in Armenia, flowing through Mesopotamia and Babylon to join the Tigris and empty into the Persian Gulf.

Θαψακηνός, -οῦ, ὁ, *a Thapsacene, man of Thapsacus.*

Θάψακος, -ου, ἡ, *Thapsacus*, a flourishing city in Syria on the west bank of the Euphrates,

called Tiphsah in *1 Kings 4:24*, where it is cited as marking the eastern boundary of Solomon's kingdom. There was a ford of the Euphrates at Thapsacus, the water being three or four feet deep.

θεῖος, -α, -ον, *divine*; τὸ θεῖον, *a portent.*

κατακαίω or κατακάω (see καίω for prin. parts), *to burn down.*

μαστός, -οῦ, ὁ, *breast.*

*μεστός, -ή, -όν, *filled, abounding in* or *with*, with gen.

οὐπώποτε, *never.*

πάνυ, *very.*

πεζῇ, *on foot.*

πεντήκοντα indecl., *fifty.* PENTE-COST.

σαφῶς, *clearly.*

*σῖτος, -ου, ὁ, *wheat, food, provisions.*

ὑποχωρέω (see χωρέω for prin. parts), *to give way before.*

φύω, φύσω, ἔφυσα or ἔφυν, πέφυκα, ἐφύην, *to bring forth, produce.* PHYSICAL.

## 356. Principal parts to be memorized

ἕπομαι, ἕψομαι, ἑσπόμην, *to follow.*

**357. Reading passage** (*Anabasis 1.4.10.1–1.4.11.5 and 1.4.17.4–1.4. 19.4*)

Ἐντεῦθεν ἐξελαύνει σταθμοὺς πέντε παρασάγγας τριά- 　10
κοντα ἐπὶ τὰς πηγὰς τοῦ Δάρδατος ποταμοῦ, οὗ τὸ εὖρος
πλέθρου. ἐνταῦθα ἦσαν τὰ Βελέσυος βασίλεια τοῦ Συρίας
ἄρξαντος, καὶ παράδεισος πάνυ μέγας καὶ καλός, ἔχων
5　πάντα ὅσα ὧραι φύουσι. Κῦρος δ' αὐτὸν ἐξέκοψε καὶ τὰ
βασίλεια κατέκαυσεν. ἐντεῦθεν ἐξελαύνει σταθμοὺς τρεῖς 　11
παρασάγγας πεντεκαίδεκα ἐπὶ τὸν Εὐφράτην ποταμόν,
ὄντα τὸ εὖρος τεττάρων σταδίων· καὶ πόλις αὐτόθι ᾠκεῖτο
μεγάλη καὶ εὐδαίμων Θάψακος ὄνομα. ἐνταῦθα ἔμεινεν
10　ἡμέρας πέντε. . . .
　　Ταῦτα δὲ ποιήσας διέβαινε· συνείπετο δὲ καὶ τὸ ἄλλο 17.4
στράτευμα αὐτῷ ἅπαν. καὶ τῶν διαβαινόντων τὸν ποταμὸν
οὐδεὶς ἐβρέχθη ἀνωτέρω τῶν μαστῶν ὑπὸ τοῦ ποταμοῦ. οἱ 　18
δὲ Θαψακηνοὶ ἔλεγον ὅτι οὐπώποθ' οὗτος ὁ ποταμὸς δια-
15　βατὸς γένοιτο πεζῇ εἰ μὴ τότε, ἀλλὰ πλοίοις, ἃ τότε Ἀβροκόμας προϊὼν κατέκαυσεν, ἵνα μὴ Κῦρος διαβῇ. ἐδόκει δὴ

2. τὸ εὖρος: understand ἐστί.

3. πλέθρου: genitive of measure (502). Βελέσυος: Belesys the satrap had apparently fled on Cyrus' approach and was considered as an enemy by the latter.

4. ἄρξαντος: from ἄρχω. Like λύσας (182, find the form λύσαντος). This word translates literally, *the one having ruled*; more freely, *the ruler*.

5. πάντα ὅσα: literally, *all things as many as*; more freely, *all things which*. ἐξέκοψε: from ἐκκόπτω in today's list. See principal parts of κόπτω.

6. κατέκαυσε(ν): from κατακαίω in today's list. See καίω for principal parts.

8. ᾠκεῖτο: imperfect passive of οἰκέω, *to inhabit*.

9. ὄνομα: accusative of specification, *by name* (529).

10. At this point is omitted the account of the final disclosure that the expedition was really against the great king, and the manner in which the Greek general Menon helped to influence the Greeks to agree to follow Cyrus in spite of the now apparent magnitude of the venture.

11. συνείπετο: imperfect of συνέπομαι. τὸ ἄλλο στράτευμα: *the rest of the army*, besides Menon's contingent, which had taken the initiative and crossed the river while the rest of the Greeks were still deliberating, thus gaining favor with Cyrus.

12. αὐτῷ: dative of accompaniment (525). It also follows a verb compounded with σύν (515).

13. ἐβρέχθη: from βρέχω in today's list. ὑπὸ τοῦ ποταμοῦ: genitive of agent with ὑπό, in passive construction. οἱ δὲ Θαψακηνοὶ ἔλεγον: the statement of the Thapsacenes seems to have been a mere flattery of Cyrus, for this appears to have been a regularly used ford of the Euphrates, where the water was not over 3 or 4 feet deep.

15. γένοιτο: second aorist optative of γίγνομαι, in indirect discourse after ὅτι. The original statement was therefore second aorist, ἐγένετο, (*it*) *became*. εἰ μή: except.

16. προϊών: from πρόειμι. See development of εἶμι (233). ἵνα μὴ Κῦρος διαβῇ: this purpose clause coming after a past tense (κατέκαυσε) would be expected to use the optative διαβαίη instead of the subjunctive. For these forms, see the development of βαίνω (211). Find βῇ.

θεῖον εἶναι καὶ σαφῶς ὑποχωρῆσαι τὸν ποταμὸν Κύρῳ ὡς
βασιλεύσοντι. ἐντεῦθεν ἐξελαύνει διὰ τῆς Συρίας σταθμοὺς   19
ἐννέα παρασάγγας πεντήκοντα· καὶ ἀφικνοῦνται πρὸς τὸν
20   Ἀράξην ποταμόν. ἐνταῦθα ἦσαν κῶμαι πολλαὶ μεσταὶ σίτου
καὶ οἴνου. ἐνταῦθα ἔμειναν ἡμέρας τρεῖς καὶ ἐπεσιτίσαντο.

17. **ὑποχωρῆσαι τὸν ποταμόν**: that the river had made way. ὑποχωρῆσαι is like λῦσαι, an aorist.
18. **βασιλεύσοντι**: future participle, being about to reign.
21. **ἐπεσιτίσαντο**: from ἐπισιτίζομαι.

## 358. Writing exercise

1. *L. 8* brings the form ᾠκεῖτο, passive of οἰκέω, *to inhabit, dwell.* Conjugate this ε-contract verb in the present system, referring if necessary to ποιέω (164). Remember that initial οι when augmented becomes ᾠ. Underscore the form ᾠκεῖτο.

2. In *l. 3* the genitive Βελέσυος, *of Belesys,* is like that of ἰχθύς, *fish,* 152. Decline Βέλεσυς in the singular and also in the plural, though the latter would seldom if ever be used. Watch the quantity of the final syllables to determine placement of accent (see 25 for note on persistent accent). Note from ἰχθύς that the ultima of the accusative plural is long.

# LESSON 66

# Hunting in the Desert

## 359. New word list

ἀπαγορεύω, ἀπηγόρευσα, ἀπηγόρευκα, ἀπηγόρευμαι, to *forbid*;
mid., *to renounce, give up* or *out.*

ἁπαλός, -ή, -όν, *tender, soft.*

ἀποσπάω (see σπάω for prin. parts),
*to draw off, withdraw.*

Ἀραβία, -ας, ἡ, *Arabia.*

ἄρωμα, -ατος, τό, a *spice.* AROMA.

ἀψίνθιον -ου, τό, *wormwood.* AB-
SINTHE.

διαδέχομαι (see δέχομαι for prin.
parts), *to relieve, receive at intervals.*

διίστημι (see ἵστημι for prin. parts),

*to set apart;* intrans., *to open ranks,
stand at intervals.*

δορκάς, -άδος, ἡ, a *gazelle, antelope.*
DORCAS.

ἐλάφειος, -ον, *of deer;* κρέα ἐλάφεια,
*venison.*

ἔνειμι, *to be in, be there.*

ἐνίοτε, *sometimes.*

εὐώδης, -ες, *sweet-smelling.*

*ἥδιστος, -η, -ον, *sweetest, very
sweet,* superl. of ἡδύς.

*ἡδύς, -εῖα, -ύ, *sweet.*

θηράω, θηράσω, ἐθήρασα, τεθήρακα,
ἐθηράθην, *to hunt, chase.*

ἱστίον, -ου, τό, *a sail.*
κάλαμος, -ου, ὁ, *a reed, stalk.*
κρέας, κρέως, τό, *flesh, meat.*
ὁμαλής, -ές, *level.*
ὄνος, -ου, ὁ, *ass, weight-bearing pulley, upper millstone.*
παντοῖος, -α, -ον, *of all sorts.*
πέρδιξ, -ικος, ὁ or ἡ, *partridge.* PARTRIDGE.
πέτομαι, πτήσομαι or πετήσομαι, ἐπτόμην, *to fly.*
πλησιάζω, πλησιάσω, ἐπλησίασα, πεπλησίακα, *to approach, draw near.*

προτρέχω (see τρέχω for prin. parts), *to run ahead, outrun.*
πτέρυξ, -υγος, ἡ, *wing.*
σπάω, σπάσω, ἔσπασα, ἔσπακα, ἔσπασμαι, ἐσπάσθην, *to draw, draw tight.* SPASM.
στρουθός, -οῦ, ὁ or ἡ, *sparrow*; with μέγας, *an ostrich.*
*τρέχω, δραμοῦμαι, ἔδραμον, δεδράμηκα, δεδράμημαι, *to run.*
ὕλη, -ης, ἡ, *wood, woody growth.*
ὠτίς, -ίδος, ἡ, *bustard,* a bird related to the crane and the plover.

**360. Principal parts to be memorized**

τρέχω, δραμοῦμαι, ἔδραμον, δεδράμηκα, δεδράμημαι, *to run.*

**361. Reading passage** (*Anabasis 1.5.1.1–1.5.3.6*)

*Chapter 5.* Ἐντεῦθεν ἐξελαύνει διὰ τῆς Ἀραβίας, τὸν Εὐφράτην   1
ποταμὸν ἐν δεξιᾷ ἔχων, σταθμοὺς ἐρήμους πέντε παρασάγγας
τριάκοντα καὶ πέντε. ἐν τούτῳ δὲ τῷ τόπῳ ἦν μὲν ἡ γῆ
πεδίον ἅπαν ὁμαλὲς ὥσπερ θάλαττα, ἀψινθίου δὲ πλῆρες· εἰ
5   δέ τι καὶ ἄλλο ἐνῆν ὕλης ἢ καλάμου, ἅπαντα ἦσαν εὐώδη
ὥσπερ ἀρώματα· δένδρον δ' οὐδὲν ἐνῆν, θηρία δὲ παντοῖα,   2
πλεῖστοι ὄνοι ἄγριοι, πολλαὶ δὲ στρουθοὶ αἱ μεγάλαι· ἐνῆσαν
δὲ καὶ ὠτίδες καὶ δορκάδες· ταῦτα δὲ τὰ θηρία οἱ ἱππεῖς ἐνίοτε ἐδίωκον. καὶ οἱ μὲν ὄνοι, ἐπεί τις διώκοι, προδραμόντες

2. σταθμοὺς ἐρήμους: *desert days' journey.*

5. ἐνῆν: from ἔνειμι in today's list. This word occurs several times in this passage. ὕλης ἢ καλάμου: called *partitive genitives* (sometimes *genitive of the whole*). With τι, translate, *anything of bush or stalk* (498). εὐώδη: compare the declension of ἀληθής (157).

7. πλεῖστοι: superlative of πολύς. Translate, *very many.* στρουθοὶ αἱ μεγάλαι: literally, *sparrows, the big ones.* Here is a good example of the typically Greek humor of litotes or understatement. This name for the ostrich was doubtless coined originally by Greek soldiers or travelers who had never seen anything like these birds before and who called them 'big sparrows'.

8. οἱ ἱππεῖς: compare declension of ἱερεύς (151).

9. ἐδίωκον: *used to hunt,* imperfect denoting repeated action (548). ἐπεί τις διώκοι . . . ἔστασαν: first locate ἔστασαν in the development of ἵστημι (216). Remember that the pluperfect of ἵστημι is often used as an imperfect. So here is a conditional relative as follows: protasis, relative (ἐπεί) plus optative διώκοι; apodosis, imperfect indicative (or equivalent ἔστασαν). A past general supposition (600). The same situation obtains below in the construction εἰ πλησιάζοιεν . . . ἐποίουν and so also for οὐκ ἦν λαβεῖν εἰ μὴ . . . θηρῷεν. In this last, the apodosis precedes the protasis. προδραμόντες: δραμόντες is second aorist participle of τρέχω, whose principal parts are part of today's lesson. δραμών is declined like ὤν, οὖσα, ὄν (180).

10 ἔστασαν· πολὺ γὰρ τῶν ἵππων ἔτρεχον θᾶττον· καὶ πάλιν,
ἐπεὶ πλησιάζοιεν οἱ ἵπποι, ταὐτὸν ἐποίουν, καὶ οὐκ ἦν
λαβεῖν εἰ μὴ διαστάντες οἱ ἱππεῖς θηρῷεν διαδεχόμενοι. τὰ
δὲ κρέα τῶν ἁλισκομένων ἦν παραπλήσια τοῖς ἐλαφείοις,
ἁπαλώτερα δέ. στρουθὸν δὲ οὐδεὶς ἔλαβεν· οἱ δὲ διώξαντες    3
15 τῶν ἱππέων ταχὺ ἐπαύοντο· πολὺ γὰρ ἀπέσπα φεύγουσα,
τοῖς μὲν ποσὶ δρόμῳ, ταῖς δὲ πτέρυξιν αἴρουσα, ὥσπερ ἱστίῳ
χρωμένη. τὰς δὲ ὠτίδας ἄν τις ταχὺ ἀνιστῇ ἔστι λαμβάνειν·
πέτονται γὰρ βραχὺ ὥσπερ πέρδικες καὶ ταχὺ ἀπαγορεύουσι.
τὰ δὲ κρέα αὐτῶν ἥδιστα ἦν.

10. **πολύ**: adverbial, *much* (530). **τῶν ἵππων**: genitive of comparison (507).
11. **ταὐτόν**: irregular for τὸ αὐτό, *the same thing*. **οὐκ ἦν**: *it was not possible*.
12. **λαβεῖν**: from λαμβάνω. **διαστάντες**: from διίστημι in today's list. Find *στάς* in the
chart of ἵστημι (216). **θηρῷεν**: from θηράω in today's word list. See development of
γεννάω (173). Find *γεννῷεν*.
16. **τοῖς μὲν ποσί**: dative with χρωμένη, present participle of χράομαι. ποσί is dative
plural of πούς. Compare the declension of ἀσπίς (146). **δρόμῳ**: *for running*. **πτέρυξι(ν)**:
compare the declension of σάρξ (145). **αἴρουσα**: present participle of αἴρω.
17. **ἄν τις ταχὺ ἀνιστῇ ἔστι λαμβάνειν**: ἀνιστῇ is from ἀνίστημι. Find *ἰστῇ* in the
chart of ἵστημι (216). Here is seen in the protasis ἐάν (ἄν) plus subjunctive ἀνιστῇ;
apodosis, ἔστι. A present general supposition (599). ἔστι is accented thus to show
possibility (128).
19. **τὰ . . . κρέα**: see declension of τὸ κρέας in 139.

## 362. Writing exercise

1. The participle προδραμόντες (*l. 9*) is from the second aorist of
προτρέχω, a compound of τρέχω, *to run*. Conjugate the second aorist
προέδραμον, using ἤγαγον (118) as a model. Augment only the indicative
forms, of course.

2. From the conjugation above take the participle προδραμών and
decline it (use ὤν, οὖσα, ὄν for endings, 180). Underscore προδραμόντες.

## LESSON 67

# The Grim Pinch of Famine

## 363. New word list

ἀλέτης, -ου, *mill-*, an adjective used
only with ὄνος to mean *mill stone*.

ἄλευρον, -ου, τό, *wheat flour*, usually
plural.

ἄλφιτον, -ου, τό, *barley meal*, used in
plural.

ἀνταγοράζω (see ἀγοράζω for prin.
parts), *to buy in exchange*.

Ἀττικός, -ή, -όν, *Attic, of Attica,* the country in Greece of which Athens was and is the principal city.

Βαβυλών, -ῶνος, ἡ, *Babylon,* capital of Babylonia.

διαγίγνομαι (see γίγνομαι for prin. parts), *to get through, exist.*

διατελέω (see τελέω for prin. parts), *to bring to an end, complete.*

ἐνενήκοντα, indecl., *ninety.*

ἐπιλείπω (see λείπω for prin. parts), *to fail, leave off.*

ἐπριάμην (second aorist only), *to buy.* Used for aorist of ὠνέομαι, ὠνήσομαι, ἐώνημαι, *to buy.*

ἡμιωβόλιον, -ου, τό, a *half-obol,* worth about three cents.

καπίθη, -ης, ἡ, *the capith,* about two quarts dry measure.

Κορσωτή, -ῆς, ἡ, *Corsote,* a large city of Mesopotamia on the Euphrates.

*κύκλος, -ου, ὁ, *a circle.* CYCLE.

λιμός, -οῦ, ὁ, *hunger, famine.*

Λύδιος, -α, -ον, *Lydian.*

*μακρός, -ά, -όν, *long.* MACRON.

Μάσκας, -α, ὁ, *the Mascas,* called a river, really a canal around the city of Corsote on the Euphrates.

ὀβολός, -οῦ, ὁ, *the obol,* an Attic coin worth about six cents.

ὀρύττω, ὀρύξω, ὤρυξα, ὀρώρυχα, ὀρώρυγμαι, ὠρύχθην, *to dig, quarry.*

περιρρέω (see ῥέω for prin. parts), *to flow around.*

πλεθριαῖος, -α, -ον, *of a plethron.*

Πύλαι, -ῶν, αἱ, *Pylae,* a fortress on the border between Mesopotamia and Babylonia. Literally, 'The Gates.'

σίγλος, -ου, ὁ, *the siglus, shekel,* a Persian coin worth about a half dollar.

τελέω, τελῶ, ἐτέλεσα, τετέλεκα, τετέλεσμαι, ἐτελέσθην, *to complete.*

τρεισκαίδεκα, indecl., *thirteen.*

χιλός, -οῦ, ὁ, *provender, fodder.*

χοῖνιξ, -ικος, ἡ, *the choenix,* an Attic dry measure containing nearly a quart.

ψιλός, -ή, -όν, *naked, bare, barren.*

### 364. Principal parts to be memorized

ἀπόλλυμι, ἀπολῶ, ἀπώλεσα and ἀπωλόμην, ἀπόλωλα or ἀπολώλεκα, *to destroy*: middle and passive, *to perish.*

### 365. Reading passage (*Anabasis* 1.5.4.1–1.5.7.3)

Πορευόμενοι δὲ διὰ ταύτης τῆς χώρας ἀφικνοῦνται ἐπὶ τὸν    4
Μάσκαν ποταμόν, τὸ εὖρος πλεθριαῖον. ἐνταῦθα ἦν πόλις
ἐρήμη, μεγάλη, ὄνομα δ' αὐτῇ Κορσωτή· περιερρεῖτο δ'
αὕτη ὑπὸ τοῦ Μάσκα κύκλῳ. ἐνταῦθ' ἔμειναν ἡμέρας τρεῖς

3. ὄνομα δ' αὐτῇ: understand ἦν. περιερρεῖτο: imperfect indicative passive of περιρρέω in today's list. Literally, *it was flowed around, surrounded.*

4. Μάσκα: a Doric genitive, usually found only with foreign proper names. κύκλῳ: *in a circle,* dative of manner (522).

5    καὶ ἐπεσιτίσαντο. ἐντεῦθεν ἐξελαύνει σταθμοὺς ἐρήμους    5
τρεισκαίδεκα παρασάγγας ἐνενήκοντα τὸν Εὐφράτην ποταμὸν
ἐν δεξιᾷ ἔχων, καὶ ἀφικνεῖται ἐπὶ Πύλας. ἐν τούτοις τοῖς
σταθμοῖς πολλὰ τῶν ὑποζυγίων ἀπώλετο ὑπὸ λιμοῦ· οὐ γὰρ
ἦν χόρτος οὐδὲ ἄλλο οὐδὲν δένδρον, ἀλλὰ ψιλὴ ἦν ἅπασα ἡ
10   χώρα· οἱ δὲ ἐνοικοῦντες ὄνους ἀλέτας παρὰ τὸν ποταμὸν
ὀρύττοντες καὶ ποιοῦντες εἰς Βαβυλῶνα ἦγον καὶ ἐπώλουν
καὶ ἀνταγοράζοντες σῖτον ἔζων. τὸ δὲ στράτευμα ὁ σῖτος    6
ἐπέλιπε, καὶ πρίασθαι οὐκ ἦν εἰ μὴ ἐν τῇ Λυδίᾳ ἀγορᾷ ἐν τῷ
Κύρου βαρβαρικῷ, τὴν καπίθην ἀλεύρων ἢ ἀλφίτων τεττά-
15   ρων σίγλων. ὁ δὲ σίγλος δύναται ἑπτὰ ὀβολοὺς καὶ ἡμιωβόλιον Ἀττικούς· ἡ δὲ καπίθη δύο χοίνικας Ἀττικὰς ἐχώρει.
κρέα οὖν ἐσθίοντες οἱ στρατιῶται διεγίγνοντο. ἦν δὲ τούτων    7
τῶν σταθμῶν οὓς πάνυ μακροὺς ἤλαυνεν, ὁπότε ἢ πρὸς ὕδωρ
βούλοιτο διατελέσαι ἢ πρὸς χιλόν.

8. ἀπώλετο: singular verb with neuter plural subject. From ἀπόλλυμι.

10. οἱ ἐνοικοῦντες: the inhabitants.

12. ἔζων: imperfect of ζάω. Compare ἐγέννων from γεννάω (173).

13. ἐπέλιπε: from ἐπιλείπω in today's list. See principal parts of λείπω. πρίασθαι: see ἐπριάμην in today's list. Understand σῖτον. οὐκ ἦν: it was not possible.

14. τὴν καπίθην: accusative following the idea of πρίασθαι, which is carried over here. ἀλεύρων . . . ἀλφίτων: genitives of contents (501). τεττάρων σίγλων: genitive of price or value (503).

15. δύναται: is worth.

16. ἐχώρει: held. The choenix of meal or flour, about a quart, was thus costing about one dollar here in the desert—some fifty or sixty times its cost in Athens.

17. κρέα: see declension of κρέας (139). ἦν δὲ . . . οὓς: past tense of the idiomatic ἔστιν οἵ, there are those who . . . . The verb retains singular number in this expression. τούτων τῶν σταθμῶν: partitive genitive, or genitive of the whole (498).

18. ὁπότε . . . βούλοιτο . . . ἤλαυνε: conditional relative with past general supposition (600).

19. διατελέσαι: understand τὴν ὁδόν, the journey.

## 366. Writing exercise

1. ἀπόλλυμι, today's verb, has a first aorist active and a second aorist middle. Conjugate these, remembering that this is a compound verb and the ω is an augmented ο and that the unaugmented ο occurs in all but the indicative forms. See λύω (97) and ἄγω (118). Underscore ἀπώλετο, which occurs in *l. 8* today.

2. *L. 16* brings χοίνικας, accusative plural of ἡ χοῖνιξ, the choenix, a quart. Decline ἡ χοῖνιξ referring to ἡ σάρξ (145). Remember that χοῖνιξ is not a monosyllabic stem like σάρξ, hence does not accent the ultima in genitive and dative, singular and plural. Underscore χοίνικας.

# LESSON 68

## An Example of Good Discipline

### 367. New word list

*ἄμαξα, -ης, ἡ, wagon.
ἀναξυρίδες, -ίδων, αἱ, trousers.
γήλοφος, -ου, ὁ, hill.
Γλοῦς, -οῦ, ὁ, Glus, son of Tamos, a noble Egyptian.
δυσπόρευτος, -ον, hard to get through, difficult of passage.
εἰσπηδάω (see πηδάω for prin. parts), to jump into.
ἐκκομίζω (see κομίζω for prin. parts), to get out.
ἔνιοι, -αι, -α, some, several.
εὐθύς, -εῖα, -ύ, straight; as adv., straightway, immediately.
εὐταξία, -ας, ἡ, good discipline.
κάνδυς, -υος, ὁ, caftan, a Persian cloak.
*κομίζω, κομιῶ, ἐκόμισα, κεκόμικα, κεκόμισμαι, ἐκομίσθην, to provide, get.
*κράτιστος, -η, -ον, best, noblest, bravest, superl. of ἀγαθός.
*μέρος, -ους, τό, part, example.
μετέωρος, -ον, raised up from the ground, in the air. METEOR.

*νίκη, -ης, ἡ, victory; περὶ νίκης, for victory, 'to win'.
ὀργή, -ῆς, ἡ, anger.
πηδάω, πηδήσομαι, ἐπήδησα, πεπήδηκα, to leap.
πηλός, -οῦ, ὁ, mud, miry clay.
ποικίλος, -η, -ον, many-colored.
πολυτελής, -ές, expensive, costly.
πορφυροῦς, -ᾶ, -οῦν, purple, dark red. PURPLE.
ποτε, once, ever.
πρανής, -ές, headlong, steep. PRONE.
ῥίπτω, ῥίψω, ἔρριψα, ἔρριφα, ἔρριμμαι, ἐρρίφθην or ἐρρίφην, to throw, throw off.
στενοχωρία, -ας, ἡ, a narrow pass.
στρατός, -οῦ, ὁ, army, force.
συνεκβιβάζω (see βιβάζω for prin. parts), to help push out.
συνεπισπεύδω (see σπεύδω for prin. parts), to help hurry forward.
σχολαίως, slowly; comp., σχολαίτερον.
τράχηλος, -ου, ὁ, neck, throat.

### 368. Principal parts to be memorized

φαίνω, φανῶ, ἔφηνα, πέφηνα, πέφασμαι, ἐφάνην, to show: middle, to appear.

### 369. Reading passage (*Anabasis 1.5.7.4–1.5.8.10*)

Καὶ δή ποτε στενοχωρίας καὶ πηλοῦ φανέντος ταῖς
ἁμάξαις δυσπορεύτου, ἐπέστη ὁ Κῦρος σὺν τοῖς περὶ αὐτὸν
ἀρίστοις καὶ εὐδαιμονεστάτοις καὶ ἔταξε Γλοῦν καὶ Πίγρητα

1. **ποτε**: one time, once. **φανέντος**: see the second passive system of φαίνω (205). Note the participle, then see it declined in 184 as λυθείς. The construction in this passage is genitive absolute denoting time (582). **ταῖς ἁμάξαις**: dative of disadvantage (517).
2. **ἐπέστη**: from ἐφίστημι. See development of ἵστημι (216). Find the form ἔστη.
3. **ἔταξε**: from τάττω. Translate, he ordered. **Γλοῦν**: compare this with the declension of νοῦς (243).

λαβόντας τοῦ βαρβαρικοῦ στρατοῦ συνεκβιβάζειν τὰς ἁμάξας.

5   ἐπεὶ δ' ἐδόκουν αὐτῷ σχολαίως ποιεῖν, ὥσπερ ὀργῇ ἐκέλευσε   8
τοὺς περὶ αὐτὸν Πέρσας τοὺς κρατίστους συνεπισπεῦσαι τὰς
ἁμάξας. ἔνθα δὴ μέρος τι τῆς εὐταξίας ἦν θεάσασθαι.
ῥίψαντες γὰρ τοὺς πορφυροῦς κάνδυς ὅπου ἔτυχεν ἕκαστος
ἑστηκώς, ἵεντο ὥσπερ ἂν δράμοι τις περὶ νίκης καὶ μάλα
10   κατὰ πρανοῦς γηλόφου, ἔχοντες τούς τε πολυτελεῖς χιτῶνας
καὶ τὰς ποικίλας ἀναξυρίδας, ἔνιοι δὲ καὶ στρεπτοὺς περὶ
τοῖς τραχήλοις καὶ ψέλια περὶ ταῖς χερσίν· εὐθὺς δὲ σὺν
τούτοις εἰσπηδήσαντες εἰς τὸν πηλὸν θᾶττον ἢ ὥς τις ἂν
ᾤετο μετεώρους ἐξεκόμισαν τὰς ἁμάξας.

4. **τοῦ βαρβαρικοῦ στρατοῦ**: partitive genitive. Translate, (*part*) *of the barbarian army* (498).
5. **ὀργῇ**: dative of manner (522).
7. **ἦν**: *it was possible.*
8. **πορφυροῦς**: compare the declension of the contract adjective χρυσοῦς (244). **κάνδυς**: for the case, compare the declension of ἰχθύς (152). The accent here is on a different syllable, of course. **ἔτυχον**: from τυγχάνω.
9. **ἑστηκώς**: from ἵστημι (216). The form here used is the longer form, derived from ἕστηκα. Translate, *wherever each happened to stand.* **ἵεντο**: from ἵημι. See its conjugation in 233. **ὥσπερ ἂν δράμοι τις περὶ νίκης**: δράμοι is from ἔδραμον, the second aorist of τρέχω. A potential optative (567). **μάλα**: *very.*
10. **κατά**: *down.* **πρανοῦς**: genitive. Compare with the declension of ἀληθής (157).
13. **ὥς τις ἂν ᾤετο**: the verb is the imperfect indicative of οἴομαι, *to think.* The construction is related to the contrary-to-fact condition in present time. Omit ὥς, *as.* Translate, *quicker than one would think,* i.e. if he were thinking about it (601).

### 370. Writing exercise

1. The participle φανέντος in *l. 1* is aorist passive of φαίνω, *to show.* Conjugate the second passive system of φαίνω, whose personal endings are the same as those of the first passive system of λύω. See 205, then 97.

2. From the above, take the aorist passive participle of φαίνω and decline it (see λυθείς, 184). Underscore φανέντος (masculine) as seen in *l. 1.*

## LESSON 69

# Shopping by River Raft

### 371. New word list

ἀγείρω, ἀγεροῦμαι, ἤγειρα, ἀγήγερκα, ἀγήγερμαι, ἠγέρθην, *to gather.*
ἀναγκαῖος, -α, -ον, *necessary.*

ἅπτω, ἅψω, ἦψα, ἦμμαι, ἥφθην, *to
lay hold of*; mid., *to touch,* with
gen.

ἀσθενής, -ές, *weak.* NEURASTHENIC.

βάλανος, -ου, ἡ, *acorn, date.*

διασπάω (see σπάω for prin. parts), *to draw apart, separate.*

διφθέρα, -ας, ἡ, *a tanned skin, leather bag.* DIPHTHERIA.

ἐπισιτισμός, -οῦ, ὁ, *the collecting of provisions, foraging.*

ἰσχυρός, -ά, -όν, *strong, fortified.*

καθέζομαι, *to sit down, halt, encamp.*

κάρφη, -ης, ἡ, *hay.*

κοῦφος, -η, -ον, *light, dry.*

μῆκος, -ους, τό, *length.*

*νοῦς, νοῦ, ὁ, *mind;* τὸν νοῦν προσέχειν, *to give thought* or *attention.*

προσέχω (see ἔχω for prin. parts), *to apply.*

στέγασμα, -ατος, τό, *tent covering.*

συναγείρω (see ἀγείρω for prin. parts), *to gather, assemble.*

συνοράω (see ὁράω for prin. parts), *to see at the same time, at once.*

συσπάω (see σπάω for prin. parts), *to draw together, sew together.*

σχεδία, -ας, ἡ, *a raft.*

φοῖνιξ, -ικος, ὁ, *the date palm, palm.*

Χαρμάνδη, -ης, ἡ, *Charmande,* a city of northeastern Arabia on the Euphrates.

## 372. Principal parts to be memorized

σπάω, σπάσω, ἔσπασα, ἔσπακα, ἔσπασμαι, ἐσπάσθην, *to draw.*

## 373. Reading passage (*Anabasis 1.5.9.1–1.5.10.9*)

Τὸ δὲ σύμπαν δῆλος ἦν Κῦρος ὡς σπεύδων πᾶσαν τὴν   9
ὁδὸν καὶ οὐ διατρίβων ὅπου μὴ ἐπισιτισμοῦ ἕνεκα ἢ τινος
ἄλλου ἀναγκαίου ἐκαθέζετο, νομίζων, ὅσῳ μὲν θᾶττον ἔλθοι,
τοσούτῳ ἀπαρασκευοτέρῳ βασιλεῖ μαχεῖσθαι, ὅσῳ δὲ σχολαί-
5   τερον, τοσούτῳ πλέον συναγείρεσθαι βασιλεῖ στράτευμα. καὶ
συνιδεῖν δ' ἦν τῷ προσέχοντι τὸν νοῦν ἡ βασιλέως ἀρχὴ

1. **τὸ δὲ σύμπαν**: *but on the whole.* Adverbial accusative (530). **πᾶσαν τὴν ὁδόν**: accusative of extent of space, *all the way* (531).

2. **μή**: *not.* Used instead of οὐκ because referring to the idea or thinking of Cyrus. Same force as εἰ μή, *if not, unless.*

3. **ὅσῳ ... τοσούτῳ**: datives of degree of difference, *by how much ... by so much* (524). See also below in *l. 5.* **ὅσῳ μὲν θᾶττον ἔλθοι ... μαχεῖσθαι**: here quoted indirectly after a past tense, the original thought of Cyrus was ὅσῳ θᾶττον ἂν ἔλθω ... μαχοῦμαι, *by how much more quickly I come ... I will fight,* etc. Here is a future more vivid conditional relative. In 603 note that when a future more vivid condition is quoted after a secondary tense, ἐάν drops ἄν to become εἰ. Similarly in a conditional relative sentence, a relative plus ἄν plus subjunctive becomes relative plus optative. In the apodosis here the future indicative (μαχοῦμαι) changes to future infinitive μαχεῖσθαι. Translate, *thinking by how much more quickly he came ... he would fight,* etc.

6. **συνιδεῖν**: from συνοράω in today's list. ἰδεῖν is the infinitive of εἶδον from ὁράω. **ἦν**: *it was possible.* **τῷ προσέχοντι τὸν νοῦν**: *for the one applying his mind, or giving attention.* Dative of relation or reference (513). **ἡ βασιλέως ἀρχὴ ... οὖσα**: this construction should logically be in the accusative case as object of συνιδεῖν, *to see.* Instead the construction changes to nominative as though the idea were ἡ βασιλέως ἀρχὴ δήλη ἦν, etc. Translate this group of words as though accusative.

πλήθει μὲν χώρας καὶ ἀνθρώπων ἰσχυρὰ οὖσα, τοῖς δὲ μήκεσι
τῶν ὁδῶν καὶ τῷ διεσπάσθαι τὰς δυνάμεις ἀσθενὴς εἴ τις
διὰ ταχέων τὸν πόλεμον ἐποιεῖτο. πέραν δὲ τοῦ Εὐφράτου    10
10   ποταμοῦ κατὰ τοὺς ἐρήμους σταθμοὺς ἦν πόλις εὐδαίμων
καὶ μεγάλη, ὄνομα δὲ Χαρμάνδη· ἐκ ταύτης οἱ στρατιῶται
ἠγόραζον τὰ ἐπιτήδεια, σχεδίαις διαβαίνοντες ὧδε. διφθέρας
ἃς εἶχον στεγάσματα ἐπίμπλασαν χόρτου κούφου, εἶτα συν-
ῆγον καὶ συνέσπων, ὡς μὴ ἅπτεσθαι τῆς κάρφης τὸ ὕδωρ·
15   ἐπὶ τούτων διέβαινον καὶ ἐλάμβανον τὰ ἐπιτήδεια, οἶνόν τε
ἐκ τῆς βαλάνου πεποιημένον τῆς ἀπὸ τοῦ φοίνικος καὶ σῖτον
μελίνης· τοῦτο γὰρ ἦν ἐν τῇ χώρᾳ πλεῖστον.

7. **πλήθει**: dative of respect, *in quantity* or *multitude*. Similarly with μήκεσι and τῷ
διεσπάσθαι in *ll.* 7 and 8 (523).
8. **τῷ διεσπάσθαι**: here is an articular infinitive, and διεσπάσθαι is the perfect infinitive, as the ε shows. τὰς δυνάμεις, *the forces*, is subject. Translate (*the realm was weak*)
*in its forces having been separated*. εἴ τις . . . ἐποιεῖτο: εἰ plus imperfect indicative, the
protasis of a condition contrary to fact in present time, *if anyone were making* (601).
9. **διὰ ταχέων**: *through rapid* (*measures*). Idiomatic expression meaning *with speed.*
For the form of ταχέων see βαθύς (156).
10. **κατά**: *along, during.*
11. **ὄνομα**: understand ἦν.
12. **σχεδίαις**: dative of means (520).
13. **ἐπίμπλασαν**: from πίμπλημι, which is conjugated in the present system as is
ἵστημι. Locate ἵστασαν in the chart of ἵστημι (216). **χόρτου κούφου**: genitive with
word denoting fullness (501).
14. **συνέσπων**: imperfect of συσπάω. ἔσπων is like ἐγέννων from γεννάω (173). **ὡς**: for
ὥστε. Translate, *so as* or *so that.*

## 374. Writing exercise

1. The form διεσπάσθαι in' *l.* 8 is the perfect passive infinitive of
διασπάω, *to draw apart, separate*, a compound of today's σπάω, *to draw.*
Conjugate the perfect middle and passive of διασπάω, getting a start from
the appropriate principal part of σπάω, and then using βεβάπτισμαι
(113) as model. Remember that the initial epsilon in this system of σπάω
is *reduplication*, and it occurs throughout the system. In the pluperfect it
stands for both reduplication and augment. Underscore διεσπάσθαι.
2. In *ll.* 8 and 9 is seen διὰ ταχέων, *through rapid things* (neuter) or
*measures*, meaning *with speed.* Conjugate this adjective ταχύς, *rapid* (cf.
βαθύς, 156). Underscore the proper instance of ταχέων.

# LESSON 70

## Cyrus' Estimate of Civil Freedom

### 375. New word list

*ἀμείνων, -ον, better, braver, comp. of ἀγαθός.

ἀνέχω (see ἔχω for prin. parts), to hold up; mid., to restrain one's self, stand firm against.

αὐτόμολος, -ου, ὁ, a deserter.

Βαβυλωνία, -ας, ἡ, Babylonia.

διατάττω (see τάττω for prin. parts), to draw up in array.

ἐλευθερία, -ας, ἡ, freedom, liberty.

εὐδαιμονίζω, εὐδαιμονιῶ, ηὐδαιμόνισα, to count happy, congratulate, with gen. of the cause.

ἕως, ἕω, ἡ, daybreak, dawn. EOS.

ζηλωτός, -ή, -όν, envied, deemed happy. ZEALOT, JEALOUS.

θαρρύνω, to encourage.

*κέρας, κέρατος or κέρως, τό, horn, wing of an army. RHINOCEROS.

*κρείττων, -ον, better, braver, comp. of ἀγαθός.

κτάομαι, κτήσομαι, ἐκτησάμην, κέκτημαι, ἐκτήθην, to win or procure for one's self; perf., to possess.

λοχαγός, -οῦ, ὁ, company leader, captain.

*οἷος, -α, -ον, of what sort.

παραινέω (see αἰνέω for prin. parts), to praise.

πολλαπλάσιος, -α, -ον, many times more.

προσλαμβάνω (see λαμβάνω for prin. parts), to take besides.

ὦ, interjection, o, frequently with vocative.

### 376. Principal parts to be memorized

εἴδω, εἴσομαι, εἶδον, οἶδα, to see, (perf.) to know.

Between the last lesson and today's is omitted an interesting account of a dangerous quarrel between Clearchus and Menon, two of the Greek commanders, which threatened to break out into an armed clash between their contingents and which was stopped by the personal intervention of Cyrus. Also omitted is an account of the treachery of Orontas, one of Cyrus' noble Persian lieutenants, followed by the trial and condemnation of the traitor to death.

### 377. Reading passage (Anabasis 1.7.1.1–1.7.4.8)

Chapter 7. Ἐντεῦθεν ἐξελαύνει διὰ τῆς Βαβυλωνίας σταθμοὺς    1
τρεῖς παρασάγγας δώδεκα. ἐν δὲ τῷ τρίτῳ σταθμῷ Κῦρος
ἐξέτασιν ποιεῖται τῶν Ἑλλήνων καὶ τῶν βαρβάρων ἐν τῷ
πεδίῳ περὶ μέσας νύκτας· ἐδόκει γὰρ εἰς τὴν ἐπιοῦσαν ἔω

4. μέσας νύκτας: the expression μέσαι νύκτες is idiomatic for midnight. ἐδόκει: here used personally, he thought. εἰς: into, towards, at. ἐπιοῦσαν: from ἔπειμι. See development

LESSON 70 Cyrus' estimate of civil freedom 211

5 ἥξειν βασιλέα σὺν τῷ στρατεύματι μαχούμενον· καὶ ἐκέλευε
Κλέαρχον μὲν τοῦ δεξιοῦ κέρως ἡγεῖσθαι, Μένωνα δὲ τοῦ
εὐωνύμου, αὐτὸς δὲ τοὺς ἑαυτοῦ διέταξε. μετὰ δὲ τὴν 2
ἐξέτασιν ἅμα τῇ ἐπιούσῃ ἡμέρᾳ ἥκοντες αὐτόμολοι παρὰ
μεγάλου βασιλέως ἀπήγγελλον Κύρῳ περὶ τῆς βασιλέως
10 στρατιᾶς. Κῦρος δὲ συγκαλέσας τοὺς στρατηγοὺς καὶ λοχα-
γοὺς τῶν Ἑλλήνων συνεβουλεύετό τε πῶς ἂν τὴν μάχην
ποιοῖτο καὶ αὐτὸς παρῄνει θαρρύνων τοιάδε· Ὦ ἄνδρες 3
Ἕλληνες, οὐκ ἀνθρώπων ἀπορῶν βαρβάρων συμμάχους
ὑμᾶς ἄγω, ἀλλὰ νομίζων ἀμείνους καὶ κρείττους πολλῶν
15 βαρβάρων ὑμᾶς εἶναι, διὰ τοῦτο προσέλαβον. ὅπως οὖν
ἔσεσθε ἄνδρες ἄξιοι τῆς ἐλευθερίας ἧς κέκτησθε καὶ ἧς
ὑμᾶς ἐγὼ εὐδαιμονίζω· εὖ γὰρ ἴστε ὅτι τὴν ἐλευθερίαν
ἑλοίμην ἂν ἀντὶ ὧν ἔχω πάντων καὶ ἄλλων πολλαπλασίων.
ὅπως δὲ καὶ εἰδῆτε εἰς οἷον ἔρχεσθε ἀγῶνα, ὑμᾶς εἰδὼς 4
20 διδάξω. τὸ μὲν γὰρ πλῆθος πολὺ καὶ κραυγῇ πολλῇ ἐπίασιν·
ἂν δὲ ταῦτα ἀνάσχησθε, τὰ ἄλλα καὶ αἰσχύνεσθαί μοι δοκῶ

of εἰμι (233). ἔω: accusative singular of ἔως, dawn, a noun of the rare 'Attic' declension, which inflects as follows: nom. ἔως, gen. ἔω, dat. ἔῳ, acc. ἔω (its accusative is an
exception to the more regular -ων, accusative singular ending of the Attic declension).
5. ἥξειν: future infinitive of ἥκω. The original thought was, 'The king will come'.
μαχούμενον: future participle expressing purpose, to fight (581).
6. κέρως: from κέρας in today's list. Declined in 139. ἡγεῖσθαι: ἡγέομαι takes the
genitive when the idea of command or superiority is implied.
7. τοὺς ἑαυτοῦ: his own troops.
8. ἅμα τῇ ἐπιούσῃ ἡμέρᾳ: along with the coming day, idiomatic for at daybreak.
11. πῶς ἂν τὴν μάχην ποιοῖτο: with ἂν the optative is potential, how he might conduct
(make) the battle (567).
12. παρῄνει: imperfect of παραινέω. τοιάδε: as follows.
13. ἀνθρώπων . . . βαρβάρων: verbs signifying lack or fullness take the genitive (501).
14. ἀμείνους: from ἀμείνων. See declension of ἡδίων (157). Find ἡδίους. The same
comparison applies to κρείττους in the same line.
15. πολλῶν βαρβάρων: genitive of comparison (507). ὅπως . . . ἔσεσθε: ὅπως with
future indicative is sometimes used to indicate a command (553). It is closely related
to the object clause composed of ὅπως plus future indicative, as though the idea were
(take care, or see) that you shall be. Translate it this way.
16. ἧς κέκτησθε: perfect of κτάομαι, which you have obtained. ἧς is attracted to the
case of its antecedent. The second ἧς is genitive with εὐδαιμονίζω, to congratulate. It is
a genitive of cause. Translate, for which I congratulate you (509).
17. ἴστε: locate this form in the development of the perfect system of εἴδω (199). So
also for εἰδῆτε and εἰδώς in l. 19.
18. ἑλοίμην ἄν: potential optative (567). ἑλοίμην is from αἱρέω.
19. ὅπως . . . εἰδῆτε: purpose clause, ὅπως plus subjunctive (562).
20. τὸ . . . πλῆθος: understand ἐστί. κραυγῇ πολλῇ: dative of manner (522). ἐπίασι(ν):
from ἔπειμι. Find ἴασι in the conjugation of εἰμι (233).
21. ἂν δὲ ταῦτα ἀνάσχησθε: protasis of a future more vivid condition, but if you stand
firm against. For ἀνάσχησθε, note the principal parts of ἔχω. The second aorist indicative

οἵους ἡμῖν γνώσεσθε τοὺς ἐν τῇ χώρᾳ ὄντας ἀνθρώπους.
ὑμῶν δὲ ἀνδρῶν ὄντων καὶ εὖ τῶν ἐμῶν γενομένων, ἐγὼ
ὑμῶν τὸν μὲν οἴκαδε βουλόμενον ἀπιέναι τοῖς οἴκοι ζηλωτὸν
25 ποιήσω ἀπελθεῖν, πολλοὺς δὲ οἶμαι ποιήσειν τὰ παρ᾽ ἐμοὶ
ἑλέσθαι ἀντὶ τῶν οἴκοι.

is ἔσχον. With augment dropped the subjunctive active would be σχῶ, σχῇς, σχῇ, etc.,
the middle σχῶμαι, σχῇ, σχῆται; σχώμεθα, σχῆσθε, σχῶνται. τὰ ἄλλα: accusative of
specification, *in the other respects* (529).
  22. γνώσεσθε: see γιγνώσκω. οἵους ἡμῖν ... ὄντας ἀνθρώπους: literally, *what sort of
men being to us.* ἡμῖν is dative of possessor. More freely, *what sort of men we have* ....
  23. τῶν ἐμῶν: genitive of τὰ ἐμά, *my affairs.* γενομένων: *becoming,* in the sense of
*turning out.* Here are two genitive absolutes implying condition, *if* (582).
  24. ἀπιέναι: from ἄπειμι. Find ἰέναι in the conjugation of εἶμι (233).
  25. ἀπελθεῖν: from ἀπέρχομαι. οἶμαι ποιήσειν: *I think that I will make.*
  26. ἑλέσθαι: from αἱρέω.

## 378. Writing exercise

  1. Give the conjugation of οἶδα, second perfect of εἴδω, *to know* (199),
underscoring the forms of this verb which occur in *ll. 17* and *19* of today's passage. Is ἴστε indicative or imperative?
  2. In *l. 14* is seen the form ἀμείνους, a comparative of ἀγαθός (238).
Taking the nominative from today's word list (it is a two-ending adjective), decline it, referring, as needed, to ἡδίων (157). Include the alternative shortened forms. Underscore ἀμείνους, determining from context
whether it is nominative or accusative.

# LESSON 71

# The Call to Battle Stations

## 379. New word list

Ἀριαῖος, -ου, ὁ, *Ariaeus,* one of
  Cyrus' Persian generals.
ἄτακτος, -ον, *not in battle array, in
  disorder.*
αὐτίκα, *at once, immediately.*
βαρβαρικῶς, *in the Persian tongue.*
διακινδυνεύω (see κινδυνεύω for
  prin. parts), *to run a risk* or
  *risks.*
ἑλληνικῶς, *in the Greek tongue.*

ἐνδύω (see δύω for prin. parts), *to
  clothe one's self in, put on.*
ἑξακόσιοι, -αι, -α, *six hundred.*
ἐξοπλίζω (see ὁπλίζω for prin.
  parts), *to arm fully.*
ἐπιπίπτω (see πίπτω for prin.
  parts), *to fall upon, attack.*
ἡνίκα, *at which time, when.*
*θώραξ, -ακος, ὁ, *breastplate, cuirass.*
  THORAX.

ἱδρόω, ἵδρωσα, to sweat.
καταπηδάω (see πηδάω for prin. parts), to jump down.
καταφανής, -ές, in plain sight, evident.
*κεφαλή, -ῆς, ἡ, head. ENCEPHALITIS.
*κράτος, -ους, τό, strength, power; ἀνὰ or κατὰ κράτος, up to strength, at full speed.
μάχαιρα, -ας, ἡ, saber.
ὁπλίζω, ὥπλισα, ὥπλισμαι, ὡπλίσθην, to arm, equip.
*παλτόν, -οῦ, τό, javelin.
παραμηρίδια, -ων, τά, thigh armor.
Πατηγύας, -α, ὁ, Pategyas, a Persian loyal to Cyrus.

Παφλαγών, -όνος, ὁ, a Paphlagonian.
πελταστικός, -ή, -όν, of the peltasts; τὸ πελταστικόν, the light-armed force.
*πιστός, -ή, -όν, faithful, trusted, loyal, reliable; comp., πιστότερος; superl., πιστότατος.
πλήθω, πέπληθα, to be full; ἀγορὰ πλήθουσα, full market, forenoon.
προμετωπίδιον, -ου, τό, a frontlet or face armor worn by horses.
προστερνίδιον, -ου, τό, a breastplate for horses.
προφαίνω (see φαίνω for prin. parts), to bring to light; mid., to come into sight.
σπουδή, -ῆς, ἡ, eagerness, haste.
τάραχος, -ου, ὁ, confusion.

## 380. Principal parts to be memorized

πίπτω, πεσοῦμαι, ἔπεσον, πέπτωκα, to fall.

Between the previous lesson and today's is the omission of two or three random events and an accounting of the numbers of the opposing forces. Cyrus' army is said to comprise 10,400 Greek hoplites, 2,500 Greek peltasts, 100,000 barbarians, and about 20 scythe-bearing chariots. The king's army numbered 1,200,000 foot soldiers, 6,000 cavalry, and 200 scythe-bearing chariots.

## 381. Reading passage (*Anabasis 1.8.1.1–1.8.7.3*)

*Chapter 8.* Καὶ ἤδη τε ἦν ἀμφὶ ἀγορὰν πλήθουσαν καὶ πλησίον    1
ἦν ὁ σταθμὸς ἔνθα ἔμελλε καταλύειν, ἡνίκα Πατηγύας ἀνὴρ
Πέρσης τῶν ἀμφὶ Κῦρον πιστῶν προφαίνεται ἐλαύνων ἀνὰ
κράτος ἱδροῦντι τῷ ἵππῳ, καὶ εὐθὺς πᾶσιν οἷς ἐνετύγχανεν
ἐβόα καὶ βαρβαρικῶς καὶ ἑλληνικῶς ὅτι βασιλεὺς σὺν στρα-    5
τεύματι πολλῷ προσέρχεται ὡς εἰς μάχην παρεσκευασμένος.

1. ἀγορὰν πλήθουσαν: the four periods of the day were πρῴ, early morning; ἀγορὰ πλήθουσα, forenoon; μέσον ἡμέρας or μεσημβρία, midday; and δείλη, late day.
2. σταθμός: stopping place. καταλύειν: to stop for breakfast.
4. ἱδροῦντι τῷ ἵππῳ: dative of manner (522).
5. ἐβόα: imperfect of βοάω.
6. προσέρχεται: quoted indirectly with ὅτι after a past tense (ἐβόα); one might have expected the optative προσέρχοιτο. παρεσκευασμένος: from παρασκευάζω. Both reduplication and accent mark this as a perfect participle.

ἔνθα δὴ πολὺς τάραχος ἐγένετο· αὐτίκα γὰρ ἐδόκουν οἱ Ἕλ-        2
ληνες καὶ πάντες δὲ ἀτάκτοις σφίσιν ἐπιπεσεῖσθαι· Κῦρός
τε καταπηδήσας ἀπὸ τοῦ ἅρματος τὸν θώρακα ἐνέδυ καὶ        3
10    ἀναβὰς ἐπὶ τὸν ἵππον τὰ παλτὰ εἰς τὰς χεῖρας ἔλαβε, τοῖς
τε ἄλλοις πᾶσι παρήγγελλεν ἐξοπλίζεσθαι καὶ καθίστασθαι
εἰς τὴν ἑαυτοῦ τάξιν ἕκαστον. ἔνθα δὴ σὺν πολλῇ σπουδῇ        4
καθίσταντο, Κλέαρχος μὲν τὰ δεξιὰ τοῦ κέρατος ἔχων πρὸς
τῷ Εὐφράτῃ ποταμῷ, Πρόξενος δὲ ἐχόμενος, οἱ δ' ἄλλοι
15    μετὰ τοῦτον. Μένων δὲ καὶ τὸ στράτευμα τὸ εὐώνυμον κέρας
ἔσχε τοῦ Ἑλληνικοῦ. τοῦ δὲ βαρβαρικοῦ ἱππεῖς μὲν Παφλα-        5
γόνες εἰς χιλίους παρὰ Κλέαρχον ἔστησαν ἐν τῷ δεξιῷ καὶ τὸ
Ἑλληνικὸν πελταστικόν, ἐν δὲ τῷ εὐωνύμῳ Ἀριαῖός τε ὁ
Κύρου ὕπαρχος καὶ τὸ ἄλλο βαρβαρικόν. Κῦρος δὲ καὶ οἱ        6
20    ἱππεῖς τούτου ὅσον ἑξακόσιοι ὡπλισμένοι θώραξι μὲν αὐτοὶ
καὶ παραμηριδίοις καὶ κράνεσι πάντες πλὴν Κύρου· Κῦρος
δὲ ψιλὴν ἔχων τὴν κεφαλὴν εἰς τὴν μάχην καθίστατο· λέγεται
δὲ καὶ τοὺς ἄλλους Πέρσας ψιλαῖς ταῖς κεφαλαῖς ἐν τῷ
πολέμῳ διακινδυνεύειν. οἱ δ' ἵπποι πάντες οἱ μετὰ Κύρου        7
εἶχον καὶ προμετωπίδια καὶ προστερνίδια· εἶχον δὲ καὶ
μαχαίρας οἱ ἱππεῖς Ἑλληνικάς.

7. **ἐδόκουν**: here used personally, *they thought*.
8. **σφίσιν**: *(upon) them*. See 72 for this pronoun. **ἐπιπεσεῖσθαι**: from ἐπιπίπτω, *to fall upon, attack*. See principal parts of πίπτω. Understand αὐτόν *(the king)* as subject of this infinitive.
9. **ἐνέδυ**: from ἐνδύω. Compare the conjugation of δείκνυμι (222). Find ἐδείκνυ.
10. **ἀναβάς**: from ἀναβαίνω. Find βάς in the chart of βαίνω (211).
11. **καθίστασθαι**: in the chart of ἵστημι (216) locate the corresponding form, ἵστασθαι; also ἵσταντο for καθίσταντο in *l. 13*; and ἵστατο for καθίστατο in *l. 22*.
13. **τὰ δεξιά**: understand μέρη, *parts*.
14. **ἐχόμενος**: *holding to, next*.
16. **ἔσχε**: from ἔχω. **τοῦ δὲ βαρβαρικοῦ**: genitive of source, for ἱππεῖς (509).
17. **ἔστησαν**: from ἵστημι.
20. **οἱ ἱππεῖς**: understand ἔστησαν. **ὅσον**: adverbial accusative, *about* (530). **θώραξι**: compare the declension of σάρξ (145). Dative of means or instrument (520).
21. **κράνεσι**: compare the declension of ἔτος (139).
22. **εἰς τὴν μάχην**: *for the battle*.

## 382. Writing exercise

1. Today's verb πίπτω, *to fall*, is deponent in its future system. The form ἐπιπεσεῖσθαι (*l. 8*) is from the compound verb ἐπιπίπτω, *to fall upon, attack*. Conjugate the future middle system of ἐπιπίπτω, underscoring the form ἐπιπεσεῖσθαι. Note from the accent and form of the future of πίπτω that it conjugates like the liquid-stem futures, that is, like the *present* system of the ε-contract verb (see ποιέω, 164).

2. Complete the declension of θώραξι (*l. 20*). Find its stem from the word list. Note σάρξ (145) but remember that the latter differs in accent pattern because it is a monosyllabic stem.

# LESSON 72

## 'Terrible as an Army with Banners'

### 383. New word list

ἀνυστός, -όν, *possible*; ὡς ἀνυστόν, *as possible.*

ἄξων, -ονος, ὁ, *axle*. AXLE.

ἀποτείνω (see τείνω for prin. parts), *to extend.*

ἀστράπτω, ἤστραψα, *to flash, glitter.*

βραδέως, *slowly, steadily.*

γερροφόρος, -ου, ὁ, *one carrying a wicker shield*; pl., *troops with wicker shields.*

δείλη, -ης, ἡ, *afternoon,* sometimes *evening.*

διακόπτω (see κόπτω for prin. parts), *to cut to pieces.*

διαλείπω (see λείπω for prin. parts), *to leave a gap between, stand apart.*

δίφρος, -ου, ὁ, *body* of a chariot.

δρεπανηφόρος, -ον, *scythe-bearing.*

δρέπανον, -ου, τό, *scythe.*

ἔθνος, -ους, τό, *a nation*. ETHNOLOGY.

ἥσυχος, -ον, *still, quiet*; ἡσυχῇ, *quietly.*

κονιορτός, -οῦ, ὁ, *a dust column.*

λευκοθώραξ, -κος, m. and f. adj., *with white cuirass.*

λόγχη, -ης, ἡ, *spear point, spear.* LANCE.

μελανία, -ας, ἡ, *blackness*. MELANCHOLY.

νεφέλη, -ης, ἡ, *a cloud.*

ξύλινος, -η, -ον, *wooden.*

παρακελεύομαι (see κελεύω for prin. parts), *to encourage.*

πλάγιος, -α, -ον, *sideways, slanting*; εἰς πλάγιον, *sideways.*

πλαίσιον, -ου, τό, *a square, rectangle.*

ποδήρης, -ες, *reaching to the feet.*

πρόσειμι, *to come on, approach, advance.*

*σιγή, -ῆς, ἡ, silence.*

συχνός, -ή, -όν, *much, considerable*; of time, *long.*

τάχα, *presently, soon, perhaps.*

τείνω, τενῶ, ἔτεινα, τέτακα, τέταμαι, ἐτάθην, *to stretch, extend, hasten.* TENSION, TONE.

χαλκός, -οῦ, ὁ, *bronze, bronze armor.*

### 384. Principal parts to be memorized

κόπτω, κόψω, ἔκοψα, κέκοφα, κέκομμαι, ἐκόπην, *to cut, beat.*

### 385. Reading passage (*Anabasis 1.8.8.1–1.8.11.5*)

Καὶ ἤδη τε ἦν μέσον ἡμέρας καὶ οὔπω καταφανεῖς ἦσαν     8
οἱ πολέμιοι· ἡνίκα δὲ δείλη ἐγίγνετο, ἐφάνη κονιορτὸς

1. **μέσον ἡμέρας**: for this and for δείλη in the next line, see note on 381, *l. 1.*
2. **ἐφάνη**: from φαίνω.

ὥσπερ νεφέλη λευκή, χρόνῳ δὲ συχνῷ ὕστερον ὥσπερ μελανία
τις ἐν τῷ πεδίῳ ἐπὶ πολύ. ὅτε δὲ ἐγγύτερον ἐγίγνοντο, τάχα
5 δὴ καὶ χαλκός τις ἤστραπτε καὶ αἱ λόγχαι καὶ αἱ τάξεις καταφανεῖς ἐγίγνοντο. καὶ ἦσαν ἱππεῖς μὲν λευκοθώρακες ἐπὶ     9
τοῦ εὐωνύμου τῶν πολεμίων· Τισσαφέρνης ἐλέγετο τούτων
ἄρχειν· ἐχόμενοι δὲ γερροφόροι, ἐχόμενοι δὲ ὁπλῖται σὺν
ποδήρεσι ξυλίναις ἀσπίσιν. Αἰγύπτιοι δ᾽ οὗτοι ἐλέγοντο εἶναι·
10 ἄλλοι δ᾽ ἱππεῖς, ἄλλοι τοξόται. πάντες δ᾽ οὗτοι κατὰ ἔθνη
ἐν πλαισίῳ πλήρει ἀνθρώπων ἕκαστον τὸ ἔθνος ἐπορεύετο.
πρὸ δὲ αὐτῶν ἅρματα διαλείποντα συχνὸν ἀπ᾽ ἀλλήλων τὰ     10
δὴ δρεπανηφόρα καλούμενα· εἶχον δὲ τὰ δρέπανα ἐκ τῶν
ἀξόνων εἰς πλάγιον ἀποτεταμένα καὶ ὑπὸ τοῖς δίφροις εἰς γῆν
15 βλέποντα, ὡς διακόπτειν ὅτῳ ἐντυγχάνοιεν. ἡ δὲ γνώμη ἦν
ὡς εἰς τὰς τάξεις τῶν Ἑλλήνων ἐλῶντα καὶ διακόψοντα. ὃ     11
μέντοι Κῦρος εἶπεν ὅτε καλέσας παρεκελεύετο τοῖς Ἕλλησι
τὴν κραυγὴν τῶν βαρβάρων ἀνέχεσθαι, ἐψεύσθη τοῦτο· οὐ γὰρ
κραυγῇ ἀλλὰ σιγῇ ὡς ἀνυστὸν καὶ ἡσυχῇ ἐν ἴσῳ καὶ βραδέως
20 προσῇσαν.

3. **χρόνῳ**: dative of degree of difference with ὕστερον. Literally, *later by a considerable time* (524).

4. **ἐπὶ πολύ**: *for a great (distance)*. **ἐγγύτερον**: comp. of ἐγγύς, *near*.

5. **χαλκός τις ἤστραπτε**: *some bronze flashed*. The idea is that at first there was a flash of bronze armor here and there.

8. **ἐχόμενοι**: *next*. Cf. the note on 381, *l. 14* in yesterday's lesson.

9. **ποδήρεσι**: compare declension of ἀληθής (157). **ἀσπίσιν**: see declension of ἀσπίς in 146.

10. **ἄλλοι . . . ἄλλοι**: *some . . . others*. Understand ἦσαν. **ἔθνη**: for declension of τὸ ἔθνος see ἔτος (139).

12. **ἅρματα**: for declension of ἅρμα see 146. **διαλείποντα συχνόν**: *leaving a considerable space*.

14. **ἀποτεταμένα**: from ἀποτείνω, *to extend*. See τείνω for principal parts. **εἰς γῆν βλέποντα**: literally, *looking to (the) ground*.

15. **ὡς διακόπτειν**: *to cut to pieces*. Compare ὡς μὴ ἅπτεσθαι in 373, *l. 14*, and the note. **ὅτῳ ἐντυγχάνοιεν**: *whomever they met* or *happened upon*. Relative plus optative, a past general supposition (600). ὅτῳ is dative singular of ὅστις, ὅ τι, *whoever, whatever*. Short form of ᾧτινι. See 158.

16. **ὡς . . . ἐλῶντα καὶ διακόψοντα**: from ἐλαύνω *to drive*, and διακόπτω, *to cut to pieces*. These future participles with ὡς denote purpose. **ὃ . . . Κῦρος εἶπεν**: relative clause used as accusative of specification (529, 540). Translate, *as to what (that which) Cyrus said*.

18. **ἐψεύσθη**: from ψεύδω. **τοῦτο**: accusative of specification, *as to this* (529).

19. **κραυγῇ, σιγῇ**: datives of manner (522). **ἐν ἴσῳ**, *evenly*.

20. **προσῇσαν**: from πρόσειμι. Find ἦσαν in the conjugation of εἰμί (233).

## 386. Writing exercise

1. Today's verb κόπτω, *to cut*, is shown by its principal parts to have a π-mute stem. In *l. 16* the participle διακόψοντα from the future system

of διακόπτω, *to cut to pieces*, expresses purpose. Conjugate διακόπτω in the future system. The π-mute γράφω (124) will serve as reference. If more detail as to endings is needed, see λύω.

2. From the above take the future active participle of διακόπτω and decline it (same endings as present participle of λύω, 181). Underscore διακόψοντα, which as seen in *l. 16* is neuter plural nominative, referring to τὰ δρέπανα, *the scythes*, in *l. 13*.

# LESSON 73
## The Caution of Clearchus

### 387. New word list

Ἀθηναῖος, -α, -ον, *an Athenian*.
ἀποβλέπω (see βλέπω for prin. parts), *to look away, look*.
ἑκατέρωθεν, *from* or *on both sides*.
ἑκατέρωσε, *in both directions, both ways*.
ἔρομαι, ἐρήσομαι, ἠρόμην, *to ask, enquire*.
Ζεύς, Διός, ὁ, *Zeus*, to the Greeks 'father of gods and men.'
θόρυβος, -ου, ὁ, *noise, murmur*.
ἱερός, -ά, -όν, *holy, sacred*; τὸ ἱερόν, *a sacred place, temple* (153); τὰ ἱερά, *the auspices* or *omens* obtained from inspecting the vitals of a sacrificed victim, *internal omens*.
καταθεάομαι (see θεάομαι for prin. parts), *to look down on, survey thoroughly*.

κυκλόω, κυκλώσω, ἐκύκλωσα, κεκύκλωμαι, ἐκυκλώθην, *to encircle, surround*.
*μέλει, μελήσει, ἐμέλησε, μεμέληκε, *it is a care, it concerns*.
Ξενοφῶν, -ῶντος, ὁ, *Xenophon*, author of the *Anabasis*. An Athenian and a pupil of Socrates, he joined the expedition as a friend of Proxenus.
ὁμαλῶς, *evenly, on an even front*.
πελάζω, πελάσω or πελῶ, ἐπέλασα, ἐπελάσθην, *to draw near, approach*.
περίειμι (see εἰμί for prin. parts), *to excel, exceed, be greater*.
στῖφος, -ους, τό, *a close array*.
σύνθημα, -ατος, τό, *an agreement, sign, watchword*.
σφάγιον, -ου, τό, *sacrifice, external omen* from a sacrifice.

### 388. Principal parts to be memorized

ἐθέλω, ἐθελήσω, ἠθέλησα, ἠθέληκα, *to be willing, wish*.

### 389. Reading passage (*Anabasis 1.8.12.1–1.8.17.2*)

Καὶ ἐν τούτῳ Κῦρος παρελαύνων αὐτὸς σὺν Πίγρητι τῷ    12
ἑρμηνεῖ καὶ ἄλλοις τρισὶν ἢ τέτταρσι τῷ Κλεάρχῳ ἐβόα ἄγειν

1. ἐν τούτῳ: *meanwhile*.

τὸ στράτευμα κατὰ μέσον τὸ τῶν πολεμίων, ὅτι ἐκεῖ βασιλεὺς
εἴη· κἂν τοῦτ', ἔφη, νικῶμεν, πάνθ' ἡμῖν πεποίηται. ὁρῶν δὲ ὁ     13
5   Κλέαρχος τὸ μέσον στῖφος καὶ ἀκούων Κύρου ἔξω ὄντα τοῦ
εὐωνύμου βασιλέα—τοσοῦτον γὰρ πλήθει περιῆν βασιλεὺς
ὥστε μέσον τῶν ἑαυτοῦ ἔχων τοῦ Κύρου εὐωνύμου ἔξω ἦν—
ἀλλ' ὅμως ὁ Κλέαρχος οὐκ ἤθελεν ἀποσπάσαι ἀπὸ τοῦ ποταμοῦ τὸ δεξιὸν κέρας, φοβούμενος μὴ κυκλωθείη ἑκατέρωθεν,
10   τῷ δὲ Κύρῳ ἀπεκρίνατο ὅτι αὐτῷ μέλοι ὅπως καλῶς ἔχοι.
καὶ ἐν τούτῳ τῷ καιρῷ τὸ μὲν βαρβαρικὸν στράτευμα     14
ὁμαλῶς προῄει, τὸ δὲ Ἑλληνικὸν ἔτι ἐν τῷ αὐτῷ μένον συνετάττετο ἐκ τῶν ἔτι προσιόντων. καὶ ὁ Κῦρος παρελαύνων
οὐ πάνυ πρὸς αὐτῷ τῷ στρατεύματι κατεθεᾶτο ἑκατέρωσε
15   ἀποβλέπων εἴς τε τοὺς πολεμίους καὶ τοὺς φίλους. ἰδὼν δὲ     15
αὐτὸν ἀπὸ τοῦ Ἑλληνικοῦ Ξενοφῶν Ἀθηναῖος, πελάσας ὡς
συναντῆσαι ἤρετο εἴ τι παραγγέλλοι· ὁ δ' ἐπιστήσας εἶπε
καὶ λέγειν ἐκέλευε πᾶσιν ὅτι καὶ τὰ ἱερὰ καλὰ καὶ τὰ σφάγια
καλά. ταῦτα δὲ λέγων θορύβου ἤκουσε διὰ τῶν τάξεων     16

4. **εἴη**: originally ἐστί, here quoted indirectly with ὅτι after a past tense. **κἂν**: for
καὶ ἐάν. Here is a future more vivid condition (603). The apodosis, πάντα πεποίηται,
*all things have been accomplished,* clearly has future force as though to say, *all will have
been accomplished.* **ἡμῖν**: dative of agent, *by us* (519).

5. **Κύρου**: genitive of source (509).

6. **τοσοῦτον**: *so much, this much.* Adverbial accusative (530). **πλήθει**: dative of respect
(523). **περιῆν**: see περίειμι in today's word list.

7. **μέσον τῶν ἑαυτοῦ ἔχων**: the participle here expresses concession, *although holding
(the) center of his own men* (581).

8. **ἀποσπάσαι**: from ἀποσπάω. See principal parts of σπάω.

9. **φοβούμενος μὴ κυκλωθείη**: a clause of fearing in past time (569). For the form
κυκλωθείη compare λυθείη in the chart of λύω (97).

10. **αὐτῷ μέλοι**: μέλει is often, as here, used impersonally. Here it becomes optative
because quoted with ὅτι after a past tense. Translate, *it was a care to him* or *he was taking
care.* **ὅπως καλῶς ἔχοι**: purpose clause after a past tense, using ὅπως with optative,
*that it might be well* (568). Recall that καλῶς ἔχειν means *to be well.* It is generally agreed
that if Clearchus had been willing to run the chance of following Cyrus' advice, the
entire outcome would probably have been different.

12. **προῄει**: from πρόειμι. In 233 find the form ᾔει. **ἐν τῷ αὐτῷ μένον**: *remaining in the
same (position).* **συνετάττετο**: imperfect of συντάττω. Translate, *was being drawn up.*

14. **πρός**: with dative, translate, *near to.*

15. **ἰδών**: from ὁράω.

16. **πελάσας**: from πελάζω. In the chart of βαπτίζω (113) locate the form βαπτίσας.
**ὡς συναντῆσαι**: *to meet.*

17. **ἤρετο**: imperfect of ἔρομαι in today's list. **εἴ τι παραγγέλλοι**: εἰ, *whether,* here
introduces an indirect question after a past tense. Hence the optative. Translate,
*whether he commanded anything,* or *was giving any command.* **ἐπιστήσας**: in the chart of
ἵστημι (216) locate the form στήσας.

18. **τὰ ἱερὰ καλά**: understand εἴη.

19. **θορύβου**: ἀκούω often uses the genitive (499).

20    ἰόντος, καὶ ἤρετο τίς ὁ θόρυβος εἴη. ὁ δὲ Κλέαρχος εἶπεν ὅτι
σύνθημα παρέρχεται δεύτερον ἤδη. καὶ ὃς ἐθαύμασε τίς
παραγγέλλει, καὶ ἤρετο ὅ τι εἴη τὸ σύνθημα. ὁ δ' ἀπεκρίνατο,
Ζεὺς σωτὴρ καὶ νίκη. ὁ δὲ Κῦρος ἀκούσας, Ἀλλὰ δέχομαί    17
τε, ἔφη, καὶ τοῦτο ἔστω.

21. **δεύτερον**: adverbial accusative, *a second time* (530). **καὶ ὅς**: *and he.*
23. **ἀλλά**: translate, *well.*
24. **ἔστω**: locate this form in the chart of εἰμί (132).

## 390. Writing exercise

1. In *l. 9* of today's reading passage is seen the form κυκλωθείη,
from the first passive system of κυκλόω, *to encircle.* Conjugate the first
passive system of this verb (cf. λύω, 97). Consult the vocabulary for its
principal parts. Underscore the form κυκλωθείη.

2. In *l. 2* occurs the form ἑρμηνεῖ from ὁ ἑρμηνεύς, *the interpreter.* Decline
this noun with its article. See vocabulary first, then note ἱερεύς (151).
Underscore the form used in the lesson.

# LESSON 74

# The Test of Battle

## 391. New word list

ἀντίος, -α, -ον, *against, face to face;*
   ἐκ τοῦ ἀντίου, *from the opposite side.*
διέχω (see ἔχω for prin. parts), *to
hold apart;* intrans., *to be distant,
be separated.*
δόρυ, -ατος, τό, *spear.*
δουπέω, ἐδούπησα, *to make a din.*
ἐκκλίνω (see κλίνω for prin. parts),
*to bend, give ground, break.*
ἐκκυμαίνω, *to billow out, surge forward.*
ἐκπλήττω,   ἐκπλήξω,   ἐξέπληξα,
   ἐκπέπληγμαι, ἐξεπλήχθην or ἐξεπλάγην, *to strike out of one's senses,
startle.*
ἐλελίζω, ἠλέλιξα, *to raise the war-cry.*
Ἐννάλιος, -ου, ὁ, *Ares, god of war.*

ἐξάγω (see ἄγω for prin. parts),
*to lead out, induce.*
ἐξικνέομαι (see ἱκνέομαι for prin.
parts), *to reach;* of missiles, *to do
execution, gain the range.*
ἐπικάμπτω (see κάμπτω for prin.
parts), *to bend towards, wheel.*
ἥμισυς, -εια, -υ, *half;* also as substantive, ἥμισυ or ἡμίσεα, *the half.*
ἡνίοχος, -ου, ὁ, *driver, charioteer.*
*θέω, θεύσομαι, *to race, charge.*
ἱππόδρομος, -ου, ὁ, *a horse race, race
course.* HIPPODROME.
κάμπτω, κάμψω, ἔκαμψα, κέκαμμαι,
   ἐκάμφθην, *to bend.*
κενός, -ή, -όν, *empty, vacant,* sometimes with gen.

κλίνω, κλινῶ, ἔκλινα, κέκλιμαι, ἐκλίθην or ἐκλίνην, *to bend.* DECLINE.
κύκλωσις, -εως, ἡ, *an encircling,
encirclement.*
παιανίζω, ἐπαιάνισα, *to sing the
paean.* This was a song in honor
of Apollo or Artemis. Before a
battle, the paean followed the
prayer and preceded the battle
cry and attack. PAEAN.
προοράω (see ὁράω for prin. parts),
*to foresee, see before, see coming.*

συσπειράομαι, συνεσπείραμαι, συνεσπειράθην, *to be formed in close
array.*
τόξευμα, -ατος, τό, *an arrow.*
τοξεύω, ἐτόξευσα, τετόξευμαι, ἐτοξεύθην, *to shoot, shoot at* or *hit* with
bow and arrow.
φθέγγομαι, φθέγξομαι, ἐφθεγξάμην,
ἔφθεγμαι, *to utter a sound, shout.*
DIPHTHONG.
*ὥς, adv. of manner, *thus,* like
οὕτως.

## 392. Principal parts to be memorized

πάσχω, πείσομαι, ἔπαθον, πέπονθα, *to suffer.*

## 393. Reading passage (*Anabasis 1.8.17.3–1.8.23.5*)

Ταῦτα δ' εἰπὼν εἰς τὴν αὐτοῦ χώραν ἀπήλαυνε· καὶ
οὐκέτι τρία ἢ τέτταρα στάδια διειχέτην τὼ φάλαγγε ἀπ'
ἀλλήλων ἡνίκα ἐπαιάνιζόν τε οἱ Ἕλληνες καὶ ἤρχοντο
ἀντίοι ἰέναι τοῖς πολεμίοις. ὡς δὲ πορευομένων ἐξεκύμαινέ    18
5   τι τῆς φάλαγγος, τὸ ὑπολειπόμενον ἤρξατο δρόμῳ θεῖν· καὶ
ἅμα ἐφθέγξαντο πάντες οἷον τῷ Ἐνυαλίῳ ἐλελίζουσι, καὶ
πάντες δὲ ἔθεον. λέγουσι δέ τινες ὡς καὶ ταῖς ἀσπίσι πρὸς τὰ
δόρατα ἐδούπησαν φόβον ποιοῦντες τοῖς ἵπποις. πρὶν δὲ
τόξευμα ἐξικνεῖσθαι ἐκκλίνουσιν οἱ βάρβαροι καὶ φεύγουσι·    19
10   καὶ ἐνταῦθα δὴ ἐδίωκον μὲν κατὰ κράτος οἱ Ἕλληνες, ἐβόων
δὲ ἀλλήλοις μὴ θεῖν δρόμῳ, ἀλλ' ἐν τάξει ἕπεσθαι. τὰ δ'    20

1. **αὐτοῦ**: for ἑαυτοῦ (73).
2. **τρία ἢ τέτταρα στάδια**: accusative of extent of space (531). **διειχέτην τὼ φάλαγγε**:
dual number, quite unusual in prose. One would have expected διεῖχον αἱ φάλαγγες.
3. **ἤρχοντο**: imperfect middle of ἄρχω, *they began.*
4. **πορευομένων**: understand αὐτῶν. Genitive absolute expressing attendant circumstances, *while they were proceeding* (582) **ἐξεκύμαινε**: from ἐκκυμαίνω in today's list.
5 **ἤρξατο**: from ἄρχω. **δρόμῳ**: dative of manner (522). **θεῖν**: from θέω in today's list.
6. **ἐφθέγξαντο**: from φθέγγομαι in today's list. **οἷον**: adverbial accusative, *such as,* or
*just as* (530).
8. **πρὶν δὲ τόξευμα ἐξικνεῖσθαι**: a type of futurity is sometimes indicated by πρίν plus
infinitive (575). Translate, *and before a bowshot reached* (*them*). The idea is *before they
came within bowshot.*
10. **κατὰ κράτος**: *at full speed.*

ἅρματα ἐφέροντο τὰ μὲν δι᾽ αὐτῶν τῶν πολεμίων, τὰ δὲ
καὶ διὰ τῶν Ἑλλήνων κενὰ ἡνιόχων. οἱ δ᾽ ἐπεὶ προΐδοιεν,
διίσταντο· ἔστι δ᾽ ὅστις καὶ κατελήφθη ὥσπερ ἐν ἱπποδρόμῳ
15 ἐκπλαγείς· καὶ οὐδὲν μέντοι οὐδὲ τοῦτον παθεῖν ἔφασαν, οὐδ᾽
ἄλλος δὲ τῶν Ἑλλήνων ἐν ταύτῃ τῇ μάχῃ ἔπαθεν οὐδεὶς
οὐδέν, πλὴν ἐπὶ τῷ εὐωνύμῳ τοξευθῆναί τις ἐλέγετο. Κῦρος   21
δ᾽ ὁρῶν τοὺς Ἕλληνας νικῶντας τὸ καθ᾽ αὑτοὺς καὶ διώκον-
τας, ἡδόμενος καὶ προσκυνούμενος ἤδη ὡς βασιλεὺς ὑπὸ
20 τῶν ἀμφ᾽ αὐτόν, οὐδ᾽ ὣς ἐξήχθη διώκειν, ἀλλὰ συνεσπειραμένην ἔχων τὴν τῶν σὺν ἑαυτῷ ἑξακοσίων ἱππέων τάξιν
ἐπεμελεῖτο ὅ τι ποιήσει βασιλεύς. καὶ γὰρ ᾔδει αὐτὸν ὅτι
μέσον ἔχοι τοῦ Περσικοῦ στρατεύματος. καὶ πάντες δ᾽ οἱ   22
τῶν βαρβάρων ἄρχοντες μέσον ἔχοντες τὸ αὐτῶν ἡγοῦνται,
25 νομίζοντες οὕτω καὶ ἐν ἀσφαλεστάτῳ εἶναι ἢν ᾖ ἡ ἰσχὺς
αὐτῶν ἑκατέρωθεν, καὶ εἴ τι παραγγεῖλαι χρῄζοιεν, ἡμίσει
ἂν χρόνῳ αἰσθάνεσθαι τὸ στράτευμα. καὶ βασιλεὺς δὴ τότε   23
μέσον ἔχων τῆς αὑτοῦ στρατιᾶς ὅμως ἔξω ἐγένετο τοῦ
Κύρου εὐωνύμου κέρατος. ἐπεὶ δ᾽ οὐδεὶς αὐτῷ ἐμάχετο ἐκ
30 τοῦ ἀντίου οὐδὲ τοῖς αὐτοῦ τεταγμένοις ἔμπροσθεν, ἐπέ-
καμπτεν ὡς εἰς κύκλωσιν.

12. τὰ μὲν ... τὰ δέ: *some ... others.*
13. ἐπεὶ προΐδοιεν, διίσταντο: relative plus optative in the protasis, a past indicative tense (imperfect) in the apodosis. A past general supposition (600).
14. διίσταντο: from διίστημι. Find ἵσταντο in the chart of ἵστημι (216). ἔστι δὲ ὅστις: instead of *whoever*, ὅστις here has the force of *someone* or *one who* .... κατελήφθη: from καταλαμβάνω. See principal parts of λαμβάνω.
15. ἐκπλαγείς: from ἐκπλήττω in today's word list. Compare this form with φανείς in the chart of φαίνω (205). παθεῖν: see πάσχω. Also for ἔπαθε(ν) in next line. ἔφασαν: see the imperfect of φημί (233).
18. τὸ καθ᾽ αὑτούς: understand πλῆθος or στράτευμα.
20. οὐδ᾽ ὥς: emphatic, *not even so.* ἐξήχθη: find the form ἤχθην in the chart of ἄγω in 118. ἤχθη is the third person singular of this. συνεσπειραμένην: perfect middle participle of συσπειράομαι in today's list.
22. ποιήσει: quoted following a past tense this way, ποιήσοι might have been expected. ᾔδει: see οἶδα, perfect of εἴδω (199).
24. τὸ αὐτῶν: *that of themselves, their own.* ἡγοῦνται: see ἡγέομαι.
25. ἀσφαλεστάτῳ: understand some word like τόπῳ, *in the safest place.* ἢν (for ἐάν) ᾖ ...: present general supposition (599).
26. εἴ τι παραγγεῖλαι χρῄζοιεν, ... ἄν ... αἰσθάνεσθαι: here is a future less vivid condition quoted indirectly (604). The protasis contains εἰ plus optative χρῄζοιεν, the mood unchanged from direct discourse. In the apodosis, ἄν plus present infinitive stands for ἄν plus present optative in the direct form. ἡμίσει ... χρόνῳ: dative of time when, or within which, an action takes place (526).
30. ἐπέκαμπτε(ν): *was wheeling* or *beginning to wheel.*
31. εἰς: purpose, *for.*

### 394. Writing exercise

1. Twice in today's reading passage are seen forms from the second aorist of today's verb πάσχω, *to suffer.* Give the second aorist system of πάσχω, noting this principal part first, and following the endings of ἤγαγον from ἄγω if needed (118). Underscore the two forms found in *ll. 15, 16.*

2. The participle νικῶντας, *conquering,* in *l. 18* is from the present system of νικάω, an α-contract. Decline the present participle of this verb, using the present participle of γεννάω as a model (195). Underscore νικῶντας.

## LESSON 75

# The Charge and Death of Cyrus

### 395. New word list

ἀκοντίζω, ἀκοντιῶ, to hurl the javelin, shoot at or hit with a javelin.

Ἀρταγέρσης, -ου, ὁ, Artagerses, one of King Artaxerxes' generals.

Ἀρταπάτης, -ου, ὁ, Artapates, an attendant of Cyrus.

βιαίως, with force or violence.

διασπείρω (see σπείρω for prin. parts), to scatter. DISPERSE.

ἑκάτερος, -α, -ον, each, each other, both.

ἑξακισχίλιοι, -αι, -α, six thousand.

ἐπισφάττω (see σφάττω for prin. parts), to slay upon.

εὔνοια, -ας, ἡ, goodwill, affection.

ἰατρός, -οῦ, ὁ, physician. PODIATRIST.

καθοράω (see ὁράω for prin. parts), to look down on, get sight of, observe.

Κτησίας, -ου, ὁ, Ctesias, a famous Greek physician of Cnidus, captured by the Persians and made personal physician to Darius II and then to his son Artaxerxes. He wrote a history of Persia in twenty-three volumes.

*ὀλίγος, -η, -ον, little, a little, few. OLIGARCHY.

ὁμοτράπεζος, -ον, ὁ, a table companion.

*ὄπισθεν, from behind, behind.

παίω, παίσω, ἔπαισα, πέπαικα, ἐπαίσθην, to strike, beat.

περιπίπτω (see πίπτω for prin. parts), to fall around, throw one's self upon.

πιστότης, -τητος, ἡ, faithfulness, loyalty.

σκηπτοῦχος, -ου, ὁ, scepter bearer, chamberlain, high court official.

στέρνον, -ου, τό, breast. STERNUM.

σφάττω, σφάξω, ἔσφαξα, ἔσφαγμαι, ἐσφάγην, to slay.

σχεδόν, nearly, about, chiefly.

τιτρώσκω, τρώσω, ἔτρωσα, τέτρωμαι, ἐτρώθην, to wound.

τραῦμα, -ατος, τό, wound. TRAUMATIC.

τροπή, -ῆς, ἡ, a turning, rout. HELIOTROPE, TROPIC.

φορέω, φορήσω, ἐφόρησα, πεφόρηκα, πεφόρημαι, ἐφορήθην, to wear.

φυγή, -ῆς, ἡ, flight, rout. FUGITIVE.

*Alexander's Victory at Issus, 333 B.C.*

Just sixty-eight years after Cyrus passed through Issus with his army of
13,000 Greeks and 100,000 Persians, Alexander of Macedon came that
way with 30,000 foot and 5,000 horse. Another Darius (surnamed Codo-
mannus), leading an army estimated at 300,000 of whom 30,000 were
tough Greek mercenaries, came up behind him in the small plain of the
Pinarus just south of Issus. Alexander with his cavalry attacked and
routed the Persian hoplites where Darius himself was stationed, winning
the battle decisively. This mosaic, found in Pompeii and moved to the
Naples museum, shows Alexander with bare head driving in upon
Darius, whose army is in rout. A noble Persian officer of Darius' staff
has just been slain. Alexander himself received a serious leg wound in
this battle. Darius fled in his chariot and was able to escape to near-by
Mt. Amanus.

## 396. Principal parts to be memorized

θνῄσκω, θανοῦμαι, ἔθανον, τέθνηκα, to die.

## 397. Reading passage (*Anabasis 1.8.24.1–1.8.29.6*)

Ἔνθα δὴ Κῦρος δείσας μὴ ὄπισθεν γενόμενος κατακόψῃ      24
τὸ Ἑλληνικὸν ἐλαύνει ἀντίος· καὶ ἐμβαλὼν σὺν τοῖς ἑξακο-
σίοις νικᾷ τοὺς πρὸ βασιλέως τεταγμένους καὶ εἰς φυγὴν
ἔτρεψε τοὺς ἑξακισχιλίους, καὶ ἀποκτεῖναι λέγεται αὐτὸς τῇ
5    ἑαυτοῦ χειρὶ Ἀρταγέρσην τὸν ἄρχοντα αὐτῶν. ὡς δ' ἡ τροπὴ      25
ἐγένετο, διασπείρονται καὶ οἱ Κύρου ἑξακόσιοι εἰς τὸ διώκειν
ὁρμήσαντες, πλὴν πάνυ ὀλίγοι ἀμφ' αὐτὸν κατελείφθησαν,
σχεδὸν οἱ ὁμοτράπεζοι καλούμενοι. σὺν τούτοις δὲ ὢν      26
καθορᾷ βασιλέα καὶ τὸ ἀμφ' ἐκεῖνον στῖφος· καὶ εὐθὺς οὐκ
10   ἠνέσχετο, ἀλλ' εἰπὼν Τὸν ἄνδρα ὁρῶ ἵετο ἐπ' αὐτὸν καὶ
παίει κατὰ τὸ στέρνον καὶ τιτρώσκει διὰ τοῦ θώρακος, ὥς
φησι Κτησίας ὁ ἰατρός, καὶ ἰᾶσθαι αὐτὸς τὸ τραῦμά φησι.
παίοντα δ' αὐτὸν ἀκοντίζει τις παλτῷ ὑπὸ τὸν ὀφθαλμὸν      27
βιαίως· καὶ ἐνταῦθα μαχόμενοι καὶ βασιλεὺς καὶ Κῦρος καὶ
15   οἱ ἀμφ' αὐτοὺς ὑπὲρ ἑκατέρου, ὁπόσοι μὲν τῶν ἀμφὶ βασιλέα
ἀπέθνῃσκον Κτησίας λέγει· παρ' ἐκείνῳ γὰρ ἦν· Κῦρος δὲ
αὐτός τε ἀπέθανε καὶ ὀκτὼ οἱ ἄριστοι τῶν περὶ αὐτὸν
ἔκειντο ἐπ' αὐτῷ. Ἀρταπάτης δ' ὁ πιστότατος αὐτῷ τῶν      28
σκηπτούχων λέγεται, ἐπειδὴ πεπτωκότα εἶδε Κῦρον, κατα-
20   πηδήσας ἀπὸ τοῦ ἵππου περιπεσεῖν αὐτῷ. καὶ οἱ μέν φασι      29

1. **δείσας**: from δείδω. **γενόμενος**: from γίγνομαι. The idea is, *becoming* or *getting behind* the Greeks. **κατακόψῃ**: from κατακόπτω. See principal parts of κόπτω. λύσῃ is the corresponding form of λύω (97).

4. **ἔτρεψε**: from τρέπω. **ἀποκτεῖναι**: from ἀποκτείνω. See principal parts of κτείνω.

6. **τὸ διώκειν**: articular infinitive, *the to pursue,* or simply *pursuit.*

7. **ὁρμήσαντες**: from ὁρμάω. **κατελείφθησαν**: from καταλείπω. See principal parts of λείπω.

10. **ἠνέσχετο**: from ἀνέχω. See principal parts of ἔχω. ἀνέχω sometimes, as here, augments both prefix and simple verb. **ἵετο**: see expansion of ἵημι (233).

12. **φησι**: see expansion of φημί (233). **ἰᾶσθαι**: the present infinitive is here used in indirect discourse to represent the imperfect indicative in the original statement. Recall that the imperfect indicative is in the present system. The subject of ἰᾶσθαι is the same as that of the final φησι.

15. **ὑπὲρ ἑκατέρου**: *on behalf of each.*

16. **ἀπέθνῃσκον**: from ἀποθνῄσκω. See principal parts of θνῄσκω. So also for ἀπέθανε in next line.

18. **ἔκειντο**: locate this form in the expansion of κεῖμαι (233).

19. **πεπτωκότα**: see principal parts of πίπτω, *to fall.* **εἶδε**: from ὁράω.

20. **περιπεσεῖν**: second aorist infinitive of περιπίπτω. See principal parts of πίπτω. **αὐτῷ**: dative with a compound verb (515). **οἱ μέν ... οἱ δέ**: *some ... others.*

βασιλέα κελεῦσαί τινα ἐπισφάξαι αὐτὸν Κύρῳ, οἱ δ᾽ ἑαυτὸν
ἐπισφάξασθαι σπασάμενον τὸν ἀκινάκην· εἶχε γὰρ χρυσοῦν·
καὶ στρεπτὸν δ᾽ ἐφόρει καὶ ψέλια καὶ τἆλλα ὥσπερ οἱ ἄριστοι
Περσῶν· ἐτετίμητο γὰρ ὑπὸ Κύρου δι᾽ εὔνοιάν τε καὶ
25    πιστότητα.

21. **ἐπισφάξαι, ἐπισφάξασθαι** (*l. 22*): the aorist active and the aorist middle infinitive of ἐπισφάττω. Compare with λῦσαι and λύσασθαι (97). **Κύρῳ**: dative after ἐπι- of the compound verb (515).

24. **ἐτετίμητο**: from τιμάω, of which the perfect middle is τετίμημαι.

## 398. Writing exercise

1. The form ἀπέθνησκον seen in *l. 16* today is from ἀποθνήσκω, *to die* (*off*), a bit more emphatic than the simple form of today's verb θνήσκω, *to die*. Give the present system of ἀποθνήσκω, underscoring the proper instance of the form ἀπέθνησκον. Consult the context as to person and number.

2. The form πεπτωκότα in *l. 19* is from the perfect active participle of πίπτω, *to fall*. Decline this participle (follow λελυκώς, 183). Underscore πεπτωκότα. Is it masculine or neuter as used today?

# LESSON 76

# Subsequent Maneuvers

## 399. New word list

ἀμείβω, ἀμείψω, ἤμειψα, ἠμείφθην, *to change.* AMOEBA.

Ἀμφιπολίτης, -ου, ὁ, *an Amphipolitan.* Amphipolis was an Athenian settlement in Macedonia.

ἀμφοτέρωθεν, *from both sides.*

ἀναλαμβάνω (see λαμβάνω for prin. parts), *to take up, pick up.*

ἀναπτύσσω (see πτύσσω for prin. parts), *to fold back, unfold.*

ἀπαλλάττω (see ἀλλάττω for prin. parts), *to change, abandon, depart*; pass., *to come off.*

ἀρήγω, ἀρήξω, ἤρηξα, *to help, save.*

αὖθις, *again.*

αὐτομολέω, αὐτομολήσω, ηὐτομόλησα, *to desert.*

διελαύνω (see ἐλαύνω for prin. parts), *to drive through, charge through.*

Ἐπισθένης, -ους, ὁ, *Episthenes* of Amphipolis, leader of the peltasts in Cyrus' army.

καίνω, κανῶ, ἔκανον, κέκονα, *to kill, slay.*

κατακαίνω (see καίνω for prin. parts), *to kill, cut down.*

*μείων, -ον, comp. of μικρός, less, worse, fewer, weaker.

ὁμοῦ, together, at the same place or time.

παραμείβομαι (see ἀμείβω for prin. parts), to change one's position.

παρατάττω (see τάττω for prin. parts), to draw up side by side. PARATAXIS.

περιπτύσσω (see πτύσσω for prin. parts), to fold around, enfold, outflank.

προσάγω (see ἄγω for prin. parts), to lead against, attack.

πτύσσω, πτύξω, ἔπτυξα, ἔπτυγμαι, ἐπτύχθην, to fold.

σύνειμι, to come together, attack.

σύνοδος, -ου, ἡ, meeting, encounter. SYNOD.

συντυγχάνω (see τυγχάνω for prin. parts), to fall in with, meet.

σχῆμα, -ατος, τό, pattern, formation. SCHEME.

φρόνιμος, -ον, prudent.

### 400. Principal parts to be memorized

στρέφω, στρέψω, ἔστρεψα, ἔστροφα, ἔστραμμαι, ἐστρέφθην or ἐστράφην, to twist, turn.

Omitted, between the last lesson and today's, is a lengthy and interesting tribute to the character, personality, and accomplishments of Cyrus as assessed by Xenophon.

### 401. Reading passage (*Anabasis 1.10.4.1–1.10.10.5*)

*Chapter 10. 4.* Ἐνταῦθα διέσχον ἀλλήλων βασιλεύς τε καὶ οἱ   4
"Ελληνες ὡς τριάκοντα στάδια, οἱ μὲν διώκοντες τοὺς καθ'
αὑτοὺς ὡς πάντας νικῶντες, οἱ δ' ἁρπάζοντες ὡς ἤδη πάντες
νικῶντες. ἐπεὶ δ' ᾔσθοντο οἱ μὲν "Ελληνες ὅτι βασιλεὺς σὺν   5
5    στρατεύματι ἐν τοῖς σκευοφόροις εἴη, βασιλεὺς δ' αὖ ἤκουσε
Τισσαφέρνους ὅτι οἱ "Ελληνες νικῷεν τὸ καθ' αὑτοὺς καὶ εἰς
τὸ πρόσθεν οἴχονται διώκοντες, ἔνθα δὴ βασιλεὺς μὲν ἀθροίζει
τε τοὺς ἑαυτοῦ καὶ συντάττεται, ὁ δὲ Κλέαρχος ἐβουλεύετο

1. **διέσχον**: from διέχω. See principal parts of ἔχω. **ἀλλήλων**: genitive of separation (504).

2. **ὡς**: *about.* **τριάκοντα στάδια**: accusative of extent of space (531). **τοὺς καθ' αὑτούς**: *those against themselves, their opponents.*

4. **ᾔσθοντο**: see principal parts of αἰσθάνομαι.

5. **ἐν τοῖς σκευοφόροις**: after the death of Cyrus, the Persian force of Cyrus, led by Ariaeus, broke and fled to the rear, passing by the camp and supply depot of Cyrus. King Artaxerxes moved after them, capturing the camp and supplies in spite of the resistance of the Greek guard. The main Greek army finally heard that their camp was taken and that the king's army was *among their baggage animals,* or *in their baggage train.*

6. **Τισσαφέρνους**: genitive of source (509). **νικῷεν**: from νικάω. Find γεννῷεν in the chart of γεννάω (173). Optative in indirect discourse with ὅτι, after a past tense.

Πρόξενον καλέσας, πλησιαίτατος γὰρ ἦν, εἰ πέμποιέν τινας
10  ἢ πάντες ἴοιεν ἐπὶ τὸ στρατόπεδον ἀρήξοντες. ἐν τούτῳ      6
καὶ βασιλεὺς δῆλος ἦν προσιὼν πάλιν ὡς ἐδόκει ὄπισθεν.
καὶ οἱ μὲν Ἕλληνες στραφέντες παρεσκευάζοντο ὡς ταύτῃ
προσιόντος καὶ δεξόμενοι. ὁ δὲ βασιλεὺς ταύτῃ μὲν οὐκ ἦγεν,
ᾗ δὲ παρῆλθεν ἔξω τοῦ εὐωνύμου κέρατος ταύτῃ καὶ ἀπῆγεν,
15  ἀναλαβὼν καὶ τοὺς ἐν τῇ μάχῃ πρὸς τοὺς Ἕλληνας αὐτο-
μολήσαντας καὶ Τισσαφέρνην καὶ τοὺς σὺν αὐτῷ. ὁ γὰρ      7
Τισσαφέρνης ἐν τῇ πρώτῃ συνόδῳ οὐκ ἔφυγεν, ἀλλὰ διήλασε
παρὰ τὸν ποταμὸν κατὰ τοὺς Ἕλληνας πελταστάς· διελαύνων
δὲ κατέκανε μὲν οὐδένα, διαστάντες δ' οἱ Ἕλληνες ἔπαιον
20  καὶ ἠκόντιζον αὐτούς· Ἐπισθένης δὲ Ἀμφιπολίτης ἦρχε τῶν
πελταστῶν καὶ ἐλέγετο φρόνιμος γενέσθαι. ὁ δ' οὖν Τισσα-     8
φέρνης ὡς μεῖον ἔχων ἀπηλλάγη, πάλιν μὲν οὐκ ἀναστρέφει,
εἰς δὲ τὸ στρατόπεδον ἀφικόμενος τὸ τῶν Ἑλλήνων ἐκεῖ
συντυγχάνει βασιλεῖ, καὶ ὁμοῦ δὴ πάλιν συνταξάμενοι ἐπο-
25  ρεύοντο. ἐπεὶ δ' ἦσαν κατὰ τὸ εὐώνυμον τῶν Ἑλλήνων      9

9. **εἰ πέμποιέν . . . ἢ . . . ἴοιεν**: an indirect question introduced by εἰ, *whether*, after a
past tense. The original thought was a deliberative subjunctive, πέμπωμεν . . . ἢ . . .
ἴωμεν, *should we send . . . or . . . should we go?* (560). It is changed to optative because
introduced by a past tense, ἐβουλεύετο.

10. **ἀρήξοντες**: future participle expressing purpose, *to save, to the rescue* (581).
**ἐν τούτῳ**: understand τῷ χρόνῳ, *at this time*.

12. **στραφέντες**: see principal parts of στρέφω in today's lesson. For the declension of
the aorist passive participle, see λυθείς (184). **ταύτῃ**: understand ὁδῷ. So also in *l. 13* and
with ᾗ in *l. 14*.

13. **προσίοντος**: understand αὐτοῦ. A genitive absolute of cause (582). **δεξόμενοι**:
future participle expressing purpose, *to receive* (581).

14. **τοῦ εὐωνύμου κέρατος**: *the left wing* of the Greeks. The Greeks had charged
through the king's left wing, having the river on their right. To their extreme right,
next the river, Tissaphernes had charged through the Greek peltasts; to their left the
king had outflanked them and captured their camp. Now the king and Tissaphernes
have joined forces and are reversing their direction and marching back against the
Greeks. This reference to the *left wing* of the Greeks goes back before the Greeks wheeled
around to meet the king. Actually, in their reversed position, it was now their *right
wing* which the king seemed to be outflanking. The river was now *at their left*.

17. **διήλασε**: from διελαύνω in today's list. See principal parts of ἐλαύνω.

19. **κατέκανε**: from κατακαίνω in today's list. See principal parts of καίνω. **διαστάντες**:
from διίστημι. Find στάς in the chart of ἵστημι (216). στάντες is nominative plural,
masculine.

20. **ἦρχε**: imperfect of ἄρχω, *was leader*. This verb when signifying leadership or
superior status takes the genitive (506).

21. **γενέσθαι**: *to have become*, in the sense of *to have shown himself*. **δ' οὖν**: has the force,
*but certainly, at all events*.

22. **ἀπηλλάγη**: from ἀπαλλάττω in today's list. See principal parts of ἀλλάττω.

23. **ἀφικόμενος**: from ἀφικνέομαι. See principal parts of ἱκνέομαι.

25. **τὸ εὐώνυμον . . . κέρας**: see again the note on *l. 14* above. As is now seen, the

κέρας, ἔδεισαν οἱ ῞Ελληνες μὴ προσάγοιεν πρὸς τὸ κέρας καὶ
περιπτύξαντες ἀμφοτέρωθεν αὐτοὺς κατακόψειαν· καὶ ἐδόκει
αὐτοῖς ἀναπτύσσειν τὸ κέρας καὶ ποιήσασθαι ὄπισθεν τὸν
ποταμόν. ἐν ᾧ δὲ ταῦτα ἐβουλεύοντο, καὶ δὴ βασιλεὺς παρα-    10
30    μειψάμενος εἰς τὸ αὐτὸ σχῆμα κατέστησεν ἀντίαν τὴν φάλαγγα ὥσπερ τὸ πρῶτον μαχούμενος συνῄει. ὡς δὲ εἶδον οἱ
῞Ελληνες ἐγγύς τε ὄντας καὶ παρατεταγμένους, αὖθις παιανί-
σαντες ἐπῇσαν πολὺ ἔτι προθυμότερον ἢ τὸ πρόσθεν.

king finally did not by-pass the Greeks for an encirclement, but brought his army into
position facing them as before, with the directions exactly reversed.

26. **μὴ προσάγοιεν, κατακόψειαν** (*l. 27*): optatives in a clause of fearing after a past
tense (569). It was not the king's intent to outflank them as they feared. And they never
executed the contemplated maneuver of bringing their line parallel to the river. Find
λύσειαν in the chart of λύω (97).

29. **ἐν ᾧ**: *while.* **καὶ δὴ βασιλεύς**: *the king also indeed.*

30. **εἰς τὸ αὐτὸ σχῆμα**: i.e. the same as at the first onset of the battle. **κατέστησε(ν)**:
from καθίστημι. Here transitive, *he placed.*

31. **τὸ πρῶτον**: adverbial accusative, *at the first* (530). **μαχούμενος**: future participle
expressing purpose, *to give battle* (581). **συνῄει, ἐπῇσαν** (*l. 33*): find ᾔει and ᾖσαν in the
conjugation of εἶμι (233).

## 402. Writing exercise

1. The form στραφέντες in *l. 12* is from the second passive system of
today's verb στρέφω, *to twist, turn.* Conjugate this system, using γράφω
(124) and λύω (97) for reference.

2. Using λυθείς (184) as a reference, decline the second aorist passive participle of στρέφω. Underscore the form στραφέντες, seen in today's lesson.

## LESSON 77

# Victorious but Marooned

## 403. New word list

ἄδειπνος,-ον, *without supper, supperless.*
ἀθρόος, -α, -ον, *in a body, in crowds or masses.*
ἀετός, -οῦ, ὁ, *eagle.*
ἀναβιβάζω (see βιβάζω for prin. parts), *to make go up, lead up.*
ἀναπαύω (see παύω for prin. parts), *to make cease*; mid., *to rest.*

ἀνάριστος, -ον, *without breakfast.*
ἀνατείνω (see τείνω for prin. parts), *to stretch up, hold up*; of a bird, ἀνατεταμένος, *with wings extended.*
ἄριστον, -ον, τό, *breakfast.*
δορπηστός, -οῦ, ὁ, *supper time.*

εἰκάζω, εἰκάσω, εἴκασα or ἤκασα, εἴκακα, εἴκασμαι or ἤκασμαι, εἰκάσθην or ἠκάσθην, *to liken to, conjecture, guess.*

ἔνδεια, -ας, ἡ, *need, scarcity.*

ἐπιδιώκω (see διώκω for prin. parts), *to follow hard, pursue.*

ἥλιος, -ου, ὁ, *the sun.* HELIOTROPE.

λόφος, -ου, ὁ, *ridge, hill.*

Λύκιος, -ου, ὁ, *Lycius,* a Syracusan.

μέχρι, *up to, until,* often with gen.

ξύλον, -ου, τό, *wood, a piece* or *bar of wood.* XYLOPHONE.

οὐδαμοῦ, *nowhere.*

πέλτη, -ης, ἡ, *a small shield, target.*

πότον, -ου, τό, *drink.*

σιτίον, -ου, τό, *food.*

σφοδρός, -ά, -όν, *extreme, violent.*

τέλος, -ους, τό, *end, purpose;* τέλος as adv., *finally.* TELEOLOGY.

ψιλόω, ψιλώσω, ἐψίλωσα, ἐψίλωθην, *to strip, make bare, clear.*

### 404. Principal parts to be memorized

πίμπλημι, πλήσω, ἔπλησα, πέπληκα, πέπλησμαι, ἐπλήσθην, *to fill.*

### 405. Reading passage (*Anabasis 1.10.11.1–1.10.19.4*)

Οἱ δ᾽ αὖ βάρβαροι οὐκ ἐδέχοντο, ἀλλὰ ἐκ πλείονος ἢ τὸ      11
πρόσθεν ἔφευγον· οἱ δ᾽ ἐπεδίωκον μέχρι κώμης τινός· ἐνταῦθα
δ᾽ ἔστησαν οἱ Ἕλληνες· ὑπὲρ γὰρ τῆς κώμης γήλοφος ἦν,      12
ἐφ᾽ οὗ ἀνεστράφησαν οἱ ἀμφὶ βασιλέα, πεζοὶ μὲν οὐκέτι, τῶν
5   δὲ ἱππέων ὁ λόφος ἐνεπλήσθη, ὥστε τὸ ποιούμενον μὴ
γιγνώσκειν. καὶ τὸ βασίλειον σημεῖον ὁρᾶν ἔφασαν, ἀετόν τινα
χρυσοῦν ἐπὶ πέλτῃ ἐπὶ ξύλου ἀνατεταμένον. ἐπεὶ δὲ καὶ      13
ἐνταῦθ᾽ ἐχώρουν οἱ Ἕλληνες, λείπουσι δὴ καὶ τὸν λόφον οἱ
ἱππεῖς· οὐ μὴν ἔτι ἀθρόοι ἀλλ᾽ ἄλλοι ἄλλοθεν· ἐψιλοῦτο δ᾽ ὁ
10  λόφος τῶν ἱππέων· τέλος δὲ καὶ πάντες ἀπεχώρησαν. ὁ οὖν      14
Κλέαρχος οὐκ ἀνεβίβαζεν ἐπὶ τὸν λόφον, ἀλλ᾽ ὑπ᾽ αὐτὸν
στήσας τὸ στράτευμα πέμπει Λύκιον τὸν Συρακόσιον καὶ
ἄλλον ἐπὶ τὸν λόφον καὶ κελεύει κατιδόντας τὰ ὑπὲρ τοῦ

1. ἐκ πλείονος: *at greater distance.*

2. οἱ δέ: article used as substantive, *and they . . .* (486).

4. ἀνεστράφησαν: from ἀναστρέφω. See principal parts of στρέφω. Literally, *were turned back* or *rallied.* τῶν . . . ἱππέων: genitive with a verb of fullness (501).

5. ἐνεπλήσθη: from ἐμπίπλημι. See principal parts of πίμπλημι. μὴ γιγνώσκειν: understand τοὺς Ἕλληνας as subject, *so that the Greeks did not know that (which was) being done,* or *what was going on.*

7. ἐπὶ ξύλου: *upon wood,* or *upon a wooden bar* or *perch.* ἀνατεταμένον: from ἀνατείνω. See principal parts of τείνω. Translate, *with wings extended.*

8. ἐχώρουν: imperfect of χωρέω.

9. ἄλλοι ἄλλοθεν: (*some from one direction and) others from another.* ἐψιλοῦτο: compare the conjugation of ὑψόω (177). Find ὑψοῦτο.

10. τῶν ἱππέων: genitive with a verb denoting want (501).

11. ὑπ᾽ αὐτόν: *under it, at the foot of it.*

12. στήσας: from ἵστημι. It is transitive here, *halting his (the) army.*

13. κατιδόντας: from καθοράω. See principal parts of ὁράω. So also ἰδών in *l. 14* below.

λόφου τί ἐστιν ἀπαγγεῖλαι. καὶ ὁ Λύκιος ἤλασέ τε καὶ ἰδὼν   15
15   ἀπαγγέλλει ὅτι φεύγουσιν ἀνὰ κράτος. σχεδὸν δ᾿ ὅτε ταῦτα   16
ἦν καὶ ἥλιος ἐδύετο. ἐνταῦθα δ᾿ ἔστησαν οἱ Ἕλληνες καὶ
θέμενοι τὰ ὅπλα ἀνεπαύοντο· καὶ ἅμα μὲν ἐθαύμαζον ὅτι
οὐδαμοῦ Κῦρος φαίνοιτο οὐδ᾿ ἄλλος ἀπ᾿ αὐτοῦ οὐδεὶς παρείη·
οὐ γὰρ ᾔδεσαν αὐτὸν τεθνηκότα, ἀλλ᾿ εἴκαζον ἢ διώκοντα
20   οἴχεσθαι ἢ καταληψόμενόν τι προεληλακέναι· καὶ αὐτοὶ   17
ἐβουλεύοντο εἰ αὐτοῦ μείναντες τὰ σκευοφόρα ἐνταῦθα
ἄγοιντο ἢ ἀπίοιεν ἐπὶ τὸ στρατόπεδον. ἔδοξεν αὐτοῖς ἀπιέναι·
καὶ ἀφικνοῦνται ἀμφὶ δορπηστὸν ἐπὶ τὰς σκηνάς. ταύτης   18
μὲν τῆς ἡμέρας τοῦτο τὸ τέλος ἐγένετο. καταλαμβάνουσι δὲ
25   τῶν τε ἄλλων χρημάτων τὰ πλεῖστα διηρπασμένα καὶ εἴ τι
σιτίον ἢ ποτὸν ἦν, καὶ τὰς ἁμάξας μεστὰς ἀλεύρων καὶ οἴνου,
ἃς παρεσκευάσατο Κῦρος, ἵνα εἴ ποτε σφοδρὰ τὸ στράτευμα
λάβοι ἔνδεια, διαδοίη τοῖς Ἕλλησιν—ἦσαν δ᾿ αὗται τετρα-
κόσιαι ὡς ἐλέγοντο ἅμαξαι—καὶ ταύτας τότε οἱ σὺν βασιλεῖ
30   διήρπασαν. ὥστε ἄδειπνοι ἦσαν οἱ πλεῖστοι τῶν Ἑλλήνων·   19
ἦσαν δὲ καὶ ἀνάριστοι· πρὶν γὰρ δὴ καταλῦσαι τὸ στράτευμα
πρὸς ἄριστον βασιλεὺς ἐφάνη. ταύτην μὲν οὖν τὴν νύκτα οὕτω
διεγένοντο.

14. **ἀπαγγεῖλαι:** from ἀπαγγέλλω. See principal parts of ἀγγέλλω. **ἤλασε:** see principal parts of ἐλαύνω.
17. **θέμενοι:** locate θέμενος in the conjugation of τίθημι (229). Translate θέμενοι τὰ ὅπλα, *grounding their arms.* It refers to each soldier's laying his shield and spear on the ground in front of him.
18. **φαίνοιτο, παρείη:** present optatives in indirect discourse with ὅτι after a past tense (589).
19. **ᾔδεσαν:** locate this form in the expansion of the perfect system of εἴδω (199). **τεθνηκότα:** see principal parts of θνῄσκω. For the declension of the perfect participle see λελυκώς (183). Verbs *to see* or *know* often use the participle in indirect discourse (591).
20. **καταληψόμενον:** future participle of καταλαμβάνω. See principal parts of λαμβάνω. This participle expresses purpose (581). **προεληλακέναι:** from προελαύνω. See principal parts of ἐλαύνω.
21. **αὐτοῦ:** adverb, *there, in the same place.* **μείναντες:** see principal parts of μένω. **εἰ . . . ἄγοιντο ἢ ἀπίοιεν:** these optatives represent original deliberative subjunctives ἀγώμεθα ἢ ἀπίωμεν, *should we bring . . . or should we depart?* (560). Quoted indirectly, or as an indirect question after a past tense, *they took counsel whether they should bring . . . or whether they should depart.* Compare the note on 401, *l. 9.*
24. **καταλαμβάνουσι:** *they find.*
25. **διηρπασμένα:** from διαρπάζω. See principal parts of ἁρπάζω.
27. **παρεσκευάσατο:** pluperfect of παρασκευάζω.
28. **λάβοι:** from λαμβάνω. **διαδοίη:** from διαδίδωμι. Find δοίη in chart of δίδωμι (227).
32. **ἐφάνη:** from φαίνω.

**406. Writing exercise**

1. The form ἐνεπλήσθη in *l. 5* today is from the first passive system of ἐμπίπλημι, *to fill up*, a compound of today's verb πίμπλημι, *to fill*. ἐμπίπλημι is so spelled in the present system, except imperfect forms, to avoid the pronunciation of two μ's so close together. The other tense systems, however, are built upon the principal parts of πίμ-πλημι, compounded with ἐν- before vowels, ἐμ- before consonants. Conjugate ἐμπίπλημι in the first passive system, underscoring the form ἐνεπλήσθη.

2. The nouns βασιλεύς, *king*, and ἱππεύς, *horseman*, are both similar to ἱερεύς (151) in their declension. Decline them both, underscoring the forms of βασιλεύς seen in *ll. 4, 29*, and *32* today, and the forms of ἱππεύς seen in *ll. 5* and *9*.


## LESSON 78

# Review

**407.** REVIEW the reading passages covered in the *Anabasis*, the principal parts of all verbs which have been assigned for memorization in the daily lessons, and the meanings of all vocabulary words marked for special attention.

# APPENDIX

# TRANSLATION OF THE
# READING PASSAGES

## 408. Using the translation

THE translation for use with the daily reading passages follows very closely the word order and primary meaning of the Greek text in order that the student may most easily see its connection therewith. Thus the translation is said to be quite 'literal', and might at first thought be judged 'awkward' by comparison with a smooth English style.

But this is how the ancients actually thought and spoke, and the reading of a foreign language is at its best when the mind of the reader follows most closely the thought patterns of the writer, so that he no longer keeps trying to fit the language into his own mold but follows with appreciation the mold of the language. He then ceases to 'translate' and becomes a 'reader', actually thinking the thoughts of the writer in the medium of the writer's own language.

In this translation, parentheses are used in three ways: (1) To indicate a thought which, though not carried in the original words, is *implied* by them; (2) to indicate a thought which more literally and exactly translates the original words, but was not considered suitable in even a fairly literal English translation; and (3) to indicate explication of the thought. It is felt that the reader will have no difficulty in catching the purpose of these insertions as he reads.

The reader should first take in hand the actual Greek text, using the translation only to help him resolve difficulties or as a check after he has read the Greek passage. It is felt that on no condition should the student write the translation into the Greek text, as the tendency to read the English instead of the Greek is then almost inescapable, and will greatly impede progress in the Greek. The student should stay with the Greek text as exclusively as possible.

## WORKING TRANSLATION FROM ST. JOHN

### Chapter 1. The Incarnate Word

## 409. Lesson 2 (verses 1–3)

¹ In (the) beginning was the Word, and the Word was with (towards) God, and God was the Word. ² This one was in (the) beginning with

(towards) God. ³ All things through him came to be (became), and apart from him came to be (became, was made) not even one thing which has been made (has come to be).

## 410. Lesson 3 (*verses 4–6*)

⁴ In him was life, and the life was the light of men. ⁵ And the light in the darkness shines, and the darkness did not grasp it. ⁶ There was (came to be) a man having been sent forth from God, his name (name to him), John.

## 411. Lesson 4 (*verses 7, 8*)

⁷ This one came for a witness, that he might witness concerning the light, that all (men) might believe through him. ⁸ That one was not the light, but that he might witness about the light.

## 412. Lesson 5 (*verses 9–12*)

⁹ He was the true light which lightens every man coming into the world. ¹⁰ In the world he was, and the world through him was made, and the world did not know him. ¹¹ To his own things he came, and his own men did not receive him.¹² But as many as received him, he gave to them (the) right to become children of God, to the ones believing on his name,

## 413. Lesson 6 (*verses 13, 14*)

¹³ who not from blood (bloods) nor from the will of flesh nor from the will of man but from God were born. ¹⁴ And the Word became flesh and tented among us—and we beheld his glory, glory as of the only-begotten from the Father—full of grace and truth.

## 414. Lesson 7 (*verses 15–17*)

¹⁵ John witnesses about him, and he cried (has cried) saying, This was the one (of) whom I said, The one coming after me has become before me, because he was before me (first of me). ¹⁶ For out of the fullness of him we all received, and grace for (instead of) grace. ¹⁷ For the law through Moses was given; grace and truth through Jesus Christ came to be.

## 415. Lesson 8 (*verses 18, 19*)

¹⁸ God no one has ever seen. (The) only-begotten God, the one being in (into) the bosom of the Father, that one declared (him).

¹⁹ And this is the witness of John when the Jews sent to him out of Jerusalem priests and Levites that they might ask him, You, who are you?

**416. Lesson 9** *(verses 20–23)*

²⁰ And he confessed and did not deny, and confessed (that), I am not the Christ. ²¹ And they asked him, What then? Are you Elijah? And he says, I am not. Are you the prophet? And he replied, No. ²² They said then to him, Who are you? that we may give an answer to those having sent us. What do you say about yourself? ²³ He said, I (am) a voice of one shouting in the desert, Make straight the highway of (the) Lord, according as Isaiah the prophet said.

**417. Lesson 10** *(verses 24–28)*

²⁴ And they had been sent from the Pharisees. ²⁵ And they asked him and said to him, Why then do you baptize if you are not the Christ nor Elijah nor the prophet? ²⁶ John answered them saying, I baptize in water. (In the) midst of you stands (he) whom you do not know, ²⁷ the one coming after me, of whom I am not worthy that I should loose the lacing of his sandal. ²⁸ These things took place in Bethany beyond the Jordan where John was baptizing.

**418. Lesson 11** *(verses 29–32)*

²⁹ On the morrow he sees Jesus coming to him and says, Behold, the lamb of God, the one bearing the sin of the world. ³⁰ This one is (he) concerning whom I said, After me is coming a man who has come to be before me, for he was before me (the first of me). ³¹ And I did not know him, but that he might be shown to Israel, on account of this I came baptizing in water. ³² And John witnessed saying (that), I have seen the Spirit coming down as a dove out of heaven, and (he) remained upon him.

**419. Lesson 13** *(verses 33–38)*

³³ And I did not know him, but the one having sent me to baptize in (with) water, that one said to me, Upon whom you see the Spirit coming down and remaining upon him, this is the one baptizing in the Holy Spirit. ³⁴ And I have seen and have borne witness that this is the Son of God.

³⁵ On the morrow again stood John and two (out) of his disciples, ³⁶ and having looked upon Jesus as he walked (walking) he says, Behold, the lamb of God. ³⁷ And the two disciples heard him speaking and they followed Jesus. ³⁸ And Jesus, having (been) turned about, and having seen them following, says to them, What do you seek? And they said to him, Rabbi,—which is said, being interpreted, Teacher,—where do you abide?

### 420. Lesson 14 (*verses 39–42*)

³⁹ He says to them, Come, and you will see. They came then and saw where he abode (abides), and with him they remained that day. (The) hour was about (the) tenth. ⁴⁰ Andrew, the brother of Simon Peter, was one of the two having heard from John and having followed him. ⁴¹ This one finds first his own brother Simon and says to him, We have found the Messiah—which is, being interpreted, Christ. ⁴² He brought him to Jesus. Having looked upon him, Jesus said, You are Simon the son of John; you shall be called Cephas, which is interpreted, Peter.

### 421. Lesson 15 (*verses 43–47*)

⁴³ On the morrow he wished to go out into Galilee, and he finds Philip. And Jesus says to him, Follow me. ⁴⁴ And Philip was from Bethsaida, out of the city of Andrew and Peter. ⁴⁵ Philip finds Nathanael and says to him, We have found him (of) whom Moses wrote in the law, and the prophets, Jesus son of Joseph from Nazareth. ⁴⁶ And Nathanael said to him, Out of Nazareth can any good (thing) be? Philip says to him, Come and see. ⁴⁷ Jesus saw Nathanael coming to him and he says about him, Behold, truly an Israelite in whom is no deceit.

### 422. Lesson 16 (*verses 48–51*)

⁴⁸ Nathanael says to him, Whence do you know me? Jesus answered and said to him, Before Philip's calling you (before the Philip to call you) when you were (being) under the fig tree, I saw you. ⁴⁹ Nathanael answered him, Rabbi, you are the son of God; you are king of Israel. ⁵⁰ Jesus answered and said to him, Because I said to you that I saw you under the fig tree, do you believe? Greater things than these you will see. ⁵¹ And he says to him, Verily, verily, I say to you, you will see the heaven (having) opened, and the angels of God ascending and descending upon the Son of man.

### *Chapter 2. The Marriage at Cana*

### 423. Lesson 18 (*verses 1–5*)

¹ And on the third day a wedding took place in Cana of Galilee, and the mother of Jesus was there. ² And both Jesus was called and his disciples to the wedding. ³ And (the) wine having run short, the mother of Jesus says to him, They have no wine. ⁴ And Jesus says to her, What (is that) to me and to you, ma'am? Not yet is my hour come. ⁵ His mother says to the servants, Whatever he says to you, do.

**424. Lesson 19** (*verses 6–9*)

⁶ And there were in the place six stone water jars, sitting according to the purifying of the Jews, holding two or three measures apiece. ⁷ Jesus says to them, Fill the jars with (of) water. And they filled them up to the top. ⁸ And he says to them, Draw out now, and carry to the master of ceremonies. And they carried (it). ⁹ And when the master of ceremonies tasted the water which had been made (having become) wine, and he did not know whence it was (is), but the servants knew, the ones having drawn out the water, the master of ceremonies calls the bridegroom.

**425. Lesson 20** (*verses 10–14*)

¹⁰ And he says to him, Every man first serves the good wine, and when they are drunk, the inferior. (But) you have kept the good wine until just now. ¹¹ This beginning of signs Jesus did in Cana of Galilee and showed his glory, and his disciples believed on him.

¹² After this he went down to Capernaum himself and his mother and brothers and his disciples, and there they remained not many days.

¹³ And the passover of the Jews was near, and Jesus went up to Jerusalem. ¹⁴ And he found in the temple those selling oxen and sheep and doves, and the money changers sitting,

**426. Lesson 21** (*verses 15–17*)

¹⁵ and having made a scourge out of cords he cast (out) all out of the temple, both the sheep and the oxen, and he poured out the small change of the money changers and overturned the tables; and to those selling the doves he said, Take away these things from here. Do not make the house of my Father a house of marketing. ¹⁷ His disciples remembered that it had (has) been written, The zeal for (of) your house will devour me.

**427. Lesson 22** (*verses 18–25*)

¹⁸ The Jews then answered and said to him, What sign do you show to us because you are doing these things? ¹⁹ Jesus answered and said to them, Destroy this temple, and in three days I will raise it up. ²⁰ The Jews then said, In forty and six years this temple was built, and will you in three days raise it up? ²¹ But he (that one) was speaking about the temple of his body. ²² When, then, he was raised from the dead, his disciples remembered that he (had) said this, and they believed the scripture and the word which Jesus spoke.

²³ And when he was in Jerusalem in the passover, on the feast day, many believed on his name, seeing his signs which he did. ²⁴ But Jesus himself did not entrust himself to them, on account of his knowing (him to know) all men, ²⁵ and because he did not have need that anyone witness concerning man, for he himself knew what was in man.

## Chapter 3. *Jesus and Nicodemus*

### 428. Lesson 23 *(verses 1–11)*

¹ And there was a man from the Pharisees, Nicodemus his name (name to him), a leader of the Jews. ² This one came to him by night (of a night) and said to him, Rabbi, we know that from God you have come (as) a teacher, for no one can (is able to) do these signs which you are doing unless God is with him. ³ Jesus answered and said to him, Verily, verily, I say to you, unless one is born from above, he cannot (is not able to) see the kingdom of God. ⁴ Nicodemus says to him, How can a man be born being an old man? Can he a second time enter into the womb of his mother and be born? ⁵ Jesus answered, Verily, verily, I say to you, unless one is born from water and from (the) Spirit, he cannot enter into the kingdom of God. ⁶ That which has (having) been born from the flesh is flesh, and that which has been born (out of) from the Spirit is spirit. ⁷ Do not be surprised that I said to you, It is necessary for you to be born from above. ⁸ The wind blows wherever it wishes, and you hear the sound of it, but you do not know whence it is coming and where it is going. So is everyone who has (having) been born of the Spirit. ⁹ Nicodemus answered and said to him, How can these things happen? ¹⁰ Jesus answered and said to him, Are you the teacher of Israel and you do not know these things? ¹¹ Verily, verily, I say to you that what we know we are speaking and what we have seen we are witnessing, and you are not receiving our witness.

### 429. Lesson 24 *(verses 12–21)*

¹² If I told you (the) earthly things and you do not believe, how, if I tell you (the) heavenly things, will you believe? ¹³ And no one has gone up into (the) heaven except the one having come down out of heaven, the Son of man. ¹⁴ And according as Moses lifted up the serpent in the desert, so must (it is necessary) the Son of man be lifted up, ¹⁵ in order that everyone believing in him may have life eternal.

¹⁶ For so did God love the world that he gave his only-begotten Son, that everyone believing on him might not perish but might have life eternal. ¹⁷ For God did not send forth his Son into the world that he might judge the world, but that the world might be saved through him. ¹⁸ The one believing on him is not judged; the one not believing already has been judged, because he has not believed on the name of the only-begotten Son of God. ¹⁹ And this is the judgment, that the light has come into the world and men loved rather the darkness than the light, for their works were evil. ²⁰ For everyone doing contemptible things hates the light and does not come to the light, in order that his deeds may not

be cross-examined. ²¹ But the one doing the truth comes to the light, that his works may be shown that they have been wrought in God.

**430. Lesson 25** (*verses 22–36*)

²² After these things came Jesus and his disciples into the land of Judaea (Judaean land), and there he discoursed with them and baptized. ²³ And John also was baptizing in Aenon near (from) Salim, for there was much water (many waters) there, and they were coming and were being baptized. ²⁴ For not yet had John been cast into (the) prison. ²⁵ There came to be, then, a questioning from the disciples of John with a Jew concerning purification. ²⁶ And they came to John and said to him, Rabbi, (he) who was with you beyond the Jordan, to whom you have borne witness, behold this one is baptizing and all are coming to him. ²⁷ John answered and said, A man cannot receive anything (nothing) unless it has been given to him from heaven. ²⁸ You yourselves bear me witness that I said, I am not the Christ, but that I have been sent forth before that one. ²⁹ The one having the bride is the bridegroom. But the friend of the groom, the one standing and hearing him, rejoices with delight because of the voice of the groom. This, then, my joy has been fulfilled. ³⁰ It is necessary for him (that one) to increase but for me to decrease.

³¹ The one coming from above is above all; the one being from the earth is of the earth and speaks from the earth. The one coming from heaven is above all. ³² What he has seen and (what) he heard, this he witnesses, and his witness no one receives. ³³ The one receiving his witness sets his seal that God is true. ³⁴ For (he) whom God sent speaks the sayings of God, for not by (out of) measure he gives the Spirit. ³⁵ The Father loves the Son and has given all things into (in) his hand. ³⁶ The one believing on the Son has life eternal; but the one disbelieving the Son will not see life, but the anger of God remains upon him.

## Chapter 4. The Woman at the Well

**431. Lesson 26** (*verses 1–8*)

¹ When (as) then the Lord knew that the Pharisees heard that Jesus was (is) making and baptizing more disciples than John— ² although Jesus himself was not baptizing but his disciples— ³ he left Judaea and went back again into Galilee. ⁴ And it was necessary for him to go through Samaria. ⁵ He comes then into a city of Samaria called Sychar, near (from) the place which Jacob gave to Joseph his son. ⁶ And there was in that place a well of Jacob. Jesus, then, having been wearied from the journey, was sitting thus upon the well. The hour was about the sixth.

⁷ There comes a woman out of Samaria to draw water. Jesus says to her, Give me to drink. ⁸ For his disciples had gone away into the city that they might buy provisions.

**432. Lesson 27** (*verses 9–18*)

⁹ The Samaritan woman says, then, to him, How do you being a Jew ask to drink from me being a Samaritan woman? For Jews do not have dealings with Samaritans. ¹⁰ Jesus answered and said to her, If you knew the gift of God, and who is the one saying to you, Give me to drink, you would have asked him and he would have given to you living water. ¹¹ She says to him, Sir, you do not have a vessel for drawing, and the well is deep. Whence, then, do you have the living water? ¹² Are you greater than our father Jacob, who gave to us the well, and himself drank out of it and his sons and his cattle? ¹³ Jesus answered and said to her, Everyone drinking from this water will thirst again. ¹⁴ But (he) who drinks from the water which I shall give to him will never thirst forever, but the water which I will give to him will become in him a well of water bubbling up into life eternal. ¹⁵ The woman says to him, Sir, give me this water, that I may not thirst nor come frequently hither to draw. ¹⁶ He says to her, Go, call your husband, and come hither. ¹⁷ The woman answered and said, I do not have a husband. Jesus says to her, You well said (that), I do not have a husband; ¹⁸ For you had five husbands, and now (he) whom you have is not your husband. This you have spoken truly (true).

**433. Lesson 28** (*verses 19–34*)

¹⁹ The woman says to him, Sir, I see that you are a prophet. ²⁰ Our fathers in this mountain worshiped; and you say that in Jerusalem is the place where it is necessary to worship. ²¹ Jesus says to her, Believe me, ma'am, that an hour is coming when neither in this mountain nor in Jerusalem will you worship the Father. ²² You worship (that) which you do not know; we worship (that) which we know, for salvation is from the Jews. ²³ But there comes an hour, and now is, when the true worshipers will worship the Father in spirit and (in) truth. And (well they may) for the Father is seeking such as his worshipers (those worshiping him). ²⁴ A spirit, is God; and it is necessary for the ones worshiping (him) to worship in spirit and in truth. ²⁵ The woman says to him, I know that Messiah is coming, the one called Christ. When that one comes, he will proclaim to us all things. ²⁶ Jesus says to her, I—the one speaking to you—am (he).

²⁷ And at this (point) came his disciples, and they marveled that he was talking with a woman. However, no one said, What do you seek?

or, Why are you talking with her? ²⁸ The woman, then, left her waterjar and went away into the city and says to the men, ²⁹ Come here, see a man who told to me everything (all things which) I did; is not this one the Christ? ³⁰ They went out of the city and were coming to him. ³¹ In the meantime the disciples were asking him, saying, Rabbi, eat. ³² But he said to them, I have food to eat which you do not know. ³³ The disciples then said to one another, Has anyone brought (something) to him to eat? ³⁴ Jesus says to them, My food is that I do the will of the one having sent me and (that) I complete his work.

### 434. Lesson 29 *(verses 35–45)*

³⁵ Do not you say that yet it is a four-months and the harvest is coming? Behold, I say to you, Lift up your eyes and see the fields, that they are white for harvest. ³⁶ Already the one harvesting is receiving pay and is gathering fruit to life eternal, in order that the one sowing may rejoice together with (and) the one reaping. ³⁷ For in this the saying is true that one is the sower (the one sowing), and another the reaper (the one reaping). ³⁸ I sent you to reap (that upon) which you have not labored; others have labored, and you have entered into the labor of them.

³⁹ And out of that city many of the Samaritans believed on him on account of the word of the woman witnessing (that), He told me all things which I did. ⁴⁰ As then the Samaritans came to him, they asked him to remain with them. And he remained there two days. ⁴¹ And many (much) more believed on account of his word. ⁴² And to the woman they said (that), No longer on account of your speech do we believe, for we ourselves have heard and we know that this one is truly the Savior of the world.

⁴³ And after (the) two days he went out thence into Galilee. ⁴⁴ For Jesus himself witnessed that a prophet does not have honor in his own country. ⁴⁵ When, therefore, he came into Galilee, the Galileans received him, having seen all things which (as many as) he did in Jerusalem on the feast. And (this was possible) for (they) themselves went to the feast.

### 435. Lesson 30 *(verses 46–54)*

⁴⁶ He went back, then, into Cana of Galilee where he made the water wine. And there was a certain nobleman whose son was sick in Capernaum. ⁴⁷ This one, having heard that Jesus is come from Judaea into Galilee, went away to him and asked that he come down and heal his son, for he was about to die. ⁴⁸ Jesus then said to him, Unless you see signs and wonders, you will never believe. ⁴⁹ The nobleman says to him, Lord, come down before my little boy dies. ⁵⁰ Jesus says to him, Go on

your way; your son lives. The man believed the word which Jesus spoke to him, and he went on his way. ⁵¹ And while he was yet going down, his slaves met him saying that his child is alive. ⁵² He enquired, then, the hour from them in which he got better. They said, then, to him (that), Yesterday, the seventh hour, the fever left him. ⁵³ The father knew, then, that (it was) in that hour in which Jesus said to him, Your son lives. And he himself believed, and his whole household. ⁵⁴ And this second miracle, again, Jesus did coming out of Judaea into Galilee.

## Chapter 5. *Jesus Heals on the Sabbath*

**436. Lesson 31** (*verses 1–12*)

¹ After these things there was a feast of the Jews, and Jesus went up to Jerusalem. ² And there is in Jerusalem at the sheep (gate) a swimming pool, the one called in the Hebrew language Bethesda, having five porticos. ³ In these lay a multitude of the infirm—blind, lame, withered [awaiting the moving of the water. ⁴ For an angel from time to time went down in(to) the pool and disturbed the water. The one, then, first going in after the disturbing of the water became well of that ailment by which (by which ailment soever) he was held]. ⁵ And there was a certain man there being thirty and eight years in his infirmity. ⁶ Jesus, seeing this one lying, and knowing that for a long time now he is (thus), says to him, Are you willing to become well? ⁷ The infirm (man) answered him, Sir, I do not have a man in order that when the water is disturbed he may put (throw) me into the pool. But while (in the time in which) I am coming, another goes down in front of me. ⁸ Jesus says to him, Rise, take up your mat, and walk. ⁹ And immediately the man became well, and he took up his mat and walked. And it was (the) sabbath on that day.

¹⁰ The Jews, therefore, said to the one having been healed, It is sabbath; and it is not permissible (possible) for you to take up your mat. ¹¹ But he answered them, The one having made me well, that one said to me, Take up your mat and walk. ¹² They asked him, Who is the man saying to you, Take (it) up and walk?

**437. Lesson 32** (*verses 13–29*)

¹³ But the one having been healed did not know who it was (is). For Jesus slipped out, a crowd being in the place. ¹⁴ After these things Jesus finds him in the temple and said to him, See, you have become well; sin no longer lest something worse happen (become) to you. ¹⁵ The man went away and said to the Jews that Jesus was (is) the one having made him well. ¹⁶ And on account of this the Jews persecuted Jesus, because he was doing these things on the sabbath. ¹⁷ But he answered them, My Father

until now is working, and I am working. [18] On account of this, therefore, (all the) more the Jews sought to kill him, because not only did he break the sabbath, but also he called God (his) own Father, making himself equal to God.

[19] Jesus, then, answered and said to them, Verily, verily, I say to you, the Son cannot do anything of himself, unless he sees the Father doing something; for what things that one does, these things also the Son does likewise. [20] For the Father loves the Son and shows to him all things which he himself does; and greater works than these he will show him, in order that you may marvel. [21] For just as the Father raises the dead and makes (them) alive, so also the Son makes alive (those) whom he wishes. [22] For indeed the Father does not judge anyone (no one), but he has given all judgment to the Son, [23] that all may honor the Son even as they honor the Father. The one not honoring the Son does not honor the Father, the one having sent him. [24] Verily, verily, I say to you that the one hearing my word and believing the one having sent me has life eternal, and is not going into judgment, but has crossed over out of death into life. [25] Verily, verily, I say to you, that an hour is coming and now is when the dead will hear the voice of the Son of God, and those having heard will live. [26] For just as the Father has life in himself, so also he granted to the Son to have life in himself. [27] And he gave him authority to make judgment, because he is (the) Son of man. [28] Do not be surprised (at) this, for an hour is coming in which all those in the tombs will hear his voice, [29] and they will come out, the ones having done the good (things) to a resurrection of life, the ones having done the evil (things) to a resurrection of judgment.

### 438. Lesson 33 (*verses 30–47*)

[30] I am not able to do anything (nothing) of myself. According as I hear I judge, and my judgment is just, because I do not seek my will but the will of the one having sent me. [31] If I witness about myself, my witness is not true. [32] Another is the one witnessing concerning me, and I know that true is the witness which he witnesses about me. [33] You have sent forth to John and he has witnessed to the truth. [34] But I do not receive (the) witness from man, but these things I say that you may be saved. [35] He (that one) was the burning and shining lamp, and you were willing to be gladdened for a season (hour) in his light. [36] But I have (the) witness greater than John's. For the works which the Father has given to me that I might finish them, the very works which I am doing bear witness concerning me that the Father has sent me. [37] And the Father who sent (having sent) me, he (that one) has witnessed concerning me. Neither have you ever heard his voice, nor have you seen his appearance, [38] and his word you do not have remaining in you, for

(he) whom that one sent forth, this one you do not believe. [39] You search the scriptures, for you think in them to have life everlasting. And those are the ones witnessing about me. [40] And you are not willing to come to me that you may have life. [41] I do not receive glory from men. [42] But I know you that you do not have the love of God in yourselves. [43] I have come in the name of my Father and you do not receive me. If another comes in his own name, that one you will receive. [44] How can you believe, receiving glory from one another, and the glory from the only God you do not seek? [45] Do not think that I shall accuse you to the Father. The one accusing you is Moses, on whom you have hoped. [46] For if you believed Moses, you would believe me; for that one wrote about me. [47] But if you do not believe his writings, how will you believe my sayings?

## *Chapter 6. The Bread of Life*

### 439. Lesson 34 *(verses 1–15)*

[1] After these things Jesus went away beyond the sea of Galilee, (that is) Tiberias. [2] And there followed him a great crowd, because they saw the signs which he was doing upon the infirm. [3] And Jesus went up into the mountain and there he sat with his disciples. [4] And the passover was near, the feast of the Jews. [5] Jesus, then, raising his eyes and seeing that a great crowd is coming to him, says to Philip, Whence are we to (should we) buy loaves that these may eat? [6] And this he said testing him, for (he) himself knew what he was about to do. [7] Philip answered him, Loaves worth two hundred denarii are not enough for them that each may take some small (portion). [8] One of his disciples says to him, Andrew the brother of Simon Peter, [9] There is a small boy here who has five barley loaves and two sardines. But these—what are they for so many? [10] Jesus said, Make the men to recline. And there was much grass in the place. The men, therefore, reclined, as to number about five thousand. [11] Jesus then took the loaves and, having given thanks, he distributed to those reclining; similarly also of the sardines as much as they wished. [12] And when they were filled, he says to his disciples, Gather together the fragments remaining over, lest anything be lost. [13] They gathered (them), then, and they filled twelve baskets with fragments from the five barley loaves which remained over to the ones who had eaten. [14] The men, therefore, seeing the sign which he did, said (that), This is truly the prophet, the one coming into the world.

[15] Jesus, then, knowing that they are about to come and seize him that they may make (him) a king, withdrew again into the mountain himself alone.

## 440. Lesson 35 *(verses 16–34)*

[16] And as it became late afternoon, his disciples went down to the sea, [17] and, entering into a boat, they were going across the sea to Capernaum. And darkness had already fallen (become), and Jesus had not yet come to them. [18] And the sea was thoroughly whipped up because a great wind was blowing. [19] Having proceeded, then, about twenty-five or thirty stades, they see Jesus walking on the sea and coming (becoming) near the boat, and they were frightened. [20] But he says to them, It is I (I am); do not fear. [21] They wanted, then, to take him into the boat, and immediately the boat arrived (became) at the land to which they were going.

[22] On the morrow the crowd which had (having) stayed (stood) on the other side of the sea saw that no other boat was there except one, and that Jesus did not enter with his disciples into the boat but his disciples went away alone— [23] (although) other boats came from Tiberias near the place where they ate the bread, the Lord having given thanks— [24] When, therefore, the crowd saw that Jesus was (is) not there nor his disciples, they themselves entered into (the) boats and came to Capernaum, seeking Jesus. [25] And finding him on the other side of the sea, they said to him, Rabbi, when did (have) you come here? [26] Jesus answered them and said, Verily, verily, I say to you, you are seeking me not because you saw signs, but because you ate of the loaves and were filled. [27] Do not work (for) the perishable (perishing) food, but (for) the food abiding to life eternal which the Son of man will give to you; for this one God the Father sealed. [28] They said, then, to him, What should we do that we may work the works of God? [29] Jesus answered and said to them, This is the work of God, that you believe on (him) whom he (that one) sent forth. [30] They said, then, to him, What sign, then, do you make, that we may see and believe you? What do you work? [31] Our fathers ate the manna in the desert according as it has been written, Bread from heaven he gave them to eat. [32] Jesus said, then, to them, Verily, verily I say to you, Moses did not give (has not given) to you the bread from heaven, but my Father gives you the true bread from heaven. [33] For the bread of God is the one coming down out of heaven and giving life to the world. [34] They said, then, to him, Lord, ever give us this bread.

## 441. Lesson 36 *(verses 35–52)*

[35] Jesus said to them, I am the bread of life. The one coming to me will never hunger, and the one believing on me will not thirst ever. [36] But I told you that you have also seen me and do not believe. [37] All that (which) the Father gives me will come to me, and the one coming to me I will never cast out, [38] for I came down from heaven not that I might do my will, but the will of the one having sent me. [39] And this is the will of the one having sent me, that everything which he has given to me,

I should not lose (ought) from it, but I will raise it up in the last day. [40] For this is the will of my Father, that everyone seeing the Son and believing on him may have life everlasting, and I will raise him up in the last day. [41] The Jews, then, murmured about him because he said, I am the bread coming down (having come down) out of heaven, [42] and they said, Is not this Jesus the son of Joseph, whose father and mother we know? How now does he say (that), I have come down out of heaven? [43] Jesus answered and said to them, Do not murmur with one another. [44] No one is able to come to me unless the Father who sent (the one having sent) me draws him; and I will raise him up in the last day. [45] It has been written in the prophets, And they shall all be taught of God. Everyone hearing and learning from the Father comes to me. [46] Not that anyone has seen the Father, except the one who is (being) from God, this one has seen the Father. [47] Verily, verily, I say to you, the one believing has life eternal. [48] I am the bread of life. [49] Your fathers ate the manna in the desert and died. [50] This is the bread coming down out of heaven, that one may eat of it and may not die. [51] I am the living bread which came (that having come) down out of heaven. If anyone eats of this bread, he will live forever. And my flesh also is the bread which I shall give for the life of the world.

[52] The Jews, then, contended with one another saying, How can this one give us his flesh to eat?

## 442. Lesson 37 (*verses 53–71*)

[53] Jesus said, then, to them, Verily, verily, I say to you, unless you eat the flesh of the Son of man and drink his blood, you do not have life in yourselves. [54] The one eating my flesh and drinking my blood has life eternal, and I will raise him up in the last day. [55] For my flesh is true food, and my blood is true drink. [56] The one eating my flesh and drinking my blood dwells in me and I in him. [57] According as the living Father sent me forth and I live through the Father, (also) the one eating me, that one, too, will live through me. [58] This is the bread that came down (having come down) from heaven, not according as the fathers ate and died; the one eating this bread shall live for ever. [59] These things he said while teaching in a synagogue in Capernaum.

[60] Many, then, of his disciples hearing (it) said, This is a harsh word; who is able to hear it? [61] But Jesus, knowing in himself that his disciples are murmuring about this, said to them, Does this scandalize you? [62] (What) then if you see the Son of man ascending where he was before? [63] The Spirit is the life giver (making alive); the flesh does not help at all (nothing). The sayings which I have spoken to you are spirit and are life. [64] But there are (some) of you who do not believe. For Jesus knew

from the beginning who were (are) the ones not believing and who was (is) the one about to betray him. ⁶⁵ And he said, Because of this I have said to you that no one can come to me unless it has been given to him from the Father.

⁶⁶ From this (time) many of his disciples went back and no longer walked with him. ⁶⁷ Jesus said, then, to the twelve, Are you also wanting to go? ⁶⁸ Simon Peter answered him, Lord, to whom shall we go away? You have the sayings of life eternal. ⁶⁹ And we have believed and know that you are the holy one of God. ⁷⁰ Jesus answered them, Did I not choose you the twelve? And of you one is a devil. ⁷¹ He meant Judas (son) of Simon Iscariot. For this one was about to betray him, (being) one of the twelve.

## WORKING TRANSLATION OF SELECTIONS FROM THE *ANABASIS* OF XENOPHON

### Book 1

**443. Lesson 39** (*1.1.1.1–1.1.2.7*). *Darius nears the End of Life*

*Chapter 1.* Of Darius and Parysatis are born two boys, (the) elder, Artaxerxes, and (the) younger, Cyrus. And when Darius was sick and suspected (the) end of his life, he wished for both the boys to be present. Now the older happened to be present. And he summons Cyrus from the province of which he (had) made him satrap. And he (had) appointed him general of all as many as are mustered into the plain of Castolus. Cyrus goes inland, then, taking Tissaphernes as friend; and he went up, having of the Greeks three hundred hoplites, moreover as leader of them Xenias the Parrhasian.

**444. Lesson 40** (*1.1.3.1–1.1.5.5*). *Trouble between Cyrus and Artaxerxes*

And when Darius died and Artaxerxes succeeded into the kingdom, Tissaphernes slandered (slanders) Cyrus to his (the) brother, (saying) that he was plotting against him. And he is persuaded and arrests Cyrus to kill (him). But their (the) mother, having interceded for him, sends him back again to his province. But he, as he went away having been in danger and having been disgraced, plans that never again shall he be in the power of his brother, but if he can he will reign instead of him (that one). Now Parysatis, indeed, their (the) mother, supported Cyrus, loving him rather than the ruling Artaxerxes. And whoever of those from the king came to him, he sent (them) all away, so treating (them) (so) as to be friends to him rather than to the king. And he took care of the barbarians (Persians) with himself, that they might be able to make war and that they might be well-disposed to him.

### 445. Lesson 41 (*1.1.6.1–1.1.7.3*). *Cyrus arms against the King*

And his Greek force he collected as secretly as he could (concealing as much as he could) that he might catch the king as unprepared as possible. In the following way, then, he made his gathering. As many garrisons as he had in the cities, he sent word to each of the commanders to take Peloponnesian men as many and as brave as possible, on the grounds that Tissaphernes (was) plotting against his cities. And (this was plausible) for the Ionic cities were Tissaphernes', having been given him of old from the king. But at that time they had revolted to Cyrus, all except Miletus. But in Miletus Tissaphernes, discerning that they were planning these same things, to revolt to Cyrus, killed some and expelled others.

### 446. Lesson 42 (*1.1.7.4–1.1.8.9*). *A Ruse to deceive the King*

But Cyrus, taking under his protection those who were exiled, having gathered an army, besieged Miletus both by land and by sea, and attempted to restore those who had been exiled (those having fallen out). And this again was another excuse to him for collecting an army. And, sending to the king, he asked, being a brother of him, for these cities to be given to him rather than for Tissaphernes to be ruler of them, and his mother helped him in doing (did with him) these things. So that the king did not perceive the plot against himself, but thought him, because making war with Tissaphernes, to be spending money upon (about) the armies, so that he was nothing distressed by their warring. And (there was further reason for him to feel satisfied) for Cyrus sent back to the king the tribute moneys accruing from the cities of Tissaphernes which he happened to have (having).

### 447. Lesson 43 (*1.1.9.1–1.1.9.10*). *Cyrus' Friendship with Clearchus*

And another army was collected for him in the Chersonese over against Abydus in the following fashion. Clearchus was a Lacedemonian exile. And Cyrus, becoming acquainted with him (this one), both admired him and gave (gives) to him ten thousand darics. And he, taking the gold, gathered an army with (from) this money and made war, setting forth from the Chersonese, with the Thracians, those dwelling (settling) above the Hellespont, and he helped the Greeks. So that also the Hellespontine cities willingly contributed money to him towards the support of his soldiers. And this army again was thus secretly supported (escaped notice being supported) for him.

**448. Lesson 44** (*1.1.10.1–1.1.11.8*). *The Contingent in Thessaly*

And Aristippus the Thessalian happened to be a guest-friend to him, and, being hard-pressed by his party opponents at home, he comes to Cyrus and asks him (for) up to two thousand mercenaries and three months' pay, (saying) that thus he would get the better of his opponents. And Cyrus gives to him up to four thousand (mercenaries) and six months' pay, and asks of him not to make peace with (towards) his opponents until he consults with him. And thus, again, the army in Thessaly was secretly supported for him.

And Proxenus the Boeotian he commanded, being a guest-friend, taking as many men as possible, to come (to become present), as wishing to make an expedition against (the) Pisidians, as (on the grounds that) the Pisidians (were) causing trouble to his own country. And Sophaenetus the Stymphalian and Socrates the Achaean, these also being guest-friends, he commanded, taking as many men as possible, to come, as purposing to (being about to) make war against Tissaphernes with the exiles of the Milesians. And these did so.

**449. Lesson 45** (*1.2.1.1.–1.2.2.6*). *Massing for the Big Push*

*Chapter 2.* And when it seemed best to him now to proceed up-country, he made the excuse that (he was) wishing to expel the Pisidians entirely from his country. And he gathers as against these both the Persian (barbarian) and the Greek (army). And there he sends word to Clearchus, taking whatever army he had (was to him), to come; and to Aristippus, making peace with (toward) those at home, to send back to himself the army which he had (what army he had); and to Xenias the Arcadian, who for him was in command of the mercenary force in the cities, he sends word to come, taking the rest except as many as were sufficient to guard the citadels. And he called also those besieging Miletus, and the exiles he commanded to make the expedition with him, promising them, if he should well accomplish (the things) for which he was making the expedition, not to stop until he brought them back home (homewards). And they gladly obeyed, for they trusted him. And, taking their arms, they came (were present) to Sardis.

**450. Lesson 46** (*1.2.3.1–1.2.5.2*). *The Roster of the Troops*

Xenias, indeed, taking the hoplites from the cities up to four thousand, came to Sardis. And Proxenus came (was present), having up to fifteen hundred (five hundred and a thousand) hoplites and five hundred light-armed troops. And Sophaenetus the Stymphalian (came), having a thousand hoplites, and Socrates the Achaean, having about five hundred hoplites, and Pasion the Megarian came, having three hundred hoplites and three hundred peltasts. And both he (this one) and Socrates were (was) also of those making the expedition about Miletus.

These came to him to Sardis. But Tissaphernes, having observed these things and having considered the preparation to be greater than as against (the) Pisidians, proceeds to the king as rapidly as he could (in what way he could most quickly), having about five hundred horsemen. And the king, indeed, when he heard from Tissaphernes (about) the expedition of Cyrus, made counter-preparations.

**451. Lesson 47** (*1.2.5.3–1.2.7.3*). *The Expedition reaches Celaenae in Phrygia*

And Cyrus, having (those) whom I have mentioned, started out from Sardis. And he marches through Lydia three days' journey, twenty-two parasangs, to the Maeander river. Of this the width (is) two plethra. And a bridge was upon (it), yoked together on (by) seven boats. Crossing this, he marches through Phrygia one day's march, eight parasangs, to Colossae, an inhabited city, prosperous and great. There he remained seven days. And Menon the Thessalian came, having a thousand hoplites and five hundred peltasts, Dolopians and Aenianians and Olynthians. Thence he marches three days' journey, twenty parasangs, to Celaenae, an inhabited city of Phrygia, great and prosperous.

**452. Lesson 48** (*1.2.7.4–1.2.9.3*). *The Palace and Game Preserve at Celaenae*

There Cyrus had (there was to Cyrus) a palace and a great park full of wild beasts, which he (that one) used to hunt (hunted) on horseback whenever he wished to exercise himself and also the horses. And through (the) midst of the park flows the Maeander river. And the source of it is (springs of it are) from the palace. And it flows also through the city of Celaenae. And there is also a palace of the great king in Celaenae, fortified upon the source (the springs) of the Marsyas river at the foot of the acropolis. And this also flows through the city and empties into the Maeander. And of the Marsyas the width is (of) twenty-five feet. There Apollo is said to have flayed Marsyas, having surpassed (him) contending with him concerning (musical) skill, and to have hung the skin in the cave whence (is) the source. And because of this the river is called (the) Marsyas. There Xerxes, when he was retreating from Greece having been defeated in the battle, is said to have built both this palace and the acropolis of Celaenae.

**453. Lesson 49** (*1.2.9.4–1.2.10.7*). *The Halt at Celaenae*

There Cyrus remained thirty days. And Clearchus came, having a thousand hoplites and eight hundred Thracian peltasts and two hundred

Cretan bowmen. And at the same time also came Sosis the Syracusan, having three hundred hoplites, and Sophaenetus the Arcadian, having a thousand hoplites. And there Cyrus held (made) a review and numbering of the Greeks in the park, and the total was (were, became, turned out to be) eleven thousand hoplites and peltasts about two thousand. Thence he marches two days' journey, ten parasangs, to Peltae, an inhabited city. There he remained three days, during (in) which Xenias the Arcadian celebrated with sacrifices the Lycaean festival (sacrificed the Lycaea) and set up a contest. And the prizes were golden flesh-scrapers. And Cyrus also watched the contest. Thence he marches two days' journey, twelve parasangs, to Ceramon-agora (Market of the Ceramians), an inhabited city, furthest toward the country (of) Mysia.

**454. Lesson 50** (*1.2.11.1–1.2.12.6*). *A Financial Crisis*

From there he marches three days' journey, thirty parasangs, to Cayster-field, an inhabited city. There he remained five days. And to the soldiers there was owed more than three months' pay, and, going to headquarters frequently, they asked (for it). And he, speaking hopes, passed time and was evidently troubled (evident being troubled). For it was not according to (characteristic of) the character of Cyrus, having (money), not to pay. In this place Epyaxa the wife of Syennesis king of the Cilicians comes to Cyrus. And she was said to have given to Cyrus much money. And so at that time Cyrus paid out to the army four months' pay. And the Cilician woman had a guard about herself, Cilicians and Aspendians. And it was also said that Cyrus had relations with the Cilician woman.

**455. Lesson 51** (*1.2.13.1–1.2.16.6*). *Review of the Armies at Tyriaeum*

Thence he marches two days' journey, ten parasangs, to Thymbrium, an inhabited city. In this place there was beside the road a spring called the (spring) of Midas the king of (the) Phrygians, at which Midas is said to have hunted the satyr, mixing it with wine. From there he marches two days' journey, ten parasangs, to Tyriaeum, an inhabited city. There he remained three days. And the Cicilian (queen) is said to have asked of Cyrus to display the army to her (to herself). Wishing, then, to display (it), he holds (makes) in the plain a review of the Greeks and of the Persians (barbarians). And he commanded the Greeks as (was) their (to them) custom (to be drawn up) for battle, so to be drawn up and to stand, and for each (general) to marshal his own (men). So they were drawn up four deep (upon fours). And Menon and those with him held the right (wing), and the left (wing) Clearchus and his men (those of that one), and the center the other generals. Cyrus, then, reviewed first the Persians. And they marched past, having been arrayed by (according to) companies and by divisions. And afterward (he reviewed) the Greeks, riding by on a chariot, and the Cilician (queen) in (on) a covered carriage. And all had bronze helmets and purple tunics and greaves and their shields uncovered.

**456. Lesson 52** (*1.2.17.1–1.2.18.6*). *Military Prestige of the Greeks*

And when he had ridden (rode) past all, stopping his chariot in front of the middle of the battle-line (the middle battle-line), sending Pigres the interpreter to the generals of the Greeks, he ordered (them) to put forward their arms and for the entire phalanx to charge. And they announced this (proclaimed these things) to the soldiers, and when the trumpet sounded, putting forward their arms, they charged. And thereupon (from this), as (they) went forward more rapidly with a shout, as though by common consent (of their own accord), the soldiers broke into a run (a running became to the soldiers) toward the tents. And the fear of the barbarians (was) great. And the Cilician (queen) fled upon her closed carriage, and those out of the market place fled, leaving behind their wares. And the Greeks with laughter came to their tents. And the Cilician (queen), seeing the brilliance and the order of the army, was amazed. And Cyrus was glad, seeing the fear caused by (from) the Greeks upon the barbarians.

**457. Lesson 53** (*1.2.19.1–1.2.20.9*). *The March through Lycaonia and Cappadocia*

Thence he marches three days' journey, twenty parasangs, to Iconium, furthest city of Phrygia. There he remained three days. Thence he marches through Lycaonia five days' journey, thirty parasangs. This country he turned over to the Greeks to plunder as being hostile. Thence Cyrus sends back the Cilician (queen) into Cilicia (by) the quickest way. And he sent with her the soldiers whom Menon had and (Menon) himself. And Cyrus with the rest marches through Cappadocia four days' journey, twenty and five parasangs, to Dana (Tyana), an inhabited city, great and prosperous. There they remained three days. During which (time) Cyrus put to death a Persian man Megaphernes, a wearer of the royal purple (a royal purple-wearer), and a certain other mighty man of his subordinates, charging (them) with (to be) plotting against him.

**458. Lesson 54** (*1.2.21.1–1.2.22.6*). *Syennesis abandons the Cilician Pass*

Thence they tried to enter into Cilicia. But the pass was a wagon road extremely steep, and difficult of access (impracticable to enter) for an army if anyone was hindering. And also Syennesis was said to be on the heights, guarding the pass. Wherefore they remained a day in the plain. And on the next day there came a messenger, saying that Syennesis had left the heights when he perceived that the army of Menon already was in Cilicia inside of the mountains, and because (that) he heard triremes were sailing around from Ionia into Cilicia, those of the Lacedemonians and of Cyrus himself. And Cyrus, therefore, went up upon the mountains, no one hindering, and he saw the tents where the Cilicians had been (were) guarding. And thence he descended into a plain vast and beautiful, well-watered, and quite full of all manner of trees and of vines. And it also bears much sesame and millet and millet grass and wheat and barley.

**459. Lesson 55** (*1.2.22.7–1.2.26.3*). *Cyrus finds Tarsus deserted*

And a mountain impregnable and lofty hems it in everywhere from sea to sea. And having descended, he marched through this plain four days' journey, five and twenty parasangs, into Tarsus, a city of Cilicia great and prosperous, where was the palace of Syennesis. And through the midst of the city flows a river, Cydnus by name, in width (of) two plethra. This city the inhabitants abandoned, (going) with Syennesis into a fortified place (stronghold) upon the mountains, except those having the shops. And also those dwelling beside the sea in Soli and in Issus remained. And Epyaxa the wife of Syennesis arrived at (came to) Tarsus five days earlier than Cyrus. And in the pass over (of) the mountains into the plain two companies of the army of Menon were destroyed. Some said that, while plundering something, they had been cut down by the Cilicians, and others that, having been left behind and not being able to find the rest of the (the other) army nor the roads, wandering about, they then perished. At any rate, these were a hundred hoplites. And the others, when they came, plundered the city and the palace in it, being angry because of the destruction of their fellow soldiers.

**460. Lesson 56** (*1.2.26.4–1.3.1.6*). *Cyrus and Syennesis reach an Agreement*

And Cyrus, after (when) he (had) marched into the city, summoned Syennesis to himself. But he said that neither did he ever before come into the hands of (to) anyone superior to (stronger than) himself, nor then was he willing to go (into the hands) to Cyrus, until his wife persuaded him and he received pledges. And after these things, when they were together with each other, Syennesis gave to Cyrus much money for his army, and Cyrus (gave) to him (that one) gifts which are considered precious at court (with the king), a gold-bridled horse and a gold collar and armlets and a golden short-sword and a Persian robe, and (he gave his word) no longer to plunder his country, and (granted him) to take back the captives who had been (having been) seized if they happen upon (them) anywhere.

*Chapter 3.* There Cyrus and his army remained twenty days. For the soldiers said they would not go forward. For they now suspected they were going against the king. And they said they had not been hired (to have been hired) for this. And Clearchus first tried to force (was forcing) his own soldiers to proceed. But they pelted both him and his baggage animals whenever they began to go forward.

**461. Lesson 57** (*1.3.2.1–1.3.5.7*). *Speech of Clearchus to his Men*

And Clearchus at that time narrowly (by a little) escaped being stoned to death (not to be stoned to death), and later, when he knew that he would not (will not) be able to compel (them), he brought together an assembly of his own soldiers. And first he wept a long time, standing. And they, seeing, marveled and were silent. And then he spoke as follows (of the following sort):

'Fellow soldiers, do not be surprised that I am grieved at the present affairs. For to me Cyrus became a guest-friend and he both honored me, being exiled from my fatherland, in respect to other things, and he gave (me) ten thousand darics. Taking which, I did not lay them up for my own use nor did I waste (them) in luxury, but I spent (them) upon you.

'And first I made war against the Thracians, and on the behalf of Greece I punished (them) with you, driving them out of the Chersonese (when they were) wanting to take away the land from the Greeks dwelling in (it). But when Cyrus called, taking you, I went, in order that if he should need anything I might help him in return for (instead of) the things in which I was well treated (I suffered well) by him.

'But since you do not wish to proceed with (me), it is necessary indeed for me either, betraying you, to use the friendship of Cyrus, or, having been false toward him (that one), to be with you. Now whether, indeed, I shall do right I do not know, but I will choose you, then, and with you I will suffer whatever is necessary. And never shall anyone (no one) say that I, having led Greeks among (into) the barbarians, giving over the Greeks, chose the friendship of the barbarians.'

**462. Lesson 58** (*1.3.6.1–1.3.10.5*). *Double-talking Orator*

'But since you are not willing to obey me, I will follow with you and whatever is necessary I will suffer. For I consider that you are to me both fatherland and friends and allies. And with you I think that I would be honored wherever I am, but, being deprived of you, that I would not be able either (neither) to help a friend or (nor) to ward off an enemy. On the basis, then, of (as) my going wherever you also (go), just so (thus) you have my intention.'

These things he said, and the soldiers, both his own (those of that one himself) and the others, having heard these things, applauded (praised). And from Xenias and Pasion more than two thousand, taking their arms and their baggage animals, pitched camp over with Clearchus. But Cyrus, being distressed and also grieving at these things, sent for Clearchus. And he was not willing to go, but, sending to him a messenger unknown to (secretly from) the soldiers, he told (him) to be of good cheer as these things would turn out for the good. And he bade him to summon (him), but himself said he would not go.

And after these things, having brought together both his own soldiers and those having come over to him, and of the others the one wishing (to come), he spoke as follows: 'Fellow soldiers, as to the (affairs) of Cyrus, indeed, (it is) evident that they are (related) toward us just as our affairs (are related) toward him. For neither are we any longer (yet) his soldiers (of that one), since, at any rate, we are not following with him, nor is that one any longer (yet) a paymaster to us. However, that he considers that he is being wronged (to be wronged) by us I know. So that, even though he summons, I do not want to go, being ashamed chiefly because I am conscious (with myself) that I have deceived (having deceived) him in all respects, and furthermore fearing lest, taking me, he inflict punishment for the things in which (of what things) he considers he has been (to have been) wronged by me.'

**463. Lesson 59** (*1.3.11.1–1.3.14.8*). *Clearchus warns of Cyrus' Wrath*

'To me, then, it seems not to be a time (an hour) for us to sleep nor to be neglectful of ourselves, but to plan whatever it is necessary to do next (out of these). And as long as we remain here, it seems to me that we ought to take thought (to be necessary to take thought) that we may remain as safely as possible. And if now it seems best to depart, that we shall depart as safely as possible and that we shall have supplies. For without these things there is no use (neither) of general nor of private soldier.

'And the man is a friend worthy of much to whom (ever) he is a friend, but a most harsh personal enemy to whom (ever) he is hostile. And he has power, both infantry and cavalry and naval, which we all alike see and also know. And (well we may) for we do not seem to me to be situated far from him. So that it is time (an hour) to say whatever anyone knows (feels convinced) to be best.' Having said these things, he ceased. And next (from this) there stood up some of their own accord to say what they were convinced, and others also, prompted by him (that one), showing of what sort was the difficulty both to remain and to depart without the will of Cyrus.

And one indeed said, pretending to be eager to proceed as quickly as possible to Greece, to choose other generals as quickly as possible, unless Clearchus wants to lead (them) back, and to buy for themselves provisions—but the market was in the barbarian army—and to pack up. And going, to ask Cyrus (for) boats that they might sail away. And if he does not give these, to ask Cyrus (for) a guide who(ever) will lead (them) back through friendly country.

**464. Lesson 60** (*1.3.14.9–1.3.17.6*). *The Democratic Process*

And if he does not even give a guide, to draw themselves up (in battle array) forthwith (the quickest way), and to send also (men) to capture first the heights, in order that neither Cyrus nor the Cilicians may get the start (of us) seizing (them), of whom we have many (persons) and much money, having plundered (these). This man spoke such things. And after this man Clearchus spoke this much:

'Let no one of you mention me as being about to command this strategy. For I see in (it) many things on account of which this ought not to be done by me. But (let him say) that the man whom you choose I will obey in what (way) it is most possible, that you may know that I also know how to take orders (to be commanded), as also any other man (of men) in the world (especially, at all).' After this (man) another stood up showing the folly of the one bidding to ask for the boats, just as if Cyrus were making the expedition back, and showing that it was foolish to ask a guide from this (man) whose undertaking we are spoiling (for whom we are spoiling the undertaking). 'And if also we shall trust the guide whom Cyrus gives, what hinders even to bid Cyrus to occupy beforehand the heights for us? For I would dread to enter into the boats which he should give to us, lest he sink us with his warships. And I would fear to follow the guide whom he should give, lest he lead us whence it will not be possible to get (go) out. But I would wish, departing with Cyrus unwilling, to go away without his knowledge (to escape his notice going away), which is not possible.'

**465. Lesson 61** (*1.3.18.1–1.3.21.7*). *Collective Bargaining*

'But I say that these things are nonsense. But I move (it seems best to me) for men going to Cyrus, whoever (are) suitable, with Clearchus, to ask him (that one) what use he wishes to make of us (what he wishes to use us). And if the undertaking is like to that for which (of what sort) he also previously used the mercenaries, for us also to follow and not to be more cowardly than those previously having journeyed up-country with him (this one). But if the undertaking appears greater than the former, and more toilsome and more dangerous, to ask (him) either to lead us having persuaded us (e.g. with money), or having been persuaded, to send (us) away on terms of friendship. For thus, both following we would follow as friends to him and eager, and departing we would depart safely. And to report back hither whatever he says to these things. And (I move) for us, having heard, to make plans with reference to (toward) these things.'

These things were voted (seemed best), and, choosing men, they send (them) with Clearchus, who asked Cyrus the things voted by (having seemed best to) the army. And he replied that he heard (hears) that Abrocomas, a hostile man, is at the Euphrates river, being distant twelve days' journey. To this one, then, he said he wished to go. And if he is there, he said he desired to impose punishment upon him, but if he flees, we will there take counsel regarding (toward) these things. And, having heard these things, the ones chosen report to the soldiers. And they had a suspicion (to them was a suspicion) that he was (is) leading against the king, but, nevertheless, it was voted (seemed best) to follow. And they ask for more pay (ask in addition pay). And Cyrus promises to give to all a half more than that which they previously earned (carried), instead of a daric, three half-darics each month per soldier (of the month, to the soldier). But that he was leading against the king no one heard there, at least in the open.

**466. Lesson 62** (*1.4.1.1–1.4.4.7*). *Arrival of Reinforcements at Issus*

*Chapter 4.* Thence he marches two days' journey, ten parasangs, to the Psarus river, of which the width was three plethra. Thence he marches one day's journey, five parasangs, to the Pyramus river, of which the width was a stade. Thence he marches two days' journey, fifteen parasangs, to Issus, farthest city of Cilicia, situated (inhabited) on the sea, great and prosperous. There they remained three days. And to Cyrus there came the ships from the Peloponnesus, thirty-five, and as admiral over them Pythagoras the Spartan. And Tamos, an Egyptian, piloted them from Ephesus, having twenty-five other ships of Cyrus, with which he was blockading Miletus. And there came also Chirisophus the Spartan upon the ships, summoned by Cyrus, having seven hundred hoplites, of which he was general on Cyrus' side. And the ships came to anchor alongside the tent of Cyrus. And in that place also the Greek mercenaries, deserting from Abrocomas, came over to Cyrus, four hundred hoplites, and joined the expedition (made the expedition with) against the king.

Thence he marches one day's journey, five parasangs, to (the) gates of Cilicia and Syria. And these were two walls, and the one on the inside, towards Cilicia, Syennesis was holding and a garrison of Cilicians. But the one outside, towards Syria, a garrison of the king was said to be guarding. And through the space between (midst of) these flows a river, Carsus by (as to) name, in width a plethron. And the entire space between the walls was (were) three stades. And it was not possible to pass through by force.

**467. Lesson 63** (*1.4.4.8–1.4.7.9*). *The Strange Retreat of Abrocomas*

For the passage was narrow and the walls extending down to the sea. And overhead were steep cliffs. And commanding (at, upon) both the walls there stood gates. On account of this passage Cyrus sent for the ships, in order that he might land hoplites inside and outside of the gates to force the enemy if they were guarding at the Syrian gates, which Cyrus thought that Abrocomas would do, having a large army. But Abrocomas did not do this, but when he heard that Cyrus was in Cilicia, turning back, he marched away from Phoenicia to the king, having, as was said, an army of three hundred thousand (thirty ten thousands of army).

Thence he marches through Syria one day's journey, five parasangs, to Myriandus, a city on the sea inhabited by Phoenicians. And the place was a market, and many freighters anchored there. Here they remained seven days. And Xenias the Arcadian and Pasion the Megarian, embarking into a boat and putting in their most valuable things (their things worth most), sailed away, as it (they) seemed to most (men), being piqued because the soldiers of theirs, the ones going over to Clearchus as going back to Greece again and not against the king, Cyrus allowed Clearchus to keep (to have). And when they were out of sight, word went around that Cyrus was pursuing them with warships. And some wished for them to be caught (taken) as being cowards. But some felt sorry for (them) if they should be captured.

**468. Lesson 64** (*1.4.8.1–1.4.9.8*). *Cyrus tactfully spares the Deserters*

But Cyrus, having called together the generals, said, 'Xenias and Pasion have deserted us. But at least let them well know, however, that they have not gotten clean away, for I know where they are gone. Nor have they escaped, for I have warships so as to seize their boat (the boat of those ones). But by the gods, I, for my part, shall not pursue them, nor shall anyone say that I, as long as anyone is present, use (him), but whenever he wishes to depart, arresting (him), I both abuse them and despoil their goods. But let them go, knowing that they are more dastardly concerning us than we (are) concerning them (those ones). And yet I at least have both their children and wives in Tralles under observation (being watched or guarded). But neither shall they be deprived of these, but they shall receive (them) back on account of their previous loyalty for (concerning) me.' And he, on his part, said these things. And the Greeks, if anyone was even somewhat discouraged toward the march inland, hearing the goodness of Cyrus, (they) accompanied (him) more gladly and more eagerly.

After these things Cyrus marches four days' journey, twenty parasangs, to the Chalus river, being a plethron in width and full of large and tame fishes which the Syrians considered gods and did not allow (anyone) to harm, nor the pigeons. And the villages in which they tented were Parysatis', having been given (her) for pin money (girdle money).

**469. Lesson 65** (*1.4.10.1–1.4.11.5 and 1.4.17.4–1.4.19.4*). *The Crossing of the Euphrates*

Thence he marches five days' journey, thirty parasangs, to the springs of the Dardas river, of which the width (was) a plethron. In this place was the palace of Belesys, the one having ruled Syria, and a park very great and beautiful, having all things which (as many as) the seasons produce. And Cyrus cut it down and burned up the palace. Thence he marches three days' journey, fifteen parasangs, to the Euphrates river, being four stades in width. And a city was inhabited there, great and prosperous, Thapsacus by name. There he remained five days. . . .

And, having done these things, he crossed over. And there followed with him also all the rest of the army (the other army altogether). And of those crossing the river no one got wet higher than the chest (the breasts) by the river. And the Thapsacenes said that never had this river become (never did it become) crossable on foot except (unless) then, but by boats, which at that time Abrocomas, going before, burned up in order that Cyrus might (may) not cross. It seemed indeed to be a portent and that the river clearly had given way to Cyrus as about to be king. Thence he marches through Syria nine days' journey, fifty parasangs. And they arrive at (to) the Araxes river. In this place were many villages full of food and wine. There they remained three days and got provisions.

**470. Lesson 66** (*1.5.1.1–1.5.3.6*). *Hunting in the Desert*

*Chapter 5.* Thence he marches through Arabia, having the Euphrates river on the right, five days' journey through the desert (five desert days' journey), thirty and five parasangs. In this place the earth was altogether a plain, level just as a sea, and full of wormwood. And also if there was in (it) anything else of bush or of stalk, all were sweet-smelling just as spices. And no tree was in (it), but all manner of wild beasts, very many wild asses, and many ostriches. And there were (in it) also bustards and gazelles. And these wild animals the horsemen sometimes chased. And the asses, when anyone pursued, running ahead, came to a stop. For they ran much faster than the horses. And again when the horses drew near they did the same thing. And it was not possible to catch (them) unless, standing at intervals, the horsemen hunted relieving (each other). And the meat of the ones (being) caught was like to venison, but more tender. But no one caught an ostrich. For (those of) the horsemen pursuing quickly gave up (ceased). For it drew away far (much) in flight (fleeing), using its feet for running and its wings, raising (them) just as a sail. And the bustards, if one suddenly rouses (them), it is possible to catch. For they fly short, just as partridges, and quickly give out. And the meat of them was very tasty (sweet).

**471. Lesson 67** (*1.5.4.1–1.5.7.3*). *The Grim Pinch of Famine*

And, proceeding through this country, they arrive at (to) the Mascas river, a plethron in width. In this place was a desert city, great, and named Corsote (and name to it Corsote). And this was surrounded (was flowed about) by the Mascas in a circle. There they remained three days and got provisions. Thence he marches thirteen days' journey through the desert (thirteen desert days' journey), ninety parasangs, having the Euphrates river on the right, and he arrives at Pylae. In these days' marches many of the baggage animals perished by hunger. For there was no fodder nor any (other) tree, but the whole country was barren. And the inhabitants, quarrying millstones along the river and making (them), carried (them) to Babylon and sold (them) and, buying food in exchange, they lived. And the food failed the army, and it was not possible to buy (it) except (unless) in the Lydian market in the barbarian (army) of Cyrus, the capith of wheat flour or barley meal for four shekels. And the shekel is worth seven and a half Attic obols. And the capith held two Attic choenixes. Eating meat, then, the soldiers got through. And there were (some) of these days' journeys which he marched very long, whenever he wished to complete (the march) either to water or to fodder.

**472. Lesson 68** (*1.5.7.4–1.5.8.10*). *An Example of Good Discipline*

And, indeed, once, when a narrow passage and mud appeared difficult of traverse (hard to get through) for the wagons, Cyrus halted with the noblest and wealthiest (young men) of his staff (around him) and ordered Glus and Pigres, taking (some) of the barbarian army, to help push out the wagons. And when they seemed to him to act (to do) slowly, as though in anger he commanded the Persians of his staff (about him), the nobles (noblest), to help hurry forward the wagons. There, indeed, it was possible to behold an (a certain) example of good discipline. For throwing off their purple caftans wherever each happened (to be) standing, they rushed just as anyone would run to win a race (for victory), and down a very steep hill, with (having) their expensive tunics and their many-colored trousers, and several also collars around their necks and armlets about their arms (hands). And immediately jumping into the mud with these, quicker than one would think, they got out the wagons, raising them off the ground (suspended in the air).

**473. Lesson 69** (*1.5.9.1–1.5.10.9*). *Shopping by River Raft*

And on the whole Cyrus was evidently hastening (evident as hastening) all the way and not spending time unless where (wherever not) he tarried (sat) on account of collecting provisions, or (of) some other necessary (thing), thinking that the quicker he came, he would catch (fight with) the king the more unprepared (by how much more quickly he came, he would fight with the king by so much more unprepared), but the more slowly (he came), the greater an army was being gathered for the king (by how much more slowly, by so much more an army was being collected for the king). And it was possible for the one giving attention (applying his mind) to realize that the king's domain was strong in quantity of country and of men, but in the distances of the roads and the resources being separated (to have been separated) (it was) weak if anyone were waging the war speedily. And on the other side of the Euphrates river during the desert days' journeys was a city prosperous and great, and its name (was) Charmande. Out of this the soldiers bought provisions, crossing with rafts as follows. Tanned skins which they had as tent coverings they filled with dry grass. Then they drew (them) together and sewed (them) together, so that the water did not touch the hay. Upon these they crossed and got provisions, both wine made out of the date from the palm tree, and millet bread. For this was very abundant (very much) in the country.

**474. Lesson 70** (*1.7.1.1–1.7.4.8*). *Cyrus' Estimate of Civil Freedom*

*Chapter 7.* Thence he marches through Babylonia three days' journey, twelve parasangs. And in the third day's march Cyrus holds (makes) a review of the Greeks and of the barbarians in the plain about midnight. For he thought that at daybreak (on the coming dawn) the king would come with his army to fight. And he commanded Clearchus to be leader of the right wing and Menon of the left (wing), and he himself marshalled his own men (those of himself). But after the review, at daybreak (along with the coming day), deserters coming from the great king brought word to Cyrus concerning the king's army. And Cyrus, having called together the generals and captains of the Greeks, both took counsel how he should conduct (make) the battle and himself praised (them), encouraging (them) as follows:

'O men of Greece (men Greeks), not because lacking barbarian men do I lead you as allies, but considering you to be better and braver than many barbarians, on account of this I took you besides. See, then, that you shall be men worthy of the freedom which you possess (have procured) and for which I congratulate you. For know you well that I would choose freedom instead of all (things) which I have and other things manifold more. But that you also may know into what sort of contest you are coming, knowing, I will teach you. For the multitude is great and they attack with much shouting. But if you stand firm against these, in the other respects I even seem to myself to be ashamed (of) what sort you will learn (know) the men are in our country (in the country to us). But if you are men (you being men) and if my affairs turn out (my affairs becoming) well, I will make the one of you wishing to depart homeward to go away an object of envy to those at home, but I think that I will make many to choose the things with me instead of those at home.

**475. Lesson 71** (*1.8.1.1–1.8.7.3*). *The Call to Battle Stations*

*Chapter 8.* And already (also) it was about mid-morning (full market) and the stopping place was near where he was about to halt (for breakfast), when Pategyas, a Persian man of the faithful ones about Cyrus, comes into sight riding at full speed, with his horse sweating, and immediately he shouted to all whom he met (on whom he happened) both in the barbarian tongue and in the Greek tongue that the king with a great army is coming on, (having been) prepared as for battle. Thereupon indeed great confusion arose (became). For immediately the Greeks and also all thought (he) would attack them (when they were) not in battle formation. And Cyrus, jumping down from his chariot, put on his breastplate and, getting upon his horse, took his javelins into his hands, and he passed along the word to all the others to arm themselves and for each one to take position in (into) his own station.

There, indeed, with great haste they took their positions, Clearchus having the right (parts) of the wing toward the Euphrates river, and Proxenus next, and the others after him (this one). And Menon and his army held the left wing of the Greek force. And from the barbarian army Paphlagonian horsemen up to a thousand stood beside Clearchus on the right, and (so did) the Greek light-armed force. And on the left also (stood) Ariaeus the lieutenant of Cyrus, and the rest of the (the other) barbarian army. And Cyrus and his horsemen (the horsemen of this one), about six hundred, (stood) armed with breastplates themselves and with thigh armor and helmets all but Cyrus. But Cyrus, having his head bare, took his position for the battle. And it is said also that (the) other Persians with their heads bare run risks in war. But the horses, all those with Cyrus, had both frontlets and breastplates. And the horsemen had also Greek sabers.

**476. Lesson 72** (*1.8.8.1.–1.8.11.5*). *'Terrible as an Army with Banners.'*

And already (also) it was midday and not yet were the enemy in sight. But when it was becoming afternoon, there appeared a dust column just as a white cloud, and a considerable time later (there appeared) just as a certain blackness in the plain for a great (distance). And when they were becoming nearer, presently indeed (also) some bronze flashed and the spears and the divisions became visible. And there were horsemen in white cuirasses upon the left (wing) of the enemy. Tissaphernes was said to be in command of these. And next (were) wicker-shield bearers, and next hoplites with wooden shields reaching to the feet. And these were said to be Egyptians. And some were horsemen, others bowmen. And all these were proceeding according to nations, each nation (proceeded) in a square full of men. And in front of them chariots (proceeded), leaving a considerable (interval) from each other, indeed the so-called scythe-bearing (chariots). And they had the scythes extending out of the axles sideways, and under the chariot bodies reaching (looking) toward the ground, so as to cut to pieces whomever they happened upon. And their purpose was to drive into the divisions of the Greeks and to cut (them) to pieces. However, as to what Cyrus said when, having called (them together), he encouraged the Greeks to stand firm against the outcry of the barbarians, he was deceived in this. For not with a cry but (as) silently as possible and quietly, evenly, and steadily they came on.

**477. Lesson 73** (*1.8.12.1–1.8.17.2*). *The Caution of Clearchus*

And at this time Cyrus, riding along himself, with Pigres the herald and three or four others, shouted to Clearchus to lead his army against the center of the enemy, (saying) that the king was there. 'And if', he said, 'we conquer this, all things have been done by us.' But Clearchus, seeing the center mass and hearing from Cyrus that the king was outside (beyond) of his left wing,—for so much did the king exceed in number that, though having the center of his own troops, he was outside the left wing of Cyrus—but, nevertheless, Clearchus was not willing to draw away from the river his right wing, fearing lest he be encircled from both sides, and he replied to Cyrus that he was taking care (it was a care to him) that it should be well (that everything should be all right).

And during (in) this time the barbarian army was coming forward on an even front, but the Greek force, remaining yet in the same (place), was putting itself into array from those yet coming up. And Cyrus, riding along not very near (towards) to the army itself, was making a survey, looking in either direction, both toward the enemy and toward his friends. And seeing him from the Greek force, Xenophon the Athenian, drawing near to meet (him), asked whether he had any word to pass along (whether he passed along anything). And he, halting, said and commanded to say to all, that both the internal omens (were) good and the external omens (were) good. And, saying these things, he heard a murmur going through the ranks, and he asked what the sound was. And Clearchus said that (the) watchword was (is) passing along a second time already. And he wondered who was (is) passing (it) out, and he asked what was the watchword. And he answered, 'Zeus savior and victory'. And Cyrus, having heard, said, 'Well, I both accept (it), and let this be (it)'.

**478. Lesson 74** (*1.8.17.3–1.8.23.5*). *The Test of Battle*

And, having said these things, he rode off to his own place. And no longer three or four stades were the two battle lines distant from each other, when the Greeks (both) raised the paean and began to go against the enemy. And as, while they proceeded, a part (some) of the battle line billowed out, the (part) left behind began to charge on the run. And at the same time they all gave a shout just as (soldiers) raise the war cry to Ares, and (also) all ran. And some say that they also made a din with their shields against their spears, causing (making) fright to the horses. And before an arrow (could) reach (them), the barbarians break and flee. And there, indeed, the Greeks pursued at full speed, and they shouted to one another not to charge on the run but to follow in array. And the chariots were carried some through the enemy themselves, and some also through the Greeks, empty of charioteers. And they, when they saw them coming (foresaw them), stood apart. But there is one who was even caught just as (one) startled out of his senses in a horse race. And yet they said that not even this one suffered anything. Nor did any (no one) other of the Greeks suffer anything in this battle, except (that) on the left wing someone was said to have been shot (with an arrow).

And Cyrus, seeing the Greeks conquering and pursuing the (force) against themselves, being glad and being hailed already as king by those about him, not even thus was led out to pursue. But holding in close formation the detachment of the six hundred horsemen with himself, he took care what the king would (will) do. And (well he might), for he knew (him) that he held the center of the Persian army. And all the leaders of the barbarians lead holding their own center (the center of themselves), considering that thus they are both in the safest (place), if their force is on both sides of them, and if they should need to send any order, in half the time the army would learn it. And the king, indeed, at that time, although holding the center of his own army, nevertheless came (became) outside the left wing of Cyrus. And since nobody gave battle to him from the opposite side, nor to those arrayed in front of him, he was bending (his line) as for an encirclement.

**479. Lesson 75** (*1.8.24.1–1.8.29.6*). *The Charge and Death of Cyrus*

Thereupon (indeed) Cyrus, fearing lest, getting (becoming) behind, he (the king) cut down the Greek force, rides against (him). And joining battle with his six hundred, he conquers those marshaled in front of the king, and turned to flight the six thousand. And he himself is said to have killed with his own hand Artagerses the leader of them. And as the rout took place (became), also the six hundred of Cyrus are scattered, rushing into pursuit, except (that) a very few were left around him, chiefly the ones called (his) table companions. And, being with these, he spies the king and the close array around him (that one). And immediately he did not restrain himself, but saying, 'I see the man', he charged on him and strikes against his chest and wounds (him) through his breastplate, as says Ctesias the physician, and he says that he himself treated (healed) the wound.

And as he strikes (the king), someone hits him with a javelin below the eye with force. And fighting there, both the king and Cyrus and those about them on behalf of each, how many of those about the king died, Ctesias tells. For he was with him (that one). And both Cyrus himself died, and eight nobles (the eight noblest) of his staff (those about him) lay (dead) upon him. And Artapates, the most loyal to him of the scepter bearers, is said, when he saw Cyrus fallen, jumping from his horse, to have fallen about him. And some say that the king commanded someone to slay him upon Cyrus, but others that he slew himself, drawing his sword. For he had a golden (sword). And he wore a collar and armlets and the other things just as the nobles of the Persians. For he had been honored by Cyrus on account of (his) goodwill and also trustworthiness.

**480. Lesson 76** (*1.10.4.1–1.10.10.5*). *Subsequent Maneuvers*

*Chapter 10.4.* In this place (both) the king and (also) the Greeks were distant from each other about thirty stades, the one (group) pursuing those opposite themselves as conquering all, the other plundering as though already all-conquering. But when the Greeks learned that the king with his army was among their baggage animals, and the king in turn heard from Tissaphernes that the Greeks were conquering the (force) opposite themselves and (that) they were (are) gone forward pursuing, thereupon, indeed, the king both collects and marshals his own men (those of himself), and Clearchus took counsel, calling Proxenus, for he was nearest, whether they should send some or (whether) all should go to the camp to the rescue. At this (time) also the king was in sight coming on again, as it seemed, from the rear. And the Greeks, facing about, made preparations as though (he were) coming on this way, and to receive (him). But the king did not lead by this way, but by that which passed along outside of the (former) left wing, by this way (also) he led off, taking up those also who had (having) deserted to the Greeks in the battle and Tissaphernes and those with him.

For Tissaphernes in the first onset did not flee but charged (through) along the river against the Greek peltasts. But, charging through, he killed nobody, but the Greeks, opening their ranks (standing apart), struck and shot at them (with javelins). And Episthenes an Amphipolitan was leader of the peltasts, and he was said to have shown himself (to have become) a prudent (man). Tissaphernes, at any rate, got off as having the worse. He does not turn back again but, arriving at (into) the camp of the Greeks, there he falls in with the king, and, indeed, drawing themselves up in array together, they again proceeded.

But when they were opposite the (former) left wing of the Greeks, the Greeks feared lest they lead on against the wing and (lest), enfolding it on both sides, they (should) cut them down. And it seemed best to them to fold back the wing and to put (to make) the river behind (them). But while they were counseling these matters, indeed the king (also), changing into the same formation, halted his battle line opposite (them), just as he came together to give battle at the first. And when the Greeks saw (them) both being near and being drawn up beside them, again raising the paean, they charged, still much more eagerly than at the first.

**481. Lesson 77** (*1.10.11.1–1.10.19.4*). *Victorious but Marooned*

And the barbarians again did not receive (them), but at a greater distance than before they fled. And they pursued up to (until) a certain village. And there the Greeks halted. For over the village was a hill upon which those about the king rallied (turned back), no longer on foot, but the hill was filled with (the) horsemen, so that (the Greeks) did not know what was being done (the thing being done). And they said they saw the royal standard (signal, sign), a certain golden eagle upon a wood (perch) upon a shield, with wings extended. And when (also) the Greeks advanced there, the horsemen, indeed, also leave the hill, not any longer in a body but some in (from) one direction, and some another. And the hill was cleared of the horsemen. And finally (also) all withdrew. Clearchus, then, did not push up on the hill, but, halting his army at the foot of it, he sends Lycius the Syracusan and another upon the hill and orders (them), observing (the) things on top of the hill, to report back what goes on (what they are). And Lycius rode, and (also), having seen, he brings back word that they are fleeing at full speed.

And about when these things were (happening), the sun also was setting. And there the Greeks stopped, and, grounding their arms, they rested. And at the same time they marveled that Cyrus nowhere appeared nor any other came from him. For they did not know that he was dead, but they conjectured that either he was off pursuing or that he had gone forward to capture some (objective). And they themselves took counsel whether, remaining on the spot (there), they should bring (lead) the baggage animals thither, or (whether) they should go back to the camp. It seemed best to them (they voted) to go back. And they arrive at their tents about supper time. This was the end of this day. And they find (take over) most of their other goods plundered and (particularly) if there was any food or drink. And the wagons full of wheat and wine which Cyrus had prepared in order that, if ever serious need should take the army, he might distribute (them) to the Greeks—and these were four hundred wagons, as they were reported (said)—these too at that time the king's army (those with the king) plundered. So that the most of the Greeks were supperless. And they were also without breakfast, for, before the army halted for breakfast, the king appeared. So they passed this night thus.

# SYNTACTICAL SUMMARY

THE rules of Greek syntax, that is, the principles for combining and using words for the expression of thought, are stated in the footnotes to the reading passages from time to time as required. For convenience of reference a connected summary of these principles has been prepared.

This recapitulation is by no means calculated to be complete and exhaustive. For example, there is no discussion of adverbs and prepositions as such. It was felt that the initial presentation of these, together with the guidance given by the cumulative vocabulary, is sufficient for the purposes of this course. As the student goes into advanced reading he will naturally want a good systematic grammar which thoroughly covers Greek syntax.

### 482. Grammatical and syntactical variations of the κοινή

Since the reading passages used during the first semester are taken from the κοινή Greek of St. John's Gospel, and those for the second semester from the Attic Greek of Xenophon's *Anabasis*, it is felt that somewhere in this textbook there should be made available for the student's convenient reference a list of the most important points of divergence between these dialects. Some of these relate to orthography and grammar, some to syntax. In view of their miscellaneous nature it was thought that these should not be placed in the body of the syntactical summary, but that they might be listed in the introduction. The following variations of the κοινή from the ordinary Attic usage are suggested, most of them from the list given by A. T. Robertson (*A Grammar of the Greek New Testament*, pp. 62 ff.) :

*Items of spelling or of grammar*

1. The use of ν-movable before consonants.
2. Use of γίνομαι for γίγνομαι, γινώσκω for γιγνώσκω.
3. Extended use of η instead of ει in the personal endings of the indicative mood middle and passive (seen occasionally in the classical period, especially in the tragic poets).
4. Use of -ην instead of -η in accusative singular of adjectives in -ης.
5. Use of -ου instead of -ους in genitive singular, consonant declension.

6. Use of -εs instead of -αs in accusative plural.
7. Use of Alexandrian α for ο/ε in the second aorist endings.
8. Disappearance of the dual forms.
9. Use of periphrastics (participle with forms of εἰμί) instead of regular conjugation.
10. Disuse of temporal and syllabic augment, especially in compound verbs.
11. Disuse of reduplication.

*Items of syntax*

12. Disuse of the optative mood and constructions.
13. Disuse of the future participle.
14. Preference for superlatives over comparatives.
15. Use of ἐν, *in*, to denote instrumentality
16. Use of ἴδιος as a personal pronoun.
17. Revived use of τόν as a relative pronoun.
18. Use of ἵνα and finite verb in non-final (i.e. non-purpose) clauses, for example, to introduce indirect discourse.
19. Use of ἑαυτῶν (third personal direct reflexive, *of themselves*) for all three persons (replacing ἡμῶν αὐτῶν, and ὑμῶν αὐτῶν, etc.).

## THE DEFINITE ARTICLE

**483.** The definite article in Greek is ὁ, ἡ, τό, *the*. Originally a demonstrative pronoun, in Attic Greek and in later Greek it corresponds to the English article, *the*, and is used to limit the application of a noun, as ὁ ἄνθρωπος, *the man*.

**484. With proper names.** Proper names sometimes take the article, as ὁ Ἰησοῦς, *Jesus*; ὁ Ἀρταξέρξης, *Artaxerxes*.

**485. With abstract qualities.** Nouns denoting qualities and abstractions often take the definite article in Greek, as ἡ χάρις καὶ ἡ ἀλήθεια, *grace and truth*.

**486. With substantive force.** The article often retains its original demonstrative force and is used as a substantive in the place of an understood noun or pronoun, sometimes with another substantive, as τοὺς ἑαυτοῦ, *his own (men)*; sometimes with an adverb, as τοὺς οἴκοι, *those at home*; sometimes with a qualifying phrase, as οἱ ἀμφὶ βασιλέα, *those about the king* (i.e. *of Persia*); sometimes with an adjective, as τὰ ἴδια, *his own (things)*, οἱ ἴδιοι, *his own (men)*; or with a participle, as τὸ γεγεννημένον, *that which has been born*; or in the expression οἱ μέν . . . οἱ δέ, *some . . . others.*

**487. Showing possession.** As in English and in some other languages, possession is often shown by the use of the definitive article, as τῷ προσέχοντι τὸν νοῦν, *for the one giving his attention.*

**488. With distributive meaning.** The article sometimes has distributive force, *each,* e.g. τρία ἡμιδαρεικὰ . . . τῷ στρατιώτῃ, *three halfdarics to the (each) soldier.*

**489. With attributive or predicate modifier.** An attributive adjective, when used with a noun and article, commonly stands between the article and its noun, as αἱ Ἑλλησποντιακαὶ πόλεις, *the Hellespontine cities.* Sometimes it follows the noun, with the article repeated, as τὸ φῶς τὸ ἀληθινόν, *the true light.* When the adjective precedes the article, or follows the noun without taking an article, it is always a predicate adjective, as ἦν γὰρ ἡ πάροδος στενή or ἦν γὰρ στενὴ ἡ πάροδος, *the passage was narrow.*

**490. With demonstrative pronoun modifier, also πᾶς or ὅλος.** A noun when modified by a demonstrative pronoun regularly takes the definite article, thus: οὗτος ὁ ἄνθρωπος or ὁ ἄνθρωπος οὗτος, *this man.* In other words, the demonstrative occupies a predicate position, as explained in the preceding paragraph. Adjectives πᾶς, *all,* or ὅλος, *whole,* used with a noun and article, generally occupy the predicate position: πᾶσαν τὴν κρίσιν or τὴν κρίσιν πᾶσαν, *all judgment;* ὅλη ἡ οἰκία or ἡ οἰκία ὅλη, *his whole household.* But when these words emphatically denote the sum total, they stand between the article and its noun, using the attributive position.

## NOUNS—*The Nominative Case*

**491. Subject or predicate.** The nominative case finds its principal use as subject of a finite verb, as ἐμνήσθησαν οἱ μαθηταὶ αὐτοῦ, *his disciples remembered.* It is also frequently used in the predicate after verbs meaning *to be, become, be considered,* and the like, as Κλέαρχος Λακεδαιμόνιος φυγὰς ἦν, *Clearchus was a Spartan exile,* or ὁ ποταμὸς καλεῖται Μαρσύας, *the river is called (the) Marsyas.*

**492. Apposition.** A noun joined with another to describe and qualify it is said to be in *apposition* with the other, and agrees with it as to case, e.g. Παρύσατις μὲν δὴ ἡ μήτηρ ὑπῆρχε τῷ Κύρῳ, *Parysatis, indeed, his mother, was supporting Cyrus.*

## *The Genitive Case*

**493. The attributive or predicate function.** The genitive case is used to limit and qualify the meaning of a noun (sometimes of a pronoun, adjective, or adverb). It may be used as a straight attributive as ὁ τοῦ Κύρου φίλος, *the friend of Cyrus,* or in the predicate, as τὸ εὖρος (ἐστι) πλέθρου, *the width is a plethron.* Many of the uses of the genitive may be expressed in English by the preposition *of.*

**494. Possessive genitive.** The genitive is often used to show possession or close relationship, as τὸ Μένωνος στράτευμα, *Menon's army,* or ἦν Ἀνδρέας ὁ ἀδελφὸς Σίμωνος Πέτρου, *it was Andrew the brother of Simon Peter.*

**495. The subjective genitive.** The genitive is sometimes used to designate the *subject* of an action or feeling, as τῶν δὲ βαρβάρων φόβος πολὺς (ἦν), *the fear of the barbarians* (i.e. the fear which the barbarians had or felt) *was great.*

**496. The objective genitive.** Sometimes the genitive designates the *object* of an action or feeling, as τὴν ἀγάπην τοῦ Θεοῦ οὐκ ἔχετε ἐν ἑαυτοῖς, *you do not have the love of God* (i.e. love for God) *in yourselves.*

**497. The genitive with verbs of judicial action.** Somewhat related to the objective genitive is the use of the genitive with verbs meaning *to accuse, prosecute, acquit, condemn,* or *punish* to indicate the crime for which the action is taken, with the accusative of the person, as δεδιὼς μὴ λαβών με δίκην ἐπιθῇ ὧν νομίζει ὑπ᾽ ἐμοῦ ἠδικῆσθαι, *fearing that, taking me, he will inflict punishment for the things (in) which he considers he has been wronged by me.*

**498. The partitive genitive.** The partitive genitive is used with verbs where the substantive is affected *only in part* by the action of the verb. Any verb may take a partitive genitive when its action affects the object only in part. For example, ἔταξε Γλοῦν καὶ Πίγρητα λαβόντας τοῦ βαρβαρικοῦ στρατοῦ συνεκβιβάζειν τὰς ἁμάξας, *he ordered Glus and Pigres, taking* (part) *of the Persian force, to help push out the wagons.*

Used with substantives or adjectives which denote a part of the whole, this partitive genitive is called *the genitive of the whole*; μέρος τι τῆς εὐταξίας, *a sample of good discipline.*

**499. With verbs of partial effect.** Certain verbs signifying *to taste, smell, hear, touch, perceive, remember* or *forget, desire, care for* or *neglect, spare, admire, despise* take the partitive genitive. For example, καὶ ἤκουσαν οἱ δύο μαθηταὶ αὐτοῦ λαλοῦντος καὶ ἠκολούθησαν τῷ Ἰησοῦ, *and the two disciples heard him speaking and they followed Jesus*; συνέσπων ὡς μὴ ἅπτεσθαι τῆς κάρφης τὸ ὕδωρ, *they sewed (them) together so that the water did not touch the hay*; καὶ τῶν παρ᾽ ἑαυτῷ δὲ βαρβάρων ἐπεμελεῖτο, *and he took care (also) of the Persians at his court*; ἐμοὶ οὖν δοκεῖ οὐχ ὥρα εἶναι ἡμῖν καθεύδειν οὐδ᾽ ἀμελεῖν ἡμῶν αὐτῶν, *to me then it seems not to be a time for us to sleep or to be neglectful of ourselves.*

**500.** Sometimes a verb of hearing takes the accusative of the thing heard, with the genitive of the person from whom it is heard. This is probably a *genitive of source* (509). For example: καὶ βασιλεὺς μὲν δὴ ἐπεὶ ἤκουσε Τισσαφέρνους τὸν Κύρου στόλον, ἀντιπαρεσκευάζετο, *and the king, indeed, when he heard of (from) Tissaphernes the expedition of Cyrus, made counter-preparation.*

**501. The genitive of material or contents; with words denoting fullness or want.** The genitive is used to express material or contents, as σῖτος μελίνης, *millet bread (bread of millet)*; ἡ καπίθη ἀλεύρων, *the capith of wheat.* Closely related to the foregoing is the use of the genitive with words signifying fullness or want. For example, Γεμίσατε τὰς ὑδρίας ὕδατος, *Fill the water jars with water*; οὐκ ἀνθρώπων ἀπορῶν βαρβάρων συμμάχους ὑμᾶς ἄγω, *not because (of my) lacking Persian men do I lead you as allies*; παράδεισος μέγας ἀγρίων θηρίων πλήρης, *a great park full of wild animals.*

**502. The genitive of measure.** The genitive without a preposition is used to express the concept of measure. For example, τοῦ δὲ Μαρσύου τὸ εὖρός ἐστιν εἴκοσι καὶ πέντε ποδῶν, *and of the Marsyas the width is twenty-five feet.*

**503. The genitive of price or value.** The genitive is also used to express price or value, as διακοσίων δηναρίων ἄρτοι οὐκ ἀρκοῦσιν αὐτοῖς, *two hundred denarii's worth of loaves* (loaves worth two hundred denarii) *are not sufficient for them.*

**504. The genitive of separation.** Another group of uses of the genitive centers about its function as an *ablative*, a case expressive of that from which anything is *separated* or *distinguished.* Verbs signifying *to remove, be distant, restrain, release, cease, fail, give up,* and the like often use the genitive. For example, ἐνταῦθα διέσχον ἀλλήλων βασιλεύς τε καὶ οἱ Ἕλληνες ὡς τριάκοντα στάδια, *in that place the king and the Greeks were distant from each other about thirty stades.*

**505. The genitive of comparison** is used with verbs meaning *to surpass* or *be inferior,* as αἰτεῖ αὐτὸν εἰς δισχιλίους ξένους ... ὡς οὕτως περιγενόμενος ἂν τῶν ἀντιστασιωτῶν, *he asks him for up to two thousand mercenaries as thus he would get the better of his political opponents.*

**506. The genitive with verbs meaning to rule, lead, direct.** Somewhat analogous to the preceding is the principle that the genitive is often used with verbs meaning *to rule, lead,* or *direct,* as καὶ Ξενίας ὁ Ἀρκὰς αὐτῷ προειστήκει τοῦ ἐν ταῖς πόλεσι ξενικοῦ, *and Xenias the Arcadian* *was in command of the mercenary force in the cities for him*; καὶ ἐκέλευε Κλέαρχον μὲν τοῦ δεξιοῦ κέρως ἡγεῖσθαι, *and he ordered Clearchus to be leader of the right wing.*

**507. The genitive of comparison with adjectives.** Adjectives and adverbs of the comparative degree, or implying a distinction, may use the genitive of comparison, as μείζονα τούτων ὄψῃ, *greater things than these you shall see*; νομίζων ἀμείνους καὶ κρείττους πολλῶν βαρβάρων ὑμᾶς εἶναι, διὰ τοῦτο προσέλαβον, *considering you to be better and braver than many Persians, on this account I took you besides*; ὁ ὀπίσω μου ἐρχόμενος ἔμπροσθέν μου γέγονεν, *the one coming after (behind) me has become before me.*

**508. The genitive of separation with adverbs of place.** Certain adverbs of place often take the genitive of separation. For example, ἦν δὲ καὶ ᾽Ιωάννης βαπτίζων ἐν Αἴνων ἐγγὺς τοῦ Σαλείμ, *and John also was baptizing in Aenon near (from) Salim*; χωρὶς αὐτοῦ ἐγένετο οὐδὲ ἕν ὃ γέγονε, *apart from him came to be not even one thing which has come into being*; ταῦτα ἐν Βηθανίᾳ ἐγένετο πέραν τοῦ ᾽Ιορδάνου, *these things happened in Bethany beyond the Jordan.* The foregoing seem clear in their relationship to the genitive of separation. Perhaps the following with εἴσω and ἔξω is in the same analogy: Κῦρος τὰς ναῦς μετεπέμψατο ὅπως ὁπλίτας ἀποβιβάσειεν εἴσω καὶ ἔξω τῶν πυλῶν, *Cyrus sent for the ships that he might land hoplites inside and outside of the gateways* (i.e. mountain barriers).

**509. The genitive of source or cause.** The genitive is used to denote the source or cause from which a given entity, action, or attitude comes. This, too, is an ablative function, a use of the genitive of separation. For example, Δαρείου καὶ Παρυσάτιδος γίγνονται παῖδες δύο, *from* (we should say 'to') *Darius and Parysatis are born two boys*; καὶ λέγεται δεηθῆναι ἡ Κίλισσα Κύρου ἐπιδεῖξαι τὸ στράτευμα αὐτῇ, *and the Cilician queen is said to have requested of Cyrus to show his army to her.* The following instance of the causal genitive might be considered analogous to the use of the genitive with verbs of judicial action: ὅπως οὖν ἔσεσθε ἄνδρες ἄξιοι τῆς ἐλευθερίας ἧς κέκτησθε καὶ ἧς ὑμᾶς ἐγὼ εὐδαιμονίζω, *see, then, that you (shall) be men worthy of the freedom which you possess and because of which I congratulate you.*

**510. Genitive of time.** The genitive is sometimes used to signify *time within which* an action occurs or applies, as οὗτος ἦλθεν πρὸς αὐτὸν νυκτός, *this man came to him at night*; ὁ δὲ Κῦρος ὑπισχνεῖται . . . ἀντὶ δαρεικοῦ τρία ἡμιδαρεικὰ τοῦ μηνὸς τῷ στρατιώτῃ, *and Cyrus promised . . . instead of a daric, three half-darics per (of the) month to each (the) soldier.*

**511. Genitive of place.** The genitive is sometimes used to denote place. This is most often encountered in poetry, but the following from

*Anabasis 1.3.1* is probably a case in point: οἱ γὰρ στρατιῶται οὐκ ἔφασαν ἰέναι τοῦ πρόσω, *for the soldiers said they would not go forward.*

**Genitive absolute.** See 582.

## The Dative Case

**512. The dative as indirect object.** The dative without preposition is used as the indirect object of a transitive verb, a relationship generally expressed in English by the words *to* or *for*, as Σύεννεσις μὲν ἔδωκε Κύρῳ χρήματα πολλὰ εἰς τὴν στρατιάν, *Syennesis, for his part, gave to Cyrus much money for the army.*

**513. The dative of relation, or reference.** The dative is sometimes used of the person or entity to whose case a statement is limited (relation), or in whose opinion a statement holds good (reference). Illustrative of both, because of a shift in mid-sentence, is the following: συνιδεῖν δ' ἦν τῷ προσέχοντι τὸν νοῦν ἡ βασιλέως ἀρχὴ . . . ἰσχυρὰ οὖσα, *and it was possible for the one giving attention to see at once that the king's realm . . . was strong.* Here the main statement, συνιδεῖν δ' ἦν, *and it was possible to see,* is limited to τῷ προσέχοντι τὸν νοῦν (hence, dative of relation). But the rest of the sentence does not follow the construction of indirect discourse after συνιδεῖν, else the accusative casting, τὴν βασιλέως ἀρχὴν . . . ἰσχυρὰν οὖσαν, would have been used. Instead the writer proceeds as though he had started, δήλη ἦν τῷ προσέχοντι τὸν νοῦν, followed by the nominative construction. This would give the sense, *to the one giving attention the king's realm was evidently (evident being) strong.* Here the element of opinion on the part of the observer is predominant (hence, dative of reference).

**514. The dative with words of benefit or detriment.** Certain words denoting *to benefit, serve, obey, advise,* and so on, or their opposites, and words indicating *friendliness* or *hostility* (of attitude) take the dative. Frequently these are verbs, as τοῦ μηκέτι δουλεύειν ἡμᾶς τῇ ἁμαρτίᾳ (*to the end*) *of our no longer being slaves to sin*; τῷ ἀνδρὶ ὃν ἂν ἕλησθε πείσομαι, *the man whom you choose, I will obey*; οἱ δὲ ἡδέως ἐπείθοντο· ἐπίστευον γὰρ αὐτῷ, *and they gladly obeyed, for they trusted him*; ἡγεῖτο δ' αὐταῖς Ταμὼς Αἰγύπτιος ἐξ Ἐφέσου, *and Tamos the Egyptian was conducting them* (the ships) *from Ephesus.* ἡγέομαι seems to take the dative where *service* or *benefit* are in focus, the genitive where the idea of *command* or *rank* predominates. The thought of friendliness is often conveyed by the adjective or substantive φίλος, *friendly, friend,* as πάντας οὕτω διατιθεὶς ἀπεπέμπετο ὥστε αὐτῷ μᾶλλον φίλους εἶναι ἢ βασιλεῖ, *he sent away all, so treating* (them) *that they were friends to him rather than to the king.*

**515. The dative after compound verbs.** The dative follows certain verbs compounded with ἐν, σύν, and ἐπί; and a few compounds with

πρός, παρά, περί, and ὑπό. For example, δεῖται αὐτοῦ μὴ πρόσθεν καταλῦσαι
. . . πρὶν ἂν αὐτῷ συμβουλεύσηται, *he asks of him not to make peace until he
consults with him*; Παρύσατις μὲν δὴ ἡ μήτηρ ὑπῆρχε τῷ Κύρῳ, *Parysatis the
mother, indeed, was supporting Cyrus.*

**516. The dative of likeness or unlikeness.** The ideas of likeness
and unlikeness often call for the dative of the entity to which the
subject is like or unlike, as καὶ ἐὰν μὲν ἡ πρᾶξις ᾖ παραπλησία οἷαπερ
καὶ πρόσθεν ἐχρῆτο τοῖς ξένοις, (δοκεῖ μοι) ἔπεσθαι, *and if the undertaking
be similar to (that for) which he also previously used the mercenaries, (I vote) to
follow.*

**517. The dative of advantage or disadvantage.** The dative is used to
indicate the person or thing for whose *advantage* or *disadvantage* an action
takes place or a situation exists, as στενοχωρίας καὶ πηλοῦ φανέντος ταῖς
ἁμάξαις δυσπορεύτου, *when a narrow pass and mud appeared difficult of traverse
for the wagons* . . .; ἄλλο δὲ στράτευμα αὐτῷ συνελέγετο ἐν Χερρονήσῳ, *and
another army was being collected for him in the Chersonese.*

**518. The dative of the possessor.** Possession is sometimes indicated by
verbs signifying *to be* or *become*, with the dative of the one holding possession, as ἐνταῦθα Κύρῳ βασίλεια ἦν, *in that place Cyrus had a palace (a palace
was to Cyrus).*

**519. The dative of agent.** The dative is sometimes used to denote the
*agent* of a given action. When this construction is used with finite verbs,
the verb almost always is in the perfect or pluperfect passive, as κἂν
τοῦτ᾽, ἔφη, νικῶμεν, πάνθ᾽ ἡμῖν πεποίηται, *and if, he said, we conquer this,
all has been done (finished) by us.* With verbal adjectives in -τέος agency,
if expressed, is regularly indicated by the dative, as πολλὰ γὰρ ἐνορῶ δι᾽
ἃ ἐμοὶ τοῦτο οὐ ποιητέον, *for I see in it (the plan) many reasons why this must
not be done by me.*

**520. The dative of instrument or means.** The instrumental dative
represents a lost instrumental case in Greek, and includes a group of uses
such as the denoting of *means, cause, manner, respect, accompaniment* (called
*sociative dative*), *agreement,* and the like. The dative of means expresses the
*means* or *instrument* by which an action or effect is accomplished, as
διῆλθε λόγος ὅτι διώκοι αὐτοὺς Κῦρος τριήρεσι, *a rumor went around that
Cyrus was pursuing them with warships.*

The dative after χράομαι is in reality a dative of means, as the thought
of this verb is *to serve one's self by,* and so *to use,* as ἐχρῆτο τοῖς ξένοις, *he
used the mercenaries.*

**521. The dative of cause.** The dative is used to express *cause*, as μὴ θαυμάζετε ὅτι χαλεπῶς φέρω τοῖς παροῦσι πράγμασιν, *do not be surprised that I am grieved because of the present affairs.*

**522. The dative of manner.** Again in the instrumental group, the dative is used to express *manner*, as οὐ γὰρ κραυγῇ ἀλλὰ σιγῇ ὡς ἀνυστὸν καὶ ἡσυχῇ ἐν ἴσῳ καὶ βραδέως προσῇσαν, *for not with shouting but (as) silently as possible and quietly, evenly, and steadily they came on.*

**523. The dative of respect.** Essentially like the foregoing dative of manner is the use of the dative to show the *respect* in which a statement is made or is true, as ἡ βασιλέως ἀρχὴ πλήθει μὲν χώρας καὶ ἀνθρώπων ἰσχυρὰ (ἦν), τοῖς δὲ μήκεσι τῶν ὁδῶν καὶ τῷ διεσπάσθαι τὰς δυνάμεις ἀσθενής, *the realm of the king in abundance of country and of men was strong, but in the distances of the roads, and in (the fact that) its resources were scattered, weak.*

**524. The dative of degree of difference.** The use of the dative with comparatives to denote *degree of difference* is also closely analogous with the dative of manner. For example, Ἐπύαξα δὲ . . . προτέρα Κύρου πέντε ἡμέραις εἰς Ταρσοὺς ἀφίκετο, *and Epyaxa . . . arrived at Sardis five days sooner (before by five days) than Cyrus.*

**525. The dative of accompaniment.** The dative is used with words (especially verbs) denoting association or accompaniment (also called *comitative* or *sociative* dative). For example, the verb ἕπομαι, *to follow,* and its compounds invariably take the dative, as, συνείπετο δὲ καὶ τὸ ἄλλο στράτευμα αὐτῷ ἅπαν, *and also all the rest of the army followed (joined in following) him.*

**525A. The dative with words implying agreement or disagreement in contact or association.** This is basically a dative of association or accompaniment (525), although sharing the qualities of the dative with words indicating friendliness or hostility of attitude (514). Here belong μάχομαι, *to fight,* πολεμέω, *to make war.* For example, ἐπολέμει . . . τοῖς Θραξί, *he made war with the Thracians.*

**526. The dative of time when.** The dative without preposition is used to designate *time when,* as τῇ ἐπαύριον (ἡμέρᾳ), *on the following day*; ἐκείνῃ τῇ ὥρᾳ, *in that hour.*

## The Accusative Case

**527. The accusative as direct object.** The principal function of the accusative case is to serve as the direct object of a transitive verb, as τὸν ἄνδρα ὁρῶ, *I see the man.*

**528. The cognate accusative.** When a verb and its direct object are of related meaning, the object repeating the thought contained in the verb, the object is said to be a *cognate* (related) *accusative*. For example, ὡς μὲν στρατηγήσοντα ἐμὲ ταύτην τὴν στρατηγίαν μηδεὶς ὑμῶν λεγέτω, *let no one of you mention me as being about to take charge of this plan of command* (*general this generalship*).

**529. The accusative of specification.** An accusative may be used to limit or qualify the meaning of a verb, adjective, noun, or entire phrase or sentence. For example, πάντα ἐψευσμένος αὐτόν, *having cheated him in all respects*; διὰ μέσου δὲ τῆς πόλεως ῥεῖ ποταμὸς Κύδνος ὄνομα, εὖρος δύο πλέθρων, *and through the center of the city flows a river Cydnus by name, in width two plethra*; ἀνέπεσαν οὖν οἱ ἄνδρες τὸν ἀριθμὸν ὡς πεντακισχίλιοι, *so the men sat down, in number about five thousand*.

**530. The adverbial accusative.** In certain settings the accusative is used as an adverb, as τόνδε τὸν τρόπον, *in the following manner*; μικρὸν ἐξέφυγε, *he narrowly escaped*; τὸ μὲν μέγιστον αἰσχυνόμενος, ὅτι . . ., *being ashamed chiefly because* . . .; τὴν ταχίστην ὁδόν, *by the quickest route*.

**531. The accusative of extent of time or space.** The accusative is regularly used to express duration of time, and extent of space, as in the oft-repeated ἐντεῦθεν ἐξελαύνει σταθμοὺς τρεῖς παρασάγγας εἴκοσιν, *thence he marches three days' journey, twenty parasangs*; ἐνταῦθα ἔμεινε τρεῖς ἡμέρας, *there he remained three days*.

**532. The double accusative.** Verbs denoting *to ask, teach, remind, clothe* or *unclothe, conceal,* and *to take away* may take a double accusative as object, as ἡγεμόνα αἰτεῖν Κῦρον, *to ask Cyrus (for) a guide*; βουλομένους ἀφαιρεῖσθαι τοὺς ἐνοικοῦντας Ἕλληνας τὴν γῆν, *wishing to take away the land (from) the Greeks dwelling there*.

**533. The predicate accusative.** Verbs meaning *to name, appoint, make, regard,* and the like may take a predicate accusative in addition to the direct object, as καὶ στρατηγὸν δὲ αὐτὸν ἀπέδειξε, *and he also appointed him general*.

**534. The accusative in oaths.** The adverbs of swearing νή (affirmative) and μά (negative) take the accusative of the person or thing sworn by, as ἀλλὰ μὰ τοὺς θεοὺς οὐκ ἔγωγε αὐτοὺς διώξω, *but, by the gods, I for my part shall not pursue them.*

## The Vocative Case

**535.** The vocative case is used to indicate a person or thing being addressed. The interjection ὦ may or may not be used. For example, *Τί ἐμοὶ καὶ σοί, γύναι; what (is it) to me and to you, madam?* ; *Ὦ ἄνδρες Ἕλληνες, O men of Greece.*

## THE PRONOUN

**536.** It is felt that the treatment of pronouns presented in *Lessons 8* and *9* is fairly adequate for the purposes of this course, and convenient for reference. That material is not repeated here. There are, however, a few observations which need to be made available for reference.

**537. The reflexive pronouns.** These characteristically refer to the subject of the clause in which they stand. In this usage they are direct reflexives, as *συνήγαγεν ἐκκλησίαν τῶν αὐτοῦ στρατιωτῶν, he called a meeting of his own soldiers.* Occasionally in a dependent clause they refer to the subject of the main verb, and thus become *indirect reflexives.*

The New Testament often uses the single form for the plurals, and sometimes substitutes the third personal reflexive ἑαυτοῦ for the second personal σεαυτοῦ, as *τὴν ἀγάπην τοῦ θεοῦ οὐκ ἔχετε ἐν ἑαυτοῖς, the love of God you have not in yourselves.*

**538. Indirect reflexives.** The third personal pronouns, οὗ, οἷ, ἕ, and so on, are generally used as indirect reflexives in Attic prose, that is, they are used in a dependent clause and refer to the subject of the main verb. For example, *ἠξίου . . . δοθῆναι οἷ ταύτας τὰς πόλεις, he asked for these cities to be given to him.*

**539. Relative pronoun as subject.** The relative pronoun ὅς may stand by itself as subject of a main verb, almost like a demonstrative but with reference to someone already mentioned, as *ὃς δὲ ἀπεκρίθη αὐτοῖς, but he answered them.*

**540. Relative without antecedent.** The Greek usually omits a pronominal antecedent of a relative pronoun, making it necessary to derive both antecedent and relative from the Greek relative pronoun when translating, as *οὗτος ἦν ὃν εἶπον, this was (he of) whom I said . . .* ; *εἰ καλῶς καταπράξειεν ἐφ' ἃ ἐστρατεύετο, if he accomplished well (the things) for which he was making the expedition.*

Such a relative clause becomes, in effect, a substantive having unitary status in the sentence. When such a relative clause with omitted antecedent precedes the main clause, the latter often contains a demonstrative referring back with emphasis to the omitted antecedent. For example, ὃ μέντοι Κῦρος εἶπεν . . . ἐψεύσθη τοῦτο, *however, as to what (that which) Cyrus said . . . he was deceived in this.* Here the entire clause ὃ . . . Κῦρος εἶπεν (and not simply the relative ὅ) has status as an accusative of specification (cf. 529).

**541. Relative attracted to case of antecedent.** A relative pronoun regularly agrees with its antecedent in number and gender, but its case is determined by its use in its own clause. Sometimes, however, a relative which should regularly stand in the accusative case is *attracted* or *assimilated* to the case of an antecedent which is genitive or dative. For example, ὅπως οὖν ἔσεσθε ἄνδρες ἄξιοι τῆς ἐλευθερίας ἧς κέκτησθε, *see, then, that you be men worthy of the freedom which you possess.*

## The Adjective

**542. Agreement with nouns.** The principal function of an adjective is to modify or qualify the meaning of a noun. With this noun the modifying adjective agrees in number, gender, and case. Pronouns and participles often are used as noun modifiers, and agree in the same manner as do adjectives.

**543. Attributive and predicate function.** An adjective may be used as attributive to its noun, as παράδεισος μέγας, *a great park*, or it may stand in predicate relationship, with the noun expressed or understood, as τὰ δὲ κρέα αὐτῶν ἥδιστα ἦν, *and their meat was very sweet*; or κακίους εἰσὶ περὶ ἡμᾶς ἢ ἡμεῖς περὶ ἐκείνους, *they are more dastardly about us than we about them.* For the relative position of attributive and predicate adjectives when the article is used, see the discussion of the definite article in 489.

**544. Adjectives as substantives.** An adjective or a participle through frequent usage often assumes the functions of a noun, as οἱ ἄριστοι, *the nobles*; οἱ φίλοι, *the friends*; ἐκ τῶν νεκρῶν, *from the dead.*

## The Verb

**545. Agreement with subject.** A verb agrees with its subject in person and number, except that a *neuter plural* subject usually has its verb in the *singular.*

*The Tenses*

**546.** The tenses of the Greek verb, with their ordinary significance, are as follows:

*The primary (principal) tenses*

Present: Indicative—action going on in present time.
   Other than indicative—action going on.
Future: Indicative—action (simple or progressive) in future time.
   Other—replacing future indicative in dependent constructions.
Perfect: Indicative and Imperative—action now completed.
   Other—completed action in dependent constructions.
Future Perfect: Indicative—action viewed as completed in future time.
   Other (rare)—replacing future perfect in dependent constructions.

*The secondary (historical) tenses*

Imperfect: Indicative only—action going on in past time.
Aorist:   Indicative—action simply occurring in past time.
    Other—action simply occurring.
Pluperfect: Indicative only—completed action in past time.

**547. The historical present.** In spirited narration the present is sometimes used for the aorist tense and is called the *historical present*. Since the English usage is similar, it may often be translated as a present. There are several examples of this in *Anabasis 1.1.1–4*. Where a dependent construction in the optative is involved, it is necessary to translate the historical present as an aorist, as Τισσαφέρνης διαβάλλει τὸν Κῦρον πρὸς τὸν ἀδελφὸν ὡς ἐπιβουλεύοι αὐτῷ, *Tissaphernes slandered Cyrus to his brother (saying) that he was plotting against him.*

**548. Repeated present or past action.** The present and the imperfect often indicate customary or repeated action in present and in past time respectively.

**549. Attempted present or past action.** The present and the imperfect often express attempted action in present and in past time respectively, as Κλέαρχος τοὺς αὑτοῦ στρατιώτας ἐβιάζετο ἰέναι, *Clearchus was trying to force his own soldiers to go.*

**550. Future sense of εἶμι.** The present εἶμι, *I am going*, often has future significance and replaces ἐλεύσομαι, the future of ἔρχομαι, as οὐκ ἔφασαν ἰέναι τοῦ πρόσω, *they said they would not go forward.*

**551. Perfect sense of certain presents.** The present tense verbs ἥκω, *I am come*, and οἴχομαι, *I am gone*, have perfect, or completed, significance and their imperfects have pluperfect significance.

**552. Present sense of certain perfects.** While the general significance of the perfect tense is somewhat that of the present tense with action completed, there are some perfects as δέδοικα, *I fear*, οἶδα, *I know*, which characteristically translate as presents, and their pluperfects as imperfects.

**553. Future indicative in commands.** The future indicative with ὅπως or ὅπως μή is sometimes used colloquially to express a command, as ὅπως οὖν ἔσεσθε ἄνδρες, *see, then, that you be men.*

**554. Future indicative in object clauses.** Verbs meaning *to strive for, care for, effect* sometimes have object clauses using ὅπως or ὅπως μή with the future indicative, as βουλεύεται ὅπως μήποτε ἔτι ἔσται ἐπὶ τῷ ἀδελφῷ, *he plans that never again he shall be in his brother's power.*

**555. Gnomic aorist.** Although the present tense in Greek, as in English, is used to express a general truth, in sententious language the aorist is used in this sense, and is called the *gnomic aorist.* It is generally translated by the present in English. For example, ὁ λαβὼν αὐτοῦ τὴν μαρτυρίαν ἐσφράγισεν ὅτι ὁ θεὸς ἀληθής ἐστιν, *the one receiving his witness sets his seal that God is true.*

## The Moods

**556. The indicative mood.** The indicative is the mood of simple direct statement, question, or supposition. It alone of the moods has tenses with which to express every variety of time relationship known to the Greek language. Despite exceptions, it is characteristically the mood for the main, or independent, clause of a Greek sentence, as contrasted with the other moods, often called the 'dependent' moods.

**557. The subjunctive mood.** Although spoken of as a 'dependent' mood it has several independent uses as the main verb of a sentence. For the most part the subjunctive employs but two tenses, the present to express continuing action regardless of time (past, present, future), and the aorist to express simple action regardless of time. Characteristically the subjunctive is used in dependent sequence after the primary tenses of the indicative, and its personal endings are the primary personal endings. Below are listed in summary form the principal uses of the subjunctive mood:

*Independent uses of the subjunctive*

**558.** In exhortations: First person (generally plural) subjunctive, as γρηγορῶμεν, *let us watch.*

**559.** In prohibitions: Second or third person aorist subjunctive with μή, as μὴ θαυμάσῃς, *do not be surprised.*

**560.** In deliberations: First person singular or plural subjunctive, as πόθεν ἀγοράσωμεν ἄρτους; *whence shall we buy loaves?*

**561.** In strong future negations: οὐ μή with subjunctive (generally aorist) or future indicative, as ὁ ἐρχόμενος πρὸς ἐμὲ οὐ μὴ πεινάσῃ, *the one coming to me shall never hunger.*

*Dependent uses of the subjunctive*

**562.** In purpose clauses, usually after primary tenses (after both primary and secondary in N.T.): ἵνα, ὡς, or ὅπως with subjunctive, as ὅπως δὲ εἰδῆτε, ὑμᾶς διδάξω, *but that you may know, I will teach you.* (The negative is μή).

**563.** In clauses of fearing after primary tenses: μή with subjunctive, as δέδοικα μὴ λαβών με δίκην ἐπιθῇ, *I fear that seizing me he will inflict punishment.*

**564.** In present general and future more vivid conditions and conditional relatives: See 599 and 603 for explication.

**565. The optative mood.** The optative, too, although known as a 'dependent mood' has certain independent uses. Characteristically it is used in dependent sequence after the secondary tenses of the indicative, and its tenses are used to identify the tenses of the subordinate indicatives or subjunctives which it replaces in indirect discourse. The N.T. has relatively few optatives and the functions of the optative are almost (see below, 566, for exception) entirely taken over by the subjunctive. The personal endings of the optative are similar to the secondary endings of the indicative. Below are summarized its principal uses:

*Independent uses of the optative*

**566.** In a wish or prayer referring to future: Simple optative, as μὴ γένοιτο, *may it not happen,* or *God forbid!*

**567.** In a potential statement (potential optative): ἄν with optative, as βουλοίμην ἂν λαθεῖν αὐτὸν ἀπελθών, *I should wish to depart without his knowledge (to escape his notice departing).*

*Dependent uses of the optative.*

**568.** In purpose clauses after secondary tenses: ἵνα, ὡς, or ὅπως with optative, as τὰς ναῦς μετεπέμψατο ὅπως ὁπλίτας ἀποβιβάσειεν, *he sent for the ships that he might land hoplites.* (The negative is μή.)

**569.** In clauses of fearing after secondary tenses: μή with optative, as Κλέαρχος οὐκ ἤθελεν ἀποσπάσαι τὸ κέρας, φοβούμενος μὴ κυκλωθείη, *Clearchus was unwilling to draw off his wing, fearing he would be encircled.*

**570.** In past general and future less vivid conditions and conditional relatives: See 600 and 604 for explication.

In indirect discourse after secondary tenses. See 586, 589.

**571. The imperative mood.** The imperative mood is used for the expression of commands or entreaties. The present tense signifies a continuing action, the aorist a simple action. The negative is μή. For example, μὴ ἐργάζεσθε τὴν βρῶσιν τὴν ἀπολλυμένην, *do not work for the perishable food*; εὖ ἐπιστάσθων ὅτι οὐκ ἀποδεδράκασιν, *let them know well that they have not gotten clean away.* For prohibitions using the aorist tense, the Greek regularly employs μή with aorist subjunctive instead of μή with aorist imperative.

### The Infinitive

**572. A verbal substantive.** Although listed with the forms of the verb, and receiving its basic structure and spelling from its verb, the infinitive is by its origin a neuter substantive. It often uses the article, which may appear in the various cases according to use (it is then called an *articular infinitive*). Its accent frequently does not conform to the recessive principle applying to verbs. It may stand as the subject, direct object, or in the predicate of a verb, or as the object of a preposition. For example δεῖται αὐτοῦ μὴ καταλῦσαι, *he asks of him not to make peace*; οὐκ ἦν λαβεῖν τοὺς ὄνους, *it was not (possible) to catch the wild asses*; πρὸ τοῦ σε Φίλιππον φωνῆσαι, *before Philip called you (before the Philip to call you).* Yet the infinitive partakes of the functions of a verb in that it has tense and voice, it may itself have a subject, object, or predicate, and it is qualified by adverbs, not adjectives.

**573. The infinitive in result clauses.** The relative adverb ὥστε (sometimes ὡς), *so as, so that,* is sometimes used with the infinitive to express *result*, as ἔχω τριήρεις ὥστε ἑλεῖν τὸ ἐκείνων πλοῖον, *I have triremes so as to capture their boat.*

**574. The epexegetic infinitive.** An infinitive may serve to limit or qualify the meaning of an adjective or adverb, and is then called an *epexegetic infinitive*, as ἡ δὲ εἰσβολὴ ἦν ἀμήχανος εἰσελθεῖν στρατεύματι, *the pass was impossible of access (to enter) for an army.*

**575. The infinitive with πρίν.** After an affirmative clause, the infinitive with πρίν signifies *before*, as κατάβηθι πρὶν ἀποθανεῖν τὸ παιδίον μου, *come down, before my child dies!*

**576. The infinitive of purpose.** With certain words, the infinitive is used to express *purpose*, as ἔρχεται γυνὴ ἀντλῆσαι ὕδωρ, *there comes a woman to draw water;* τὴν χώραν ἐπέτρεψε διαρπάσαι τοῖς Ἕλλησιν, *he turned the country over to the Greeks to plunder.*

### The Participle

**577. A verbal adjective.** The participle retains the action qualities of the verb. For example, it can take a predicate or an object (depending upon whether it is intransitive or transitive), and it is modified by adverbs. Yet it is also adjectival in character and serves to modify and qualify nouns and pronouns and, when used in the genitive absolute construction, even entire clauses. It does not have forms to show person, as do the finite moods—indicative, subjunctive, optative, and imperative —and its accent often does not conform to the recessive principle. It varies its form to agree with substantives in number, gender, and case, that is, it is *declined* like an adjective.

**578. Attributive and predicate function.** Like an adjective, the participle often stands in simple attributive relationship to a substantive, as ὁ βασιλεύων Ἀρταξέρξης, *the ruling Artaxerxes.* It is also frequently used as predicate, as Κῦρος δῆλος ἦν ἀνιώμενος, *Cyrus was evidently distressed (evident being distressed).*

**579. The participle in periphrasis.** As can easily be seen, the predicate use of participles readily opens the possibility for a roundabout equivalent to finite forms of the Greek verb. This is called *periphrasis* (Gk. περίφρασις, *a circumlocution*) and occurs frequently in the κοινή of the N.T. period. For example, γεγραμμένον ἐστίν, *it is having been written,* is a periphrasis for γέγραπται, *it is (has been) written.*

**580. The participle as substantive.** Like an adjective, the participle, usually with the definite article, is used as a substantive. So, οἱ ἐνοικοῦντες, *the inhabitants.*

**581. The circumstantial participle.** The participle, in its function as the modifier of a substantive expressed or understood, often serves to define the *circumstances* of an action or state. It is then called a *circumstantial participle* and it may express the following relationships:

*Time* (with relation to the time of the principal verb), as ἔλαβεν τοὺς ἄρτους καὶ εὐχαριστήσας διέδωκεν, *he took the loaves and, having given thanks (when he had given thanks), he distributed (them).*

*Cause*, as οὐκ ἀνθρώπων ἀπορῶν βαρβάρων συμμάχους ὑμᾶς ἄγω, *not lacking (because I lack) Persian men, do I lead you as allies.*

*Condition* ('if'), as βασιλεὺς ὤν, τοὺς φίλους ἂν τιμῴην, *being king (if I should be king), I would honor my friends.*

*Concession* ('although'), as μέσον τῶν ἑαυτοῦ ἔχων, ἔξω ἦν τοῦ Κύρου εὐωνύμου, *although holding the center of his own troops, he was outside the left flank of Cyrus.*

*Attendant Circumstances* ('while', 'meanwhile'), as τούτῳ συγγενόμενος ὁ Κῦρος ἠγάσθη αὐτόν, *associating with this man, Cyrus admired him.*

*Means or Manner*, as ἐμβάντες εἰς πλοῖον ἀπέπλευσαν, *getting into a boat, they sailed off*; καὶ οἱ Ἕλληνες στραφέντες παρεσκευάζοντο δέχεσθαι, *and the Greeks, facing about, prepared to receive (the attack).*

*Purpose* ('to', 'in order to'), as ἐκ δὲ τούτου ἀνίσταντο οἱ μὲν λέξοντες ἃ ἐγίγνωσκον, *and thereupon some stood up to say what they thought.*

**582. The genitive absolute.** The circumstantial participle is often attached to a substantive (expressed or implied), both standing in the genitive case and without grammatical connection with the main structure of the sentence. Such a grouping is called a *genitive absolute*. It may be used to denote the various relationships expressed by the circumstantial participle (see 581). But the principal, and almost exclusive, scope of the genitive absolute is in representations of *time, cause, condition, concession*, and *attendant circumstances*. These are illustrated as follows:

*Time* ('when'), ὑστερήσαντος οἴνου, *when (the) wine had run out.*

*Cause* ('because'), οὐδὲν ἤχθετο αὐτῶν πολεμούντων, *he was nothing distressed because of their warring.*

*Condition* ('if'), εὖ τῶν ἐμῶν γενομένων, *my affairs turning out well*, or *if my affairs turn out well.*

*Concession* ('although'), καὶ μεταπεμπομένου αὐτοῦ, οὐκ ἐθέλω ἐλθεῖν, *even though he keeps on sending for (me), I do not want to go.*

*Attendant Circumstances*, ὁ γὰρ Ἰησοῦς ἐξένευσεν ὄχλου ὄντος ἐν τῷ τόπῳ, *for Jesus slipped out, there being a crowd in the place.*

**583. The participle of leading action.** With the verbs τυγχάνω, *to happen*, λανθάνω, *to lie hidden, escape notice*, and φθάνω, *to get the start, do* *before*, the participle carries the leading thought, the finite verb taking the role of qualifier. In translation the participle is sometimes placed as main verb. For example, Ἀρίστιππος δὲ ὁ Θετταλὸς ξένος ὢν ἐτύγχανεν αὐτῷ, and *Aristippus the Thessalian happened being (was by chance) a guest-friend to him*; τοῦτο τὸ στράτευμα τρεφόμενον ἐλάνθανεν αὐτῷ, *this army escaped notice being supported (was secretly supported) for him.*

## INDIRECT DISCOURSE

**584. Direct and indirect discourse.** Direct discourse, including the direct statement, direct question, and direct command, gives the words of the speaker just as he is supposed to have stated them, with verbs in the same person, number, tense, and mood as originally used. For example, Κῦρος οὖν ἔλεξε ὧδε· ἥδομαι ἐπεὶ οἱ φίλοι τιμῶνται, *Cyrus, then, spoke thus:* '*I am glad because my friends are honored.*'

Indirect discourse, including the indirect question, gives the words of the speaker from the point of view of the person reporting. The quoted verbs are often changed as to person, not usually as to number. The original tense is characteristically retained. The mood conforms to the structure of the sentence in which the quotation appears. For example, Κῦρος οὖν ἔλεξεν ὅτι ἥδοιτο ἐπεὶ οἱ φίλοι τιμῷντο, *Cyrus, then, said that he was glad because his friends were honored.*

**585. Simple and complex sentences.** A sentence containing but one clause is called a *simple sentence*; a *complex sentence* is one containing a main clause (corresponding to the single clause of a simple sentence), upon which one or more subordinate clauses depend. For example, Κῦρος ἥδεται, *Cyrus rejoices*, is a simple sentence; Κῦρος ἥδεται ἐπεὶ οἱ φίλοι τιμῶνται, *Cyrus is glad because his friends are honored*, is a complex sentence, in which ἥδεται is the *main verb*, and τιμῶνται is the verb of the subordinate or dependent clause and is called the *dependent verb*. In indirect quotation the same rules and principles apply to a simple sentence and to the main clause of a complex sentence.

**586. Tense of the verb of quotation.** As in English, the tense of the verb of quotation makes a crucial difference in the form of the verbs of the sentence *indirectly quoted*. This is because the quoted sentence becomes in reality a subordinate construction to the verb of quotation 'he says that . . .', or 'he said that . . .', and so the tenses of the quoted sentence must be considered *from the viewpoint* of the tense of quotation. In English this relationship is indicated by changing *the tenses* of the quoted statement. For example, a direct statement in the present tense by Cyrus, '*I am* glad because my friends *are* honored', if quoted indirectly after a past tense *Cyrus said*, would be changed to read, 'that he *was* glad because his friends *were* honored'. No such changes would be necessary if the indirect quotation were after a present tense verb, as *Cyrus says that he is glad because his friends are honored*. And with a future we would write, *Cyrus will say that he is glad because his friends are honored*. Exactly so in Greek. After primary tenses the quoted sentence remains unchanged as to tense and mood of verbs, but after secondary tenses the quoted verbs are generally changed. And the Greek shows the difference not by changing *tenses*, as we do, but characteristically by shifting the verbs into the *same tense of the optative mood*. There are some matters of detail which need to be watched, of course, as these changes are made.

**587. Three methods of indirect quotation.** A simple sentence, or the main clause of a complex sentence, may be quoted indirectly in one of three ways: (1) after ὅτι or ὡς with a finite verb, (2) with the infinitive replacing the original verb, (3) with the participle replacing the original verb.

**588. Indirect quotation after ὅτι or ὡς.** After a *primary tense* in the verb of quotation both main and dependent verbs of the quoted statement retain their original tense and mood, as Κῦρος λέγει ὅτι ἥδεται ἐπεὶ οἱ φίλοι τιμῶνται, *Cyrus says that he is glad because his friends are honored*.

**589.** After a *secondary tense* in the verb of quotation (using ὅτι or ὡς) the main and dependent verbs of the quoted statement *may* retain their original tense and mood but usually change as follows:

Main verb (except optatives, or indicatives with ἄν, which do not change) changes to same tense of optative.

Dependent verb (except optatives and secondary tenses of indicative, which do not change) changes to same tense of optative (ἐάν, if present, becomes εἰ), for example,

Original statement: ἥδομαι ἐπεὶ οἱ φίλοι τιμῶνται, *I am glad because my friends are honored*.

After secondary tense: Κῦρος ἔλεξεν ὅτι ἥδοιτο ἐπεὶ οἱ φίλοι τιμῶντο, *Cyrus said that he was glad because his friends were honored*.

**590. Indirect quotation using the infinitive.** A main verb may be quoted indirectly after primary or secondary tenses by changing it to the *same tense of the infinitive*. The subject, if expressed, stands in the accusative. A dependent verb follows the rule stated in the preceding paragraphs. For example,

Original statement: ὁ Κῦρος ἥδεται ἐπεὶ οἱ φίλοι τιμῶνται, *Cyrus is glad because his friends are honored*.

After λέγεται, *it is said*: λέγεται τὸν Κῦρον ἥδεσθαι ἐπεὶ οἱ φίλοι τιμῶνται, *it is said that Cyrus is glad (Cyrus to be glad) because his friends are honored.*

After ἐλέγετο, *it was said*: ἐλέγετο τὸν Κῦρον ἥδεσθαι ἐπεὶ οἱ φίλοι τιμῶντο, *it was said that Cyrus was glad (Cyrus to be glad) because his friends were honored.*

**591. Indirect quotation using the participle.** A main verb may be quoted indirectly after primary or secondary tenses of verbs signifying *to see, know* or *be ignorant of, hear* or *learn*, and the like, and of ἀγγέλλω, *to announce*, by changing it to the *same tense of the participle*. A dependent verb follows the rule stated in 589 above. For example,

Original statement: ὁ Κῦρος ἥδεται ἐπεὶ οἱ φίλοι τιμῶνται, *Cyrus is glad because his friends are honored.*

After οἶδε, *he knows*: οἶδε τὸν Κῦρον ἡδόμενον ἐπεὶ οἱ φίλοι τιμῶνται, *he knows that Cyrus is glad (Cyrus being glad) because his friends are honored.*

After ᾔδει, *he knew*: ᾔδει τὸν Κῦρον ἡδόμενον ἐπεὶ οἱ φίλοι τιμῶντο, *he knew that Cyrus was glad (Cyrus being glad) because his friends were honored.*

**592. Three verbs 'to say'.** Of the three common verbs of quotation, (1) φημί regularly takes the infinitive in indirect discourse, (2) εἶπον regularly takes ὅτι or ὡς with indicative or optative, (3) λέγω takes either, but in the active voice it usually takes ὅτι or ὡς, in the passive the infinitive. Most verbs signifying *to think* or *believe* take the infinitive in indirect discourse.

## THE CONDITIONAL SENTENCE

**593. Definition.** A complete conditional sentence is one which sets forth a supposed condition (called the *condition*, or *protasis*) upon the basis of which a given conclusion (called the *conclusion*, or *apodosis*) is to be expected. For example, *If Cyrus arrives, he will deliver us.* Both condition and conclusion, or protasis and apodosis, as they will be called, may carry varying degrees of certainty or probability. For example, the above sentence could be framed with less vivid probability as follows: *If Cyrus should come, he would deliver us.* The straight conditional sentence is characterized by the word *if*, or in the Greek, εἰ.

**594. The conditional relative sentence.** A very closely related variation of the conditional sentence is the *conditional relative* sentence, wherein the supposed condition is a relative clause introduced by a relative particle. The above sentence can, with practically no change of meaning, be stated, *When Cyrus arrives, he will deliver us* or *When Cyrus should arrive, he would deliver us.* This relative particle is sometimes a relative adverb like ὅτε, or ὁπότε, *whenever*; sometimes a pronoun like ὅ τι, *whatever*; sometimes a noun–adjective combination like ὁπόσοι ἄνθρωποι, *however many men.* The conditional relative sentence is characterized by the substitution of a relative for the word εἰ, *if.* Otherwise it follows exactly the same rules and principles as does the straight conditional sentence. The English has a corresponding conditional or conditional relative sentence which translates naturally and accurately the thought in each type of condition found in the Greek.

**595. The conditional sentence a complex sentence.** The conditional sentence is nothing more or less than a complex sentence in which the apodosis, or conclusion, is the main clause and the protasis, or condition, the dependent clause. A conditional sentence tends to reverse the order in which the main and the dependent clause appear, placing the protasis, or dependent clause, first. But in actual use, the order of protasis and apodosis is varied frequently. In identifying a conditional sentence the student cannot depend upon the order. He must look for the tell-tale εἰ, *if*, or ἐάν or ἤν (εἰ plus ἄν) with subjunctives, or for the relative particle in order to be sure that he is looking at the protasis.

### *Rules for Conditional and Conditional Relative Sentences*

**596.** The following somewhat tabular presentation gives the various types of conditional sentences with the rules governing the structure of each. In each case the corresponding conditional relative sentence is also shown. It is also felt that the student will be helped by a demonstration of the sample condition as it would appear quoted indirectly after a verb of quotation in a secondary tense (after primary tenses there are no changes in tense or mood of the quoted condition). For the principles governing this indirect quotation, the student is referred to paragraphs 584 ff.

For the sake of clearness and easy comparison, a single simple condition is used throughout. Likewise the same verbs of quotation are used throughout. In deference to Greek usage, ἔλεξε, *he said*, is indicated for use with ὅτι or ὡς; ἐλέγετο, *it was said*, for use with the infinitive; and ᾔδει, *he knew*, for use with the participle.

TABLE OF RULES FOR CONDITIONAL SENTENCES
(The bracketed verbs of quotation belong *respectively* with the bracketed quoted verbs.)

**Particular suppositions** (no affirmative or negative implications)

**597. In present time** (*'present particular'*)

| | |
|---|---|
| *Conditional* | Protasis: εἰ with present indicative. Apodosis: any indicative tense. |
| | εἰ Κῦρος κελεύει, καλῶς ἔχει (εἶχε or ἕξει). |
| | *If Cyrus is commanding, it is (was or will be) well.* |
| *Conditional relative* | Protasis: relative with present indicative. Apodosis: any indicative tense. |
| | ὅ τι Κῦρος κελεύει, καλῶς ἔχει (εἶχε or ἕξει). |
| | *Whatever Cyrus (now) commands, it is (was or will be) well.* |

*Conditional indirectly quoted* (after secondary tense)

ἔλεξεν ὅτι
ἐλέγετο ⎫, εἰ Κῦρος κελεύοι, καλῶς ⎧ ἔχοι.
ᾔδει ⎭ ⎨ ἔχειν.
⎩ ἔχον.

He said
It was said ⎫ that, if Cyrus commanded, it was well.
He knew ⎭

**598. In past time** (*'past particular'*)

| | |
|---|---|
| *Conditional* | Protasis: εἰ with past indicative. Apodosis: any indicative tense. |
| | εἰ Κῦρος ἐκέλευσε, καλῶς εἶχε (ἔχει or ἕξει). |
| | *If Cyrus commanded, it was (is or will be) well.* |
| *Conditional relative* | Protasis: relative with past indicative. Apodosis: any indicative tense. |
| | ὅ τι Κῦρος ἐκέλευσε, καλῶς εἶχε (ἔχει or ἕξει). |
| | *Whatever Cyrus commanded, it was (is or will be) well.* |

*Conditional indirectly quoted* (after secondary tense)

ἔλεξεν ὅτι
ἐλέγετο ⎫, εἰ Κῦρος ἐκέλευσε, καλῶς ⎧ ἔχοι.
ᾔδει ⎭ ⎨ ἔχειν.
⎩ ἔχον.

He said
It was said ⎫ that, if Cyrus had (previously) commanded, it
He knew ⎭ was (had been) well.

*Note*: In the apodosis here an original εἶχε, changing to 'same tense' of optative, would change to ἔχοι present optative, because there is no imperfect optative, and the imperfect indicative is in the *present system*. Present, ἔχει, would also change to present optative. ἕξει would change to ἕξοι, future optative.

## General suppositions (usualness implied)

### 599. In present time (*'present general'*)

| | |
|---|---|
| Conditional | Protasis: ἐάν with subjunctive. Apodosis: present indicative. |

ἐὰν Κῦρος κελεύῃ, καλῶς ἔχει.
*If Cyrus (ever) commands, it is (always) well.*

| | |
|---|---|
| Conditional relative | Protasis: relative plus ἄν with subjunctive. Apodosis: present indicative. |

ὅ τι Κῦρος ἂν κελεύῃ, καλῶς ἔχει.
*Whatever Cyrus commands (in general), it is (always) well.*

Conditional indirectly quoted (after secondary tense)

ἔλεξεν ὅτι
ἐλέγετο ⎱, εἰ Κῦρος κελεύοι, καλῶς ⎰ἔχοι.
ᾔδει         ⎰                               ⎱ἔχειν.
                                              ἔχον.

Note that ἐάν becomes εἰ (cf. 589).

He said
It was said ⎱ *that, if Cyrus (ever) commanded, it was (al-*
He knew    ⎰ *ways) well.*

### 600. In past time (*'past general'*)

| | |
|---|---|
| Conditional | Protasis: εἰ with present optative. Apodosis: past (usually imperfect) indicative. |

εἰ Κῦρος κελεύοι, καλῶς εἶχε.
*If Cyrus (ever) commanded, it was (always) well.*

| | |
|---|---|
| Conditional relative | Protasis: relative with present optative. Apodosis: past (usually imperfect) indicative. |

ὅ τι Κῦρος κελεύοι, καλῶς εἶχε.
*Whatever Cyrus commanded, it was (always) well.*

Conditional indirectly quoted (after secondary tense)

ἔλεξεν ὅτι
ἐλέγετο ⎱, εἰ Κῦρος κελεύοι, καλῶς ⎰ἔχοι.
ᾔδει         ⎰                               ⎱ἔχειν.
                                              ἔχον.

He said
It was said ⎱ *that, if Cyrus (ever) commanded, it was (al-*
He knew    ⎰ *ways) well.*

*Note*: Imperfect indicative goes to present tense optative (compare note to 598). Observe also that the distinction in form between a present general and a past general supposition disappears when these are quoted indirectly after a past tense.

**Contrary-to-fact suppositions** (implying unfulfilled condition)

**601. In present time** (*'present contrary-to-fact'*)

| | |
|---|---|
| Conditional | Protasis: εἰ with imperfect indicative. Apodosis: ἄν with imperfect indicative. |
| | εἰ Κῦρος ἐκέλευε, καλῶς ἂν εἶχε. |
| | *If Cyrus were (now) commanding, it would (now) be well.* |
| Conditional relative | Protasis: relative with imperfect indicative. Apodosis: ἄν with imperfect indicative. |
| | ὅ τι Κῦρος ἐκέλευε, καλῶς ἂν εἶχε. |
| | *Whatever Cyrus were (now) commanding, it would (now)· be well.* |

| | | | |
|---|---|---|---|
| Conditional indirectly quoted (after secondary tense) | ἔλεξεν ὅτι<br>ἐλέγετο<br>ᾔδει | εἰ Κῦρος ἐκέλευε, καλῶς ἂν | εἶχε.<br>ἔχειν.<br>ἔχον. |
| | *He said*<br>*It was said*<br>*He knew* | that, if Cyrus were (then) commanding, it would (then) be well. | |

**602. In past time** (*'past contrary-to-fact'*)

| | |
|---|---|
| Conditional | Protasis: εἰ with aorist indicative. Apodosis: ἄν with aorist (occasionally imperfect) indicative. |
| | εἰ Κῦρος ἐκέλευσε, καλῶς ἂν ἔσχε. |
| | *If Cyrus had (in the past) commanded, it would have been well.* |
| Conditional relative | Protasis: relative with aorist indicative. Apodosis: ἄν with aorist (occasionally imperfect) indicative. |
| | ὅ τι Κῦρος ἐκέλευσε, καλῶς ἂν ἔσχε. |
| | *Whatever Cyrus had commanded, it would have been well.* |

| | | | |
|---|---|---|---|
| Conditional indirectly quoted (after secondary tense) | ἔλεξεν ὅτι<br>ἐλέγετο<br>ᾔδει | εἰ Κῦρος ἐκέλευσε, καλῶς ἂν | ἔσχε.<br>σχεῖν.<br>σχόν. |
| | *He said*<br>*It was said*<br>*He knew* | that, if Cyrus had commanded, it would have been well. | |

Note that in quoting indirectly these contrary-to-fact conditional sentences after a secondary tense there is no change in the verbs, except that the infinitive or participle may be substituted for the main verb.

**603. Future more vivid supposition** (*implying vivid degree of probability*)

Conditional      Protasis: ἐάν with subjunctive. Apodosis: future
                 indicative or equivalent.
                 ἐὰν Κῦρος κελεύσῃ, καλῶς ἕξει.
                 *If Cyrus commands (in future), it will be well.*

Conditional     Protasis: relative plus ἄν with subjunctive. Apodosis:
relative            future indicative or equivalent.
                 ὅ τι Κῦρος ἂν κελεύσῃ, καλῶς ἕξει.
                 *Whatever Cyrus commands (in future), it will be well.*

Conditional     ἔλεξεν ὅτι                              ἕξοι.
indirectly      ἐλέγετο     }, εἰ Κῦρος κελεύσειε, καλῶς   { ἕξειν.
quoted (after   ᾔδει                                  ἕξον.
secondary             Note that ἐάν becomes εἰ (cf. 589).
tense)            *He said*
                 *It was said* } *that, if Cyrus commanded (in future), it would*
                 *He knew*      *be well.*

*Note*: The future indicative with εἰ is sometimes used in the protasis
of a future more vivid condition.

**604. Future less vivid supposition** (*less vivid probability; should–would*)

Conditional     Protasis: εἰ with optative. Apodosis: ἄν with optative.
                 εἰ Κῦρος κελεύσειε, καλῶς ἂν ἔχοι.
                 *If Cyrus should command, it would be well.*

Conditional     Protasis: relative with optative. Apodosis: ἄν with
relative            optative.
                 ὅ τι Κῦρος κελεύσειε, καλῶς ἂν ἔχοι.
                 *Whatever Cyrus should command, it would be well.*

Conditional     ἔλεξεν ὅτι                              ἔχοι.
indirectly      ἐλέγετο     }, εἰ Κῦρος κελεύσειε, καλῶς ἂν { ἔχειν.
quoted (after   ᾔδει                                  ἔχον.
secondary      *He said*
tense)            *It was said* } *that, if Cyrus should command, it would be well.*
                 *He knew*

Note that the future less vivid does not change in quotation after
a secondary tense, except that the infinitive or participle may be substituted for the main verb.

# VOCABULARY

## GREEK-ENGLISH

### A

ά-, called *alpha-privative*; inseparable particle giving negative force to the word to which it is prefixed. When prefixed to words beginning with a vowel, its usual form is ἀν-. Like the Latin *in-*. For example, ἀδιάβατος, *uncrossable*.

ἅ, from ὅς.

Ἀβροκόμας, -α, ὁ, *Abrocomas*, satrap of Phoenicia and Syria and commander of one fourth of Darius' army, some 300,000 men.

Ἄβυδος, -ου, ἡ, *Abydus*, a city of Troas.

ἀγαγεῖν, ἀγάγῃ, ἀγαγών, from ἄγω.

ἀγαθός, -ή, -όν, *good, brave*. (Comparisons in 238).

ἀγαλλιάω, ἀγαλλιάσομαι, ἠγαλλίασα, ἠγαλλιάθην or ἠγαλλιάσθην, *to rejoice*.

ἄγαμαι, ἠγασάμην, ἠγάσθην, *to admire*.

ἀγαπάω, ἀγαπήσω, ἠγάπησα, ἠγάπηκα, ἠγάπημαι, ἠγαπήθην, *to regard with affection, love spiritually*.

ἀγάπη, -ης, ἡ, *divine love, love, affection*. AGAPĒ.

ἄγγελος, -ου, ὁ, *messenger, angel*. ANGEL.

ἀγγέλλω, ἀγγελῶ, ἤγγειλα, ἤγγελκα, ἤγγελμαι, ἠγγέλθην, *to announce, report*. EVANGELIZE.

ἀγείρω, ἀγεροῦμαι, ἤγειρα, ἀγήγερκα, ἀγήγερμαι, ἠγέρθην, *to gather*.

ἅγιος, -α, -ον, *holy*. HAGIOLATRY.

ἀγορά, -ᾶς, ἡ, *market place, market*.

ἀγοράζω, ἀγοράσω, ἠγόρασα, ἠγόρακα, ἠγοράσθην, *to buy in the market, buy*.

ἄγριος, -α, -ον, *wild*.

ἄγω, ἄξω, ἤγαγον, ἦχα, ἦγμαι, ἤχθην, *to lead, drive*. (Expanded in 118).

ἀγών, -ῶνος, ὁ, *an assembly, game, contest, struggle*. AGONIZE. (Declined in 147).

ἄδειπνος, -ον, *without supper, supperless*.

ἀδελφός, -οῦ, ὁ, *brother*. PHILADELPHIA.

ἀδικέω, ἀδικήσω, ἠδίκησα, ἠδίκηκα, ἠδίκημαι, ἠδικήθην, *to be unjust, to wrong, harm*.

---

ἀετός, -οῦ, ὁ, *eagle*.

Ἀθηναῖος, -α, -ον, *an Athenian*.

ἆθλον, -ου, τό, *prize*. ATHLETE.

ἀθροίζω, ἀθροίσω, ἤθροισα, ἤθροικα, ἤθροισμαι, ἠθροίσθην, *to collect, gather, muster*.

ἀθρόος, -α, -ον, *in a body, in crowds* or *masses*.

ἄθυμος, -ον, *dispirited*; comp., ἀθυμότερος.

αἱ, from ὁ.

αἵ, from ὅς.

Αἰγύπτιος, -ου, ὁ, *an Egyptian*.

αἷμα, -ατος, τό, *blood*. HEMOPHILIA.

αἰνέω, αἰνέσω, ᾔνεσα, ᾔνεκα, ᾔνημαι, ᾐνέθην, *to praise*.

Αἰνιάν, -ᾶνος, ὁ, *an Aenianian*, from southwestern Thessaly.

Αἰνών, ἡ, indecl., *Aenon*.

αἱρετός, -ή, -όν, *chosen*.

αἱρέω, αἱρήσω, εἷλον, ᾕρηκα, ᾕρημαι, ᾑρέθην, *to take, seize*; mid., *to choose, prefer*. HERESY.

αἴρω, ἀρῶ, ἦρα, ἦρκα, ἦρμαι, ἤρθην, *to lift up, bear, take away, hold in suspense*.

αἰσθάνομαι, αἰσθήσομαι, ᾐσθόμην, ᾔσθημαι, *to perceive, learn, observe*. AESTHETIC.

αἰσχύνω, αἰσχυνῶ, ᾔσχυνα, ᾐσχύνθην, *to dishonor, shame*; mid., *to be ashamed*.

αἰτέω, αἰτήσω, ᾔτησα, ᾔτηκα, ᾔτημαι, *to ask, demand, beg*.

αἰτιάομαι, αἰτιάσομαι, ᾐτιασάμην, ᾐτίαμαι, ᾐτιάθην, *to blame, accuse*.

αἰών, -ῶνος, ὁ, *age, eternity*. EON.

αἰώνιος, -ον, *lasting, eternal*. (Declined in 57).

ἀκηκόαμεν, from ἀκούω.

ἀκινάκης, -ου, ὁ, *a short-sword*.

ἀκολουθέω, ἀκολουθήσω, ἠκολούθησα, ἠκολούθηκα, *to follow*. ANACOLUTHON.

ἀκοντίζω, ἀκοντιῶ, *to hurl the javelin, shoot at* or *hit with a javelin*.

ἀκούω, ἀκούσομαι, ἤκουσα, ἀκήκοα, ἠκούσθην, *to hear*. ACOUSTIC.

## Vocabulary

ἀκρόπολις, -εως, ἡ, upper city, citadel. ACROPOLIS.

ἄκρος, -α, -ον, at the peak, highest; τὸ ἄκρον, height, summit. AKRON. (Note: Akron, Ohio, is in Summit County).

ἄκων, -ουσα, -ον, unwilling.

ἀλέξω, ἀλέξομαι, ἠλεξάμην, to ward off; mid., to defend. ALEXANDER.

ἀλέτης, -ου, an adjective used only with ὄνος to mean mill stone.

ἄλευρον, -ου, τό, wheat flour, usually plural.

ἀλήθεια, -ας, ἡ, truth. (Declined in 43.)

ἀληθής, -ές, true, honest. (Declined in 157.)

ἀληθινός, -ή, -όν, true.

ἀληθῶς, truly.

ἁλίσκομαι, ἁλώσομαι, ἑάλων or ἥλων, ἑάλωκα or ἥλωκα, to be caught, be captured.

ἀλλά, but.

ἀλλάττω, ἀλλάξω, ἤλλαξα, ἤλλαχα, ἤλλαγμαι, ἠλλάχθην or ἠλλάγην, to change, reconcile. HYPALLAGE.

ἀλλήλων, ἀλλήλοις, of or to one another. (Declined in 74.)

ἅλλομαι, ἁλοῦμαι, ἡλάμην or ἡλόμην, to leap, spring up.

ἄλλος, -η, -ο, other, another, remaining, rest of. ALLOPATHY.

ἄλφιτον, -ου, τό, barley meal, used in plural.

ἁλώσοιντο, from ἁλίσκομαι.

ἅμα, at the same time.

ἅμαξα, -ης, ἡ, wagon.

ἁμαξιτός, -όν, for wagons.

ἁμαρτάνω, ἁμαρτήσω, ἡμάρτησα or ἥμαρτον, ἡμάρτηκα, ἡμάρτημα, ἡμαρτήθην, to err, miss the mark, be wrong, sin.

ἁμαρτία, -ας, ἡ, error, sin. HAMARTIOLOGY.

ἀμείβω, ἀμείψω, ἤμειψα, ἠμείφθην, to change. AMOEBA.

ἀμείνων, -ον, better, braver, comp. of ἀγαθός.

ἀμελέω, ἀμελήσω, ἠμέλησα, ἠμέληκα, to neglect, be negligent of.

ἀμήν, surely, assuredly, certainly. AMEN.

ἀμήχανος, -ον, impossible, impracticable. MECHANICAL.

ἀμνός, -οῦ, ὁ or ἡ, lamb.

ἄμπελος, -ου, ὁ, vine.

ἀμφί (much the sense of περί but rarer) with gen., about, concerning; with acc., about, around. AMPHITHEATER.

Ἀμφιπολίτης, -ου, ὁ, an Amphipolitan. Amphipolis was an Athenian settlement in Macedonia.

ἀμφότερος, -α, -ον, rare in singular, each or both of two; usually plural, both.

ἀμφοτέρωθεν, from both sides.

ἀν-, see ἀ-.

ἄν, a postpositive particle without English equivalent, used chiefly as an auxiliary in conditional sentences, and to denote potentiality with the optative.

ἄν, contraction for ἐάν in future more vivid or present general suppositions.

ἀνά, with gen., on board; with dat., on, upon; with acc., up, throughout, up to. ANALYSIS.

ἀναβαίνω (see βαίνω for prin. parts), to go up, ascend, go inland.

ἀναβάς, from ἀναβαίνω.

ἀνάβασις, -εως, ἡ, an expedition up-country, into the interior. ANABASIS.

ἀναβέβηκε, from ἀναβαίνω.

ἀναβιβάζω (see βιβάζω for prin. parts), to make go up, lead up.

ἀναγγέλλω (see ἀγγέλλω for prin. parts), to carry back tidings, report.

ἀνάγκη, -ης, ἡ, necessity, distress; ἀνάγκη ἐστί, or with ἐστί understood, it is necessary.

ἀναγκαῖος, -α, -ον, necessary.

ἀνάκειμαι (see κεῖμαι for prin. parts), to recline at table, dine.

ἀναλαβών, from ἀναλαμβάνω.

ἀναλαμβάνω (see λαμβάνω for prin. parts), to take up, pick up.

ἀναξυρίδες, -ίδων, αἱ, trousers.

ἀναπαύω (see παύω for prin. parts), to make to cease; mid., to rest.

ἀναπεσεῖν, from ἀναπίπτω.

ἀναπίπτω (see πίπτω for prin. parts), to fall back, lie back, recline (for a meal).

ἀναπτύσσω (see πτύσσω for prin. parts), to fold back, unfold.

ἀνάριστος, -ον, without breakfast.

ἀναρπάζω (see ἁρπάζω for prin. parts), to snatch up, carry off as booty.

ἀνάστασις, -εως, ἡ, resurrection. ANASTASIA.

ἀναστήσω, from ἀνίστημι.

ἀναστρέφω (see στρέφω for prin. parts), *to turn back, reverse.* ANASTROPHE.

ἀναστρέψας, from ἀναστρέφω.

ἀνάσχησθε, from ἀνέχω.

ἀνατείνω (see τείνω for prin. parts), *to stretch up, hold up*; ἀνατεταμένος, of a bird, *with wings extended.*

ἀνατρέπω (see τρέπω for prin. parts), *to overturn, overthrow.*

ἀναχωρέω (see χωρέω for prin. parts), *to go back, withdraw, retire.*

ἄνδρα, from ἀνήρ.

ἀνδράποδον, -ου, τό, *slave, captured person, captive.*

ἀνέβη, from ἀναβαίνω.

ἄνεμος, -ου, ὁ, *wind.* ANEMOMETER.

ἀνέπεσαν, from ἀναπίπτω.

ἀνέρχομαι (see ἔρχομαι for prin. parts), *to ascend, go up.*

ἀνέστη, from ἀνίστημι.

ἀνεστράφησαν, from ἀναστρέφω.

ἀνέχω (see ἔχω for prin. parts), *to hold up*; mid., *to restrain one's self, stand firm against.*

ἀνεῳγότα, from ἀνοίγω.

ἀνῆλθε, from ἀνέρχομαι.

ἀνήρ, ἀνδρός, ὁ, *man.* PHILANDER. (Declined in 138.)

ἀνθ' by elision for ἀντί before a rough vowel.

ἄνθρωπος, -ου, ὁ, *man.* ANTHROPOLOGY. (Declined in 49.)

ἀνιάω, ἀνιάσω, ἠνίασα, ἠνιάθην, *to grieve, distress.*

ἀνίσταντο, ἀνιστῆ, from ἀνίστημι.

ἀνίστημι (see ἵστημι for prin. parts), *to make stand up, raise up, arouse*; mid., *to stand up.*

ἀνοίγω, ἀνοίξω, ἀνέῳξα, ἀνέῳγα, ἀνέῳγμαι, ἀνεῴχθην, *to open.*

ἀντ', by elision for ἀντί.

ἀνταγοράζω (see ἀγοράζω for prin. parts), *to buy in exchange.*

ἀντί, with gen., *instead of, in return for.* ANTIPHONAL.

ἀντίος, -α, -ον, *against, face to face*; ἐκ τοῦ ἀντίου, *from the opposite side.*

ἀντιπαρασκευάζομαι (see παρασκευάζω for prin. parts), *to prepare one's self in return, make counter-preparations.*

ἀντιπέρας or ἀντιπέραν, *over against, on the opposite side of.*

ἀντιστασιώτης, -ου, ὁ, *one of the opposite faction, a party opponent.*

ἀντλέω, ἀντλήσω, ἤντλησα, ἤντληκα, *to bail out, draw out.*

ἄντλημα, -ατος, τό, *vessel for drawing water, bucket.*

ἄντρον, -ου, τό, *cave.* ANTRUM.

ἀνυστός, -όν, *possible*; ὡς ἀνυστόν, *as possible.*

ἄνω, *up, upwards, on high, into the interior, up-country.*

ἄνωθεν, *from above, anew.*

ἀνωτέρω, *higher than, higher, above.*

ἄξιος, -α, -ον, *worthy, worth,* often with gen. of value.

ἀξιόω, ἀξιώσω, ἠξίωσα, ἠξίωκα, ἠξίωμαι, ἠξιώθην, *to deem proper, expect, ask as right.* AXIOM.

ἄξων, -ονος, ὁ, *axle.* AXLE.

ἀπ', by elision for ἀπό.

ἀπαγγέλλω (see ἀγγέλλω for prin. parts), *to bring back word.*

ἀπαγορεύω, ἀπηγόρευσα, ἀπηγόρευκα, ἀπηγόρευμαι, *to forbid*; mid., *to renounce, give up or out.*

ἀπάγω (see ἄγω for prin. parts), *to lead back, away.*

ἀπαιτέω (see αἰτέω for prin. parts), *to ask from, ask back, demand.*

ἀπαλλάττω (see ἀλλάττω for prin. parts), *to change, abandon*; pass., *to come off.*

ἁπαλός, -ή, -όν, *tender, soft.*

ἀπαράσκευος, -ον, *unprepared.*

ἅπας, ἅπασα, ἅπαν, strengthened form of πᾶς, *quite all, all together.*

ἀπέδειξε, from ἀποδείκνυμι.

ἀπέδωκε, from ἀποδίδωμι.

ἀπέθανον, from ἀποθνήσκω.

ἀπειθέω, ἀπειθήσω, ἠπείθησα, *to be unbelieving, disobedient.*

ἄπειμι, *to go away.*

ἀπέκτεινε, from ἀποκτείνω.

ἀπεκρίθη, ἀπεκρίθησαν, from ἀποκρίνω.

ἀπελαύνω (see ἐλαύνω for prin. parts), *to march away, ride away.*

ἀπελευσόμεθα, ἀπεληλύθεισαν, ἀπελθεῖν, ἀπελθόντας, ἀπελθών, from ἀπέρχομαι.

ἀπέρχομαι (see ἔρχομαι for prin. parts), *to go away.*

ἀπεστάλκατε, ἀπεσταλμένοι, ἀπέστειλα, from ἀποστέλλω.

ἀπέχω (see ἔχω for prin. parts), to be distant.

ἀπῆλθε, ἀπῆλθον, from ἀπέρχομαι.

ἀπηλλάγη, from ἀπαλλάττω.

ἀπιέναι, ἄπιμεν, ἀπίοιμεν, ἀπιόντες, ἀπιών, from ἄπειμι.

ἁπλοῦς, -ῆ, -οῦν, simple, sincere. (Declined in 244.)

ἀπό, with gen., from.

ἀποβιβάζω (see βιβάζω for prin. parts), to cause to go off, push off, land.

ἀποβλέπω (see βλέπω for prin. parts), to look away, look.

ἀποδεδράκασι, from ἀποδιδράσκω.

ἀποδείκνυμι (see δείκνυμι for prin. parts), to appoint.

ἀποδιδόναι, from ἀποδίδωμι.

ἀποδιδράσκω, ἀποδράσομαι, ἀπέδραν, ἀποδέδρακα, to run away, get fully away.

ἀποδίδωμι (see δίδωμι for prin. parts), to give back, deliver, pay off, pay. APODOSIS.

ἀποθανεῖν, ἀποθάνῃ, from ἀποθνῄσκω.

ἀποθνῄσκω (see θνῄσκω for prin. parts), to die off, die.

ἀποκρίνω (see κρίνω for prin. parts), to reply, answer.

ἀπόκρισις, -εως, ἡ, a separating, an answer. (Declined in 152.)

ἀποκτείνω (see κτείνω for prin. parts), to kill, put to death.

ἀπολείπω (see λείπω for prin. parts), to desert, abandon.

ἀπολελοίπασι, from ἀπολείπω.

ἀπολέσθαι, ἀπόληται, from ἀπόλλυμι.

ἀπολήψονται, from ἀπολαμβάνω.

ἀπόλλυμι, ἀπολῶ or ἀπολέσω, ἀπώλεσα or ἀπωλόμην, ἀπόλωλα and ἀπολώλεκα, to destroy; mid. and pass., to perish. APOLLYON.

Ἀπόλλων, -ωνος, ὁ, Apollo.

ἀποπέμπω (see πέμπω for prin. parts), to send back, away.

ἀποπεφεύγασι, from ἀποφεύγω.

ἀποπλέω (see πλέω for prin. parts), to sail away.

ἀπορέω, ἀπορήσω, ἠπόρησα, ἠπόρηκα, ἠπόρημαι, ἠπορήθην, to be at a loss, be puzzled, lack (with gen.).

ἀπορία, -ας, ἡ, difficulty.

ἀποσπάω (see σπάω for prin. parts), to draw off, withdraw.

ἀποστάντες, from ἀφίστημι.

ἀποστέλλω (see στέλλω for prin. parts), to send forth. APOSTLE.

ἀποστῆναι, from ἀφίστημι.

ἀποσυλάω (see συλάω for prin. parts), to despoil, plunder.

ἀποτείνω (see τείνω for prin. parts), to extend.

ἀποτεταμένα, from ἀποτείνω.

ἀποφεύγω (see φεύγω for prin. parts), to flee away, make an escape.

ἀποχωρέω (see χωρέω for prin. parts), to withdraw, retreat.

ἅπτω, ἅψω, ἧψα, ἧμμαι, ἥφθην, to lay hold of; mid., touch, with gen. SYNAPSE.

ἀπώλετο, ἀπώλοντο, from ἀπόλλυμι.

Ἀραβία, -ας, ἡ, Arabia.

Ἀράξης, -ου, ὁ, the Araxes, a river flowing into the Euphrates between Thapsacus and Corsote.

ἄρατε, ἆρον, from αἴρω.

ἀργυροῦς, -ῆ, -οῦν, of silver, silver. ARGYROL. (Declined in 244.)

ἀρετή, -ῆς, ἡ, valor, loyalty, excellence.

ἀρήγω, ἀρήξω, ἤρηξα, to help, save.

Ἀριαῖος, -ου, ὁ, Ariaeus, one of Cyrus' Persian generals.

ἀριθμός, -οῦ, ὁ, number, an enumeration. ARITHMETIC.

Ἀρίστιππος, -ου, ὁ, Aristippus, a Thessalian mercenary general.

ἄριστον, -ου, τό, breakfast.

ἄριστος, -η, -ον, best, bravest, noblest, superl. of ἀγαθός. ARISTOCRACY.

Ἀρκάς, -άδος, ὁ, Arcadian, native of Arcadia.

ἀρκέω, ἀρκέσω, ἤρκεσα, ἤρκεσμαι, ἠρκέσθην, to ward off, be strong enough, suffice.

ἅρμα, -ατος, τό, chariot. (Declined in 146.)

ἁρμάμαξα, -ης, ἡ, closed carriage.

ἀρνέομαι, ἀρνήσομαι, ἠρνησάμην, ἤρνημαι, ἠρνήθην, to deny, refuse.

ἆρον, aor. imper. active of αἴρω.

ἁρπάζω, ἁρπάσω, ἥρπασα, ἥρπακα, ἥρπασμαι, ἡρπάσθην, to seize, plunder, ravish, carry off. HARPY.

Ἀρταγέρσης, -ου, ὁ, Artagerses, one of King Artaxerxes' generals.

Ἀρταξέρξης, -ου, ὁ, Artaxerxes, king of

Persia.

Ἀρταπάτης, -ου, ὁ, *Artapates, an attendant of Cyrus.*

ἄρτι, *exactly, just now.*

ἄρτος, -ου, ὁ, *a wheat loaf, loaf of bread, bread.*

ἀρχαῖος, -α, -ον, *ancient, from of old*; τὸ ἀρχαῖον, *formerly.* ARCHAIC.

ἀρχή, -ῆς, ἡ, *beginning, supreme power, realm.* OLIGARCHY. (Declined in 43.)

ἀρχιτρίκλινος, -ου, ὁ, *toastmaster, master of ceremonies.*

ἄρχω, ἄρξω, ἦρξα, ἦρχα, ἦργμαι, ἤρχθην, *to be first, begin, lead, rule, be in command* (often with gen.). MONARCH.

ἄρχων, ἄρχοντος, ὁ, *leader, commander, ruler.* ARCHON. (Declined in 146.)

ἄρωμα, -ατος, τό, *a spice.* AROMA.

ἀσθένεια, -ας, ἡ, *weakness, infirmity, sickness.* NEURASTHENIA.

ἀσθενέω, ἠσθένησα, ἠσθένηκα, *to be infirm, be sick.* NEURASTHENIA.

ἀσθενής, -ές, *weak.* ASTHENIC.

Ἀσπένδιος, -ου, ὁ, *an Aspendian, native of Aspendus, a Greek colony in Pamphylia.*

ἀσπίς, -ίδος, ἡ, *shield.* (Declined in 146.)

ἀστράπτω, ἤστραψα, *to flash, glitter.*

ἀσφαλέστατα, ἀσφαλέστερος, *from* ἀσφαλής.

ἀσφαλής, -ές, *safe, secure, 'non-slipping'*; comp., ἀσφαλέστερος; superl., ἀσφαλέστατος.

ἀσφαλῶς, *safely.*

ἄτακτος, -ον, *not in battle array, in disorder.*

ἀτιμάζω, ἀτιμάσω, ἠτίμασα, ἠτίμακα, ἠτίμασμαι, ἠτιμάσθην, *to dishonor, disgrace, hold lightly.*

Ἀττικός, -ή, -όν, *Attic, of Attica, the country in Greece of which Athens was and still is the principal city.*

αὖ, *again, furthermore.*

αὖθις, *again.*

αὐξάνω, αὐξήσω, ηὔξησα, ηὔξηκα, ηὔξημαι, ηὐξήθην, trans., *to augment*; intrans. (late Gk.), *to grow.* AUGMENT.

αὕτη, *from* οὗτος.

αὐτήν, *from* ἑαυτοῦ.

αὐτίκα, *at once, immediately.*

αὐτόθι, *in this or that place, there.*

αὐτόματος, -η, -ον, *self-impelled, spontaneous*; ἀπὸ or ἐκ τοῦ αὐτομάτου, *unbidden,*

*of own accord, by chance.* AUTOMATIC.

αὐτομολέω, αὐτομολήσω, ηὐτομόλησα, *to desert.*

αὐτόμολος, -ου, ὁ, *a deserter.*

αὐτός, αὐτή, αὐτό, gen. αὐτοῦ, αὐτῆς, αὐτοῦ, *in other than nom. case, him, her, it*; between the noun and its article, *the same* (ὁ αὐτὸς λόγος, *the same word*); in predicate position, intensive, *himself,* etc. (ὁ λόγος αὐτός or αὐτὸς ὁ λόγος, *the word itself*). AUTOGRAPH. See 66 for declension and discussion.

αὐτοῦ, *here.*

ἀφ', *by elision for* ἀπό *before a rough vowel.*

ἀφαιρέω (see αἱρέω for prin. parts), *to take away.* Sometimes with acc. of thing taken and acc. of person deprived.

ἀφανής, -ές, *out of sight, hidden, doubtful.*

ἀφαρπάζω (see ἁρπάζω for prin. parts), *to plunder, pillage.*

ἀφειστήκεσαν, *from* ἀφίστημι.

ἀφῆκε, ἀφιέναι, *from* ἀφίημι.

ἀφίημι (see ἵημι for prin. parts), *to send forth, let go, leave, remit.*

ἀφικνέομαι (see ἱκνέομαι for prin. parts), *to arrive at, come to, reach.*

ἀφίκοντο, *from* ἀφικνέομαι.

ἀφίστημι (see ἵστημι for prin. parts), trans., *to separate, lead to revolt*; intrans., *to revolt.*

Ἀχαιός, -οῦ, ὁ, *an Achaean.*

ἄχθομαι, ἀχθέσομαι, ἠχθέσθην, *to be distressed, angry.*

ἀψίνθιον, -ου, τό, *wormwood.* ABSINTHE.

# Β

Βαβυλών, -ῶνος, ἡ, *Babylon, capital of Babylonia.*

Βαβυλωνία, -ας, ἡ, *Babylonia.*

βαθύς, -εῖα, -ύ, *deep.* BATHYSCAPHE. (Declined in 156.)

βαίνω, βήσομαι, ἔβην, βέβηκα, βέβαμαι, ἐβάθην, *to go.* ANABASIS. (Expanded in 211.)

βάλανος, -ου, ἡ, *acorn, date.*

βάλλω, βαλῶ, ἔβαλον, βέβληκα, βέβλημαι, ἐβλήθην, *to throw, throw at, pelt.*

βαπτίζω, βαπτίσω, ἐβάπτισα, βεβάπτισμαι, ἐβαπτίσθην, *to baptize.* BAPTIZE.

(Expanded in 113.)

βαρβαρικός, -ή, -όν, barbarian, i.e., Persian; τὸ βαρβαρικόν, the Persian force of Cyrus. BARBARIC.

βαρβαρικῶς, in the Persian tongue.

βάρβαρος, -ον, not Greek, foreign; as subst., a barbarian, Persian.

βασιλεία, -ας, ἡ, kingdom.

βασίλειος, -ον, royal, noble; τὰ βασίλεια, palace.

βασιλεύς, -έως, ὁ, king. BASIL.

βασιλεύω, βασιλεύσω, to be king, reign.

βασιλικός, -οῦ, ὁ, a nobleman, courtier. BASILICA.

βεβλημένος, from βάλλω.

Βέλεσυς, -υος, ὁ, Belesys, satrap of Syria and Assyria.

βέλτιστος, -η, -ον, superl. of ἀγαθός, good, brave.

Βηθανία, -ας, ἡ, Bethany.

Βηθζαθά, ἡ, indecl., Bethzatha or Bethesda.

Βηθσαϊδά, ἡ, indecl. except for acc. Βηθσαϊδάν, Bethsaida.

βία, -ας, ἡ, force, violence.

βιάζομαι, βιάσομαι, ἐβιασάμην, βεβίασμαι, to compel, force, use force upon.

βιαίως, with force or violence.

βιβάζω, βιβάσω or βιβῶ, ἐβίβασα, causal of βαίνω, to make go, push.

βιβρώσκω, βρώσομαι, ἔβρωσα, βέβρωκα, βέβρωμαι, ἐβρώθην, to eat.

βίος, -ου, ὁ, life. BIOLOGY.

βλέπω, βλέψω, ἔβλεψα, βέβλεφα, βέβλεμμαι, ἐβλέφθην, to look, see, face or point.

βοάω, βοήσω, ἐβόησα, βεβόηκα, βεβόημαι, ἐβώσθην, to shout.

Βοιώτιος, -ου, ὁ, a Boeotian, a Greek from Boeotia.

βουλεύω, βουλεύσω, ἐβούλευσα, βεβούλευκα, βεβούλευμαι, ἐβουλεύθην, to plan; mid., to consider.

βούλομαι, βουλήσομαι, βεβούλημαι, ἐβουλήθην, to wish, will.

βοῦς, βοός, ὁ or ἡ, an ox or cow. BUCOLIC. (Declined in 151.)

βραδέως, slowly, steadily.

βραχύς, -εῖα, -ύ, short, little; pl., few. BRACHYPOD.

βρέχω, βρέξω, βέβρεγμαι, ἐβρέχθην, to wet.

βρῶμα, -ατος, τό, food. BROMA.

βρῶσις, -εως, ἡ, eating, meat, food.

## Γ

Γαλιλαία, -ας, ἡ, Galilee.

Γαλιλαῖος, -α, -ον, Galilean; also subst., a Galilean.

γάμος, -ου, ὁ, wedding, marriage. POLYGAMY.

γὰρ, postpositive, for.

γε, enclitic postpositive, at least, at any rate, even.

γεγεννημένον, from γεννάω.

γέγονε, γεγενημένον, from γίγνομαι.

γεγραμμένον, from γράφω.

γέλως, -ωτος, ὁ, laughter.

γεμίζω, γεμιῶ, ἐγέμισα, ἐγεμίσθην, to fill, load.

γενέσθαι, from γίγνομαι.

γεννάω, γεννήσω, ἐγέννησα, γεγέννηκα, γεγέννημαι, ἐγεννήθην, to beget, bear. (Expanded in 173, present active participle γεννῶν declined in 195.)

γένοιτο, γενόμενος, from γίγνομαι.

γερροφόρος, -ου, ὁ, one carrying a wicker shield; pl., troops with wicker shields.

γέρων, γέροντος, ὁ, old man.

γεύω, γεύσω, ἔγευσα, γέγευμαι, to give a taste; mid., to taste. DISGUST.

γέφυρα, -ας, ἡ, bridge.

γῆ, γῆς, ἡ, earth. GEOGRAPHY. (Declined in 243.)

γήλοφος, -ου, ὁ, hill.

γίγνομαι, γενήσομαι, ἐγενόμην, γέγονα, to be, become, show one's self. GENESIS.

γιγνώσκω, γνώσομαι, ἔγνων, ἔγνωκα, ἔγνωσμαι, ἐγνώσθην, to know, get to know. (Second aorist ἔγνων conjugated in 209.) AGNOSTIC, KNOW.

γίνομαι, N.T. form of γίγνομαι.

γινώσκω, N.T. form of γιγνώσκω.

Γλοῦς, -οῦ, ὁ, Glus, son of Tamos, a noble Egyptian on Cyrus' staff.

γνούς, from γιγνώσκω.

γνώμη, -ης, ἡ, opinion, intention, mind, idea. GNOMIC.

γνώσεσθε, from γιγνώσκω.

γογγύζω, ἐγόγγυσα, to murmur, grumble, mutter.

γράμμα, -ατος, τό, a mark, written charac-

*ter, letter.* GRAMMAR.

γραφή, -ῆς, ἡ, *a writing, scripture.* GRAPH.

γράφω, γράψω, ἔγραψα, γέγραφα, γέγραμμαι, ἐγράφην, *to write.* (Expanded in 124.)

γυμνάζω, γυμνάσω, ἐγύμνασα, *to exercise.* GYMNASIUM.

γυμνής, -ῆτος, or γυμνήτης, -ου, ὁ, *light-armed foot soldier.* A general term including slingers, bowmen, javelin throwers, and even shield-carrying peltasts.

γυνή, γυναικός, ἡ, *woman, wife.* GYNECOLOGY. (Declined in 145.)

**Δ**

δακρύω, δακρύσω, ἐδάκρυσα, δεδάκρυμαι, *to weep.*

Δάνα, -ων, τά, *Dana,* also *Tyana,* a city of Cappadocia north of Tarsus, on the highway to Cilicia and Syria.

δαπανάω, δαπανήσω, ἐδαπάνησα, δεδαπάνηκα, δεδαπάνημαι, ἐδαπανήθην, *to spend.*

Δάρδας, -ατος, *the Dardas,* a little river in Syria.

δαρεικός, -οῦ, ὁ, *daric,* a Persian gold coin worth about ten dollars (1954 values).

Δαρεῖος, -οῦ, ὁ, *Darius.*

δασμός, -οῦ, ὁ, *tribute, tax.*

δέ, postpositive conjunction, *but, and.*

δεδιώς, from δείδω.

δεδομένον, δέδωκε, from δίδωμι.

δεῖ, δεήσει, ἐδέησε, 3rd person verb, *it is necessary.*

δείδω, δείσομαι, ἔδεισα, δέδοικα or δέδια, *to fear.* Perf. used as pres.

δείκνυμι or δεικνύω, δείξω, ἔδειξα, δέδειχα, δέδειγμαι, ἐδείχθην, *to show, exhibit.* EPIDEICTIC. (Expanded in 222.)

δείλη, -ης, ἡ, *afternoon,* sometimes *evening.*

δειλός, -ή, -όν, *cowardly.*

δείξει, from δείκνυμι.

δείσας, from δείδω.

δέκατος, -η, -ον, *tenth.*

δένδρον, -ου, τό, *tree.* PHILODENDRON.

δεξιός, -ά, -όν, *right, right side;* ἐν τῇ δεξιᾷ understands χειρί, *on the right.* DEXTROUS.

δέον, from δέω.

δέρμα, -ατος, τό, *skin, hide.* DERMATOLOGY.

δέρω, δερῶ, ἔδειρα, δέδαρμαι, ἐδάρην, *to flay, skin.*

δεῦρο, *here, hither, hither!*

δεῦτε, pl. of δεῦρο, *hither! come hither!*

δεύτερος, -α, -ον, *second;* ἐκ δευτέρου, also δεύτερον or τὸ δεύτερον, *for the second time.* DEUTERONOMY.

δέχομαι, δέξομαι, ἐδεξάμην, δέδεγμαι, *to receive, accept, withstand* an attack.

δέω, δεήσω, ἐδέησα, δεδέηκα, δεδέημαι, ἐδεήθην, *to lack, need;* as passive deponent δέομαι, *to desire, request, beg.* τὸ δέον, *the needful, the good.*

δή, a postpositive emphatic particle, *indeed,* etc. Sometimes not translated in words.

δῆλος, -η, -ον, *plain, evident, manifest.*

δηνάριον, -ου, τό, *denarius,* a Roman coin.

δήποτε, *once, ever.*

διά, with gen., *through;* with acc., *through, on account of.* DIATHERMY.

διαβαίνω (see βαίνω for prin. parts), *to cross over.*

διαβάλλω (see βάλλω for prin. parts), *to slander, accuse.* DEVIL.

διαβάς, διαβῇ, from διαβαίνω.

διαβατός, -όν, *crossable, fordable.*

διάβολος, -ου, ὁ, *slanderer, the devil.* DIABOLIC.

διαγίγνομαι (see γίγνομαι for prin. parts), *to get through, exist.*

διάγω (see ἄγω for prin. parts), *to pass* or *spend time, tarry.*

διαδέχομαι (see δέχομαι for prin. parts), *to relieve, receive at intervals.*

διαδίδωμι (see δίδωμι for prin. parts), *to distribute.*

διαδοίη, from διαδίδωμι.

διακινδυνεύω (see κινδυνεύω for prin. parts), *to run a risk* or *risks.*

διάκονος, -ου, ὁ or ἡ, *servant, minister.* DEACON, ARCHIDIACONAL.

διακόπτω (see κόπτω for prin. parts), *to cut in pieces.*

διακόσιοι, -αι, -α, *two hundred.*

διαλείπω (see λείπω for prin. parts), *to leave a gap between, stand apart.*

διαρπάζω (see ἁρπάζω for prin. parts), *to plunder thoroughly, sack.*

διασπάω (see σπάω for prin. parts), to draw apart, separate.

διασπείρω (see σπείρω for prin. parts), to scatter. DISPERSE.

διαστάντες, from διίστημι.

διατάττω (see τάττω for prin. parts), to draw up in array.

διατελέω (see τελέω for prin. parts), to bring to an end, complete the march.

διατιθείς, from διατίθημι.

διατίθημι (see τίθημι for prin. parts), to arrange, treat.

διατρίβω, (see τρίβω for prin. parts), to wear away, spend time, tarry, discourse. DIATRIBE.

διδακτός, -ή, -όν, taught. DIDACTIC.

διδάσκαλος, -ου, ὁ, teacher.

διδάσκω, διδάξω, ἐδίδαξα, δεδίδαχα, δεδίδαγμαι, ἐδιδάχθην, to teach.

διδούς, διδῷ, from δίδωμι.

δίδωμι, δώσω, ἔδωκα, δέδωκα, δέδομαι, ἐδόθην, to give. DOSE. (Expansion in 227.)

διεγείρω (see ἐγείρω for prin. parts), to rouse thoroughly.

διεγένοντο, from διαγίγνομαι.

διέδωκε, from διαδίδωμι.

διελαύνω (see ἐλαύνω for prin. parts), to drive through, charge through.

διέρχομαι (see ἔρχομαι for prin. parts), to go through, be circulated.

διέσχον, from διέχω.

διέχω (see ἔχω for prin. parts), to hold apart; also intrans., to be apart, be separated.

διήλασε, from διελαύνω.

διῆλθε, from διέρχομαι.

διίσταντο, from διίστημι.

διίστημι (see ἵστημι for prin. parts), to set apart; intrans., to open ranks, stand at intervals.

δίκαιος, -α, -ον, just, right.

δίκη, -ης, ἡ, justice, punishment, penalty.

διό, for διὰ ὅ, on account of which, wherefore.

δισχίλιοι, -αι, -α, two thousand.

διφθέρα, -ας, ἡ, a tanned skin, leather bag. DIPHTHERIA.

δίφρος, -ου, ὁ, body of a chariot.

διψάω, διψήσω, ἐδίψησα, δεδίψηκα, to thirst, suffer from thirst.

διώκω, διώξω, ἐδίωξα, δεδίωχα, δεδίωγμαι, ἐδιώχθην, to pursue, persecute.

δοθῆναι, δοίη, from δίδωμι.

δοκέω, δόξω, ἔδοξα, δέδογμαι, ἐδόχθην or ἐδοκήθην, to consider, think, seem; impers., δοκεῖ, it seems best, is decided, voted. DOGMA.

δόλος, -ου, ὁ, deceit, treachery.

Δόλοψ, -οπος, ὁ, a Dolopian. Dolopia was a small country near Aetolia.

δόξα, -ης, ἡ, opinion, reputation, glory. DOXOLOGY.

δορκάς, -άδος, ἡ, a gazelle, antelope. DORCAS.

δορπηστός, -οῦ, ὁ, suppertime.

δόρυ, -ατος, τό, spear.

δός, from δίδωμι.

δοῦλος, -ου, ὁ, slave.

δοῦναι, from δίδωμι.

δουπέω, ἐδούπησα, to make a din.

δράμοι, from τρέχω.

δρεπανηφόρος, -ον, scythe-bearing.

δρέπανον, -ου, τό, scythe, sickle.

δρόμος, -ου, ὁ, a running, run, race, gallop, 'double-quick'. PALINDROME.

δύναμαι, δυνήσομαι, δεδύνημαι, ἐδυνήθην, to be able, be worth. DYNAMIC.

δύναμις, -εως, ἡ, power, force, army. DYNAMO.

δυνάστης, -ου, ὁ, a mighty man, nobleman. DYNASTY.

δυνατός, -ή, -όν, able, possible.

δύο, gen. and dative δυοῖν, two. DUAL.

δυσπόρευτος, -ον, hard to get through.

δύω, δύσω, ἔδυσα or ἔδυν, δέδυκα, δέδυμαι, ἐδύθην, to enter, sink, put on; of the sun, to set.

δώδεκα, indecl., twelve. DODECANESE.

δῶ, δῶμεν, δώσω, δώσειν, from δίδωμι.

δωρεά, -ᾶς, ἡ, gift.

δῶρον, -ου, τό, gift. DOROTHY, THEODORE.

## E

ἐάν, if (for εἰ, if, plus ἄν). Conditional conjunction used principally in present general and future more vivid suppositions.

ἑαυτοῦ, -ῆς, -οῦ, of himself, herself, itself. (Declined in 73).

300    Vocabulary

ἐάω, ἐάσω, εἴασα, εἴακα, εἴαμαι, εἰάθην, to permit, allow.

ἕβδομος, -η, -ον, seventh. HEBDOMADAL.

Ἑβραϊστί, in the Hebrew tongue.

ἐγγύς, near, near from (with gen.); comp., ἐγγύτερον.

ἐγεγόνει, from γίγνομαι.

ἐγείρω, ἐγερῶ, ἤγειρα, ἐγήγερκα or ἐγρήγορα, ἐγήγερμαι, ἠγέρθην, to raise, arouse.

ἐγένετο, from γίγνομαι.

ἐγερεῖς, ἐγερῶ, from ἐγείρω.

ἐγκέλευστος, -ον, prompted.

ἔγνω, ἔγνωκα, from γιγνώσκω.

ἐγώ, ἐμοῦ, I. EGO. (Declined in 72.)

ἔγωγε, emphatic for ἐγώ, I for my part.

ἔδει, imperf. indic. active of δεῖ.

ἔδεισαν, from δείδω.

ἐδόθη, ἔδωκε, from δίδωμι.

ἐθέλω, ἐθελήσω, ἠθέλησα, ἠθέληκα, to be willing, wish, want.

ἔθνος, -ους, τό, a nation. ETHNOLOGY.

εἰ, if, whether.

εἴ, from εἰμί.

εἶδαν, εἶδε, εἴδετε, from ὁράω.

εἴδητε, from εἴδω.

εἶδος, -ους, τό, form, species.

εἴδω, εἴσομαι, εἶδον, οἶδα, to see; οἶδα (perf. as pres.; ᾔδη, pluperf. as imperf.), to know. (οἶδα conjugated in 199.)

εἰδώς, perf. act. partic. of εἴδω.

εἴη, εἴησαν, from εἰμί.

εἰκάζω, εἰκάσω, εἴκασα or εἴκακα, εἴκασμαι or ἤκασμαι, εἰκάσθην or ἠκάσθην, to liken to, conjecture, guess.

εἴκοσι, indecl., twenty.

εἱλόμην, from αἱρέω.

εἰμί, ἔσομαι, to be, be possible. (Expanded in 132, participle ὤν declined in 180.)

εἶμι, to go. (Conjugated in 233.)

εἶναι, from εἰμί.

εἶπαν, εἶπε, εἶπον, εἰπών, εἴρηκας, from εἴρω.

εἴρετο, from ἔρομαι.

εἴρω, ἐρῶ, εἶπον, εἴρηκα, εἴρημαι, ἐρρήθην, to say.

εἰς, with acc., into, up to, against, for, upon.

εἷς, μία, ἕν, gen. ἑνός, μιᾶς, ἑνός, one. HENDIADYS. (Declined in 156.)

εἰσβάλλω (see βάλλω for prin. parts), to throw into, invade; of rivers, to empty.

εἰσβολή, -ῆς, ἡ, an inroad, invasion, a pass.

εἰσελαύνω (see ἐλαύνω for prin. parts), to march into.

εἰσελθεῖν, εἰσεληλύθατε, from εἰσέρχομαι.

εἰσέρχομαι (see ἔρχομαι for prin. parts), to go or come in or into, enter.

εἰσήλασε, from εἰσελαύνω.

εἰσπηδάω (see πηδάω for prin. parts), to jump into.

εἱστήκει, from ἵστημι.

εἴσω, inside. ESOTERIC.

εἶτα, then, afterwards.

εἶχε, εἶχον, from ἔχω.

ἐκ, ἐξ, with gen. out of. ECCENTRIC.

ἕκαστος, -η, -ον, each, every, all.

ἑκάτερος, -α, -ον, each, both.

ἑκατέρωθεν, from or on both sides.

ἑκατέρωσε, in both directions, both ways.

ἑκατόν, indecl., one hundred.

ἐκβαλεῖν, from ἐκβάλλω.

ἐκβάλλω (see βάλλω for prin. parts), to cast out.

ἐκδέρω (see δέρω for prin. parts), to strip off the skin, flay.

ἐκδέχομαι (see δέχομαι for prin. parts), to receive, expect, await.

ἐκεῖ, there, in that place.

ἐκεῖθεν, from there, thence.

ἐκεῖνος, ἐκείνη, ἐκεῖνο, gen. ἐκείνου, ἐκείνης, ἐκείνου, demonstrative, that. (Declined in 68.)

ἔκειντο, from κεῖμαι.

ἐκκαλύπτω (see καλύπτω for prin. parts), to uncover. Cf. APOCALYPSE.

ἐκκεκαλυμμένας, from ἐκκαλύπτω.

ἐκκλησία, -ας, ἡ, a called assembly, meeting, church. ECCLESIASTICAL.

ἐκκλίνω (see κλίνω for prin. parts), to bend, give ground, break.

ἐκκομίζω (see κομίζω for prin. parts), to get out.

ἐκκόπτω (see κόπτω for prin. parts), to cut out, cut down.

ἐκκυμαίνω, to billow out, surge forward.

ἐκλέγω (see λέγω for prin. parts), to choose, pick out. ECLECTIC.

ἐκλείπω (see λείπω for prin. parts), to

*leave off, abandon.* ECLIPSE.

ἐκλήθη, from καλέω.

ἐκνεύω, ἐκνεύσω, ἐξένευσα, *to incline the head, nod, slip away, 'bow out.'*

ἐκπεπτωκότας, from ἐκπίπτω.

ἐκπίπτω (see πίπτω for prin. parts), *to fall out, be exiled.*

ἐκπλαγείς, from ἐκπλήττω.

ἐκπλήττω, ἐκπλήξω, ἐξέπληξα, ἐκπέπληγμαι, ἐξεπλήχθην or ἐξεπλάγην, *to strike out of senses, startle.*

ἐκπορεύομαι (see πορεύομαι for prin. parts), *to go or proceed forth.*

ἔκτος, -η, -ον, *sixth.*

ἐκφεύγω (see φεύγω for prin. parts), *to evade, escape.*

ἐκχέω (see χέω for prin. parts), *to pour out.*

ἐκών, -οῦσα, -όν, *willing.* Often best translated adverbially, *willingly.*

ἔλαβε, ἐλάβομεν, ἔλαβον, from λαμβάνω.

ἐλάσσων, ἔλασσον, same as ἐλάττων, ἔλαττον.

ἐλαττόω or ἐλασσόω, ἠλάττωσα, ἠλάττωκα, ἠλάττωμαι, ἠλαττώθην, *to make less or inferior, decrease.*

ἐλάττων, ἔλαττον, or ἐλάσσων, ἔλασσον, *smaller, fewer, worse.*

ἐλαύνω, ἐλῶ, ἤλασα, ἐλήλακα, ἐλήλαμαι, ἠλάθην, *to ride, drive, march, proceed.* ELASTIC.

ἐλάφειος, -ον, *of deer;* κρέα ἐλάφεια, *venison.*

ἐλέγχω, ἐλέγξω, ἤλεγξα, ἐλήλεγμαι, ἠλέγχθην, *to cross-examine, refute, reprove, convict.*

ἐλεῖν, ἐλέσθαι, from αἱρέω.

ἐλελίζω, ἠλέλιξα, *to raise the war cry.*

ἐλευθερία, -ας, ἡ, *freedom, liberty.*

ἔλησθε, from αἱρέω.

ἐληλακότες, from ἐλαύνω.

ἐλήλυθας, ἐληλύθει, ἦλθε, ἔλθῃ, ἐλθεῖν, ἔλθοι, ἐλθών, from ἔρχομαι.

ἕλκω or ἑλκύω, ἑλκύσω, εἵλκυσα, εἵλκυκα, εἵλκυσμαι, εἱλκύσθην, *to draw, drag.*

Ἑλλάς, -άδος, ἡ, *Hellas, the Greek mainland, Greece.*

Ἕλλην, -ηνος, ὁ, *a Greek.* HELLENE.

Ἑλληνικός, -ή, -όν, *Greek.* HELLENIC.

ἑλληνικῶς, *in the Greek tongue.*

Ἑλλησποντιακός, -ή, -όν, *of the Hellespont, Hellespontine.*

ἐλοίμην, ἑλόμενοι, from αἱρέω.

ἐλπίζω, ἐλπιῶ, ἤλπισα, ἤλπικα, ἤλπισμαι, ἠλπίσθην, *to hope, expect.*

ἐλπίς, -ίδος, ἡ, *hope.*

ἐλῶντα, from ἐλαύνω.

ἐμαυτοῦ, ἐμαυτῆς, *of myself.* Reflexive pronoun. (Declined in 73.)

ἐμβαίνω (see βαίνω for prin. parts), *to enter, go in.*

ἐμβάλλω (see βάλλω for prin. parts), *to empty, throw one's self in, attack.* EMBOLISM.

ἐμβάς, ἐμβάντες, from βαίνω.

ἐμβλέπω (see βλέπω for prin. parts), *to look upon.*

ἔμεινε, from μένω.

ἐμνήσθησαν, from μιμνήσκω.

ἐμός, -ή, -όν, *my, mine.*

ἐμπίπλημι (for ἐμπίμπλημι; see πίμπλημι for prin. parts), *to fill up, fill to the full.* In the present system all but the imperfect tense use the stem ἐμπιπ-, dropping the second μ for the sake of euphony.

ἐμπόριον, -ου, τό, *market, market place, merchandise.* EMPORIUM.

ἔμπροσθεν, *before, in front of* (often with gen.).

ἐν, *with dat., in.* IN.

ἔν, from εἷς.

ἐνέβησαν, from ἐμβαίνω.

ἔνειμι, *to be in, be there.*

ἐνεπλήσθη, ἐνεπλήσθησαν, from ἐμπίπλημι.

ἔνδεια, -ας, ἡ, *need, scarcity.*

ἐνδύω (see δύω for prin. parts), *to clothe one's self in, put on.*

ἕνεκα, *with gen., on account of.*

ἐνενήκοντα, indecl., *ninety.*

ἐνῆν, ἐνῆσαν, from ἔνειμι.

ἔνθα, *where, whither, there, thereupon.*

ἐνθάδε, *thither, here, now.*

ἐνθέμενοι, from ἐντίθημι.

ἔνιοι, -αι, -α, *some, several.*

ἐνίοτε, *sometimes.*

ἐννέα, indecl., *nine.*

ἐνοικέω (see οἰκέω for prin. parts), *to inhabit.*

ἐνοράω (see ὁράω for prin. parts), *to see in something.*

ἐνταῦθα, *in that place, there.*

ἐντεῦθεν, *from there, thence.*

ἐντίθημι (see τίθημι for prin. parts), *to put in or into.*

ἐντυγχάνω (see τυγχάνω for prin. parts), *to chance upon, find.*

Ἐνυάλιος, -ου, ὁ, *Ares, god of war.*

ἕξ, indecl., *six.* HEXAGON.

ἐξάγω (see ἄγω for prin. parts), *to lead out, induce.*

ἐξαιτέω (see αἰτέω for prin. parts), *to demand of one*; mid., *to intercede, beg off.*

ἑξακισχίλιοι, -αι, -α, *six thousand.*

ἑξακόσιοι, -αι, -α, *six hundred.*

ἐξέβαλε, from ἐκβάλλω.

ἐξελαύνω (see ἐλαύνω for prin. parts), *to march forth, march on, drive out.*

ἐξελθεῖν, from ἐξέρχομαι.

ἐξέλιπον, from ἐκλείπω.

ἐξέρχομαι (see ἔρχομαι for prin. parts), *to come or go out.*

ἔξεστι, impers., *it is possible, it is permissible.*

ἐξέτασις, -εως, ἡ, *examination, inspection, review.*

ἐξέφυγε, from ἐκφεύγω.

ἐξηγέομαι (see ἡγέομαι for prin. parts), *to lead out, tell out, declare.* EXEGESIS.

ἐξῆλθε, from ἐξέρχομαι.

ἐξήχθη, from ἐξάγω.

ἐξικνέομαι (see ἱκνέομαι for prin. parts), *to reach*; of missiles, *to do execution, gain the range.*

ἔξομεν, from ἔχω.

ἐξοπλίζω (see ὁπλίζω for prin. parts), *to arm fully.*

ἐξουσία, -ας, ἡ, *power, freedom, right.*

ἔξω, *outside, without.* EXOTERIC, EXOTIC.

ἑορτή, -ῆς, ἡ, *feast, festival.*

ἔπαθον, from πάσχω.

ἐπαινέω (see αἰνέω for prin. parts), *to praise, approve.*

ἐπαίρω (see αἴρω for prin. parts), *to lift up, raise on high.*

ἐπάνω, *above.*

ἐπάρατε, ἐπάρας, from ἐπαίρω.

ἐπαύριον, *on the morrow.*

ἐπεί, *when, since.*

ἐπειδή, *when, after, since.*

ἔπειμι (see εἰμί for prin. parts), *to be on or upon.*

ἔπειμι (see εἶμι for prin. parts), *to go on, move forward, charge, attack.*

ἐπέλιπε, from ἐπιλείπω.

ἐπέστη, from ἐφίστημι.

ἐπῆν, from ἔπειμι, *to be on or upon.*

ἐπῆσαν, from ἔπειμι, *to go on,* etc.

ἐπί, with gen., *on, upon*; with dat., *at, upon, for, in the power of*; with acc., *against, upon.* EPIGLOTTIS.

ἐπίασι, from ἔπειμι, *to go on,* etc.

ἐπιβουλεύω (see βουλεύω for prin. parts), *to plot against,* with dat.

ἐπιβουλή, -ῆς, ἡ, *plot.*

ἐπίγειος, -ον, *on or of the earth, earthy.*

ἐπιδείκνυμι (see δείκνυμι for prin. parts), *to show, display.* EPIDEICTIC.

ἐπιδιώκω (see διώκω for prin. parts), *to follow hard, pursue.*

ἔπιεν, from πίνω.

ἐπιθεῖναι, ἐπιθῇ, from ἐπιτίθημι.

ἐπικάμπτω (see κάμπτω for prin. parts), *to bend towards, wheel.*

ἐπικίνδυνος, -ον, *dangerous*; comp., ἐπικινδυνότερος.

ἐπικρύπτω (see κρύπτω for prin. parts), *to conceal thoroughly*; mid., *to do secretly.*

ἐπιλέγω (see λέγω for prin. parts), *to call by name, say further.* EPILOGUE.

ἐπιλείπω (see λείπω for prin. parts), *to fail, leave off.*

ἐπιμελέομαι, ἐπιμελήσομαι, ἐπιμεμέλημαι, ἐπεμελήθην, *to take care*; with gen., *to take care of, attend to.*

ἐπίμπλασαν, from πίμπλημι.

ἐπιοῦσαν, ἐπιούσῃ, from ἔπειμι, *to go on.*

ἐπιπεσεῖσθαι, from ἐπιπίπτω.

ἐπιπίπτω (see πίπτω for prin. parts), *to fall upon, attack.*

ἐπίπονος, -ον, *toilsome*; comp., ἐπιπονώτερος.

ἐπίρρυτος, -ον, *well-watered.*

Ἐπισθένης, -ους, ὁ, *Episthenes of Amphipolis, leader of the peltasts of Cyrus' army.*

ἐπισιτίζομαι, ἐπισιτιοῦμαι, ἐπεσιτισάμην, *to collect supplies, forage.*

ἐπισιτισμός, -οῦ, ὁ, the collecting of provisions, foraging.

ἐπίσταμαι, ἐπιστήσομαι, ἠπιστήθην, to know, know how. EPISTEMOLOGY.

ἐπιστήσας, from ἐφίστημι.

ἐπισφάττω (see σφάττω for prin. parts), to slay upon.

ἐπιτήδειος, -α, -ον, suitable, fitting; τὰ ἐπιτήδεια, provisions, supplies.

ἐπιτίθημι (see τίθημι for prin. parts), to put upon, set upon, attack, inflict upon. EPITHET.

ἐπιτρέπω (see τρέπω for prin. parts), to turn over to, entrust.

ἐπιχωρέω (see χωρέω for prin. parts), to move forward, move against, charge.

ἕπομαι, ἕψομαι, ἑσπόμην, to follow, often with dat.

ἐπουράνιος, -α, -ον, of or in heaven, heavenly.

ἐπριάμην (2nd aorist only), to buy; used for aorist of ὠνέομαι, ὠνήσομαι, ἐώνημαι, to buy.

ἑπτά, indecl., seven.

ἑπτακόσιοι, -αι, -α, seven hundred.

Ἐπύαξα, -ης, ἡ, Epyaxa, wife of Syennesis, king of Cilicia.

ἐπύθετο, from πυνθάνομαι.

ἐραυνάω or ἐρευνάω, ἠρεύνησα, to search.

ἐργάζομαι, ἐργάσομαι, εἰργασάμην, εἴργασμαι, to work, do, trade, work for.

ἔργον, -ου, τό, work, deed. ERG, ENERGY.

ἐρεῖ, from εἴρω.

ἔρημος or ἐρῆμος, -η, -ον, or -ος, -ον, deserted, deprived of, through desert, desert-; with χώρα understood, ἐρῆμος, -ου, a desert. HERMIT.

ἐρίζω, ἤρισα, to strive, vie with. ERISTIC.

ἑρμηνεύς, -έως, ὁ, interpreter, herald.

ἑρμηνεύω, ἑρμηνεύσω, to explain, interpret. HERMENEUTICS.

ἔρομαι, ἐρήσομαι, ἠρόμην, to ask, enquire.

ἐρυμνός, -ή, -όν, fortified.

ἔρχομαι, ἐλεύσομαι, ἦλθον, ἐλήλυθα, to come, go. (Present participle ἐρχόμενος declined in 58).

ἐρωτάω, ἐρωτήσω, ἠρώτησα, ἠρώτηκα, ἠρώτημαι, ἠρωτήθην, to ask.

ἔσεσθε, from εἰμί.

ἐσθίω, ἔδομαι or φάγομαι, ἔφαγον, ἐδήδοκα, ἐδήδεσμαι, ἠδέσθην, to eat. EDIBLE, ESOPHAGUS.

ἔσονται, ἔσται, from εἰμί.

ἕστασαν, ἕστηκε, ἑστηκώς, ἕστησαν, ἑστῶσα, from ἵστημι.

ἐστί, ἔστι, ἔστω, from εἰμί.

ἔσχατος, -η, -ον, furthest, utmost, last, worst. ESCHATOLOGY.

ἔσχες, from ἔχω.

ἔσωθεν, from inside; τὸ ἔσωθεν, the inside.

ἕτερος, -α, -ον, the other, another, other, different. HETERODOX.

ἔτι, yet, again, still.

ἔτος, ἔτους, τό, year. (Declined in 139.)

ἔτυχε, from τυγχάνω.

εὖ, well. EUPHONY.

εὐδαίμων, εὔδαιμον, fortunate, prosperous, wealthy. EUDAEMONISM. (Declined in 157.)

εὐδαιμονίζω, εὐδαιμονιῶ, ηὐδαιμόνισα, to count happy, congratulate, with gen. of the cause.

εὐήθεια, -ας, ἡ, foolishness, silliness.

εὐήθης, -ες, silly, foolish.

εὐθέως, straightway, at once.

εὐθύνω, ηὔθυνα, to make straight, lead straight.

εὐθύς, -εῖα, -ύ, straight; as adv., straightway, immediately.

εὔνοια, -ας, ἡ, goodwill, affection.

εὐνοϊκῶς, with good will; with ἔχειν, to be well-disposed.

εὗρεν, 2nd aor. of εὑρίσκω.

εὑρίσκω, εὑρήσω, ηὗρον, ηὕρηκα, ηὕρημαι, ηὑρέθην (often with augment or redup. εὑ-), to find. EUREKA.

εὑρόντες, 2nd aor. act. partic. of εὑρίσκω.

εὖρος, -ους, τό, width.

εὑρών, 2nd aor. act. partic. of εὑρίσκω.

εὐταξία, -ας, ἡ, good discipline.

Εὐφράτης, -ου, ὁ, the Euphrates, the great river of western Asia, rising in Armenia, flowing through Mesopotamia and Babylon to join the Tigris and empty into the Persian gulf.

εὐχαριστέω, ηὐχαρίστησα, to give thanks. EUCHARIST.

εὔχομαι, εὔξομαι, εὐξάμην or ηὐξάμην, to pray, wish for.

εὐώδης, -ες, sweet-smelling.

εὐώνυμος, -ον, left, left side.

ἔφαγον, ἐφάγετε, from ἐσθίω.

ἐφάνη, ἐφάνησαν, from φαίνω.

ἔφασαν, from φημί.

ἐφειστήκεσαν, from ἐφίστημι.

Ἔφεσος, -ου, ἡ, Ephesus, oldest of the twelve ancient cities of Ionia, famed for its temple of Ephesian Artemis, and scene of missionary activities of St. Paul.

ἔφη, from φημί.

ἐφίστημι (see ἵστημι for prin. parts), to make stop, set in command; in 2nd aor., perf., and pluperf. act., to stand, be set, halt.

ἐξέφυγε, from φεύγω.

ἐχάρη, 2nd aor. ind. pass. (with act. signif.) of χαίρω.

ἐχθές, yesterday.

ἐχθρός, -οῦ, ὁ, enemy, personal foe.

ἔχω, ἕξω, ἔσχον, ἔσχηκα, ἔσχημαι, to have, hold; ἐχόμενος, adjoining, next.

ἑωράκαμεν, ἑώρακε, ἑωρακότες, ἑώρων, from ὁράω.

ἕως, ἕω, ἡ, daybreak, dawn. EOS.

ἕως, as long as; with ἄν plus subjunctive, until.

## Z

ζάω, ζήσω, ἔζησα, ἔζηκα, to live. ZOOLOGY.

ζεύγνυμι, ζεύξω, ἔζευξα, ἔζευγμαι, ἐζεύχθην or ἐζύγην, to yoke, bind together. ZEUGMA.

Ζεύς, Διός, ὁ, Zeus, to the Greeks 'father of gods and men'.

ζῆλος, -ου, ὁ, jealousy, zeal. ZEAL.

ζηλωτός, -ή, -όν, envied, deemed happy. ZEALOT, JEALOUS.

ζητέω, ζητήσω, ἐζήτησα, ἐζήτηκα, ἐζητήθην, to seek, ask.

ζήτησις, -εως, ἡ, inquiry, investigation.

ζωή, -ῆς, ἡ, life, means of living. (Declined in 43.)

ζώνη, -ης, ἡ, belt, girdle, 'girdle money' or 'pin money'. ZONE.

ζωοποιέω (see ποιέω for prin. parts), to make alive, quicken.

## H

ἤ, or, than; ἤ . . . ἤ, either . . . or.

ᾗ, from ὅς.

ἤγαγε, ἤγαγον, from ἄγω.

ἠγάσθη, from ἄγαμαι.

ἡγεμών, ἡγεμόνος, ὁ, leader, guide. HEGEMONY.

ἡγέομαι, ἡγήσομαι, ἡγησάμην, ἥγημαι, to lead, be in command of; of mental action, to consider.

ἠγέρθη, from ἐγείρω.

ἦγμαι, from ἄγω.

ᾔδει, ᾔδειν, ᾔδεις, ᾔδεισαν, ᾔδεσαν, from εἴδω.

ἡδέως, gladly, adverb from ἡδύς; comp., ἥδιον.

ἤδη, already, now.

ἥδιον, more gladly, comp. of ἡδέως.

ἥδιστος, -η, -ον, sweetest, very sweet, superl. of ἡδύς.

ἥδομαι, ἡσθήσομαι, ἥσθην, to be glad, delight in, enjoy. HEDONISM.

ἡδύς, -εῖα, -ύ, sweet. (Comp., ἡδίων, declined in 157.)

ἤκουσαν, ἤκουσε, from ἀκούω.

ἥκω, ἥξω, ἧξα, ἧκα, to have come, come, be present.

ἤλασε, from ἐλαύνω.

Ἠλίας, -ου, ὁ, Elias, Elijah. (Declined in 44.)

ἦλθε, ἦλθον, from ἔρχομαι.

ἠλίβατος, -ον, high, steep.

ἥλιος, -ου, ὁ, the sun. HELIOTROPE.

ἠλπίκατε, from ἐλπίζω.

ἡμᾶς, ἡμεῖς, from ἐγώ.

ἡμέρα, -ας, ἡ, day. EPHEMERAL.

ἡμέτερος, -α, -ον, our, ours.

ἡμιδαρεικόν, -οῦ, τό, a half-daric.

ἡμῖν, from ἐγώ.

ἡμιόλιος, -α, -ον, half as much again.

ἥμισυς, -εια, -υ, half; also as subst., ἥμισυ or ἡμίσεα, the half.

ἡμιωβόλιον, -ου, τό, a half-obol, worth about three cents.

ἦν, imperf. indic. act. of εἰμί.

ἤν, a form of ἐάν, if.

ἤνεγκαν, ἤνεγκε, from φέρω.

ἠνέσχετο, from ἀνέχω.

ἠνεῴχθησαν, aor. pass. indic. of ἀνοίγω.

ἡνίκα, at which time, when.

ἡνίοχος, -ου, ὁ, driver, charioteer.

ἠντληκότες, from ἀντλέω.

ἦραν, aor. ind. act. of αἴρω.

ἠρνήσατο, from ἀρνέομαι.

ἠρώτησαν, from ἐρωτάω.

ἦσαν, from εἰμί.

ἤσθετο, ἤσθοντο, from αἰσθάνομαι.

ἤσθη, from ἤδομαι.

ἥσυχος, -ον, *still, quiet*; ἡσυχῇ, *quietly*.

ἡττάομαι, ἡττήσομαι, ἥττημαι, ἡττήθην, *to be inferior, be defeated*.

ἦχα, ἤχθην, from ἄγω.

## Θ

θάλαττα or θάλασσα, -ης, ἡ, *sea*.

θάνατος, -ου, ὁ, *death*. THANATOPSIS.

θαρρέω, θαρρήσω, ἐθάρρησα, τεθάρρηκα, *to be of courage, be of good cheer*.

θαρρύνω, *to encourage*.

θᾶττον, *faster*, comp. adv. of ταχύς.

θαυμάζω, θαυμάσομαι, ἐθαύμασα, τεθαύμακα, ἐθαυμάσθην, *wonder, be surprised*.

Θαψακηνός, -οῦ, ὁ, *a Thapsacene, man of Thapsacus*.

Θάψακος, -ου, ἡ, *Thapsacus*, a flourishing Syrian city on the west bank of the Euphrates, called *Tiphsah* in *1 Kings 4:24*, where it is cited as marking the eastern boundary of Solomon's kingdom. There was a ford of the Euphrates at Thapsacus, the water being three or four feet deep.

θεάομαι, θεάσομαι, ἐθεασάμην, τεθέαμαι, *to look upon, behold*. THEATER.

θεῖος, -α, -ον, *divine*; τὸ θεῖον, *portent*.

θέλημα, -ατος, τό, *will*.

θέλω, θελήσω, shortened form of ἐθέλω, *to will, be willing*.

θέμενοι, from τίθημι.

θεός, -οῦ, ὁ, *god*. THEOLOGY. (Declined in 49.)

θεραπεύω, θεραπεύσω, ἐθεράπευσα, τεθεράπευμαι, ἐθεραπεύθην, *to serve, heal*. THERAPEUTIC.

θερίζω, θερίσω, ἐθέρισα, ἐθερίσθην, *to reap, harvest*.

θερισμός, -οῦ, ὁ, *a mowing, reaping, harvest*.

Θετταλός, -οῦ, ὁ, *a Thessalian*.

θέω, θεύσομαι, *to race, charge*.

θεωρέω, θεωρήσω, ἐθεώρησα, τεθεώρηκα, τεθεώρημαι, ἐθεωρήθην, *to behold, review, contemplate*. THEORIZE.

θηράω, θηράσω, ἐθήρασα, τεθήρακα, ἐθηράθην, *to hunt, chase*.

θηρεύω, θηρεύσω, ἐθήρευσα, ἐθηρεύθην, *to hunt*.

θηρίον, -ου, τό, *beast, animal*.

θνῄσκω, θανοῦμαι, ἔθανον, τέθνηκα, *to die*.

θόρυβος, -ου, ὁ, *noise, murmur*.

Θρᾷξ, -κός, ὁ, *a Thracian*.

θρέμμα, -ατος, τό, *that which is reared*; pl., *young stock, domestic animals*.

Θύμβριον, -ου, τό, *Thymbrium*, a city of southern Phrygia.

θύρα, -ας, ἡ, *door*; pl., *a residence, headquarters*.

θύω, θύσω, ἔθυσα, τέθυκα, τέθυμαι, ἐτύθην, *to kill, sacrifice, celebrate with sacrifices*.

θώραξ, -κος, ὁ, *breastplate, cuirass*. THORAX.

## I

ἰαθείς, from ἰάομαι.

Ἰακώβ, ὁ, indecl., *Jacob*.

ἰάομαι, ἰάσομαι, ἰασάμην, ἴαμαι, ἰάθην, *to heal, cure, treat*. IATRIC.

ἰατρός, -οῦ, ὁ, *physician*. PODIATRIST.

ἴδε, ἰδεῖν, ἴδετε, ἴδῃς, ἴδητε, from ὁράω.

ἴδιος, ἰδία, ἴδιον, *one's own, peculiar*. IDIOSYNCRASY. (Declined in 56.)

ἰδιώτης, -ου, ὁ, *private soldier, person in private status*.

ἰδόντες, ἰδοῦ, ἰδοῦσα, from ὁράω.

ἱδρόω, ἵδρωσα, *to sweat*.

ἴδωμεν, ἰδών, from ὁράω.

ἰέναι, from εἶμι.

ἵεντο, ἵετο, from ἵημι.

ἱερεύς, -έως, ὁ, *priest*. (Declined in 151.)

ἱερός, -ά, -όν, *holy, sacred*; τὸ ἱερόν, *sacred place, temple*; τὰ ἱερά, *the auspices* or *omens* obtained from inspecting the vitals of a sacrificial victim, *internal omens*. HIERARCHY. (τὸ ἱερόν is declined in 50.)

Ἱεροσόλυμα, -ων, τά, *Jerusalem*.

ἵημι, ἥσω, ἧκα, εἷκα, εἷμαι, εἵθην, *to send, throw*; mid., *rush*. (Pres. system declined, 233.)

Ἰησοῦς, -οῦ (dat. -οῦ, acc. -οῦν), ὁ, *Jesus*.

ἱκανός, -ή, -όν, *sufficient, able*.

ἱκνέομαι, ἵξομαι, ἱκόμην, ἷγμαι, *to come, go*.

'Ικόνιον, -ου, ό, *Iconium*, a city anciently in Phrygia near the border, later on the edge of Lycaonia. Paul and Barnabas ministered there on their first missionary journey.

ἴλη, -ης, ή, *a flock, troop, band.*

ἱμάς, ἱμάντος, ό, *strap, thong, lacing.*

ἵνα, *in order that, that.*

ἴοιεν, ἰόντες, ἰόντος, ἰόντων, from εἶμι.

'Ιορδάνης, -ου, ό, *Jordan.*

'Ιουδαῖος, -α, -ον, *Jewish*; as substantive, *Jew.*

'Ιούδας, gen. -α, dat. -ᾳ, acc. -αν, ό, *Judas.*

ἱππεύς, -έως, ό, *a horseman, cavalryman.*

ἱππικός, -ή, -όν, *on horse, cavalry.*

ἱππόδρομος, -ου, ό, *a horse race, race course.* HIPPODROME.

ἵππος, -ου, ό, *horse.* HIPPOPOTAMUS.

'Ισκαριώτης, -ου, ό, *Iscariot, citizen of Carioth* in Judaea.

ἴσος, -η, -ον, *equal to, equal, the same as*; ἐν ἴσῳ, *in equal step, in step.* ISOSCELES.

'Ισραήλ, ό, indecl., *Israel.*

'Ισραηλείτης, -ου, ό, *Israelite.*

'Ισσοί, -ῶν, οἱ, *Issus*, a large city in south-eastern Cilicia, site of the defeat of Darius by Alexander in 333 B.C.

ἴστε, from εἶδω.

ἵστημι, στήσω, ἔστησα or ἔστην, ἕστηκα, ἕσταμαι, ἐστάθην, trans. and causal, *to make stand, make halt, set*; mid. forms, as well as 2nd aor., 1st and 2nd perfs. act., usually intrans., *to stand, come to a stand, halt.* The perf. and pluperf. act. are usually translated as pres. and imperf., *I stand, was standing.* STAND. (Expanded in 216.)

ἱστίον, -ου, τό, *a sail.*

ἰσχυρός, -ά, -όν, *strong, fortified*; χωρίον ἰσχυρόν, *a fortress, fort.*

ἰσχυρῶς, *strongly, harshly, extremely, very.*

ἰσχύς, -ύος, ή, *strength, force.*

ἰχθύς, -ύος, ό, *fish.* ICHTHYOLOGY. (Declined in 152.)

'Ιωάννης, -ου, ό, *John.*

'Ιωνία, -ας, ή, *Ionia*, the Greek territory of coastal Asia Minor from Phocaea south to Miletus, generally considered.

'Ιωνικός, -ή, -όν, *Ionian, of Ionia.*

'Ιωσήφ, ό, indecl., *Joseph.*

## Κ

καθαρισμός, -οῦ, ό, *a cleansing, purifying.* CATHARTIC.

καθέζομαι, *to sit down, halt.*

καθεύδω, καθευδήσω, ἐκαθεύδησα, κεκαθεύδηκα, *to sleep, go to sleep.*

καθηδυπαθέω, καθηδυπάθησα, *to waste in luxury.*

καθήκω (see ἥκω for prin. parts), *to come* or *extend down.*

κάθημαι, καθήσομαι, *to sit, be seated, be located.*

καθίζω, καθίσω, ἐκάθισα, κεκάθικα, *to seat, sit.*

καθίσταντο, καθίστασθαι, καθίστατο, from καθίστημι.

καθίστημι (see ἵστημι for prin. parts), *to set down, station, appoint*; 2nd aor. and pluperf., *to succeed, begin to reign*; *to settle down, take one's place, turn out.*

καθοράω (see ὁράω for prin. parts), *to look down on, get sight of, observe.*

καθώς, *according as, as.*

καί, *and, also, even.*

καίνω, κανῶ, ἔκανον, κέκονα, *to kill, slay.*

καιρός, -οῦ, ό, *right time, due time, time.*

καίτοιγε, *and yet, although.*

καίω, καύσω, ἔκαυσα, κέκαυκα, κέκαυμαι, ἐκαύθην, *to burn.* CAUSTIC.

κακός, -ή, -όν, *bad, cowardly, dastardly.* CACOPHONY. (Comparisons in 238.)

κάλαμος, -ου, ό, *reed, stalk.*

καλέω, καλῶ, ἐκάλεσα, κέκληκα, κέκλημαι, ἐκλήθην, *to call.* CALL.

καλός, -ή, -όν, *beautiful, good, fine.* CALLIGRAPHY. (Comparisons in 238.)

καλύπτω, καλύψω, ἐκάλυψα, κεκάλυμμαι, ἐκαλύφθην, *to cover, veil.* APOCALYPSE.

καλῶς, *well*, from καλός.

κάμπτω, κάμψω, ἔκαμψα, κέκαμμαι, ἐκάμφθην, *to bend.*

Κανά, ή, *Cana.*

κάνδυς, -υος, ό, *caftan*, a Persian cloak.

καπηλεῖον, -ου, τό, *a shop, store.*

καπίθη, -ης, ή, *the capith*, about two quarts

dry measure.

Καππαδοκία, -ας, ἡ, *Cappadocia*, a country in central Asia Minor.

καρπός, -οῦ, ὁ, *fruit*. POLYCARP.

Κάρσος or Κέρσος, -ου, ὁ, *the Carsus* or *Cersus* river, between Syria and Cilicia.

κάρφη, -ης, ἡ, *hay*.

Καστωλός, -οῦ, ἡ, *Castolus*, a village near Sardis.

κατά, with gen., *down towards, in opposition to*; with acc., *down along, according to*. CATACLYSM.

καταβαίνω (see βαίνω for prin. parts), *to descend, come or go down*.

καταβάντες, καταβάς, καταβέβηκα, καταβῇ, κατάβηθι, from καταβαίνω.

καταγαγεῖν, καταγάγοι, from κατάγω.

κατάγω (see ἄγω for prin. parts), *to lead down, bring to port, restore*.

καταδύω (see δύω for prin. parts), *to sink, make sink*.

καταθεάομαι (see θεάομαι for prin. parts), *to look down on, survey thoroughly*.

κατακαίνω (see καίνω for prin. parts), *to kill, cut down*.

κατακαίω or κατακάω (see καίω for prin. parts), *to burn down*.

κατάκειμαι (see κεῖμαι for prin. parts), *to recline, lie down*.

κατακοπῆναι, from κατακόπτω.

κατακόπτω (see κόπτω for prin. parts), *to cut down, cut to pieces*.

καταλαβόντες, from καταλαμβάνω.

καταλαμβάνω (see λαμβάνω for prin. parts), *to seize upon, discover, grasp, find, catch*. CATALEPSY.

καταλείπω (see λείπω for prin. parts), *to leave behind*.

καταληψόμενον, from καταλαμβάνω.

καταλιπόντες, from καταλείπω.

καταλύω (see λύω for prin. parts), *to dissolve, end, make peace, unyoke, make a halt*. CATALYST.

κατανοέω (see νοέω for prin. parts), *to perceive, observe*.

καταπετρόω (see πετρόω for prin. parts), *to stone to death*.

καταπηδάω (see πηδάω for prin. parts), *to jump down*.

καταπράττω (see πράττω for prin. parts), *to accomplish*.

καταστησομένων, from καθίστημι.

κατατίθημι (see τίθημι for prin. parts), *to put down, deposit, lay up*.

καταφάγεται, from κατεσθίω.

καταφανής, -ές, *in plain sight, evident*.

κατέβη, κατέβησαν, from καταβαίνω.

κατεθέμην, from κατατίθημι.

κατειλημμένην, perf. mid. and pass. participle of καταλαμβάνω.

κατείχετο, from κατέχω.

κατέκανε, from κατακαίνω.

κατελείφθησαν, from καταλείπω.

κατελήφθη, from καταλαμβάνω.

κατεσθίω (see ἐσθίω for prin. parts), *to devour, eat up*.

κατέστησε, from καθίστημι.

κατέχω (see ἔχω for prin. parts), *to restrain, hold completely*.

κατηγορέω, κατηγορήσω, κατηγόρησα, *to accuse, assert*. CATEGORIZE.

κατιδόντας, from καθοράω.

Καΰστρου πεδίον, τό, *Cayster-plain*, or *Cayster-field*. A crossroads city in Phrygia.

Καφαρναούμ, ἡ, indecl., *Capernaum*.

κέγχρος, -ου, ὁ, *millet grass*, useful for fodder.

κεῖμαι, κείσομαι, *to lie, be situated*. (Present system conjugated in 233.)

κέκραγε, from κράζω.

Κελαιναί, -ῶν, αἱ, *Celaenae*, a flourishing city of Phrygia, at the sources of the Marsyas and the Maeander rivers.

κελεύω, κελεύσω, ἐκέλευσα, κεκέλευκα, κεκέλευσμαι, ἐκελεύσθην, *to command, bid*.

κενός, -ή, -όν, *empty, vacant*, sometimes with gen.

Κεράμων ἀγορά, *Ceramon-agora*, a town in Phrygia. The name means, 'Market of the Ceramians.'

κεράννυμι, ἐκέρασα, κέκραμαι, ἐκεράσθην or ἐκράθην, *to mix, dilute*. CRASIS.

κέρας, κέρατος or κέρως, τό, *horn, wing* of an army. RHINOCEROS. (Declined in 139.)

κεράσας, from κεράννυμι.

κέρμα, -ατος, τό, *small change, coins*.

κερματιστής, -οῦ, ὁ, *money changer*.

κεφαλή, -ῆς, ἡ, *head*. ENCEPHALITIS.

*Κηφᾶς, -ᾶ, ὁ, Cephas.*

*Κιλικία, -ας, ἡ, Cilicia.* The country in Asia Minor where the apostle Paul was born. Tarsus was its chief city.

*Κίλιξ, -κος, ὁ, a Cilician.*

*Κίλισσα, -ης, ἡ, a Cilician woman.*

*κινδυνεύω, κινδυνεύσω, ἐκινδύνευσα, κεκινδύνευκα, κεκινδύνευμαι, ἐκινδυνεύθην, to face danger, run a risk.*

*κίνησις, -εως, ἡ, a moving, motion.* KINETIC.

*κλάσμα, -ατος, τό, fragment, piece, morsel.*

*Κλέαρχος, -ου, ὁ, Clearchus,* one of Cyrus' Greek generals.

*κληθήσῃ* from *καλέω.*

*κλίνω, κλινῶ, ἔκλινα, κέκλιμαι, ἐκλίθην* or *ἐκλίνην, to bend.* DECLINE.

*κλώψ, κλωπός, ὁ, thief.* (Declined in 145.)

*κνημίς, -ῖδος, ἡ, greave,* for the protection of the shins.

*κοιλία, -ας, ἡ, belly, womb, inner self.*

*κολλυβιστής, -οῦ, ὁ, money changer.*

*Κολοσσαί, -ῶν, αἱ, Colossae,* a city on the Lycus river in Phrygia. One of the early Christian churches was here, addressed by Paul in his Epistle to the Colossians.

*κόλπος, -ου, ὁ, bosom.*

*κολυμβήθρα, -ας, ἡ, swimming pool, bath.*

*κομίζω, κομιῶ, ἐκόμισα, κεκόμικα, κεκόμισμαι, ἐκομίσθην, to provide, get.*

*κομψός, -ή, -όν, fine, elegant, well* (of health).

*κομψότερος, -α, -ον, better,* comp. of *κομψός.*

*κοπιάω, κοπιάσω, ἐκοπίασα, κεκοπίακα, to be tired, toil until weary.*

*κόπος, -ου, ὁ, toil and trouble, labor.*

*κόπτω, κόψω, ἔκοψα, κέκοφα, κέκομμαι, ἐκόπην, to cut, knock.* SYNCOPATE.

*Κορσωτή, -ῆς, ἡ, Corsote,* a large city of Mesopotamia on the Euphrates, surrounded by a canal called the *Mascas* river.

*κόσμος, -ου, ὁ, order, ornament, universe, world.* COSMETIC, COSMIC.

*κοῦφος, -η, -ον, light, dry.*

*κόφινος, -ου, ὁ, basket.* COFFIN.

*κράβατος, -ου, ὁ, couch.*

*κράζω, κράξω, ἔκραξα* or *ἔκραγον, κέ-*

*κραγα, to cry.*

*κράνος, -ους, τό, helmet.* CRANIUM.

*κράτιστος, -η, -ον, best, noblest,* superl. of *ἀγαθός.*

*κράτος, -ους, τό, strength, power; ἀνὰ* or *κατὰ κράτος, up to strength, at full speed.*

*κραυγή, -ῆς, ἡ, shout, outcry.*

*κρέας, κρέως, τό, flesh, meat.* (Declined in 139.)

*κρείττων, -ον, better, braver,* comp. of *ἀγαθός.*

*κρεμάννυμι, κρεμῶ, ἐκρέμασα, ἐκρεμάσθην, to hang.*

*κρήνη, -ης, ἡ, spring, fountain.*

*Κρής, -τός, ὁ, a Cretan.*

*κριθή, -ῆς, ἡ, barley,* plural in *Anab.*

*κρίθινος, -η, -ον, made of barley.*

*κρίνω, κρινῶ, ἔκρινα, κέκρικα, κέκριμαι, ἐκρίθην, to judge, distinguish.*

*κρίσις, -εως, ἡ, decision, judgment.* CRISIS.

*κτάομαι, κτήσομαι, ἐκτησάμην, κέκτημαι, ἐκτήθην, to win* or *procure for one's self;* perf., *to possess.*

*κτείνω, κτενῶ, ἔκτεινα, ἔκτονα, to kill.* Usually found in compounds, *ἔκτονα* always so.

*Κτησίας, -ου, ὁ, Ctesias,* a famous Greek physician of Cnidus, captured by the Persians and made personal physician to Darius II and then to his son Artaxerxes. He wrote a history of Persia in twenty-three volumes.

*Κύδνος, -ου, ὁ, the Cydnus,* a river rising in the Taurus mountains and flowing through Cilicia. Tarsus was on this river.

*κύκλος, -ου, ὁ, a circle.* CYCLE.

*κυκλόω, κυκλώσω, ἐκύκλωσα, κεκύκλωκα, ἐκυκλώθην, to encircle, surround.*

*κύκλωσις, -εως, ἡ, an encircling, encirclement.*

*κύριος, -ου, ὁ, lord;* vocative, *κύριε,* often *sir.*

*Κῦρος, -ου, ὁ, Cyrus.*

*κωλύω, κωλύσω, ἐκώλυσα, κεκώλυκα, κεκώλυμαι, ἐκωλύθην, to hinder.*

*κώμη, -ης, ἡ, village.*

## Λ

*λαβεῖν, λάβοι, λαβόντα, λαβών,* from *λαμβάνω.*

*λαθεῖν,* from *λανθάνω.*

λάθρᾳ, *secretly*; with gen., *without the knowledge of.*

Λακεδαιμόνιος, -ου, ὁ, *a Lacedemonian, Spartan.*

λαλέω, λαλήσω, ἐλάλησα, λελάληκα, λελάλημαι, ἐλαλήθην, *to converse, talk, say.*

λαλιά, -ᾶς, ἡ, *speech, talk.*

λαμβάνω, λήψομαι or λήμψομαι, ἔλαβον, εἴληφα, εἴλημμαι, ἐλήφθην, *to take, receive, grasp.* EPILEPSY.

λαμπρότης, -τητος, ἡ, *brightness, splendor.* LAMP.

λανθάνω, λήσω, ἔλαθον, λέληθα, λέλησμαι, *to lie hidden, escape the notice of*; with partic., *to be secret, forgotten.* LETHE.

λέγω, λέξω, ἔλεξα, λέλεγμαι, ἐλέχθην, *to say, call, mean.* LECTURE, DIALECTIC.

λέγω, ἔλεξα, εἴλοχα, εἴλεγμαι, ἐλέγην, *to choose, gather.* Practically always in compound form. SELECT.

λείπω, λείψω, ἔλιπον, λέλοιπα, λέλειμμαι, ἐλείφθην, *to leave.* ELLIPSIS.

λελοιπὼς εἴη, from λείπω.

Λευείτης, -ου, ὁ, *Levite.*

λευκοθώραξ, -κος, m. and f. adj., *with white cuirass.*

λευκός, -ή, -όν, *brilliant, white.* LEUCOCYTE.

λήμψεσθε (for λήψεσθε), fut. ind. mid. of λαμβάνω.

ληφθῆναι, from λαμβάνω.

λίθινος, -η, -ον, *of stone, stony.*

λιμός, -οῦ, ὁ, *hunger, famine.*

λόγος, -ου, ὁ, *word.* LOGOMACHY.

λόγχη, -ης, ἡ, *spear point, spear.* LANCE.

λόφος, -ου, ὁ, *ridge, hill.*

λοχαγός, -οῦ, ὁ, *company leader, captain.*

λόχος, -ου, ὁ, *a company*, generally about 100 men, sometimes less.

Λυδία, -ας, ἡ, *Lydia.*

Λύδιος, -α, -ον, *Lydian.*

Λύκαια, -ων; τά, the *Lycaea*, a festival of the Arcadians in honor of Zeus.

Λυκαονία, -ας, ἡ, *Lycaonia*, a country north of Cilicia in Asia Minor.

Λύκιος, -ου, ὁ, *Lycius*, a Syracusan.

λυμαίνομαι, λυμανοῦμαι, ἐλυμηνάμην, λελύμασμαι, ἐλυμάνθην, *to outrage, spoil.*

λυπέω, λυπήσω, ἐλύπησα, λελύπηκα, λελύπημαι, ἐλυπήθην, *to grieve, vex, give pain.*

λύχνος, -ου, ὁ, *light, lamp.*

λύω, λύσω, ἔλυσα, λέλυκα, λέλυμαι, ἐλύθην, *to loose, destroy, break.* ANALYSIS. (Synopsis in 82, complete conjugation in 97; participles λύων, λύσας, λελυκώς, λυθείς declined 180–184.)

# M

μά, introduces a negative oath, *no* or *not, by!*

μαθητής, -οῦ, ὁ, *learner, disciple.* MATHEMATICS.

μαθών, from μανθάνω.

Μαίανδρος, -ου, ὁ, the *Maeander*, a winding river rising in Celaenae and flowing through Phrygia and between Lydia and Caria to the Aegean sea. MEANDER.

μακρός, -ά, -όν, *long.* MACRON.

μάλα, *very, exceedingly*; μάλιστα, superl. of μάλα; ὡς μάλιστα, *as much as possible.*

μᾶλλον, *more, rather.*

μανθάνω, μαθήσομαι, ἔμαθον, μεμάθηκα, *to learn.*

μάννα, τό, indecl., *manna.*

Μαρσύας, -ου, ὁ, the *Marsyas*, a river of Phrygia named from the satyr Marsyas.

μαρτυρέω, μαρτυρήσω, ἐμαρτύρησα, μεμαρτύρηκα, μεμαρτύρημαι, ἐμαρτυρήθην, *to bear witness, witness.*

μαρτυρία, -ας, ἡ, *witness, testimony.*

Μάσκας, -α, ὁ, the *Mascas*, called a river, really a canal around the city of Corsote on the Euphrates.

μαστός, -οῦ, ὁ, *breast.*

μάχαιρα, -ας, ἡ, *saber.*

μάχη, -ης, ἡ, *battle, fight.* LOGOMACHY.

μάχομαι, μαχοῦμαι, ἐμαχεσάμην, μεμάχημαι, *to fight, give battle, fight with.*

Μεγαρεύς, -εως, ὁ, *a Megarian*, from Megara, a Greek city between Athens and Corinth.

μέγας, μεγάλη, μέγα, *great, large.* MEGAPHONE. (Declined in 189, comparisons in 238.)

Μεγαφέρνης, -ου, ὁ, *Megaphernes.*

μέγιστος, -η, -ον, *greatest*, superl. of μέγας.

μεθερμηνεύω, μεθερμηνεύσω, *to translate, interpret.*

μεθύσκω, μεθύσω, ἐμέθυσα, μεμέθυσμαι,

ἐμεθύσθην, *to intoxicate, make drunk.*

μείζων, -ον, *greater,* comp, of μέγας.

μεῖναι, μεινάντες, from μένω.

μείων, -ον, *less, worse, fewer, weaker,* comp. of μικρός.

μελανία, -ας, ἡ, *blackness.* MELANISM.

μέλας, μέλαινα, μέλαν, *black,* MELANCHOLY. (Declined in 191.)

μέλει, μελήσει, ἐμέλησε, μεμέληκε, impers., *it is a care, it concerns.*

μελίνη, -ης, ἡ, *millet,* a kind of grain.

μέλλω, μελλήσω, ἐμέλλησα, *to intend, be going* to do something.

μέλω, *to be an object of care* or *thought*; mid., *to take care of* (with gen.).

μεμαθηκώς, perf. act. partic. of μανθάνω.

μεμαρτύρηκα, from μαρτυρέω.

μὲν ... δέ, particles used to set off contrasting items. In English the contrast is often expressed by mere emphasis in the reading.

μέντοι, *however.*

μένω, μενῶ, ἔμεινα, μεμένηκα, *to remain.*

μέρος, -ους, τό, *a part, example.*

μέσος, -η, -ον, *middle, in the middle.* MESOZOIC.

Μεσσίας, -ου, ὁ, *Messiah.*

μεστός, -ή, -όν, *filled, abounding in* or *with,* with gen.

μετά, with gen., *in company with, with*; with dat., *in midst of*; with acc., *after.* METAPHYSICAL.

μεταβαίνω (see βαίνω for prin. parts), *to pass over, cross over.* METABASIS.

μεταβέβηκε, from μεταβαίνω.

μεταξύ, *between*; τὸ μεταξύ, *the time* or *space between, the meantime.*

μετάπεμπτος, -ον, *summoned.*

μεταπέμπω (see πέμπω for prin. parts), *to send for.*

μετέωρος, -ον, *raised up from the ground.* METEOR.

μετρητής, -οῦ, ὁ, *a measure* (about 9 gallons).

μέτρον, -ου, τό, *measure.* METRIC.

μέχρι, *up to,* sometimes with gen.

μή, *not.* Used to negate commands, conditions, purpose clauses. Also introduces clauses of fearing in the sense of *lest, that.*

μηδέ, *and not, not even, neither.*

μηκέτι, *no longer.*

μῆκος, -ους, τό, *length.*

μήν, μηνός, ὁ, *month.* MOON. (Declined in 147.)

μήποτε, *never.*

μήτηρ, μητρός, ἡ, *mother.* MOTHER. (Declined in 138.)

μήτι, interrog. particle, often untranslated. Expects a neg., often with sense, *Can it be that ...?*

Μίδας, -ου, ὁ, *Midas,* king of the Phrygians.

μικρός, -ά, -όν, *small*; as adv., μικρόν, *by a little, little, just.* MICROSCOPE.

Μιλήσιος, -ου, ὁ, *a Milesian.*

Μίλητος, -ου, ἡ, *Miletus,* a city in Ionia.

μιμνήσκω, μνήσω, ἔμνησα, μέμνημαι, ἐμνήσθην, *to remind*; mid. and pass., *to remember.* MNEMONICS.

μισέω, μισήσω, ἐμίσησα, μεμίσηκα, μεμίσημαι, ἐμισήθην, *to hate.* MISANTHROPE.

μισθοδότης, -ου, ὁ, *paymaster, employer.*

μισθός, -οῦ, ὁ, *pay, wages.*

μισθοφόρος, -ου, ὁ, *a mercenary, professional soldier.*

μισθόω, μισθώσω, ἐμίσθωσα, μεμίσθωκα, μεμίσθωμαι, ἐμισθώθην, *to let out, hire.*

μνᾶ, μνᾶς, ἡ, *mina,* one-sixtieth of the Greek silver talent, worth 100 drachmas. (Declined in 243.)

μνημεῖον, -ου, τό, *monument, tomb.*

μοί, μοι, from ἐγώ.

μονογενής, -ές, *only-begotten.*

μόνος, -η, -ον, *only, alone*; μόνον as adv., *only.* MONOGAMY.

μοῦ, μου, from ἐγώ.

Μυριάνδος, -ου, ἡ, *Myriandus,* a Syrian city on the gulf of Issus.

μυριάς, -άδος, ἡ, *a ten thousand.* MYRIAD.

μύριοι, -αι, -α, *ten thousand.*

Μύσιος, -α, -ον, *Mysian, of Mysia,* a country in Asia Minor between Lydia and Phrygia.

Μωϋσῆς, -έως, ὁ (also Μωσῆς), *Moses.*

# N

Ναζαρέθ, ἡ, indecl., *Nazareth.*

Ναθαναήλ, ὁ, indecl., *Nathanael.*

ναός, -οῦ, ὁ, *temple.*

ναύαρχος, -ου, ὁ, *fleet commander, admiral.*

## Vocabulary

ναῦς, νεώς, ἡ, ship. NAVY. (Declined in 151.)

ναυτικός, -ή, -όν, naval. NAUTICAL.

νεκρός, -ά, -όν, dead; νεκρός, -οῦ, ὁ, corpse, dead body. NECROTIC.

νέος, -α, -ον, new, young. NEON.

νεφέλη, -ης, ἡ, a cloud.

νεώτερος, -α, -ον, comparative of νέος.

νικάω, νικήσω, ἐνίκησα, νενίκηκα, νενίκημαι, ἐνικήθην, to conquer, surpass. NICODEMUS.

νίκη, -ης, ἡ, victory; περὶ νίκης, for victory, to win.

Νικόδημος, -ου, ὁ, Nicodemus.

νοέω, νοήσω, ἐνόησα, νενόηκα, νενόημαι, ἐνοήθην, to observe, think, plan.

νομίζω, νομιῶ, ἐνόμισα, νενόμικα, νενόμισμαι, ἐνομίσθην, to consider, think.

νόμος, -ου, ὁ, law, custom. NOMOLOGY.

νόσημα, -ατος, τό, sickness, malady.

νοῦς, νοῦ, ὁ, mind; τὸν νοῦν προσέχειν, to give thought or attention. NOUS. (Declined in 243.)

νύμφη, -ης, ἡ, bride. NYMPH.

νυμφίος, -ου, ὁ, bridegroom, husband.

νῦν, now. NOW.

νύξ, νυκτός, ἡ, night; μέσαι νύκτες, midnight. NYCTALOPIA.

## Ξ

Ξενίας, -ου, ὁ, Xenias, a Greek general in Cyrus' army.

ξενικός, -ή, -όν, foreign, mercenary.

ξένος, -ου, ὁ, a foreigner, guest-friend, mercenary soldier. XENOPHOBIA.

Ξενοφῶν, -ῶντος, ὁ, Xenophon, author of the Anabasis. An Athenian and a pupil of Socrates, he joined the expedition as a friend of Proxenus.

Ξέρξης, -ου, ὁ, Xerxes, king of Persia.

ξηρός, -ά, -όν, dry, parched, withered.

ξύλινος, -η, -ον, wooden.

ξύλον, -ου, τό, wood, a piece or bar of wood. XYLOPHONE.

## Ο

ὁ, ἡ, τό, gen. τοῦ, τῆς, τοῦ, def. article, the; sometimes used by itself (chiefly with μέν and δέ) as pronoun, the one, the ones. (Declined in 63.)

ὅ, from ὅς.

ὀβολός, -οῦ, ὁ, the obol, an Attic coin worth about six cents.

ὅδε, ἥδε, τόδε, this, the following. (Declined in 65.)

ὁδοιπορία, -ας, ἡ, journey.

ὁδός, -οῦ, ἡ, road, way. EXODUS.

ὅθεν, from where, whence.

οἱ, from ὁ.

οἷ, οἵ, from οὗ, οὖ.

οἶδα, οἴδαμεν, οἴδατε, perf. of εἴδω with present sense. (Conjugated in 199.)

οἴκαδε, homeward, home.

οἰκέω, οἰκήσω, ᾤκησα, ᾤκηκα, ᾤκημαι, ᾠκήθην, to dwell, inhabit. ECUMENICAL.

οἰκία, -ας, ἡ, house, household. ECONOMY.

οἴκοι, at home.

οἰκοδομέω, οἰκοδομήσω, ᾠκοδόμησα, ᾠκοδόμημαι, ᾠκοδομήθην, to build.

οἶκος, -ου, ὁ, house, abode.

οἰκτείρω, οἰκτερῶ, ᾤκτειρα, to pity, feel sorry for.

οἶνος, -ου, ὁ, wine. WINE.

οἴομαι or οἶμαι, οἰήσομαι, ᾠήθην, to think, believe.

οἷος, -α, -ον, of what sort.

οἷόσπερ, -απερ, -όνπερ, just such as.

οἴχομαι, οἰχήσομαι, to be gone, to have gone.

ὀκνέω, ὀκνήσω, ᾤκνησα, to hesitate, dread.

ὀκτακόσιοι, -αι, -α, eight hundred.

ὀκτώ, indecl., eight. OCTAGON.

ὄλεθρος, -ου, ὁ, destruction, death, loss.

ὀλίγος, -η, -ον, little, a little, few. OLIGARCHY. (Comparisons in 238.)

ὁλκάς, -άδος, ἡ, merchant ship, freighter.

ὅλος, -η, -ον, whole, entire. HOLOCAUST.

Ὀλύνθιος, -ου, ὁ, an Olynthian. Olynthus was an Athenian colony on the peninsula of Chalcidice adjoining Macedonia.

ὁμαλής, -ές, level.

ὁμαλῶς, evenly, on an even front.

ὁμοίως, similarly, alike. HOMOEOPATHY.

ὁμολογέω, ὁμολογήσω, ὡμολόγησα, ὡμολόγηκα, ὡμολόγημαι, ὡμολογήθην, to say the same thing, agree, confess. HOMOLOGOUS.

ὁμοτράπεζος, -ου, ὁ, a table companion.

312    *Vocabulary*

ὁμοῦ, *together, at the same place or time.*

ὅμως, *nevertheless.*

ὅν, from ὅς.

ὄνομα, -ατος, τό, *name.* ONOMATOPOEIA.

ὄνος, -ου, ὁ, *an ass, a weight-bearing pulley, upper millstone.*

ὄντας, ὄντος, from εἰμί.

ὅπη, *whither, where, in what way or direction.*

ὄπισθεν, *from behind, behind.*

ὀπίσω, *behind, backwards.*

ὁπλίζω, ὥπλισα, ὥπλισμαι, ὡπλίσθην, *to arm, equip.*

ὁπλίτης, -ου, ὁ, *a hoplite, heavy-armed soldier.*

ὅπλον, -ου, τό, *instrument, weapon.* PANOPLY.

ὁπόσος, -η, -ον, *as much as, as many as, how much or many.*

ὁπότε, *whenever.*

ὅπου, *where, wherever.*

ὅπως, *in what way, how.* Also in purpose clauses, same as ἵνα, ὡς, *in order that.* With future indic. used for exhortation; ὅπως ἔσεσθε, *see that you be.*

ὁράω, ὄψομαι, εἶδον, ἑώρακα, ἑώραμαι or ὦμμαι, ὤφθην, *to see.* (εἶδον is borrowed from εἴδω.) OPTICAL.

ὀργή, -ῆς, ἡ, *anger, wrath.*

ὀργίζω, ὀργιοῦμαι, ὥργισα, ὥργισμαι, ὠργίσθην, *to anger;* mid. and pass., *to be angry.*

ὄρθιος, -α, -ον, *straight up, steep.*

ὁρμάω, ὁρμήσω, ὥρμησα, ὥρμηκα, ὥρμημαι, ὡρμήθην, *to start out, rush.* HORMONE.

ὁρμέω, ὁρμήσω, *to be moored, come to anchor.*

ὄρος, ὄρους, τό, *mountain.* OROGRAPHY.

ὀρύττω, ὀρύξω, ὥρυξα, ὀρώρυχα, ὀρώρυγμαι, ὠρύχθην, *to dig, quarry.*

ὅς, ἥ, ὅ, gen. οὗ, ἧς, οὗ, relative pronoun, *who, which.* (Declined in 64.)

ὅσος, ὅση, ὅσον, *as much as, as many as, as great as;* as adverb ὅσον with numerals, *about.*

ὅσπερ, ἥπερ, ὅπερ, intensive for ὅς, ἥ, ὅ, *who indeed, which indeed.*

ὅστις, ἥτις, ὅ τι, gen. οὗτινος, ἧστινος, οὗτινος, *whoever, anyone who.* (Declined in 158.)

ὅτε, *when, whenever;* ὅταν equals ὅτε plus ἄν.

ὅτι, conjunction *that.*

ὅτου, gen. sing. of ὅστις.

οὐ, οὐκ, οὐχ, *not.*

οὗ, *where.*

οὗ, οὑ, *of him,* third personal pronoun, also used as indirect reflexive. See 72.

οὗ, from the relative pronoun ὅς.

οὐδαμοῦ, *nowhere.*

οὐδέ, *but not.*

οὐδείς, οὐδεμία, οὐδέν, gen. οὐδενός, οὐδεμιᾶς, οὐδενός, *no one, none.*

οὐδέν, οὐδένα, from οὐδείς.

οὐκέτι, *no longer.*

οὖν, postpositive, *then, therefore.*

οὔποτε, *never.*

οὔπω, *not yet.*

οὐπώποτε, *never.*

οὐρανός, -οῦ, ὁ, *heaven.* URANUS.

οὖς, from ὅς.

οὖσαν, οὔσης, from ὤν, participle of εἰμί.

οὗτος, αὕτη, τοῦτο, gen. τούτου, ταύτης, τούτου, *this, the preceding.* (Declined in 67.)

οὕτως or οὕτω, *thus, in this way.*

ὀφείλω, ὀφειλήσω, ὠφείλησα or ὤφελον, ὠφείληκα, ὠφειλήθην, *to owe.*

ὄφελος, -ους, τό, *help, advantage, use.*

ὀφθαλμός, -οῦ, ὁ, *eye.* OPHTHALMOLOGY.

ὄφις, -εως, ὁ, *snake, serpent.*

ὄχλος, -ου, ὁ, *throng, crowd.* OCHLOCRACY.

ὀχυρός, -ά, -όν, *impregnable, strong.*

ὀψάριον, -ου, τό, *small fish, sardine.*

ὄψεσθε, ὄψεται, from ὁράω.

ὄψιος, -α, -ον, *late;* ὀψία (sc. ὥρα), *the latter part of the day, evening.*

## Π

παθεῖν, from πάσχω.

παιανίζω, ἐπαιάνισα, *to sing the paean.* This was a song in honor of Apollo or Artemis. Before a battle the paean followed the prayer and preceded the battle cry and attack. PAEAN.

παιδάριον, -ου, τό, *little boy, lad.* Dimin. of παῖς.

παιδίον, -ου, τό, *child.*

παῖς, -δός, ὁ or ἡ, child. PEDAGOGUE.

παίω, παίσω, ἔπαισα, πέπαικα, ἐπαίσθην, to strike, beat.

πάλιν, again, back. PALINDROME.

παλτόν, -οῦ, τό, javelin.

πάντα, πάντες, from πᾶς.

παντάπασι, wholly, altogether.

πάντῃ, everywhere, on all sides.

παντοδαπός, -ή, -όν, manifold, of all sorts.

παντοῖος, -α, -ον, of all sorts.

πάντοτε, always.

πάνυ, very.

παρά, with gen., from beside; with dat., beside; with acc., to, towards, beyond. PARALLEL.

παραγγέλλω (see ἀγγέλλω for prin. parts), to send word.

παραγίγνομαι or παραγίνομαι (see γίγνομαι for prin. parts), to become near, come, be present.

παράδεισος, -ου, ὁ, a park, game preserve. PARADISE.

παραδιδόναι, from παραδίδωμι.

παραδίδωμι (see δίδωμι for prin. parts), to give over, surrender, betray.

παραδώσων, from παραδίδωμι.

παραινέω (see αἰνέω for prin. parts), to praise, applaud.

παρακελεύομαι (see κελεύω for prin. parts), to encourage.

παραλαμβάνω (see λαμβάνω for prin. parts), to receive.

παραμείβομαι (see ἀμείβω for prin. parts), to change one's position.

παραμηρίδια, -ων, τά, thigh armor.

παραπλήσιος, -α, -ον, like, resembling.

παρασάγγης, -ου, ὁ, parasang, a Persian road measure equal to thirty stadia or 18,000 Greek feet; roughly 3½ miles.

παρασκευάζω, παρασκευάσω, παρεσκεύασα, παρεσκεύασμαι, παρεσκευάσθην, to provide for, prepare; mid. and pass., to be ready.

παρασκευή, -ῆς, ἡ, preparation.

παρατάττω (see τάττω for prin. parts), to draw up side by side. PARATAXIS.

παρείη, from πάρειμι.

πάρειμι (see εἰμί for prin. parts), to be present, come.

παρεῖναι, from πάρειμι.

παρέλαβον, from παραλαμβάνω.

παρελαύνω (see ἐλαύνω for prin. parts), to march along, ride past.

παρελθεῖν, from παρέρχομαι.

παρέρχομαι (see ἔρχομαι for prin. parts), to pass by or through.

παρέχω (see ἔχω for prin. parts), to afford, provide, offer, furnish.

παρήλασε, from παρελαύνω.

παρῆλθε, from παρέρχομαι.

παρῆν, παρῆσαν, from πάρειμι.

πάροδος, -ου, ἡ, passage, roadway.

Παρράσιος, -ου, ὁ, a Parrhasian, from Parrhasia, a district in Arcadia.

Παρύσατις, -ιδος, ἡ, Parysatis, wife of Darius II.

παρών, from πάρειμι.

πᾶς, πᾶσα, πᾶν, gen. παντός, πάσης, παντός, the whole, entire, all. PAN-AMERICAN. (Declined in 156.)

Πασίων, -ωνος, ὁ, Pasion of Megara, one of Cyrus' Greek generals.

πάσχα, τό, indecl., passover, paschal lamb. PASCHAL.

πάσχω, πείσομαι, ἔπαθον, πέπονθα, to experience, suffer, be treated. PATHOLOGY.

πατέω, πατήσω, ἐπάτησα, πεπάτηκα, πεπάτημαι, to tread, walk.

Πατηγύας, -α, ὁ, Pategyas, a Persian loyal to Cyrus.

πατήρ, πατρός, ὁ, father. PATERNAL. (Declined in 138.)

πατρίς, -ίδος, ἡ, native land, home country. PATRIOTIC.

παύω, παύσω, ἔπαυσα, πέπαυκα, πέπαυμαι, ἐπαύθην, to make cease, stop; mid., to cease, stop. PAUSE.

Παφλαγών, -όνος, ὁ, a Paphlagonian.

πεδίον, -ου, τό, plain.

πεζῇ, on foot.

πεζός, -ή, -όν, on foot, infantry.

πείθω, πείσω, ἔπεισα, πέπεικα or πέποιθα, πέπεισμαι, ἐπείσθην, to persuade; mid. and pass., to be persuaded, obey, often with dative.

πεῖν, from πίνω.

πεινάω, πεινήσω, ἐπείνησα, πεπείνηκα, to hunger.

πειράζω, ἐπείρασα, πεπείρασμαι, ἐπειράσθην, to make trial of, test.

πειράομαι, πειράσομαι, ἐπειρασάμην, πεπείραμαι, ἐπειράθην, to try, attempt. EMPIRICAL.

πείσομαι, from πάσχω.

πείσομαι, from πείθω.

πελάζω, πελάσω or πελῶ, ἐπέλασα, ἐπελάσθην, to draw near, approach.

Πελοποννήσιος, -α, -ον, Peloponnesian.

Πελοπόννησος, -ου, ἡ, the Peloponnesus, southern portion of Greece.

Πέλται, -ῶν, αἱ, Peltae, a city in Phrygia on the Maeander river.

πελταστής, -οῦ, ὁ, peltast, a light-armed soldier carrying a small shield or target, probably several spears for throwing or hand use, and perhaps a sword.

πελταστικός, -ή, -όν, of the peltasts; τὸ πελταστικόν, the light-armed force.

πέλτη, -ης, ἡ, a small shield, target.

πέμπω, πέμψω, ἔπεμψα, πέπομφα, πέπεμμαι, ἐπέμφθην, to send. POMP.

πεντακισχίλιοι, -αι, -α, five thousand.

πεντακόσιοι, -αι, -α, five hundred.

πέντε, indecl., five. PENTAGON.

πεντεκαίδεκα, indecl., fifteen.

πεντήκοντα, indecl., fifty. PENTECOST.

πεπτωκότα, from πίπτω.

πέραν, beyond, on the other side of, usually with gen.

πέρδιξ, -ικος, ὁ or ἡ, partridge. PARTRIDGE.

περί, with gen., about, concerning; with dat., round, about; with acc., around, all around. PERISCOPE.

περιγενόμενος, from περιγίγνομαι.

περιγίγνομαι (see γίγνομαι for prin. parts), to be superior, get the better of (with gen.).

περίειμι (see εἰμί for prin. parts), to excel, exceed, be greater.

περιέχω (see ἔχω for prin. parts), to surround, hem in.

περιῆν, from περίειμι.

περιπατέω (see πατέω for prin. parts), to walk about, walk. PERIPATETIC.

περιπεσεῖν, from περιπίπτω.

περιπίπτω (see πίπτω for prin. parts), to fall or throw one's self around or upon.

περιπλέω (see πλέω for prin. parts), to sail around.

περιπτύσσω (see πτύσσω for prin. parts), to fold around, enfold, outflank.

περιρρέω (see ῥέω for prin. parts), to flow around.

περισσεύω, περισσεύσω, ἐπερίσσευσα, ἐπερισσεύθην, to abound, exceed, be over or remain.

περιστερά, -ᾶς, ἡ, dove, pigeon.

Πέρσης, -ου, ὁ, a Persian.

Περσικός, -ή, -όν, Persian.

πέτομαι, πτήσομαι or πετήσομαι, ἐπτόμην, to fly.

πέτρα, -ας, ἡ, rock, cliff. PETRIFY.

Πέτρος, -ου, ὁ, Peter.

πετρόω, ἐπέτρωσα, ἐπετρώθην, to turn to stone; pass., to be stoned.

πηγή, -ῆς, ἡ, spring, well; pl. αἱ πηγαί, source of a river.

πηδάω, πηδήσομαι, ἐπήδησα, πεπήδηκα, to leap.

πηλός, -οῦ, ὁ, mud, miry clay.

Πίγρης, -ητος, ὁ, Pigres, Cyrus' herald and interpreter.

πιέζω, πιέσω, ἐπίεσα, ἐπιέσθην, to press hard.

πίῃ, πίητε, from πίνω.

πίμπλημι, πλήσω, ἔπλησα, πέπληκα, πέπλησμαι, ἐπλήσθην, to fill.

πίνω, πίομαι, ἔπιον, πέπωκα, πέπομαι, ἐπόθην, to drink. πεῖν is for πιεῖν, 2nd aor. infin.

πίπτω, πεσοῦμαι, ἔπεσον, πέπτωκα, to fall.

Πισίδαι, -ῶν, οἱ, the Pisidians.

πιστεύω, πιστεύσω, ἐπίστευσα, πεπίστευκα, πεπίστευμαι, ἐπιστεύθην, to trust, believe, with dative of person trusted.

πίστις, -εως, ἡ, trust, trustworthiness, a pledge, assurance of good faith.

πιστός, -ή, -όν, faithful, trusted, loyal, reliable.

πιστότης, -τητος, ἡ, faithfulness, loyalty.

πλάγιος, -α, -ον, sideways, slanting; εἰς πλάγιον, sideways.

πλαίσιον, -ου, τό, a square, rectangle.

πλανάω, πλανήσω, ἐπλάνησα, πεπλάνημαι, ἐπλανήθην, to cause to stray, deceive; mid., to wander, straggle. PLANET.

πλεθριαῖος, -α, -ον, of a plethron.

πλέθρον, -ου, τό, plethron, a measure equivalent to 100 Greek feet, about 97 feet 1 inch.

πλεῖστος, -η, -ον, superl. of πολύς, very much, very many, most.

## Vocabulary

πλείων, πλεῖον, comp. of πολύς, more. PLEONASM.

πλέω, πλεύσομαι or πλευσοῦμαι, ἔπλευσα, πέπλευκα, πέπλευσμαι, to sail.

πλῆθος, -ους, τό, great mass or number, multitude, crowd. PLETHORA.

πλήθω, πέπληθα, to be full; ἀγορὰ πλήθουσα, full market, forenoon.

πλήν, except, except that.

πλήρης, πλῆρες, full, full of, with gen.

πληρόω, πληρώσω, ἐπλήρωσα, πεπλήρωκα, πεπλήρωμαι, ἐπληρώθην, to fill, fulfill.

πλήρωμα, -ατος, τό, a filling, fullness.

πλησιάζω, πλησιάσω, πεπλησίακα, to approach, draw near.

πλησίος, -α, -ον, hard by, near, 'near from' (with gen.) ; superl., πλησιαίτατος ; as adv., πλησίον, near by.

πλοιάριον, -ου, τό, a skiff, boat.

πλοῖον, -ου, τό, a boat, pontoon.

πνεῦμα, -ατος, τό, breath, spirit.

πνέω, πνεύσομαι, ἔπνευσα, πέπνευκα, πέπνευσμαι, ἐπνεύσθην, to breathe, blow. PNEUMATIC.

ποδήρης, -ες, reaching to the feet.

πόθεν, from where, whence.

ποιέω, ποιήσω, ἐποίησα, πεποίηκα, πεποίημαι, ἐποιήθην, to do, make. POET. (Expanded in 164, present active participle declined in 195.)

ποιητέος, -α, -ον, to be made or done, necessary to do, verbal adj. from ποιέω.

ποικίλος, -η, -ον, many-colored.

πολεμέω, πολεμήσω, ἐπολέμησα, πεπολέμηκα, πεπολέμημαι, ἐπολεμήθην, to make war. POLEMICS.

πολέμιος, -α, -ον, hostile; οἱ πολέμιοι, the enemy; τὰ πολέμια, matters of war.

πολιορκέω, πολιορκήσω, ἐπολιόρκησα, πεπολιόρκημαι, ἐπολιορκήθην, to besiege, blockade.

πόλις, πόλεως, ἡ, city. METROPOLIS. (Declined in 152.)

πολλάκις, many times, often.

πολλαπλάσιος, -α, -ον, many times more.

πολύς, πολλή, πολύ, gen. πολλοῦ, πολλῆς, πολλοῦ, much, many. POLYGON. (Declined in 188, comparison in 238.)

πολυτελής, -ές, expensive, costly.

πονηρός, -ά, -όν, painful, evil, wicked.

πορεύομαι, πορεύσομαι, ἐπορευσάμην, πεπόρευμαι, ἐπορεύθην, to proceed, go.

πόρρω, afar, far off, far from.

πορφυροῦς, -ᾶ, -οῦν, purple, dark red.

πόσις, -εως, ἡ, a drinking, drink. POTION.

ποταμός, -οῦ, ὁ, river. HIPPOPOTAMUS.

πότε, interrog. adv., when?

ποτέ, enclitic particle, once, ever.

πότον, -ου, τό, drink. POTION.

που, anywhere, somewhere.

ποῦ, where?

πούς, ποδός, ὁ, foot. As a measure, about 11·65 inches. PODIATRY.

πρᾶγμα, -ατος, τό, an affair, doing, business; in a bad sense, πράγματα παρέχειν, to cause trouble. PRAGMATIC.

πρανής, -ές, headlong, steep. PRONE.

πρᾶξις, -εως, ἡ, a doing, undertaking, enterprise. PRAXIS.

πρᾷος, -εῖα, -ον, tame.

πράττω or πράσσω, πράξω, ἔπραξα, πέπραχα, πέπραγμαι, ἐπράχθην, to do. PRACTICAL.

πρεσβύτερος, -α, -ον, older, elder. PRESBYTER.

πρίασθαι, from ἐπριάμην.

πρίν, before, until; sometimes with ἄν plus subjunctive, sometimes with infinitive.

πρό, with gen., before.

προαισθάνομαι (see αἰσθάνομαι for prin. parts), to perceive beforehand, foresee.

προαισθόμενος, from προαισθάνομαι.

προβάλλω (see βάλλω for prin. parts), to throw before; mid., to hold before one's self, hold forward. PROBLEM.

προβατικός, -ή, -όν, of or for sheep; ἡ προβατική, sheep gate.

πρόβατον, -ου, τό, sheep; pl., cattle.

προδίδωμι (see δίδωμι for prin. parts), to give over, abandon, desert.

προδόντα, προδούς, from προδίδωμι.

προδραμόντες, from προτρέχω.

πρόειμι (see εἶμι for prin. parts), to go forward.

προεῖπον (2nd aorist only; cf. εἶπον from εἴρω), to tell before, give orders, proclaim.

προειστήκει, from προΐστημι.

προεληλακέναι, from προελαύνω.

προῄει, from πρόειμι.

316     *Vocabulary*

πρόθυμος, -ον, *willing, eager*; comp., προθυμότερος.

προΐδοιεν, from προοράω.

προϊέναι, προϊόντων, from πρόειμι.

προΐστημι (see ἵστημι for prin. parts), to *put in command, be in command*.

προκαταλαμβάνω (see λαμβάνω for prin. parts), to *seize before or first*.

προκαταληψομένους, from προκαταλαμβάνω.

προμετωπίδιον, -ου, τό, a *frontlet*, or face armor worn by horses.

Πρόξενος, -ου, ὁ, *Proxenus*, a Boeotian friend of Cyrus.

προοράω (see ὁράω for prin. parts), to *foresee, see before, see coming*.

πρός, with gen., *from, characteristic of*; with dat., *toward, at*; with acc., *to, toward, against*. PROSELYTE.

προσάγω (see ἄγω for prin. parts), to *lead against, attack*.

προσαιτέω (see αἰτέω for prin. parts), to *ask besides, ask more, beg hard*.

πρόσειμι, to *come on, approach, advance*.

προσέλαβον, from προσλαμβάνω.

προσελθόντας, from προσέρχομαι.

προσέρχομαι (see ἔρχομαι for prin. parts), to *go over to, join, come on, approach*.

προσέχω (see ἔχω for prin. parts), to *apply*.

προσῇσαν, from πρόσειμι.

πρόσθεν, *earlier, before*; πρόσθεν ... ἤ or πρόσθεν ... πρίν, *sooner than, before*; εἰς τὸ πρόσθεν, *forward*; τὸ πρόσθεν, *before*.

προσιόντος, προσιόντων, προσιών, from πρόσειμι.

προσκυνέω, προσκυνήσω, προσεκύνησα, προσκεκύνηκα, προσεκυνήθην, to *fall down and worship, adore, hail*.

προσκυνητής, -οῦ, ὁ, *worshiper*.

προσλαμβάνω (see λαμβάνω for prin. parts), to *take besides*.

προσποιέομαι (see ποιέω for prin. parts), to *pretend*.

προστερνίδιον, -ου, τό, a *breastplate* for horses.

πρόσω and τοῦ πρόσω, *forward*.

πρότερος, -α, -ον, *former, earlier, preceding*; adverbially, πρότερον and τὸ πρότερον, *before, in time past*.

προτρέχω (see τρέχω for prin. parts), to *run ahead, outrun*.

προφαίνω (see φαίνω for prin. parts), to *bring to light*; mid., to *come in sight*.

πρόφασις, -εως, ἡ, *excuse, pretext*.

προφήτης, -ου, ὁ, *prophet*. PROPHET. (Declined in 44).

πρῶτος, -η, -ον, *first*; adv. πρῶτον, *at first, first*. PROTOTYPE. (Declined in 56.)

πτέρυξ, -υγος, ἡ, *wing*.

πτύσσω, πτύξω, ἔπτυξα, ἔπτυγμαι, ἐπτύχθην, to *fold*.

Πυθαγόρας, -ου, ὁ, *Pythagoras*, a Spartan admiral.

Πύλαι, -ῶν, αἱ, *Pylae*, a fortress on the border between Mesopotamia and Babylonia. Literally, 'The Gates'.

πύλη, -ης, ἡ, *gate, pass*. PYLON.

πυνθάνομαι, πεύσομαι, ἐπυθόμην, πέπυσμαι, to *inquire, learn*.

Πύραμος, -ου, ὁ, the *Pyramus*, a large river rising in Cappadocia and flowing through Cilicia to the sea.

πυρετός, -οῦ, ὁ, *heat, fever*. PYRETIC.

πυρός, -οῦ, ὁ, *wheat*, generally plural.

πώ, *yet*, used after a negative.

πωλέω, πωλήσω, ἐπώλησα, πεπώληκα, ἐπωλήθην, to *barter, sell*.

πώποτε, *ever, ever yet*.

πῶς, *how?*

## Ρ

Ῥαββί, title of respect, *Rabbi, honorable Sir*.

ῥέω, ῥεύσω, ἔρρευσα, ἐρρύηκα, to *flow*. RHEUMATIC.

ῥῆμα, -ατος, τό, *word, saying*.

ῥίπτω, ῥίψω, ἔρριψα, ἔρριφα, ἔρριμμαι, ἐρρίφθην or ἐρρίφην, to *throw, throw off*.

## Σ

σάββατον, -ου, τό, *sabbath*.

Σαλείμ, τό, indecl., *Salim*.

σαλπίζω, ἐσάλπιγξα, to *blow the trumpet*; impers., *the trumpet sounds*.

Σαμαρίτης, -ου, ὁ, a *Samaritan*.

Σαμαρῖτις, -τιδος, ἡ, *Samaritan woman*.

Σαμαρεία, -as, ἡ, Samaria.

Σάρδεις, -εων, αἱ, Sardis, capital of Lydia.

σάρξ, σαρκός, ἡ, flesh. SARCOPHAGUS. (Declined in 145.)

σατράπης, -ου, ὁ, satrap, viceroy.

Σάτυρος, -ου, ὁ, the satyr Silenus. The satyrs were wood sprites specially associated with Dionysus.

σαφῶς, clearly.

σεαυτοῦ, σεαυτῆς, also σαυτοῦ, σαυτῆς, of thyself, of yourself. (Declined in 73.)

σημεῖον, -ου, τό, sign, token, proof.

σήσαμον, -ου, τό, the sesame, an oriental plant from which is made an oil useful for food and for medicine.

σιγή, -ῆς, ἡ, silence.

σίγλος, -ου, ὁ, the siglus, a Persian silver coin worth about a half-dollar.

Σίμων, -ωνος, ὁ, Simon. (Declined in 147.)

σιτίον, -ου, τό, food.

σῖτος, -ου, ὁ, grain, food, provisions; σῖτος μελίνης, millet bread.

σιωπάω, σιωπήσομαι, ἐσιώπησα, σεσιώπηκα, ἐσιωπήθην, to be silent.

σκανδαλίζω, ἐσκανδάλισα, ἐσκανδαλίσθην, to cause to stumble, offend. SCANDALIZE.

σκέπτομαι, σκέψομαι, ἐσκεψάμην, ἔσκεμμαι, to view, search out, deliberate. SCEPTIC.

σκευοφόρος, -ον, baggage-carrying; τὰ σκευοφόρα, the baggage animals.

σκηνή, -ῆς, ἡ, awning, tent. SCENE.

σκηνόω, σκηνώσω, ἐσκήνωσα, to tent, tabernacle.

σκηπτοῦχος, -ου, ὁ, scepter bearer, a chamberlain or high court official.

σκληρός, -ά, -όν, harsh, austere, stern. SCLEROTIC.

σκοτία, -as, ἡ, darkness. (Declined in 43.)

σκότος, -ους, τό, darkness.

Σόλοι, -ων, οἱ, Soli, a Cilician coastal city.

σός, σή, σόν, your, yours.

σοφία, -as, ἡ, wisdom, skill. SOPHOMORE.

Σοφαίνετος, -ου, ὁ, Sophaenetus, of Stymphalus in Arcadia.

σπάω, σπάσω, ἔσπασα, ἔσπακα, ἔσπασμαι, ἐσπάσθην, to draw, draw tight. SPASM.

σπείρω, σπερῶ, ἔσπειρα, ἔσπαρμαι, ἐσπάρην, to sow. SPARSE.

σπεύδω, σπεύσω, ἔσπευσα, to urge, be

eager, hasten.

σπουδή, -ῆς, ἡ, eagerness, haste.

στάδιον, -ου, τό, a stade, six hundred Greek feet. The Greek foot was about 11·65 inches. In the plural also οἱ στάδιοι. STADIUM.

σταθμός, -οῦ, ὁ, a stopping place, day's march, stage.

στέγασμα, -ατος, τό, tent covering.

στέλλω, στελῶ, ἔστειλα, ἔσταλκα, ἔσταλμαι, ἐστάλην, to send.

στενός, -ή, -όν, narrow, small. STENOGRAPHY.

στενοχωρία, -as, ἡ, a narrow pass.

στερέω, στερήσω, ἐστέρησα, ἐστέρηκα, ἐστέρημαι, ἐστερήθην, to deprive of, rob. STERILE.

στέρνον, -ου, τό, breast. STERNUM.

στῆναι, στήσας, from ἵστημι.

στῖφος, -ους, τό, a close array.

στλεγγίς, -ίδος, ἡ, flesh scraper, used by athletes.

στοά, -ᾶς, ἡ, colonnade, portico, cloister. STOIC.

στολή, -ῆς, ἡ, a garment, robe. STOLE.

στόλος, -ου, ὁ, expedition, host.

στράτευμα, -ατος, τό, army.

στρατεύω, στρατεύσω, ἐστράτευσα, ἐστράτευμαι, to make an expedition, take the field.

στρατηγέω, στρατηγήσω, ἐστρατήγησα, ἐστρατήγηκα, to be general, command, manage.

στρατηγία, -as, ἡ, plan of command. STRATEGY.

στρατηγός, -οῦ, ὁ, general. STRATEGIC.

στρατιά, -ᾶς, ἡ, army.

στρατιώτης, -ου, ὁ, soldier.

στρατοπεδεύω, ἐστρατοπεδευσάμην, ἐστρατοπέδευμαι, to pitch camp.

στρατός, -οῦ, ὁ, army, force.

στραφείς, στραφέντες, from στρέφω.

στρεπτός, -ή, -όν, twisted; ὁ στρεπτός, necklace, collar. STREPTOCOCCUS.

στρέφω, στρέψω, ἔστρεψα, ἔστροφα, ἔστραμμαι, ἐστράφην, to twist, turn, face about.

στρουθός, -οῦ, ὁ or ἡ, sparrow; with μέγας, an ostrich, a good example of Greek humor of understatement.

Στυμφάλιος, -ου, ὁ, a Stymphalian, native of

*Stymphalus.*

σύ, σοῦ, *thou, you.* (Declined in 72.)

συγγενέσθαι, from συγγίγνομαι.

συγγίγνομαι (see γίγνομαι for prin. parts), *to be with, meet, become acquainted with.* Used sometimes of sexual relations.

συγκαλέω (see καλέω for prin. parts), *to call together.*

Συέννεσις, -ιος, ὁ, *Syennesis,* a king or viceroy of Cilicia. Probably a hereditary title, used by Xenophon as a proper name.

συκῆ, συκῆς, ἡ, *fig tree.* SYCOPHANT.

συλάω, συλήσω, ἐσύλησα, ἐσυλήθην, *to spoil, strip off the spoil,* as from a slain enemy.

συλλαβών, from συλλαμβάνω.

συλλαμβάνω (see λαμβάνω for prin. parts), *to arrest.*

συλλέγω (see λέγω for prin. parts), *to gather, collect.*

συλλογή, -ῆς, ἡ, *a gathering, levy.*

συμβάλλω (see βάλλω for prin. parts), *to throw together, contribute, collect.* SYMBOLIZE.

συμβουλεύω (see βουλεύω for prin. parts), *to advise, counsel;* mid., *to consult with, ask advice.*

σύμμαχος, -ον, *allied;* ὁ σύμμαχος, *an ally.*

σύμπας, -ασα, -αν, *all together, all taken collectively.*

συμπέμπω (see πέμπω for prin. parts), *to send with.*

σύμπλεως, -ων, gen. -ω, *quite full,* with gen.

συμπορεύομαι (see πορεύομαι for prin. parts), *to proceed with, go along with, accompany.*

συμπράττω (see πράττω for prin. parts), *to help in doing,* with dat. of the one helped.

σύν, with dat., *with.*

συναγείρω (see ἀγείρω for prin. parts), *to gather, assemble.*

συνάγω (see ἄγω for prin. parts), *to gather together, gather, bring together.*

συναγωγή, -ῆς, ἡ, *synagogue.* SYNAGOGUE.

συναλλαγέντι, from συναλλάττω.

συναλλάττω (see ἀλλάττω for prin. parts), *to change, reconcile with.*

συναναβαίνω (see βαίνω for prin. parts), *to march inland with.*

συνεγένοντο, from συγγίγνομαι.

σύνειμι, *to come together, attack.*

συνείπετο, from συνέπομαι.

συνεισέρχομαι (see ἔρχομαι for prin. parts), *to enter with, get in with.*

συνεισῆλθε, from συνεισέρχομαι.

συνεκβιβάζω (see βιβάζω for prin. parts), *to help push out.*

συνεπισπεύδω (see σπεύδω for prin. parts), *to help hurry forward.*

συνέπομαι (see ἕπομαι for prin. parts), *to follow with.*

συνήγαγε, συνήγαγον, from συνάγω.

σύνθημα, -ατος, τό, *an agreement, sign, watchword.*

συνιδεῖν, from συνοράω.

σύνοδος, -ου, ἡ, *meeting, encounter.* SYNOD.

σύνοιδα (perf. only, as present; see εἴδω), *to share in knowledge;* with reflexive pron., *to be conscious.*

συνοράω (see ὁράω for prin. parts), *to see at the same time, at once.*

συντάττω (see τάττω for prin. parts), *to arrange together, form together, marshal.* SYNTAX.

συντυγχάνω (see τυγχάνω for prin. parts), *to fall in with, meet.*

συγχράομαι or συγχράομαι (see χράομαι for prin. parts), *to use jointly, have dealings with.*

Συρακόσιος, -ου, ὁ, *a Syracusan, native of Syracuse.*

Συρία, -ας, ἡ, *Syria.*

Σύριος, -α, -ον, *Syrian.*

Σύρος, -ου, ὁ, *a Syrian.*

συσκευάζω, συσκευάσω, συνεσκεύασα, συνεσκεύασμαι, *to pack up.*

συσπάω (see σπάω for prin. parts), *to draw together, sew together.*

συσπειράομαι, συνεσπείραμαι, συνεσπειράθην, *to be formed in close array.*

συστρατεύομαι (see στρατεύω for prin. parts), *to take the field with, join an expedition.*

συστρατιώτης, -ου, ὁ, *fellow soldier.*

Συχάρ, ἡ, indecl., *Sychar.*

συχνός, -ή, -όν, *much, considerable;* of time, *long.*

σφάγιον, -ου, τό, *sacrifice, external omen* from a sacrifice.

σφάττω, σφάξω, ἔσφαξα, ἔσφαγμαι, ἐσφάγην, *to slay.*

σφοδρός, -ά, -όν, *extreme, violent.*

σφραγίζω, σφραγίσω, ἐσφράγισα, ἐσφράγικα, ἐσφράγισμαι, *to seal, confirm.*

σχεδία, -ας, ἡ, *a raft.*

σχεδόν, *nearly, about, chiefly.*

σχῆμα, -ατος, τό, *pattern, formation.*
SCHEME.

σχοινίον, -ου, τό, *rope, cord.*

σχολαίως, *slowly*; comp. σχολαίτερον.

σῴζω, σώσω, ἔσωσα, σέσωκα, σέσωμαι or
σέσωσμαι, ἐσώθην, *to save, keep safe.*
(N.T. omits ι subscript.)
σωθῆτε, aor. pass. subjunct. of σῴζω.

Σωκράτης, -ους, ὁ, *Socrates,* an Achaean
friend of Cyrus.

σῶμα, -ατος, τό, *body.* SOMATIC.

Σῶσις, -ιος, ὁ, *Sosis,* a Greek from Syracuse.

σωτήρ, σωτῆρος, ὁ, *savior.* SOTERIOLOGY.

σωτηρία, -ας, ἡ, *salvation, safety.*

**T**

Ταμώς, Ταμώ, ὁ, *Tamos,* an Egyptian pilot.

τάξις, -εως, ἡ, *an arrangement, division,
station.* TAXIDERMY.

ταράττω or ταράσσω, ταράξω, ἐτάραξα,
τετάραχα, τετάραγμαι, ἐταράχθην, *to
disturb, trouble.*

ταραχή, -ῆς, ἡ, *disturbance, troubling.*

τάραχος, -ου, ὁ, *confusion.*

Ταρσοί, -ῶν, οἱ, *Tarsus.* The capital of
Cilicia, birthplace of St. Paul.

τάττω, τάξω, ἔταξα, τέταχα, τέταγμαι,
ἐτάχθην, *to arrange, draw up, marshal,
assign, order.* TACTICS.

ταῦτα, ταύτης, etc., from οὗτος.

τάχα, *presently, soon, perhaps.*

τάχιστος, -η, -ον, superl. of ταχύς.

ταχύς, -εῖα, -ύ, *quick, swift.* As adverb,
ταχύ, *speedily*; θᾶττον, *faster*; τάχιστα,
*most swiftly.* διὰ ταχέων, *with speed,
rapidity.* TACHOMETER.

τε, postpositive enclitic, *and.*

τεθνηκότα, from θνῄσκω.

τείνω, τενῶ, ἔτεινα, τέτακα, τέταμαι,
ἐτάθην, *to stretch, extend, hasten.* TENSION,
TONE.

τεῖχος, -ους, τό, *wall.*

τέκνον, -ου, τό, *child.* (Declined in 50.)

τελείόω, τελειώσω, ἐτελείωσα, τετελείωκα,

τετελείωμαι, ἐτελειώθην, *to bring to
completion, finish, carry through, make
perfect.*

τελευτάω, τελευτήσω, ἐτελεύτησα, τετελεύτηκα, ἐτελευτήθην, *to end, die.*

τελέω, τελῶ, ἐτέλεσα, τετέλεκα, τετέλεσμαι, ἐτελέσθην, *to complete.*

τελευτή, -ῆς, ἡ, *end.*

τέλος, -ους, τό, *end*; τέλος as adverb,
*finally.* TELEOLOGY.

τέρας, -ατος, τό, *sign, portent, marvel.*

τεσσαράκοντα, same as τετταράκοντα.

τεταγμένοι, τεταγμένους, from τάττω.

τετρακισχίλιοι, -αι, -α, *four thousand.*

τετράμηνος, -ον, *of four months.*

τετταράκοντα or τεσσαράκοντα, indecl.,
*forty.*

τέτταρες, -α, *four.* TETRAGON.

τηρέω, τηρήσω, ἐτήρησα, τετήρηκα, τετήρημαι, ἐτηρήθην, *to watch over, keep.*

Τιβεριάς, -άδος, ἡ, *Tiberias.*

τίθημι, θήσω, ἔθηκα, τέθηκα or τέθεικα,
τέθειμαι, ἐτέθην, *to put, place, set, institute
or hold.* THESIS. (Expanded in 229.)

τιμάω, τιμήσω, ἐτίμησα, τετίμηκα, τετίμημαι, ἐτιμήθην, *to honor, value.*

τιμή, -ῆς, ἡ, *honor, value.*

τίμιος, -α, -ον, *esteemed, precious, honored.*
TIMOCRACY.

τιμωρέω, τιμωρήσομαι, ἐτιμωρησάμην,
τετιμώρημαι, *to avenge, take vengeance on,
punish.*

τίς, τί, gen. τίνος, τίνος, interrogative *who?
what?* τί also has sometimes the force
of *why?* (Declined in 158.)

τὶς, τὶ, gen. τινός or του, *someone, anyone,
anything, a certain.* (Declined in 158.)

Τισσαφέρνης, -ους, ὁ, *Tissaphernes,* a Persian noble.

τιτρώσκω, τρώσω, ἔτρωσα, τέτρωμαι,
ἐτρώθην, *to wound.*

τοιόσδε, τοιάδε, τοιόνδε, *of this kind, as
follows.*

τοιοῦτος, τοιαύτη, τοιοῦτο, *of this kind,
such as this,* referring to something already mentioned.

τοῖς, τόν, from ὁ.

τόξευμα, -ατος, τό, *an arrow.*

τοξεύω, ἐτόξευσα, τετόξευμαι, ἐτοξεύθην,
*to shoot, shoot at* or *hit with bow and
arrow.* TOXIC.

τοξότης, -ου, ὁ, *bowman, archer.*
τόπος, -ου, ὁ, *place.* TOPOGRAPHY.
τοσοῦτος, τοσαύτη, τοσοῦτον, *so much, so great, so many, so much only.*
τότε, *then, at that time.*
τοῦ, τούς, from ὁ.
τούτου, τούτῳ, etc., from οὗτος.
Τράλλεις, -εων, οἱ, *Tralles,* a city in northern Caria.
τράπεζα, -ης, ἡ, *table.* TRAPEZE. (Declined in 43.)
τραῦμα, -ατος, τό, *wound.* TRAUMATIC.
τράχηλος, -ου, ὁ, *neck, throat.*
τρεῖς, τρία, gen. τριῶν, τριῶν, *three.* TRIGONOMETRY.
τρεισκαίδεκα, *thirteen.*
τρέπω, τρέψω, ἔτρεψα, τέτροφα, τέτραμμαι, ἐτράπην, *to turn.* TROPISM.
τρέφω, θρέψω, ἔθρεψα, τέτροφα, τέθραμμαι, ἐθρέφθην or ἐτράφην, *to nurture, feed, support, nourish.* DYSTROPHY.

*arrow.* TOXIC.
τοξότης, -ου, ὁ, *bowman, archer.*
τόπος, -ου, ὁ, *place.* TOPOGRAPHY.
τοσοῦτος, τοσαύτη, τοσοῦτον, *so much, so great, so many, so much only.*
τότε, *then, at that time.*
τοῦ, τούς, from ὁ.
τούτου, τούτῳ, etc., from οὗτος.
Τράλλεις, -εων, οἱ, *Tralles,* a city in northern Caria.
τράπεζα, -ης, ἡ, *table.* TRAPEZE. (Declined in 43.)
τραῦμα, -ατος, τό, *wound.* TRAUMATIC.
τράχηλος, -ου, ὁ, *neck, throat.*
τρεῖς, τρία, gen. τριῶν, τριῶν, *three.* TRIGONOMETRY.
τρεισκαίδεκα, *thirteen.*
τρέπω, τρέψω, ἔτρεψα, τέτροφα, τέτραμμαι, ἐτράπην, *to turn.* TROPISM.
τρέφω, θρέψω, ἔθρεψα, τέτροφα, τέθραμμαι, ἐθρέφθην or ἐτράφην, *to nurture, feed, support, nourish.* DYSTROPHY.

τρέχω, δραμοῦμαι, ἔδραμον, δεδράμηκα, δεδράμημαι, *to run.*
τριάκοντα, indecl., *thirty.*
τριακόσιοι, -αι, -α, *three hundred.*
τρίβω, τρίψω, ἔτριψα, τέτριφα, τέτριμμαι, ἐτρίβην, *to rub, wear.*

τριήρης, -ους, ἡ, *trireme, galley, warship propelled by three banks of oarsmen, an estimated total of 174 men.* (Declined in 139.)
τρίτος, -η, -ον, *third.*
τροπή, -ῆς, ἡ, *a turning, rout.* HELIOTROPE, TROPIC.
τρόπος, -ου, ὁ, *a turning, way, manner, character.* TROPISM.
τροφή, -ῆς, ἡ, *nourishment, food, support.* HYPERTROPHY.
τρώγω, τρώξω, ἔτρωξα, τέτρωγμαι, *to chew, eat.* TROGLODYTE.
τυγχάνω, τεύξομαι, ἔτυχον, τετύχηκα, *to hit the mark, attain, happen.*
Τυριαῖον, Τυραῖον, or Τυριάειον, -ου, τό, *Tyriaeum,* a city in southern Phrygia.
τυφλός, -ή, -όν, *blind.*

Υ

ὑγιής, -ές, *sound, healthy, well.* HYGIENIC.
ὑδρία, -ας, ἡ, *water pot, water jar.*
ὕδωρ, ὕδατος, τό, *water.* HYDRAULIC. (Declined in 146.)
υἱός, -οῦ, ὁ, *son.*
ὕλη, -ης, ἡ, *wood, woody growth.*
ὑμεῖς, ὑμῖν, ὑμῶν, from σύ.
ὑπάγω (see ἄγω for prin. parts), *to lead slowly, go slowly, go.*
ὑπαντάω, ὑπαντήσομαι, ὑπήντησα, *to go to meet, meet.*
ὕπαρχος, -ου, ὁ, *underofficer, lieutenant.*
ὑπάρχω (see ἄρχω for prin. parts), *to begin, be under as a foundation;* with dat., *to support.*
ὑπέρ, with gen., *over, concerning, for the sake of;* with acc., *over, more than, beyond.* HYPER-.
ὑπερβολή, -ῆς, ἡ, *a passing over, an exceeding.* HYPERBOLE.
ὕπερθεν, *from above, overhead.*
ὑπισχνέομαι, ὑποσχήσομαι, ὑπεσχόμην, ὑπέσχημαι, *to promise.*
ὑπό, with gen., *under, by* (indicating agent); with dat., *under, at the base or foot of* (place where); with acc.,

## Vocabulary

ὑπολαμβάνω (see λαμβάνω for prin. parts), to take up the conversation, reply, to receive under one's protection.

ὑστερέω, ὑστερήσω, ὑστέρησα, ὑστέρηκα, ὑστερήθην, to be behind, be deficient, insufficient, lacking.

### Φ

φαίνω, φανῶ, ἔφηνα, πέφηνα, πέφασμαι, ἐφάνην, to show; mid. and pass., to appear. PHENOMENON. (Expanded in 205.)

φανερόω, φανερώσω, ἐφανέρωσα, πεφανέρωμαι, ἐφανερώθην, to make visible, show forth.

Φαρισαῖος, -ου, ὁ, a Pharisee.

φέρω, οἴσω, ἤνεγκα, ἐνήνοχα, ἐνήνεγμαι, ἠνέχθην, to carry, bear, receive (of wages). PHOSPHORUS.

φεύγω, φεύξομαι or φευξοῦμαι, ἔφυγον, πέφευγα, πέφυγμαι, to flee, be exiled. FUGUE.

φημί, φήσω, ἔφησα, to say. EUPHEMISM. (Present system conjugated in 233.)

φθάνω, φθήσομαι, ἔφθην or ἔφθασα, to get the start of, do first, usually with participle. φθάσωσι, from φθάνω.

φιλέω, φιλήσω, ἐφίλησα, πεφίληκα, πεφίλημαι, ἐφιλήθην, to love as a friend. PHILIP.

Φίλιππος, -ου, ὁ, Philip.

φιλοτιμέομαι, φιλοτιμήσομαι, πεφιλοτίμημαι, ἐφιλοτιμήθην, to be jealous, feel piqued.

φοβέω, φοβήσω, ἐφόβησα, ἐφοβήθην, to frighten, terrify; pass., to be frightened, be afraid.

Φοινίκη, -ης, ἡ, Phoenicia.

Φοῖνιξ, -ικος, ὁ, a Phoenician.

Φρυγία, -ας, ἡ, Phrygia.

Φρύξ, -υγός, ὁ, a Phrygian.

φυλάττω, φυλάξω, ἐφύλαξα, πεφύλαχα, πεφύλαγμαι, ἐφυλάχθην, to keep watch, guard. PROPHYLACTIC.

φύω, φύσω, ἔφυσα or ἔφυν, πέφυκα, ἐφύην, to bring forth, produce. PHYSICAL.

# X

χαίρω, χαιρήσω, ἐχάρησα, κεχάρηκα, κεχάρημαι, ἐχάρην, *to rejoice, be of good cheer.*

χαλεπός, -ή, -όν, *difficult, harsh, grievous;* superl., χαλεπώτατος.

χαλκός, -οῦ, ὁ, *bronze, bronze armor.*

χαλκοῦς, -ῆ, -οῦν, *bronze.*

Χάλος, -ου, ὁ, *the Chalus,* a river in the northern part of Syria.

χαρά, -ᾶς, ἡ, *joy, delight.*

χαρίεις, χαρίεσσα, χαρίεν, *graceful.* (Declined in 190.)

χάρις, χάριτος, ἡ, *grace, favor;* χάριν ἔχειν, *to give thanks.* EUCHARIST. (Declined in 146.)

Χαρμάνδη, -ης, ἡ, *Charmande,* a city of northeastern Arabia on the Euphrates.

χείρ, -ός, ἡ, *hand.* CHIROGRAPH.

Χειρίσοφος, -ου, ὁ, *Chirisophus,* a Spartan general of Cyrus' mercenary force.

χείρων, -ον, *worse,* comp. of κακός.

Χερρόνησος, -ου, ἡ, *the Chersonese,* a Thracian peninsula.

χέω, χέω or χεῶ, ἔχεα, κέχυκα, κέχυμαι, ἐχύθην, *to pour, let flow.*

χίλιοι, -αι, -α, *a thousand.* KILOGRAM.

χιλός, -οῦ, ὁ, *fodder, provender.*

χιτών, -ῶνος, ὁ, *undergarment, tunic.*

χοῖνιξ, -ικος, ἡ, *the choenix,* an Attic dry measure containing nearly a quart.

χορτάζω, χορτάσω, ἐχόρτασα, ἐχορτάσθην, *to feed to the full, fatten.*

χόρτος, -ου, ὁ, *pasture, grass.*

χράομαι, χρήσομαι, ἐχρησάμην, κέχρημαι, ἐχρήσθην, *to use,* with dat.

χρεία, -ας, ἡ, *advantage, use, need, necessity.*

χρή, χρήσει (imperf. ἐχρῆν or χρῆν), impersonal, *it is necessary.*

χρῄζω, χρήσω, *to need, desire.*

χρῆμα, -ατος, τό, *a thing of use, goods;* τὰ χρήματα, *money, goods.*

Χριστός, -οῦ, ὁ, *Christ, the Anointed.*

χρόνος, -ου, ὁ, *time.* CHRONOLOGY.

χρυσίον, -ου, τό, *gold, money.*

χρυσοῦς, -ῆ, -οῦν, *of gold, golden.* CHRYSANTHEMUM. (Declined in 244.)

χρυσοχάλινος, -ον, *gold-bridled.*

χωλός, -ή, -όν, *lame, crippled.*

χώρα, -ας, ἡ, *country, land, farm, place, field.*

χωρέω, χωρήσω, ἐχώρησα, κεχώρηκα, κεχώρημαι, ἐχωρήθην, *to make room for, hold, contain, give place, withdraw, move, advance.*

χωρίον, -ου, τό, *place, locality.*

χωρίς, with gen., *without, apart from.*

# Ψ

Ψάρος, -ου, ὁ, *the Psarus,* a river rising in Cataonia and flowing through Cilicia to the sea.

ψέλιον or ψέλλιον, -ου, τό, *armlet.*

ψεύδω, ψεύσω, ἔψευσα, ἔψευσμαι, ἐψεύσθην, *to lie, cheat, deceive, behave falsely.* PSEUDONYM.

ψιλός, -ή, -όν, *naked, bare, barren.*

ψιλόω, ψιλώσω, ἐψίλωσα, ἐψιλώθην, *to strip, make bare, clear.*

# Ω

ὦ, interjection, *o,* frequently with vocative.

ὦ, from εἰμί.

ᾧ, from ὅς.

ὧδε, adverb from ὅδε, *in the following manner, as follows, hither, here.*

ὤν, present participle of εἰμί. (Declined in 180.)

ὤνιος, -α, -ον, *for sale, saleable;* τὰ ὤνια, *wares.*

ὥρα, -ας, ἡ, *hour, season.* HOROSCOPE.

ὥς, adv. of manner (like οὕτως), *so, thus.*

ὡς, basically a rel. adv. of manner, *as, as if, on the ground that*; of degree, strengthening the superlative, as ὡς βέλτιστος, *as fine (noble, brave) as possible, the finest possible*; with number, *approximately, about.*

Developed as a conj., of time, *as, when*; introducing purpose clauses (like ἵνα, ὅπως), *in order that, that*; introducing indirect discourse (like ὅτι), *that.*

Developed as a preposition (equivalent to εἰς, probably for ὡς εἰς, *as to* or *toward*), used only with persons, *to.*

ὥσπερ, *just as, just as though.*

ὥστε, *so that, so as.*

ὠτίς, -ίδος, ἡ, *bustard,* a bird related to the crane and the plover.

ὠφελέω, ὠφελήσω, ὠφέλησα, ὠφέληκα, ὠφέλημαι, ὠφελήθην, *to help, be of use* or *service to.*

# INDEX

ALL references are to sections. For Greek references, see the desired word in the Greek–English vocabulary above.

Abstract qualities, article with, 485.
Accents, 24; location of, 25; kinds used, 26; value of final οι and αι, 44, 51, 99; in α-declension, 44; in o-declension, 51; apparent irregularities with infinitives and participles, 99, 112.
Accompaniment, dative of, 525.
Accusative case, syntax of, 527 ff.
Acute accent, 24, 26.
Adjectives, 13; agreement of, 55; a- and o-declension, 56; two-ending o-declension, 57; consonant and a-declension, 156; two-ending consonant declension, 157; certain irregulars, 188 ff.; regular comparison, 237; certain irregular comparisons, 238; contract adjectives, 244; agreement, 542; attributive and predicate, 543; as substantives, 544.
Advantage, dative of, 517.
Adverbial accusative, 530.
Adverbs, 15; comparison of, 239.
Agent, dative of, 519.
Agreement, adjectives, 55, 542; verbs, 545; participles, 578.
Alphabet, 1.
*Anabasis*, brief synopsis of, 249; the Greek of, 250.
Antepenult, 23 ff.
Aorist tense, gnomic 555; see also *First aorist, Second aorist.*
Apodosis, see *Conditional sentences*, 593 ff.
Apposition of nouns, 492.
Article, 10; declension of, 63; syntax of, 483 ff.
Articular infinitive, 572.
Attendant circumstances, with participles, 581; genitive absolute, 582.
Attribute and predicate position, adjectives, 55; demonstratives, 65; article, 489.
Augment, 107.

Benefit and detriment, dative in, 514.
Breathings, 5.

Cases, 35; see also *Nominative, Genitive, Dative, Accusative, Vocative.*
Cause, with genitive, 509; with participles, 581; genitive absolute, 582.
Circumflex accent, 24, 26; in α-declension, 45; in o-declension, 51.
Circumstantial participle, 581.
Cognate accusative, 528.
Cognate mutes, 106.
Commands, with future indicative, 553; imperative, 571.
Comparison, genitive of, 505 ff.
Complex sentence, 585.
Compound verbs, with dative, 515; augment and reduplication of, 107 f.
Concession, with participles, 581; genitive absolute, 582.
Condition, with participles, 581; genitive absolute, 582.
Conditional and conditional relative sentences, 593 ff.
Conditional relatives, see *Conditional and conditional relative sentences.*
Conjunctions, 17.
Consonants, 2; mutes, 106.
Contract adjectives, 244.
Contract nouns, 243.
Contract participles, 195.
Contract verbs, 163 ff., 170, 173, 175, 177; declension of active participles, 195.
Contrary-to-fact suppositions, 601 f.
Co-ordinate mutes, 106.

Dative case, syntax of, 513 ff.
Declension, 34; see also *Nouns.*
Definite article, see *Article.*
Degree of difference, dative of, 524.
Deliberative subjunctive, 560.
Dependent clauses, 585; in indirect discourse, 589.
Deponent verbs, 131.
Diphthongs, 4.
Double accusative, 532.
Dual number, 37.

MARCH
OF THE TEN
THOUSAND

Route of the Ten Thousand

Route of the Persian Royal Road

Scale of Parasangs
0, 5, 10, 15, 20, 25, 30,

Scale of Miles
0, 50, 100, 150, 200,